REIMAGINING SOUTH ASIA

Multilateralism in the Contemporary Times

Editor

Prof. Nagalaxmi M. Raman

Foreword by

Ambassador Anil Trigunayat

IFS Retd.

PENTAGON PRESS LLP

Reimagining South Asia: Multilateralism in the Contemporary Times
Editor: **Prof. Nagalaxmi M. Raman**

ISBN 978-93-90095-51-3

First Published in 2022

Published by
PENTAGON PRESS LLP
206, Peacock Lane, Shahpur Jat,
New Delhi-110049
Phones: 011-64706243, 26491568
Telefax: 011-26490600
email: rajan@pentagonpress.in
website: www.pentagonpress.in

Printed at Aegean Offset Printers, Greater Noida, U.P.

Contents

Foreword

I am happy to see the book 'Reimagining South Asia: Multilateralism in the Contemporary Times 'edited by Professor Nagalaxmi M Raman. The book presents a much broader landscape on developments in South Asia and is timely and relevant. The contributions by eminent academicians and scholars delve deep into the emerging intricacies of ideational strategies, survival instincts during the pandemic, existential threats like Climate change, sovereign considerations and big power play in the region as the Covid, Counter Terrorism and Chinese expansionism continue to remain the big challenges for India and others and even for regional bonhomie and way forward.

Even after more than 35 years SAARC has not been able to achieve its full potential and has in fact been stunted by binary between India and Pakistan whose bilateral relations remain at their lowest despite the fact that a ceasefire of sorts and occasional collaboration is witnessed. Islamabad's 'Zero sum' game with India and adherence to cross border terrorism as an instrument of its foreign policy remain major challenges. However, the Covid 19 pandemic provided a unique opportunity for cooperation and joint action among South Asian countries, since the virus knows no boundaries. India rose to the occasion, having been the largest country and economy and the vaccine hub and pharmacy of the world. It prioritised its neighbours and has emerged as a first responder to natural calamities and endemics and pandemics following her nonreciprocal 'Neighbourhood First policy'. Regional countries are also beginning to follow their own instincts and national interests while navigating their bilateral relations with China and India whose affections are lavished on them.

At the same time due to the lack of integration and progress on the SAARC track, India began its outreach and connectivity to South East Asia with ASEAN countries as the focus in accordance with her 'Act East Policy'. We see the emergence and renewed focus on achievable projects under the rubric of BBIN (Bangladesh, Bhutan, India and Nepal) and BIMSTEC (Bay of Bengal Initiative for Multi Sectoral Technical and Economic Cooperation) with the participation of Bangladesh, Bhutan, India, Myanmar, Nepal, Thailand and Sri Lanka comprising of 21% of the global population. These alternative sub regional multilateral efforts are witnessing a merging of India's Neighbourhood and Act East policies to some extent. As developments in Myanmar indicate that even that track has its own challenges. But India maintains the centrality of Asean on alternative tracks as a strategic choice. Moreover, for India the Indo-Pacific obviously includes West Asia and Africa as its natural contours of interest and importance.

Developments in Afghanistan with the sudden vacation of strategic space by USA and onset of Taliban have created an immense challenge and threat of centrifugal expanse of terrorism, extremism and radicalism from various groups like ISIS (Khorasan) and Al Qaeda has become a reality. India and other countries in the region and the world are rightly concerned as the Islamic Emirate struggles to find its feet and comply with the expectations and red lines of the international community. It has also engineered an opportunity for China with the help of Pakistan to fill the strategic void created by the ignominious departure of the US. This could have its own adverse dynamic especially for New Delhi which was heavily invested in the welfare and development of Afghans for over two decades. Hence, greater focus on retrieving and developing new networks of connectivity and critical alignments will become increasingly important as the geo-strategic and geo-economic competition in the region becomes intense.

At the same time Sino-US rivalry often being referred to as Cold War 2.0 of a different kind but worse consequences has created an intense theatre of competition in the Indo-Pacific where South Asia especially India have acquired critical importance that has been clearly articulated in the US policy towards South Asia and the Indo-Pacific. Evolution and maturing of the QUAD (USA, Australia, Japan and India) and AUKUS (USA, Australia and UK) will have far reaching consequences in the security semantics of the region. India's approach and Indo-Pacific strategy remains non-confrontational, inclusive and international law driven despite her bilateral complexities with China. Even though India preferred the Competition with Cooperation matrix in her engagement with her largest neighbour ensuing conflict on the borders and beyond may lead to accentuation of red lines. Both countries seem to be working to alleviate that through their collaboration in organisations and mechanisms like the BRICS, RIC and the SCO in which Moscow appears to be playing cupid for their own geo political considerations.

Multilateralism and several strands of regional and sub regional tracks will continue to have their complementary and cross cutting nuances and utility as the UN and other multilateral organisations will reassert their relevance and enforceability of a collective action to retrieve their credibility and prestige. India indeed has a key role to play through her humanitarian assistance, soft power approaches, firm choices in foreign policy and quest for stronger presence in the multilateral domain. It has already shown its leadership during her Presidency of BRICS, RIC, the UNSC and will take the mantle forward in 2023 at the G20. However, leadership in Asia is her ordained destiny and a priority since neighbours are a gift of geography and not choice.

As the new global order remains in transition, I am confident that this book will provide and inform the readers and researchers about the in-depth dimensions of global challenges like the pandemic, terrorism and climate change and ensuing collaborative opportunities for a multilateral governance effort as well as focus on many under currents across South Asia and the Asian straits.

Ambassador Anil Trigunayat
(IFS Retd.)

Preface

South Asia is at a critical juncture of history. A world of opportunity is beckoning us. We should not hold regional prosperity hostage to the interests of individual states, which may obstruct all efforts aimed at regional cooperation. In regions like ours, which is emotionally connected by historical memories and inerasable cultural linkages, but separated by zero-sum politics and misgivings, it requires careful articulation of ideas. We need to seriously ponder over these issues and evolve ways of circumventing them. We need to identify areas where our initiatives have a greater chance of succeeding.

Even at the best of times, when there was great power cooperation rather than great power rivalry like now, multilateralism has belied the ability to update swiftly. For example, Resolution 50/52 adopted unanimously during the 50th session of the United Nations, "to initiate the procedure set out in Article 108 of the Charter of the United Nations to amend the Charter, with prospective effect, by the deletion of the 'enemy State' clauses from Articles 53, 77 and 107 at its earliest appropriate future session" awaits action, nearly 25 years later.

Multilateralism 0.1

The COVID-19 pandemic has placed all international institutions under a magnifying glass. By any measure, most have performed below par. Such is the caution espoused that multilateralism today seems to have reverted to version 0.1. The General Assembly now passes resolutions through the 'no objection' procedure. The Security Council has been found wanting in no small measure. The 75th session's 'leaders' week' runs the risk of being reduced to a video playback session.

It is true that the functioning of multilateral institutions, like much else, requires reform. They need to adapt to new realities, just as their headquarters staff have quickly adopted the new normal of 'work from home'. However, the pursuit of change by threatening to leave multilateral institutions is a phenomenon witnessed only during the period of the League of Nations. One state followed another in bidding goodbye, until the League's final demise.

The post-World War II multilateral institutions have survived such departures. The United Nations Educational, Scientific and Cultural Organization (UNESCO) in Paris and the Human Rights Council in Geneva have survived the departure of the USA. The United Nations Industrial Development Organization (UNIDO) in Vienna continues to function despite the withdrawal of the USA and many others. The World Health Organization (WHO), notwithstanding its visible shortcomings, will survive U.S. threats. The reasons are simple. Multilateral organisations serve the desperately-felt global needs of their vast membership. The pandemic has reinforced the desire for greater global cooperation amongst most states.

India has Emerged as a Leader of 'New Multilateralism' Amid COVID-19

Since COVID-19 broke as a global pandemic, Prime Minister Narendra Modi has been on a leadership offensive. He organised a teleconference with the South Asian Association of Regional Cooperation (SAARC) countries in mid-March and declared a regional emergency fund, to which India committed USD10 million. He reached out to Saudi Arabia, this year's G20 host, to urge a virtual G20 Summit to coordinate the economic fallout of COVID-19 containment measures, which was also held in March. At the meeting, Modi articulated the importance of 'new multilateralism' principles and a more humane approach to globalisation. He also staunchly supported the WHO, calling for other G20 leaders to strengthen its powers in the wake of Trump's halting of U.S. funding. Most recently, Modi addressed the Virtual Non-Alignment Movement (NAM) Summit of more than 120 countries to discuss global management of COVID-19. Speaking at NAM, Modi called for solidarity: "In the post-COVID world, we need a new template of globalisation, based on fairness, equality, and humanity."

Modi has also made a slew of bilateral calls, including with the leaders of Australia, Russia, Israel, Japan, Canada, France, Germany, Indonesia, Singapore, the UK, Ethiopia, and the USA. Though most calls were about pledging assistance and coordinating consular support and medical research efforts, the calls with French President Emmanuel Macron and German Chancellor Angela Merkel also included commitments to 'a new human-centric concept of globalisation'.

The USA, having drawn a hard line against soft power, created an opening for the international leadership role it decisively vacated. Conjecture initially had China filling this void: China was initially commended by the WHO for its effective domestic measures and proactively shared its national experience to help other countries, while Chinese entrepreneur Jack Ma funded global vaccine efforts and exports of personal protective equipment (PPE). Meanwhile, at the beginning of the year, Modi was being criticised for his government's controversial Citizenship Amendment Act (CAA) and other legislation thought to be aimed at creating anti-Muslim sentiment, with members of the European Parliament drafting a resolution against the CAA, fearing it could cause the 'largest statelessness crisis in the world'.

In this context, Modi's cooperation with France and Germany and a rise to global responsibility may seem unexpected. However, in a matter of months, Beijing is now on the back foot as it excludes the WHO from investigation efforts into the origin of the virus. Washington's constant criticism of China and calls for compensation are unconstructive and detracts from cooperative efforts. The global crisis has shifted the focus from India's domestic human rights challenges as India engages in 'saviour diplomacy', exporting PPE and—reportedly—the hydroxychloroquine drug and other needed medicines and food. Prime Minister Modi's efforts at global coordination at a time when others are abandoning multilateralism have been well received by defenders of the international order. India's reputation as the largest democracy in the world and as a longstanding defender of development also holds it in good stead for inclusive leadership.

India is Uniquely Qualified to Play an International Leadership Role in a New Global Order

There are few countries with which India does not have good relations. India's broad-based friendships stem from its non-aligned philosophy. Arriving on the international stage in the aftermath of WW II with unapologetic autonomy, India refused to trade its hard-fought freedom from Britain for a false dichotomy of communism versus capitalism. As a newly independent state with a poor population of 350 million, a partitioned territory and a global share of GDP of just 3 per cent, India nevertheless became a leader on its own terms. Leading the Non-Alignment Movement of emancipation for emerging states in support of Third World solidarity, India has remained a steadfastly autonomous political power.

As a result of its strategically autonomous foreign policy, India has maintained a wide array of relationships including those with Saudi Arabia, Israel, Iran, the USA, the UK, the EU and Russia while continuing its third world solidarity role as leader of the 'Group of 77' of least-developed and developing economies. India also has a workable relationship with China, its number one trading partner, as evidenced by its founding-member status of China's Asia Infrastructure Investment Bank (AIIB) and Prime Minister Modi's famous 'power selfie' with then Premier Li in 2015.

I express my deep sense of gratitude and congratulate all the contributors who put in their effort to analyse and give their insights on the upcoming concerns in South Asia.

This book will undoubtedly be useful to researchers and others interested in the study of South Asia.

Finally, I would also like to express my sincere thanks to Mr. Rajan Arya of Pentagon Press LLP, for arranging the publication of this volume in record time as committed.

Prof. Nagalaxmi M. Raman
Editor

Contributors

Anuska Saxena, Researcher, Lady Shri Ram College for Women Delhi, India.

Astha Chadha, PhD Scholar, Ritsumeikan Asia Pacific University, Japan.

Gargi Sharma, Research Assistant, Amity Institute of International Studies, AUUP Noida.

Garima Lal, Research Scholar, JNU, New Delhi.

Dr. Sujit Kumar Datta, Chairman and Associate Professor in the Department of International Relations at the University of Chittagong, Chittagong-4331, Bangladesh.

Dr. Pamreihor Khashimwo, ICSSR Post-Doctoral Fellow (PDF) at University of Delhi and former Research Associate (RA) at Centre for Air Power Studies, New Delhi. He completed MA (Political Science) from University of Delhi, M.Phil, and Ph.D from Jawaharlal Nehru University, New Delhi. He was visiting scholar in Freie University in Berlin, Germany, in 2013 (under Konrad Adenauer Foundation (KAS) fellowship) and awarded Indian Council for Social Science Research (ICSSR) Doctoral Fellowship in 2016. He is currently working on "India's energy engagement with Africa."

Dr. Mohan Singh, Assistant Professor, Economics, Army Cadet College Wing, Indian Military Academy, Dehradun

Prof. (Dr) Nagalaxmi M. Raman, Director & Head, Amity Institute of International Studies, AUUP, Noida.

Ms Rachel C. Walter, Media Analysts, Kanalytics.

Ms. Samprity Biswas, Research Scholar, Centre for Russian and Central Asian Studies, School of International Studies, Jawaharlal Nehru University, New Delhi.

Ms. Hsin Yen Phoebe Mok, Research Assistant, Soka University, Japan

Sanchita Borah, Ph.D. Scholar, Latin American Studies Programme, CCUSLAS, SIS, Jawaharlal Nehru University, New Delhi.

Sandeep Singh, Research Assistant, Amity Institute of International Studies, AUUP, Noida.

Nancy Puri, Research Scholar, Amity Institute of International Studies, Amity University Uttar Pradesh,, Noida.

Dr. C. R. Akhouri, Offg. Director, Amity Humanity Foundation, Noida

Sandhya Rani, Research Scholar, JNU, Delhi

Haridass S., Research Assistant, Amity Institute of International Studies, AUUP Noida.

Lobzang Dorji, Department of Arts and Humanities, Sherubtse College, Royal University of Bhutan.

Paljor Galey, Department of Arts and Humanities, Sherubtse College, Royal University of Bhutan.

Tashi Jamtsho, Department of Social Science, Sherubtse College, Royal University of Bhutan.

1

ASEAN Outlook on the Indo-Pacific Narrative: Prospects for Regional Hegemony

Anuska Saxena

Introduction

The Association of Southeast Asian Nations (ASEAN), as an international forum for cooperation among Southeast Asian nations, has been through a lot ever since its inception. When it was formed in 1967, it aimed to create a cohesive group of non-communist nations willing to counter China's increasing interests in communism in Southeast Asia and seek regional political and economic support in a post-colonial setup. Today, the ASEAN sits in the centre of one of the world's most geo-strategically vital regions, the Indo-Pacific.

For a long time, the term 'Asia-Pacific' was used to describe the region encompassing the Asia that lay in the Western Pacific Ocean (including East Asia, South and Southeast Asia, and Oceania). However, the term 'Indo-Pacific' was coined later to define a priority towards the Indian Ocean Region. The Indo-Pacific can be understood as a framework for maritime cooperation, marked by the presence of the ASEAN at the centre and stretching up to the ends of the maritime routes that connect this centre with India, Africa, Australia, West Asia (Iran and Syria) and Northeast Asia (North Korea). The Indo-Pacific strategy sits at the underbelly of ASEAN's maritime power. It serves as the big thing that will drive the world's attention away from the transatlantic, projecting it towards the rising giant that is 'Asia'. However, the region comes with its contentions—with China's rising maritime aggression and its long-term ambition of becoming the world number one, as well as with the emergence of a power rivalling the ASEAN, called the 'Quad' (short for Quadrilateral Security Dialogue), there is significant uncertainty as to what the Indo-Pacific means for the region and the world, and who gets to be the leader in the Indo-Pacific narrative.

The Many Players of the Game

The Indo-Pacific is home to 60 per cent of the world's transit trade, making it a strategic hub and a central location for maritime connectivity. The Straits of Malacca, one of the world's most important chokepoints for maritime oil trade, lies here. It also houses the vision for an Indo-Pacific Economic Corridor, aiming to create a transnational trade network connecting South and Southeast Asian nations with each other and with the world. Many of the countries that can be found in the Indo-Pacific are allies to the Asia Pacific Economic Corridor (APEC) and China's Belt and Road Initiative (BRI).

At the same time, the region also faces volatilities due to the presence of pirates on the seas, fear of massive interference from the USA and China, and a general lack of dynamic leadership, which has been the case primarily because of conflicting Indo-Pacific strategies from the three important players in the region—China, the USA and the ASEAN—and the various alliances they bring with them.

In 2016, Japanese President Shinzo Abe first talked about a "Free and Open Indo-Pacific Strategy" (hereon addressed as FOIP), which has come to be an essential part of the US and the Quad approach to the region. The Quad, comprising the USA, Japan, Australia and India, follows this somewhat cohesive strategy of creating an Indo-Pacific that is 'free' and 'open' for the partners and is modelled on good regional governance and freedom of navigation. The FOIP has emerged as somewhat of a counter-argument to the ASEAN's "Open and Inclusive Indo-Pacific", a strategy that the Association has been working on since January 2018. The 'inclusivity' that the ASEAN talks about and the USA opposes refers to China's inclusion in the region.

It must be noted here that the ASEAN's engagements with China have been on the rise ever since the two became signatories to a Free-Trade Agreement (FTA) in 2002. Owing to the failed efforts of some ASEAN nations in being able to follow an FTA among themselves and their increasing dependence on China for infrastructural, trade and economic support, it has led them to become much closer to China than they would like. At the same time, China's increasing presence in Southeast Asia, either through the BRI or through its maritime aggressiveness (as evident in its 'String of Pearls' strategy or its bullying mechanisms in the disputed South China Sea), threatens the stability of the Indo-Pacific. Vietnam has complained time and again about China's military interference in the Paracel and the Spratly (islands which are claimed by both China and Vietnam), and despite being the chair of the ASEAN, Vietnam has been unable to unite ASEAN member-states against China in the South China Sea. The ASEAN faces a similar dilemma in dealing with the USA, primarily because the US-ASEAN economic ties are on the rise, but the intense relations of certain ASEAN nations (such as Thailand and The Philippines) with China are a bone of contention for the USA. The balancing game that ASEAN member-states are attempting to play, both with China and the USA, is a significant reason why the global fate of the Indo-Pacific narrative is yet to be determined.

The ASEAN Outlook on Indo-Pacific, which was released as a strategy document in 2019, defined the efforts the ASEAN will be making in creating an Indo-Pacific based on the values of mutual trust, openness, inclusivity, transparency, good governance, respect for sovereignty, a rule-based order, and, most importantly, non-intervention (there is no direct mention of China or the USA in this context). At the same time, it agrees with the "freedom of navigation" that the USA emphasises as well. However, there is no mention of any military or defence strategy that the ASEAN will be collectively undertaking to deal with threats in the Indo-Pacific, nor does it talk about the tensions created by the USA-China adversity in the region, the nuclear ambitions of North Korea, or the internal factors within the ASEAN that may act as obstacles to the success of this strategy.

The fact that the charting of this Outlook was an endeavour undertaken by Indonesia, a member-state that is known to be the representative mediating party of the ASEAN, may work well in emancipating its image to China or the USA (especially since the country wished to generate an Outlook that neither challenged the US FOIP nor China's BRI or String of Pearls). The effort may also reiterate the idea that the role the Indo-Pacific and the ASEAN play in Jakarta's foreign policy are vital.

Analysis of ASEAN's Indo-Pacific Outlook

The ASEAN Indo-Pacific Outlook document, released in 2019, is a comprehensive document that states that the vision of the ASEAN, as defined in the document, is not to replace a pre-existing mechanism or provide a new one but to envisage an Indo-Pacific where the ASEAN is central to regional architecture. The emphasis on ASEAN'S centrality towards the development of Indo-the Pacific infrastructure can be seen in its promotional strategies for the East Asia Summit, which is a dialogue held among 18 states parties from the Asia-Pacific on matters pertaining to regional dynamics. We see that the first EAS, held in 2005 in Malaysia, led to the formulation of the Kunming Declaration, which essentially focused on the development of communication and transport networks, as well as other forms of infrastructure, with the backing of the ASEAN. It gives us a clear idea as to how the ASEAN envisions itself, as well as ASEAN-led mechanisms (including the EAS, the ASEAN Defence Ministers Meeting or the ASEAN Regional Forum), in the light of the Indo-Pacific strategy.

Another essential aspect that Outlook focuses on is "non-intervention" and, at the same time, "amicable cooperation". The South China Sea aspect figures vividly here. In 2013, The Philippines, a member-state of the ASEAN, filed a case against the People's Republic of China in the Public Court of Arbitration, stating that China's 9-Dash Line map has no historical relevance; therefore, it becomes a matter of exploitation of the sovereignty of the Philippines, since it is a claimant of the islands nearest to it in the South China Sea, but China's 9-Dotted line depictions show otherwise. The Declaration of Code of Conduct in the South China Sea, which was signed between China and the ASEAN in November of 2002, highlighted that any differences in the

South China Sea were to be resolved using bilateral dialogue mechanisms. With the Philippines violating the Code in filing the case, the China-Philippines relations deteriorated and were revived only after Robert Duterte assumed the latter's leadership. Similar sentiments can be observed in Vietnam (which is also an ASEAN member), wherein the country is seen strengthening security and infrastructure relations with the USA to counter China in the South China Sea, something that also violates the 2002 Code, simply because it brings a third party into a bilateral dispute. The perspective on cooperation and negotiation, significantly emphasised in the ASEAN Outlook document, faces challenges at the member-state level. On the other hand, it would not be unfair to call China an external threat to the harmony this document seeks to promote, considering the fact that the country has repeatedly violated the Treaty of Amity and Cooperation (TAC) by the ASEAN (which was ratified by China as a non-ASEAN state in 2003), and continues its hostilities in the South China Sea.

The US 'Free and Open' Indo-Pacific strategy, though resonating with some of the political ideals of ASEAN's Outlook, such as sovereign rights of countries and the rule of law, the larger is security and counter-terrorism oriented. The 2019 US-FOIP document claims to work side-by-side with the sovereign states in the Indo-Pacific. However, its strategic military and security influence can be clearly seen in the case of Australia, Japan, or Vietnam. These countries are in dynamic defence partnerships with the USA and ensure that US military presence is felt in the region.

In this context, the China factor figures again. We see US aircraft and naval sorties in South China and the Philippine sea regions almost every day. US sorties with large reconnaissance aircraft, bomber aircraft, warships and Navy passenger ships have become a common affair in the ea. While some may say it is indicative of the US exercising freedom of navigation, the counter-China symbolism is apparent.

The US FOIP strategy emphasises infrastructural development and maritime trade and countering transnational crime, restricting activities of miscreant non-state actors (especially pirates) in the Indo-Pacific, establishing networks to counter cybercrime and the use of the internet for terrorism, promoting nuclear non-proliferation, and cooperating on provisions such as naval bases, aircraft and dual-use carriers, and alternative energy sources. The ASEAN Outlook merely states the extensive detailing of US-ASEAN partnership in these aspects in a list of possible areas of cooperation. US funding for, say, programs such as the Department of State's Southeast Asia Maritime Security Initiative (SAMSI) and the Bay of Bengal Initiative (which amount to a total of US$ 356 million), or even in the form of foreign assistance provided to the region by the US Agency for International Development (which has accounted for US$ 4.5 billion), overwhelms the ASEAN call for cooperation primarily because the economic and political stature that the USA has managed to create for itself, especially with certain individual Indo-Pacific and ASEAN states. While the ASEAN Outlook clearly states it means no harm to another outlook, its emphasis on ASEAN centrality can hardly bear fruit with the presence of the US on one side and China on the other.

Reforms in the Outlook must look at not just diversifying cooperation among Indo-Pacific states but also intra-ASEAN cooperation in the Indo-Pacific. To prioritise this Outlook, ASEAN states must exchange among themselves the military or technical support they are obtaining from other countries today. They need to be assured that their stringent alliance with the ASEAN will fulfil not just their purpose in the region but their national economic and military demands too. In this context, it is also important for the ASEAN Outlook to provide frameworks for the governance of piracy, transnational criminality, and cybercrime in the region to emerge central to the security dynamics of the region. Naval interoperability systems, logistical support agreements, intelligence and surveillance networks and exchange of military personnel for training will be an essential step in this regard.

What is also important is Climate Change cooperation. It is well understood that the smaller littoral states of the Indo-Pacific, such as Fiji, Seychelles, Mauritius, or East Timor, face unprecedented sinking conditions at the hands of global warming and melting glaciers. Fijian Prime Minister Frank Bainimarama has begun planning to shift 40 Fijian villages to a greater height amidst the rising sea levels in the Indo-Pacific. In this context, the ASEAN can set up mechanisms to provide shelter to refugees of climate change from small states of the

Indo-Pacific and can facilitate an ASEAN-led rapid response or HADR (Humanitarian Assistance and Disaster Relief) mechanism for hostilities inflicted by natural calamities or climate change. This would also further the security and defence status of the entity in the region.

In this regard, in its Indo-Pacific Outlook, the ASEAN must also attempt to act as the upholder of the United Nations Convention on the Law of the Sea (UNCLOS). Its capacity to uphold norms levied on commercial and warships in the South China Sea, through political or legal action, may further its image as a rightful hegemon in the sea. In the context of both, Article 34 of the UNCLOS, which speaks of the legal status of waters which comprise of the straits used for international passage, and Article 38 on the Right of Transit passage, can be well applied by the ASEAN to assert its idea of freedom of navigation and sovereignty, while it fulfils the code of conduct in the sea, as defined by international law. Various other aspects of the UNCLOS can be well used by the entity to enhance its geopolitical agenda.

Conclusion

The ASEAN as a forum is yet to decide what it exactly is. Is it an economic cooperative among Southeast Asian nations, aiming to create a mutual economic boom and reduce inequalities? Does it wish to emerge as a hegemon in the Indo-Pacific, having countered the shenanigans of China and the USA successfully? Does it want to act as the centre of trade and maritime connectivity for the world? Or is it a legal, social, and political order for Southeast Asian nations that aims to resolve disputes and take necessary action against threats to the region? In my opinion, the ASEAN is yet to define the priority of its existence, despite its achievements. The mandate and the limited funding of the grouping will make it difficult for the entity to progress beyond its current scope, and its understaffed Secretariat bears a significant burden. The ten nations that comprise the ASEAN represent a diverse spectrum of identities and political affiliations in the forum. The economic and military capacities of member-nations also stand at the disparity. While Singapore remains one of the most developed free-market economies, Cambodia is one of the poorest nations in the world. Poverty, inequality and a lack of focus on Sustainable Development continue to ail ASEAN member countries. The inability of the ASEAN in being able to bring about the consent of all members in policymaking and to take action on issues that concern the region, in this light, can be seen as a consequence of intra-ASEAN disparities.

Suggestively, the first step ASEAN must take is to diversify sources of its funding because clearly, national contributions shall not be enough for reform and rigorous implementation of its Indo-Pacific Outlook. Secondly, the need to increase staffing of the ASEAN governing body (the Secretariat), with experts from diverse fields (which may include economists, security specialists, cyber specialists, climate experts and logistical staff), stems from the need for ASEAN to progress in its agenda. Thirdly, the ASEAN must develop a framework to enable a European Union-style customs union and promote the idea of a single market in the forum so that the economic and commercial growth of one nation state of the ASEAN directly leads to growth for the other. This can be done through the creation of Special Economic Zones (SEZs) in the Indo-Pacific, through multilateral Free-Trade Agreements or by the establishment of maritime economy initiatives such as the IORA (Indian Ocean Rim Association). Lastly, for further cooperation with the small states, the ASEAN Indo-Pacific Outlook must robustly encourage and provide support for them to adopt a Blue Economy model of governance and legislature that prioritises the preservation of their marine resources on the basis of ecosystem-based management of resources.

The ability of the ASEAN to address its internal conflicts and reach a consensus among member-nations on how to deal with the hindrances in its Indo-Pacific Strategy is yet to be determined. The bi-annual ASEAN Summit held in Thailand in November 2019 and the consequent joint statement released in March 2020 proved fruitful in charting a collective strategy on how the ASEAN would deal with COVID-19 in the region. In the context of the Indo-Pacific, the ASEAN must adopt a similar approach of discussion, debate, accommodation of dissent and rigorous implementation of the blueprint that emerges forthwith by all members. Amid the current COVID-19 pandemic, the need for increased regional and international cooperation has been realised, and the ASEAN has the potential to emerge as exemplary for cooperation around the world. This potential can only be achieved through collective action in the grouping on dealing with China and the USA, creating a joint action plan that addresses the economic inequalities in the region, and attempting to resolve them through cooperation restricted among ASEAN members itself.

REFERENCES

Acharya, Amitav (2019). Why ASEAN's Indo-Pacific Outlook Matters. East Asia Forum [online]. Available at https://www.eastasiaforum.org/2019/08/11/why-aseans-indo-pacific-outlook-matters/

ASEAN (1976). Treaty of Amity and Cooperation in Southeast Asia Indonesia. Available at https://asean.org/treaty-amity-cooperation-southeast-asia-indonesia-24-february-1976

ASEAN (2019). ASEAN Outlook on the Indo-Pacific. Available at https://asean.org/storage/2019/06/ASEAN-Outlook-on-the-Indo-Pacific_FINAL_22062019.pdf

ASEAN (2019). ASEAN's Outlook on the Indo-Pacific. Available at https://asean.org/storage/2019/06/ASEAN-Outlook-on-the-Indo-Pacific_FINAL_22062019.pdf

Department of State, United States of America (2019). A Free and Open Indo-Pacific: Advancing a Shared Vision. Available at https://www.state.gov/wp-content/uploads/2019/11/Free-and-Open-Indo-Pacific-4Nov2019.pdf

Kuo, Mercy A. (2018). The Origin of 'Indo-Pacific' as Geopolitical Construct. *The Diplomat* [online]. Available at https://thediplomat.com/2018/01/the-origin-of-indo-pacific-as-geopolitical-construct

Kurlantzick, Joshua (2012). ASEAN's Future and Asian Integration. Council on Foreign Relations [online]. Available at https://www.cfr.org/sites/default/files/pdf/2012/10/IIGG_WorkingPaper10_Kurlantzick.pdf

Parameswaran, Prashanth (2018). ASEAN's Role in a U.S. Indo-Pacific Strategy. Wilson Centre [online]. Available at https://www.wilsoncenter.org/sites/default/files/media/documents/publication/2018-09_aseans_role_parameswaran.pdf

PTI (2019). ASEAN backs India's rising role in Indo-Pacific region. *The Economic Times* [online]. Available at https://economictimes.indiatimes.com/news/defence/asean-backs-indias-rising-role-in-indo-pacific-region/articleshow/71881250.cms?from=mdr

Saha, Premesha (2019). ASEAN's Indo-Pacific outlook: An analysis. Observer Research Foundation [online]. Available at https://www.orfonline.org/expert-speak/aseans-indo-pacific-outlook-an-analysis-52542

2

India's Relations with Africa: Evaluating Changes in India's Africa Policy during COVID-19

Astha Chadha

ABSTRACT

Africa has been a key strategic partner of India through its cultural policy as well as South-South development cooperation. The tackling of the COVID-19 pandemic has been taken up by India as another opportunity to deepen its relations as well as engagement with the African nations. However, India's objectives regarding its Africa policy have been only partly successful despite several Africa-focused policies in the past few decades. This paper raises the question of what are the key trends in India's Africa policy. How have India's COVID-19 policies strengthened its relations with Africa amid the COVID-19 pandemic? In order to address these questions, this paper will employ a qualitative examination of India's policies against the coronavirus pandemic towards the African continent as well as its implications for India's foreign policy of Extended Neighbourhood under the SAGAR Doctrine of the current Modi administration. Through the empirical analysis, this paper argues that India's Africa policy, despite its intended successes, is fragmented while being challenged by the increasing presence of Chinese development projects in that continent. Thus, triangular or multilateral cooperation in Africa's development is better equipped to boost African development while positioning India as a key player in Africa. New Delhi's COVID-19 strategy has offered an immense opportunity for India to make an essential contribution in the development of Africa in the key sectors of health, infrastructure and science and technology; however, the post-pandemic strategy lacks focus and a clear blueprint towards India's strategic presence in the continent. This paper concludes that India needs to reformulate its Africa policy by engaging with more Indo-Pacific players in joint development projects through institutional mechanisms (such as AAGC) in order to give Africa an alternative route to development alongside China-led infrastructure development for its economic and political security in a post-COVID-19 world.

Keywords: *COVID-19, India, Africa, Medical Diplomacy.*

1. Introduction

India and Africa have a long-shared history of civilizational contact that has lasted through centuries and even coincided in the recent past with the engagement of Mahatma Gandhi in Africa's struggle against apartheid and imperialism, while India was fighting its own battle for independence. Even in the post-independence era, New Delhi maintained cordial relations in the continent through its huge Diaspora in Africa and through the Non-Alignment Movement (NAM), which marked a key point in the Cold War policy of the Third World. In the post-Cold War era, New Delhi's Africa policy has been founded on enhancing economic ties, cooperating on anti-terrorism initiatives, assisting peace promotion and security in Africa (Beri, 2008). However, since India adopted its path towards post-1991 liberalisation and globalization-fueled economic growth, India-Africa relations have not fructified to their optimum potential due to the lack of a proactive Africa policy in New Delhi as well as increasing political unrest in Africa. While India maintained cordial contact with Africa through business ventures, several African nations had already vanished from India's foreign policy priorities, despite their geographical proximity.

It was only in the past two decades that there has been a resurgence in India's Africa focus, with the launch of several new initiatives by the Indian government to increase its assistance and aid to African nations while also establishing New Delhi as an emerging regional power in the Indian Ocean. India's Africa focus increased during the COVID-19 pandemic; however, due to the lack of a precedent in India's Africa policy for consistency, it would be difficult to predict if India could maintain the momentum of its deepening engagement in the continent even after the pandemic. Additionally, India's objectives regarding its Africa policy have been only party successful despite several Africa-focused policies in the past two decades. This paper raises the question of the key factors driving the Africa-focused foreign policy of India in recent years. How India's COVID-19 policies are working to strengthen its relations with Africa amid the COVID-19 pandemic?

To address these questions, the next section offers a background highlighting the trends in India's Africa policy in recent decades, followed by a brief theoretical framework of the paper. The succeeding sections discuss the factors affecting India's recent upsurge in African engagement during the pandemic, offer a qualitative examination of India's policies towards the African continent as well as its implications for India's foreign policy of Extended Neighbourhood under the SAGAR Doctrine of the current Modi administration, and lastly, followed by a conclusion.

Through empirical analysis, this paper argues that India's Africa policy, despite its intended successes, is quite fragmented while being challenged by the increasing presence of Chinese development projects in the continent. Thus, triangular or multilateral cooperation in Africa's development is better equipped to boost African growth while positioning India as a key player in Africa. New Delhi's COVID-19 strategy has offered an immense opportunity for India to make an essential contribution in the development of Africa in key sectors of health, infrastructure and science and technology; however, the post-pandemic strategy lacks focus and a clear blueprint towards India's strategic presence in the continent. This paper concludes that India needs to reformulate its Africa policy by engaging with more Indo-Pacific players in joint development projects through institutional mechanisms (such as AAGC) in order to give Africa an alternative route to development alongside China-led infrastructure development for its economic and political security in a post-COVID-19 world.

2. Africa in New Delhi's Foreign Policy

South-South Cooperation to Indo-Pacific Vision

For New Delhi, Africa has been a potential partner for exemplary South-South cooperation among nations accounting for nearly 2.3 billion of the total world population. India-Africa bilateral trade amounts to US$ 70 billion with good trade relations with Nigeria, Egypt, Angola, South Africa, Ghana, etc., accompanied by US$ 7.5 billion of total Indian infrastructure development assistance to 40 Africa countries (Table 2.1).

Table 2.1: India's Select Key Development Projects in Africa

Country	*Project Name*	*Value (US$)*	*Date*
Ghana	Ghana State House/Presidential House	$ 30 mn	Nov 2008
Gambia	National Assembly Building Complex	$ 16.65 mn	Sep 2014
Rwanda	Nyaborongo Hydro Power Project	$ 80 mn	Nov 2014
Mozambique	IT Park Project	$ 25 mn	Nov 2014
Mauritius	Offshore Patrol Vessel	$ 48.5 mn	Mar 2015
Seychelles	Coastal Surveillance Radar System	$ 14.12 mn	Mar 2015
Sudan	Kosti Power Plant	$ 350 mn	Oct 2015
Zambia	Hydel Power Project	$ 29.03 mn	Apr 2016
Mauritania	Milk Processing Plant	$ 11.3 mn	May 2016
Swaziland	IT Park Project	$ 20mn	Sep 2016
Ghana	Komenda Sugar Plant	$ 35 mn	Nov 2016
Cameroon	Maize & Rice Plantation projects	$ 37.46 mn	Sep 2017
Mauritius	ENT Hospital Project	$ 24.24 mn	Mar 2018
Mauritius	Light Rail Transit Phase I·	$ 546.11 mn	Oct 2019
Niger	Mahatma Gandhi International Convention Centre	Undisclosed	Jan 2020
Mauritius	New Supreme Court Building	$ 30 mn	(In progress)
Tanzania	Water Supply Schemes to Dar-es-Salam	$ 178.13 mn	(In progress)

Source: Prepared by author from several open-access materials of Ministry of External Affairs.

The 1964 launch of the Indian Technical and Economic Cooperation (ITEC) programme aimed at human resource development saw African nations as the major beneficiaries of India's technological assistance program for South-South Cooperation (Indian Technical & Economic Cooperation, 2020). However, the 1991 economic reforms in India compelled it to 'Look East', which faded the South-South cooperation rhetoric in the new millennium (Haokip, 2011).

Naidu (2013) has noted that as Africa has garnered increasing attention due to its huge untapped economic potential, there is increased participation of nations like India and China that hold varying degrees of capabilities as well as strategic interests to invest in and develop the continent. While China is one of the dominant players in Africa's rapid development that has increased manifold under the Beijing-led BRI, India has felt the need in the past two decades to shift the basis of its Africa policy from anti-colonialism to contemporary strategic imperatives such as India-Africa economic partnership, assisting in Africa's political stability and institution-building. Amidst an increasing Chinese presence in Africa and New Delhi's fading Africa diplomacy, India initiated the Pan African e-network Project in 2009 (approx. US$ 200 million) to upgrade and spread telecommunication technology to 48 nations in the African Union, making access to education and healthcare possible in the conflict-ridden continent (Ministry of External Affairs, 2009).

Table 2.2: India's Peacekeeping Forces in Africa

Country	*UN Mission*	*Indian Forces*
Somalia	UN Assistance Mission in Somalia (UNSOM)	1
Morocco	UN Mission for the Referendum in Western Sahara (MINURSO)	2
Sudan	UN Interim Security Force for Abyei (UNISFA)	3
Cyprus	UN Peacekeeping Force in Cyprus (UNFICYP)	6
Syria	UN Disengagement Observer Force (UNDOF)	186
DRC (Congo)	UN Organization Stabilization Mission in DR of Congo (MONUSCO)	2,030
South Sudan	UN Mission in South Sudan (UNMISS)	2,423

Source: Prepared by author from several open-access materials of Ministry of External Affairs.

India presently maintains its United Nations peacekeeping forces in several African nations, with a total of 5,621 Indian personnel deployed globally as of April 2020 (Table 2.2). India's recent response to the pressing geopolitical needs has been New Delhi's Indo-Pacific vision that encompasses its own Indian Ocean policy. India's Free Open and Inclusive Indo-Pacific (FOIIP) includes the West Coast of Africa in the Eastern Indian Ocean (Chadha, 2020a). Moreover, under the Extended Neighbourhood under the SAGAR Doctrine, India aims at including African nations under the development programmes and partnerships or mutual development in the realms of trade, medical infrastructure, education, etc. Mboce (2019) has argued that amid the evolving security threats in the Indian Ocean for both New Delhi and the African member-nations of the Indian Ocean Rim Association (IORA), mutual cooperation needs to be reviewed for being insufficient to handle the emerging security crisis in the region.

India's commitment to a rule-based maritime order in the Indian Ocean and a Free and Open Indo-Pacific are the foundations of India's new pragmatic policy towards Africa since India's Indo-Pacific policy cannot be truly inclusive without accounting for the vast development potential of Africa, as well as maintaining a comprehensive policy to combat the new conventional and non-conventional security threats emanating from fragile African nations. So, what drives India's renewed interest in Africa? This paper argues that security calculations driving India's Africa policy are mainly the intensifying India-China conflict and India's own aim to be a net security provider in its extended neighbourhood. However, that also raises the question of how the security calculations driving India's present Africa policy have impacted this Africa policy, especially during the pandemic.

Pillars of India-Africa Relations towards Combating the COVID-19 Crisis

India and Africa have shared cultural and colonial history, apart from being part of substantial movements such as those related to anti-colonial struggles, non-alignment and anti-apartheid. Though the relationship slowed while India went on the path of its own development, the recent shifts in the global economy and power equations have been well-noted by both India and Africa, who embarked on a collective journey of growth through partnerships when India hosted the India-Africa Forum Summit for the first time in 2008. Africa is not only blessed with abundant natural resources, but also young human capital, with over 60 per cent of its population being under 35 years of age. Africa as a continent is estimated to reach a collective $ 3 trillion Gross Domestic Product by the end of 2020 (estimated before the pandemic).

When the pandemic began affecting parts of the world in 2020, the African continent was of key concern owing to the severe lack of adequate health infrastructure to deal with the COVID-19 crisis on a massive scale. By the third quarter of the year, Africa had collectively reported 1.4 million cases and about 35,000 deaths. As the first pillar of its pandemic outreach, the Indian government acted swiftly to not only assist Africa during the pandemic by despatching the required medicines, followed by vaccines, but also by sending medical personnel, as well as training African healthcare professionals through its ITEC programmes online (Chadha, 2021). New Delhi also aimed its COVID-19 diplomacy towards the Indian Diaspora in Africa's East and South (Ibid.).

The second pillar of India's pandemic diplomacy regarding Africa can be termed mainly as an expansion of development partnerships in the African continent with other nations. These partnerships were aimed at playing a four-fold role in India's own SAGAR (Security And Growth for All in the Region) policy—first, to establish India as a reliable development partner in the African continent alongside other players like China; second, to enhance existing and new partnerships for with other nations and emerging regional powers for like-minded development cooperation adhering to international standards in the Indo-Pacific region; third, to bring in Africa into the larger Indo-Pacific region since New Delhi sees it as encompassing the entire Indian Ocean and the east coast of Africa; and fourth, to establish the African continent as part of New Delhi's own extended neighbourhood, where it could prioritise its relations with geo-strategically important nations like Seychelles and Mauritius—both of which have been crucial for strengthening India's own security close to its maritime backyard where China maintains a considerable presence (Chadha, 2020a, 2020b).

3. Theoretical and Analytical Framework

This paper employs the International Relations theory of Realism, particularly the concept of balance of power, to examine India's COVID-19 strategy, geopolitical factors affecting India's COVID-19 process and evaluates India's key policies towards Africa in the recent decades leading up to the pandemic.

Classical realism dates back to 1939 with *The Twenty Years in Crisis* (Carr, 2016) and *Politics among Nations: The Struggle for Power and Peace* by Hans Morgenthau, which became the key for political realism after the 1950s. Classical realism assumed the flawed nature of humanity, which is power-hungry, and a constant struggle among states to increase capabilities due to their anarchic nature. The last three decades before the twenty-first century saw the emergence of Neorealism (Waltz, 1979) which brought the focus of international relations on the states as the centre point rather than on individuals, as in classical realism, because international relations are conflicting as states pursue greater power due to the anarchical characteristic of the international system. Realism as an IR theory explains the nation-state as being the centre for all decision making in a country. Realism is bound by the assumption that all nation-states are guided by national interests and try to achieve them by way of building sufficient military capabilities to guard their respective states against any threat by outside powers.

Within the realist thought, the balance of power theory, which basically is a theory of equilibrium among great powers, is based on works of Thucydides, Hobbes and Rousseau, and have been extended into the classical realist theory by Carr (1964) and Morgenthau (1963). The theory suggests that possession and concentration of military and material capabilities with the great powers are kept in check and balanced due to the major powers trying to survive and maintain their supremacy in the international system, thus restoring the equilibrium. According to the theory, balance can be achieved through internal military capacity building (when economic wealth is transformed into military prowess), forging offsetting alliances, 'passing the buck' of balancing to other states, etc. It is more plausible for the less powerful states to bandwagon or join the more powerful states or a group of states instead of balancing against them. According to Waltz (1979), the international system is under a recurring balancing phenomenon due to shifts in the relative distribution of capabilities. So, while in a bipolar international system, the power is balanced by states through internal military strengthening, in a multi-polar world, the balancing is done by states through forging of counterbalancing alliances. Thus, inherently, realists assume that states are competitive and would always prefer balancing.

In this regard, India's COVID-19 policy, through the pillars of medical diplomacy and development-based engagements, show India's foreign policy becoming more balancing in nature and expressive of India's ambition to be a greater and more significant power in the world's geopolitical calculations. With China becoming aggressive in the seas and on the borders around India, and the US policy becoming more anti-China, it has instilled a security threat for India amid the pandemic aimed at preventing China from achieving regional hegemony even if it includes counterbalancing by allying with the USA. The theory is helpful in explaining why China's strategic rival, India, is striving to mark its presence, especially in Africa, through diplomatic measures, including medical diplomacy and development partnerships. The theory helps explain how India has made health and economic security objectives a strategic driver in its COVID-19 policy.

Analytical Framework

	Key Factors through lens of Realism		Pillars of India's COVID-19 Policy		
1.	India-China conflict	→	Medical Diplomacy and		Africa (Extended
2.	India's role as net security provider	→	Development-based partnerships	→	Neighbourhood policy under the SAGAR Doctrine)

This paper analyses critical factors affecting India's Africa policy through the lens of Realism, i.e., the India-China conflict and India's aim to be a net security provider in its extended neighbourhood. It then establishes the link between these factors and their impact on the pillars of India's Africa policy during the pandemic as identified in the previous section, i.e., Medical Diplomacy and Development-based partnerships and studies the impact of these policies on India's relations with Africa through its key policy under PM Modi, i.e., the policy of Extended Neighbourhood under the SAGAR Doctrine, which complements India's larger Indo-Pacific vision.

4. India-China Conflict and Impact on Relations with Africa

India-China relations post-independence were cordial as India's first Prime Minister, Nehru, eventually joined the Non-Aligned Movement (NAM). However, the 1962 military action by China took India by surprise, while only a handful of African nations took a pro-India stance on Beijing's military offensive (Naidu, 2013). The choice between India and China was a difficult one but several African nations sided with China over its aggressive anti-imperialist stance as several global powers like the USA and the UK voiced support for India against Chinese aggression (Ibid.). While India proceeded to gradually mend relations with both African nations as well as China diplomatically, Beijing had already pioneered its Africa diplomacy and economic cooperation by the early 2000s while India began taking measured steps for its Africa policy in 2003 through LoCs, and in 2008 through the India-Africa Forum Summit to be held once every three years, quite similar to China's Forum on China-Africa Cooperation (FOCAC) established in 2000.

The recent India-China clashes along the Line of Actual Control (LAC) in 2013 (Depsang) and 2017 (Doklam) have not only impacted New Delhi's strategic partnership with Beijing but has instilled a deepening mistrust among the two nuclear powers as more clashes have followed during the COVID-19 pandemic (Chadha, 2021). Amid this worsening security situation, India and China have been ramping up their military presence on land and in the seas while seeking partnerships with a different set of like-minded nations—China through its BRI, and India through its Indo-Pacific vision alongside Japan, the USA, Australia, Canada, and European countries. The cumulative impact on Africa has been that India and China have not cooperated on their Africa policy, and African nations while welcoming India's development aid, have wholeheartedly participated in the BRI framework due to their urgent infrastructure needs.

Economic Partnership and Investments in Africa

In 2000, China launched the Forum on China-Africa Cooperation (FOCAC) at the ministerial level, held every three years between Beijing and 53 African states. Within a few years of expanded engagement, the 3rd FOCAC (2006) in Beijing and the 6th FOCAC (2015) in Johannesburg were upgraded to summit meetings (Forum on China-Africa Cooperation, n.d.). The 2012 Beijing Declaration at the fifth edition of the FOCAC called for a 'reasonable' global order stating, "The balance of power in the world is moving towards more of an equilibrium" (Forum on China-Africa Cooperation, 2012).

By 2009, China had not only overtaken the USA and Europe as Africa's largest trading partner, but its total trade with Africa in 2015 also stood at US$ 300 billion from US$ 10 billion in 2000 (Ibid.). By 2012, China's FDI (Foreign Direct Investment) in Africa reached US$ 15.3 billion, with Chinese companies increasing from 2,000 to about

Table 4.1: Forum on China-Africa Cooperation (FOCAC) (China's policy towards Africa)

Meetings	*Theme/Objectives*	*Date*
FOCAC I	Developing new, stable long-term partnerships	Oct 2000
FOCAC II	Pragmatic and Action-Oriented Cooperation	Dec 2003
FOCAC III Summit	Bilateral visits, Trade, Investment, Youth exchange, Agriculture	Nov 2006
FOCAC IV	Sharm el-Sheikh declaration and human resources development, agriculture, infrastructure development, investment, and trade	Nov 2009
FOCAC V	Beijing Declaration for a "more just and reasonable international order", Economic cooperation, trade, people-to-people and cultural exchanges	Jul 2012
FOCAC VI Summit	Xi Jinping's "New type of international relations", peacekeeping, conflict resolution and humanitarian intervention in Africa	Dec 2015
FOCAC VII Summit	China-Africa solidarity and cooperation, BRI in Africa, US$ 15 billion of grants, interest-free loans, and concessional loans to Africa	Sep 2018

Source: Prepared by author from FOCAC Mechanism website and open-access information.

10,000 between 2012 and 2017 in fifty African countries (Jayaram et al., 2017). In the next three years, the China-Africa cooperation moved from an Africa-oriented China policy to integration of Africa in China's more extensive view of "new type of international relations" as stated by President Xi Jinping in his United Nations General Assembly high-level debate in 2015, affirming his support for greater representation and say of the developing countries, especially African countries, in the international governance system (*FOCAC Mechanisms*, n.d.; *Spotlight: China-Africa Ties Testify to New Type of International Relations*, n.d.; Table 4.1). The 2018 FOCAC Summit further gathered African support for the second edition of the BRI, with President Xi Jinping stating that "Inadequate infrastructure is believed to be the biggest bottleneck to Africa's development" (Reuters, 2018).

Against this backdrop, India's key challenge in Africa has been a lack of first-mover diplomacy. In 2008, the Indian government launched the India-Africa Forum Summit to set frameworks for India's Africa policy (Table 4.2). India-Africa total trade stood only at US$ 6.8 billion in 2003 when India launched concessional lines of credit (LoCs) towards increased economic aid for development projects in agriculture, railways, energy projects, etc. (Chakrabarty, 2021). However, while China has retained its spot as the top trading partner (value of trade in goods) of Africa, India moved from being the continent's second-largest partner behind China in 2015 at US$ 51.1 billion and is currently standing at the third spot in 2018 at US$ 76.9 billion. India's 180 LoC projects in Africa amount to about US$ 10.5 billion (Ibid.).

Table 4.2: India-Africa Forum Summit (India's Policy Towards Africa)

Summits	*Main Outcomes/Areas of Cooperation*	*Date*
IAFS I	14 countries of Africa chosen by the African Union (AU) participated to discuss India-Africa cooperation in agriculture trade, peace, security, science and technology	Apr 2008
IAFS II	15 countries of Africa chosen by the AU; US$ 15 bn LoCs for next 3 years by India and US$ 700 mn for new institutions and 22,000 training positions; US$ 2 mn for AU Mission in Somalia (AMISOM); discussion on agriculture, trade, capacity building and promoting businesses	May 2011
IAFS III	Delhi Declaration; US$ 600 mn for development projects in African countries; sustainable development, agriculture, access to energy, education and skill development, blue economy, peace and security	Oct 2015

Source: Prepared by author from several open-access materials of Ministry of External Affairs.

India-China Conflict and Africa's Infrastructure Development in Recent Decade

India's approach towards the 2013 China-led Belt and Road Initiative has been not to be part of the ambitious project since it views the Beijing project as a threat to the sovereignty of nations, such as its flagship China-Pakistan Economic Corridor (CPEC), which passes through disputed territory in Kashmir (Bajpai, 2017). The key SLOCs (Sea Lines of Communication) in the Indian Ocean are crucial for the global energy trade but are now a greater geopolitical challenge for India as it seeks to balance the Chinese naval presence in its own strategic maritime backyard. Moreover, the China-led BRI has been actively engaging in development projects in several African nations, but not without concerns regarding the financial burden and lack of transparency in funding for these development projects (Onjala, 2018). As more African countries are debt-ridden with huge unpaid Chinese loans, India has steadily been earning goodwill for financing demand-driven projects in poor African nations.

New Delhi unveiled the AAGC (Asia Africa Growth Corridor) in 2017 along with Japan for a quality infrastructure initiative as a counter to the BRI. The AAGC was an outcome of the confluence of India's SAGAR doctrine to provide security and development in the neighbourhood, as well as Japan's EPQI (Extended Partnership for Quality Infrastructure) initiative, that clearly distinguished itself from the Chinese BRI with its emphasis on quality infrastructure based on international norms.[1] The AAGC aimed at promoting how the benefit of an India-based partnership to the African continent is not only better technology and reliable infrastructure from Japan but also more significant employment opportunities with the AAGC relying on local labour instead of bringing workers from home, as done under the Beijing BRI model (Chadha, 2020a; Thankachan, 2017).

The COVID-19 pandemic exacerbated the need for urgent health infrastructure development, besides required economic projects in Africa. The pandemic provided a new opportunity to New Delhi to establish new strategic partnerships in the extended neighbourhood through more trilateral and multilateral agreements with nations seeking to invest in Africa's health, infrastructure and technology (Chadha, 2021). Several European countries began talks with India to unveil joint development projects in Africa while acknowledging India's goodwill created by funding demand-driven projects. India also extended US$ 11 billion LoCs to 41 African nations in 2020, making Africa the largest recipient of India's foreign aid. India, along with Morocco (among Africa's five largest economies), launched the India-Arab energy forum in July 2021 to undertake a trilateral joint rural electrification project in several African nations (Chaudhury, 2021a).

5. India's Role as Net Security Provider in its Extended Neighbourhood

Having established India's aim to be a "leading power, and not just a balancing power" in 2015 during the Indian Foreign Secretary's address in Singapore, New Delhi reshaped its foreign policy to accommodate its own aim to be a net security provider in the extended neighbourhood (MEA of India, 2015). Since net security provider would mean India would have to commit more to its global role, Indian PM Modi's 2018 speech in the Parliament of Uganda laid down ten guiding principles of India's cooperation with Africa. Unlike the previous pan-Africa policy of New Delhi, PM Modi adopted a more individual state-priority based engagement with nations in the African continent, stating "India will work with you, and for you" with a focus on agriculture, FDI, trade, security, counter-terrorism, climate change, digitalization and infrastructure (MEA of India, 2018).

Even during the COVID-19 pandemic, India's Africa engagement falls within these ten guiding principles as New Delhi committed itself to combat the pandemic in and beyond its extended neighbourhood through the collective collaboration for health security digitally. Early in March 2020, India's e-ITEC training sessions were aimed at healthcare assistance for medical personnel and professionals of the developing world, of which close to two-fifths were African professionals. Besides, there were programmes for various nations, with about 40 per cent of the participants being African medical personnel and professionals (Indian Technical & Economic Cooperation, 2020). After 18 new African diplomatic missions were established in 2019, India announced four new embassies by 2021 in the continent (BBC News, 2020).

Since the COVID-19 pandemic affected developing nations more, India stepped up into its role as a responsible regional power by extending humanitarian assistance to African countries despite surging infection domestically. PM Modi launched Mission Sagar (SAGAR—Security and Growth for All in the Region) to provide medical equipment and medicines to West Africa as well as African nations in the Indian Ocean (Ministry of External Affairs, 2020). Meanwhile, India has been employing its *Atmanirbhar Bharat* (Self-Reliant India Initiative) and Make in India policy to make necessary medical supplies available to Africa besides other nations. India's vaccine assistance (Vaccine Maitri Initiative) saw New Delhi extending medical supplies of 150 metric tonnes to 25 African states while providing over 25 million India-made vaccines to 42 African countries. Even during the second wave of infections in mid-2021, India continued to supply vaccines with

Africa under the global COVAX vaccine-sharing facility (Chaudhury, 2021b).

The maiden India-Africa Defence Ministers meeting was held in February 2020 on the sidelines of the Defence Expo 2020.[2] That year also saw India's External Affairs Minister prioritizing Seychelles and Comoros in combating both the COVID-19 pandemic as well as increased securitization of the Indian Ocean by China (Bhaumik, 2020; Press Trust of India, 2020). However, India still faces some roadblocks in its defence relations with African nations that clearly seek greater economic engagement with India. For instance, the African Indian Ocean island nation, Seychelles, despite its geographical proximity to India, does not have direct trade routes with India (Chadha, 2020b). India pledged military training and capacity building for Africa's military personnel in India. The Ministry of External Affairs in India, while discussing development projects in Burkina Faso, Mali, Nigeria, Niger, and Uganda in April 2020, also signed a Memorandum of Understanding on space exploration with Nigeria, with India eventually aiming to enter the remote sensing domain in the country (Chaudhury, 2020b, 2020a). The e-inauguration of an ENT facility in Mauritius was coupled with telemedicine and online training to medical professionals in Mauritius (Chadha, 2021; Chaudhury, 2020a; Hindustan Times, 2020). As recent as August 2020, India announced a plan to execute the Free Trade Agreement with Africa in order to capitalize on the vast trade opportunities in the continent.

While several developed nations continued to support patents for vaccine development, India partnered with South Africa to lead the developing world's voice for a patent waiver from the World Trade Organization to enable local production of COVID-19 vaccines in 2021 (Chaudhury, 2021b). Renewing the momentum of its Africa policy, India's External Affairs Minister, S. Jaishankar, visited Kenya in June 2021 for the India-Kenya Joint Commission to discuss bilateral development projects, healthcare assistance and maritime security in the Indian Ocean, with the joint statement reiterating prioritization of "Manufacturing, Affordable Housing, Universal Health and Food Security, and underlining that India will further build upon its partnership taking these into account" (MEA of India, 2021).

New Delhi's relations with African island-nations, especially

Mauritius, Seychelles and Comoros, are crucial for protecting India's national economic and security interests, which is reflected in New Delhi's increased development aid to these nations since 2015. The pandemic assistance created a massive momentum for India's Africa policy, which could set the stage for the next step towards deepening India-Africa ties based on economic, defence and security partnerships. However, with new emerging security threats during the second wave of COVID-19 infections, the recent US withdrawal from Afghanistan, the rise of the Taliban and increased terrorist activities in both Africa and Asia, burgeoning maritime security threats are the new reality that India needs to tackle with increased cooperation with Africa in the post-pandemic world.

Conclusion

This paper examined key factors affecting India's policy towards Africa through the lens of Realism, i.e., the India-China conflict and India's aim to be a net security provider in the extended neighbourhood. It showed the impact of these factors in shaping India's COVID-19 policy based on India's foreign policy in its neighbourhood through PM Modi's Extended Neighbourhood policy under the SAGAR Doctrine. India's Africa policy was founded on its deepening triangular partnerships in Africa, which increased during the pandemic, and secondly, on India's healthcare diplomacy to assist African nations during the COVID-19 pandemic.

The India-China conflict has sent their bilateral relations for a toss while also impacting Africa's priorities for a mutually beneficial economic, strategic partnership for its development. While China remains Africa's top trading and investment partner, India is gradually catching up as a key collaborator in the continent, earning goodwill for its demand-driven projects in African nations burdened with huge Chinese debt at the commencement of the COVID-19 pandemic. While China has increased aggression close to India's borders and seas in 2021, India has retaliated by employing its diplomacy amid the COVID-19 pandemic to build development-based partnerships among nations and has become closer to the USA and other like-minded Indo-Pacific powers. Though India's financial capabilities amid the pandemic are much more limited than China's, India aims to assert its position as an influential power in the Indian Ocean by forging new partnerships in Africa during the pandemic with third world nations.

India's role as a net security provider is more apparent as it explored medical diplomacy and development-based partnerships to extend its influence further in African nations that are more committed to India-based development than in the past. Against the backdrop of constantly changing relations among states and high geopolitical volatility, aiming at a multi-faceted and robust relationship with Africa post-pandemic will help India establish clear visibility and significance in the Indian Ocean region and even beyond to unlock the true potential of this erstwhile South-South partnership, now within India's larger Indo-Pacific vision through the SAGAR doctrine. India's presently fragmented Africa policy and untapped potential of its Africa relations are insufficient to deal with the complex security challenges in the Indo-Pacific, and partnering with other like-minded nations in Africa could synergize India's Africa policy while establishing New Delhi in its desired position as the net security provider in its extended neighbourhood.

Overall, despite its intended successes, India's Africa policy is very fragmented while being challenged by the increasing presence of Chinese development projects in the continent. A new development has been on the defence front, with the India-Africa defence Forum being established further to enhance synergy between IAFS and Africa's Agenda 2063. Triangular or multilateral cooperation in Africa's development is better equipped to boost African growth while positioning India as a key player in Africa. New Delhi's COVID-19 strategy has offered an immense opportunity for India to make an essential contribution in the development of Africa in key sectors of health, infrastructure and science and technology; however, the post-pandemic strategy lacks focus and a clear blueprint towards India's strategic presence in the continent. India needs to continue the reformulation and updating of its Africa policy based on the individual needs of African nations by engaging with more Indo-Pacific players in joint development projects through institutional mechanisms (such as AAGC) in order to give Africa an alternative route to development alongside China-led infrastructure development for its economic and political security in a post-COVID-19 world.

NOTES

1. Aizawa (2019) has noted the transition of Japan's Partnership for Quality Infrastructure (PQI) in 2015 to EPQI in 2017, to clearly differentiate between Asian Infrastructure Investment Bank (AIIB, which is majorly Beijing-controlled), and Japan's US$ 200 billion Indo-Pacific infrastructure initiative that would emphasize higher quality and adherence to international standards (Aizawa, 2019).
2. The first India-Africa Defence Ministers meeting at India's Defence Expo 2020 was the long-awaited next step for India-Africa military ties. Indian military vehicle makers supplied 1,200 vehicles to six African nations in 2015, with the major recipients being Zimbabwe Defence Forces, Tanzanian People's Defence Force, four African armies in UN Multidimensional Integrated Stabilization Mission in Mali (MINUSMA), etc. (Ranjan, 2016)

REFERENCES

Aizawa, M. (2019). Sustainable development through quality infrastructure: emerging focus on quality over quantity. *Journal of Mega Infrastructure & Sustainable Development*, 1(2), 171–187. https://doi.org/10.1080/24724718.2019.1706922

Bajpai, K. (2017). Narendra Modi's Pakistan and China Policy: Assertive Bilateral Diplomacy, Active Coalition Diplomacy. *International Affairs*, 93(1), 69–91.

BBC News. (2020). *Narendra Modi: India pledges $600m to help Africa*. BBC News. https://www.bbc.com/news/world-asia-india-34664626

Beri, R. (2008). India's Africa policy in the postcold war Era: An assessment. Https://Doi.Org/10.1080/09700160308450084, 27(2), 216–232. https://doi.org/10.1080/09700160308450084

Bhaumik, A. (2020). *S. Jaishankar in Seychelles, Doval in Colombo: India ups outreach to Indian Ocean region to counter China. Deccan Herald*. https://www.deccanherald.com/national/s-jaishankar-in-seychelles-doval-in-colombo-india-ups-outreach-to-indian-ocean-region-to-counter-china-920645.html

Carr, E. H. (2016). *The Twenty Years' Crisis, 1919-1939*. M. Cox (ed.). 1st edn. Palgrave Macmillan UK.

Chadha, A. (2020a). *India's Strategy towards Japan & FOIP amid Regional Transformations: Analysis from the Realist and Constructivist Perspectives* [Ritsumeikan Asia Pacific University]. https://doi.org/http://doi.org/10.34382/00013844

——(2020b). *India and the Seychelles: Economics First, Defense Later. The Diplomat*. https://thediplomat.com/2020/12/india-and-the-seychelles-economics-first-defense-later/

——(2021). India's COVID-19 Strategy and implications for its relations in the Indian Ocean. *Ritsumeikan Journal of Asia Pacific Studies*, 39(1), 81–104.

Chakrabarty, M. (2021). India-Africa relations: Partnership, COVID-19 setback and the way forward. Observer Research Foundation. https://www.orfonline.org/expert-speak/india-africa-relations-partnership-covid19-setback-way-forward/#_ednref23

Chaudhury, D. R. (2020a). India continues to support Mauritius to contain Covid. *The Economic Times*. https://economictimes.indiatimes.com/news/politics-and-nation/india-continues-to-support-mauritius-to-contain-covid/articleshow/75920352.cms

—— (2020b). *India to despatch key medicines to 25 African states on goodwill mission. The Economic Times.* https://economictimes.indiatimes.com/news/politics-and-nation/india-to-despatch-key-medicines-to-25-african-states-on-goodwill-mission/articleshow/75422868.cms?from=mdr

—— (2021a). India-Morocco to explore joint electrification projects in Africa; focus on renewables. *The Economic Times.* https://economictimes.indiatimes.com/industry/renewables/india-morocco-to-explore-joint-electrification-projects-in-africa-focus-on-renewables/articleshow/84612759.cms?from=mdr

—— (2021b, August 7). India's burgeoning engagements with Africa. *The Economic Times.* https://economictimes.indiatimes.com/news/india/indias-burgeoning-engagements-with-africa/articleshow/85121299.cms?from=mdr

Forum on China-Africa Cooperation. (n.d.). *FOCAC Mechanisms.* Forum on China-Africa Cooperation. Retrieved October 26, 2021, from http://www.focac.org/eng/ltjj_3/ltjz/

—— (2012). *FOCAC Beijing Declaration calls for more just and reasonable international order.* Forum on China-Africa Cooperation. http://www.focac.org/eng/ljhy_1/dwjbzjjhys/hyqk/t954303.htm

Haokip, T. (2011). India's Look East Policy. *South Asian Survey*, 18(2), 239–257. https://doi.org/10.1177/0971523113513368

Hindustan Times. (2020). India sends equipment, personnel to Mauritius to contain oil spill - India news - *Hindustan Times*.. https://www.hindustantimes.com/india-news/india-sends-equipment-personnel-to-mauritius-to-contain-oil-spill/story-I3NtjaMPJT1Wso85ljTmlN.html

Indian Technical & Economic Cooperation. (2020). *ITEC/:Indian Technical and Economic Cooperation.* Indian Technical & Economic Cooperation Programme. https://itecgoi.in/index

Jayaram, K., Kassiri, O., & Yuan Sun, I. (2017). *The closest look yet at Chinese economic engagement in Africa.* https://www.mckinsey.com/featured-insights/middle-east-and-africa/the-closest-look-yet-at-chinese-economic-engagement-in-africa

Mboce, H. N. (2019). India–Africa Co-Operation on Maritime Security: Need for Deeper Engagement. Https://Doi.Org/10.1080/09700161.2019.1623496, 43(4), 261–277. https://doi.org/10.1080/09700161.2019.1623496

MEA of India. (2015). IISS Fullerton Lecture by Dr. S. Jaishankar, Foreign Secretary in Singapore. Ministry of External Affairs of India. https://www.mea.gov.in/Speeches-Statements.htm?dtl/25493/iiss+fullerton+lecture+by+ dr+ s+ jaishankar+foreign+secretary+in+singapore

—— (2018). Prime Minister's address at Parliament of Uganda during his State Visit to Uganda. Ministry of External Affairs of India. https://mea.gov.in/Speeches-Statements.htm?dtl/30152/Prime+Ministers+address+at+Parliament+ of+ Uganda+during+his+State+Visit+to+Uganda

—— (2021). India-Kenya Joint Statement on the Visit of External Affairs Minister to Kenya (June 12-14, 2021). Ministry of External Affairs of India. https://www.mea.gov.in/bilateral-documents.htm?dtl/33918/IndiaKenya_ Joint_ Statement_on_ the_ Visit_of_External_Affairs_Minister_ to_ Kenya_June_ 1214_ 2021

—— (2009). *Pan African e-Network Project (PAENP).* Government of India.

—— (2020). Mission Sagar: India's helping hand across the Indian Ocean. Ministry of External Affairs, India. https://mea.gov.in/press-releases.htm?dtl/32678/Mission_Sagar_Indias_helping_hand_across_the_Indian_Ocean

Naidu, G. V. C. (2013). India, Africa and the Indian Ocean. Http://Dx.Doi.Org/10.1080/19480881.2013.847557, 9(2), 189–207. https://doi.org/10.1080/19480881.2013.847557

Onjala, J. (2018). China's development loans and the threat of debt crisis in Kenya. *Development Policy Review*, 36, O710–O728. https://doi.org/10.1111/DPR.12328

Press Trust of India. (2020). Seychelles holds "particular priority" for India in fight against the Covid-19: S Jaishankar. *Times of India*. https://timesofindia.indiatimes. com/india/seychelles-holds-particular-priority-for-india-in-fight-against-the-covid-19-s-jaishankar/articleshow/79447030.cms

Ranjan, S. (2016). India–Africa defence cooperation against the backdrop of the 'Make in India' initiative. Http://Dx.Doi.Org/10.1080/10246029.2016.1225586, 25(4), 407–419. https://doi.org/10.1080/10246029.2016.1225586

Reuters. (2018, September 3). China's Xi says funds for Africa not for "vanity projects." *Reuters*. https://www.reuters.com/article/china-africa/chinas-xi-says-funds-for-africa-not-for-vanity-projects-idUSL3N1VO018

Spotlight: China-Africa ties testify to new type of international relations. (n.d.). Retrieved October 26, 2021, from http://www.focac.org/eng/ljhy_1/dwjbzjjhys_1/pw/t1320675.htm

Thankachan, S. (2017). Japan's "Free and Open Indo-Pacific Strategy": Reality before the rhetoric? *Maritime Affairs: Journal of the National Maritime Foundation of India*, 13(2), 84–91. https://doi.org/10.1080/09733159.2017.1414831

Waltz, K.N. (1979). Theory of International Politics. In *Random House*. Random House.

3

China's Strategic Gameplay and the Indo-Pacific Region

Gargi Sharma

ABSTRACT

In the last couple of months, the world faced a deadly pandemic that killed over twenty-five million people and brought even the most powerful and rapidly growing economies to a standstill. However, one country whose economy has not stopped growing, and that is China. In fact, in these mean times when other countries are coming together in order to support each other, China's neighbours have seen significant changes in its recent behaviour. It has turned more hostile and aggressive towards other nations.

Some countries like the USA and Australia called for an investigation into the origin of the COVID-19 pandemic. China fears that the investigation could damage its reputation globally; therefore, in an attempt to cover up and create strategic flashpoints, the Asian Dragon started lashing out at all countries. However, this aggression is not new. Its neighbours have faced it multiple times in the past seven decades. This aggressive avatar also has its roots in the history of China.

However, this growing aggression is being taken very seriously now because we are entering a new era of greater geopolitical realignment in the world order where China is trying to replace the USA as a world hegemon. As a result, Chinese aggression is gradually bringing the countries in the Indo-Pacific together and strengthening their ties. The countries are also compelled to make changes in their policies towards China. This paper looks into its complex history in order to find the reasons for its recurring aggression towards the outside world. It also analyses how this aggression is remoulding the Indo-Pacific and how the coming together of countries against China may impact the world order.

Keywords: *Indo-Pacific, Chinese belligerence, COVID-19, QUAD, multilateral cooperation, diplomacy, neighbours*

Introduction

The year 2020 witnessed a global pandemic that affected billions of lives and brought even the most powerful and rapidly growing economies to a standstill. The virus unleashed a miserable health crisis, social disruption, and economic devastation on the world. China's Wuhan was the city where the transmission is said to have started. Some countries also accused China of manufacturing the COVID-19 virus, but ironically, China was also quick to "manage to suppress local outbreaks and return to some form of normalcy"[1] (Krishnan, 2020). Moreover, in these mean times when other countries came together in order to support each other, China's neighbours have seen significant changes in its recent behaviour. It has turned more hostile and aggressive towards the other nations.

China's Assertive Behaviour Against Neighbours

Along with the Sino-India border, this aggression was also seen in the East, South China Sea, and Indo-Pacific region in 2020. China was breathing fire on its neighbours, and it had tense geopolitical confrontations with a growing array of its neighbours. It clashed with India in areas near Pangong Tso and Galwan Valley in one of the worst border flare-ups in decades. The two countries have been fighting the worst border conflict in four decades in Eastern Ladakh, with the India-China border witnessing bloodshed for the first time since 1975. The armies of India and China engaged in violent standoffs on the Himalayan borders in the first quarter of 2020, which also led to the killing of 20 Indian soldiers[2] in Galwan Valley in Ladakh. The number of Chinese casualties was kept unrevealed.

In December 2020, the Indian External Affairs Minister, S. Jaishankar, delivered a statement that "India is probably at the most difficult phase of its relationship with China certainly in the last three-four decades. China is India's second trade partner after the USA. We engaged with each other in pretty much every domain. So, the direction of the ties probably was positive. Despite having several agreements, the People's Liberation Army (PLA) has literally brought tens of thousands of soldiers in full military preparation mode right up to the Line of Actual Control in Ladakh. Naturally, the relationship would be profoundly disturbed by this" (Basu, 2020).[3]

Figure 1: Galwan Valley: China and India Clash

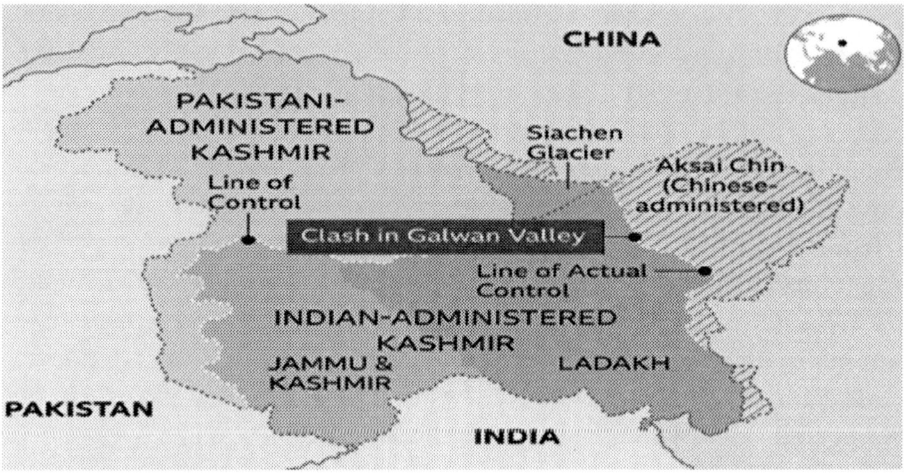

Source: BBC Asia, 2019

Vietnam, Malaysia, the Philippines, Taiwan, and Brunei have territorial claims in the South China Sea. China also claims almost all the waters as historical rights based upon the "nine-dash line". In the first quarter of 2020, there were reports of escalated standoffs of the Chinese navy with Vietnam and Malaysia[4] in the South China Sea and pressure on Taiwan with night-time drills in the Taiwan Strait (Ananthalakshmi *et.al.*, 2020). China has been accused of bullying its neighbours and attempting to build a "maritime empire" by the USA, which has carried out patrols close to Chinese islands throughout the Obama and Trump administrations. In January 2021, when Biden was sworn in as President, China responded by passing a law "permitting the coastguard to open fire on foreign vessels, demolishing foreign structures on claimed reefs, to board and inspect foreign vessels in China-claimed waters".[5] The US Navy responded by deploying the US aircraft carrier group in the South China Sea to promote the "freedom of the seas".

As part of its 'shadow trade war',[6] China also attempted to threaten its close trade partner, Australia, with its virus-weakened economy with boycotts of wine, beef, barley, and Chinese students when Australia demanded an investigation about the origin of the virus. This step deteriorated the "China-Australia relationship"[7] and brought Australia even closer to other countries that are also facing the brunt of Chinese belligerence. There has been a bitter trade war with the USA since Trump entered office, and it is expected to stay the same throughout the Biden presidency. Several rifts occurred in the South China Sea, which has angered the USA. In May 2020, a US vessel conducting routine operations was expelled by the Chinese navy in the South China Sea waters. As a result, in June this year, the US Mission to the United Nations formally submitted a note arguing that China's maritime claims in the South China Sea are "inconsistent with international laws"[8] (Mohan, 2020). The USA formally rejected China's "historical rights" claims in the South China Sea. Meanwhile, China's "wolf warrior" diplomats—a moniker taken from a particularly nationalistic Rambo-Esque movie—engaged in a vigorous cyber campaign to defend Communist Party interests and offer thinly veiled threats if countries drifted away from the "correct stance" on important issues.

Salami Slicing at Work

China's 'Salami Slicing'[9] strategy was highlighted by Indian Army Chief General Bipin Rawat after the Doklam standoff when he asserted, "India cannot afford to let its guard down against China (Dutta, 2017). As far as northern adversaries are concerned, the flexing of muscle has started. The salami slicing, taking over territory in a very gradual manner, and testing our limits of threshold is something we have to be wary about and remain prepared for situations emerging which could gradually emerge into conflict." Despite the region being far removed from any population centre, the Doklam plateau is of great significance to India as it "slopes down to the Siliguri Corridor which is a narrow strip of Indian territory dividing the Indian mainland from its North-Eastern states" (Macaes, 2019).[10] China was spotted constructing a road in the area in 2017, which was condemned by India as it was an unacceptable change to the status quo. If China would occupy the plateau, it could block off the corridor and isolate India's North-Eastern region from the mainland.

With the aid of its expansionist policy, China has been expanding its territorial jurisdiction both in territorial and maritime regions at the expense of its neighbours in the last couple of years and has successfully acquired Tibet and doubled the Chinese territory in 1962,

Figure 2: Salami Slicing in Arunachal Pradesh

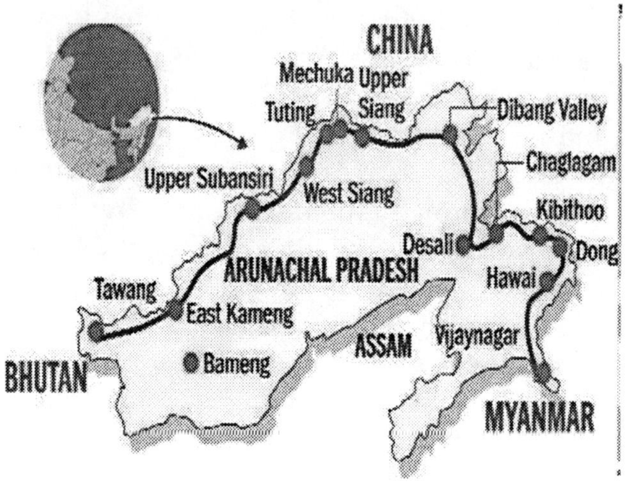

Source: The Viyug, 2020.

Figure 3: Cabbage Strategy in Paracel Islands, South China Sea

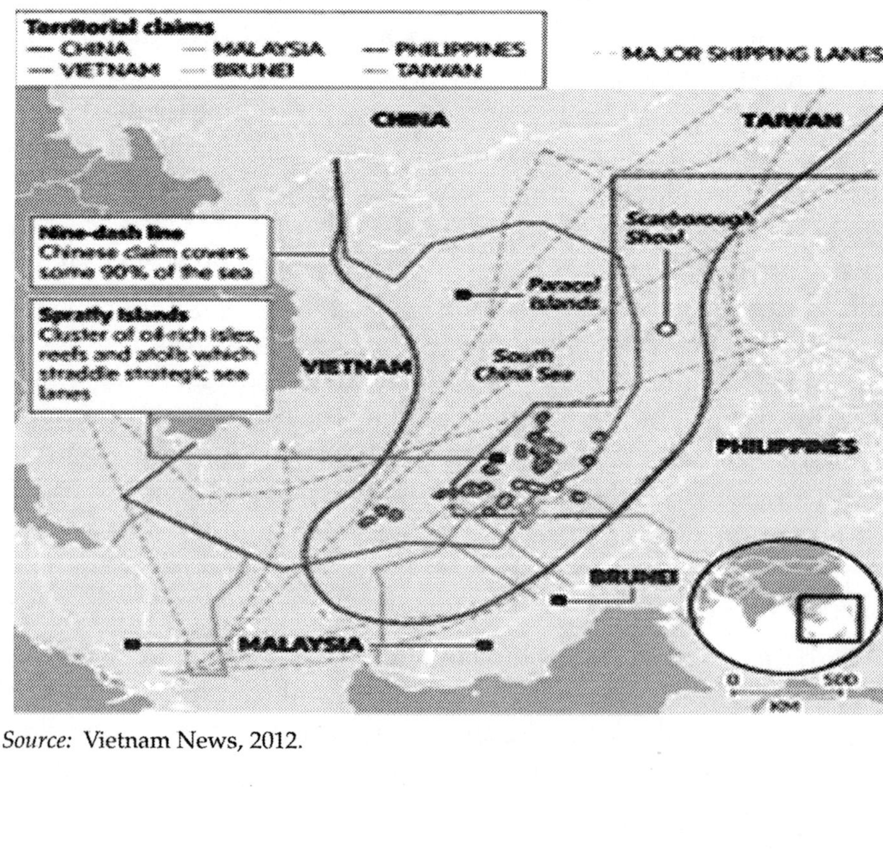

Source: Vietnam News, 2012.

then captured Aksai Chin after the attack on India in the 1962 war and annexed Paracel Islands in 1974 from Vietnam. The strategy is still at work in some places, including India's Arunachal Pradesh, which China calls 'South Tibet' and the Japanese 'Senkaku Island'. It is also known as the 'Cabbage Strategy' in some areas of the South China Sea.

China's Troubled History

China's relationship is getting worse not just with India but with other neighbouring and distant countries. Interestingly one can catch a glimpse of Chinese assertiveness and hostility at present from its history. China, which appears to be a mega-power and aspires to be a regional and global hegemon, has a troubled past. It was in a much better state in terms of transportation, production, military, and trade and possessed much better technological capacities and capabilities than the advanced imperialist nations around the 12th century[11] (Murthy, 2020). The Asian dragon had double the production capacity of steel than England;[12] however, despite being powerful, prosperous, and advanced, the Chinese empires never expected any threats from the outside world and did not work enough to strengthen their security measures which in turn helped the imperial powers like England and Japan to pave their way into the Chinese land (Murthy, 2020).

The colonial powers even went on to deploy dubious methods like using opium to conquer the nation when they could not do so with the help of the military. The kingdom tried to resist later, but the last Chinese monarchy under the Qing dynasty collapsed in 1912, leading to a weak republic. Japan took advantage of the situation and led the country to its worst position in history. The land that used to flourish at one point in time was now on its knees. The humiliation, poverty, and famine caused by the colonialist powers gave birth to the communist movement, which would later shape the country's policy in the future. Communist China, under Mao Tse Tung's leadership, cocooned itself and focussed on rebuilding the country's economy, infrastructure, and military.

When it opened itself back to the world, it brought an assertive and aggressive approach to avoid the repetition of history. In the last few decades, China has put huge investments into numerous countries in the disguise of its Belt and Road Initiative to connect to the outside world and to spread its influence all over the globe. It had exercised aggression not just on the Indo-China borders but also in the South China Sea and in the Indo-Pacific region with the construction of artificial islands to extend its Exclusive Economic Zone and claiming the rights of those islands which the Japanese had occupied in the past and even exercising military power to assert its claims. In the wake of becoming the greatest superpower, China's leadership took the "Great Leap Forward"[13] in the late 1950s to surpass industrial countries like Great Britain in production (Pandeya, 2020). Unfortunately, the plan failed miserably, leading to the most considerable artificial starvation period in human history and taking millions of lives. To contain the backlash, the leadership diverted attention by waging war against India in 1962 in the name of "China's rightful retaliation against India's three years of armed intrusion"[14] between 1958 and 1961 (Pandeya, 2020). Even today, China is aspiring to rule the world and become a world superpower but simultaneously faces several internal and external challenges.

Indo-Pacific: Origin and Significance

The term 'Indo-Pacific' is not really new to India, as the Indian Maritime Doctrine referred to "the shift in global maritime focus from the Atlantic-Pacific combine to the Pacific-Indian"[15] in 2004 (Scott, 2012), but the term gained momentum three years later when it was used by former Japanese PM Shinzo Abe in the strategic domain for the first time in 2007 to denote "maritime space comprising the Indian Ocean and the Western Pacific. Littoral to it are the states of Asia (including Western Asia/Middle East) and eastern Africa".[16] He referred to the region during his speech in the Indian Parliament as 'Confluence of the two seas' featuring the interconnectedness of the Pacific and the Indian oceans (Banerjee, 2020).

The region holds a greater strategic, geopolitical, and economic significance as two-thirds of the world's total trade volume passes through this region; some of the emerging economies (including India, China, South Korea, Japan, etc.) are highly dependent on the region for maritime trade, resources, and energy supply,[17] and it also comprises several chokepoints and egresses; hence, security becomes

Figure 4: From Asia-Pacific to Indo-Pacific

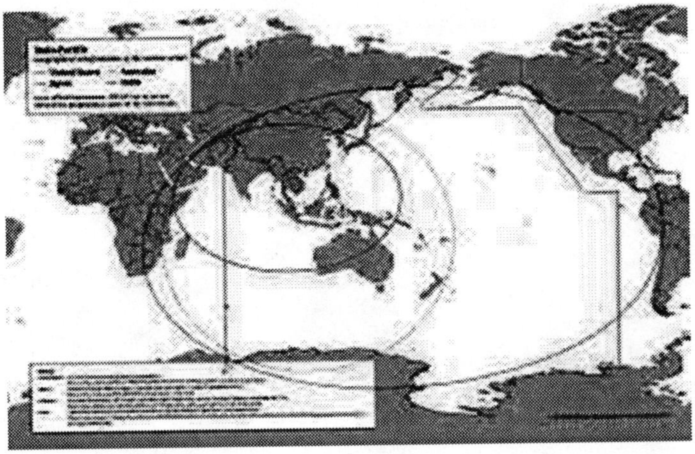

Source: SWP Berlin, 2020.

more critical for the region due to increased piracy and maritime crimes (Banerjee, 2020). The region also comprises many International Shipping Lanes and Sea Lines of Communications through which half the global containerized cargo and a third of the world's bulk cargo passes. The region connects trade and energy routes spanning from the Suez Canal and the Strait of Hormuz at one end to the Malacca, Sunda, and Lombok straits leading into the South China Sea. It contributes to a combined GDP of almost $ 20 trillion. Nearly 80 per cent of the world's total population is directly or indirectly dependent on the Indo-Pacific region for its survival, which increases the region's significance even more.

The Dragon's International Investment Strategy

China has invested heavily in several Asian and African economies in the form of aid and investments and creating alternative institutions like the AIIB, SRF, and the New Development Bank (NDB) to expand its influence all over the region with the help of economic inducement and infrastructural capacity building. Chinese investments in various countries as part of the Belt and Road Initiative (launched in 2013; earlier known as 'One Belt, One Road') as well as the Maritime Silk Route also seek to revive its ancient silk route legacy and expand its network all over the world.

Figure 5: China's BRI and MSR Trade Routes

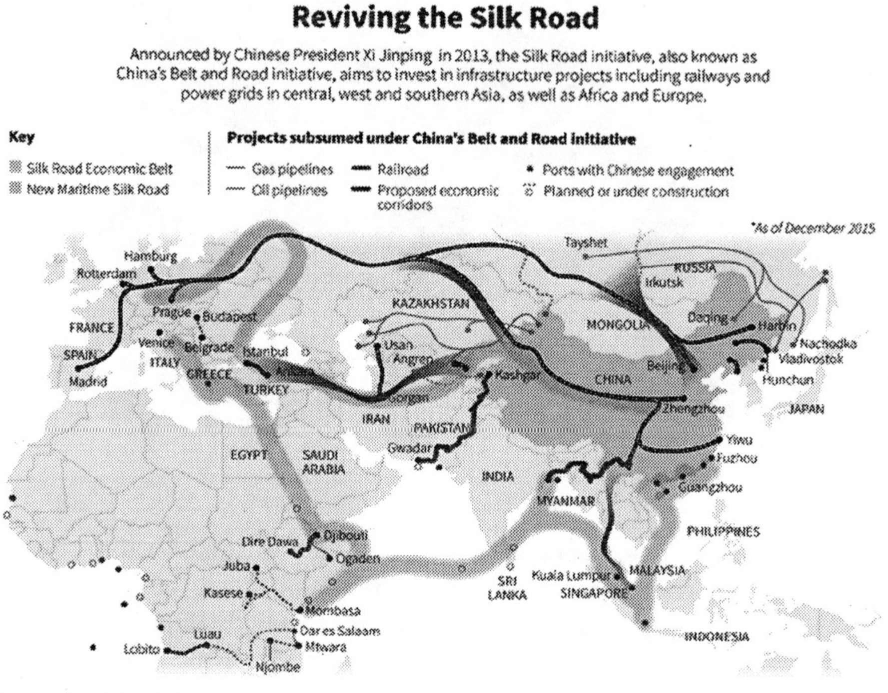

Source: MICS, 2017.

India has never accepted the idea of becoming a part of the Chinese BRI and MSR projects due to "sovereignty and territorial integrity issues"[18] (Kondapalli, 2017). One of the BRI projects, termed as the China-Pakistan Economic Corridor (CPEC), passes through Pakistan-Occupied Kashmir, which has been illegally occupied by Pakistan since 1947. Former Indian Minister of External Affairs Minister Sushma Swaraj made very clear to her Chinese counterpart in 2014 that India's "One China" policy had to be congruent to China's "One India"[19] policy (Kondapalli, 2017). The Chinese must also respect India's claims in Pakistan-Occupied Kashmir if they want India to do the same in other regions.

China has always perceived the idea of the Indo -Pacific as a means to its containment strategy; however, it seeks to expand its control and influence over the region due to its great significance in 21st-century trade. In the last few years, there have been several instances of China's increased belligerence and assertiveness in the Indo-Pacific, which have compelled "like-minded democracies"[20] to come together to ensure an open, free and peaceful Indo-Pacific anchored on a rule-based order (Scott, 2020). These countries seek a "liberal order system in the Indo-Pacific to retain peace, stability, and freedom of navigation in these waters"[21] (Scott, 2020).

Emerging Multilateral Cooperation

As a result of the belligerence, the Indo-Pacific powers became cautious of the Chinese threat. Defending the Southeast Asian region, the USA issued a statement that the international community would not allow Beijing "to treat the South China Sea as its maritime empire".[22] Indo-Pacific partners are trying to decrease their reliance on China and achieve closer coordination among themselves (Ford *et.al*, 2020). The Indian, Japanese, Malaysian, and Australian governments[23] undertook concrete steps to reduce their economic exposure to Beijing, ranging from investment and manufacturing to technology (Ford *et.al*, 2020). The External Affairs Ministers of all ASEAN[24] nations (Association of Southeast Asian Nations) also issued a statement, which is being perceived as one of their strongest statements to date on the South China Sea, insisting that maritime disputes should be resolved according to the UN Law of the Sea Treaty. The former External Affairs Minister of Indonesia, Marty Natalegwa, in 2013 proposed to ASEAN and other states concerned to sign an Indo-Pacific Treaty of Friendship and Cooperation;[25] the proposal, however, could not become successful at a later stage (Georgieff, 2013). The countries are wary of China's assault on maritime security and freedom of navigation in the Indo-Pacific region. Hence, they are coming up with different initiatives to promote a rule-based, open, free, and inclusive Indo-Pacific.

US Approach towards Indo-Pacific Concept

Earlier, the term 'Asia-Pacific', was more prevalent in the vocabulary of Western leadership. The former US President Barack Obama had adopted an enhanced engagement with the Asia-Pacific region during his presidency in his declared 'Pivot to Asia' policy. This policy shift was mostly undertaken in order to address the neo-containment of an expansionist and revisionist China. Later, the Trump administration switched to the Indo-Pacific and blamed previous US administrations for misreading the strategic intentions of China. The current American vision[26] of the Indo-Pacific is closely in line with other democratic nations and their policies towards Chinese assertiveness (including Free and Open Indo-Pacific concept of Japan, Act East Policy of India, Indo-Pacific concept of Australia, Republic of Korea's New Southern Policy, and Taiwan's New Southbound Policy).

Washington also enhanced bilateral and trilateral cooperation in order to achieve maritime security with the help of joint military exercises (such as Talisman Saber (USA-Australia) and the Malabar trilateral naval exercise (Japan-India-USA). Several logistics-sharing agreements (e.g., Logistics Exchange Memorandum of Agreement (LEMOA) in 2016, Communications Compatibility and Security Agreement (COMCASA) in 2018 with India, have also been signed.

India's Approach towards the Indo-Pacific Concept

The Indian subcontinent has one of the best maritime geographies in the world and is centrally located in Indo-Pacific. It enjoys the maximum reach possible across the Indian Ocean Region (IOR). It has a great history of prosperous kingdoms situated along the Indian Ocean, but after the Chinese aggression in the 1960s, India started focussing inwards and reactivated involvement with coastal neighbours only after the post-Cold War period. It began with 'Look East' in 1991, which later turned into 'Act East. The Act East policy came into being during the Modi era in 2014 and focused on expanding the Indian Ocean Region's vision of action and included the Pacific as the nation's economic and strategic interests.

The Indo-Pacific came to life once again in 2018 during Indian Prime Minister Narendra Modi's speech at the Shangri-La Dialogue,[27] where he emphasized the need for a "free, open and inclusive Indo-Pacific region, resting on territorial integrity and sovereignty of all nations and amicable settlement of disputes based on dialogue and adherence to international law".[28] The Indian Ocean and the Indo-Pacific region play a vital role in the country's economic well-being, and even a bit of disruption in the region causes a great deal of difference to the country. Hence, Indo-Pacific's importance for safeguarding our national security and economic prosperity was also highlighted in the speech.

Fig. 6: India's Indo-Pacific Strategy

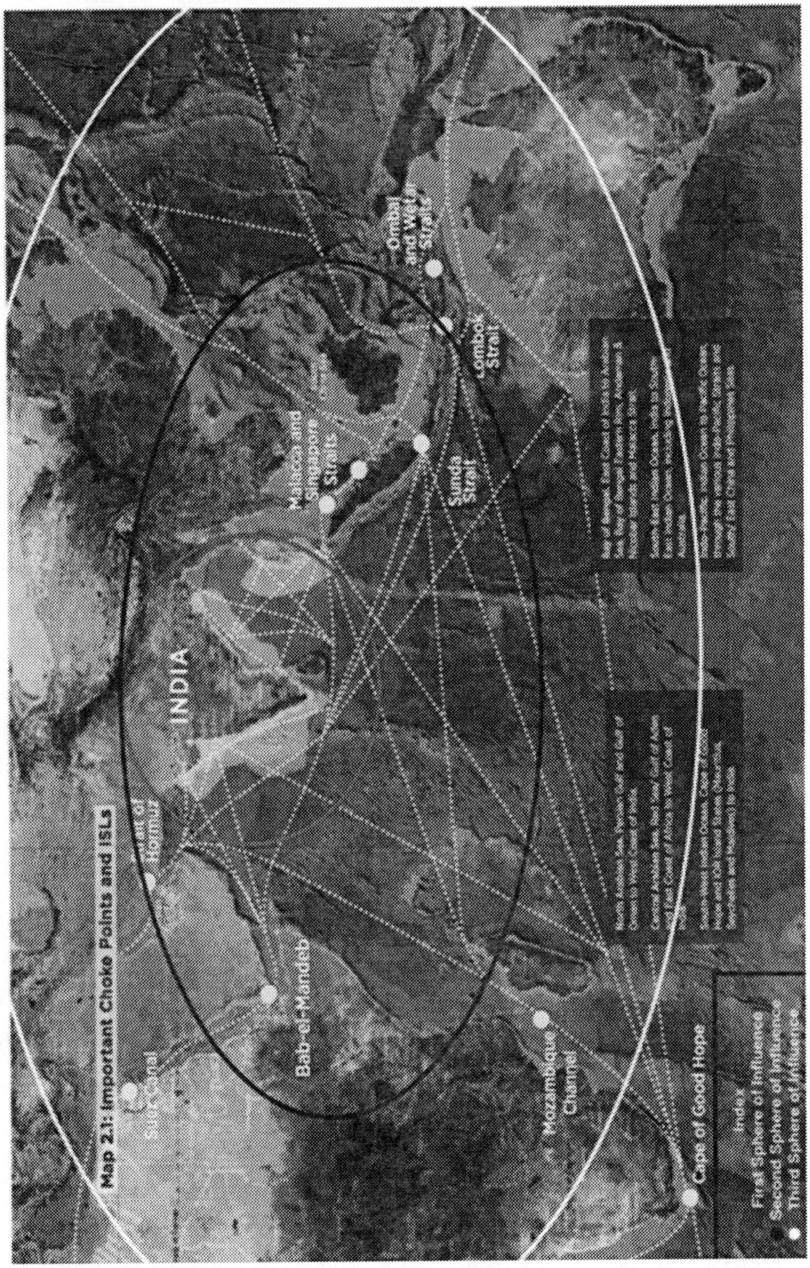

Source: defencyclopedia.com (2016).

India actively worked on the matter, and an Indo-Pacific division was set up in the Ministry of External Affairs. In 2019, the Indo-Pacific Oceans' Initiative (IPOI) was launched by India during the East Asia Summit to collaborate on issues related to maritime security, marine ecology, disaster reduction and management, trade connectivity and maritime transport. In order to strengthen ties with neighbouring countries, India sought to work on several issues.

The Indian leadership worked closely with its southern neighbours, The Maldives and Sri Lanka, providing monetary support to reduce their debt burden to China. It made investments in three projects of The Maldives (development centre at Addu city, water supply and sewage treatment in 36 islands and a small and medium enterprises development financing project) and in Sri Lanka (solar projects, counter-terrorism, housing and medical sectors). It also resolved border disputes with Bangladesh to improve India-Bangladesh relations. India launched SAGAR (Security and Growth for All in the Region) in order to promote inclusive all-round development of the region as a whole and Project Mausam in 2014 to renew cultural links among IOR countries.

India and Australia recently signed a new military logistics agreement allowing Indian and Australian military ships and aircraft to refuel and access maintenance facilities at each other's bases. Similar agreements between Delhi and Tokyo were signed in the first week of September 2020. India has also signed new military logistics agreements with Australia and Japan recently. The "Military Logistics Agreement" (MLA) named Acquisition, and Cross-Servicing Agreement (ACSA) will help the armed forces of both nations to work closely in the field of services and supplies. India has similar agreements with the USA, France, Oman and Singapore.

India's Vaccine Diplomacy

Due to the COVID-19 pandemic, India, which was severely affected, still continuously tried to help countries in the Indian Ocean region by providing medical aid and masks. In an attempt to showcase itself as the "net security provider,"[29] it sent ample supplies of hydroxychloroquine (HCQ) tablets to South Asian countries, including Sri Lanka, Bhutan, Afghanistan and Bangladesh and to island nations including The Maldives, Seychelles and Mauritius lying towards India's southern coast (Brewster, 2020).

As soon as the two COVID-19 vaccines, Covaxin (India's first indigenous COVID-19 vaccine produced by Bharat Biotech developed in collaboration with the Indian Council of Medical Research (ICMR)—National Institute of Virology (NIV)—and Covishield (produced by India's Serum Institute, the world's largest producer of vaccines and developed by Oxford University and AstraZeneca), were approved in India, the country announced that it would send 10 to 20 million doses to its neighbours for free. As one of the world's top producers of drugs, India has already started delivering Covishield vaccines to Nepal, Bhutan, The Maldives, Mauritius, Seychelles, Bangladesh and Myanmar as part of mission "Vaccine Maitri"[30] (Bhaumik, 2021).

India's vaccine diplomacy seeks to curb China's growing influence in South Asia. The effort has not gone unnoticed in the neighbourhood. Bangladesh's leadership which was unsure about the arrival of vaccines from India now seems content, and the vaccine diplomacy will "help Delhi recover the ground it has lost"[31] due to prickly matters in the recent past (Bhaumik, 2021). The vaccines sent to Kathmandu have also helped "swing popular sentiment towards India". India certainly lacked Beijing's ability to offer loans and military equipment to win over its neighbours. India's attempt to use what instruments it had to use its vaccines to gain friends and influence in the region cannot be ignored. "The impact of vaccine diplomacy will surely last for a while, but much follow-up action is needed after this is over"[32] (Bhaumik, 2021).

QUAD 2.0

QUAD is a grouping of four democracies, namely, India, the USA, Japan and Australia, working to achieve common goals (including maritime domain awareness, cyber security, counter-terrorism, information sharing, connectivity and infrastructure). The QUAD traces its roots to nearly two decades ago in 2004 when Australia, India, Japan and the USA came together in order to coordinate relief activities after the deadliest tsunami, which swept away entire communities around the Indian Ocean and killed and affected millions of lives. Born as a collective response to the cause, it was shelved in 2007 and revived in 2017 as QUAD 2.0. Three of the four countries, namely Australia, Japan and the USA, stayed together even after the incident and went on to form an enhanced security partnership. The countries were said to be "like-minded democracies with common goals and interests". India also came along, and the QUAD members met for the first time in 2007 during the ASEAN Regional Forum summit in Manila. They have been increasing cooperation on common issues of concern incrementally. The formation of QUAD is a very significant step strategically. It may seek to control the belligerence of the rogue Chinese Navy in the South China Sea (SACS) and bring in checks and balances for their naval operations in the IOR (Indo Pacific Region).

China has recently targeted all the member countries of QUAD in one or the other way; hence, for the first time in Quad's history, the implications of going forward could be significant as the countries take a determined path. QUAD is on the verge of taking actions that would strengthen its position as a security group. In November 2020, the Indo-Pacific Quad countries—India, Japan, Australia, and the USA took part in a series of joint naval exercises as part of the Malabar exercise[33] in the Indian Ocean, with the first part conducted in the Bay of Bengal and the second in the Arabian Sea. Australia was a part of the exercise after 13 years (Babones, 2020).

Figure 7: Chinese and QUAD Naval Forces in Indo-Pacific

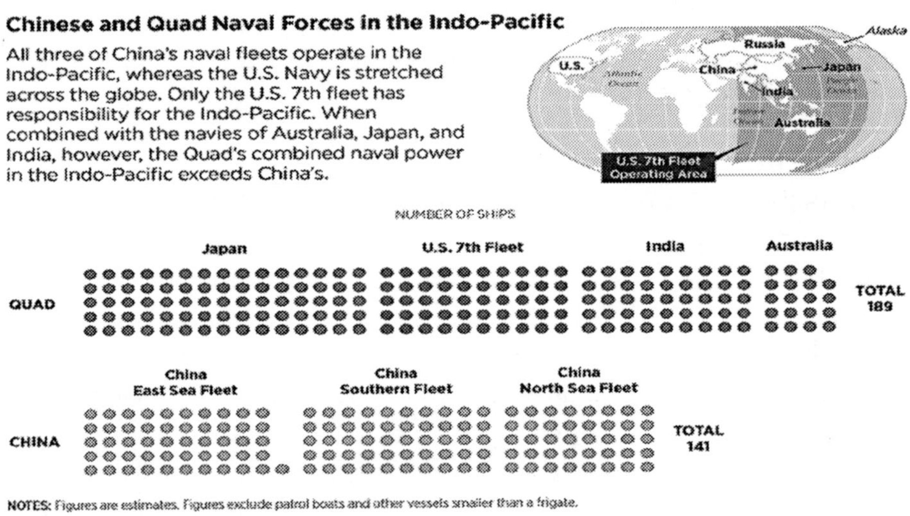

Source: IISS, Heritage Foundation (2019).

In January 2021, the four QUAD members jointly participated in a fortnight-long anti-submarine warfare exercise, 'Sea Dragon 2021' in Andersen Air Force Base in Guam. Canada also took part with the Royal Australian Air Force, Royal Canadian Air Force, Indian Navy, and Japan Maritime Self-Defence Force. QUAD views this development as a "significant step forward"[34] with a "political nod to the Quad and moving towards Quad Plus" amidst rising concerns over China (Bhattacharyya, 2021).

In Chinese Foreign Minister Wang Yi's opinion, QUAD was not an attempt to contain or counter China, but just a headline-grabbing idea. However, not every other statesman had the same views. Some also viewed the grouping as a "mini" NATO whose plan at one point of time revolved around countering communism.

Pacific Deterrence Initiative

The USA is a bit more cautious and took more concrete steps to counter Chinese aggression and expansionism in the region. The Pentagon is going to establish a Pacific Deterrence Initiative[35] modelled after the European Deterrence Initiative, which was created in response to Russia's military intervention in Ukraine and the annexation of Crimea in 2014 (Inhofe *et.al.*, 2020). The relevant bill would authorize $ 1.4 billion to go toward capabilities such as missile defence, enhancing forward posture and improving interoperability with allies and partners.

The initiative attempts to convince and deter adversaries by making them doubt their own capacities and capabilities to sustain a war. With China's continuously increasing belligerence in the Indo-Pacific, the foundation of deterrence is weakening; however, America's "competitive edge has eroded in every domain of warfare...and it is continuing to erode". Hence, in order to create a credible balance of military power, the Pacific Deterrence Initiative is going to be established by the National Defence Authorization Act[36] for Fiscal Year 2021 (Inhofe *et. al*, 2020). The Pacific Deterrence Initiative seeks to:

- enhance budgetary transparency and congressional oversight;
- focus resources on modernisation of logistics and infrastructure;
- reassure allies and partners of America's commitment to the Indo-Pacific region; and

- help deter Chinese aggression by strengthening the credibility of American deterrence by focussing resources on deterring China (Inhofe *et. al*, 2020).

The Pacific Deterrence Initiate is not an adequate solution to the current problem. It is focussed regionally, but there is a need to take initiatives that are global in nature. This initiative is military-based, but there is a need to focus upon economic security, international development, diplomacy, human rights and democratic norms, and multilateral cooperation. Hence, it can be concluded that the Pacific Deterrence Initiative is just a step and not a full-fledged solution.

Indo-Pacific Coordination Group

Then there is another group termed the Indo-Pacific Coordination Group by the US government, which includes selected countries including India, the USA, Australia, Japan, South Korea, New Zealand, and Vietnam and promotes cooperation among them in order to fight the pandemic. It seeks to achieve closer collaboration between countries in the Indo-Pacific and bring them on the same page.

Indo-Pacific Oceans Initiative

In November 2019, Indian PM Modi proposed an "Indo-Pacific Oceans Initiative"[37] for a safe, secure and stable maritime domain (Chaudhury, 2019). The focus areas include creating partnerships among interested states in enhancing maritime security, sustainably using marine resources, and disaster prevention and management. India has consistently been indicating that it was keen on playing a more prominent role in the Indo-Pacific region. With this in mind, India is stepping up its interactions with the Pacific Island countries. The USA has also been pushing for a more significant role for India in the Indo-Pacific in an effort to contain China's growing clout in the region.

India has been an active participant in mechanisms like the Indian Ocean Rim Association (IORA), in ASEAN-led frameworks like the East Asia Summit, the ASEAN Defence Ministers' Meeting Plus, the ASEAN Regional Forum as well as the Bay of Bengal Initiative for Multi-Sectoral Technical and Economic Cooperation and the Mekong-Ganga Economic Corridor.

Indian Ocean Rim Association

The Indian Ocean Rim Association[38] or IORA, is another means to increase cooperation in the Indian Ocean. It was formerly known as the Indian Ocean Rim Association for Regional Cooperation (IOR-ARC). It is a grouping of 23 countries and ten dialogue partners. Established in 1997, its first summit was held 20 years later in 2017 in Indonesia.

Figure 8: IORA's Priority Areas of Cooperation

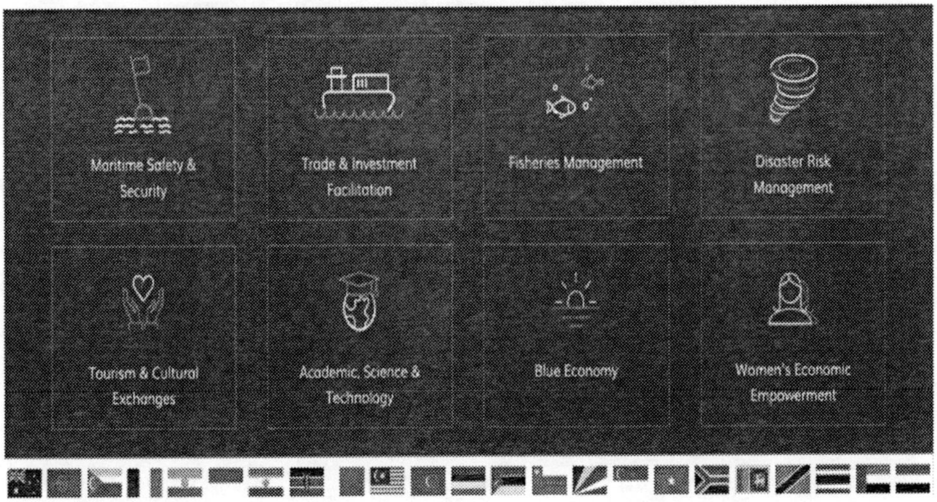

Source: IORA, 2021.

India received the IORA chairmanship from 2011 to 2013 and made a serious effort to revitalise the dormant institution by providing direction and determination to strengthen institutions and capacities within the IORA. The six priority areas[39] and two focus areas, i.e., Maritime Safety and Security; Trade and Investment Facilitation; Fisheries Management; Disaster Risk Management; Tourism and Cultural Exchanges; Academic, Science and Technology; Blue Economy and Women's Economic Empowerment were identified during the period in order to promote sustained growth and balanced development in the Indian Ocean Region. With this initiative, India seeks to build enhanced cooperation with the island nations and other countries in various sectors in the region.

Impact on Current and Future World Order

The COVID-19 outbreak has created an unprecedented situation and challenged the existing world order. No other crisis has been so severe. It is the first global pandemic, whereas all other outbreaks such as Plague or Spanish Flu were localized affairs. Even the Gulf War did not disrupt the global economy and lives of people, in one go, like this, and there was no worldwide lockdown and disruption in the economic activities of nations. In those instances, the nations were still powerful because of their ability to spend on their military force. However, in 2020, a nation's economic power and excess money available to invest in other nations is a solid factor to win over the allegiance of those nations in international institutions.

The countries of the world, big and small, are facing major economic and health-related crises and a crisis of institutional legitimacy as well, all at a time of increasing geopolitical rivalry. China has an economic leverage[40] and it will certainly go ahead with this option (Saran, 2020). It may also think of taking over present institutions like the WHO or UN, where it can create rules that benefit its own interests. Since it claims that it was able to contain the spread of COVID-19 ahead of other nations, it might use this fact to buttress its claim that its own political system is superior to that of other nations. It might hold up its political system as a model for the rest of the world to follow. To create a win-win situation, China may go ahead with both economic and political options. It can also create a proper atmosphere and work for establishing new, parallel international institutions and become a dominant nation globally by becoming the rule-maker while other nations are rule-followers, or it can seek parity with the USA on global platforms. China's one-word agenda has been 'global dominance'[41] (Mauldin, 2019). The race to achieve the top slot in the emerging world order will go on for some time; we may see China replacing the USA as a global hegemon.

However, there is a strong anti-China sentiment in the world now, and Beijing has been taking up both economic and military conflicts, as has been witnessed with Australia, India and other countries in recent months. China has a firm grip over the South China Sea and ASEAN, among a few other international organisations. However, it is also grappling with internal demands for democracy. It is suspected that the USA might use the strong anti-China sentiment and the recession to create a social upheaval in the country. The international collective of nations might be successful against China's military strength. The anti-China sentiment is prevailing in the world today, and other nations can cash in on this chance to create political instability and help usher in democracy in that country.

However, these are just premature predictions. What we are witnessing today is a very sharp contest between the USA and China for the Number One spot to guide economic interests and dictate the world order. This strong contest will last for some time. China's challenge to the USA is real but premature. The country is behaving in a frustrating manner, which is both unpredictable and dangerous, but its forward march has been disrupted by COVID-19. A new coalition of democratic countries in opposition to China's hegemony is already in the process of coming together. However, to what extent this coalition will be able to tame China's assertiveness and expansionist strategy is unclear. There will be a new, emerging world order in the foreseeable future. An economic and diplomatic cold war might erupt between the current global power, the USA, and the aggressive competitor, China. Whatever the new dynamics are, India will have to determine a clear strategy to handle China. It will have to align with nations in the Indo-Pacific region facing a similar challenge from Beijing and form new security architecture to counterbalance Chinese aggressive behaviour. If the Chinese Dragon continues to breathe fire in a similar fashion, the Indian Elephant should and will not stay behind.

Conclusion

The concept of the Indo-Pacific region emerged in the recent past due to its geostrategic and geo-economic significance to the major players in the world. A stark increase in Chinese investments and belligerence in the region, especially amidst the COVID-19 pandemic and the resulting crisis, has alerted the "like-minded democracies" who have now come together to ensure a free and open Indo-Pacific region. It will be interesting to see how the tables turn due to policy shifts and changes in approaches of various state actors towards the Indo-Pacific region; what new institutions are constructed; how the existing regional and global structures are utilised to change the condition in one's favour; and which new dynamics emerge in the foreseeable future.

NOTES

1. Krishnan, Ananth. 2020. "How China is controlling COVID-19". *The Hindu*, November 28, 2020. https://www.thehindu.com/news/international/coronavirus-how-china-is-controlling-covid-19/article33201851.ece
2. "India-China clash: 20 Indian troops killed in Ladakh fighting." 2020. BBC. https://www.bbc.com/news/world-asia-53061476
3. Basu, Nayanima. 2020. "'Most difficult phase' — Jaishankar says India-China ties 'significantly damaged' this year." *The Print*, December 9, 2020. https://theprint.in/diplomacy/most-difficult-phase-jaishankar-says-india-china-ties-significantly-damaged-this-year/563425/
4. Ananthalakshmi, A. and Rozanna Latiff. 2020. "Chinese and Malaysian ships in South China Sea standoff." Reuters. https://www.reuters.com/article/us-malaysia-china-southchinasea-idUSKBN21Z1TN
5. *The Times of India*. 2021. "South China Sea tension flares again as Joe Biden Takes Charge." January 25, 2021. https://timesofindia.indiatimes.com/world/china/south-china-sea-tension-flares-again-as-joe-biden-takes-charge/articleshow/80445933.cms
6. *Economic Times*. 2020. "China's 'shadow trade war' threatens Australia." November 27, 2020. https://economictimes.indiatimes.com/news/international/business/chinas-shadow-trade-war-threatens-australia/articleshow/79445948.cms?from = mdr
7. Ibid.
8. Mohan, Geeta. 2020. "China's growing territorial aggression amid corona virus crisis." *India Today*. https://www.indiatoday.in/mail-today/story/china-growing-territorial-aggression-amid-covid-crisis-1692787-2020-06-26.
9. Dutta, Prabhash K. 2017. "What is China's salami slicing tactic?" *India Today*. https://www.indiatoday.in/india/story/doklam-china-salami-slicing-army-chief-general-bipin-rawat-1039864-2017-09-07
10. Macaes, Bruno. 2019. "How China's Belt and Road strategy threatens India." *The Telegraph*. https://www.telegraphindia.com/culture/books/how-chinas-belt-and-road-strategy-threatens-india/cid/1683827.
11. Murthy, K.S.D. 2020. "China's paranoia, aggression stem from its troubled past." *The Federal*. https://thefederal.com/opinion/chinas-paranoia-aggression-stem-from-its-troubled-past/
12. Ibid.
13. Pandeya, Maneesh. 2020. "China's anti-India aggression rooted in failing US-China ties." *Sunday Guardian* Live. https://www.sundayguardianlive.com/world/chinas-anti-india-aggression-rooted-failing-us-china-ties.
14. Ibid..
15. Scott, David. 2012. "The "Indo-Pacific"—New Regional Formulations and New

Maritime Frameworks for US-India Strategic Convergence." *Asia-Pacific Review* 19, no. 2 (November): 85-109. 10.1080/13439006.2012.738115

16. Banerjee, Udita. 2020. "US and India: Paving the road to ensuring Peace and Prosperity in the Indo-Pacific region." *Electronic Journal of Social and Strategic Studies*, (December), 215-237. 10.47362/EJSSS.2020.1205
17. Ibid.
18. Kondapalli, Srikanth. 2017. "Why India is not part of the Belt and Road Initiative summit." *Indian Express*, May 15, 2017. https://indianexpress.com/article/opinion/why-india-is-not-part-of-the-belt-and-road-initiative-summit-4656150/
19. Ibid.
20. Scott, Jason. 2020. "Australia Seeks to Build Defence Ties to Counter China Squeeze." *Bloomberg Quint*. https://www.bloombergquint.com/global-economics/australia-seeks-to-build-defense-ties-to-counter-china-squeeze.
21. Ibid.
22. Ford, Lindsey W. and Julian Gewirtz. 2020. "China's post-COVID aggression is reshaping Asia." *The Hindu*. https://www.thehindu.com/opinion/lead/chinas-post-covid-aggression-is-reshaping-asia/article32095103.ece
23. Ibid.
24. "Asean leaders cite 1982 UN treaty in South China Sea dispute." 2020. *The Guardian*. https://www.theguardian.com/world/2020/jun/27/asean-leaders-cite-1982-un-treaty-in-south-china-sea-dispute
25. Georgieff, Jack. 2013. "An Indo-Pacific Treaty: An Idea Whose Time Has Come?" *The Diplomat*, May 17, 2013, 1-7.
26. "A Free And Open Indo-Pacific: Advancing a Shared Vision." 2019. US Report. https://www.state.gov/wp-content/uploads/2019/11/Free-and-Open-Indo-Pacific-4Nov2019.pdf
27. "Modi sends out a clear message at the Shangri-La Dialogue." 2018. *Hindustan Times*. https://www.hindustantimes.com/editorials/modi-sends-out-a-clear-message-at-the-shangri-la-dialogue/story-VZx9KOod8dPxSkFKcDtd8I.html
28. Ibid.
29. Brewster, David. 2020. "Covid contest in Indian Ocean region: India, China jostle for top spot." Lowy Institute. https://www.lowyinstitute.org/the-interpreter/covid-contest-indian-ocean-region-india-china-jostle-top-spot
30. Bhaumik, Subir. 2021. "Can India outshine China with Covid-19 vaccine diplomacy?" *South China Morning Post*. https://www.scmp.com/week-asia/health-environment/article/3119194/can-india-outshine-china-covid-19-vaccine-diplomacy
31. Ibid.
32. Ibid.
33. Babones, Salvatore. 2020. "The Quad's Malabar Exercises Point the Way to an Asian NATO." *Foreign Policy*. https://foreignpolicy.com/2020/11/25/india-japan-australia-u-s-quad-alliance-nato/
34. Bhattacharyya, Anirudh. 2021. "Canada joins Quad joint naval exercise in Pacific Ocean." *Hindustan Times*, January 25, 2021. https://www.hindustantimes.com/india-news/canada-to-join-quad-joint-naval-exercise-in-pacific-ocean-101611556512917.html

35. Inhofe, Jim and Jack Reed. 2020. "The Pacific Deterrence Initiative: Peace Through Strength in the Indo-Pacific." War On The Rocks. https://warontherocks.com/2020/05/the-pacific-deterrence-initiative-peace-through-strength-in-the-indo-pacific/?utm_source=Sailthru&utm_medium=email&utm_campaign=EBB%2005. 29.20&utm_term=Editorial%20-%20Early%20Bird%20Brief
36. Ibid.
37. Chaudhury, Dipanajan R. 2019. "PM Modi proposes Indo-Pacific Oceans Initiative." *The Economic Times*, November 5, 2019. https://economictimes.indiatimes.com/news/politics-and-nation/pm-modi-proposes-indo-pacific-oceans-initiative/articleshow/71915838.cms
38. "Priorities & Focus Areas." 2020. Indian Ocean Rim Association - Official Website. https://www.iora.int/en/priorities-focus-areas/overview
39. Ibid.
40. Saran, Shyam. 2020. "China's strategy of economic self-reliance, under label of 'dual circulation', has been sharpened by pandemic." *The Indian Express*.
41. Mauldin, John. 2019. "China's Grand Plan To Take Over The World." Forbes. https://www.forbes.com/sites/johnmauldin/2019/11/12/chinas-grand-plan-to-take-over-the-world/?sh=63691d4d5ab5

REFERENCES

Ananthalakshmi, A. and Rozanna Latiff. 2020. "Chinese and Malaysian ships in South China Sea standoff." Reuters. https://www.reuters.com/article/us-malaysia-china-southchinasea-idUSKBN21Z1TN.

"Asean leaders cite 1982 UN treaty in South China Sea dispute." 2020. *The Guardian*. https://www.theguardian.com/world/2020/jun/27/asean-leaders-cite-1982-un-treaty-in-south-china-sea-dispute.

Babones, Salvatore. 2020. "The Quad's Malabar Exercises Point the Way to an Asian NATO." *Foreign Policy*. https://foreignpolicy.com/2020/11/25/india-japan-australia-u-s-quad-alliance-nato/.

Banerjee, Udita. 2020. "US and India: Paving the road to ensuring Peace and Prosperity in the Indo-Pacific region." *Electronic Journal of Social and Strategic Studies*, (December), 215-237. 10.47362/EJSSS.2020.1205

Basu, Nayanima. 2020. "'Most difficult phase'—Jaishankar says India-China ties 'significantly damaged' this year." *The Print*, December 9, 2020. https://theprint.in/diplomacy/most-difficult-phase-jaishankar-says-india-china-ties-significantly-damaged-this-year/563425/

Bhattacharyya, Anirudh. 2021. "Canada joins Quad joint naval exercise in Pacific Ocean." *Hindustan Times*, January 25, 2021. https://www.hindustantimes.com/india-news/canada-to-join-quad-joint-naval-exercise-in-pacific-ocean-101611556512917.html

Bhaumik, Subir. 2021. "Can India outshine China with Covid-19 vaccine diplomacy?" *South China Morning Post*. https://www.scmp.com/week-asia/health-environment/article/3119194/can-india-outshine-china-covid-19-vaccine-diplomacy

Brewster, David. 2020. "Covid contest in Indian Ocean region: India, China jostle for top spot." Lowy Institute. https://www.lowyinstitute.org/the-interpreter/covid-contest-indian-ocean-region-india-china-jostle-top-spot

Chaudhury, Dipanajan R. 2019. "PM Modi proposes Indo-Pacific Oceans Initiative." *The Economic Times*, November 5, 2019. https://economictimes.indiatimes.com/news/politics-and-nation/pm-modi-proposes-indo-pacific-oceans-initiative/articleshow/71915838.cms

Dutta, Prabhash K. 2017. "What is China's salami slicing tactic?" *India Today*. https://www.indiatoday.in/india/story/doklam-china-salami-slicing-army-chief-general-bipin-rawat-1039864-2017-09-07

Economic Times. 2020. "China's 'shadow trade war' threatens Australia." November 27, 2020. https://economictimes.indiatimes.com/news/international/business/chinas-shadow-trade-war-threatens-australia/articleshow/79445948.cms?from=mdr

Ford, Lindsey W. and Julian Gewirtz. 2020. "China's post-COVID aggression is reshaping Asia." *The Hindu*. https://www.thehindu.com/opinion/lead/chinas-post-covid-aggression-is-reshaping-asia/article32095103.ece

"A Free And Open Indo-Pacific: Advancing a Shared Vision." 2019. US Report. https://www.state.gov/wp-content/uploads/2019/11/Free-and-Open-Indo-Pacific-4Nov2019.pdf

Georgieff, Jack. 2013. "An Indo-Pacific Treaty: An Idea Whose Time Has Come?" *The Diplomat*, May 17, 2013, 1-7.

"India-China clash: 20 Indian troops killed in Ladakh fighting." 2020. BBC. https://www.bbc.com/news/world-asia-53061476.

Inhofe, Jim and Jack Reed. 2020. "The Pacific Deterrence Initiative: Peace Through Strength in the Indo-Pacific." War On The Rocks, *Texas National Security Review*. https://warontherocks.com/2020/05/the-pacific-deterrence-initiative-peace-through-strength-in-the-indo-pacific/?utm_source=Sailthru&utm_medium=email&utm_campaign=EBB%2005.29.20&utm_term=Editorial%20-%20Early%20Bird%20Brief

Krishnan, Ananth. 2020. "How China is controlling COVID-19." *The Hindu*, November 28, 2020. https://www.thehindu.com/news/international/coronavirus-how-china-is-controlling-covid-19/article33201851.ece

Kondapalli, Srikanth. 2017. "Why India is not part of the Belt and Road Initiative summit?" *Indian Express*, May 15, 2017. https://indianexpress.com/article/opinion/why-india-is-not-part-of-the-belt-and-road-initiative-summit-4656150/

Macaes, Bruno. 2019. "How China's Belt and Road strategy threatens India." *The Telegraph*. https://www.telegraphindia.com/culture/books/how-chinas-belt-and-road-strategy-threatens-india/cid/1683827

Mauldin, John. 2019. "China's Grand Plan to Take Over the World." Forbes. https://www.forbes.com/sites/johnmauldin/2019/11/12/chinas-grand-plan-to-take-over-the-world/?sh=63691d4d5ab5

"Modi sends out a clear message at the Shangri-La Dialogue." 2018. *Hindustan Times*. https://www.hindustantimes.com/editorials/modi-sends-out-a-clear-message-at-the-shangri-la-dialogue/story-VZx9KOod8dPxSkFKcDtd8I.html.

Mohan, Geeta. 2020. "China's growing territorial aggression amid corona virus crisis." *India Today*. https://www.indiatoday.in/mail-today/story/china-growing-territorial-aggression-amid-covid-crisis-1692787-2020-06-26

Murthy, K.S.D. 2020. "China's paranoia, aggression stem from its troubled past." *The Federal*. https://thefederal.com/opinion/chinas-paranoia-aggression-stem-from-its-troubled-past/

Pandeya, Maneesh. 2020. "China's anti-India aggression rooted in failing US-China ties." *Sunday Guardian* Live. https://www.sundayguardianlive.com/world/chinas-anti-india-aggression-rooted-failing-us-china-ties

"Priorities & Focus Areas." 2020. Indian Ocean Rim Association - Official Website. https://www.iora.int/en/priorities-focus-areas/overview

Saran, Shyam. 2020. "China's strategy of economic self-reliance, under label of 'dual circulation', has been sharpened by pandemic." *The Indian Express*.

Scott, David. 2012. "The "Indo-Pacific"—New Regional Formulations and New Maritime Frameworks for US-India Strategic Convergence." *Asia-Pacific Review* 19, no. 2 (November): 85-109. 10.1080/13439006.2012.738115

Scott, Jason. 2020. "Australia Seeks to Build Defence Ties to Counter China Squeeze." *Bloomberg Quint*. https://www.bloombergquint.com/global-economics/australia-seeks-to-build-defense-ties-to-counter-china-squeeze

The Times of India. 2021. "South China Sea tension flares again as Joe Biden Takes Charge." January 25, 2021. https://timesofindia.indiatimes.com/world/china/south-china-sea-tension-flares-again-as-joe-biden-takes-charge/articleshow/80445933.cms

4

The Global Powers Pivot to Asia: Exploring the Rise of China, Sino-US Competition and the Role and Implications for India

Garima Lal

ABSTRACT

Since the beginning of the twenty-first century, various spheres of international relations have witnessed a gradual shift. The rise of China has been viewed as one of the most significant emerging powers, which carry the potential to effectively pose a challenge to the US pre-eminence in global affairs in general and in Asia-Pacific in particular. Although there is some fluidity and ambiguity in the demarcation and conceptualisation of the region of Asia-Pacific, the region has arguably attained prominence in an evolving international order, more so in the post-Cold War period. Importantly, the USA, which has been the dominant power in the region in the post-1945 period, has been essentially confronted with an increasingly assertive China, which is rapidly growing on both economic and military fronts in the Asia-Pacific. The growing clout of China has been propelled by the launch of the massive BRI strategy. Moreover, Beijing's military assertiveness with regard to the territorial and maritime disputes in the South China Sea has also influenced the power structure in the region. At the same time, one cannot overlook the continued salience of the region for the USA, which is manifested in its policy formulations like the 'Pivot to Asia' strategy. In this context, several key questions arise. What has propelled the rise of China in the Asia-Pacific? How does its growing assertiveness stand with respect to the hitherto dominant power, the USA? Does it pose a challenge to the US hegemony and thereby has implications for the power, security and peace in the region? Where does India, an important power centre in the region, fit in this picture? Notably, this paper seeks to assess this growing power of China with respect to the continued influence and clout of the USA. A discussion of the Sino-US competition in the Asia-Pacific region, which straddles the aspects of political and economic rise, military strength, power balancing and alliances with various great powers and middle powers, particularly the role and implications for India, is made. In this context of a shifting power balance and alliance politics in the region, what is also discussed is the Quadrilateral Security Dialogue (Quad), which has become increasingly proactive in the pandemic era that has raised myriad new challenges with implications for the international order. This paper argues that the rise of China, particularly in the context of its BRI strategy, the burgeoning Sino-US competition and the evolving role and strategies of other important powers like India, has been central to shaping and reshaping the power dynamics in Asia-Pacific, a region that has clearly emerged as a theatre of complex global power manoeuvrings. The contours of power dynamics in the Asia-Pacific thus hold significance in determining the future global order as the region has essentially emerged as the pivot for the interactions of the major global powers.

***Keywords**: China, USA, India, global power, middle powers, great powers, Quad, pandemic, BRI, South China Sea*

Introduction

In the evolving international order, the Asia-Pacific has emerged as one of the most critical regions. Although there remains some fluidity and ambiguity in the demarcation and conceptualisation of the region of Asia-Pacific, the region has arguably attained prominence in an evolving international order, more so in the post-Cold War period. In defining the contours of the region of the Asia-Pacific, Liselotte Odgaard argues that the four sub-regions, namely, Southeast Asia, Central Asia, Northeast Asia, and South Asia, are regions where an external dominant power, that is, the USA, is challenged by one great internal power, that is China (Odgaard, 2007, p. 21). Brian L. Job notes that the manner in which the major powers in this region interact with one another and their interactions within the international system have become a critical factor in deciding the nature and operationalisation of the system at large (Job, 2009, p. 31). From the point of view of the present study, the focus is on two of the world's emerging great powers that are a part of the region, namely, China and India, and external power, the USA, that lies just beyond its peripheries and interacts with it extensively. It is the peculiar interactions of these three powers, along with the role of other middle powers, which shape and reshape the power dynamics, peace and stability in this crucial region.

Notably, the USA, which has been the pre-eminent power in the Asia-Pacific in the post-1945 period, has been essentially confronted with a progressively forceful China, which is rapidly gaining prominence on both the economic and military fronts in the region. It is this very narrative of the rapid ascent of China in the Asia-Pacific and its purported eclipsing of the USA that forms the fundamental question that this paper seeks to address. It is important to note here that this paper aims to assess this growing power of China with respect to the continued influence and clout of the USA. It is here that the role of other vital powers in the region, particularly India, and initiatives like the Quadrilateral Security Dialogue (Quad or QSD) attain massive salience. In this context, this paper then seeks to address the following key questions: What has propelled the rise of China in the Asia-Pacific? How does the growing assertiveness of China stand with respect to the hitherto dominant power, the USA? Does it pose a challenge to the US hegemony and thereby has implications for the power, security and peace in the region? Where does India, a significant power centre in the region, fit in this picture?

The working proposition of this paper is that power dynamics and stability in the region of the Asia-Pacific is largely a function of the behaviour and interactions amongst the three major powers, namely the USA, China and India. Thus, it is the interactions of these three powers that form the core of the discussion that follows. This paper consists of four broad sections. The first attempts to trace the rise of China in the Asia-Pacific, particularly focussing on its grand BRI strategy, rapid economic rise and its growing assertiveness in military and territorial disputes. The second section discusses the burgeoning competition between the rapidly-rising China and the dominant and formidable force, the USA. In discussing the Sino-US rivalry, the discussion straddles the domains of political and economic rise, military strength, power balancing and alliances with various great powers and middle powers, particularly the role and implications for India. In this context of a shifting power balance and alliance politics in the region, what is also discussed is the Quadrilateral Security Dialogue (Quad), which has become increasingly proactive in the pandemic era, a period that has raised myriad new challenges with implications for the international order. The final concluding section underscores the salience of the Asia-Pacific as an emerging power centre in the rapidly evolving international order.

Tracing the Rise of China in the Asia-Pacific

In the rapidly evolving international order, the rise of China has been one of the most significant developments, which is often thought to be carrying the potential to effectively challenge the US pre-eminence in both the Asia-Pacific region and also in the global arena. The primary feature that distinguishes the contemporary world order from that of its Cold War counterpart is the fact that China has ceased to exist as a middle power which alternated between the major alliances and its foreign policy today rather holds resemblance with "a dominant power *in spe*" (Odgaard, 2007, p. 231).

Debates on the shifts in the balance of power have swiftly followed this rapid ascent of China in the Asia-Pacific (Fels, 2017, p. 10). The rise of China, the potential challenge it raises to the US hegemony in the region and its increasing assertiveness in economic and military affairs in the region is thought to be by many scholars as having an indelible imprint on the security and power balance in the region (ibid). While isolated actions taken by Beijing across the Asia-Pacific may seem of little or no strategic significance when viewed in unanimity, it becomes clear that China is indeed marching ahead on an effective plan to propagate its power and clout in the long run, which is undoubtedly proving to be effective irrespective of the name assigned, be it "charm offensive, smile strategy, peaceful rise, or development" (Committee on Foreign Relations, 2005). Indeed, tracing the rise of China is critical to comprehending the evolving views on the salience of the Asia-Pacific in the international order and also the "shifting power structure within the region itself" (Fels, 2017, p. 6).

Simultaneously with the rise of China has been a growing concern about the manner in which Beijing seeks to wield its massive economic and military strength (Vaughn & Morrison, 2006, p. 3). It becomes important to realise here that China is a rising power that is witnessing swift transformations in its economic standing, expanding its clout in the region, seeking the regard and acceptance of other key powers, all at the same time (Ikenberry & Mastanduno, 2003, p. 2). This has led to several predictions about the emerging power structure. While some consider the emergence of a new great power in the international arena as leading to a probable disordering of the abiding power structure, thereby opening up the possibility of a conflict, others accept the possibility of managing such a transition in power in a conflict-free harmonious fashion (Vaughn & Morrison, 2006, p. 3). It thus becomes crucial to trace the rise of China in the Asia-Pacific region in order to make sense of the power dynamics in the region and also the future of the world order.

Notably, when analysing Beijing's foreign policy in the Asia-Pacific region, it becomes important to consider several internal and external factors such as energy security, national interests, etc. (Saeed, 2017, p. 501). The safety and freedom of maritime routes in the Pacific Ocean and the Indian Ocean are critical to China's energy security, more so in the context of rapid economic growth, which demands an uninterrupted energy supply (ibid). Also, the national interests of China, which can be categorised as the sustenance of the Communist Party of China's reign in the country, protecting its sovereignty and territorial integrity; and, ensuring continued economic and social progress for which a sustained availability of energy and mineral resources along with a continued hold on the market is critical are all factors in shaping the foreign policy of the country (Braun *et.al.*, 2016, p. 19). China's foreign policy is steered mainly towards bolstering it economically and militarily, which can propel it to attain regional hegemony in the region of the Asia-Pacific (Pant, 2007, p. 56).

China's growing clout in the region of Asia-Pacific can be broadly understood by mapping its rapid economic rise and growing military strength. In this context, it becomes crucial to examine China's Belt and Road (BRI) strategy launched in 2013, which is an important pillar of its rapidly expanding influence. Also, the growing assertiveness of Beijing regarding territorial and maritime disputes in the South and the East China Seas needs to be closely examined in order to understand the rise of China in the Asia-Pacific and its impact on the regional order in the particular and global order in general.

China's Economic Rise and the Grand BRI Strategy

China has been undertaking relentless initiatives in order to augment its power and influence in global affairs, and the Belt and Road

Initiative (BRI), by far, is one of the most determined steps in this direction. Owing to the enormous strategic salience of the region of the Asia-Pacific, China has been undertaking stringent measures to ensure safe trade and maritime routes and amalgamate its regional clout, and the BRI is an important pivot in this effort (Saeed, 2017, p. 505). Conceived in 2013, subsequent to the transition of power from President Hu Jintao to President Xi Jinping, the BRI is undoubtedly "the most ambitious foreign policy approach" espoused by Beijing to date (Mayer, 2018, p. 2). The project was initially called the "One Belt, One Road (OBOR)" Initiative but was subsequently named "the Belt and Road Initiative (BRI)". The BRI can be most aptly summarised in the following words of Chinese President Xi Jinping, "China will actively promote international co-operation through the Belt and Road Initiative. In doing so, we hope to achieve policy, infrastructure, trade, financial, and people-to-people connectivity and thus build a new platform for international cooperation to create new drivers of shared development" (Jinping, 2017, p. 16). Aimed towards enhancing investment and collaboration, this unprecedented initiative seeks to "link China to the Asia-Pacific economic circle in the east and the European economic circle to its west" (Saeed, 2017, p. 505).

The BRI is a vast project that entails the financing and construction of a network of roads, railways, natural gas and oil pipelines, fibre-optics, communication systems, ports, and airports (Alon, Zhang, & Lattemann, 2018, p. 3). Its aim initiative is to enhance Asia's connectivity to Europe, the Middle East and Africa through both land and sea, which means through "the belt" and "the road", respectively (Wolf, 2020, p. 6). The BRI is aimed at utilising "the Belt" to connect China to Europe through Central Asia and Russia, to the Middle East through Central Asia, and also to South Asia, Southeast Asia, and the Indian Ocean (Schortgen, 2018, p. 25). Moreover, "the Road" intends to connect China with Europe and with the South Pacific Ocean through the South China Sea and the Indian Ocean, respectively (ibid). The project is frequently understood as a twenty-first-century Silk Road, comprising of a "belt of overland corridors and a maritime road of shipping lanes" (Kuo & Kommenda, 2018). The land-based Silk Road Economic Belt (SREB) and the sea-based Maritime Silk Route Economic Belt (CMSR) thus represent the two broad development proposals that form what is known as the BRI. The initiative then seeks effectively to re-establish the ancient Silk Road in linking Southeast Asia with Africa and Europe via the construction of infrastructure and ports in the states alongside the coastlines (Saeed, 2017, p. 505). The BRI has, therefore, become a blanket term to cover China's trade and overseas investment initiatives (Andersen & Jiang, 2018, p. 19).

Francis Schortgen argues that the BRI is "the most ambitious example of global economic statecraft in the twenty-first century" as it covers 65 countries, aims to reach around 62 per cent of the world population, accounts for almost a third of the global GDP and about 35 per cent of the global trade in goods and commodities (Schortgen, 2018, p. 25). China has been rapidly increasing its foreign direct investment through the Belt and Road Initiative (BRI) (Satake, 2020, p. 45). The funding of this massive enterprise called the BRI, which has an estimated cost of around US$ 800 billion, is spearheaded by China and through the Asian Infrastructure Investment Bank (AIIB) and the New Development Bank (NDB) (Alon, Zhang, & Lattemann, 2018, p. 3). In this respect, Schortgen contends that the push is ahead given to the AIIB and the BRICS-led NDB is not merely a manifestation of Beijing's resolve to contribute an increased share in financial governance at the global level; it is at the same time an indication of the country's exasperation with the constant domination by the West of the World Bank and the International Monetary Fund (IMF) and also the Japanese dominance of the Asian Development Bank (ADB) (Schortgen, 2018, p. 25). The BRI then seems to be China's blueprint for erecting "a new world order" in place of the current international system, which has been led mainly by the USA (Macaes, 2019, p. 208).

Without a doubt, the considerable investment, together with China's growing power, has inevitably generated significant geostrategic repercussions in regions where geopolitical contestations between China and the USA are already on the rise (Gong, 2020, p. 39). In the eyes of many Chinese analysts, however, the BRI is more for defensive purposes, primarily serving as a direct response to the Obama Administration's "strategic rebalance" in the Asia-Pacific region in 2011. Regardless of the motivations behind the BRI, be they domestic, economic or geopolitical, it has produced significant regional strategic repercussions. Although China's BRI could potentially contribute to the development of several Indo-Pacific countries, there have been growing concerns over the openness, economic efficiency, soundness and transparency of BRI projects (Satake, 2020, p. 45). Lai-Ha Chan asserts that the BRI, on the whole, can be inferred as "a regional (re)ordering project" which seeks to challenge or constrict the USA as the reigning dominant power subtly and work out new standards and arrangements of (regional) public goods to countries across Asia and Europe to achieve their acceptance of Chinese power and authority (Chan, 2020, p. 200). Alternatively stated, the strategic purpose of the BRI is "to remake the regional order" (ibid). Erico Fels argues that owing to the astounding economic growth of China, the regional economic structure in the Asia-Pacific has turned out to be increasingly Sino-centric (Fels, 2017, p. 7).

China's economic advancement is a challenge to the existing world order as it poses a challenge to the US financial authority and thereby imperils the US strategic pre-eminence, first regionally in Asia and subsequently in the international order possibly (White & Taylor, 2009, p. 88). Moreover, alongside its spectacular economic development, China has also managed to erect an extraordinary military build-up, which forms another crucial aspect of China's increasing clout in the Asia-Pacific region.

Chinese Assertiveness in Military and Territorial Disputes

In the previous two decades, China has been swiftly enhancing its military system and potential (Saeed, 2017, p. 507). Though the steps to modernise the military were undertaken in the early 1980s, it was subsequent to witnessing an alluring conquest and the overpowering strength of the USA and its allies during the Gulf War of 1991 that acceleration in these efforts took place (ibid). Over the past few years particularly, China has frequently reported new advances in military modernisation, such as in the Pacific, the country has installed an aircraft carrier laced with all modern technological features; also, a more progressive carrier is under construction, which ought to give strength to Beijing's strategic standing in the region (Saeed, 2017, pp. 507-508). Besides, Beijing has been providing Islamabad with the newest submarines and other naval vessels, and the two frequently carry out regular joint military exercises in the Indian Ocean (ibid, p.

508). Although there have been repeated assertions of the peaceful and defensive character of its military pursuits by China, there has been a concomitant demand for the acceptance of Beijing's "absolutist (but ambiguous) positions on a variety of highly contentious territorial, maritime, and resource disputes" (Malik, 2012, p. 164).

In present times, Beijing gives high importance to the territorial disputes in the East China Sea (ECS) and the South China Sea (SCS). The conflicts between China and other states over the issues of territorial sovereignty and resource claims in these strategically essential seas form crucial sets of concerns for the region (Swaine, 2013). Importantly, six countries have laid overlapping claims to the ECS and the SCS, an area that is a powerhouse of reserves of hydrocarbons and natural gas and which also serves as a passage for trillions of dollars of global trade flow (Council on Foreign Relations, n.d.). It seems that Beijing associates the assertiveness and defence of its maritime territorial claims in these two seas and gives strength to its standing in the South China Sea to its national priorities (Members and Committees of Congress, 2021, p. 8).

Notably, many key factors have led China to become much more assertive in the maritime domain in a quest to safeguard its rapidly growing interests (Braun., *et.al* 2016, pp. 19-20). These are an increased focus on the ECS and the SCS; a belief that the US rebalance is targeted towards China, which accords Beijing's assertion as largely a response to the US strategic rebalance towards the Asia-Pacific; puts the blame on the USA for giving "wrong signals to China's neighbours", particularly to those who seek to take exception to China's territorial claims in the SCS and the ECS; challenges posed by the Chinese pursuit for maritime strength and; the heavy dependence of the rapidly developing Chinese economy on the trade and resources via the sea route (ibid).

Beijing has continued to assert its territorial claims and sovereignty in both the East China Sea and the South China Sea while slowly "stepping up its grey zone activities in air and sea in these areas" (Satake, 2020, p. 44). Over the last few years, China has resorted to some extreme steps in order to lay claim to thousands of square feet in the SCS (Council on Foreign Relations, n.d.). For instance, the PLA's submarines and other naval vessels have, from time to time, approached and even infiltrated the contiguous zone around the Senkaku Islands of Japan since 2015 (Satake, 2020, p. 44). Moreover, as per the U.S. Department of Defence, Beijing has positioned anti-ship and anti-aircraft missile systems on the Spratly Islands and also built military architecture like runways, support buildings, loading piers, and communications facilities on many artificial islands (Council on Foreign Relations, n.d.). Despite the July 2016 ruling of an arbitration tribunal constituted under Annex VII of the United Nations Convention on the Law of the Sea (UNCLOS) against China's maritime claims made on the basis of a nine-dash line in the SCS, China has continued the construction of military facilities and deployment of military means in both the Spratly and Paracel Islands (Satake, 2020, pp. 44-45).

With such a rapid expansion in China's maritime claims and infrastructure deployment on artificial islands, there has been increasing assertions from other claimants in the region like Japan, the Philippines, and Vietnam, which has transformed the ECS and the SCS into theatres of escalating territorial disputes (Council on Foreign Relations, n.d.). The increasingly assertive posture displayed by China has also ignited apprehensions over an armed conflict and given rise to concerns about US security commitments in the region (ibid). China's extensive military overtures in the South China Sea have raised apprehensions amongst several US observers that China is acquiring an "effective control of the SCS", which is an area that carries immense strategic, political, and economic value for the USA and its associates (Members and Committees of Congress, 2021, p. 1). It is important to note here that simultaneously with the increased Chinese assertion in this crucial area, the USA, which has important stakes in the dispute, has concomitantly enhanced its military activities and naval presence in the seas, which, if not dealt with in a wise manner, carries the risk of turning the maritime areas of the Asia-Pacific from a vital passage of trade into conflict-zones (Council on Foreign Relations, n.d.).

The evolving shape of security and strategy in the Asia-Pacific, according to several analysts, will be largely defined by Beijing's political, economic, and military progression. This view, on the one hand, is propelled by the undoubtable realities of China's size, geographic location, historical past, and inherent power potential, and on the other hand, it is the great economic development, military build-up, and assertiveness towards its claims in the ECS, SCS and Taiwan that make these concerns all the more alluring (Pollack, 1998, p. 1). The appearance of China as "a major power in the Western Pacific" alongside its increasing military assertion can possibly be a marker of "the end of the Vasco da Gama epoch of Western dominance in the Western Pacific" (Fels, 2017, p. 11). Jonathan D. Pollack argues that although the military abilities of China ought not to be overrated, its enrichment and strategic intentions behind them shall be instrumental in defining the future security framework of the region of Asia-Pacific in either positive or negative ways (Pollack, 1998, p. 1). Clearly, the USA is confronted with the growing assertiveness of China in both economic and military terms in the region of the Asia-Pacific (Fels, 2017, p. 5). Beijing's passion in chasing its interests in the Western Pacific has essentially strained Sino-US relations, more so when both the powers are grappling with a phase of evolving power dynamics (Braun *et.al.*, 2016, p. 20). Given the undeniable rise of China, the Sino-US competition has become an important feature of the Asia-Pacific order. It becomes crucial to assess the rapid rise of China in the context of the continued clout and presence of the USA in the region and the role of the middle powers and alliance systems.

Assessing Sino-US Competition in the Asia-Pacific

The striking happenings in the post-Cold War era and China's pursuits and outlook to become a global power to pose a challenge to US primacy and outstrip it in due course has implications for the power structure, peace and stability in not only the region but also the world at large. Enrico Fels argues that the theme of the burgeoning competition between the USA and China and a transition in power owing to China's impressive economic development has been widely discussed and debated; however, there has been a lack of a holistic and well-structured study of the purported connection between economic development and a real power shift in the Asia-Pacific region (Fels, 2017, p. 57). In studying the Sino-US competition, the aim here is to probe whether a transition in power in favour of China, thereby diminishing the US clout, has actually taken place in the region.

Importantly, the policy orientation, approach and understanding of the regional order of the two powers, the USA and China, differ in various aspects. The position of the USA in the evolving international order has witnessed significant changes in the post-Cold War period after it enjoyed a short phase of true global unipolarity subsequent to the collapse of the Soviet Union in 1991 (Fels, 2017, p. 2). The USA seems wary of an increasingly assertive China, which seeks to dominate the regional order in the Asia-Pacific with its spectacular economic growth, massive connectivity initiatives like the BRI and strengthening military prowess, which carries the potential to eventually "exclude" the USA from regional affairs (Saeed, 2017, p. 501). Therefore, successive US administrations have sought to adopt highly confrontational strategies such as the "Pivot to Asia" strategy and revitalisation of initiatives such as the Quadrilateral Security Dialogue. The USA pursues a comparatively forthright policy of executing measures of "pre-emption, unilateralism and hegemony assisted by its alliance system with the purpose of spreading liberal democracy and the rule of law", which is largely guided by a conviction that its massive economic and military strength provides it with the means to impose the form of governance and ideals of state conduct preferred by it (Odgaard, 2007, p. 215), whereas China is "the shadow boxer", which means that its desires and policies are relatively unclear, which leads to "the fear of the great unknown" and thereby causes resentment to a "Sino-centric order" (ibid, p. 216). In explaining the essentially competing conceptions of regional order advocated by Washington and Beijing, Liselotte Odgaard states:

Washington advocates an order predominantly based on military instruments in contrast to Beijing, which promotes an order founded in the instruments of diplomacy. This difference means that the USA concentrates on activities such as the reorganisation of its military presence to increase the credibility of flexible response and preventive first-use, the involvement of US armed forces in the domestic security policies of other states, and the maintenance of its Cold War alliance system as the basis of permanent security arrangements in the Asia-Pacific. For its part, China increasingly focuses on the forging of compromises with states that are, at least partially, supportive of Chinese interim demands for respect for the absolute sovereignty of states, acceptance of political authorities with a proven record of control over geographically delimited territories and people, and institutionalized security arrangements founded in the UN system of the Cold War. (Odgaard, 2007, p. 222)

Evidently, Washington and Beijing's interests and pursuits in the Asia-Pacific differ largely from each other. Arguably, given such essentially conflictual and divergent standpoints regarding regional order, Washington and Beijing seem to have delegated a substantial responsibility for the maintenance of stability in the region to middle powers with significant economic and military capabilities to stay partly autonomous of the strategies adopted by the great powers (Odgaard, 2007, p. 222). The question then arises whether the states in Asia will be ready to displease their giant neighbour, China, in order to promote the US cause. (Committee on Foreign Relations, 2005). Walter C. III Ladwig contends that on the one hand, the US ideals of regional order premised on the rule of law and democracy do not indubitably attract every country in the region, although it is not possible to dismiss the US military and political clout in the region; on the other hand, China also has not been able to provide an appealing Sino-centric order, albeit it holds desires to use its economic development to present itself as an alternative to America in the region (Ladwig III, 2009, p. 105). In such a rapidly evolving scenario, the possibility of other regional powers playing a significant role in moulding the regional security structure is huge (ibid). The role of middle powers, great powers and the alliance system thus becomes crucial in deciding the fate of the burgeoning Sino-US competition in the Asia-Pacific and the contours of the regional security architecture.

Understanding the Role of Middle Powers, Great Powers and the Alliance System

The rapid advance in Chinese power holds massive value for the global scenario owing to its equation with the USA and not because it is a contender for global dominance (White & Taylor, 2009, p. 97). In the burgeoning competition between the USA and China, other important powers in the Asia-Pacific have an influential role to play. It, however, becomes crucial to note here that the middle powers have vastly varying security interests, and their relationship with the major powers differs in significant ways (Odgaard, 2007, p. 5). It is the respective relationship of the two powers, the USA and China, with the middle powers that is crucial in deciding the power balance in the Asia-Pacific.

It is the role played by the middle powers in the Asia-Pacific that makes it evident that even though it might first appear that a power transition in the region has occurred in favour of China, it is not actually a clear shift but only a reduction in the gap with the USA as although the ties between Beijing and the middle powers have witnessed some improvement, primarily on the economic front and not in terms of security and strategic cooperation, with Pakistan and Thailand being the only deviations from this trend, these powers have not simultaneously downgraded their ties with Washington (Fels, 2017, pp. 759-760). Moreover, even though a strategic shift favouring Beijing has been seen in Pakistan's stance, it is however important to note that Islamabad nonetheless has not been willing to cease its relations with Washington as in spite of some cynicism displayed by the elites in Pakistan, the many interests fulfilled from cooperation with the USA are immensely desirable. Additionally, the USA has established improved cooperation, particularly in terms of security relations (a concept that is immensely important to the realist framework) with several regional middle powers like Australia, Japan and South Korea (ibid, p. 759). Most of the states in the Asia-Pacific region, more so those that are central to the US alliance system such as the ASEAN member-states, South Korea, India, Taiwan, Japan, Australia and New Zealand, continue to count on the USA for security guarantees and would not want to depend on China even if it acquired the military abilities to do so because, if the choice becomes inevitable, these states would go for a *Pax Americana* instead of a Sino-centric order (Odgaard, 2007, p. 230). Thus the up-gradation in the Chinese position vis-à-vis the middle powers is not a singular factor in analysing the power dynamics in Asia-Pacific as the position of the USA has continued to be indisputably stronger in the domain of security ties as no middle power has substituted it for China. It would then not be an exaggeration to argue that Washington remains the "first among equals" (Odgaard, 2007, p. 230).

Evidently, the USA has been the preferred choice for most of the states in the Asia Pacific when it comes to providing security guarantees as it helps them to reckon with the increasing Chinese strength (Odgaard, 2007, p. 217). The USA, which is a "distant hegemon", continues to be the "balancing power of choice" for a majority of states in the region that form the Chinese neighbourhood (Malik, 2012, p. 165). It can then be argued, in adherence to the realist interpretation of the future balance of power, that the current patterns of allying with the USA in the security domain are expected to continue as the middle powers strive to balance a materially strong China (Fels, 2017, p. 762). While the prolongation of the alliance system with the USA is a thinkable possibility, what is also possible is that the middle powers decide to withhold allegiance to both the USA and China and rather pursue a hedging strategy, albeit continuing some degree of political, economic and security cooperation with both (ibid). Given the failure of both Washington and Beijing to reach an agreement on the core rules of state conduct, the middle powers have so far not been willing to choose between the two outright (Odgaard, 2007, p. 227). Such an evolving equation between the USA and China and the dynamic role played by the middle powers is bound to have an impact on the future structure of power in the Asia-Pacific region and also the global order.

Emerging Power Dynamics in Asia-Pacific: Is there a Shift in the Balance of Power?

The alliance system and the preferences of the middle powers in the region of Asia-Pacific have shown that a true and concrete shift in the balance of power is not observable in the region as although Beijing has improved its ties with the middle powers, it has mostly been limited to the field of economics, and when it comes to the domain of security, which is an important parameter in the realist understanding of international relations, the USA has continued to be stronger and the preferred choice. In the region of the Asia-Pacific, the alliance politics of the USA has helped it to sustain an alliance-based power balance in its favour (Fels, 2017, p. 762). Although there has been a relative decline in the position of the USA in the region, nonetheless, it continues to be "the most sought-after power" as a majority of countries in the region hold the desire to reap the fruits from economic engagements with China, but, at the same time, they do not look forward to a region dominated by Chinese hegemony or their policy choices being circumscribed by it (Malik, 2012, p. 165). Liselotte Odgaard argues that while its policy of "shadow boxing" may render Beijing with the political influence that is over what can be justified by its abilities, nevertheless, it fails to garner loyal allies and partners, which could ultimately allow it to triumph in the contest for influence in the global order (Odgaard, 2007, p. 217). Given the continued salience of the USA in the political affairs of the region, it would be an oversimplification to state that a power shift favouring China has taken place in the Asia-Pacific where the latter has managed to either crowd out the former or initiate a great power war although there have been some impressive material developments displayed by it (Fels, 2017, p. 761).

Although a clear shift in the balance of power has not been observable in the region of the Asia-Pacific so far, however, what cannot be denied is the fact that China has risen as a massive force in the region with the potential to alter the future regional security framework. Here it becomes interesting to look at four alternative strategic scenarios for the Asia-Pacific as laid down by Mohan Malik in analysing the geopolitical implications of Beijing's impressive growth. These are: firstly, "Weak Unipolarity" where the USA remains the pre-eminent power, while its ties with Beijing are characterised by security competition and economic cooperation; secondly, a "Concert of Powers in a Multipolar Asia," where the forces of economic interconnectedness and regional connectivity propagated by multilateral institutions allow the various powers active in the region like the USA, China, Japan, India, and Russia to work together in order to manage the economic and security affairs of the region; thirdly, the scenario is "Bipolar Asia: A New Cold War?" where Beijing attempts to attain predominance in the region as a harbinger to rival Washington in the international order at large ; and, last but not the least, the fourth scenario is a "China-Led Asian Co-Prosperity Sphere: Back to the Future?" which proposes conditions that may cause Asia to accommodate itself to the astonishing rise in Chinese power and thereby trigger it to accept China's supremacy in the region (Azizian & Lukin, 2012, p. 15). Of the four possible schemes discussed above, it is an amalgamation of weak unipolarity at the global and regional levels and bipolarity in Asia characterised by "geopolitical competition and selective partnership on transnational issues of mutual interest" that carry the highest probability in the near future (Malik, 2012, p.

177). Liselotte Odgaard argues that coexistence between the two major powers in the Asia-Pacific, namely, Beijing and Washington, is not a possibility, and thus, "an unstable balancing situation" is likely to prevail (Odgaard, 2007, p. 4). Diverse cultures, different political regime types, historic estrangements, shifting balance of power, and rapid economic changes are some of the distinguishing characteristic features of the Asia-Pacific region that have led many to visualise the region as a future theatre for rivalry with security dilemmas, prestige competition, territorial clashes, nationalist resentments, and economic disputes expected to swell and envelop the region (Ikenberry & Mastanduno, 2003, p. 2). The significant economic and military growth and the rising influence of China have essentially triggered a process of "power transition competition" between the USA and China, which has a revisionist nature (Braun *et.al.*, 2016, p. 7). Power transition competition implies a struggle between the "big and powerful" states, where "big" is understood in respect of territory, demographics, and developmental state; and "powerful" means influence in global matters, not merely on particular issues but aimed to shape the future world order and the rules of state conduct (ibid, pp. 7-8). It is argued that the myriad variables of this struggle between Washington and Beijing make it difficult to concretely predict a clear shift in power from the USA to China or an extension of the US pre-eminence; however, what it actually triggers is a modification in the very norms through which various states interact in international affairs, thereby leading to the possibility of change in the existing global system (ibid, p. 8).

It is thus the manner in which the Sino-US ties are marked by a growing strategic evolving competition that is expected to singularly be the most important political factor in deciding not just the future of the region of the Asia-Pacific but also the contours of an international security framework (White & Taylor, 2009, pp. 97-98). Positive developments in Sino-US ties are expected to help in the continuation of peace and prosperity in global affairs (ibid, p. 97). However, what cannot be denied at the same time is the possibility of the ties becoming adverse given the fact that Beijing's increasing influence is posing an effective challenge to US dominance (ibid, p. 98). Considering the severe implications in case of an eruption of either a hot or cold war between the USA and China, not merely for them but even for other states in the region of the Asia-Pacific and beyond, it becomes crucial to explore new avenues for enhanced cooperation between the two important powers (Fels, 2017, p. 767).

The rise of China is one of the most critical developments in the contemporary scene of international affairs in general and the Asia-Pacific region in particular. The management of Beijing's increasing power and influence and moulding its behaviour has erupted as one of the most significant challenges being faced by the Asia-Pacific and international order in recent times (Malik, 2012, p. 165). From the point of view of Beijing, Washington holds the intention to function in tandem with its allies and security partners in the region, such as New Delhi, in order to reinforce its strategic pre-eminence (Saeed, 2017, p. 501). In this context, it becomes crucial to map the engagement of India in the Asia-Pacific region.

India in the Asia-Pacific Region: Role, Implications and Relevance of the Quadrilateral Security Dialogue

While it is the theme of unipolarity that broadly defines the global order, the regional order in the Asia-Pacific is displaying trends of multi-polarity as, although the USA continues to be the pre-eminent power in the region, what cannot be overlooked is the significant rise of other important power centres, particularly China, India and Japan (Pant, 2007, p. 56). Besides the powers like the USA, China and Japan, India too has emerged as an important player in the balance of power in the region of the Asia-Pacific (ibid, p. 57). Over the years, New Delhi has been progressively working on expanding its strategic focus from the South Asian region to the Pacific region (Ladwig III, 2009, p. 105). Notably, various strategic objectives such as expanding its sphere of influence, achieving strategic autonomy, advancing multi-polarity in the region and balancing against China guide India's engagement with the Asia-Pacific (Brewster, 2011). The interplay of these myriad objectives will largely shape New Delhi's role and engagement in the Asia-Pacific.

The Asia-Pacific has emerged as a crucial region where India must compete with China and balance its rising power. Beijing ultimately views New Delhi as a potential competitor in the Asia-Pacific, which leaves very little space for any compromise between the two (Odgaard, 2007, p. 223). Both the countries aspire for the same things at the same time in the same region (Malik, 2016, p. 49). As New Delhi's great-power ambitions in the region carry the potential to challenge the Chinese position, it leaves Beijing with little or no desire to establish any substantial strategic cooperation with New Delhi and rather underlines Islamabad's position as the best choice as a strategic partner of Beijing in the region (Odgaard, 2007, p. 224).

By contrast, the USA is a dominant global power that actively looks for partners and allies in the region who can effectively contribute towards its strategic predominance without posing a challenge to its core interests and in the long run, the USA intends to prioritise India, as a strategic partnership between the two is bound to propagate Washington's version of the Asia-Pacific order in the South Asian region (Odgaard, 2007, pp. 223-227). Thus, despite its cold attitude towards Washington's scheme to consolidate *Pax Americana*, New Delhi remains the first choice because of its position and influence over South Asia and the Indian Ocean (ibid, pp. 223-224). Simultaneously, India envisions utilising its strategic relations with the USA to strengthen its position vis-à-vis Beijing and also to mitigate adverse steps from Islamabad (Malik, 2016, p. 50). In the long run, by choosing *Pax Americana* over a Sino-centric order, New Delhi's policy approach in the Asia-Pacific has worked towards enhancing its own regional role and at the same time has made an attempt to hedge its ties with China (Ladwig III, 2009, p. 105). Thus the foreign policy of New Delhi in the Asia-Pacific region has sought to institute itself as a major power in the region and to curtail Beijing's influence; it is to achieve this objective that New Delhi has become closer to the USA and Japan as the three share several common and overlapping values and interests in the region (Pant, 2007, p. 68).

India has steadily attained a position to significantly influence the balance of power in the Asia-Pacific largely due to its growing economy, bolstering maritime capacities and its security relations with the USA, Japan, Australia, and several key nations in Southeast Asia (Ladwig III, 2009, pp. 104-105). Importantly, although it is often thought to be "caught in the middle" of the interests of Beijing and Washington in the region, it becomes crucial to realise that New Delhi's own strategic policy is taking shape and gaining influence as it establishes closer economic ties with the countries in the region (Carnegie Endowment for International Peace, 2012). Although India recognises the merits of the US alliance system in ensuring stability in the Asia-Pacific region and is on the same page with several countries of the East and Southeast Asia which favour the US role in the region through economic, political, and military engagement, it becomes important to realise that in adopting such a position, India is in no way willing to subordinate itself to other powers nor is it surrendering itself as a junior partner in any alliance; instead it is chasing its own goals as "an emerging great power", whose interests currently overlap those of the USA and its regional partners (Ladwig III, 2009, p. 106).

With the rise of China, the USA is drawing India into a strategic role in the Asia-Pacific. It encourages it to extend its reach into the Pacific Ocean and form strategic partnerships with its Pacific allies (Brewster, 2011). In this context, the emergence of the Quadrilateral Security Dialogue (also known as Quad or QSD) becomes a crucial development. Importantly, the QSD, as a regional mini-lateral grouping, is a step to facilitate India's involvement in the twenty-first century's great power politics in Asia by creating "a coalition of democracies against the rising revisionist power" (Satake, 2020, p. 45). The incessant emergence of alliances and counter alliances creates new regional power dynamics (Thoker & Singh, 2018, p. 82). In recent times, the Quad and its renewed presence have been a very significant development from the point of view of the power dynamics in the Asia-Pacific region. It is a manifestation of the increased cooperation between India and the USA, along with others in the region. The alliance carries the potential to pose a significant challenge to the rise and ambitions of China in the region. Notably, the changes in the international structure, primarily triggered by the rise of China and the continuous 'power shift' in the region since around 2008, has been a major contributing factor in the expanding momentum for the renewal of the Quad in the USA and India, along with Japan and Australia (Satake, 2020, p. 44). At the same time, it becomes important to note that the revival of the Quad has sparked debates about the renewed attempts to erect "a potential anti-China alliance" (Eisentraut & Gaens, 2018, p. 3). A manifestation of such an attitude is found in the criticism raised by the Chinese media that the Quad initiative is "a possible first step towards an Asian NATO" and the comparison of the idea of the revival of Quad to "sea foam, destined to dissipate soon" by the Chinese Minister of Foreign Affairs, Wang Yi (ibid).

The Quad is primarily a strategic dialogue among four countries, namely the USA, Australia, India and Japan. The framework, known as the Quadrilateral Security Dialogue (QSD) or Quad, was first taken up for discussion when its four member countries closely worked together as a core group following the tsunami disaster that struck the Indian Ocean in 2004 (Satake, 2020, p. 42). It was followed by the first informal meeting between the four countries held in 2007 on the sidelines of the ASEAN Regional Forum (ARF) in Manila, the Philippines (Thu, 2020, p. 91). Ever since the first senior official-level meeting in 2007, the Quad has been operating both as a framework for meetings of senior officials to discuss matters relating to security in the region and as a base for a single naval and tabletop exercise (Buchan & Rimland, 2020, p. 1). In the decade following its initial inception, the regional strategic scenario has become tenser, and several apprehensions have been raised about the Chinese ascent and actions in the region, which seem to justify the renewal of the initiative with a greater force (Thu, 2020, p. 92).

Notably, the Quad initiative has returned to prominence in the pandemic era, with the first Quad summit being held in March 2021, albeit through virtual mode given the limitations and resulting precautions raised due to the spread of the novel corona virus. The virtual Quad meeting was attended by leaders of all four countries, namely, US President Joe Biden, Australian Prime Minister Scott Morrison, Indian Prime Minister Narendra Modi, and Japanese Prime Minister Yoshihide Suga (Smith, 2021). As of 2021, the leadership in all the member-states of the Quad has become increasingly aligned in their common apprehensions regarding the growing Chinese assertiveness in the region and seem to be highly inclined towards defining a constructive agenda for enhanced cooperation (ibid). It has been iterated that the primary goal of the initiative is to maintain the liberal rule-based global order, which Beijing seems to be undermining in posing a revisionist challenge to the status quo and thus, the primary work of the initiative is aimed not at the erection of institutions or military alliances, but on the generation of a steady convergence of cooperation on various issues such as climate change, COVID-19 pandemic, critical and emerging technologies, counter-terrorism, cyber security and disaster recovery (D'Ambrogio).

Suppose the USA, India, Japan, and Australia are able to coordinate and co-operate their military and economic policies in an effective manner by working in close consultation. In that case, information sharing and military exercises, China's pursuit of attaining hegemony in the region can be conclusively deterred (Satake, 2020, p. 47). The QSD can effectively lay the ground for creating a parity that is crucial in maintaining stable ties between Beijing and regional powers, thereby contributing to the creation of a more stable regional balance of power (ibid, pp. 47-48).

Conclusion: Asia-Pacific as the New Power Centre of World Geopolitics?

What is evident is that the evolving architecture of power balance and security in the Asia-Pacific region is highly uncertain when compared to the outright bipolar order prevalent during the Cold War phase. While US hegemony characterised the regional order for a long time, the emergence of new powers in the region, particularly China and India, appear ready to transform the Asia-Pacific.

In recent times, the heart of global geopolitics has arguably drifted to the region of the Asia-Pacific with the rapid ascent of China and India and a marked focus being accrued by the USA in favour of the region. It becomes tempting to predict the future balance of power in this important region in such a scenario. However, given the fact that the massive rise of China has taken place in the context of the continued salience of the USA and the presence of various other powers like Japan and India, it becomes difficult to forecast a decisive shift in the balance of power in the region of the Asia-Pacific. What is, however, clear is the need and importance of creating a more stable power balance as the Sino-US competition rapidly escalates in the region and beyond. Diverse powers, including Japan, India, Australia, and member countries of the Association of Southeast Asian Nations (ASEAN), can play a more significant role in maintaining a multiple power balance in the region. In this context, initiatives like the Quad grouping can help create a more stable power balance that supports a free, open and inclusive Asia-Pacific order.

Notably, three important powers in the contemporary global order, among others, namely, the USA, China and India, interact in the Asia-Pacific region, which makes it highly probable that the evolving patterns of state conduct in the region will prove to be instrumental in determining the future world order. Moreover, other vital powers in the region like Japan, Russia, Australia, and North and South Korea, to mention a few, which have not been the focus of this study, are also critical players in the region and thereby are instrumental in shaping the regional order. The rise of China, particularly in the context of the BRI strategy, the burgeoning Sino-US competition and the evolving role and strategies of other vital powers like India, have then been central to shaping and reshaping the power dynamics in the Asia-Pacific, a region that has clearly emerged as the theatre of complex global power manoeuvrings. , the contours of power dynamics in the Asia-Pacific thus hold significance in determining the future global order as the region has emerged as the pivot for the interactions of the major global powers.

REFERENCES

Alon, I., Zhang, W. & Lattemann, C. (2018). Introduction. In I. Alon, W. Zhang, & C. Lattemann (eds.), *China's Belt and Road Initiative: Changing the Rules of Globalization* (pp. 1-14). Switzerland: Palgrave Macmillan.

Andersen, L.E. & Jiang, Y. (2018). *China's engagement in Pakistan, Afghanistan and Xinjiang*. Danish Institute for International Studies.

Azizian, R. & Lukin, A. (2012). Introduction. In R.A. Lukin (ed.), *From APEC 2011 to APEC 2012: American and Russian Perspectives on Asia-Pacific Security and Cooperation* (pp. 7-20). Honolulu and Vladivostok: Asia-Pacific Centre for Security Studies and Far Eastern Federal University.

Braun, W.G.; Lai, D.; Lee, J.A.; Asbery, T.; Ngo, D.; Conroy, J.P. and Gellert, F.J. (2016). *U.S.-China Competition: Asia-Pacific Land Force Implications*. Strategic Studies Institute and U.S. Army War College Press.

Brewster, D. (2011). *India as an Asia Pacific Power*. London: Routledge.

Buchan, P.G. & Rimland, B. (2020, March 16). *Defining the Diamond: The Past, Present, and Future of the Quadrilateral Security Dialogue*. Retrieved August 2, 2021, from Centre for Strategic and International Studies: https://www.csis.org/analysis/defining-diamond-past-present-and-future-quadrilateral-security-dialogue

Carneige Endowment for International Peace. (2012, September 27). *India's Role in the Asia Pacific*. Retrieved July 31, 2021, from https://carnegieendowment.org/2012/09/27/india-s-role-in-asia-pacific-event-3830

Chan, L.-H. (2020, June 5). Can China remake regional order? Contestation with India over the Belt and Road Initiative. *Global Change, Peace and Security*, 32(2), 199-217.

Committee on Foreign Relations. (2005, June 7). The Emergence of China throughout Asia: Security and Economic Consequences for the United States. Hearing before the Subcommittee on East Asian and Pacific Affairs of the Committee on Foreign Relations United States Senate. Washington: Government Printing Office. Retrieved from http://www.access.gpo.gov/congress/senate

Council on Foreign Relations. (n.d.). *China's Maritime Disputes*. Retrieved August 3, 2021, from cfr.org/chinas-maritime-disputes/#!/chinas-maritime-disputes?cid=otr-marketing_use-china_sea_InfoGuide

D'Ambrogio, E. (n.d.). *The Quad: An emerging multilateral security framework of democracies in the Indo-Pacific region*. Retrieved August 2, 2021, from European Parliamentary Research Service (EPRS): https://www.europarl.europa.eu/RegData/etudes/BRIE/2021/690513/EPRS_BRI(2021)690513_EN.pdf

Eisentraut, S. & Gaens, B. (2018, May). The US-Japan-India-Australia Quadrilateral Security Dialogue: Indo-Pacific Alignment or Foam in the Ocean. *FIIA Briefing Paper* 239. Finnish Institute of International Affairs.

Fels, E. (2017). *Shifting Power in Asia-Pacific? The Rise of China, Sino-US Competition and Regional Middle Power Allegiance*. Switzerland: Springer International Publishing.

Gong, X. (2020, 2020). China's Economic Statecraft: The Belt and Road in Southeast Asia and the Impact on the Indo-Pacific. *Security Challenges*, 16(3), 39-46.

Ikenberry, G.J. & Mastanduno, M. (2003). Introduction. In G. J. Ikenberry & M. Mastanduno (eds.), *International Relations Theory and the Asia-Pacific* (pp. 1-21). New York: Columbia University Press.

Job, B.L. (2009). Grappling with an elusive concept. In W. T. Tow (ed.), *Security Politics in the Asia-Pacific A Regional–Global Nexus?* New York, United States of America: Cambridge University Press.

Jinping, X. (2017, October 18). *Secure a Decisive Victory in Building a Moderately Prosperous Society in All Respects and Strive for the Great Success of Socialism with Chinese Characteristics for a New Era*. Retrieved September 10, 2020, from http://www.xinhuanet.com/english/download/Xi_Jinping%27s_report_at_19th_ CPC _ National_Congress.pdf

Kuo, L. & Kommenda, N. (2018, July 30). *What is China's Belt and Road Initiative?* Retrieved September 10, 2020, from *The Guardian*: https://www.theguardian.com/cities/ng-interactive/2018/jul/30/what-china-belt-road-initiative-silk-road-explainer

Ladwig III, W.C. (2009, May 28). Delhi's Pacific Ambition: Naval Power, "Look East," and India's Emerging Influence in the Asia-Pacific. *Asian Security*, 5(2), 87-113.

Macaes, B. (2019). *Belt and Road: A Chinese World Order*. Penguin Books.

Mayer, M. (2018). China's Rise as Eurasian Power: The Revival of the Silk Road and Its Consequences. In M. Mayer (ed.), *Rethinking the Silk Road: China's Belt and Road Initiative and Emerging Eurasian Relations* (pp. 1-42). Singapore: Palgrave Macmillan.

Malik, M. (2012). China in the Asia-Pacific in 2040: Alternative Futures. In R. Azizian & A. Lukin (eds.), *From APEC 2011 to APEC 2012: American and Russian Perspectives on Asia-Pacific Security and Cooperation* (pp. 162-177). Honolulu and Vladivostok: Asia-Pacific Centre for Security Studies and Far Eastern Federal University.

Malik, M. (2016). Balancing Act: The China-India-U.S. Triangle. *World Affairs*, 179(1).

Members and Committees of Congress. (2021). *U.S.-China Strategic Competition in South and East China Seas: Background and Issues for Congress.* Congressional Research Service.

Odgaard, L. (2007). *The Balance of Power in Asia-Pacific Security: US–China policies on regional order.* London and New York, USA and Canada: Routledge: Taylor & Francis Group.

Pant, H.V. (2007). India in the Asia–Pacific: Rising Ambitions with an Eye on China. *Asia-Pacific Review*, 14(1).

Pollack, J.D. (1998). Asian-Pacific Responses to a Rising China. In J. D. Pollack & R. H. Yang (eds.), *In China's Shadow: Regional Perspectives on Chinese Foreign Policy and Military Development.* RAND.

Saeed, M. (2017). From the Asia-Pacific to the Indo-Pacific Expanding Sino-U.S. Strategic Competition. *China Quarterly of International Strategic Studies*, 3(4), 499-512.

Satake, T. (2020). The future of the Quadrilateral Security Dialogue: Possibilities and challenges. In B. Singh & S. Teo (eds.), *Minilateralism in the Indo-Pacific: The Quadrilateral Security Dialogue, Lancang-Mekong Cooperation Mechanism, and ASEAN* (1st edn., pp. 42-56). New York: Routledge: Taylor & Francis Group.

Schortgen, F. (2018). China and the Twenty-First-Century Silk Roads: A New Era of Global Economic Leadership? In W. Zhang, I. Alon, & C. Lattemann (eds.), *China's Belt and Road Initiative: Changing the Rules of Globalization* (pp. 17-34). Switzerland: Palgrave Macmillan.

Smith, S.A. (2021, May 27). *The Quad in the Indo-Pacific: What to Know.* Retrieved August 2, 2021, from Council on Foreign Relations: https://www.cfr.org/in-brief/quad-indo-pacific-what-know

Swaine, M.D. (2013, April 4). *China's Maritime Disputes in the East and South China Seas.* Retrieved August 3, 2021, from Carnegie Endowment for International Peace: https://carnegieendowment.org/2013/04/04/china-s-maritime-disputes-in-east-and-south-china-seas-pub-51417

Thoker, P.A. & Singh, B. (2018, July-September). India In The Asia–Pacific Power Dynamics. *World Affairs: The Journal of International Issues*, 22(3), 82-93.

Thu, H.L. (2020). The Quadrilateral Security Dialogue and ASEAN centrality. In B. Singh & S. Teo (eds.), *Minilateralism in the Indo-Pacific: The Quadrilateral Security Dialogue, Lancang-Mekong Cooperation Mechanism, and ASEAN* (pp. 88-102). New York: Routledge: Taylor & Francis Group.

Vaughn, B. & Morrison, W. M. (2006). *China-Southeast Asia Relations: Trends, Issues, and Implications for the United States.* CRS Report for Congress, Congressional Research Service, The Library of Congress. Retrieved from Congressional Research Service, The Library of Congress.

White, H. & Taylor, B. (2009). A rising China and American perturbations. In W. T. Tow (ed.), *Security Politics in the Asia-Pacific: A Regional–Global Nexus?* (pp. 85-98). New York, United States of America: Cambridge University Press.

Wolf, S.O. (2020). *The China-Pakistan Economic Corridor of the Belt and Road Initiative: Concept, Context and Assessment.* Switzerland: Springer Nature Switzerland AG.

5

Transformation of Sino-Indian Relations in South Asia: A post COVID Assessment

Dr. Sujit Kumar Datta

ABSTRACT

The purpose of this paper is to search why and how Sino-Indian relations in South Asia will transform in the post COVID era. When two big neighbouring countries of comparable national power are vying for influence in South Asia and strategic space, competition is bound to occur. Geographically, India is supposed to be a South Asian provincial supremacy, but a nearer appearance exposes it in an unfavourable location vis-à-vis China in that region. The most crucial factor is that the Indian government does not have more political, financial, and martial capabilities to track the South Asian regional power's determination in the long run. So, all the South Asian small states could continuously show China to balance India's effect in their countries. However, these disagreements have evolved from a confrontation to the mixed elements of competition and cooperation in the current period. Sino-Indian relations in South Asia have undergone a transformation with momentum toward collaboration on several South Asian regional issues over the last two decades. With Chinese inspiration in the South Asian region rising day by day, it is vital that India does not fall behindhand in the South Asian area but preserves a stable dominance in that region. In brief, this paper will articulate the construction of a valuable analytical outline for the investigation of the transformation of the Sino-Indian relationship in South Asia in the post COVID era, revealing the importance of external factors in influencing Sino-Indian bilateral and multilateral interactions throughout the adjustment of the order of their political and strategic preferences.

Keywords: *COVID-19, Transformation, Rivalry, Security Dilemma, Regional power, Hegemony.*

Introduction

South Asia is a word used to denote the southern part of the Asian continent comprising the South Asian Association for Regional Cooperation (SAARC) countries. South Asia is bounded on the south by the Indian Ocean and land in West Asia, Central Asia, East Asia, and Southeast Asia (World Bank, 2018). China always wants a peaceful and development-oriented relationship with South Asian counties. Besides, South Asian small counties need more economic cooperation from China and India. The peaceful growth of China has become more pertinent against the background of South Asia as it is perceived not as a threat to neighbouring countries as the conventional International Relations theories argues concerning the rise of a hegemony; instead, the East Asian countries accommodated the rise of China than balancing it since this rise comes with an 'absence of fear (Bijan, Z., 2005).

However, this has not been the case with China's immediate big neighbour, India, also vying to be a significant, influential authority in that region. The 'geopolitical centrality' of South Asia had been recognized by mainly the British colonial administration. As a result, traditional geopolitical understanding of international relations has resurfaced where both the countries are set to construct their global identity as 'the Asian Power' (Srinivasan, T.N., 2005). In this context, this thesis argues that the South Asian state has emerged as one of the main parts to transform the Sino-Indian relationship in South Asia from 1988 to 2018. With the rising effect of China and India as Asian giants, this thesis argues that the two powers are vying for geopolitical supremacy in that area though India is far behind China in all kinds of national and international components.

The Background of Research

The steady growth of China and rising India defines the Asian century with a corresponding impact on their domestic landscapes and affecting the regional and global order. China has, for centuries, maintained connections with South Asian nations, and Chinese travellers have written extensively about the region. China shares its boundary through five South Asian states, namely, Afghanistan, Bhutan, India, Nepal, and Pakistan. On the other hand, there is a geographical link between mountains and rivers with South Asian countries and China. While India is far behind China in the ranking of the world economy, the democratic credentials of India happen to place New Delhi in the good books of the great authorities, particularly the USA. However, South Asia does not appear central to the Chinese global view. South Asia has not also been capable of creating a value chain for China in the worldwide market. China generally looks at South Asia from several perspectives. Nonetheless, geographically, India promoted South Asian-related diplomacy in the present century as its neighbourhood policy towards South Asian nations. India is a vital country of South Asia that can manage regional security.

Map 1: Countries of South Asia

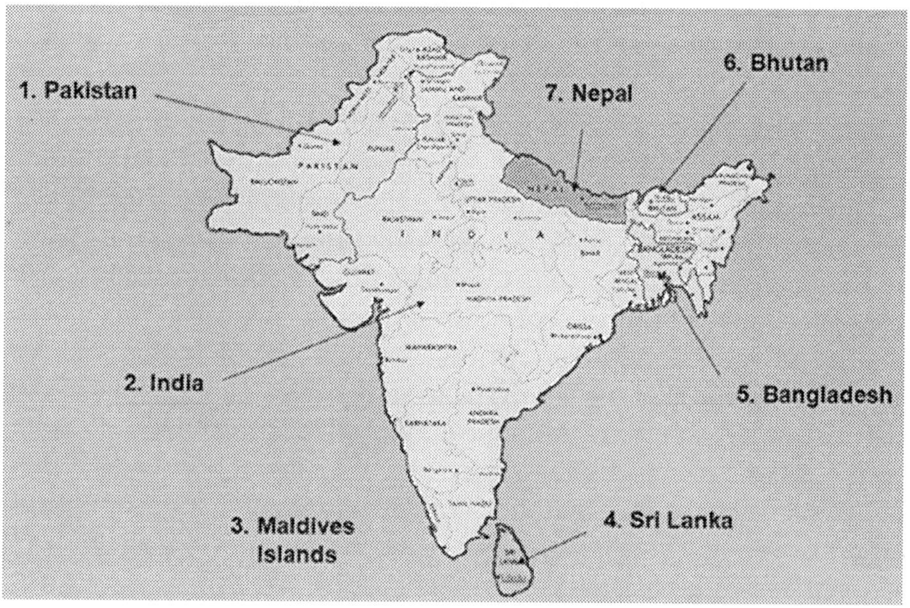

Source: www. images.wisegeek.com

During the last seven decades, China has maintained excellent relations with South Asian nations to ensure South Asian harmony and safety, and China has followed the "five principles of peaceful coexistence" policy, which is more critical for Chinese foreign policy (Chung, C.P., 2009). Nevertheless, China-India relations in South Asia have transformed to normal from 1988 to 2018. However, the two influential Asian giants still have a challenging aspect of their bilateral relationship. Additionally, extra hegemonic perceptions of India in South Asia challenge China to contain these kinds of hegemonic attitudes. For these reasons, South Asian small countries have maintained a decent relationship with China. In South Asian politics, India's neighbouring countries underscored that peace and progress are the main features of the 21st-century diplomatic vision. On the other hand, China wants to continue a close relationship with its neighbours to develop regional integration. It will create a local integration process to cooperate with its neighbouring countries. China will focus its peace and development activities with South Asian countries like Latin America and Africa to increase partnership spaces and make it additionally productive. Other South Asian nations can be benefited from both sides, like the two Asian giants—China and India.

Map 2: China and South Asia

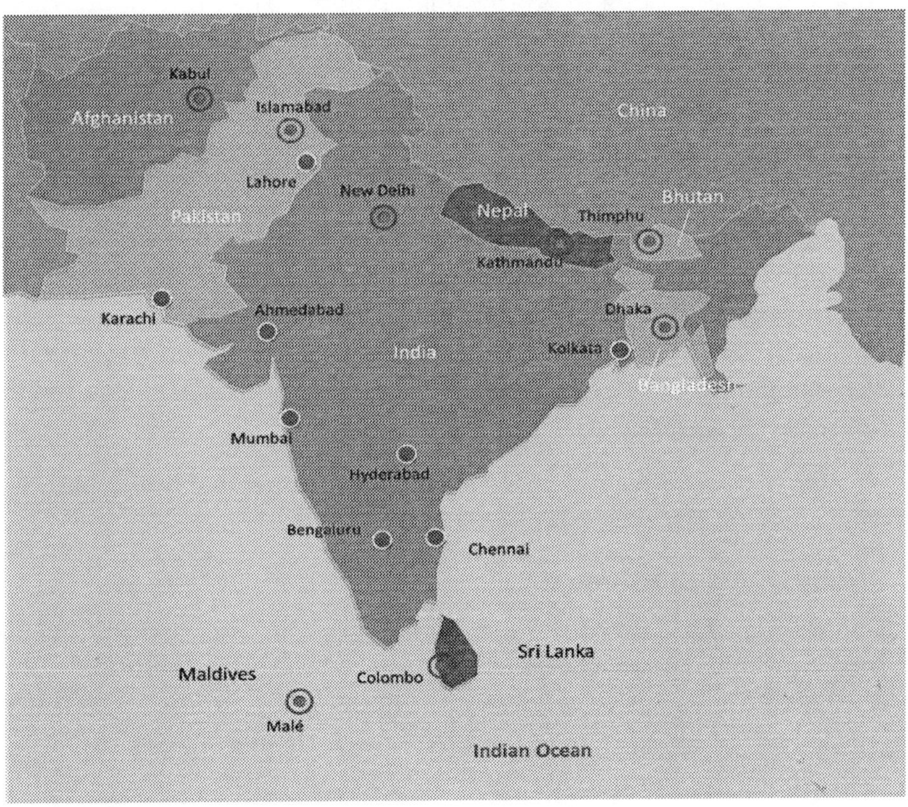

Source: https://yourfreetemplates.com

This opportunity has been accomplished by completing administrative, political, and structural constructions to bring low-tech Chinese factories to South Asian countries, making Chinese investment industrial-energy and infrastructure development, taking full advantage of the ocean-going blue economy. South Asian small states want to take advantage of the rivalry or competition between these two Asian giants, China and India (Pant, H.V., 2013).

It is essential to overcome this situation that the states of this region can come out with their national interest without hurting anyone. Increasing Chinese influence in South Asia is an excellent matter for India. India always wishes to lead South Asia, but some South Asian countries want to make and keep good relations with China. Is a 'Modi doctrine' emerging in Indian foreign policy? (Konwer, S., 2018). For these reasons, there is an unofficial conflict, cooperation, and rivalry amid China and India in South Asian politics. The other South Asian countries should maintain a balanced foreign policy towards China and India (Holslag, J., 2010).

Research Question

This paper will examine the difficulties and opportunities for transforming the Sino-Indian relationship in South Asia. Research questions related to why and how they change and the underlying determinants of the transformation in the behaviour of both the states in South Asian politics. Thus, this paper seeks to explain the transformation of the Sino-Indian relationship in South Asia for the following research question:

> "What factors have contributed to transforming the Sino-Indian relationship in the South Asian region?"

Research Methodology

Several research methods are usually employed in carrying out empirical social researches such as this research. The quantitative and statistical approach is used to conduct cross-national comparative studies based on aggregate data. Although the qualitative method is the primary tool employed in this study, quantitative and statistical methods have been used to get the public view on various issues and questions raised in different sections of this paper.

Thus, the techniques that have been followed include qualitative and interpretative analyses of primary and secondary data and materials such as books, articles, magazines, government official documents, and survey data gathered through email interviews. To explore the involvement of China and India in South Asia, I have done library research combined with an examination of historical agreements and official documents, which included each government's publications, annual reports, defence White Papers, interstate agreements, policy announcements, and speeches to obtain primary sources of information. Secondary sources included academic journal articles, books, newspapers, and information obtained from the media and the Internet. To assess the Sino-Indian transformation relationship in South Asia, I have used data from government documents, such as inter-state treaties and memorandum of understanding, legislative reports, and statistical compilations, which came in many formats, including books, periodicals, maps, and online databases, collect from Chinese, Indian and other South Asian governmental websites.

Theoretical Analysis

Regional transformation is the final category in Holsti's conceptualization of change in international politics. "It means quantitative changes that bring a new form to life when accumulated over a while. However, logically, the new forms must derive from old patterns. They can partly replace old forms, but by definition, they must include residues or legacies of the old. One cannot transform from nothing" (Holsti, K.J., 1964). In other words, transformation means that old ideas, practices, and norms may remain reasonably similar over long periods, but the functions of the institutions change. The main interest in this study will be Holsti's final category transformation for explaining the Sino-Indian transforming relationship in South Asia.

This is because while Holsti is more general and extensive and explains transformation by contextualizing International Relations theory, Paul, by contrast, is more specific and presents it in the context of a region. According to Paul, "regional transformation means 'serious alterations have occurred in relations among states and in terms of their core national interests, strategies, behavioural patterns, perceptions, and institutional structures" (Paul, T.V., 2012). Three criteria stand out as important in Paul's definition of regional transformation; first, meaningful alterations in the perceptions, core interests, and strategies; second, fundamental alterations in behavioural patterns; and third, severe modifications in relations among states. Paul's regional transformation criteria will help us explain the changing way of conflict and cooperation in South Asia and whether the region has changed at the end of the Cold War. For scrutiny in this study, three key areas have been selected: democracy, political economy, and security.

As Paul argues, "Transformational change in a region could occur through the introduction of democratic order, robust economic interdependence, or an institutional framework among the core countries that constitute a region" (Paul, T.V., 2012). This issue primarily concerns the theoretical debate within International Relations about the Sino-Indian transformative relationship in South Asia from 1988 to 2018 between neo-liberalism and realism. Neo-liberalism emphasizes democracy, economic interdependence, and institutions as a feeling of regional peace and order (Russett, Bruce and Oneal John R., 1997). Realism argues that the fundamental source of regional order is the balance of power (Paul, T.V.; Wirtz, James and Fortmann Michael, 2004). While liberalism sees regional transformation as a linear progression toward peace, eventually heading toward a local security community, realism views peace as episodic.

There are three possible scenarios of transformative Sino-Indian relationship in South Asia. These are Cooperation Scenario, Competition Scenario, and Competition with Cooperation Scenario. This thesis will test the hypothesis, arguing on which theoretical background is most appropriate to describe the transformation of the Sino-Indian relationship in South Asia. However, after reviewing the theory of Complex Interdependence and Benjamin Miller's view of significant power involvement in regional politics, this thesis aims to identify which hypotheses derive from this framework and provide the best explanations of transformations of the Sino-Indian relationship in South Asia.

China and India in South Asia are the most robust demand for all South Asian nations. China and India have both been eager to enlarge their economy and power with their neighbours in recent times. Realists and neoliberals agree that countries are the maximum significant performers on the global scene and that egoist interests under the complex interdependence mainly influence their behaviours. However, they have different ideas regarding the attitudes of the state towards the distribution of cooperative gains. According to realists, states utility functions strongly consider how the benefits of cooperation are redistributed among countries, affirming that collaboration can fail if its services change in terms of power distribution. However, great powers have been involved in South Asian politics from different dimensions. Finally, the Sino-Indian transformative relationship in South Asia is related to a complex interdependence theory.

Historical Background of Sino-Indian Relations in South Asia

The history and background of the Sino-Indian bilateral relationship in South Asia include mixed mistrust, cooperation, and competition. "The 'peaceful' rise of China has become more pertinent in the context of Asia as it is perceived not as a threat to the neighbouring countries as the conventional International Relations (IR) theories argue concerning the rise of a hegemony; instead the East Asian countries accommodated the rise of China than balancing it since this rise comes with an 'absence of fear'" (Garver, John W., 2002).

However, "this has not been the case for China's immediate big neighbour, India, also vying to become a leader in Asia. The 'geopolitical' centrality of Asia and the recognition of India and China as continental powers were long recognised by mainly the British colonial administration, especially about the British Raj's impending departure from the continent" (Brobst, Peter John and Sir Olaf Caroe, 2006). It is contended that "the term 'Great Game' was coined by a British Officer named William Connolly around 1840 and was later popularized by Rudyard Kipling to refer to the mastery of Asia" (Brobst, Peter John and Sir Olaf Caroe. 2006). As a result, the traditional geopolitical understanding of international relations has resurfaced where both the countries are set on constructing their global identity as 'the Asian Power.' In the South Asian context, this chapter argues that the South Asian region has arisen as one of the critical areas of possible Sino-Indian strategic competitive location.

Map 3: The Line of Actual Control of the Sino-Indian Border, 1959 to Date

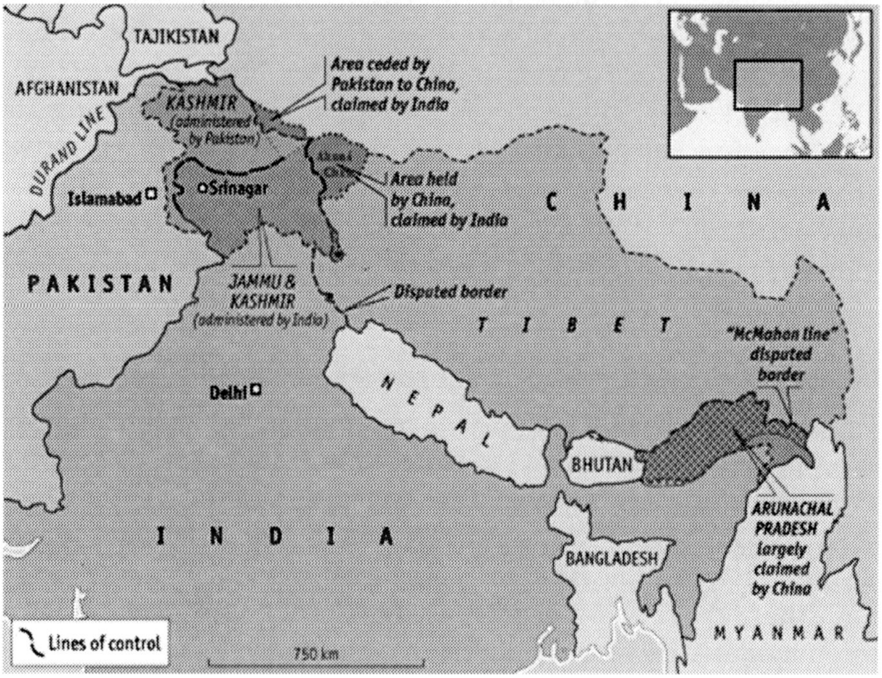

Source: The Economist (2016)

China may not become part of South Asia on the ground geographically, historically, and culturally. However, "China is with South Asia on many grounds like political, strategic, economic, and even cultural. China may not be geographically and historically part of South Asia, but its growing presence is being felt in South Asia, and it is going to keep its presence felt in the affairs of South Asian politics" (Brewster, David Gomà. 2018).

Not many people in South Asia bother much whether China geographically belongs to South Asia or not, except India. There is a discernable difference of opinion about the Chinese role in that region and its impression on the same region politics among cross-sections of people in various South Asian countries. Most people in South Asian countries shape their views of China on differing threat perceptions of different South Asian countries and how China fits into their respective threat perceptions. India perceives China's greater involvement, especially in its ties with Pakistan, Bangladesh, Sri Lanka, and partly, with Nepal, as a threat to itself in terms of security, which it tends to equate with its supremacy over the whole region. Thus, every Chinese step to make an inroad into South Asian politics is considered a threat by India (Van Ness, Peter, 2018).

Besides, all South Asian small countries welcomed China's role, presence, engagement, and greater involvement in this region in all forms and manifestations as stabilizing, favourable, necessary, and geopolitically critical; perhaps Bhutan is the only India-friendly element. (Kumar, Pranav, "Sino-Bhutanese Relations: Under the Shadow of India–Bhutan Friendship", (*China Report*, 2010)

These tiny South Asian countries see China's existence in the area as a countervailing power to India and the West. It increases their autonomy vis-à-vis India and the West too. Besides, many of these countries lament China's 'lacklustre' attitude and response to Indian and US moves in South Asia. These hardliners even urge for more forceful and multifaceted participation of China in South Asian politics. The Indian view on Chinese involvement in South Asia is inquisitive and self-contradictory because Sino-Indian trade is increasing day by day, and it is no problem at all. However, it is problematic whenever China engages in economic and other activities such as trade, aid, investment, and military assistance programs with smaller South Asian countries. Indian policy elites view that as a risk to the 'Common South Asian Identity'. However, the main reason is that China has much more to offer to these smaller South Asian countries while India cannot match it and neither wants to. Either way, there are divergent views in South Asia regarding Chinese involvement in South Asian politics. Sometimes, it is a wonder why the Indian policy elites think that what is suitable for Indians may not be right for other South Asian countries.

Smaller South Asian countries rightly or not perceive India as some threat to them. Thus, it is natural that they would welcome Chinese engagement in this region as that would give them an alternative source for development opportunities and more autonomy vis-à-vis India and the West. China also naturally wants to expand its market and investment and make it friendlier. "India's policy of opposing

Bhutanese attempts to establish diplomatic ties with China is a case in point to understand the Indian attitude towards China in the context of South Asian politics. India always fears that its smaller neighbours are a threat to it in one way or the other and would pose a greater threat if they are on good terms with China" (Gupta, Prakash C. and Ray, Cecily S., 2003).

The Indian policy elites have developed a habit of securitizing economic relations and development activities in other South Asian countries by China while it would not or could not offer economic benefits and investment to them. One wonders if the message is that no need to develop if that is going to be supported by China, the 'extra-regional country because then it will have 'security' implications for South Asia, which is what it stands for with the Indian policy elites (Gonsalves, Eric, 2018).

The Indian policy elites considered as not acceptable the neighbourhood policy as espoused by a former short-time foreign minister and Prime Minister of India, Inder Kumar (I.K.) Gujral and held that interference and meddling in the internal affairs of neighbours is the sure way to maintain influence and dominance. South Asian affairs undercut the basis of a cooperative, harmonious, shared South Asian identity, community, and organization like the SAARC (Murthy, Padmaja, 1999). There is a strong feeling among many South Asian countries that the sub-region should move beyond the present security fixation. The tendency of India, Pakistan, and even others to securitize everything and judge it from the realist security perspective must be amended, and they should refocus on cooperative, prosperous economic development efforts together. However, that would not happen excluding China, which is already involved in the affairs of the region. Whether we like it or not, China has a long border with five South Asian states and very close proximity with Bangladesh (Ali, Syed Muazzem, 2018).

As the Sino-South Asian map shows that South Asia cannot develop itself by excluding Chinese involvement and Chinese hydroelectric projects on the river Tsang Po, as the Brahmaputra is called in Tibet, and China's cooperation should not be limited between China-India and China-Pakistan. However, all countries should have a win-win economic equation and other ties with China. Only prosperous and secure neighbours can give India more security, while weak, poor, unstable, vulnerable, and dominated neighbours would create more insecurity and keep India down along with entire South Asia. China, it seems at least shortly, does not want to challenge Indian pre-eminence in South Asia. Bosworth, Barry, and Susan M. Collins state it as "Accounting for growth: comparing China and India" (Bosworth, B. & Collins, S.M., 2008).

The best possible way for the whole of South Asia would be to forge a cooperative, stabilizing, development-based relationship with a rising China rather than ostracizing it or shying away from it and securitizing its involvement in the affairs of the South Asian region. China has become a global actor as well as an actor in the South Asian sub-region. All should strive to find ways to engage China in a positive, stabilizing developmental role in South Asia and how the Sino-South Asian relationship can usher in a prosperous future for both South Asia and China.

Factors to Transform Sino-Indian Relations in South Asia in the post COVID Era

Sino-Indian transformative relations in South Asia have become increasingly involved in the last few decades. Though bilateral trade and cooperation have been growing, concerns have been increasingly strained by mutual suspicion and intermittent disputes. Given the vast influence the two Asian giants have over the global strategic environment, a critical question will be whether they can maintain a stable relationship amidst their growing distrust. This chapter will analyze the independent variables—political and economic factors which transform the Sino-Indian relationship in South Asia—with the help of the Complex Interdependence Theory in the case of their history of enmity, trade, strategic competition, and cooperation and the impact of great powers to transform the Sino-Indian relationship in South Asia; especially USA's and Russian impact on South Asia. In general, Sino-Indian relations are influenced by several factors: (1) Historical legacy and Border crisis; (2); Economy; (3) Soft power; (4) Indian nuclear test—1998; (5) Doklam standoff—2017; (6) Ladakh crisis—2020; and (7) Great powers' impact. In relation to other world areas, South Asia has not been the top priority area for either the USA or Russia since the end of their stormy conflict (Gordon, Sandy, 1995).

Though in the 1990s, India's financial risk and its explosion of the nuclear bomb injected a new dynamism and complexity to the region, South Asia still has not acquired a significant devotion in the US, Russian, and Chinese external strategy perspectives. The breakdown of the Soviet Union that ended the Cold War bipolar conflict between the USA and the USSR somewhat eased the safety situation in South Asia, thus reducing the significance of the region. However, a turnaround came after the 9/11 terror attacks that brought a decisive reorientation of the external strategy perspective of the USA on South Asia. Concomitantly, it similarly refocused China's attention to South Asia. The 9/11 era brought a convergence of interest of great powers, especially the USA, Russia, and China, on achieving a stable South Asia. Specifically, these countries preferred a resilient and steady Pakistan and sought an end to terrorism in Afghanistan. These great powers were keen to avoid the area being flattened by atomic climax between India and Pakistan. However, despite this convergence of interests in the US, Russian, and Chinese perspectives on South Asia, a critical area of divergence arose between the two on the issue of Indo-US relations. These relations altered the regional security balance. For China, in particular, this meant a grave security threat that brought the USA and Russia to China's doorstep. Remarkably, the combined role of the USA and India in the South Asian area is a significant risk for China. The major crisis of this region is not only the Sino-Indian conflict nor tension between India and Pakistan but also the presence of the great powers in South Asia. As Indo-US relations decisively impinge on China's security, South Asia has arisen as a new fulcrum of power competition among the USA, Russia, and China in the post 9/11 era.

Discussion

By exploring the transformation of the Sino-Indian relationship in South Asia, this paper has focused on a principal question—What factors have contributed to transforming the Sino-Indian relationship in the South Asian region? The outcome of this research has generally borne out on the basis of Complex Interdependence that the interconnection between the arguments and the empirical evidence corroborates the effects of independent variables. These factors have played a significant role in defining the nature of Sino-Indian relations, which is not characterized by all the elements of rivalry described in most of the literature, but as cooperation with deep engagement, diplomatically and economically, cooperation in regional issues, and competition in security arenas. This variable also offers competing explanations for local transformations.

This paper has explored the underlying factors of transforming the Sino-Indian relationship in South Asia. Here, the independent variable is "factors to transform Sino-Indian relationship in South Asia", which refers to the change from confrontation to cooperation. The main factors that transform the Sino-Indian relationship in South Asia are historical legacy, economy, soft power, Indian nuclear test—1998, Doklam standoff—2017, Ladakh crisis—2020, joint employment and social challenges, and the impact of the significant powers (the USA and Russia) on transforming the Sino-Indian relationship in South Asia. The dependent variables comprise two sets of variables: "Sino-Indian transformative relationship in South Asia" and "Sino-Indian economic and strategic cooperation and competition in South Asia". The transformation of the Sino-Indian relationship in South Asia from 1988 to 2018 is in four stages. They are Recovery Period (1988-1998), Frozen Period (1998-2003), Acceleration Period (2003-2013), and Cooperative Period (2013-2018).

The areas of cooperation and competition of the Sino-Indian transformative relationship in South Asia are trade and investment, security, the Indian Ocean, disaster management, anti-terrorism, energy, soft power, ICT, etc. By analyzing both the variables of this paper, it is clear that there is a correlation between them from several perspectives. The independent variable has different impacts on dependent variables as it results in cooperation and competition in the Sino-Indian relationship in South Asia. The variables also indicate how the Sino-Indian relationship has been transforming in South Asia and the factors that affect this transformation. The independent variable correlates with the dependent variables as it results in cooperation and competition in the Sino-Indian transformative relationship in South Asia. The independent variable of this present research is mentioned as the factor to transform the Sino-Indian relationship in South Asia, which impacts the dependent variables of the study. The transformation of the Sino-Indian relationship in South Asia has occurred in different stages.

On the other hand, another set of the dependent variables on Sino-Indian strategic and economic cooperation and competition in South Asia portrays several fields where both the countries have collaboration and, in some areas, competition in the South Asian region. Here, it is clear that in South Asia, both India and China have several fields where they are cooperating and maintaining an excellent strategic and economic relationship, which is the result of several factors. Similarly, regarding the competition between these countries in South Asia, there are some specific areas where both have their own strategic and economic interests, and this competition is also the effects of the independent variable of this research, that is, the factors to transform the Sino-Indian relationship in South Asia. However, considering the independent variable and two sets of dependent variables, this research showed the correlation among them, and it depicted that the independent variables have a significant impact on the dependent variables.

In sum, the general framework of the research variables is as described above. The research hypothesis has examined these variables to test the theory of complex interdependence and Benjamin Miller's idea of significant power involvement in regional politics to understand the Sino-Indian transformative relationship in South Asia.

Future Challenges and Recommendations

There are some significant challenges for further transforming the Sino-Indian relationship in South Asia.

Firstly, a political consensus has not yet been translated into political reality. At the meeting in Wuhan, the two countries reached several vital agreements on the policy.

Secondly, the potential for economic and trade investment still has been more expressed. The China-India industrial structure has its characteristics, with software-hardware complementary advantages. As of November 2018, China was India's third-place export destination and the largest source of imports.

Thirdly, the humanistic communication base is relatively weak.

Like the two ancient civilizations, China and India have a history of communication for more than 2,000 years. They have become a significant word in the history of the exchange of civilizations, leaving rich strains and spiritual traditions for thousands of years. Indian song and dance, astronomy, calendar, literature, architecture, and sugar technology have been introduced in China, while Chinese paper, silk, porcelain, tea, music, etc., have been introduced in India. The history of communication between the two peoples has been historical evidence of interconnected and mutual learning of their countries since ancient times.

Fourthly, third-party issues and historical legacies continue to interfere with relations between the two countries during the period. The impetus for advancing China-India relations comes from the intrinsic value of the relationship, and the relations of the two countries cannot determine a third-party factor by any means.

Some policy recommendations and potential areas may sponsor in the future other steady and supportive Sino-Indian two-sided relations in the context of South Asian politics. They are:

1. China and India should solve the boundary issues and take the Sino-Indian relationship to the heights, the most critical factor for China-India relations in South Asian politics. Both sides should realize that minor adjustments in the "Line of Actual Control (LAC)" would be an excellent initiative to end the border problem, the most critical limitation of Sino-Indian relations.

2. Eliminate negative impact from third party factors by remaining strategically determined. Facing a rapidly evolving and complex domestic and international situation, China and India must stay strategically focused. They should not let short-term ups and downs cause tunnel vision. Both China and India have firmly followed the strategy of independence and non-violent progress and cherish their strategic autonomy. India enjoys great prestige in the Non-Aligned Movement, has a strong independent national character, and upholds its values and principles in foreign exchange without following others blindly. These national characteristics are highly appreciated by the Chinese population and form an essential cornerstone for India

to build its place in a multi-polar world.

3. China and India need to transform their financial model with international trade policy. Likewise, the current global system needs to change. There are many clauses in the country's import-export law, which are obstacles for South Asian countries to invest in China and India. By correcting these policies and regulations, China and India must create open conditions for South Asian countries.
4. Both countries should talk to each other about China-Pakistan relations because the relations are another crucial factor in China-India relations. Beijing will also assure New Delhi that China's continuing ties with Pakistan are only for economic cooperation, which may serve as a helpful force to end subsidiary and more extremist actions and establish dogmatic clearance on the Kashmir issue.
5. China-India must express their misperceptions and mistakes in their strategic involvement in South Asia. Both have nuclear ballistic development programs. Beijing and New Delhi have avowed the policy of No First Use (NFU). However, India's demand that China uses this strategy only for their two-sided NFU commitment has been evaded by China. China holds enough weaponry to attack the main Indian metropolises. India's present growth of the Agni projectile programme is meant to address that tactical inequity. By then, it is likely that the Chinese replied to the US placement of projectiles that could by chance activate the Indian accumulation of its atomic and projectile militaries. Against this background, tactical discourse, and the overview of the weapons regulator instrument, a bilateral NFU would be one measure that could head off a needless weapons race.
6. The leaders of the two states ought to have the foresight to appear outside the safety prism. There are many zones in which China and India could collaborate in South Asia. Mutually, the two states should adopt the "Panchsheela or Five Principles of Peaceful Coexistence" as the basis of their foreign policy. On the other hand, the two nations face a control policy and intervention in national matters. As the two central Asian

emerging states, China and India also pursue an extra reasonable, just, and valuable global financial direction so that, worldwide, South Asia can have a better advantage from the 21st century's global economic system.

7. South Asia is the farthest significant market for both countries. China and India have great potential to enlarge trade with South Asian countries, which is unhappily insufficient. They can acquire from each other on their limited areas, which maybe help the small South Asian countries.
8. China and India should realize their mutual interests and benefits, which will cooperate in the coming decades regarding their mutual bilateral relations with other states.

Conclusion

There are ample signs that the transformation of the Sino-Indian relationship in South Asia has changed significantly in the present decade. Indian businesses are trying to intensify economic relations with China; Chinese business people are visiting India to look for investment opportunities, and Chinese officials are openly talking about wanting to invest a massive amount in South Asia. The smaller South Asian countries like Bangladesh, Nepal, and Sri Lanka have always wanted to have close relations with China. Although the prevailing discourses in international relations prefer to see this as an attempt to balance India, it is much more than that as any perceptive observer can see. Chinese President Xi Jinping has attributed quite a high degree of importance to China's relationship with India and thinks it is essential to have India walking beside China. His rhetoric makes one feel as if the Nehru era friendship is back; only this time, China is much more developed and far ahead of India. Xi thought that China and India should have direct trains encouraging regional growth and be twin announcers of provincial harmony and solidity.

When China and India join hands in collaboration, it will be advantageous for both the nations and the whole South Asian area. President Xi wanted the "Chinese 'dragon' and the Indian 'elephant' to join each other in a duet, not a dual. "A duet, not a duel: China's world view has evolved" (*The Hindustan Times*, 2018). Also, the Indian Prime Minister stated, "When India and China work together, 1+1 is not two, but eleven. I am the first Indian PM you came out of Beijing to receive: PM Narendra Modi to Xi Jinping in Wuhan" (*The Times of India*. 2018). China and India have some striking similarities. Both are ancient civilizations having a magnificent past and revived as new states in the mid-20th century. Today, "China's economy is about five times larger than India's" (*The World Fact Book*. 2019). In global politics, China's economic growth rates are higher than India's. Both the nations have re-emerged as major international and economic powers. The Sino-Indian relationship in South Asia is serious not only for those in China and India but also for the entire world.

REFERENCES

Ali, Syed Muazzem. (2018). The Current and Future State of India–Bangladesh Relations, *Strategic Analysis*, vol. 42, no. 5, pp. 529-537.

Bijan, Z. (2005). China is rising in the 21st century, *Foreign Affairs*, vol. 84, p. 18.

Bosworth, B. & Collins, S.M. (2008). Accounting for growth: comparing China and India. *Journal of Economic Perspectives*, 22(1), 45-66.

Brewster, David Gomà. (2018). China-India Relations in the Contemporary World, *Pacific Affairs*, vol. 91, no. 3, pp. 553-554.

Brobst, Peter John and Sir Olaf Caroe. (2006). *The future of the great game and India's Independence and the Defence of Asia*, Akron: The University of Akron Press, p. 12.

China Report. (2010) vol. 46, no. 3, pp. 243-252.

Chung, C. P. (2009). The Good Neighbour Policy in the Context of China's Foreign Relations, China, *An International Journal*, vol. 7, No. 1, pp. 107-123.

Garver, John W. (2002). The security dilemma in Sino-Indian relations, *India Review*, vol. 1, no. 4, pp. 1-38.

Gonsalves, Eric. (2018). India, China, and the World: A Connected History, *Indian Foreign Affairs Journal*, vol. 13, no. 2, pp. 177-181.

Gordon, Sandy. (1995). South Asia after the cold war: winners and losers, *Asian Survey*, vol. 35, no. 10, 1995, pp. 879-895.

Gupta, Prakash C. and Ray, Cecily S. (2003). Smokeless tobacco and health in India and South Asia, *Respirology*, vol. 8, no. 4, 2003, pp. 419-431.

Holslag, J. (2010). *India and China: Prospect for peace* New York, Columbia University Press, pp. 221-225.

Holsti, K.J. (1964). The concept of power in the study of international relations. *Background*, 7(4), 179-194.

Konwer, S. (2018). Hallmarks of Current Indian Foreign Policy. *Indian Foreign Affairs Journal*, 13(3), 231-241.

Murthy, Padmaja. (1999). The Gujral doctrine and beyond, *Strategic Analysis*, vol. 23, no. 4, pp. 639-652.

Pant, H.V. (2013), India and China Rising, *Cambridge Review of International Affairs*, p. 26.

Paul, T.V. (2012). *International Relations Theory and Regional Transformation* (Cambridge: Cambridge University Press, p. 5.

Paul, T.V.; James Wirtz and Michael Fortmann. (2004). The literature on Realism is vast. A relevant work for our purpose is *Balance of Power Theory and Practice in the 21st Century*, Stanford: Stanford University Press.

Peter, Van Ness. (2018). China and the Third World: patterns of engagement and indifference, In *China and the World*, Routledge, pp. 151-168.

Russet, Bruce and Oneal, John R. (1997). *Triangulating Peace: Democracy, Interdependence, and International Organizations*, New York: W. W. Norton, pp. 37-41.

Srinivasan, T.N. (2005). Productivity and Economic Growth in South Asia and China, *The Pakistan Development Review*, pp. 479-503.

The Hindustan Times, (2018). available at https://www.hindustantimes.com/analysis/a-duet-not-a-duel-china-s-world-view-has-evolved/story-ODTbJPWvi4XUmzXgfKwieI.html" (accessed 17 June 2020) *The Times of India*. (2018). "http://timesofindia.indiatimes.com/articleshow/63940029.cms?utm_source= contentofinterest&utm_medium=text&utm_campaign=cppst" (accessed 17 May 2020)

The World Bank. (2018). available at "http://www.worldbank.org/en/region/sar" (accessed 18 February 2019).

The World Fact Book. (2019). Central Intelligence Agency (USA) available at www.cia.gov/library/publications/resources/theworldfactbook/geos/in.htm. (accessed 17 March 2020).

6

India's Energy Diplomacy Towards South Asian Countries

Dr. Pamreihor Khashimwo

ABSTRACT

The current persistent economic growth highlights the fact that India has become one of the key global energy-consuming nations. The quandary of insufficient domestic energy resources and excessive reliance on international supplies has created a daunting challenge to its sustainable development and national security. Realising the possible danger of energy disruptions, India has begun to regard credible access to overseas energy resources as one of its national priorities, which requires realistic assessments of energy-related diplomatic initiatives for energy-oriented cooperation at both the bilateral and multilateral levels. India started to acknowledge energy as a crucial tool of connectivity for bolstering its relationship with South Asian countries. India faces formidable challenges in meeting its growing energy requirements; it produces only 30 per cent of its fossil fuel demand, imports over 80 per cent. Due to a lack of significant domestic reserves, India looks towards South Asian countries and geopolitically challenges the Middle East region to fulfil its rapidly increasing energy requirements. In this scenario, India urgently needs to diversify its sources and revitalise energy cooperation with its South Asian neighbouring countries. However, this requires a better and coordinated energy policy to address the issues involved by developing a mature energy policy to compete with the strong challenges from China. This paper presents India's energy-rich neighbouring South Asian countries in terms of its future energy needs, geostrategic, and geopolitical challenges highlighting the possible scope, measures, and challenges.

Keywords: *Energy Diplomacy, Energy, Energy Security, Cooperation, South Asia, Bilateral, Multilateral, Geopolitical, Challenges, and Connectivity.*

Background

India is not only becoming an economic actor but also establishing its geopolitical influence not only in South Asia but also across the world. Like any other economic power, India has been injecting market reforms into its energy sector. This has not been an easy process; there are numerous reasons for this having proved to be such an onerous task: energy regulations are divided between the central and state governments, and the ruling of inefficient state-owned energy enterprises has resulted in a sector shot through with corruption and political interests (Chaudhari, 2015). The combined dilemma of insufficient native energy resources, over-reliance on imports, chronic underinvestment in power infrastructure and technology are some of the challenges India has been facing. It has begun exploring the possibility of using foreign policy to reform long-standing distortions of the country's energy system.

The degree to which these domestic policy issues overrun the debate on the country's energy sector cannot be underestimated. India provides only transient consideration, usually just high-sounding, to the external aspect of its energy policies. Efforts at energy diplomacy, in many instances, have been often trumped by domestic political considerations. In its quest for supply diversification, many countries have been identified as key energy sources and allies. The same is true for India. Now, the country's growing energy requirements need to be defined in the nature of its relations with other countries, as India is using foreign policy to conduct its energy policy and to provide energy security (Redko, 2016). It is diversifying its energy sources to meet the growing demand of over 1.3 billion population and is now importing crude oil from Russia, Venezuela, Mexico, Algeria, Nigeria, Angola, etc. However, these countries are far away. Neighbouring countries like Myanmar, Bangladesh, Nepal, Bhutan, Sri Lanka, and Central Asian countries could be a better alternative. These countries are close to India and have rich untapped oil, natural gas, and hydropower resources.

In the past, the rationale for India's aid diplomacy in South Asia has been the focus on political, strategic, commercial, and economical. It usually has concentrated its aid to perform its vital function of promoting national security (Abrol, 1989). Today, India acknowledges that energy is a crucial tool of connectivity for bolstering its relationship with South Asian countries. Also, though it realised the importance of energy resources in the South Asian countries, it would, however, not be easy to harness this energy wealth of the region. This, nevertheless, demands an effective energy policy along with a robust foreign policy and building viable transnational energy infrastructure in the region. Energy competition among the major economies in the region has been increasing to secure their own future energy needs. Broadly, the search for energy and the military go hand in hand. Many global powers, including the USA, have adopted a strategy of 'energy and military' and have established energy footholds in many energy-rich countries. Likewise, China, with its 'String of Pearls' approach[1] adopted aggressive energy diplomacy.

For India, diversification of energy sources is crucial, as there is a shortage of native energy resources. India's energy equation realignments have been propelled by a growth trajectory fuelled by an enormous demand for energy that cannot be met by domestic production alone (Das, 2014). The centre of gravity of India's energy markets is shifting to imports. These developments are happening rapidly to diversify its import, albeit not able to move away from its dependence on Central Asia energy supplies.[2] Nevertheless, India has limitations in Central Asian policy due to the absence of direct land access and the strong challenges from China. In this circumstance, India inevitably needs to pursue all available energy options in South Asian countries immediately.

India must explore and exploit available energy resources in and outside India (Pandey, 2017). Energy diplomacy is broadly defined as "the use of foreign policy to secure access to energy supplies abroad and to promote largely through bilateral, that is, government-to-government cooperation in the energy sector". India's energy diplomacy with energy resource-rich countries like the USA, Russia, Qatar, Saudi Arabia, Iran, and Australia has been unfolding (Kar, 2017). India's Africa energy policy added new dimensions to national interest in securing energy equity in Africa and enhancing the country's energy security. Besides, South Asia is one of the key energy sources for India in the long term. India has been working on creating connectivity grids in its neighbourhood and moving beyond physical connectivity to energy as a tool of connectivity (Bagchi, 2017).

India's energy diplomacy, however, lacks a combined approach to energy and military. Besides, India is a late starter in aggressive energy diplomacy; it is still majorly confined to foreign policy. India thus needs lots of catching up to do, requiring strong effort to promote energy diplomacy. It must take the lead to promote a regional approach to energy needs and work assiduously to promote the sub-region comprising Bangladesh, Bhutan, Nepal, and Myanmar as an energy hub. Also, it needs to be aware of the challenges posed by climate change. The developments in South Asian energy security, such as the India-Nepal petroleum products pipeline and the India-Bhutan joint venture hydropower project, has revived the conversation on energy cooperation in the region. Meanwhile, these energy projects are a welcome development; like many others earlier, they have suffered logistical, bureaucratic, or political delays.

India's Gas Pipeline Projects: Prospects and Challenges

India's domestic natural gas production remains a big concern and would continue to grow its dependency on imports in the future. It imports gas only through LNG carriers and pushes for transnational pipelines. In the early 1990s and 2000s, it was involved in multilateral negotiations for building natural gas pipelines from Iran, Turkmenistan, and Myanmar.[3] However, these proposed pipeline projects failed to make any progress owing to various political and security reasons. Thus, India is less successful in creating effective energy diplomacy as compared to China. Some of the important gas pipelines that failed to make any further progress include Iran-Pakistan-India (IPI), Turkmenistan-Afghanistan-Pakistan-India (TAPI), Myanmar-Bangladesh-India (MBI), engaging Oman for Oman-India sub-sea pipeline projects, and the Bhutan-Bangladesh-India-Nepal (BBIN) sub-regional frameworks for energy cooperation.

The fundamental aim of the country is to import gas to increase the share of natural gas in the country's energy mix from 6 per cent today to 15 per cent by 2030 to meet the growing demand through the international gas pipeline project (IEA 2020). In 2010, India signed two agreements for the Turkmenistan-Afghanistan-Pakistan-India (TAPI) and Myanmar-Bangladesh-India pipelines (MBI). However, not a single project has been successfully implemented to date. The main reasons for the delay in gas pipeline projects include constant political differences between parties, existing security concerns, unaddressed commercial issues, lack of effective energy diplomacy, and thorny relations with neighbouring countries. Due to the highly politicised nature of interactions, bilateral and multilateral energy cooperation is often stalled and cannot make substantial progress.

TAPI and IPI: Challenges

The proposed 1,680-km TAPI pipeline will provide 1,341.78 million cubic feet per day of gas to India if implemented successfully. TAPI's framework agreement was signed in 2009 and states that the transnational pipeline would be built by a consortium of national oil companies from the four nations. It also provides for payment of transit fees to Afghanistan and Pakistan for allowing usage of their territories for the passage of the pipeline. Yet, the TAPI gas pipeline project has been delayed since the pipeline passes through the terror-affected areas of Kandahar and Herat in Afghanistan and Pakistan before reaching India. The project is very important for the transmission of Central Asian natural gas to the Indian market. Besides, piped gas supplies from Iran, Turkmenistan, and LNG from the Gulf region would feature prominently among India's options in the future (Mahalingam, 2004). However, the security situation in Afghanistan makes it a more distant prospect than the IPI pipeline. There are also concerns about resources. Although reserves were re-evaluated upwards in 2008 due to the South Yolatan field, Turkmenistan has committed significant volumes to Russia as well as to China under long-term contracts, which exceed by far its current production (IEA, 2020). Also, Turkmen gas production often missed the official optimistic targets.[4]

The 2,775-km IPI pipeline project started in the 1990s and continues to face an uncertain future. This transnational pipeline project could not happen due to many geopolitical pressures and security concerns, while Iranian gas could be either piped to India through deep-sea pipelines or overland through Afghanistan and Pakistan. Several issues that complicate the operationalisation of the pipeline are India's participation due to the changing nature of bilateral relations among countries involved in the project, the development of Iran's resources, as well as pricing and geopolitical issues (Kulkarni *et.al*, 2019). Geopolitical issues hampering the pipeline extension to India include concerns about safe transit through the troubled province of Baluchistan. Other concerns are historical mistrust and constant conflicts with Pakistan and security concerns regarding Baluchistan province in Pakistan, through which a portion of the pipeline is planned.

The 1,300-km transnational Iran-Oman-India pipeline is under-sea, avoiding Pakistani waters via Oman, and the Indian Ocean can transport 1,098.141 million cubic feet of gas per day. The planned pipeline from the Iranian port of Chabahar to India's Gujarat coast would compensate for the delayed IPI project; it involved fewer issues such as transit country conflict. This deep-sea pipeline will not only connect India with Iran's gas fields, but Oman is also slated to join the pipeline at a later stage. This would give India a stronghold on the gas trade in both Iran and Oman. This would boost India's stand-in comparison to China's One Belt One Road Programme (Kar, 2017). To fructify all the transitional pipeline projects, India needs strong domestic and political support and accepting Pakistan as a transit route for part of its energy imports. If not, the planned pipelines may have to await the return of peaceful political relations between India and Pakistan; this, however, is unlikely to happen in the near future. India will have to work within the existing constraints to bolster its means to further secure energy security (Taneja, 2014). In this scenario, India is urgently required to engage with energy-rich South Asian countries, including Myanmar in the east.

Myanmar-Bangladesh-India (MBI) Gas Pipeline: Outlook and Predicaments

The MBI pipeline project[5] is a 1,575-km long pipeline connecting the Shwe field to the A-1 block in Myanmar to import gas to India, passing through Bangladesh in which ONGC Videsh owns a stake of 20 per cent and GAIL a stake of 10 per cent. However, not much progress has been made on this front, while an export pipeline to China has started construction in mid-2010 (IEA, 2020). India's OVL has two fields, and it discovered a huge gas field in an offshore block in Myanmar that is estimated to hold gas equivalent to India's 40 per cent production. However, it can be accessed only after laying a deep-sea pipeline or overland through Bangladesh. Geopolitically, the MBI pipeline projects are less expensive and at a lower risk as compared to other proposed pipelines (TAPI and IPI). The advantage of this gas pipeline is its proximity to India. This pipeline, however, was held up due to Bangladesh's linking the project with its desire to obtain transit rights to Nepal and Bhutan through India (Lama, 2008). Besides, mechanisms for protecting the interests of all the parties do not exist, and there is no agreed legal framework to regulate activities in the pipeline project (Dadwal, 2011). The question is whether Bangladesh would be willing to allow the pipeline to be routed through its territory; the security of such a pipeline would be a paramount concern that would decide the pace of monetisation of this gas field (Mahalingam, 2004).

The alternative route is to bypass Bangladesh through the north-eastern states of India; this may increase the cost, but it would provide a stable and long-term gas source from Myanmar. The pipeline via Northeast India can also be used to develop the region since the development of that region has strategic importance for India's security to counter and monitor the increasing presence of China (Mohan, 2017). It will also require preparations to effectively handle any situation like the Doklam and Galwan Valley border skirmishes along the Indo-Myanmar international border. This pipeline project is significant for India to look beyond the immediate and obvious objective of achieving energy security to the long-term implications of the MBI on regional stability, security, and integration. However, this pipeline project, from its very inception, has suffered from political impediments (Huda, 2013). By adopting a cooperative approach and political consensus on a roadmap, India, Bangladesh, and Myanmar can look beyond the myopia of realpolitik that resulted in the stagnation of the energy project (Huda, 2013). The route may also involve multiple issues, including insurgency issues in the northeast region and lack of funding. India constantly encounters a lack of proper funding and coordination between public and private firms, because of which, India's intention to secure a long-term energy supply has been negatively impacted in the past.

India-Bangladesh Energy Partnership

To further strengthen and expand bilateral relations and cooperation in various sectors, India and Bangladesh have signed seven agreements, including one on hydrocarbons, in 2020. The two nations inked the Framework of Understanding (FoU) on cooperation in the hydrocarbon sector. It is deepening cooperation in the area of power and energy connectivity by speeding up various projects, including the implementation of the India-Bangladesh Friendship Pipeline and Maitree Super Thermal Power Project. This is expected to further strengthen energy cooperation by streamlining investments, promoting hydrocarbon connectivity, technology transfer, and training, and strengthening sub-regional energy cooperation, including Nepal, Myanmar, and Bhutan. The two nations focus on boosting cooperation in energy efficiency and clean energy, including solar and biofuel. Energy connectivity is one of the most dynamic sectors of cooperation in the India-Bangladesh relationship. Being the largest producer and consumer of energy in South Asia, it is natural for India to be the epicentre for an energy initiative.

India and Bangladesh bilateral relations need to devise mutual benefits by expanding in areas like the energy sector. The cooperation in the energy sector can be the hallmark of renewed engagements since there are rich opportunities for joint ventures between the two countries. India needs to elevate its relations so that Bangladesh's gas will feature in India's energy supply calculus. Bangladesh has substantial quantities of natural gas; however, there is immense domestic resistance within the country to any proposal to export gas to India. There are also some major thorny issues between India and Bangladesh, which include the demarcation of the land and maritime boundaries, bilateral trade deficits, migration, border management, and transit, among others (Reuter, 2016). India needs to engage and address its concerns and other issues and adopt formal treaties and legal frameworks to move forward with the energy project. These problems cannot be under-estimated; after all, this might impact energy cooperation.

From syncing gas grids to supplying diesel to building pipelines and gas-based power plants to help Bangladesh power up, Indian PSUs have invested in Bangladesh's energy sector, such as oil operating blocks SS-04 and SS-09 in partnership with OVL (45 per cent) and BAPEX (10 per cent). Also, the EXIM Bank of India is funding a project worth $ 1.6 billion for the construction of the 1,320-MW Maitree Power Project in Rampal. India has even pledged a total investment of $ 9 billion in the power and energy sector of Bangladesh. In the private sector, Reliance Power and Adani Power Limited have signed agreements worth $ 1 billion and $ 2 billion for the construction of the first phase of the Meghnaghat Power Plant and for supplying energy to Bangladesh from Adani's power plant in Jharkhand, respectively (Tripathi, 2017).

India-Bhutan Hydropower Collaboration

Bhutan is India's closest South Asian partner, and India has invested in developing the infrastructure for hydroelectric power in the mountainous kingdom and buying it back. India even provides grants and loans to develop the hydropower sector, which is crucial to Bhutan's economy. Bhutan exports about 6,000 kilowatts annually, earning about US$ 250 million. India has seen the significant hydropower potential of Bhutan as a source of cheap electricity. Bhutan is estimated to have a hydropower potential of 30 GW; around 1.8 GW of hydropower is imported from Bhutan annually. The first energy cooperation between India and Bhutan took place in 1961. Since then, several hydropower projects have been signed, and Indian hydropower companies actively participate in Bhutan. The India-Bhutan energy cooperation has presented itself as a model of BIMSTEC countries (Bhonsale, 2020).

India and Bhutan entered into an agreement in 2006 on hydropower with an additional protocol in 2009 stating that India would help Bhutan install 10,000 MW hydro capacity by 2020 and purchase all the surplus power generation. India certainly benefits from energy investment in renewable energy sources such as hydropower from Bhutan (Khashimwo, 2017). The Punatsangcchhu I and II and the Mandechhu projects have suffered delays due to ecological risks and funding problems from India, which will account for 2,940 MW of the total 10,000 MW to be generated. The project commissioning has been delayed, and the costs have escalated massively. According to Walker (2016), the cost of the 1,200 MW Punatsangchhu I has gone up from an estimated $ 510 million to $ 1.46 billion. For the 1,020 MW Punatsangchhu II project, the cost has gone up from $ 570 million to $ 1.1 billion, and for the 720 MW Mangdechhu project, from $ 435 million to $ 675 million.

India and Bhutan launched the first inter-governmental agreement for the 600 MW Kholongchhu hydropower joint venture in Bhutan. The Kholongchhu Hydro Electric Power (HEP) project aims to be completed in the second half of 2025. This project is one of the four additional projects agreed to in 2008, as part of India's commitment to help Bhutan create a total of 10,000 MW of installed capacity by 2020 (Haider, 2020). However, India's policy on the construction of hydropower projects in the neighbourhood seems to have changed; the amount of the grant to Bhutan has been decreased. It resulted in the prevailing undercurrent in Bhutan that India is exploring and exploiting the hydropower sector for its own benefit. There have been growing concerns among a section of the Bhutanese against India's involvement in the hydropower projects, alleging the country of increasing hydro-debts in Bhutan (Rajan, 2018). This is one of the key reasons why Bhutan has refused to sign the concession agreement for joint venture energy projects. All this affected and caused delay and reversal of the hydropower project grant provided by India. Thus, the Bhutan-India hydropower development cooperation model is unravelling and needs a substantial rethink, rather than the aggressive upscaling that is happening today (Walker, 2016). The cooperation should have a renewed emphasis on clean energy, both in terms of technological advances and large-scale adoption and deployment between the two nations.

India-Nepal Energy Trade

The atmosphere of mistrust between India and Nepal over border issues will likely impact energy sector cooperation. The 69-km existing oil pipeline, from Motihari-Raxaul in India to Amlekhgunj in Nepal, having a capacity of 2 million metric tons per annum, is South Asia's first cross-border petroleum products pipeline. This would not only be cheaper, and Nepal is insured against phases of poor relations with India that could disrupt energy supplies. In fulfilment of the commitment made under an MoU signed in 2014, Indian Oil

Corporation Ltd., has made an investment of over Rs. 324 crore in collaboration with Nepal Oil Corporation Ltd.[6] India has sought to persuade Nepal, which has an estimated 40 GW of economically viable hydroelectric potential but which had been hampered by Nepal's political instability and a broader Nepalese suspicion regarding India's intentions.

India and Nepal signed an agreement in 2014 to start selling electricity to each other, deepening energy ties between the two countries. Under the agreement, India will help to develop Nepal's vast but underexploited hydropower potential and tackle its energy shortages (Sharma, 2014). A Power Development Agreement for the 900 MW Arun III hydropower project between India's Satluj Jal Vidyut Nigam Limited and the Investment Board of Nepal was concluded in 2014. The revitalisation of the energy deal with Nepal will be an important tool to enhance its relations and challenge China's increasing influence in the Himalayan country (Chathurvedi, 2019). Since difficulties arise in quick delivery of projects, which is an area where China scores over India, India will have to use all its traditional influence and cultural links with Nepal, its diplomatic skills, and financial support to compete with China that is trying hard to gain a foothold in Nepal's hydro energy exploitation domain as they desperately want power (Chathurvedi, 2019).

The China Factor

China has been very successful in constructing pipelines in Myanmar and Central Asia. Chinese investment in the energy sector appeared to be on the rise in its quest for energy security as it started to expand its power and energy infrastructure. China's high voltage transmission technology enables it to transmit power across thousands of kilometres and thus pave the way for power exports to not only India's neighbourhood but also to faraway countries in Europe (Aneja, 2016). Technological innovation enables China to expand its footprints in the energy sector across Indian neighbouring countries. China embarked on an aggressive energy policy and has been aggressively pursuing the establishment of soft and hard power to achieve its energy interests (Arif, 2017). India's approach is significant and has implications for China because of their shared similarities (Li, 2020).

A comparative study suggests that the pattern of interaction between India and China could be a mix of cooperation and competition to secure energy supplies.

China's presence in India's backyard has been increasing in magnitude in recent decades. It has been hunting for oil equity for a longer period than India (Pathak, 2007). India and China compete in various oil and natural gas projects in many South Asian energy-rich countries. Chinese investments in Myanmar are of significance as part of its grand project for energy security, linking Kunming in Yunnan province to Kyaukphyu in the Rakhine state of Myanmar with an oil and a natural gas pipeline. The China National Petroleum Corporation operates two onshore oil and gas development and production projects in Myanmar, a deep-water exploration and development project and the construction of pipelines.[7] Myanmar concomitantly pursued bilateral negotiations with China for a gas pipeline agreement, and construction has already started and is progressing well. The Sino-Myanmar oil pipeline and the resultant Chinese presence is a matter of concern for India's energy and national security interests.

Chinese investments in Bangladesh are on the rise, and it strives hard to become a major player in the energy sector. The Chinese have signed a joint venture with Bangladesh for the construction of coal-fired power plants and the production of 1,320 MW of electricity. The units are proposed to be established at Dhankhali in the Patuakhali district of Bangladesh.[8] The Chinese began to show similar enthusiasm in Sri Lanka. The Machinery Engineering Corporation, a Chinese company, is constructing the $ 1.3 billion coal-fired power plant in Norochcholai, Sri Lanka, ostensibly to meet that country's demand for power (Bhatia *et.al*, 2016). India is a key player in the retail fuel business of Sri Lanka through IOC. India's investments and presence in the energy sector of Sri Lanka have been significant. IOC Lanka, which is a subsidiary of the IOC, dominates 43.5 per cent of the total market share and is, therefore, a major stakeholder in the oil industry of Sri Lanka. India and Sri Lanka have been jointly developing the Trincomalee oil storage tank farm. Currently, IOC Lanka operates 15 storage facilities in Trincomalee. India invested in the Floating Storage Regasification Unit (FSRU), a liquefied natural gas (LNG) terminal, and a 500-MW LNG-fired power plant in Colombo. In terms of India's contribution to the clean energy sector in Sri Lanka, India has also invested in a solar power plant at Sampur, which has a capacity of 50 MW.

India looks at developing connectivity through the energy sector so that it can be leveraged for securing its strategic interests also. Indian efforts to make its presence felt in the energy sector have been sluggish, and a lot remains to be done. India faces a dilemma in terms of strategically executing its energy projects in the neighbourhood. Unlike Beijing, New Delhi cannot instruct its private sector companies to invest their capital in a particular way and in areas of India's strategic interests. Privately-owned companies are fuelled by the profit motive rather than national security. This is in stark contrast with the Chinese model of investments, where state-owned companies are directed by the government to channelise their resources in areas of strategic interest. In China, the corporations and companies serve as an extended arm of the state and, therefore, implement its agenda with a singular focus. Cooperation between India and China on securing foreign energy resources can result in economic benefits for both countries. Unfortunately, the political differences and territorial conflicts will prevent any substantial cooperation between them on energy in the near future.

India-Japan Energy Partnership to counter China's Influence

India's neighbouring countries are energy and power deficient and demand huge investments and collaboration. India, therefore, needs to work towards energy security in its neighbourhood and ensure developmental goals through collaboration to face competition from China. In this scenario, Japan has shown noteworthy interest in the energy sector of South Asia. Japan has broadened the horizons of its collaboration with India in the energy sector; Japanese investment capital and its high level of technological innovation have made it a positive contributor to the region's quest for energy security. Japanese companies have entered into joint ventures with various coal and oil companies from India, Bangladesh, Sri Lanka, and Myanmar. Japanese has been rendering assistance in the development of the power and energy sector by using high-quality technology to develop electricity and power in Sri Lanka (Ministry of Power, Government of Sri Lanka,

2014). Japan's presence in Bangladesh has been increasing; for the power project near Cox Bazar, the Japan International Cooperation Agency (JICA) has loaned $ 3.7 billion to Coal Power Generation Company Bangladesh Ltd.

India's investments in the energy sector in South Asia to expand its presence have to compete with the massive presence and investments of the Chinese. India needs a collaborative effort to counter China's significant presence in the energy sector and strategise the building of natural gas pipelines and other energy projects. In this context, India and Japan can develop their footholds, and both countries can consider signing more joint ventures to invest in the energy sector in the region. There is a convergence of interests between the two nations in matters of infrastructure and energy security. Both nations face a common competitor from China and have unresolved territorial disputes with it. Japanese innovation will find market avenues of massive potential in South Asia. A joint venture with Japan can converge the interest of nations like Bangladesh, Myanmar, and Sri Lanka as it gives them the best techno-commercial deals to compete with the Chinese presence and pressure. Japan has made inroads into the energy sector of Myanmar. For example, it is leading by example; the JFE Engineering Corporation of Japan has completed Myanmar's first waste-to-energy power plant, which has a generation capacity of 760 KW. The Yangon Waste-to-Energy Plant Project, along with the Thilawa Industrial Zone, has emerged as a crucial Japanese investment in the country.

Conclusion

Energy, to be the core of India's foreign policy and national security architecture, is changing aspiration and ambition. Wistfully, India's failure in implementing gas pipeline and other energy projects display its weak energy diplomacy. The main reason for its ineffective attempt at pipeline projects in Central and South Asia is due to unfocused diplomatic negotiation and lack of convergence in the energy policies of the involved nations and stakeholders. Domestic policy issues often overwhelm the debate on the Indian energy sector. India's external energy policy has revolved around peripheral or transient issues (Chaudhuri, 2015). Its energy diplomacy needs to align with energy security policy convergence among the South Asian nations. Since cross-border energy projects are perceived as conduits of resources, they are vital to national security and call for a national security approach to energy diplomacy (Huda, 2020).

There are immense prospects for investment in the energy sector in Bangladesh, Nepal, Bhutan, Myanmar, and Sri Lanka. The region has now assumed the status of paramount importance for India because of the competition involved in the utilisation of energy resources. While India has historically exercised influence in its neighbouring countries, China has emerged as a key player with a slew of investments in infrastructure projects and energy collaborations. The fact that Chinese investments in the energy sector pose a threat to the security apparatus must be recognised. India must immediately collaborate in the energy sector to develop connectivity in South Asia. Both bilateral and multilateral energy diplomacy can support the long-term energy security of the country through the fostering of the foreign relationship concerning energy supply and demand (Griffiths, 2019).

India must push for effective implementation of the BIMSTEC Grid Interconnection, which was signed during the 4th BIMSTEC Summit held in 2018. The SAARC Framework on energy cooperation in electricity was signed at the 18th SAARC Summit in 2014 in Kathmandu. At the same time, India needs to look at ways to achieve a greater connection between multiple agencies such as government agencies and autonomous bodies at the regional level, as well as steps to strengthen and enhance the regulatory framework. Regional energy interconnection often involves multiple stakeholders and institutions. Ambitious plans for a pan-South Asian regional power have been encouraged by Asian development, but there has been very slow progress due to the paucity of connecting infrastructure in the region. India's National Power Corporation (NTPC) has been pursuing the feasibility of power cooperation with Sri Lanka, but with little effect.

India needs to bring systematic changes in a way that it engages with energy-rich South Asian countries by exploring the possibilities and operationalising gas pipeline interconnections in the region while analysing energy security concerns. This, however, is required to elevate energy security and energy diplomacy with energy as one of the core parts of all foreign policy and national security decisions.

India's energy policies are still a road under construction. The many problems, both regulatory and financial, that plague the Indian domestic energy sector means that medium-term Indian energy diplomacy will be about leveraging overseas capital and technology to resolve these problems on the home front. To ensure long-term energy security, India should pursue multi-pronged energy strategies and needs to engage actively with South Asian neighbouring countries. Also, building energy infrastructures like the LNG terminal and pipeline should be given the utmost priority in the region. India's renewed enthusiasm for regional energy cooperation in the region has been marked by an incongruous claim of hard borders and ethno-nationalism, which creates significant concerns for the sustainability of cross-border energy projects. There has so far been no change regarding India's external reactivity and passivity on political developments in South Asia—its main source of hydropower and gas imports.

NOTES

1. China has good naval facilities in friendly ports all around India, in the Indian Ocean, and the Bay of Bengal. The China-financed port of Gwadar in Baluchistan that sits close to the Straits of Hormuz, through which 40 per cent of the world's oil passes. Gwadar has multiple advantages for China, including potential veto power over the flow of West Asian oil through Hormuz.
2. Central Asia is the core of Asia. It stretches from the Caspian Sea to China in the East and Afghanistan in the south to Russia in the north. There are five countries: Kyrgyzstan, Turkmenistan, Uzbekistan, and Kazakhstan, all countries are rich in oil and gas.
3. See, Supply, distribution, and marketing of natural gas including CNG and LNG, 16th Report of the Standing Committee of Parliament on Petroleum and Natural Gas, Lok Sabha Secretariat, New Delhi, 2007.
4. Turkmenistan is also planning to increase exports to Iran by expanding the existing pipeline and building another one. Europe is also looking at Turkmen gas although the issue was held back by the lack of a Trans-Caspian pipeline.
5. The MBI was first discussed in 1997 by the Dhaka-based private firm, Mohona Holdings. The pipeline originates from the Shwe field off the Bay of Bengal through the Rakhine State in Southern Myanmar and turns east to enter the Indian state of Tripura. The pipeline would then cross Bangladesh at Brahmanbaria and traverse the country until it exits at Jessore and ends at the Indian state of West Bengal.
6. See Business Standard, India, Nepal to Expand Energy Cooperation, Explore New Pipeline, August 24, 2020. https://www.business-standard.com/article/economy-policy/india-nepal-to-expand-energy-cooperation-explore-new-pipeline-120082401028_1.html

7. "CNPC in Myanmar. " *China National Petroleum Corporation*. June 8, 2017. http://www.cnpc.com.cn/en/Myanmar/country_index.shtml
8. "Bangladesh-China JV to construct $1.56 bn power plant in southern Bangladesh". *Reuters*. March 30,2016. http://in.reuters.com/article/bangladesh-power-china-idINL3N1721UK

REFERENCES

12th Five Year Plan. "*Planning Commission of India* June 5, 2017. http://planning commission.gov.in/plans/planrel/fiveyr/welcome.html (accessed 7 August 2020).

Abrol, Vandana. (1989). India's Aid Diplomacy in South Asia. *Indian Journal of Asian Affairs*, 2(2): 35-48.

Aneja, Atul. (2016) "China to export electricity along the New Silk Road." *The Hindu*, April 5, 2016.

Arif, B.H. (2017). The role of soft power in China's foreign policy in the 21st century, *International Journal Social Science Education Studies* 3, pp. 94-1-1.

Bagchi, Indrani. (2017). Away from OBOR, India Pushing for 'Energy Diplomacy' in Neighbourhood, *The Economic Times*, May 15, 2017. (accessed 4 August 2020) https://economictimes.indiatimes.com/industry/energy/away-from-obor-india-pushing-for-energy-diplomacy-in-neighbourhood/articleshow/58678035.cms?from=mdr

Bangladesh-China JV to construct a $1.56 bn power plant in southern Bangladesh." *Reuters*, March 30, 2016. http://in.reuters.com/article/bangladesh-power-china-idINL3N1721UK (accessed 13 July 2020).

BD-Japan joint venture in the petroleum sector was introduced." *Dhaka Tribune* Nov. 13, 2016. http://www.dhakatribune.com/business/2016/11/13/bd-japan-joint-venture-petroleum-sector-introduced/ (accessed 17 August 2020).

Bhatia, Rajiv et al (2016), "Chinese investments in Sri Lanka," *Gateway House: Indian Council on Global Relations*. http://www.gatewayhouse.in/chinese-investments-sri-lanka/ (accessed 24 September 2020).

Bhonsale, Mihir. (2020). Prospects for Energy Cooperation Under BIMSTEC, Commentaries, June 10, 2020, Observer Research Foundation (ORF). https://www.orfonline.org/research/prospects-for-energy-cooperation-under-bimstec-67638/ (accessed 8 October 2020).

Chathurvedi, A.K. (2019). India and Nepal: Energy Cooperation, *The Peninsula Foundation*, https://www.thepeninsula.org.in/2019/10/20/indo-nepal-energy-cooperation/ (accessed 2 October 2020).

Chaudhuri, Pramit Pal. (2015). Fragmented and Fitful: India's Energy Diplomacy. March 13, 2015, Rhodium Group. https://rhg.com/research/fragmented-and-fitful-indias-energy-diplomacy/ (accessed 14 July 2020).

Dadwal, Shebonti Ray. (2011) 'Can the South Asian Gas Pipeline Dilemma be Resolved through a Legal Regime, *Strategic Analysis*, vol. 35, no. 5, p, 760. (accessed 3 September 2020): http://www.tandfonline.com/doi/pdf/10.1080/09700161.2011.591251 (accessed 9 August 2020).

Das, Pranab Kr. (2014). Central Asia: A New Avenue to India's Future Energy Needs and Geo-Strategic Challenges. *International Journal of Innovative Research & Development*, vol. 3, issue 11, pp. 48-56.

Griffiths, Steven. (2019). Energy Diplomacy in a Time of Energy Transition, *Energy Strategy Reviews* 26, (2019) 100386.

Haider, Suhasini. (2020). India, Bhutan Sign Pact for First Joint Venture Hydropower Project. *The Hindu*, June 29, 2020. https://www.thehindu.com/news/national/india-bhutan-sign-pact-for-first-joint-venture-hydropower-project/article31945878.ece (accessed 20 July 2020).

http://www.thehindu.com/news/international/China-to-export-electricity-along-the-New-Silk-Road/article14219169.ece (accessed 14 July 2020).

Huda, Mirza Sadaqat. (2013). Myanmar, Bangladesh, and India: Prospects for Energy Cooperation. *National Geographic*, July 13, 2013. https://blog.nationalgeographic.org/2013/07/13/myanmar-bangladesh-and-india-prospects-for-energy-cooperation/ (accessed 29 September 2020).

Huda, Mirza Sadaqat. (2020). *Energy Cooperation in South Asia; Utilising National Resources for Peace and Sustainable Development*. Routledge, London.

International Energy Agency (IEA), India 2020, Energy Policy Review. https://niti.gov.in/sites/default/files/2020-01/IEA-India-In-depth-review2020.pdf (accessed 18 July 2020).

Kar, Sanjay Kumar. (2017). India's Energy Supply Security: Prospects and Challenges. *Modern Diplomacy*, January 17, 2017. https://moderndiplomacy.eu/2017/01/17/india-s-energy-supply-security-prospects-and-challenges/ (accessed 25 September 2020).

Khashimwo, Pamreihor. (2017). India-Bhutan Relations: Unlocking the Hydropower Potential for Better Cooperation, Centre for Air Power Studies (CAPS), In Focus, 7th November 2017, 85/17. http://capsindia.org/files/documents/CAPS_Infocus_PK_00.pdf (accessed September 2020).

Kulkarni, Sanket Sudhir, and Pimpalkhare, Ameya. (2019). India's Import Diversification Strategy for Natural Gas: An Analysis of Geopolitical Implications. *ORF Issue Brief*, December 2019, issue. 330. https://www.orfonline.org/wp-content/uploads/2019/12/ORF_IssueBrief_330_NaturalGasImports_NEW-06Dec.pdf (accessed 5 September 2020).

Kumar, Devindra. (2012). Securing India's Energy Future, Centre for Defence and Strategic Studies, Australian Defence College.

Lama, Mahendra, K. (2008). 'Cross-border power trading in South Asia: An emerging new paradigm,' The Energy and Resources Institute (TERI), vol. 3, issue 2, p. 11. (accessed 3 September 2020); http://bookstore.teriin.org/docs/newsletters/Engery%20Sec%20Insights%20july_08.pdf (accessed 28 September 2020).

Li, Zhang. (2020), "India's Energy Diplomacy: Geo-Strategic Perceptions and Practice," https://en.cnki.com.cn/Article_en/CJFDTotal-SJJZ200501009.htm (accessed 20 October 2021).

Mahalingam, Sudha. (2004). Energy and Security in a Changing World. *Strategic Analysis*, vol. 28, no. 2, pp. 249-271.

Ministry of Power, Government of Sri Lanka, 2014, "The Government of Japan assistin the development of power sector in Sri Lanka.". http://powermin.gov.lk/english/?p=3397 (accessed 25 August 2020).

Mohan, Rakshit. (2017). India's Energy Diplomacy in the Neighbourhood: The Way

Forward. *Chennai Centre for Chinese Studies*. (accessed 16 September 2020). https://www.c3sindia.org/geopolitics-strategy/indias-energy-diplomacy-in-the-neighbourhood-the-way-forward-by-rakshit-mohan/ (accessed 3 July 2020).

Pandey, Pooran Chandra. (2017). Lessons from the BRICS: India and China push solar diplomacy, DOC Research Institute, 20 September 2017. (accessed 26 June 2020. https://doc-research.org/2017/09/lessons-india-china-solar-diplomacy/

Pathak, Vidhan. (2007). India's Energy Diplomacy in Francophone Africa: Competitive-Cooperation with China. *India Quarterly: A Journal of International Affairs*, vol. 63, issue 2, pp. 26-55.

Rajan, Amit. (2018). India-Bhutan Hydropower Projects: Cooperation and Concerns. Institute of South Asian Studies (ISAS), National University of Singapore, *Working Paper*, no. 209, 17 October 2018. https://www.isas.nus.edu.sg/wp-content/uploads/2018/10/Working-Paper-No.-309-India-Bhutan-Hydropower-Projects-2.pdf (accessed 12 June 2020).

Redko, Valerilia. (2016). The Role of Energy Diplomacy in the Indian Current External Policy. National Research University Higher School of Economics, Faculty of World Economy and International Affairs, Student Thesis. https://www.hse.ru/en/edu/vkr/182145092 (accessed 23 September 2020).

Sharma, Gopal. (2014). India and Nepal Sign Electricity Trading Pact, Reuters, October 21, 2020. https://in.reuters.com/article/nepal-india-power/india-and-nepal-sign-electricity-trading-pact-idINKCN0IA1LF20141021 (accessed 18 October 2020).

Taneja, Kabir. (2014). A Survey of India's Energy Prospects in the Middle East region, *Takshashila Discussion Document 2014-S01*, Takshashila Institutions, November 2014.

Walker, Beth. (2016). India and Bhutan's Cooperation and Hydropower are Fraying at the Edges. *Scroll*, October 0, 2016. https://scroll.in/article/818231/india-and-bhutans-cooperation-on-hydropower-needs-a-rethink (accessed 12 June 2020).

7

Asia Pacific Trade Agreement: Takeaway for India

Dr. Mohan Singh

ABSTRACT

The process of economic development is highly integrated with external economic relations in the era of globalization, and hence an array of initiatives has been taken to extend and intensify international trade. Going further, efforts have also been made to create a multilateral arrangement to facilitate greater cohesive and regionally balanced economic growth in order to enhance livelihood opportunities. Consequently, it has led to better economic harmony and coordination among different countries and repeatedly proved that economic growth is compulsorily an inclusive and mutual concern. The Asia Pacific Trade Agreement (APTA, 2005), which was incepted as the Bangkok Agreement in 1975 between India, Bangladesh, South Korea, Laos PDP and Sri Lanka (China, 2001 and Mongolia, 2020 joined later), is the oldest trade agreement between the countries of the Asia-Pacific region. Although the APTA is not a full-fledged free trade agreement, it is the first preferential trade agreement betweeri developing countries. It is considered as one of the most important trade agreements for us because it is the only trade agreement that directly links India and China, whereas the other trade agreements, which involve India and China, have them as observers or signatories but do not extend tariff preferences to each other.

If we look into the trade data of APTA member countries, it appears that India's global integration, as measured by its external trade, is low in reference to the Asia-Pacific region but is of vital importance for expanding India's economic and strategic space. The volume of India's foreign export with other members of APTA, which was Rs. 4,360,989.37 crores (India's total exports Rs. 37,533,952.62 crores) in 2004-05, increased to Rs. 23,741,473.68 crore (India's total export Rs. 221,985,418.10) in 2019-20, but the share of these countries in India's total export decreased from 11.6188 per cent to 10.6951 per cent during the last 15 years.

Similarly, India's imports from the members of APTA has also increased from Rs. 4,962,583.43 crore (total Rs. 50,106,454.02) in 2004-05 to Rs. 58,782,109.13 crore (total Rs. 336,095,445.60) in 2019-2020. It is quite encouraging that the share of these countries in India's total import also increased from 9.9041 per cent to 17.4897 per cent during the same period. Hence, it is better to work on an alternative approach against the perception of the insignificance of the APTA for India, to strengthen the cooperation for beneficial economic opportunities. India, on its part, needs to continue to enlarge its economic and strategic space in the global and regional arenas. Additionally, India has to consider the economic dividend from global trade by including more items like services and more countries from potential natural trade partners. An enhanced coalition among countries of APTA will also provide an opportunity for India in terms of science and technology, research and development, value addition in the socio-political life of the people of the country, etc., and thereby pave the path for India to get its due place in Strategic Global Positioning.

Keywords: *Asia Pacific Trade Agreement (APTA), Economic Development, Foreign Trade*

Introduction

Economic development is the natural outcome of common human activities instigated by the basic instinctive trait of being self-centric. All the individual and collective efforts of humankind targeting to attain a better materialistic life are assumed to be directly related to more production and consumption. The other attributes like inter-dependency, cooperation, and support become tools for collective utilisation of natural resources with the help of technology for enhancing mutual benefits. Not categorically wrong, market-driven human decisions have bought liveliness into the lives of many people across the globe. Hence, international interdependence has been well adjusted with the initial concept of self-sufficient, self-dependence or self-reliance, especially in the era of globalization, when countries are coming closer and breaking political boundaries in favour of economic and social drives. Nevertheless, even though the concept of free trade is accepted in every approach of economic growth, every country has been trying to protect and augment its economic welfare and, therefore, different economic and political groups have been created within the broader horizon of the global village.

India has been a founder-member of different regional economic groups like SAARC, ADB, and ASEAN, along with being a member of all world-level institutions like the World Bank, IMF, WTO, UNCTAD, etc. The main objective of forming a regional group is to capitalize on the economic dividend mutually because of localized availability and common issues pertaining to economic well-being. The Indian government initiation of energizing India's external economic relations in general, and external trade in particular, has been targeted to facilitate speed up of economic growth with the regional balance and enhance livelihood opportunities and market access. This would also lead to better economic harmony and coordination among neighbouring nations, enabling the group to deal better with the rest of the world. India, on its part, needs to continue to enlarge its economic and strategic place in local and global positioning by enhancing trade on the one hand and effective geo-political contribution on the other. The inception of the Asia Pacific Trade Agreement (APTA) in 1975 with signatories like India, Bangladesh, the Republic of Korea, the Laos People's Democratic Republic and Sri Lanka is one of its kind of proactive steps to set up the first preferential trade agreement between developing countries. It was assumed that with trade cooperation among the members of the APTA, the agreement could soon become a Comprehensive Economic Partnership Agreement of Asia and Pacific (CEPAAP). Although the APTA has been proved its worth in helping its member countries in facilitating cheap and easy trade, it has been a matter of qualm because of its low Indian trade in comparison to the total trade of the country. However, we should not enervate its role by ignoring its contribution in the long-run business and political yields for the country. This paper is an effort to evaluate the place of the APTA in India's foreign trade and regional polity.

Research Methodology

This is an analytical paper. The discussion in it is based on empirical evidence and secondary data. The main source of data is the government departmental data banks and publications and other associated documents of different organizations. Research papers and other articles, along with relevant books, served as the base of this creation. Most of the articles were accessed online. The data collected from different sources are presented in tabular form and in graphic patterns. To derive a logical interpretation, different mathematical tools are used to reproduce the inferences and conclusions. The analysis is accomplished in the form of a conclusion and suggestions, which is given at the end of this paper. Since this article is based on secondary data, it is investigative work with reviewed nature.

An Overview of APTA

Initially, five members—India, Bangladesh, the Republic of Korea, the Laos People's Democratic Republic and Sri Lanka—signed this agreement in 1975 as the Bangkok Agreement. Later, The People's Republic of China joined in 2001 and Mongolia in 2020 to become a seven-member agreement. It was renamed APTA in 2005 during its first Ministerial Council held in Beijing, China. Till now, four Ministerial Council meetings have been held; the second in Goa, India, in 2007, the third in Seoul, South Korea in 2009 and the fourth in Bangkok, Thailand, in 2017. Under the aegis of the United Nations, in 2018, the working groups on Investment, Services, and Trade Facilitation were established to improve investment among the member countries. The main objective of the APTA is to help the participating countries to speed up economic development by liberalizing trade and investment. For this, the APTA provisioned different clauses to promote inter-regional trade and strengthen the economies of the participating countries. It also aims to reduce tariff and regulatory barriers for on-trade of commodities, technology, and investments.

The APTA is a kind of open accord and accessible to all member-states and customs territories of the United Nations Economic and Social Commission for Asia and the Pacific (UNESCAP). The secretariat of the Asia-Pacific Trade Agreement was set up at the UNESCAP that assists with identifying prospective members who could participate in this trade agreement without negatively affecting their own economy. The UNESCAP, along with helping the countries to participate in the agreement, also facilitates the negotiation of terms among the participating countries. Negotiations under the APTA not only cover conventional tariff concessions but also work for the assistance of trade in services, removal of non-tariff barriers to trade and promotion of cross-border investment. The organizational structure of the Asia-Pacific Trade Agreement consists of three main bodies: (1) Ministerial Council: The highest decision-making body of the APTA, which meets once every two years. It provides overall direction to trade policy negotiations and supervises the implementation of the provisions of the agreement; (2) Standing Committee: It comprises the officials designated by each member to administer the trade agreement through national and alternative focal points created for the specific purpose; and (3) Secretariat: Since this agreement is aiming for more comprehensive efforts of the United Nations to reduce hurdles among the countries, so the Trade and Investment Division of the UNESCAP serves as the secretariat of this agreement.

India's Trade with Members of APTA

The issue of the APTA came to be debated when, in June 2016, it was notified that the Government of India was enthusiastic about expanding its trade ties with its neighbours via mutual tariff concessions under the provisions of the Asia Pacific Trade Agreement (APTA), and so intended to expand and intensify this lesser-known but very old trade agreement. In September 2016, the Cabinet, taking a very pragmatic step, approved these concessions for additional commodities. As a result of multi-level dialogues and different rounds of negotiations pertaining to APTA trade concessions, India has offered a concessional tariff on 570 items @ 23.9 per cent with 48 items @ 39.7 per cent. By September 2016, the Union Cabinet had approved concessional tariffs for an additional 3,142 items @ 28.01 per cent to expand the coverage and benefits of the Agreement. This shows that India is keen to expand trade ties with its neighbours and that it should be welcomed as its long-term trade policy.

Comparative trade data indicates the significance of APTA countries in India's foreign trade over a period of time. Since its inception in 2005, the value of the exports and imports of the members have increased drastically and can be seen as a sizable percentage of the country's total exports and imports. Data from the following tables is evidence of the importance of this preferential tariff trade Agreement in terms of incremental trade growth in comparison with other groups.

Table 1 shows a brief of the progress of India's exports to countries of the APTA. The total Indian exports to these countries were valued at Rs. 4,360,989.37 lakh in 2004-05 increased to Rs. 9,274,976.73 lakh in 2009-10, Rs. 18,205,480.86 lakh in 2014-15 and Rs. 23,741,473.68 lakh in 2019-20; hence, in the last 15, it has risen more than five times (5.444

times) of the total trade at the time of the formal inception of the APTA. If we see the countries' individual partnership in India's exports, China used to contribute about half of all India's exports to the APTA countries, followed by Bangladesh with around one-fourth of the total export.

Table 1: India's Export to APTA Countries (Values in Rs. Lakh)

S.No.	*Country*	*2004-05*	*2009-10*	*2014-15*	*2019-20*
1.	BANGLADESH PR	732,887.76	1,150,106.83	3,944,038.17	5,817,660.89
2.	CHINA P RP	2,523,296.90	5,471,392.87	7,303,043.30	11,767,331.48
3.	KOREA RP	468,043.69	1,612,681.15	2,808,473.91	3,433,765.43
4.	LAOS PD RP	1,190.39	8,120.26	41,293.77	17,737.65
5.	MONGOLIA	605.66	3,714.76	4,830.59	11,524.14
6.	SRI LANKA DSR	634,964.97	1,028,960.86	4,103,801.13	2,693,454.09
	Total	4,360,989.37	9,274,976.73	18,205,480.86	23,741,473.68

Source: Export Import Data Bank, Department of Commerce, GOI; Downloaded from https://tradestat.commerce.gov.in/eidb/default.asp on 25 June 2021.

Table 2: India's Imports to APTA Countries (Values in Rs. Lakh)

S.No.	*Country*	*2004-05*	*2009-10*	*2014-15*	*2019-20*
1.	BANGLADESH PR	26,676.51	120,528.14	379,440.83	897,514.07
2.	CHINA P RP	3,189,230.68	14,604,861.20	36,956,536.01	46,152,476.82
3.	KOREA RP	1,576,541.54	4,055,061.49	8,272,008.53	11,088,343.94
4.	LAOS PD RP	23.24	9,218.20	52,282.93	2,190.32
5.	MONGOLIA	92.40	601.30	2,629.87	920.58
6.	SRI LANKA DSR	170,019.05	185,001.57	464,275.90	640,663.40
	Total	4,962,583.43	18,975,271.90	46,127,174.08	58,782,109.13

Source: Export Import Data Bank, Department of Commerce, GOI; Downloaded from https://tradestat.commerce.gov.in/eidb/default.asp on 25 June 2021.

Not only have Indian exports to APTA countries increased sizably our country's imports from APTA countries have also increased significantly following this Agreement. It is evident from Table 2 that India's total imports from these countries increased from Rs. 4,962,583.43 lakh in 2004-05 to Rs. 18,975,271.90 lakh in 2009-10 and further to Rs. 46,127,174.08 lakh in 2014-15 and Rs. 58,782,109.13 in 2019-20; thus, in the last 15 years, it has gone up to around 12 times the total imports in 2204-05. The seriousness of India and the significance of the APTA is sufficiently highlighted in these trends. The most significant increase of imports from China (around 14.5 times) which contributes about 78.5 per cent of India's total imports from APTA countries, is a mark of India's need for this Agreement. Collectively, India's exports and imports to APTA countries increased from Rs. 9,323,572.80 in 2004-05 to Rs. 82,523,582.81 in 2019-20. This is a sizable increase in the volume of India's foreign trade to APTA counties by more than 8.85 times in the last 15 years. The most important point to note from the data is that China is not only the biggest trade partner but also the fastest-growing trade partner of the country.

Table 3: Share of APTA Countries in India's Trade
(Values in Rs. Lakh)

Year	*Export*			*Import*		
	Total	*APTA*	*% Share*	*Total*	*APTA*	*% Share*
2004-05	37,533,952.62	4,360,989.37	11.6188	50,106,454.02	4,962,583.43	9.9041
2009-10	84,553,364.38	9,274,976.73	10.9694	136,373,554.75	18,975,271.90	13.9142
2014-15	189,634,841.76	18,205,480.86	9.6003	273,708,657.82	46,127,174.08	16.8527
2019-20	221,985,418.10	23,741,473.68	10.6951	336,095,445.60	58,782,109.13	17.4897

Source: Export Import Data Bank, Department of Commerce, GOI; Downloaded from https://tradestat.commerce.gov.in/eidb/default.asp on 25 June 2021.

It is also pertinent to note the importance of APTA for India in reference to its trade partnership with the member countries vis-à-vis India's total world trade. Although the share of India's exports to APTA countries is only 10.7 per cent and that of imports only 17.5 per cent, which is very little in comparison to its given population size, the significant rise in India's import share from the APTA countries from 9.9 per cent in 2004-05 to 17.5 per cent in 2019-20 is a matter of concern as it shows the increasing partnership among the APTA countries. On this issue, we must not forget that APTA members are developing countries, making them the natural partner of our country. Importantly, the regional inter-dependency among similar countries is envisaged as part of long-term strategies of economic and political sustainability.

Table 4: Growth Rate of India's Trade with APTA Countries (Year-to-year basis)

Year	*Percentage Growth in Export*		*Percentage Growth in Import*	
	Total	*APTA*	*Total*	*APTA*
2015-16	–9.49	–14.05	–9.02	8.45
2016-17	7.75	7.94	3.51	1.08
2017-18	5.79	18.09	16.42	20.27
2018-19	17.95	24.34	19.78	3.11
2019-20	–3.81	–4.26	–6.50	–6.26

Source: Export Import Data Bank, Department of Commerce, GOI; Downloaded from https://tradestat.commerce.gov.in/eidb/default.asp on 25 June 2021.

The significance of the Asia Pacific Trade Agreement can not only be judged on the basis of the percentage of India's foreign trade merchandise commodities with APTA's member countries but also by the importance of trade of services and other invisible capital movements, which are more important from the future Indian perspective. The other important aspect of assessment of the importance of APTA is its progress in the last few years in terms of incremental growth of trade among the member countries as compared with the total world trade of a country. If we see the data of India's foreign trade growth rate, it is clear that in the last five years, India's trade with APTA member countries was faster most of the time in comparison to the total trade of the country. Although there are fluctuating figures of India's export growth rate in the last five years, India's exports to APTA member countries increased by more than 30 per cent in the last five years against only 17 per cent average growth of its total exports during the same period. India's export increase on a year-to-year basis with APTA members remained impressively high for three of the last five years, especially in 2017-18 and 2018-19. On the other hand, the growth of India's imports showed mixed results. Nevertheless, India's imports from APTA member countries has increased more than 27 per cent in the last five years in comparison to a 22.8 per cent increase in its total imports during the same period. It is amply clear that the role of the APTA is gaining importance continuously in reference to India's foreign exports and imports in particular and economic integration for economic development in general.

Conclusion and Suggestions

Economic development is a comprehensive process and the resultant of inter-related and inter-dependent efforts. Not all countries are equally endowed by nature and empowered with technology. Hence, mutual cooperation in cultivating collective economic dividends becomes a compulsion of rational behaviour. The development of regional and global integrating institutions is the outcome of the natural process of shared economic growth. The Asia Pacific Trade Agreement is one such example of regional cooperation for a common economic goal of reduction in cost and increase in output. It is the first preferential trade agreement targeted at reducing the cost and hurdles in the way of trade among the members, all of which are developing countries. Consequently, it aims to promote trade among the member countries on the principle of common objectives and similar conditions. The journey of the APTA has been encouraging on account of its enhanced integration observable from incremental trade volume over the years. The continuously increasing share of APTA countries in India's exports and imports reveals the amplified importance of the Agreement for India's future trade perceptive. Moreover, being regional and having similar economic strata, member countries enjoy the benefit of low costs and easily accessible trade, thus reducing the pressure on their limited resources.

There has been a debate on the relevance of the Asia Pacific Trade Agreement since its formation in the light of a wider concept of globalization under the close watch of international institutions and heavy-sized developed economies. Many international conventions, which are based on the principle of equality and similarity, find the local agreement to be against the concept of internationalization. Moreover, owing to its size, India needs more international market access and, eventually, it was the founder member of all-important international treaties. For the same reason, India does not lag behind in proactively participating and strengthening regional cooperation institutions like SAARC, APTA, etc.; not only to reap localized economic benefits but also to gain its own place in the regional political arena and empower itself for better bargaining in the international political and economic domains. Instead of looking back, it is time to intensify the APTA by including more commodities and services and bringing more countries on a merit basis to be part of the Agreement. India's increased capacity of a skilled labour force and manufactured goods need broader market access with low delivery costs. APTA member countries with similar socio-cultural-economic conditions can prove to be natural trade partners and will have political and economic advantages in the new world order.

REFERENCES

Das, A. (n.d.), "India's Neighbourhood Policy: Challenges and Prospects", *Jindal Journal of International Affairs*, vol. 4, issue 1, 18-37.

Department of Commerce, Government of India, "Export Import Data Bank", retrieved on 25 June 2021 from https://tradestat.commerce.gov.in/eidb/default.asp

Dr. Vadranam, Suresh and Sahoo, Jayaprada (2020), "South Asian Association for Regional Cooperation (SAARC) Countries and the Role of Regional Development", *Quest Journals, Journal of Software Engineering and Simulation*, volume 6, issue 3 (2020), pp. 18-24, www.questjournals.org

Gupta, S. (2018), "Constraints to India's Support for Regional Economic Integration", *Asia Pacific Bulletin*, July 11, 2018, retrieved on March 24, 2019 from East-West Centre.org/APB.

International Monetary Fund, "Asia Pacific: Good times, uncertain times, a time to prepare", Regional Economic Outlook, World Economic and Financial Surveys, April 2018.

Menon, Jayant. (2007), "Bilateral Trade Agreements", *Asian-Pacific Economic Literature*, vol. 21, pp. 29-47.

Siddique, A. (2007), "Regionalism, Trade and Economic Development: Theories and Evidence from the Asia-Pacific Region", in M.A.B. Siddique (ed.), *Regionalism, Trade and Economic Development in the Asia-Pacific Region* (pp. xiii-iv, 3-22), Edward Elgar Publishing, Cheltenham, UK.

Sikri, R. (2009), "India's Look East Policy", *Asia-Pacific Review*, vol. 16, issue 1, pp. 131-145.

Sundaram, D. (2013), "Look East Policy", *International Journal of Advancements in Research & Technology*, 2(5), 169-185, retrieved on March 30, 2019.

The World Bank Group, "From Containment to Recovery", East Asia and Pacific Economic Update, World Bank, October 2020.

United Nations, "Asia Pacific Trade Agreement", Economic and Social Cooperation for Asia Pacific (ESCAP), 2005.

United Nations, "Asia-Pacific Trade and Investment Report 2017: Channelling Trade and Investment into Sustainable Development", Economic and Social Cooperation for Asia Pacific (ESCAP), 2017.

8

An Analytical Study of ISIS Operations in South Asia

Prof. (Dr) Nagalaxmi M. Raman and Ms Rachel C. Walter

ABSTRACT

This paper seeks to examine ISIS from its inception to its rise in power and evolution into a "caliphate", the organisation's possible future trajectory. It scrutinizes ISIS in the context of its motives and operational strategies to chart its ideology, propaganda tactics, and financing. This paper studies the factors that led to its expansion and acted as its backbone and how it radicalised individuals through its vast spectrum of associated networks and groups. The intention is to dissect the approach taken by this terrorist organisation towards South Asia. As the shadow of its influence spread across the countries of South Asia, be it India, Pakistan, Bangladesh, Afghanistan, the Maldives, and Sri Lanka, all have the footprints of ISIS on their doorsteps. It is imperative to study the developments of ISIS that endanger the stability and security of the region. This paper also traces the counter-measures taken by security agencies to dismantle ISIS.

Keywords: *ISIS, Terrorism, Ideology, Islamic, Caliphate, Attack*

Introduction

The Islamic State of Iraq and Syria (ISIS) is the world's deadliest and powerful terrorist militant organisation. Its roots go back to 2004 when al-Qaeda in Iraq was formed. It is infamous for horrendous acts of brutal violence and assaults on civilians. The self-proclaimed Caliphate has claimed responsibility for hundreds of terrorist attacks that have destroyed priceless monuments, ancient temples, antique arts of work and important buildings and have slaughtered Shiites, Christians,

Alawites and those who not aligned to their interpretation of jihadist Sunni Islam. The organisation has institutionalised slavery and has carried out mass genocides. The group has seized control of territories of large areas of northern and eastern Syria and northern and western Iraq and has successfully imposed its ideological influence. The Islamic caliphate has even garnered fighters with a vengeance beyond their controlled areas which act as catalysts for ISIS. In 2001, the world saw the largest terror strike when al-Qaeda (less brutal in comparison to ISIS) flew a passenger plane into the Pentagon and targeted the World Trade Centre, which caused death and injury to 10,000 Americans. This led to the "War on Terror", leading to an invasion of Iraq in 2003 by US troops which subsequently led to the formation of the AQI (al-Qaeda in Iraq) by Abu Musab al Zarqawi, who was previously a part of Osama Bin Laden's al-Qaeda Network. (Sekulow, 2015).

The rapidly ongoing spread of global terrorism has challenged academicians and policymakers who are attempting to expound on the causes and consequences of this phenomenon. The emergence of the Islamic State of Iraq and Syria (ISIS), also termed Daesh and ISIL (Islamic State of Iraq and Levant), added a whole new dimension to ISIS. To exhibit its supremacy, ISIS competed with other terror networks like al-Qaeda for influence over Islamist groups operating from and in different parts of the world that have made extremism more vicious and challenged the very core of humanism. It poses a heavy burden on the international community and strategists to effectively comprehend the group's ideology and counter the threat. The impact of ISIS on South Asia is a matter of concern as the region holds geopolitical significance and is largely affected by terrorism. The ISIS has reshaped the concept of terrorism and extremism in its more abhorrent forms. It has made the world shudder because of its highly publicized atrocities on its victims. The threat looms large over the world, particularly in South Asia, due to the organization's extensive network. Because the ISIS reigns over the hearts of its sympathisers, the threat remains potent (Taneja, 2018).

The AQI implemented the most draconian Sharia law, which even created a rift between the former and the latter (the al-Qaeda and the al-Qaeda in Iraq). The AQI aimed to remove Western occupation and maintained that its killing spree would bring forth a caliphate. This new government is crucial to the ISIS. The reason for this is that Islam is claimed to be a universal religion that purports to establish a global Islamic state. This idea is embodied in the political concept of the Ummah, where all Muslims, irrespective of geographical, national and political boundaries, are destined to be joined together through a common faith. The Ummah is to be governed by the Sharia, which is the most divine and holy law that supersedes all other laws. As per the teachings of Islam, the world is divided into two spheres—dar-al-Islam (house of Islam) and Dar-al-Harb (house of war). In the jihadist interpretation, there will be a constant conflict between the house of Islam (under Muslim control) where the Sharia is the highest authority and the house of war that does not submit to it; the conflict will end only by establishing a single, global Islamic state known as the caliphate, which would rule over the entire Muslim community under a supreme leader, the Caliph. However, there is a lack of explicit guidance on how to decide on a Caliph, as the Shias believe the leader must come from the bloodline of Muhammad, and the Sunnis maintain that any true believer can qualify for the office. Although the Shias believe in the idea of the Mahdi (spiritual leader to restore religion and justice) and while looking for him, the Sunnis established their caliphate regardless of whether it ruled from Damascus, Baghdad, Istanbul or the Ottoman Empire that ruled for 500 years. It collapsed after World War I, and the title of Caliph remained just a name without any power. In addition, in 1922, Mustafa Kamal (Atatürk) prompted the Turkish assembly to abolish the caliphate, and in 1924 its significance as a universal Islami authority was removed. To re-establish the caliphate, the Muslim Brotherhood was founded in Egypt in 1928, but ultimately it failed. In 2006, al-Qaeda too sought to establish a caliphate; however, a group leader, Abu Musab-al-Zarqawi, was killed during a US airstrike. The new head of the organisation, Abu Ayyub-al-Masari launched a caliphate in Diyala Province (2007) and renamed the group as the "Islamic State of Iraq"; he died in 2010 during the Iraqi operation by the USA. The organisation was in urgent need of a new leader, and it was then that Al Baghdadi took over control.

Research Methodology

In this dissertation, the qualitative methodology was used to obtain a deep understanding of the topic. The paper is written with the help of secondary data, including books, websites, journals, etc. The websites included those of the government and reports by think tanks.

Objectives

1. To identify the origin and modus operandi of ISIS.
2. To investigate the influence and presence of ISIS in South Asia with relevance to its influence on impressionable minds.
3. To conceptualize the role of 'media jihadists' and 'lone wolves' in the ISIS social media propaganda.
4. To analyse the implications of the ISIS in South Asia.

Literature Review

The Name of Terror: Abu Bakr Al Baghdadi (Taneja, Kabir, 2018). The ISIS phenomenon in South Asia and beyond. Caliph Ibrahim was a man who held a very prestigious and respectable religious position. He was part of the armed resistance in the Iraq war but was detained in the US-run Iraqi prison. Later, after release, he joined the ISI to strike fear in "his" enemies' hearts. Ibrahim took on the name of Abu Bakr al-Baghdadi and became a skilled commander and tactician who attracted many young jihadists. During the Syrian civil war, Al-Baghdadi and his counterparts fought against Syrian forces and captured large areas throughout the region. In 2013, he changed the organisation's name from the ISI to the "Islamic State of Iraq and Syria". In the following year, he, as the leader of the ISIS., delivered a speech at the Grand Mosque at Mosulin which he proclaimed himself Allah's vice-regent on Earth, called upon the people to obey him and became a "self-proclaimed caliphate" and took control of Fallujah, Mosul and Tikrit. Under him, ISIS became more brutal than its predecessor, al-Qaeda.

The ideology of the Islamic Caliphate: The Islamic State of Iraq and Syria (ISIS) propagated the most stringent form of doctrine described as totalitarian in the millenarian view that renounces political pluralism and diversity of thought. However, contrary to the belief of ISIS, Islamic history is filled with a rich diversity of thought and interpretation that has led Muslim societies to prosper politically, economically and spiritually. The ISIS, on the other hand, dismisses this concept of development and embodies in the narrow-minded a very marginal reading of Islamic doctrine. They have cultivated their own set of scholarly authorities rather than referring to widely-recognised Muslim scholars. The ideology of the ISIS is not much rooted in traditional Islam; moreover, it is based on three current documents, the most well-known being the *Management of Savagery* (Idarat al-Tawahhush) written by Abu Bakr al-Naji (pseudonym). It is a roadmap to create an Islamic state steeped in realpolitik and departs from civilised Islamic conduct of warfare. The document is widely circulated among ISIS commanders and leaders and is considered as the first resource for mujahids to manage their areas of influence. In addition, two books are held in high regard by the ISIS, *Introduction to Jurisprudence of Jihad* by Abu Abdullah al-Muhajjer and *The Essentials of Making Ready for Jihad* by Sayyid Imam al-Sharif. These three books call for a war that advocates an offensive jihad and requires planners and lieutenants to kill with impunity and brutally punish dissenters of Islam. The ISIS also follows the ideology of a Jordanian jihadist named Abu Musab al-Zarqawi on his understanding of *takfir* (declaring someone to be a heretic). They claimed that those who reject their caliphate are automatically apostates. Islamic scholar Rashad Ali points out that beliefs regarding the Caliphate were considered as a subsidiary as they are not a fundamental aspect of Islam.

The ISIS holds its own creed according to which Islam should be cleansed from within, and Muslims who do not obey their strict interpretation of the law are deviant believers and to be killed. They profess that governments that embrace democracy and secularism are infidels, and thus their killings are legitimized. Another key aspect of the ISIS is to call upon people to join the jihad they propagate as a permanent obligation, and the Caliph must assemble armies. Certainly, in this regard, traditional Islamic scholars respond that jihad is considered a final resort when all peaceful means have been exhausted, though neither is it sanctioned for world domination nor to convert non-believers. However, jihadists of the ISIS justify their acts of indiscriminately targeting civilians, including women and children, by stating that if "anyone commits aggression against you, attack them as they did to you but be mindful to God", which makes their killings legitimate on the ground that the enemy was also involved in the same kind of activities. According to Hadith, it is forbidden to kill non-combatants as murder is considered an abomination, yet Daesh militants vigorously use it. The ISIS has successfully emerged as the most ruthless jihadist organisation that has committed heinous public executions, beheadings, videotaping killings and even posting them online. The very first publicized act was the execution of a US journalist; it was posted on YouTube. Another gruesome footage was released on social media of a Jordanian military pilot being burned and of beheadings of Egyptian Christians. Daesh jihadists also force non-Muslims to convert at gunpoint, contravening the traditional Islamic ethic of "no compulsion in religion". They also demand tribute, i.e., jizya (tax imposed on non-Muslims under a Muslim ruler) who live in the lands under their control or face death. Islamic scholars pointed out that such a tax should not be applied to individuals who have been residents for centuries. Another key tactic of the ISIS is to routinely torture its enemies in detention centres within its territories and punish those who break the law of the Sharia. These detention facilities were in Al-Raqqa, Syria, including government buildings, Mabna al-Mohafaza, a governor's palace and Qasr al-Mohafez, a transport building office. In them, captives were flogged with thick cables, generator belts, given electric shocks and even forced to remain in contorted positions, in violation of every principle of international law in which captives are entitled to at least basic nutrition and medical care. Even children as young as eight are abducted, tortured and executed. The most treacherous work of ISIS militants is to place decapitated heads in a row and use them as a trademark of trophy executions. The ISIS also believes in destroying religious sites and relics as, according to them, they violate Islamic teachings, although classical Islamic scholarship does not allow the destruction of non-Muslim places of worship. Another hideous act of the radical group is to enslave girls and women belonging to religious minorities, particularly the 'Yazidi', and use them as sex slaves or sell them into sexual servitude. A survivor of an ISIS torture camp, Nadia Murad, described how young women were forced to pray before they were raped and made to do manual labour. "These women were made to do unimaginable things". Slavery conditions for men are different; they were transported to training camps where they were indoctrinated. The ISIS has been criticised by Muslim jurists and scholars for ignoring what is written in the Sunnah of Prophet Muhammad about eliminating slavery and eradicating it. The ambitions of the ISIS have become a reality due to the organisation's self-sustained financial state.

ISIS Financial Tactics and Attacks. The ISIS is branded as the best-funded terrorist organisation in the world. This makes the radical group more dangerous than others as it possesses both the means and the will to carry out its threats. It is well-equipped and holds the richest terrorist force. The group secures a huge war chest of money and hi-tech military equipment. The ISIS has even captured American howitzers that incorporate GPS targeting systems and machine guns that fire close to 800 rounds per minute. The M1 Abrams tanks, American-made, are considered to be among the most lethal three armoured vehicles in the history of the world. The ISIS possesses radiological material to make dirty bombs and has enormous pounds of uranium compounds. So, as far as financial strategies are concerned, the ISIS is a different animal. The methods of generating funds include the sale of oil and antiquities as well as resorting to extortion and taxation. This makes the group financially diversified, meaning that if one source of funding is shut down, it can resort to other options to generate revenue. The ISIS's financial resources have grown fast to capture more territory and resources. The Islamic State revenue rose from $ 1 million per month (2008-2009) to $ 3 million per day in 2014, and in the later years, the group kept on strengthening itself. They use their resources to run training schools where they indoctrinate students, train religious police to check on those who break the Sharia law and run Islamic courts under their own code of conduct. The ISIS pays its fighters an enormous amount of $ 400 per month, and an additional amount is paid to those who bring forth trained brides who become beneficial tools for the organisation. These brides are later used as suicide bombers. The Islamic State also sets and approves the annual budget and has appointed a chief financial officer to manage its accounts; it has established its own bank and uses Iraqi dinars and Turkish liras. Although the territories under the ISIS portray a brutal, two-tiered society in which the families of terrorists live well, and the others suffer. To maintain a state of eight to ten million people, wage war along its borders, finance and carry out international attacks and manage its network cells is a task skilfully managed by the ISIS. It earns revenue through oil fields that are a major source of income. A black market oil trade flourishes along the porous borders controlled by the Islamic State; oil is sold at a steep discount rate, and smugglers even use WhatsApp to coordinate their oil sales. This particular activity has declined a bit due to the USA's extensive airstrikes on oil facilities. The Islamic State oil reserves also suffer because professional technical workers are either killed or run away. As the ISIS controls vast areas, it levies taxes on the people in them; some taxes are akin to a normal state while others are like extortion. The Islamic State levies taxes on goods sold, basic utilities like water and electricity, trucks entering its territory and loots archaeological sites and non-Muslim communities. Extortion and taxation generate as much as $ 360 million, a massive amount for a terrorist organisation. For the Islamic State, another option to generate a significant amount of income is through kidnapping for ransom, which generally goes unreported in the international press. It is estimated that the ISIS received a handsome amount of donations from wealthy business people from Saudi Arabia, Qatar, the United Arab Emirates and Kuwait. These donors channelise millions of dollars to Syrian rebel groups. Although Saudi Arabia and the UAE have criminalised financial support to terrorist organisations and have made headway in limiting the financial route, funding channels include unregistered charitable organizations that funnel money to the Islamic State of Iraq and Syria. Whenever the ISIS captures an area, it loots private collections, archaeological sites, museums and artefacts; though it considers such artwork as against Islamic ethics yet does not hesitate to use these antiquities to earn wealth.

The IS has accumulated large sums of billion dollars in cash by seizing state-owned banks of northern and western Iraq. It has also collected cash by auctioning the properties of individuals whom the organisation considers enemies, such as government officials, Iraqi police and army personnel and public prosecutors. The properties confiscated by the ISIS are even used as bases for their fighters and members. The Islamic State controls the most fertile parts of Iraq and Syria, and the crops were sold at discounted prices in the black markets, which quickly generated revenue of about 200 million (dollars). It also captured such areas that are rich in natural resources like sulphur, cement and phosphate that create income for it. The ISIS's most atrocious financial tactic is human trafficking, whereby the organisation is engaged in organ harvesting and selling of women and young girls into marriage and sexual slavery. The Islamic State has claimed responsibility for hundreds of terrorist attacks worldwide.

The well-known attacks that are linked with the ISIS include the Paris attack in November 2015, in which a series of bombers and shooters terrorised the streets of Paris by killing 130 people. In the attack on San Bernardino in December 2015, a married couple who owed allegiance to the ISIS opened fire at the Inland Regional Centre in California, causing the death of 14 people. In the March 16 Brussels bombings, the ISIS targeted Brussels airport and the nearby metro station in Belgium, killing 32 people. Another attack by the Islamic State was in June 2016 in Pulse Nightclub when a gunman entered a gay nightclub in Orlando, opened fire and was held responsible for the deaths of 49 people. In July 2016, in Nice, a truck driven by a terrorist mowed down a crowd of people in the Riviera town in France, causing the deaths of 86 people. In Berlin in December 2016, a man hijacked and drove a truck into a market on Christmas and killed himself along with 11 others. In Manchester in May 2017, a suicide bomber killed 22 people at the Manchester Arena in England during a concert.

Dwindling territory and sluggish narrative of Islamic State: On the eve of 10 July 2017, Iraq's Prime Minister, Haider al-Abadi announced, in the besieged city of Mosul, the defeat of the Islamic State, although the narrative of the demise of the Islamic State had appeared primarily in the Western discourse months earlier. The ISIS, in 2014, took control over Iraq in a relatively easy manner with their leader, Abu Bakr al-Baghdadi, announcing the institutionalisation of their proto-state from the Great Mosque. The ISIS, from 2014 to 2016, conquered territory at a dangerous pace in both Syria and Iraq while setting up a governorate (wilayat) to install its own set of rules and laws according to the Sharia and their interpretation of Islam. The fall of Mosul changed the fate of the Islamic caliphate. In 2017, the ISIS lost territorial control as the Iraqi military, backed by anti-ISIS militias and the US-led Western coalition, liberated one city after another under 'Inherent Resolve'.

The ISIS loss of its de facto capital, Raqqa, also diminished its influence. In Syria, the options were different in political terms, with Iran and Russia backing the Syrian Bashar al-Assad regime, and thus the ISIS narrative weakened. However, the narrative of the end of the ISIS is based on the false equation that defines a military victory over the group as a strategic win. Yet it is important to remember that the ISIS started merely as an insurgency born out of al-Qaeda and was able to establish a strong presence in Iraq through the al-Qaeda under the first leader and ideologue, Abu Musab al-Zarqawi. However, relinquishing territory to Syria and Iraq is a moral setback for the ISIS, and this resulted in it constantly increasing its media output to maintain the morale of its ground forces and, most importantly, the online support base that the organisation had skilfully cultivated. The ISIS has lost its critical cities and towns, which it had garnered over the past years. These include Mosul, Tikrit, Kirkuk, Fallujah, Ramadi and Raqqa. The loss of Raqqa means that it is now concentrated mainly in Syria. When faced with such a dire situation, it has no choice left but to transform itself from its proto-state structure back to the organisational form of insurgency. Even though the Iraqi military has made constructive progress against the ISIS, there are still signs emerging of a political vacuum in the country that initially led the ISIS to succeed in capturing territory. With the ISIS downturn, the situation of Syria is more complicated; the landscape is riddled with smaller insurgencies looking to set up their proto-state similar to the caliphate. This complicated web of violence and political unrest in Iraq and Syria opens up an avenue for ISIS to again re-organise and emerge again as a well-orchestrated Islamic state, but then again, it would be a little early to determine a plausible outcome.

In September 2017, the ISIS released an audio clip statement allegedly from its elusive leader Al-Baghdadi that he divided into two parts, first addressing the ideological gap in the ISIS on the issue of Takfir that has generated a lot of debates and second, on geopolitics and the ISIS which was important amidst its losses and the prolonged silence of the leader, Baghdadi, who gave a morale boost to the ISIS fighters by stating that a territorial loss should not be linked to the ideological truth and goals of the organisation. He blamed the exhaustion of the foreign policy of America in the Middle East for its failure to counter the presence of Russia in the region. He ended his speech with the statement that "the show must go on". However, despite the territorial losses of the ISIS and the various complexities of the ground situation of both Syria and Iraq, one aspect of the ISIS could not go unavoided, and that is the organisation's reach beyond the region and the group's ability and strategies to influence people to act in its name in foreign lands. The ISIS has its governorates and allegiance to other terror groups. For example, Abu Sayyaf of The Philippines is engaged in fierce fighting with the military in the southern city of Marawi. India, the South Asian state, has even donated a token amount to The Philippines in its battle against the ISIS and its affiliates in South East Asia.

South Asia: A Germination Ground

The ideology of the ISIS has steered itself towards South Asia as it offers the Islamic state an appealing choice as the region is already home ground to many insurgent movements with some of its targets as easily vulnerable to terrorism. The region consists of approximately 60 per cent of the global Muslim population, with a sizable number open to radical recruitment. They target the deep-rooted communal and sectarian fault lines, which they exploit to their advantage. Whether it is porous borders, participation of Pakistanis and Shias of Afghanistan in the Syrian conflict, Islamic insurgencies in Kashmir and Afghanistan, informal economy, self-employed people that act as tools to raise funds for their jihadist enterprise, and an easy way out to procure weapons—all make South Asia an ideal ground for ISIS expansion. Demography plays a vital role in making certain areas inaccessible, like the Tora Bora caves of Afghanistan, uninhabited islands of the Maldives, and many youth cohorts professing extremist ideology in Pakistan. It has found many sympathisers who can easily be manipulated; ISIS has mobilized new generations of radicals, some of whom are even educated belonging to the urban middle and upper-middle classes who can pose a threat to the region. These educated jihadists work in a decentralised manner, either in 'cell formation' or as 'lone wolves', making their detection challenging. The return of ISIS fighters to their countries acts as a strategic plan to galvanise network cells within the existing IS regional affiliates. This leads to promotion and expansion in the organisational and operational structure of ISIS. South Asia provides ISIS with an opening to central and Southeast Asia along with the safe passage in hiding, training, recruiting, and fundraising from different parts of the region. ISIS mentioned South Asia as pivotal towards its expansion in Myanmar and the Caucasus region.

The Media Propaganda of Islamic State

The unregulated cyberspace of South Asia provides another avenue for ISIS to propagate its ideological narrative. As the region consists of many internet users, this facilitates their online media strategy, particularly in areas where ISIS militants cannot grow physically. There, it uses cyberspace to spread its extremist ideology. The social media platform and Islamist forums have been key meeting places for Daesh recruiters to contact vulnerable disfranchised youth. The media platform is a sacrosanct feature of ISIS operations. The organisation uses Facebook, WhatsApp, Telegram and other services to a great extent to spread its ideology and for recruitment. An ISIS key document in its media strategy is Media Operative; you are a mujahid too, it is a guide to employ the group's ideas, thoughts, and propaganda. The document was published by the Al-Himma library, which is a media outlet with the task of publicising its religious pamphlets and manifestos. It is to make sure that the online support base does not feel less important in comparison to the ground troops. This shows how important the media narrative is for the ISIS. To spread itself, the ISIS has four outlets that directly or indirectly feed information. The first is Amaq, a website that directly releases ISIS statements and operational details with infographics. Another is Rumiyah magazine, which could be called the Islamic State's 'Newsweek'. It covers the activities of the ISIS. The third outlet is Dabiq, which brought to the mainstream the capabilities of the organisation towards formalizing information. It has well-produced layouts and seems like a professional media enterprise. Dabiq manifests the outward interpretation of the ISIS beyond its territorial gains (Iraq and Syria). The fourth media outlet is the most elusive one; it is the Nashir Media Foundation, the ISIS official channel, is used for directives that create a robust online sphere of influence. The organisation even uses a vast-scale Twitter platform that caters to 46,000 active pro-ISIS accounts, which results in an increase in online radicalisation. However, Twitter's suspension of many accounts and its crackdown against ISIS supporter groups made the organisation looking for an alternative. Telegram service offers a broadcast option with no user limitation; this feature allowed the ISIS to propagate itself to unlimited numbers, and with Telegram offering encryption, the organisation was able to spread information and announcements to stake claims regarding attacks around the world. YouTube is used by the ISIS to stream violent viral videos, professionally filmed and edited to target young impressionable minds. Facebook pages are used to promote hate speech, whereby they can glamorise extremism

Media Jihadists and 'lone wolves'

The online propaganda of ISIS targets the new tech-savvy overambitious generation that is unhappy and dissatisfied with the religio-political organisation. Although the motivational factors vary from individual to individual and from area to area, one thing that is common amongst these media jihadists is their obsessive belief in the idea of the caliphate and the endless narratives. This pro-ISIS South Asian breed considers organisations like Harkat ul-Jihadi al-Islami and al Qaeda of Afghanistan, Lashkar-e-Taiba and Jaish-e-Muhammad of the Kashmir militants, Pakistan's Tehrik-e-Taliban, Indian Mujahedeen or Jihad ul-Islami of Bangladesh are merely inclined to maintain their status quo. At the same time, these new generation jihadists are driven by grander objectives, and they believe that the older generation is not doing enough for the community. A rift between the new and the old leads the younger generation to jump onto the Islamic State bandwagon. These media jihadists synchronise well with the ideology of the ISIS as they are morally consequentialist and unapologetically brutal. They are not narrow or parochial like the al-Qaeda pan-Islamist approach, the Taliban Afghan-centric or the Kashmiri militants' only-Kashmir policy; rather, they are globally-oriented militants aiming for Sunni supremacy.

The South Asian affiliates of the ISIS target specifically youth who have grievances and resentment against the state due to corruption and unemployment and are in search of an ideological identity or just mere excitement such youth are exploited by recruiters. This new breed of media jihadists are non-conformists breaking the stereotype that they have been radicalised in rural madrassas whereas they are self-radicalised on the internet, through their university classmates, familial networks and some through modern religious institutions like the Hizb-ul-Tahr and Tanzeem-e-Islami. In these organisations, recruiters penetrate to establish subgroups. A bond of trust is created through spiritual discussions, and later they are exposed to the channel of a radical version of political Islam. Whether they are self-proclaimed IS network cells in Karachi, Pakistan, that targeted a bus of Ismaili Shias, the Gulshan Cafe attacker in Dhaka or the Kalyan cell in India, all hail from well-to-do families with college or university educational backgrounds. Another reason that has made the operations of the ISIS highly effective is its 'lone-wolf' jihadists. This 'lone wolf' strategy of the Islamic State is beneficial in many ways. First, it is relatively easy and cheap as it does not require much planning. Besides, such jihadists are dispensable, and there are no 'handlers' to trace. Second, 'lone wolves' frustrate preventive measures as they have no direct connection with the ISIS, and therefore, they remain sheltered. Third, the attacks carried out by them damage the psychology and leadership of the nation by creating a sense of fear among civilians and inciting alarmism that governments appear helpless and even incompetent to overcome. Fourth, the worldwide proliferation of the 'lone wolf' strategy helps to boost the image of the ISIS by demonstrating its vast area of reach that appeals to its civilian sympathisers. The strategic logic that encourages the IS to rely more on these independent actors is because, after its defeat in Iraq and Syria, the organisation is desperate for payback and motivates its inspired supporters to attack as well become an important force multiplier. To bolster its political objectives, ISIS media jihadists use anti-Islamic sentiments and feed their propaganda machine. All such media tactics and operations have proven to be highly effective. The ISIS can fuel its narrative on a global platform by reaching out to the local population to join its jihad.

Countries in the Grip of ISIS

The ISIS exploits the South Asian complex socio-cultural and socio-political structure to market its ideology. Clearly, the terrorist organisation understands the significance of the region and can make its influence in South Asia. Afghanistan, a gateway to South-West and Central Asia, shares its border with Pakistan in the south with Uzbekistan in the north and Iran in the west. The ISIS-KP (Khorasan Province) of Afghanistan has made significant inroads into the complex tribal districts. The ISIS in Pakistan is playing a significant role in the same way the Taliban regime played for the al-Qaeda in Afghanistan in late 1990. Pakistan has somehow grown into a paradise for terrorist groups. Hence it is trying to change the perception. In the case of Bangladesh, the radical group has inspired an attack in the capital city Dhaka. Even the ongoing Rohingya refugee crisis has made the region a perfect ground for ISIS recruitment that has already made attempts at radicalisation in the refugee camps. As far as India is concerned, there have been 82 reported active cases of investigation on individuals suspected of engaging in pro-ISIS activities. These involved people who went to or attempted to travel to Syria, Afghanistan, Iraq and Libya to join the ISIS or those who have shown an inclination towards it through online support and propaganda. There are cases of a handful of people who have financed ISIS activities. The most significant issue of the Indian discourse was neither an attack nor a bombing but an anonymous account on Twitter that became the most vocal proponent of the ISIS on a social media platform. The Twitter account was known as ShamiWitness (@shamiwitness) and was run by Mehdi Biswas, an engineer who worked in a multinational corporation in the IT capital of India, Bengaluru. The account gained much popularity and was even followed by its author but was not flagged by the Indian authorities; rather, a British media organisation identified the owner in an investigation. This was a failure on the part of the National Technical Research Organisation of India, which is a technical intelligence agency. The highlighted discourse here is that Biswas is a well educated and financially stable middle-class individual whose inclination towards the ISIS or radicalisation could not be traced to the traditionally accepted explanations of Lack of opportunity and poverty.

The influence of the ISIS is also prominent in Bangladesh that endangers the stability of the wider region. In July 2016, an attack on the upbeat restaurant, Holey Artisan Bakery, killed 22 people and brought the spotlight of global terrorism on Bangladesh. The attack was orchestrated by an educated Bangladeshi youth who was inspired by the ISIS violence. The organisation claimed responsibility through its media outlet, in which it highlighted Bangladesh as its Bengal governorate. The radical terror group claiming the attack showed that the local jihadist was in touch with the organisation and was keen to join and fight for the ideological vision of the ISIS. Individuals from Bangladesh and India who are pro-ISIS attempted to work together with like-minded people online to create a more extensive base and an organised entity capable of attack with direct co-option with the ISIS. In Afghanistan, the situation is worse and complicated. The Islamic State in Khorasan is the Afghan avatar of the ISIS. The terror group has a vast presence in the ungoverned borderlands between Pakistan and Afghanistan, even along the disputed Durand Line. The fighters in the ISKP were part of the former Pakistan Taliban that successfully fled from the military operation conducted by the armed forces of Pakistan in the country's tribal areas such as FATA and Waziristan. These jihadists entered the Achin district in Nangarhar province as refugees and were initially aided by local villagers who sympathised with them, thinking they were Pashtuns. The jihadists used the situation to look for new avenues but only to return to the path of terrorism. To contain the terror group, America took a hands-on approach against the ISKP in Afghanistan and launched an airstrike with GBU-43/B (the mother of all bombs) in Achin district against the group. The US media reported that the ISKP fighters even belonged to Kerala in India who had travelled to Afghanistan to join the ISIS. In recent years, the ISIS, via its news agency Amaq, claimed the killing of police officers of Srinagar, Jammu and Kashmir, by which the organisation made its first official operation in the state. ISIS presence in Pakistan came to the fore when it claimed responsibility for two attacks in 2017. The first was in February with an attack on a Sufi shrine that killed 88 people, and the second was in August when 15 people were killed in Quetta; both these attacks were in the Balochistan area.

INDIA

The first two cases of Indians getting involved in pro-ISIS activities were between 2011 and 2013. These two individuals were engaged in on-off trips from India to the Middle East and were determined to join the ISIS in Syria. However, the Indian approach towards the Syrian crisis was based on the paradigm that it would only be contained within the Middle East region. Another case that emanates from India was when four young men left their home in Kalyan, Maharashtra, to join ISIS forces in Syria. These individuals intended to expand recruitment for ISIS, for which they planned to target educational institutions. According to the National Investigation Agency, the highest number of recruiters of ISIS have come from Kerala, Maharashtra, Telangana and West Bengal. In India, the presence of the ISIS is largely on media platforms, which open an avenue for potential jihadists. Another case that was highlighted in 2015 was from the state of Telangana. Naser Mohammed from Tamil Nadu formed a pro-ISIS module using social media and mobile phones and created a group called Junood-ul-Khilafa-fil-Hind. It was used as a platform to hold intra-state meetings between the recruiters of ISIS and those interested in joining.

On 5 March, the Anti-Terrorist Squad killed a man named Saifullah, a terrorist, in the Indian state of Uttar Pradesh. The pro-ISIS media channel proclaimed Saifullah as a soldier of the Khilafah. Lately, others involved with Saifullah were also arrested. On March 7, 2017, these cell members had targeted a passenger train operating between Bhopal and Ujjain in Madhya Pradesh with an improvised explosive device, which killed nine people. It was orchestrated that the Islamic State had influenced the attack. The media reported that this was considered the first full-scale Islamic State operation in India. The men involved were in contact with each other via social media. This shows how easy it has become for the terror group to make initial contacts with like-minded people. The Islamic State has a two-fold presence in India; one is the self-radicalised individuals or cells and the other breakaway factions of existing terrorist groups that have pledged allegiance to the leader of the ISIS, Abu Bakr al-Baghdadi. These self-radicalised cell members are then trained by their handlers in Iraq and Syria. One of the self-radicalised individuals named Mehdi Masroor Biswas posted 120,000 tweets on his Twitter handle (ShamiWitness) to support the ISIS.

The two Indian militant groups that are affiliated with the ISIS include a splinter group of the Student Islamic Movement of India (SIMI) and the Indian Mujahideen (IM). An IM splinter group Ansar-ul-Tawhid-fi-Bilad al-Hind (supporters of monotheism), pledged its allegiance to the IS. The leader of this group is Sultan Armar, and soon after his death in 2014, his younger brother, Shami Armar, took over. He became the most significant link of the ISIS in India and was able to radicalise 30 individuals, including people from Karnataka and Andhra Pradesh. Shami Armar was responsible for forming another IS affiliate in India, the Junud-ul-Khilafa-e-Hind (soldiers of Indian caliphate), in 2015 that made arrangements for these radical fighters unable to travel to Iraq and Syria. He facilitated a large sum of money to operatives here in India for training purposes and to increase membership. The NIA arrested these operatives in 2016 before they could attack and cause any damage to the country. Other than these pro-IS cells, seven more such cells have been discovered or disrupted since the declaration of the caliphate in 2014. One of the cells included one in Madhya Pradesh that was later busted by the police in May 2015. In the Kalyan cell episode, four men from Mumbai travelled to Iraq, and in the one relating to the Kerala cell, its members travelled to Afghanistan and were later killed in US airstrikes in March 2017. The cell in Hyderabad was disrupted in 2016, while the one from Tamil Nadu of eight people was discovered in 2017. According to the Intelligence Bureau report of January 2017, hundreds of people have travelled to IS-controlled territories; a few have been arrested, and others are under watch.

Other than these pro-IS cells, the organisation tried to exploit the situation in Kashmir to arouse support and increase membership in India. Fear sprouted when IS flags were waved in anti-government protests in late 2015; however, Indian security forces in Kashmir claimed that these were acts of mischief and represented no serious threat. Also, the ISIS presence in Bangladesh and parts of West Bengal are a matter of concern for India. Abu Jandal al-Bangali, the leader of the IS Bengal faction, stated in an interview in *Dabiq* magazine that it planned to create fear and chaos and then capture the territory. Although it is over-ambitious, but given the population of India, any attempt to create mayhem through terror attacks would disrupt inter-religious harmony and somehow undermine social cohesion in the country. It is believed that the ISIS, to gain support, increase membership and create more network cells, could raise anti-Hindu sentiments among Muslims. Those who can be easily indoctrinated to cause communal strife between the two communities would be beneficial to the organisation. On 8 March, the National Investigation Agency stated that the attack on a passenger train in Ujjain was a precursor to a larger attack on a Sufi shrine in Uttar Pradesh. The radical group consistently targets religious shrines, and India is no exception. The plan to attack the Sufi shrine ensures that such soft institutions are potential targets. In addition, the terror group even threatened to attack a temple in February 2017 during a rally addressed by PM Narendra Modi and the Taj Mahal in March 2017. These threats provided insights into the targets of the group. The crowded train system is another significant target, and it is evident from the recovery of maps of train systems from the leader of the IS cell in Thakurganj area of Lucknow.

Protecting daily commuters and the sprawling rail network is a huge security challenge. Despite these various vulnerabilities, the ISIS has not been able to carry out any spectacular attack on Indian soil. There are multiple reasons for this. The approach of the ISIS has not been able to garner much support, firstly, due to the effective coordination between the national and international security agencies and monitoring of radicals by security forces has prevented ISIS-directed and inspired attacks. Secondly, it is unable to create an environment of breakthrough because the Muslim community has played a very dynamic role in preventing attacks by reporting radicalised individuals or suspected terrorists to the police. This was highlighted by the former Home Minister, Rajnath Singh. Another important fact is that major Muslim organisations and madrassas in India are very vocal in their opposition to terrorism and the kind of extremism propagated by these terror groups. The ISIS has not been able to influence much because the majority of Muslims here shuns the ideology of the ISIS and its interpretation and methods of the Sharia. Rather, radical Islamic thinking within India relates to regional issues and conflicts. The interesting point is that the Salafist Movement, which was criticised for its role in contributing to radicalisation globally, is divergently and relatively syncretic in India, and that provides another level of institutional buffer against the plans of the IS. Fourthly, the countries that sent Muslim volunteers in the Afghan war of 1980 had to contend with returning foreign fighters who formed jihadist networks in their own countries. India, due to its strong partnership and defence ties with Russia and the then Soviet Union, ensured that its citizens did not travel to Afghanistan to fight in the war. This decision prevented jihadist networks from establishing a solid foothold in India. The significant point here lies in the better integration of the Muslim community into mainstream society has prevented dissatisfaction and marginalisation that could be exploited by ISIS cells. The existing buffers against terrorism have been effective in preventing ISIS networks, and this amounts to the fact that those who travelled to Iraq and Syria and those who have been arrested are a very small fraction of the Muslim population that has fallen into the clutches of the ISIS. Yet the threat of the ISIS is unavoidable as transnational ambitions, sensational online media propaganda with media jihadists and 'lone wolves', and isolated cells have the potential to damage communal relations in the present trying times when alienated, vulnerable youth become susceptible to radical influences and thus creating a situation in which the threat is imminent. For India, the rise and success of the ISKP in Afghanistan and Pakistan is also a sign of grave concern. After the destruction of the caliphate, the most organised and operational success of the ISIS clone seems to have been set in Afghanistan. There are narratives that the ISKP could infiltrate the valley of Kashmir and create a second strain of jihadists that would largely be based on religion and not on politics. The Indian government has been devising a national strategy to deal with the ISIS since 2015. India increasingly incorporated soft measures in 2017, opening a new government division to counter radicalisation. This is in line with its programmes in states such as Kerala and Maharashtra, where the respective police departments undertook successful deradicalization drives involving close to 500 people. Reportedly, these individuals were radicalised by propaganda present on Facebook and were identified by the cyber security division. In Kashmir, the Centre pardoned first-time offenders arrested for pelting stones against the military, which affected 4,500 individuals. The main features of India's deradicalization efforts include avoiding wrongful arrests, prevention of social stigma and alienation associated with arrests, providing local helplines and winning the confidence of the minority community on a larger scale. The government has also created a counter-terror unit called National Security Guards though not many states have set up SWAT (Special Weapons and Tactics) or similar teams to handle the first impact of a terror strike. Looking at the trying times, it has become imperative to invest time, energy and money to create such special units capable of handling terrorist challenges. It is also necessary that court trials of all incidents of terror and communal crime move swiftly and justice is delivered. Also, to counter the threat posed by the ISIS, the government encouraged the National Investigation Agency of India to establish a research cell on the ISIS in March 2019.

AFGHANISTAN

The phenomenon of transnational terrorism in South Asia begins with Afghanistan. It has been a brewing ground for terrorism owing to certain factors like sectarianism, internal turmoil and a large Muslim population that the ISIS aims to radicalise. The radical group views the land as fertile ground to create a foothold. According to a United Nations Report, the ISIS in Afghanistan is estimated to have 4,000 militants who are responsible for 38 terrorist attacks. The ISIS wing that emerged as the ISKP or IS-K (Islamic State of Khorasan Province) in 2014 covers Afghanistan and Pakistan and has struggled to expand beyond a few Afghan and Pakistani districts, particularly in eastern Nangarhar where the group first emerged. The ISKP has recruited dissatisfied low-level commanders from the Nangarhar district and militants from Pakistan tribal areas. It has been stalled for various reasons; the internal clashes between the Afghanistan and Pakistan leaderships, the US-led coalition airstrikes and the opposition from the Taliban regime of Afghanistan.

The fighters of ISKP are from central Asia, including those associated with the Islamic Jihad Union, The Turkistan Islamic Party and others from Azerbaijan. Interestingly, the Afghans fighting for the Islamic State in Syria and Iraq were recruited from Europe after they had migrated there over the decades and who returned to Afghanistan to support the Islamic caliphate as trainers and mid-level commanders.

The IS-K influenced other districts like Nazyan, Achin and Deh Bala—all are border districts with safe passage in Khyber and Orakzai agencies of Pakistan. The largest presence of the ISKP is in Kunar, with support networks and access to both Pakistan and Afghanistan, which makes the area most suitable for the group. The IS-K strategy is to move outside the Taliban traditional areas and move northward to appoint recruits from provinces including Kunduz, Samangan, Sar-e Pol, and Faryab. The radical group also reached the Kajaki district of the southern Helmand province. The ISKP expanded by gaining control over these districts and then appealed to Salafi networks and later expanded to cross-border militant groups.

The strategy for recruitment in these areas is face-to-face outreach and preaching with the promise of regular paychecks and arms. The leadership of the organisation is dominated by the core group of the Tehrik-e-Taliban of Pakistan and the former governor of the Khorasan Province, Hafiz Saeed, who assumed the IS-K leadership until he was killed by a US drone strike. The ISKP number two leader, Shahidullah Shahid, is the primary spokesman and the leading facilitator. They linked the Islamic State to the Orakzai-based former group, the TTP, that has dominated the leadership of the ISKP. According to Afghan security officials, Shahidullah Shahid was more influential due to his close ties with the Islamic State Central and to the funding sources in the Gulf. Though it is vital to point out that the ISKP leadership is notable for its lack of Afghans even after the majority of operations occurred in Afghanistan, rather, the upper-level leadership is dominated by Pakistanis. While the other middle-level positions are captured by the former Taliban commanders, those who joined the IS-KP are considered to be the most notorious and influential members, although the Islamic State 'caliphate' seeks to eradicate the dispute between Afghanistan and Pakistan, which posed a problem for the recruitment strategy of the ISIS because of the high level of distrust on both sides of the border.

Furthermore, the IS-K began to consolidate control through mass executions. Forced displacements and target killings of clerics from Jalalabad and Kot districts. The clerics were killed because they did not support ISKP agendas and could not provide fighters from their religious congregations. In this environment of heightened violence and shifting power, displacement became a fact of life. Families and religious leaders who did not align with the IS-K relocated to the provincial capital of Jalalabad or into Taliban-controlled areas in western Nangarhar, such as the Khogiani district. The IS-K also successfully co-opted the cross-border criminal and militant network, the Lashkar-e-Islam, which operates in the Nangarhar province Khyber Agency border area. The Lashkar-e-Islam was already involved in several land conflicts straddling the Af-Pak border; by partnering with the IS-K, it was able to increase its influence on these conflicts and gain more control of strategic smuggling routes. In return, the IS-K was able to broaden its support base and increase its operational capacity. Recruiting and outreach were further augmented by an IS-K FM radio station, "The Voice of the Caliphate", broadcasting throughout the province. Earlier, segments of the community welcomed the IS-KP due to its non-violent proselytizing forms, and they even appreciated the fact that the group cadres did not demand taxes from villagers like the Taliban had done for long. However, these early benefits gave way as the IS-K executed the elders of the tribal community and announced it would ban poppy cultivation, which is an important source of livelihood at a time when markets prices are high.

The terror group also began to conduct kidnappings for ransom by holding tribal leaders, people in business and cell tower security guards hostage and demanding money and ammunition for their release. Beyond these economic and security consequences, communities also began to question the religious and social structure of life under the Islamic State, namely, the destruction of dozens of Sufi shrines in several districts and the promise that IS-K fighters would be provided brides from among the local communities. The IS-K even operates detention centres, mostly holding Taliban prisoners, in DehBala and Achin districts. The ISKP was held responsible for an offensive attack against Afghan counter-intelligence forces in the Nangarhar district. The Islamic State claimed a suicide attack on a gathering of mostly Shia demonstrators from Afghanistan's Hazara ethnic group in central Kabul, which killed nearly 80 people and wounded 231. This was the first significant IS-K attack outside Nangarhar.

It demonstrated that the group could reach outside its area of immediate control. The presence of the IS-K will remain problematic in the near future for several reasons. The group appears to be well-funded, obtaining significant sums from Islamic State Central routed through diverse channels (the Gulf, China, Turkey) and prioritizing control of areas inside Afghanistan where it can extract revenue from the control of heroin processing and trading timber smuggling, and kidnapping. The IS-K's position along the Af-Pak border is crucial to the flow of external funding from abroad through Pakistan and into Afghanistan, as well as its internal revenue streams, which depend on a porous international border. If displaced, the group will likely seek another area along the border, most likely northwards into Kunar or even Badakhshan.

A regionally supported political settlement with the Taliban should continue to be a focus. Establishing border security will be key to any serious attempt at rooting out the IS-K. Yet, the governments of both Afghanistan and Pakistan appear willing to sacrifice long-term regional security to enable their own ultimately uncontrollable militant proxies to create insecurity for their neighbour across the Durand Line. Until these short-sighted tactics are not reversed, international forces, and the international community more broadly, risk getting drawn into a fight with the Islamic State that is essentially the same mix of territorial, regional-geopolitical, and hyper-local conflicts that have characterized Afghanistan-Pakistan relations for decades. The fight against the IS-K, while important, is a distraction from the mainline of effort: peace and stability through a regionally supported political settlement with the Afghan Taliban. The capabilities and sophistication of ISKP are so alarming that the Afghan forces planned to work together with the coalition, even with the Taliban, to curb its growing influence (Taneja, K., 2015).

PAKISTAN

The influx of ISKP fighters from Afghanistan into Pakistan will increase as the group seeks to expand and attract more recruits. The IS accumulates and inspires attacks in urban centres, with religious sects being targeted as the group seeks power. They have hired highly educated youth from the universities of Lahore, Peshawar, Karachi and Multan. The radical individuals were former members of the Tehrik-e-Taliban Pakistan (TTP), which affiliated itself to the IS; however, its territorial loss in the Federally Administered Tribal Agencies (FATA) forced the jihadists to shift to the ideology of the Daesh. It is estimated that about two to three thousand Pakistanis are Daesh members recruited from urban areas.

The Daesh strategy in Pakistan also includes women as the organisation underscores the female benefits membership can offer. They are enlisted as fighters and suicide bombers as they can penetrate targets more easily than men. Affiliated groups of the ISIS in Pakistan, the Abtal-ul-Islam, draw financial support primarily through donations from Turkey and Saudi Arabia. Interestingly, other terror networks like the Lashkar-e-Taiba and the Jamaat-ud-Dawa send their members to training camps in Syria. These groups that embraced ISIS opened up the possibility of establishing massive operational ties through the local networks, which could enhance the capacity of the organisation to carry out sophisticated attacks in Pakistan. Even leaders of the Wilayat Province Shura play a significant role as they have understood the Pakistani terrain and its people. Their influence with local tribes could help the Wilayat Khorasan build a support base in Pakistan.

The Shura's networking nexus could help Daesh to develop linkages with multiple terrorist organizations and recruits from Deobandi madrasas throughout Pakistan. In the recent past, the Sawt-al-Ummah pledged allegiance to the Daesh. This group is an offshoot of the Hizb-ul-Tahrir, whose campaign of support for an Islamic caliphate could sway its members to gravitate toward the Daesh brand. The ideological appeal, global reputation, and substantial financial resources of the ISIS act as catalysts, whereas the group has found room in Pakistan's already crowded jihadi space. However, the organisation's ambitions for the region have placed it at odds with other militant groups such as the TTP of Pakistan, the most lethal one, that has not largely expressed support for Daesh elements in the region due to the TTP alliance with the Afghan Taliban, which has lost territory to the Daesh since 2015. The Pakistani efforts against Daesh are just focused militarily, although it should be multifaceted operations; however, the operations have cleared militant safe havens in the FATA. But these groups, including the Wilayat Khorasan, simply just shifted to Balochistan or Afghanistan to counter the threat. Pakistan must seek a joint effort with Afghanistan with a focus on border control to stem the flow of militants between the two countries. Both countries need to reach a final resolution over their border dispute. The National Counter Terrorism Authority is required to play a leading role to develop effective civilian organizations at the national level to assess, plan, and orchestrate the national counter-terrorism effort against the Daesh. The counter-terrorism strategy must also address the main strength of the Daesh in Pakistan, firstly, the resonance of its ideology with different segments of Pakistani society. It should focus on the sectarian divisions, which the Wilayat Khorasan has already proven that it could exploit to gain recruits.

SRI LANKA

Sri Lanka faced a security crisis in 2019 after a series of coordinated suicide attacks ripped through parts of the country on April 21, Easter Sunday. The deadliest single day of violence in the country saw more than 250 people killed and several hundred more injured. Almost 50 foreign nationals, mainly from China, India, the USA and Britain, also perished. The aftermath of the attack saw religious and ethnic tensions reignite; the government struggled to formulate an adequate response. In the Easter attacks, nine suicide bombers had struck at three churches as well as three luxury hotels. The Islamic State (IS) claimed responsibility; however, the government has blamed local jihadist militant groups, the National Thowheed Jamath (NTJ), Jammiyath-ul-Millathu Ibrahim (JMI), and Willayath-As-Seylani (WAS) that were even banned under the Prevention of Terrorism Act. They were described as self-radicalised Salafi-jihadist networks that drew inspiration and support from the IS.

Although the IS claimed responsibility for the Easter attack through its Amaq news agency, a video was released by the IS-affiliated Al-Ghuraba media, allegedly featuring the suicide bombers. Except for Zahran Hashim, the alleged mastermind, all the other bombers had their faces covered. Messages were in Arabic and Tamil visible in the video, while a caption read, "O Crusaders, this bloody day is our reward to you". The SITE Intelligence Group, which monitors jihadi networks worldwide, said the bombings were widely celebrated by IS supporters online through IS flags and labelling the attackers as commandoes. In a statement issued on Telegram, the IS said it had targeted Christians as well as citizens of countries involved in the international coalition opposing it. For the IS, the Easter attack was a significant boost as it attempted to reset the narrative about its decline. Such an attack demonstrated that the IS could form tactical alliances with low-profile local Islamist groups such as the NTJ in Sri Lanka. It is vital to point out that some of the suicide bombers belonged to a wealthy family like that of Ilham Ahmed Ibrahim, who was a prominent member of the business community in the capital, Colombo. He was one of the two bombers who targeted the luxury Shangri-La Hotel.

They believed the bombers were inspired by the IS brand, eager for the high profile that it would confer. As per reports, the first two ISIS Sri Lankan nationals were Sharfaz Nilam and Thauqeer Thajudeen, who had travelled to Syria. They were pioneering Sri Lankan jihadists and may have, along with charismatic preachers such as Zahran, inspired hundreds of other individuals towards the IS cause. Since 2012 there was a spread of the ultra-conservative Wahabbi and Salafi ideologies from the Middle East into some Muslim-majority towns. A series of anti-Muslim riots perpetrated by radical Buddhist groups in 2018, and four years earlier in 2014, further contributed to Sri Lankan Muslims feeling marginalised.

ISIS jihadists exploited such local grievances to radicalise some young Muslim men, adding a new dimension to the country's threat landscape. Violence and oppression against Rohingya Muslims in Myanmar is also a source of grievance for some local Muslims due to close links between Buddhist extremist groups in both countries and given that Sri Lanka had previously refused asylum to a group of Rohingya refugees who attempted to enter the country by boat. Sri Lanka's largely peaceful Muslim community faced a significant backlash following the attacks, with radical Sinhalese mobs attacking and destroying hundreds of Muslim properties in the North-Western province. The government says it has increased security to control communal tensions. However, Muslim women wearing traditional Islamic dress were targeted after the government banned face coverings in public following the Easter attacks, citing security reasons due to which nine Sri Lankan Muslim ministers resigned in protest against the government being unable to protect Muslim citizens. In August 2019, Sri Lanka officially ended four months of emergency rule. Emergency laws, imposed following the attacks, had given the military and police sweeping powers to arrest and detain suspects without court orders. Temporary curfews and social media blackouts were also imposed as part of comprehensive and sweeping security measures. To date, almost 300 people linked to the attacks have been arrested, with half that number still in demand. Security officials say all those directly responsible for the suicide bombings have either been killed or arrested (Mahalingam, 2019).

BANGLADESH

Since the ISIS announced the establishment of the caliphate, Bangladesh witnessed many pro-ISIS groups such as the Jund al-Tawhid and the al-Khilafah pledging allegiance to the organisation. The militants from Jama'at-ul-Mujahideen Bangladesh and Ansarullah Bangla Team have also revived their organisational capabilities and are preparing for attacks in the country, which include targeted assassinations involving individuals whom they consider obstacles or apostates to establishing an Islamic State in Bangladesh. These militant groups send their Bangladeshi recruits to fight in Syria. Bangladesh Islamist militant groups have also formed a new organisation under the rubric of the International Lion Force of Hindustan. This group aims to establish an Islamic State in Bangladesh based on Sharia law with the help of the ISIS. The pledge to Abu Bakr al-Baghdadi by these groups manifest a significant impact on the ISIS hold in Bangladesh.

In this context, a video surfaced on an internet platform with five masked individuals declaring the ISIS as their leader. In October 2014, the JTK urged Bangladeshi Muslims to participate in armed jihad and even contribute financially to the Islamic cause. So the ISIS cells in Bangladesh benefit from ties with their local parent organisations. The majority of ISIS recruits come from educated middle-class families, and some are relatively wealthy. With this overwhelming group that professes the ideology of the ISIS with the help of social media applications, radicalisation is persistent. The ISIS holds power to influence the existing militant groups of Bangladesh through its brand image, network capabilities and financing. The major claimed attack by the ISIS in Bangladesh is the assault on the Holey Artisan Bakery in July 2016 in Dhaka that caused the death of 22 civilians. The main target of the ISIS was foreigners, and the Bangladesh-affiliated group, the Dawlat -ul-Islam Bengal, claimed responsibility. The group consists of individuals who had defected from the Jamaat-ul-Mujahideen, and the other was from the Jund-at-Tawhid Wal-Khilafah that was formed in 2015 and led by Muhammad Saifullah Ozaki, who is reported to be the Leader of ISIS-Bangladesh. However, despite the ISIS claim, the Bangladeshi authorities denied that the Dhaka attacks had anything to do with the Islamic State of Iraq and Syria; instead, the Bangladesh government claimed that the perpetrators were members of the JMB, though an unavoidable fact is that the ISIS currently has mobile teams that move from district to district to pre-attack dens to highlight the group's nationwide reach with the jihadists stockpiling arms and explosives. In this view, Bangladeshi officials have highlighted the sharp increase in the recovery of suicide belts. The internal militant groups being influenced by IS strategy involves women in group activities. This is to work below the radar of law enforcement. Women are radicalised and forced to join mostly by their male family members, who are jihadists.

The Bangladesh counter-terrorism measures are at a critical juncture and its preparedness to counter is under scrutiny. Bangladesh needs to improve its cyber and digital domains, which is to build up technical capabilities for monitoring violent extremism online. The country still, however, lacks a dedicated counter-terrorism agency that can focus upon areas such as investigation, prosecution, counselling, arrest and building public awareness on counter-terrorism issues. Although Bangladesh faces a new challenge, the persecution of Rohingya Muslims in Myanmar Rakhine state has led to the influx of over 600,000 refugees in Bangladesh. The humanitarian crisis has opened up a new avenue for ISIS jihadists. Furthermore, the situation at the India-Pakistan border posed a significant challenge to counter-terrorism in Bangladesh. It all boils down to the fact that several militant groups of Bangladesh, such as the JMB, have found a haven in West Bengal where the most high-profile terrorists hide and operate.

In 2017, Indian law enforcement authorities even detained Samiun Rahman and Ibne Hasan, who was trying to set up an ISIS Bangladesh based in New Delhi to radicalise and recruit for an attack in India as well as Myanmar. Samiun revealed to Delhi police that his task was to recruit potential jihadists to fight the Myanmar military and enter Myanmar through India's north-eastern states. Another lucrative factor that drives Bangladeshi jihadists to India is the availability of small weapons through the black market. The Bangladesh-India border acts as a channel for illicit flows, which creates an environment for the militants to operate.

MALDIVES

As far as the Maldives is concerned, the over 200 nationals of the population of 400,000 that travelled to Syria to join the ISIS have contributed mainly in terms of foreign fighters on a per capita basis.

According to the Maldivian government, the National Counter-Terrorism report states that recently 69 male Maldivians had travelled abroad to join foreign wars. Issues like unemployment, organised crime and gang violence are factors that have taken the youth towards the path of radicalisation. Despite its geographical remoteness and small population, the Maldives is a fertile ground for transnational jihadist recruitment, as seen in the disproportionate number of Maldivian fighters in Syria. The growth of jihadism in the Maldives is a matter of security concern, particularly for India and other South Asian countries. In the past decade, jihadist networks of the Pakistan-based Lashkar-e-Taiba (LeT), al-Qaeda and other terrorist groups have operated in the Maldives. Terrorism has become a concern in recent times, especially in light of the 28 September 2015 attack targeting President Abdulla Yameen. The earliest cases of 50 to 100 Maldivians who attempted to travel to Iraq and Syria were reported in October 2013. Most Maldivian fighters who travelled to Syria joined the al-Qaeda affiliated group, Jabhat-al-Nusra (JN). There have been Maldivian fighters with the Islamic State of Iraq and Syria (ISIS), as well as other groups such as the Islamic Front (IF) and Free Syrian Army (FSA). Fighters have included students, those who were convicted or accused of terrorism or related to such crimes in the Maldives, as well as religious figures and former military personnel. In this context, in 2015, members of criminal gangs such as the Kuda Hanveiru in the capital, Male, have been reported to be going to Syria. The Maldivians go to Syria through Sri Lanka, India or Thailand, and travel from there to Pakistan or Turkey for training. It was also reported that about 20 individuals of the Maldivian community in the southern Indian state of Kerala had travelled to Syria to join the ISIS, although before the country faced the danger of radicalisation, it was traditionally relaxed in terms of religiosity. Recently, jihadist pamphlets disparaging Alawites and Shiite Muslims have been found in several mosques. Similarly, the Taliban style of public flogging as punishment for adultery is being propagated. Maldivian fighters are recruited through social media as well as in mosques. Several extremist Maldivian groups and preachers have online platforms like Facebook, Twitter, and Instagram, through which they propagate their jihadist intentions. In this context, a video on YouTube entitled "A Message to the Maldivian Government" featured three masked men who threatened to kill President Abdulla Yameen and Vice-President Mohamed Jameel Ahmed and tourist spots on which the Maldivian economy depends. The 200 Maldivian supporters of the ISIS even conducted an organised demonstration and called for the full implementation of Sharia Law and an end to secular rule in the Maldives. One of the most active Maldivian online groups, the Haqqu, had 1,056 members. The ISIS is even interested in drawing recruits from radicalised criminal gangs, although the majority of them were convicted for illegal activities like drug trafficking, assault and murder. Media representatives of Maldivian fighters in the group are known as Bilad al-Sham. It is anti-government and anti-democratic and has called the victory of President Abdulla Yameen 'jahiliyyah', meaning 'ignorance'. This indicates that Maldivian jihadist groups continue to disseminate ISIS ideology through their online outlets leading to radicalisation and recruitment to fight and carry out suicide attacks for the Islamic caliphate.

Over the past decades, successive Maldivian governments have failed to curb the exposure of its citizens to the ISIS. Similarly, the government have been unable to stem the flow of foreign funds or foreign radical preachers who promote jihadist ideology. In October 2015, the Maldives passed a new terrorism law defining acts of terrorism as offences and punishment for them. The law gives the authority to declare any group as a terrorist organisation and monitor conversation through telephone internet, prosecute individuals for speeches or statements encouraging terrorism, and prevent the travel of suspected ISIS sympathisers. The biggest challenge the government faced was from the Adhaalath Party (AP) that propagated the Salafist ideology and others from extremist NGOs such as the Jamiyyat-ul-Salaf (JS), Dhi Salafiyyah and the Islamic Foundation of Maldives. Presently, a strategic ally of the AP and needed to oppose the ruling government, the Maldivian Democratic Party (MDP) led by Mohamed Nasheed is also believed to lend tacit support to the spread of radicalism in the country. To contain the growth of political treason and to limit the spread of terrorist activity, the Maldivian government has reshuffled its governance and security structure. Other related challenges for the Maldives include reducing poverty and increasing employment opportunities, diversifying the economy beyond tourism and fishing, and combating drug trafficking and drug abuse, along with gang culture among the youth. With its limited resources, the Maldives cannot achieve all this on its own. A regional effort is required to dismantle the jihadist and drug-trafficking networks that span the region. International aid and cooperation are needed to counter extremism in the country and to tackle the challenges arising from socio-economic grievances that the country encounters.

Recommendation

Regional Cooperation to Counter ISIS

The ISIS is now a reality for South Asian governments, with the region facing an increasing risk of ISIS-inspired violence. Although the full extent of the threat is not yet understood, it is clear that regional counter-terrorism cooperation needs to be strengthened.

The main regional forum of South Asian countries, the South Asian Association for Regional Cooperation (SAARC), is dormant due to India's concerns over cross-border terrorism emanating from Pakistan-based groups. Therefore, in the absence of any realistic future cooperation with Pakistan, a focus on counter-terrorism in a reconstituted India-Sri Lanka Maldives trilateral grouping at the level of the country's national security advisers, as well as the Bay of Bengal Initiative For Multi-Sectoral Technical And Economic Cooperation. A grouping that includes Sri Lanka, India and Bangladesh, could be two ways to enhance regional counter-terrorism cooperation. Beyond these forums, national security operations or bilateral cooperation with strategic extra-regional powers, such as the USA, remain the only viable alternative options in each country's policy toolkit.

It is vital for South Asian countries to join hands for-off on-ground engagement between communities and governance along with a system of robust online anti-terror apparatus to keep tabs on the activities of pro-ISIS movements on social media and finances through banking, travel and other areas. Countries should make their human intelligence more robust to deter ISIS activities and have a joint online database convergence to the internet influence of the ISIS.

Conclusion

The Islamic State of Iraq and Syria; the name itself is enough to bring fear and terror in the hearts of people. It became a global terror network that conquered large areas and directed horrific attacks. The terrorist group has successfully propagated its stringent ideology in areas not only within its territorial control but also in different parts of the world. The ISIS became the deadliest terror organisation as it managed to draw tens of thousands of recruits from around a hundred countries. Its methods are the most atrocious and brought a whole new dimension to the phenomenon of terrorism. It cleverly radicalises educated youths through its media propaganda to suit the organisation's ambition. The terror network, for the sake of the Islamic caliphate, established connections with other terrorist organisations of the world. The ISIS, through ferocious acts, holds the position of the most financially equipped group that its soldiers handsomely. The terror group became known for its trophy-style mass executions and its re-establishment of sexual servitude. The organisation reached the highest peak of power under the misguided leadership and vision of Abu Bakr al-Baghdadi, a cunning enigmatic black-clad leader who transformed the flagging insurgency into a caliphate. Baghdadi made ISIS sympathisers, envisioning the world to be based on their interpretation of Sharia law. It was his idea to expand beyond its territories and spread the radical seeds to other nations; thus, South Asia is significant. The ISIS did manage to initiate its plan and radicalise a certain segment of people. However, it, in times of organisational triumph, faced diminished territory and its weakening narrative. Abu Bakr again very well played the role of a leader and motivated the organisation's on-and-off ground soldiers with a speech to continue fighting for their vision and ideology.

Abu Bakr al-Baghdadi detonated a suicide vest during a raid in north-western Syria by the United States Special Operations Forces. Soon after his death, the ISIS declared Amir Mohammed Abdul Rahman al-Mali al-Sable as its leader. Yet, it is vital to understand that even after the death of the former leader of the ISIS, the group has found different hosts and has the capacity to adapt structurally to their way of functioning. The Islamic State caliphate was never territorial; it was more of a caliphate of mind, and until the ideology of the ISIS reverberates in the minds of its disillusioned followers, it cannot be destroyed. The end of ISIS ideology is thus imperative for the peace and stability of not only the Indian subcontinent but also for the entire world.

REFERENCES

A Growing Frontier for Terrorist Groups: Unsuspecting Chat Apps. Retrieved from https://www.wired.com/story/terrorist-groups-prey-on-unsuspecting-chat-apps/ Lone

Al-Dayel, N. & Mumford, A. (27 January 2020). ISIS and Their Use of Slavery. Retrieved from https://icct.nl/publication/isis-and-their-use-of-slavery/

Badawy, A. & Ferrara, E. (n.d.). The Rise of Jihadist Propaganda on Social Networks.

Bashar, I. (n.d.). ISIS, AQIS and the Revival of Islamist Militancy in Bangladesh. *Counter Terrorist Trends and Analyses*, 7(6), 18–23. Retrieved from https://www.jstor.org/stable/10.2307/26351362

Basit, A.; Mahmood, S.; Bashar, I. & Siyech, M.S. (n.d.). South Asia: Afghanistan, Pakistan, Bangladesh, India. *Counter Terrorist Trends and Analyses*, 10(1), 31–52. Retrieved from https://www.jstor.org/stable/10.2307/26349854

Calamur, K. (24 April 2019). There's No Way ISIS Can Pay Its Bills. Retrieved from https://www.buzzfeednews.com/article/hayesbrown/us-official-theres-no-way-isis-can-pay-its-bills,——ISIS's Newest Recruiting Tool: Regional Languages. Retrieved from https://www.theatlantic.com/international/archive/2019/04/isiss-newest-recruiting-tool-tamil-and-regional-languages/587884/

'Caliphate' defeated but jihadist group remains a threat. (23 March 2019). Retrieved from https://www.bbc.com/news/world-middle-east-45547595ISIS

Chulov, M. (24 March 2019). A brief history of ISIS. Retrieved from https://theweek.com/articles/589924/brief-history-isis

Clarke, P. C. & Amarasingam. (28 October 2019). The rise and fall of the ISIS 'caliphate'. Retrieved from https://www.theguardian.com/world/2019/mar/23/the-rise-and-fall-of-the-isis-caliphate

Country Reports on Terrorism 2017-India. (19AD). Retrieved from https://www.refworld.org/docid/5bcf1fa3a.html

Cullen, David (2017). Place of publication not identified: Oxford University Press.

Cyber-Extremism: ISIS and the Power of Social Media. Retrieved from https://link.springer.com/article/10.1007/s12115-017-0114-0BBC

Dharmawardhane, I. (n.d.). Maldives. *Counter Terrorist Trends and Analyses*, 8(1), 63-69. Retrieved from https://www.jstor.org/stable/10.2307/26369568

Dhume, S. (2 May 2019). Baghdadi's Death Will Make Global Affiliates More Independent. Retrieved from https://www.rand.org/blog/2019/10/baghdadis-death-will-make-global-affiliates-more-in dependent.html

El-Sherif, A. (n.d.). Opinion | South Asia Is Islamic State's New Target. Retrieved from https://www.wsj.com/articles/south-asia-is-islamic-states-new-target-11556837481

Fast Facts. (n.d.). Retrieved from https://amp.cnn.com/cnn/2014/08/08/world/isis-fast-facts/index.htm

Feldman, N. & Lake, A. (2008). Noah Feldman's *The fall and rise of the Islamic state*. Herndon, VA: American Muslims for Constructive Engagement.

Gunaratna, R. (28 October 2016). The Egyptian Muslim Brotherhood's Failures. Retrieved from https://carnegieendowment.org/2014/07/01/egyptian-muslim-brotherhood-s-failures-pub -56046

Gunaratna, R. (28 October 2016). The Egyptian Muslim Brotherhood's Failures. Retrieved from https://carnegieendowment.org/2014/07/01/egyptian-muslim-brotherhood-s-failures-pub -56046

Hassan, H. (7 January 2019). As ISIS suffers in its heartland, South Asia ripe for its rise. Retrieved from https://www.cnn.com/2016/10/27/opinions/isis-threat-pakistan-afghanistan-south-asia/in dex.html

History.com Editors. (10 July 2017). ISIS. Retrieved fromhttps://www.history.com/topics/21st-century/isis

Hossain, S. (n.d.). History of ISIS. Retrieved from https://www.history.com/topics/21st-century/isis

How South Asia emerged as hotbed for terror attacks since 1970. Who was Abu Bakr al-Baghdadi and why is his death important? Retrieved from https://www.theguardian.com/world/2019/oct/27/who-is-abu-bakr-al-baghdadi-why-imp ortant-isis-caliphSalah_Shoaib

How the Syria conflict has spread. (21 August 2014). Retrieved from https://www.bbc.com/news/world-middle-east-28850956 (n.d.)

ISIS Fast Facts. (5 December 2019). Retrieved from https://www.cnn.com/2014/08/08/world/isis-fast-facts/index.html

ISIS in Iraq: The Impact on National, Regional and Global Peace and Security (n.d.). Retrieved from https://www.researchgate.net/publication/315787738_ISIS_in_Iraq_The_Impact_on_Na tional_Regional_and_Global_Peace_and_Security(PDF)

ISIS Lone Wolf Attacks: Implications for Indian Security. (21 June 2017). Retrieved from https://nesa-center.org/isis-lone-wolf-attacks-implications-for-indian-security/

ISIS' Lone-Wolf Strategy. Retrieved from https://www.fpri.org/article/2016/08/isis-lone-wolf-strategy/

ISIS: Its History, Ideology, and Psychology. (n.d.). Retrieved from https://www.researchgate.net/publication/324279895_ISIS_Its_History_Ideology_and_Psychology (PDF)

ISIS's New Target: South Asia. Retrieved from https://foreignpolicy.com/2019/05/02/isiss-new-target-south-asia/

Islamic State (IS) in India (Updated until 31 December 2017). (n.d.). Retrieved from https://www.satp.org/satporgtp/countries/india/database/ISIindia.htm

Islamic State in South Asia: Are Easter Bombings Validating the Region's Vulnerability? Retrieved from Mendelsohn, B. (25 August 2016) https://www.youngbhartiya.com/article/islamic-state-in-south-asia-are-easter-bombings -validating-the-region-s-vulnerability

Johnson, C.G. (n.d.). *The Rise and Fall of the Islamic State in Afghanistan.*

Jones, S.G. (3 August 2015). ISIS in South Asia. (n.d.). Retrieved from https://thediplomat.com/tag/isis-in-south-asia/

JSTOR. (n.d.). Expanding the Caliphate. Retrieved from https://www.foreignaffairs.com/articles/afghanistan/2015-06-11/expanding-caliphate

Lone Wolf Attacks: Latest News, Photos, Videos on Lone Wolf Attacks. (n.d.). Retrieved from https://www.ndtv.com/topic/lone-wolf-attacks

Mabon, S. & Royle, S.A. (2017). *The origins of ISIS: The collapse of nations and revolution in the Middle East.* London, New York, I.B. Tauris.

Mahalingam, M. (25 June 2019). Islamic State in South Asia: Are Easter Bombings Validating the Region's Vulnerability? Retrieved from https://www.youngbhartiya.com/article/islamic-state-in-south-asia-are-easter-bombings-validating-the-region-s-vulnerability

Mahalingam, M. (25 June 2019). Lone Wolf Attacks: Latest News, Photos, Videos on Lone Wolf Attacks. (n.d.). Retrieved from https://www.ndtv.com/topic/lone-wolf-attacks

Md Sazzad Hossain, 2015. Social Media and Terrorism: Threats and Challenges to the Modern Era, Retrieved from https://journals.sagepub.com/doi/abs/10.1177/0971523117753280

Misachi, J. (20 October 2016). ISIS' Lone-Wolf Strategy. Retrieved from https://www.foreignaffairs.com/articles/2016-08-25/isis-lone-wolf-strategy

Monitoring–Essential Media Insight. (n.d.). Retrieved from https://monitoring.bbc.co.uk/key-focus-area/5i6b5ehotjBrown

Nasr, S.V.R. (2001). Islamic Leviathan: Islam and the Making of the State Power.

Otten, C. (25 July 2017). The Biggest Cities In Iraq. Retrieved from https://www.worldatlas.com/articles/the-biggest-cities-in-iraq.html

Perspective (8 March 2017). Baghdadi Just Confirmed ISIS Martyrdom ... (n.d.). Retrieved from https://www.researchgate.net/publication/336880911_PERSPECTIVE_Baghdadi_Just_Confirmed_ISIS_Martyrdom_Narrative_Ensuring_ISIS_Will_LivePragativadinewsser vice.

Prospects for The Islamic State in Pakistan. (n.d.). Retrieved from https://www.researchgate.net/publication/303550903_Prospects_for_The_Islamic_State_in_Pakistan

PTI (26 April 2019). Suspected ISIS terrorist killed in Lucknow encounter: ISIS flag, train time table, explosives seized - Pragativadi: Leading Odia Daily. Retrieved from https://pragativadi.com/suspected-isis-terrorist-killed-lucknow-encounter-isis-flag-train -time-table-explosives-seized/PTI.

PTI. (26 April 2019). Easter Sunday bombings: Father of two Sri Lanka suicide bombers arrested on suspicion of aiding, abetting sons. Retrieved from https://www.thehindu.com/news/international/easter-sunday-bombings-father-of-two -sri-lanka-suicide-bombers-arrested-on-suspicion-of-aiding-abetting-sons/article2694 4467.ece

PTI. (6 November 2019). ISIS-K attempted suicide attack in India last year: US official. Retrieved from https://economictimes.indiatimes.com/news/defence/isis-k-attempted-suicide-attack-in-india-last-year-us-official/articleshow/71933009.cms

Rasheed, A. (27 October 2019). ISIS-K attempted suicide attack in India last year: US official. Retrieved from https://m.economictimes.com/news/defence/isis-k-attempted-suicide-attack-in-india-last year-us-official/articleshow/71933009.cms (27 October 2019).

Rawat, M. (11 September 2019). Islamic State's Baghdadi: a trail of horror and death. Retrieved from https://www.reuters.com/article/us-mideast-crisis-baghdadi-leader-newsma-idUSKBN1 X60AQ

Rehman, J. (2005). Islamic State Practices, International Law and the Threat from Terrorism.

Safi, M. (27 October 2019). How South Asia emerged as a hotbed for terror attacks 1970. Retrieved from https://www.indiatoday.in/world/story/terror-attacks-sri-lanka-india-pakistan-south-asi a-middle-east-1507353-2019-04-22

Salafism in India: Diversity and Challenges JSTOR. (n.d.). Retrieved from https://www.jstor.org/stable/26351510

Salafism in India—Diversity and Challenges. (n.d.). Retrieved from https://www.researchgate.net/publication/316644095_Salafism_in_India-_Diversity_and _Challenges(PDF)

Salah, Shoaib. (14 May 2019). ISIS heading towards South Asia. Retrieved from https://blogs.timesofisrael.com/isis-heading-towards-south-asia/

Salah_Shoaib. (14 May 2019). Who was Abu Bakr al-Baghdadi and why is his death important? Retrieved from https://www.theguardian.com/world/2019/oct/27/who-is-abu-bakr-al-baghdadi-why-imp ortant-isis-caliphSanchez, R. (19 February 2015). ISIS heading towards South Asia. Retrieved from https://blogs.times ofisrael.com/isis-heading-towards-south-asia/

Sekulow, J. (2015). *Rise of ISIS threat we can't ignore.* New York: Howard, Mabon, S. & Royle, S.A. (2017).

Siyech, M.S. (2017, May). The Islamic State in India: Exploring its Footprints. Retrieved from https://www.researchgate.net/publication/316998707

Siyech, M.S. (n.d.). Salafism in India-Diversity and Challenges. Retrieved from https://www.researchgate.net/publication/316644095

Slaves of ISIS: the long walk of the Yazidi women. Retrieved from https://www.theguardian.com/world/2017/jul/25/slaves-of-isis-the-long-walk-of-the-yazi di-women

Specia, M. (20 March 2019). The Evolution of ISIS: From Rogue State to Stateless Ideology. Retrieved from https://www.nytimes.com/2019/03/20/world/middleeast/isis-history-facts-islamic-state.html

Swanson, A. (18 November 2015). United Nations investigates claim of ISIS organ theft. Retrieved from https://www.cnn.com/2015/02/18/middleeast/isis-organ-harvesting-claim/index.html

Swanson, A. How the Islamic State makes its money. Retrieved from https://www.washingtonpost.com/news/wonk/wp/2015/11/18/how-isis-makes-its-money/

Taneja, K. & Taneja, K. (n.d.). How the Islamic State makes its money. Retrieved from https://www.washingtonpost.com/news/wonk/wp/2015/11/18/how-isis-makes-its-money/

Taneja, K. & Taneja, K. (n.d.). The fall of ISIS and its implications for South Asia. Retrieved from https://www.orfonline.org/research/the-fall-of-isis-and-its-implications-for-south-asia/

Taneja, K. (2 May 2019). ISIS's New Target: South Asia. Retrieved from https://foreignpolicy.com/2019/05/02/isiss-new-target-south-asia/

Taneja, K. (2 May 2019). Uncovering the influence of ISIS in India. Retrieved from https://www.orfonline.org/research/42378-uncovering-the-influence-of-isis-in-india/

Taneja, K. (2018). Uncovering the influence of ISIS in India. ORF Occasional Paper, 158, 1–42. Retrieved from www.orfonline.org

Taneja, Kabir. (23 July 2018). The ISIS Phenomenon South Asia and beyond. Retrieved from www.orfonline.org

The increasing presence of ISIS in South Asia. (n.d.). Retrieved from https://www.iiss.org/blogs/analysis/2019/06/isis-south-asia

The Islamic State (Terrorist Organization). (n.d.). Retrieved from https://www.rand.org/topics/the-islamic-state-terrorist-organization.html

The Jihadist Threat to Europe: From Al Qaeda to the Islamic State (n.d.). Retrieved from https://www.researchgate.net/publication/331592000_The_Jihadist_Threat_to_Europe_From_Al_Qaeda_to_the_Islamic_State-Al-Dayel, N., & Mumford, A. (27 January 2020). ISIS and Their Use of Slavery. Retrieved from https://icct.nl/publication/isis-and-their-use-of-slavery/An Overview of ISIS. (n.d.). Retrieved from https://ing.org/an-overview-of-isis/Arquilla, J.; Ronfeldt, D.; Bandura, A.; Christopherson, K.; Conway, M.; and Contena, B., ... Kya. (1 January 1970).

The rising specter of the Islamic State in India. (11 June 2019). Retrieved from https://nesa-center.org/the-rising-specter-of-the-islamic-state-in-india/Timeline:

The True Origins of ISIS. Retrieved from https://www.theatlantic.com/ideas/archive/2018/11/isis-origins-anbari-zarqawi/577030/ History and Editors. (10 July 2017). Origins of ISIS. (n.d.). Retrieved from https://www.ukessays.com/essays/security/history-of-isis.phpHistory.com

Uncovering the Influence of ISIS in India. (n.d.). Retrieved from https://www.orfonline.org/wp-content/uploads/2018/07/ORF_Occasional_Paper_158_ISIS-India.pd

9

Russia-Pakistan Rapprochement and its Implications for India

Samprity Biswas

ABSTRACT

The emerging geopolitical environment has presented Russia and Pakistan with unprecedented opportunities to foster bilateral cooperation. Taking cognizance of these opportunities, both the countries have demonstrated mutual willingness to cooperate across various realms that have marked a new phase in their bilateral relationship. This development has led scholars and analysts to voice concern for Russia-India ties, which in their view can suffer a setback because of the former's growing closeness towards Pakistan. However, this study argues that despite the warming of ties, a closer look at Russia's doctrinal documents reveals a fragmented policy towards Pakistan. For example, except once in 2008, Pakistan has never been mentioned in any of Russia's Foreign Policy Concepts and Doctrines, unlike India. Similarly, President Putin's article, 'Russia and the Changing World' (2012), highlights Russia's interest in Asian countries like India, China and Afghanistan, but Pakistan was not mentioned. Secondly, the joint military exercises between them known as 'Friendship exercises' are mainly counter-terrorism exercises, with most of them performed within the ambit of the Shanghai Cooperation Organization. Similarly, the military agreement signed in 2014 between them highlights their joint efforts to counter terrorism while sharing similar views on Afghanistan. Thirdly, Russia-Pakistan defence and economic ties are far below potential and face severe institutional constraints, and a Russian President is yet to visit Pakistan. In view of these limitations, the paper rationalizes that Russia's warming stance towards Pakistan is majorly driven by the former's characterization of Pakistan as a frontline state in mitigating the menace of terrorism emanating from the Afghan region that can destabilize the Central Asian region, with which Russia shares borders. Therefore, contrary to the dominant realist understanding that Russia-Pakistan rapprochement will weaken Russia-India ties and push India towards the USA, this paper argues that (i) First, Russia prioritizes its ties with India and will not turn against it as it is aware of the potentiality of the Indian markets; (ii) Second, Russia's ties with India are invested across all spheres and steeped in historical nostalgia while its relations with Pakistan is mainly based on tactical calculations. Since Pakistan has leverage over the Taliban, Russia retains an interest in recalibrating its ties with it to influence developments in Afghanistan that have a bearing on Russia's security interests; (iii) Third, as evident from past efforts of Russia to bring peace and stability to the Afghan region and its recent pragmatic stance towards the Taliban against the backdrop of the latter's takeover of Afghanistan, it is very likely that Russia will include India in any joint effort directed towards maintaining peace and stability in Afghanistan. This was evident from the past meetings of what came to be known as the 'Moscow Process' in which India was included at Russia's behest alongside Pakistan and the Taliban.

Keywords: *Russia's foreign policy, Pakistan, Taliban, terrorism, Afghanistan, India*

Introduction

The end of the Cold War presented unprecedented opportunities to the newly-established Russian Federation to foster a mutually beneficial relationship with Pakistan. Azizian and Vasilieff (2003) enumerate three such opportunities that led to a major breakthrough in Russia-Pakistan relations in the post-Cold War period. The first breakthrough came when Moscow revised its foreign policy towards South Asia. This was followed by the second opportunity that came in the late 1990s in the form of Russia's foreign policy reorientation under its Prime Minister, Yevgeny Primakov, who sought to redirect Russia's energies away from the West. Finally, the 9/11 terrorist attacks presented both countries with a common ground for strategic cooperation. Notwithstanding these unprecedented opportunities, Russia-Pakistan cooperation remained "fragile", "shaky", and "controversial" due to certain domestic and external factors (Azizian and Vasilieff, 2003: 54). The underlying assumptions in Pakistan's strategic thinking were heavily influenced by its colonial legacy, and an anti-India stance contributed to this 'shaky' relationship (Hussain, 2012). However, as major changes have begun to shape the geopolitical environment of the international system in general and the Central Asian region in particular, Russia and Pakistan are once again encountering favourable circumstances that can help strengthen their bilateral cooperation.

Russia's apprehension of the persisting instability in Afghanistan spilling over to its territory via the Central Asian Republics (The Ministry of Foreign Affairs of the RF, 2016) coupled with a shared dissatisfaction with the USA and Russia's growing comprehensive strategic partnership with Pakistan's 'all-weather friend', China, is gradually leading Russia and Pakistan to recalibrate their ties (Ballesteros, 2018). Pakistan's membership in the Shanghai Cooperation Organization (SCO), along with Russia's withdrawal of its arms embargo on Pakistan, has calculated moves that need to be analyzed within the wider framework of Russia's geopolitical logic towards the East in the face of its growing alienation from the West as well as its interests in safeguarding its territorial integrity from any threats emanating from the Taliban-ruled Afghan region, over which Pakistan has leverage.

'Pakistan' in the Russian Federation's Foreign Policy

The policymakers of New Russia in the early 1990s confined Russia's foreign policy to the "politics of the begging bowl". Russia conveniently accepted the subordination of its foreign policy to the agenda of the West, in effect failing to draw up an independent concept of its foreign policy in the new international system. This failure was most profoundly visible in Russia's relations with the countries of the East. New Russia's preoccupation with the West for potential economic assistance resulted in Russia's ignorance towards the East. However, when the 'pro-Westernism' in New Russia's foreign policy received a backlash as the free-market reforms worsened Russia's domestic conditions, the East started to feature prominently in Russia's foreign policy. From 1994 onwards, President Yeltsin undertook a relatively independent course in Russia's foreign policy that was evident from Russia's efforts to reactivate its relations with Asian countries (El Doufani, 1994). In this context, Russia's relations with Pakistan received a new boost as annual high-level bilateral visits began to take place. Pakistan, for its part, reciprocated Russia's call for cooperation in a bid to address its security dilemma in the Central Asian region. During the Cold War, Pakistan exploited the superpower rivalry to come out of its "regional handicap". However, with the disintegration of the USSR and the end of the Cold War, Pakistan's continued security dilemma in the absence of the "geopolitical opportunities of the Cold

War" intensified Pakistan's sense of insecurity. Memon (1994) rightly stated that as the end of the Cold War brought an end to Pakistan's foreign policy options, it sought to rectify its ties with the newly-formed Russian Federation.

Efforts towards the recalibration of Russia-Pakistan bilateral relations in the post-Cold War scenario were clearly evident from the high-level exchanges between both states. In 1992, Russian Vice-President Alexander Rutskoi visited Pakistan, followed by a visit by Foreign Minister Kozyrev in 1993. These visits were returned by Pakistan's Foreign Secretary Akram Zaki to Russia in October 1992, followed by Foreign Minister S.A. Ahmed Ali's visit in 1994. This was followed by the visit of a Russian parliamentary delegation to Pakistan in 1995. During these visits, a broad range of issues ranging from defence, technology, energy and abolition of visa restrictions was discussed (Owais, 2007). Apart from these bilateral visits, an international conference on developing relations between Pakistan and the CIS was held in 1992 in Moscow.

The newly-formed government in Pakistan in 1997 continued the friendly attitude towards Russia. Reports of closer relations were produced against the backdrop of the Pakistan Foreign Minister's visit to Russia in 1997. Pakistan also invited Russia to assist in bringing about a resolution on the Kashmir issue. In 1998, after the nuclear tests by India and Pakistan, Russia, unlike the West, reiterated that sanctions were not the correct answer to address the situation. Instead, Russia's Prime Minister, Primakov, initiated a three-point plan in order to ease the situation between India and Pakistan. Though the plan did not yield any concrete results, it did result in the visit of Pakistan's Prime Minister Nawaz Sharif to Moscow in 1999. This visit was significant as it marked the first visit of a Pakistani leader to Russia since 1974 (Donaldson *et al.*, 2014). Notwithstanding these incidents of cooperation in Russia-Pakistan, relations rupture soon developed due to a number of factors. The recommencement of Russia's close strategic ties with India coupled with Pakistan's support to the Taliban forces in Afghanistan and Putin's energetic approach towards enhancing Russia's influence in the Central Asian states once again rekindled tension between Moscow and Islamabad. As scholars began to doubt the possibility of any genuine cooperation between Russia and Pakistan in the face of such challenges, the events of 9/11 proved to pave the way for a new phase in their bilateral relations.

The terrorist attacks on the USA on September 11, 2001, presented the Russian leadership with the opportunity to publicly criticize the unprecedented rise of worldwide terrorism while at the same time highlighting and articulating Russia's own share of struggles with the Chechen rebels. Putin's use of Chechnya as an analogy to interpret the events of 9/11 was a well-calculated political move to justify Russia's counter-terrorism activities against the Chechen rebels while at the same time exploiting the opportunity to cooperate with the West in mitigating the menace of terrorism originating in Russia's neighbourhood. The 9/11 events thus presented Russia with circumstances that were favourable to evoke the "geopolitical spectres of fundamentalist states" along with the West. Based on this concept, the states of the Central Asian region assumed significance as both the USA and Russia attempted to bolster their presence in these states to eliminate the extremist forces. This eventually played out to Russia's wider geopolitical interests of enhancing its presence in the Central Asian region in order to safeguard Russia's territorial unity and integrity from the extremist forces emanating from the region (O'Loughlin *et.al.*, 2004). In this context, Afghanistan that shares borders with the Central Asian Republics, assumed special significance for Russia. Russia's apprehension of a spill-over of these extremist forces to its own territory via the Central Asian states of Tajikistan, Uzbekistan and Kyrgyzstan led Russia to revisit its ties with the strategically located Pakistan that in the aftermath of the 9/11 events had assumed the status of a frontline state in the US-led 'War on Terror.'

Recognizing the significant potentiality of Pakistan in regional politics along with its geostrategic position and its influence in the Muslim world, Russia sought to reorient its policies towards Pakistan post 9/11 (Morgulov, 2014). A significant manifestation of their increased mutual confidence was the establishment of the Consultative Group on Strategic Stability in April 2002, along with an agreement to tackle common issues of threats. This was followed by the visit of Aziz Ahmed Khan, additional secretary in the Ministry of Foreign Affairs, to Moscow in January 2002 to discuss economic and political matters. As a consequence of this visit, the Pakistan-Russia Business Forum was created later that year. The following year, President Pervez Musharraf visited Russia in the hope of developing interstate ties along with coordinating international efforts in the fight against terrorism (President of Russia, 2003). A joint statement was adopted by the heads of states that emphasized the importance of strengthening mutually-beneficial cooperation in sectors like energy, telecommunica-tions, metallurgy, infrastructural development and so on. A three-year period program from 2003 to 2006, recognizing the importance of developing the fields of culture, science and education, was also signed. Besides promoting bilateral cooperation, both sides held comprehensive discussions on issues of regional and global significance. Most importantly, both sides emphasized their common interests in the reintegration of Afghanistan into the international community as a "stable", "predictable", and "peaceful" state (President of Russia, 2003). This visit signalling a new direction in Russia-Pakistan bilateral ties raised hopes of an improved relationship between both countries.

In July 2004, Russian Foreign Minister Igor Ivanov visited Pakistan, which was followed by the visit of a delegation of the Russian Duma. The next year, the presidents of both the countries and the heads of government met on the sidelines of the UN General Assembly session and the SCO Heads of Governments meeting, respectively. This was followed by the visit of the Russian Foreign Minister to Pakistan in November 2006. Along with his Pakistani counterpart, Khurshid Kasuri, both sides discussed major global issues and potential areas of bilateral cooperation. Russia also showed interest in participating in the construction of the Iran-Pakistan gas pipeline. In the light of such increasing bilateral contacts, a shift in Russia's strategic perception of Pakistan was clearly evident (Hanif, 2013). This shift became even more pronounced when Russian Prime Minister Mikhail Fradkov, accompanied by a high-level entourage, paid a three-day visit to Pakistan in April 2007. This visit was significant in many ways. Firstly, it was the first visit of a Russian Prime Minister to Pakistan in 38 years. Secondly, the visit signalled the desire of both countries to intensify their ties reflected from the array of agreements signed during the visit. These agreements pertained to increasing cooperation in combating terrorism, promoting cultural cooperation through scientific and educational exchanges, along with an MOU reached on cooperating on railways of both the countries (Gul *et. al*, 2007).

Russia's reassessment of the strategic importance of Pakistan as reflected from the above-mentioned initiatives came against the backdrop of major problems that the unipolar international system was gradually confronting. The emergence of global economic divisions coupled with elements of improvisation in the foreign policy of major powers accompanied by a breakdown of the traditional regional structure compelled Russia to review its national interests and determine its place in the international arena by setting a new direction in its foreign policy. An important element introduced in Russia's foreign policy in this dynamic setting was the concept of "flexible coalitions" that Sergey Ivanov, the first vice-premier of the Russian Federation, emphasized in his speech at the Valdivia Club meeting of September 2007. He remarked that Russia would not enter into any kind of long-term alliances with any state; rather, it would prefer to keep its freedom by entering into "flexible coalitions", which devoid of any obligations, would not run counter to Russia's national interests (Zlobin, 2008: 309). This, in part, was driven by Russia's mistrust and dissatisfaction with the West that by 2008 produced a noticeable assertiveness in Russia's foreign policy orientation. President Putin's Munich speech of February 2007 had already hinted in that direction when he criticized the USA in strong terms by remarking that it had "overstepped its national borders in every way" (Katz, 2007: 29). This anti-West speech reflecting Russia's efforts towards resurgence, both in the regional and the international spheres, found expression in the subsequent foreign policy concept of 2008, which clearly listed the threats Russia was facing from the West through the latter's continuous "political and psychological policy of containing Russia". The concept further stated that the West's "unilateral action strategy" would prove detrimental for the international system (President of Russia, 2008). Russia acknowledged its own role as a major power in the international system through this concept, and a few months later, its intervention in Georgia confirmed its strong desire for the 'strategic independence" that it presents today as indispensable for confirming its status as potential global power. This goal, at its root, is not about territorial enlargement or about domination; rather, it is about Russia's "image", "respect" and "recognition" in a world that it believes is being driven by America's unilateral policies (Allison, 2008: 1171). Within this wider context of Russia's foreign policy reorientation, its turn towards Pakistan, as manifested from the mention of Pakistan for the first time in Russia's foreign policy concept, was viewed as a calculated strategic move by Moscow against the backdrop of its increasing confrontation with the West.

The above-mentioned 'systemic' factor has interplayed with other domestic and regional factors to promote Russia-Pakistan relations, the fundamental of which has been the situation in Afghanistan and Russia's stake in its stability. An analysis of Russia's foreign policy documents and other doctrinal documents pertaining to its increasing cooperative relations with Pakistan, especially in the last decade, exhibits its desire to jointly promote regional and trans-regional cooperation to maintain stability in Afghanistan. To that effect, a Quadrilateral Summit (also known as the Dushanbe Four) was proposed in 2009 between the leaders of Russia, Pakistan, Afghanistan and Tajikistan. The leaders called for increased cooperation in areas of trade and commerce, communications, energy and transportation. The primary goal was to deliberate upon feasible ways to tackle terrorism, drug trafficking and illicit arms transfer in the region (*The Nation*, 2009). The leaders called for the use of the SCO's Regional Anti-Terrorist Structure to enhance cooperation in that direction. Though the Quadrilateral Summit did not sustain after three annual summit meetings, a flurry of other high-level meetings between the dignitaries of Russia and Pakistan continued to take place, reflecting an overall consistent and steadily progressing Russia-Pakistan relations (Purushothaman, 2015). This was evident from Pakistan President Asif Ali Zardari's visit to Russia in May 2011. Both sides discussed the future prospects of their bilateral ties along with pressing international and regional issues. Talks on coordinating efforts to counter international terrorism dominated the agenda. An intergovernmental agreement was also signed pertaining to air traffic along with two MOUs on energy and agriculture (President of Russia, 2011). The subsequent year, Russia's Foreign Minister, Sergei Lavrov, paid a visit to Islamabad following the cancellation of President Putin's trip to Pakistan. This was followed by Pakistan's Chief of Army Staff, Ashfaq Pervez Kayani, 's visit to Moscow. During his visit, talks on military and technical cooperation between Russia and Pakistan made the rounds that, from the Russian perspective, resulted from two factors. The first was the diversification of India's growing military relations with other countries that compelled Russia to diversify its own markets, and the second and most important factor, as stated by the director of the Centre for Analysis of Strategies and Technologies, Ruslan Pukhov, was the situation in Afghanistan. He stated that Russia was attempting to devise ways on how to ensure the safety and security of the southern borders of the CIS post the US pull-out of combat forces from Afghanistan. Since Pakistan exerts a strong influence over Afghanistan, a continued rebuffing of Pakistan by Russia in favour of India would eventually run contrary to Russia's security interests (Strokan, 2012). Consequently, reciprocal high-level visits by Russian and Pakistani leaders have continued over the last few years, but the bilateral developments since 2014 have marked a new phase in Russia-Pakistan relations. Russian Defence Minister Sergei Shoigu's visit to Pakistan in 2014 culminated in a landmark military cooperation agreement between both countries that paved the way for further military cooperation (Syed, 2014). This development occurred against the backdrop of Russia's growing confrontation with the West following the crisis in Crimea coupled with Russia's apprehension of the situation in Afghanistan in the wake of the USA's decision to pull out its combat troops from the region by the end of 2014.

A closer look at the military cooperation agreement signed between Russia and Pakistan along with the doctrinal documents pertaining to Russia's foreign policy adopted during this time reveals that the developments in Afghanistan had been the paramount factor in driving Russia closer to Pakistan. The military cooperation agreement, for instance, talks about "exchanging information on politico-military issues, strengthening collaboration in defence and counter-terrorism sectors (and) sharing similar views on developments in Afghanistan" (Roy, 2014). On a similar note, the foreign policy concepts of the Russian Federation of 2013 and 2016 reiterates Russia's commitments to implement comprehensive measures in crisis-stricken Afghanistan along with "other interested states" to mitigate the terrorist threat emanating from the region along with reducing the illicit production and trafficking of narcotic drugs (The Ministry of Foreign Affairs of RF, 2013 and 2016). A mention of Russia's commitment to cooperate with Afghanistan and its "neighbouring states" is stressed upon in the concepts, but who these neighbouring states are is not mentioned. Moreover, in these concepts, unlike the 2008 Foreign Policy Concept, Pakistan does not even find a mention throughout the documents. This has invariably led scholars to remark that Russia is still struggling to formulate a comprehensive foreign policy towards Pakistan, unlike its policies towards other Asian countries like Afghanistan, India and China. Putin's article entitled "Russia and the Changing World", published in *Moscow News* in 2012 along with the National Security Strategy and Maritime Doctrine of the Russia Federation up to 2020, mentions Russia's interests in the South Asian countries of India, China and the situation in Afghanistan but Pakistan was not mentioned even once (Moskalenko and Topychkanov, 2014). Though the carefully worded foreign policy concepts emphasize Russia's willingness to cooperate with Afghanistan and its "neighbouring states," which implicitly hints at Pakistan, the lack of a direct mention establishes the fact that Russia's policy towards Pakistan is fragmented and it is the situation in Afghanistan that is the paramount factor driving Russia's growing engagement with Pakistan.

Factors Promoting Russia-Pakistan Rapprochement

A number of factors are contributing to the recalibration of ties between Russia and Pakistan. Foremost among them is Russia's strategic interest in Afghanistan, whose stability and security has a direct bearing on Russia's national interests. Russia's fears of a spill-over of extremist ideas and forces from Afghanistan to its own territory via the Central Asian states have propelled Russia to recognize Pakistan as a frontline state in mitigating the forces of instability in Afghanistan. Russia's anticipation intensified against the backdrop of the USA's decision to withdraw the International Security Assistance Force (ISAF) from Afghanistan by the end of 2014. Convinced of the Taliban's attempt towards a reassertion and the weakness of Afghanistan's government in quelling the Taliban forces, Russia initiated efforts to strengthen its strategic relations with Pakistan (Katz, 2014). This was reflected in the numerous doctrinal documents, including Russia's foreign policy concepts that pointed towards Russia's willingness to cooperate with 'interested states' in maintaining stability in Afghanistan. Additionally, the softening of the rhetoric of Russian authorities towards the recent Taliban takeover of Afghanistan and its pragmatism towards the Taliban once again needs to be conceptualized and understood within the broader context of Russia's apprehension of a spill-over of terrorism and drug trafficking to its own territory via the Central Asian states (Kozlov and Rynda, 2021).

Besides the situation in Afghanistan, the role of major states like India, China, and the USA has been significant in shaping the trajectory of Russia-Pakistan relations. Firstly, some scholars like Hussian (2012), Hanif (2013), Craig (2015) and others argue that India's closeness to the USA has led Russia and Pakistan to forge closer ties. They hold that India's diversification of import markets for arms has not gone down well with Russia that explains Russia's move towards diversifying its own export markets for arms as manifested from the supply of weapons to Pakistan and the joint exercises held with it. However, such analysis tends to limit bilateral relations by viewing it through the prism of zero-sum games. Extending relations with one country in the region does not mean jeopardizing relations with other countries there. In today's complex and interdependent world, states should be led by contingent interests. Russia's supply of weapons to Pakistan coming against the backdrop of the recent events that have led to strained relations between Russia and the West can be explained as an effort on Russia's part to diversify its markets recover its sanction-bound economy rather than oppose India (Jamal, 2016). Various Russian leaders, including the Russian President, have consistently reiterated that Russia values its ties with India and Russia's closeness towards Pakistan or any other country will not dilute its "trust-based" relations with India (*News 18*, 2017).

Second, the role of China in strengthening Russia-Pakistan relations has surfaced in many writings. China's relations with Russia have reached a new level of the comprehensive strategic partnership, while Pakistan has consistently occupied "a unique position in China's foreign policy calculus" (Pant, 2012). Many scholars argue that Pakistan, China's 'all-weather friend' is being drawn closer to Russia through some Chinese efforts, most notable in the case of Pakistan's membership in the SCO, in the China-Pakistan Economic Corridor (CPEC) and in the Chinese-initiated One Belt, One Road project (OBOR) (Purushothaman, 2015). Moreover, Russia, China and Pakistan are equally concerned about the developments in Afghanistan given their close proximity to the region. Maintaining stability in the region is, therefore, in the interests of all three states (Rashid, 2016). Collective efforts by these three states in various sectors are leading analysts to consider the possibility of an emerging 'Russia-China-Pakistan Axis' (Thoker and Singh, 2017; Shahid, 2017; Mitra 2015; Purushothaman, 2015).

Third, the USA has played a crucial role in shaping the trajectory of Russia-Pakistan relations today, much like in the Cold War period. Its decision to eventually pull out its combat forces from Afghanistan, coupled with the freezing of military aid under the administration of President Donald Trump, have deteriorated USA-Pakistan relations (*The Hindu*, 2018). Pakistani political analysts have expressed their anguish towards the USA, remarking that its present policies towards Pakistan will eventually lead to its loss of advantage over Pakistan.

As the USA's interests in Pakistan have begun to wane, Pakistan, in a desperate attempt, is looking forward to recalibrating its ties with other major powers, including Russia, which is facing its own deteriorating relations with the USA but has reciprocated Pakistan's call for cooperation.

Russia-Pakistan Engagement: Implications for India

The emerging geopolitical environment has presented Russia and Pakistan with unprecedented opportunities to foster bilateral cooperation. Taking cognizance of these opportunities, both the countries have demonstrated mutual willingness to cooperate across various realms that have led to a new phase in their relations. However, an analysis of Russia's foreign policy clearly exhibits that this relationship is tactical and is mainly driven by Russia's interest in the Afghan region. In the past, Russia, in a bid to step into the region to safeguard its own security interests, has played an active role in including its most trusted ally, India, in deliberations on Afghanistan. The Moscow Process meetings were privy to this as, for the first time, India and Pakistan, along with Taliban leaders, were on the same table negotiating over the future of Afghanistan. Therefore, at the behest of Russia, it is almost certain that India will be included on issues pertaining to the peace and stability of Afghanistan.

Secondly, India is an important ally for Russia in South Asia, and it is very unlikely that Russia will jeopardize its relations with the former for Pakistan. At the strategic level, both India and Russia are strategic partners, and their relationship is steeped in historical nostalgia, unlike Russia's relations with Pakistan that have on several occasions been impinged by USA-Pakistan relations. Similarly, at the economic and military levels, Russia and Pakistan's economic ties are far below potential and are unimpressive compared to Russia-India trade figures. Though the military agreement between Russia and Pakistan, signed in 2014, had stipulated the upliftment of the arms embargo and the sale of weapons to Pakistan, Russia in a recent meeting with India's Defence Minister, Rajnath Singh in September 2020, had assured that it would stop the sale of weapons to Pakistan. Russia also supported India when the chief of the NSA, Ajit Doval, walked out of a virtual meet of SCO heads of states over a distorted map shown by the Pakistani representative that violates the charter and principles of the Shanghai Cooperation Organization (*The Hindu*, 2020).

Third, Russia's warming of ties with Pakistan should be viewed within the greater context of the change in Russia's foreign policy orientation. The ideational underpinnings of Russia's foreign policy have undergone a major shift from 2007 onwards as it was categorically stated by Russian authorities that their country would enter into flexible coalitions that were devoid of any obligations. Therefore, relations between countries should not be viewed from a zero-sum game angle as cooperation on some issues can very well coexist with confrontation on other issues. Seen from this perspective, it is restrictive for scholars to assume that Russia's warming ties with Pakistan will push India closer to the USA.

Conclusion

The trajectory of Russia-Pakistan relations shows how this bilateral relation has been hostage to the influence of other states, both from within and outside the region. This has invariably thwarted Russia and Pakistan from developing their bilateral relations to its full potential as their relation was, more often than not, influenced and determined by other states, particularly the USA, India, China and Afghanistan, in the context of global and regional contestations within the South-Asian region. However, as Russia and Pakistan today stand on the threshold of a multi-polar world order confronted with an array of traditional and non-traditional threats, they are faced with similar security challenges that demand bilateral cooperation. The most profound of these challenges is the delicate situation in Afghanistan.

However, in spite of the recent warming of relations, a closer look at Russia's doctrinal documents still reflects a fragmented policy towards Islamabad. Moreover, Russia-Pakistan collaboration in fields other than security is far from impressive. This clearly reflects that Russia's warming stance towards Pakistan is majorly driven by the former's characterization of Pakistan as a frontline state in mitigating the menace of extremism and terrorism emanating from Afghanistan that can destabilize the Central Asian region, with which Russia shares borders. Therefore, it is only wise to wait and see whether the recent Russia-Pakistan bilateral cooperation will widen and deepen in the near future or, like in the Cold War period, it will once again fall hostage to the influence of external actors.

REFERENCES

Allison, R. (2008), "Russia Resurgent? Moscow's Campaign to 'Coerce Georgia to Peace'," *International Affairs*, 84(6):1145-1171.

Azizian, R. and Vasilieff, P. (2003), "Russia and Pakistan: The Difficult Path to Rapprochement," *Asian Affairs*, 30(1): 36-55.

Ballesteros, C. (2018), "Pakistan Wants to Buy Military Supplies from Russia and China after U.S. Funding Freeze", *Newsweek,* 20 January 2018, [Online: web], accessed 8 March 2020, URL: http://www.newsweek.com/pakistan-russia-china-military-supplies-us-funding-793258

Craig, T. (2015), "As the US Moves Closer to India, Pakistan looks to Russia", *The Guardian*, February 3 2015, [Online: web], accessed 22 March 2020, URL: https://www.theguardian.com/world/2015/feb/03/pakistan-russia-us-obama-india

Donaldson, R. et al, (2014), *The Foreign Policy of Russia: Changing Systems, Enduring Interests,* London: Routledge.

El Doufani, M. M. (1994), "Futile Interventions: Russia's Disengagement from the Third World," *International Journal*, 49(4): 846-873.

Gul, N. et al, (2007), "Pakistan's Foreign Policy Survey, January-June 2007", *Pakistan Horizon*, 60(3): 2-22.

Hanif, M. (2013), "Pakistan-Russia Relations: Progress, Prospects and Constraints", *IPRI Journal*, 13(2):63-86.

Hussian, N. (2012), "Pak-Russia Relations: Lost Opportunities and Future Options", *Journal of Political Studies*, 19(1): 79-89.

Jamal, U. (2016), "Russia Wants to De-hyphenate India and Pakistan. Should Delhi Worry?", *The Diplomat*, 27 September 2016, [Online: web], accessed 22 August 2020, URL: https://thediplomat.com/2016/09/russia-wants-to-de-hyphenate-india-and-pakistan-should-delhi-worry/

Katz, M. (2014), "Putin's Predicament: Russia and Afghanistan after 2014", *Asia Policy*, 17 (Jan 2014):13-17.

—— (2007), "Assertive, but Alone", *The World Today*, 63(11): 29-31.

Kozlov, P and Rynda, A. (2021), "Afghan Crisis: Russia Plans for New Era with Taliban Rule", *BBC Russian*, 21 August 2021, [Online: web], accessed 8 September 2021, URL:https://www.bbc.com/news/world-europe-58265934

Memon, M. (1994), "Reorientation of Pakistan's Foreign Policy after the Cold War," *Pakistan Horizon*, 47(2):45-61.

Ministry of Foreign Affairs (2013), Government of the Russian Federation, Ministry of Foreign Affairs, *Concept of the Foreign Policy of the Russian Federation*, [Online: web], accessed 14 September 2020, URL: http://www.mid.ru/en/foreign_policy/official_documents//asset_publisher/CptICkB6BZ29/content/id/122186

—— (2016), Government of the Russian Federation, Ministry of Foreign Affairs, *Foreign Policy Concept of the Russian Federation*, December, [Online: web], accessed 8 September 2020, URL: http://www.mid.ru/en/foreign_policy/official_documents//asset_publisher/CptICkB6BZ29/content/id/2542248

—— Ministry of Foreign Affairs (2016),Government of the Russian Federation, Ministry of Foreign Affairs, *Foreign Policy Concept of the Russian Federation*, December, [Online: web], accessed 18 August 2020, URL: http://www.mid.ru/en/foreign_policy/official_documents//asset_publisher/CptICkB6BZ29/content/id/2542248

Mitra, J. (2015), "Russia, China and Pakistan: An Emerging New Axis?" *The Diplomat*, August 18 2015, [Online: web], accessed 3 September 2020, URL: https://thediplomat.com/2015/08/russia-china-and-pakistan-an-emerging-new-axis/

Morgulov, I. (2014), "Russia and Pakistan: Prospects of Interaction", [Online: web], accessed 9 July 2020, URL: https://pakistan.mid.ru/web/pakistan_en/russia-and-pakistan-prospects-of-interaction

Moskalenko, V. and Topychkanov, P. (2014), "Shared Challenges and Common Opportunities", [Online: web], accessed 14 August 2020, URL: http://carnegieendowment.org/files/russia_and_pakistan2014.pdf.

News 18 (2017), "Growing Ties with Pakistan won't affect Russia's Relations with India, says Putin", *News 18*, June 1 2017, [Online: web], accessed 22 August 2020, URL: https://www.news18.com/news/world/ties-with-pakistan-wont-affect-russias-relations-with-india-says-putin-1419507.html

O'Loughlin, J. et al, (2004), "A 'Risky Westward Turn'? Putin's 9/11 Script and Ordinary Russians", *Europe-Asia Studies*, 56(1): 3-34.

Owais, M. (2007), "Pakistan-Russia Relations: Economic and Political Dimensions", *Pakistan Horizon*, 60(2), 125-139.

Pant, H. (2012), "The Pakistan Thorn in China-India-US Relations", *The Washington Quarterly*, 35(1): 83-95.

President of Russia (2003), "Joint Statement of the President of the Russian Federation, Vladimir Putin, and the President of the Islamic Republic of Pakistan, General Pervez Musharraf", [Online: web] Accessed 10 September 2020, URL: http://en.kremlin.ru/supplement/3657

—— (2008), "The Foreign Policy Concept of the Russian Federation", [Online: web], accessed 7 September 2020, URL: http://en.kremlin.ru/supplement/4116

—— (2011), "Meeting with President of Pakistan Asif Ali Zardari", [Online: web], accessed 14 August 2020, URL: http://en.kremlin.ru/events/president/news/page/423

Purushothaman, U. (2015), "The Russia-Pakistan Rapprochement: Should India Worry?", *ORF Issue Brief*, 117: 1-6.

Rashid, A. (2016), "Russia and Pakistan Slowly Move towards An Embrace",[Online: web], accessed 22 September 2020, URL: https://www.aljazeera.com/indepth/opinion/2016/12/russia-pakistan-slowly-move-embrace-161203083811644.html

Roy, R. (2014), "Russia's Military Cooperation Agreement with Pakistan: An Assessment", [Online: web], accessed 14 September 2020, URL: https://idsa.in/idsacomments/RussiasMilitaryCooperationAgreement_rroy_151212

Shahid, K. (2017), "Trump's Warming to Islamabad has formalized the China-Pakistan-Russia Axis", *Huffpost*, August 30 2017, [Online: web], accessed 22 August 2020, URL: https://www.huffingtonpost.in/kunwar-khuldune-shahid/trump-s-warning-to-islamabad-has-formalised-the-china-pakistan-russia-axis_a_23188832/

Strokan, S. (2012), "Pakistan and Russia Move Closer towards Military Cooperation", *Russia Beyond*, 10 October 2012, [Online: web], accessed 14 September 2020, URL: https://www.rbth.com/articles/2012/10/10/pakistan_and_russia_move_ closer_toward_military_cooperation_18965.html

Syed, S. B. (2014), "Pakistan, Russia Sign Landmark Defence Cooperation Agreement', *Dawn*, 21 November 2014, [Online: web], accessed 14 August 2020, URL: https://www.dawn.com/news/1145875

The Hindu (2018), "U.S. Freezes over USD 1.1 Billion Security Assistance to Pakistan", *The Hindu*, January 5 2018, [Online: web], accessed 22 August 2020, URL: https://www.thehindubusinessline.com/news/world/us-freezes-over-11-bn-security-assistance-to-pakistan/article10012464.ece

—— (2020), "Ajit Doval Walks Out of SCO Meet After Pakistan Shows Map", *The Hindu*, September 15 2020, [Online: web], accessed 22 July 2021, URL: https://www.thehindu.com/news/national/ajit-doval-walks-out-of-sco-meet-after-pakistan-shows-new-map/article32615026.ece

The Nation (2009), "Quadrilateral Summit to Promote Cooperation", *The Nation*, Lahore, 29 July 2009.

Thoker, P. A. and Singh, B. (2017), "The Emerging China, Pakistan and Russia Strategic Triangle: India's New Gordian Knot," *JIIR*, 21(1): 61-83.

Zlobin, N. (2008), "The New World Order: US and Russian in the Post-Soviet Space: Mutual Squeezing and Cooperation", *International Journal*, 63(2): 307-319.

10

Enhancing Indo-Pak Relations through Climate Action Activities

Hsin Yen Phoebe Mok

ABSTRACT

Since the 1947 India-Pakistan war, conflicts along the Line of Control continue to be a significant source of threat to peace and harmony in South Asia. With the COVID-19 pandemic in 2020, there are increasing fears that this would intensify sectarian violence amongst different religious and political ideologies. The consequences of senseless wars and conflicts within the region have rendered its most vulnerable communities desperate for a new way of co-existing. COVID-19 could serve as a turning point for all humanity and perhaps a final warning to act to construct a better world for all. This pandemic has exposed existing gaps on issues such as welfare inequality, resource mismanagement, and poorly-funded infrastructure. As one of the most vulnerable regions in the face of the global climate crisis, South Asia must be determined to seek global collaborations with environmental scientists and renewable energy investors to transform our planet together. This article seeks to promote deterrence of sectarian violence between the two nations and instead encourage the investment of energy into co-creating climate action activities as part of a peaceful negotiation in fixing the environmental damage that resulted from the ongoing conflicts caused by civil unrest in both nations. This article also encourages committed investments in climate change education, green jobs, and collaboration towards a green economy that will assist the nations in cultivating resilience towards climate change. By engagement in collective climate action activities, there still lies hope to overcome various forms of human insecurities that war and conflict have cost to the sanctity of all life forms.

Commitments of India and Pakistan

In India and Pakistan, heat waves have become increasingly normative. In 2018, Pakistan saw the highest official temperature recorded in the world—with 50.2 degrees Celsius in Nawabshah—and a week later, that record was broken when Jacobabad hit 51 degrees Celsius.[1] Following that event, Pakistan has made considerable efforts to enhance its climate action activities by endorsing the UN Sustainable Development Goals and determining to achieve the 2030 deadline way ahead. In 2014, Pakistan launched the "Billion Tree Afforestation Project" (BTAP) in the north-western region, which demonstrates its commitment to restore the province's depleted forests and fight the detrimental effects of global warming. The reforestation project was later extended in 2018 to the rest of Pakistan by Prime Minister Imran Khan after Pakistan's political party, the Tehreek-e-Insaf, came to power. Under the program, the government plans to plant 10 billion trees across Pakistan by 2023.[2] Similarly, under the leadership of Prime Minister Narendra Modi, India is currently one of the few countries on its way to meet its nationally determined commitments stated in the Paris Agreement back in 2015.[3] Prime Minister Modi had announced an ambitious plan for India's climate actions, including a massive scale-up of renewable energy. India is now approximately halfway towards meeting its target of achieving 175 GW of renewable energy capacity by 2022. In each nation's unique ways, both have shown awareness of the immediate crisis of climate change in the South Asian region. Yet integrated collaboration must be enforced to ensure the full-on protection of the sanctity of human life.

Expanding Climate Action Activities to Endorse Harmony along Line of Control

Traditionally, there have been various ways to enhance Indo-Pakistan relations; one of the most obvious manners of fostering friendship is the utilization of sports, for example, cricket. However, what it actually does is promote competition between nations over the endorsement of cooperation on regional issues, while there have also been various summits that seeks to enhance friendly relations, namely, the Agra Summit, the Lahore Summit, and the Shimla Summit.[4] However, these summits have proved to be inefficient, as sustainable outcomes and investments did not result from them. The possibility could be that the priorities of nations continue to be on "eternal economic growth", as criticized by Greta Thunberg during the UN Climate Summit in

2019. For change to happen, we need to educate on what kind of world we are actually living in and what we have been producing in the name of national security. Thus, governments must support climate educators working together through alignment with scientific principles to transform all the sectors of politics, economies, and social aspects of human life on the planet—building bridges at all levels of society by encouraging world beach cleanups, management for climate action teams, and put theories into action to help guide each nation's ordinary citizens towards peacebuilding.

From War Economy to Sustainable Green Economy

The continuous enabling of nuclear proliferation and the secrecy of nuclear programs pose a major threat to trust and mutual cooperation. To foster trust, there must be transparency in governance and how governments are spending money on research. While it is challenging, there are possibilities for both India and Pakistan to cooperate in expanding durable peace-building in South Asia and overcome the gap in solidarity. One policy for campaigning is the need for cooperative nuclear waste management. Both Indian and Pakistani citizens must be made aware of the wasteful results of nuclear testing and proliferation on both humans and the environment. The classification of threats to lives is based on the level of radioactivity of nuclear waste, identified under the International Atomic Energy Agency (IAEA) under various categories such as (i) Exempt waste, (ii) Very short-lived waste, (iii) Very low-level waste, (iv) Low-level waste, (v) Intermediate-level waste, and (vi) High-level waste. The prime challenge when it comes to waste management is how to sort and dispose of high-level radioactive waste (HLW).[5] With COVID-19 exposing the lack of resilient infrastructures of the South Asian region, this is the critical moment to demand the Indian and Pakistani governments respond to the need for an increased degree of collaboration among South Asian scientific communities. For years, the global scientific community has argued the severity of the impact of nuclear waste on cross-border issues.

All forms of inorganic waste contribute to unquantifiable impacts to the environment: ocean, air, and land. With the leadership of Greta Thunberg, there had been much rallying by youth climate leaders around the world to take concrete steps to raise awareness on climate issues; yet from the beginning, Greta was targeted by politicians and lobbyists as a threat to nationalistic perspectives. This has proven to show how fundamentally disconnected nation-states are from climate science and its urgency. Instead, nations with large militaries such as the USA continue to expand their military budgets year by year. It has been estimated by *Forbes* magazine that the US military emits more CO_2 than many several industrialized countries combined.[6] The expansion of military budgets also increases the legitimacy of endorsing a global war economy that affects our survival on the planet. Just for the US military alone, war and preparing for it are historically coal and fossil fuel-intensive activities. Following this up by being the single largest consumer of energy in the USA, the US Department of Defence is also the world's largest institutional consumer of petroleum.[7] It is estimated that 70 per cent of all energy is consumed by the moving and utilization of military troops and battle equipment around the world, and that involves the burning of vast quantities of jet fuel, diesel, and use of bio-hazardous materials.[8] Military equipment has never been recognized as fuel-efficient, and it has been estimated that the USA's fleet of 60,000 Humvees can only give four to eight miles per gallon of diesel.[9] Military real estate and oversees project development, also leaves a considerable carbon footprint. In the fiscal year 2017, the US Department of Defence notably spent US$ 3.5 billion on heating, cooling, and providing electricity to 560,000 buildings at 500 installations.[10] Moreover, this is just one military power on this planet. The budget of a global war economy could have been used to sustain 100 planets or more, yet very little of this funding has demonstrated the true commitment of global leaders towards peace-building initiatives, except for youthful advocates, such as Greta Thunberg and some others. It is time to put peacemakers, peacekeepers, and peace-builders of every form in the limelight and let them take the lead in directing humanity towards a sustainable, green economy future.

Climate Change Education: Focus on Peace-building

To begin fostering talents in the South Asian region, the endorsement of climate action summits, youth leadership forums, and summits of international leaders must become central platforms for harmonious dialogues in re-commitment to focus on global peace-building. There have been many summits between India and Pakistan, yet the inefficiency lies in having reached little commitment to promoting climate action activities within schools and large corporations. It is time to shift this vicious cycle of getting nothing done and instead put the investments into climate change education and youth empowerment. Youths, who are often pure at heart, tend to desire to connect with other students from diverse backgrounds. Students who are encouraged to attend study-abroad programs and cultural exchanges will cultivate a global mindset and see the connections between their local culture and that of others. Endorsements in education on food and climate change impact can also encourage awareness within agriculture practices that are historically not eco-friendly. Helping citizens to become aware of how their money is being invested, whether it is in fossil fuels or renewable energy, boosts confidence in government sectors when citizens are encouraged to be active thinkers on how their lives and their hard-earned tax dollars are regenerated back to protecting the planet.

Climate change education and environmental science are, by default, focused on evidence-based research and data. Thus, education on statistics will help students learn how to monitor and analyze data for decision-making. The centre of eco-literacy and the endorsement of a systems-thinking approach is part of the expansion of climate change education in local schools that have a global mindset. Educators must focus attention on bringing students closer to nature, learning how nature sustains life, and how to live in accordance with the rhythms of nature. They encourage schools to teach and to model sustainable practices that will make students aware of their inherent ecological consciousness. At the heart of climate change education is the promotion of freedom of action that desires peacebuilding actions; thus, that requires governments and NGOs such as the United Nations to guide students in learning about policies such as the Paris Agreement and energy policymaking. Unless we completely transform our ways of living, there will be little chance that we can globally improve the response to climate change in the years ahead.

Global Cooperation to Share Best Practices and Evidence-based Policy-making

Government officials of both nations should be encouraged to declare their commitment towards climate actions with solidarity with neighbouring countries and to expand on the significance that environmental science has in transforming the way we live today. The empowerment of the South Asian Association for Regional Cooperation (SAARC) as a trusted format for policy drafting and regional debates can create regional solidarity and friendships, endorsing the accumulation of funding to ensure mutual prosperity in the region. Such committed actions will demonstrate the sincerity of nations within South Asia to take charge in ushering the change we need to see for our planet. Lastly, the enhancement of arts and cultural exchanges will promote less antagonistic South Asian ties that see political or religious ideologies as simply one of many aspects of human experience, rather than its totality. This will discourage extremism in thought and cultivate tolerance for differences in perspectives for better dialogue opportunities. Through a commitment to solving the global climate crisis together, the prospect of mutual prosperity can hopefully be achieved within the timeframe of 2030 UNSDGs.

Policy maps such as food systems maps and carbon emission maps that are gathered through data science can help students and governmental officials to think clearer on how we can potentially reduce emissions related to human activities. Schools such as Columbia University, which hosts a Centre for Global Energy Policy and a cutting-edge Earth Institute, can promote global solidarity in tackling climate change jointly. When scientific knowledge and ecological wisdom is enhanced, the chances for the desire of a war economy will hopefully diminish, and the need to resolve issues through violent means will decrease significantly when self-interest groups recognize that they are creating more damage than benefits. Other human behaviours that many nations had historically chosen to ignore have been smoking cigarettes (the massive dumping of cigarette butts that post environmental hazards), inappropriate dumping of animal organs (an increase of zoonotic diseases), and the irresponsible consumption and production of merchandise (such as micro-plastics and chemical products). Without a comprehensive understanding of the interconnectedness and interdependence of life on earth, there will be no voluntary restriction in wasteful behaviours within nation-states.

Encouragement in Innovation

Investment in local innovations, and innovation exchanges within the South Asia region, will also greatly encourage resource recycling. Energy usage that is re-usable and the development of clean water technologies will achieve overall well-being for all populations within the region. Endorsing the desire to share scientific findings is the key to better solutions and more diversified ideas for solving regional climate crises.

Conclusion

By strategically expanding their efforts on Green Economy and Environmental Sciences, the hope exists to discourage criminal actions and mismanagement of resources along the Line of Control. The existing narco-terrorism associated with the Kashmir regional conflict promotes a considerable fear for vulnerable communities, specifically women and children, who are historically rendered powerless through the destruction caused by war. Enhancing climate action activities opens more opportunities for job-seeking citizens to find a more constructive purpose in life by contributing towards peace-building rather than efforts for war and conflict. The prevalence of sectarian violence, when faced with the reality of our global challenges, proves to be a minuscule issue against the threats of our survival as a unified species. To ensure a smooth transition towards a regenerative green economy within the South Asian region, there must be enhanced investments in the realms of environmental sciences, AI innovation, the agricultural sector, nutritional sciences, and global climate change education.

NOTES

1. Ahsan, Ahmad. Pakistan and India face common threats. Climate Change is the biggest one. Sept. 18, 2019. https://www.dawn.com/news/1505534#:~:text=The%20Pakistan%20Climate%20Change%20Act,of%20water%20flow%20in%20rivers. Website.
2. Pakistan achieves Global Climate Change Target.

3. Jaiswal, Anjali and Kwatra, Sameer. India Announces Stronger Climate Action. https://www.nrdc.org/experts/sameer-kwatra/india-announces-stronger-climate-action#:~:text=Increasing%20the%20fleet%20of%20electric,motorization%20rates%20in%20the%20world. September 23, 2019. Website.
4. Lawson, Alastair. A History of India-Pakistan Summits. http://news.bbc.co.uk/2/hi/south_asia/1434337.stm. July 11, 2001.Website.
5. Malhotra, Aditi. Nuclear Waste Management: Exploring Future Areas of India-Pakistan Cooperation. https://southasianvoices.org/nuclear-waste-management/. July 31, 2014. Website.
6. McCarthy, Niall. Report: The U.S. Military Emits More CO2 Than Many Industrialized Nations [Infographic]. https://www.forbes.com/sites/niallmccarthy/2019/06/13/report-the-u-s-military-emits-more-co2-than-many-industrialized-nations-infographic/#438d15c54372. June 13, 2019. Website.
7. Ibid.
8. Ibid.
9. Ibid
10. Ibid.

11

A Race for Water Security: Constructivist Understanding of Sino-India Relations over the River Brahmaputra

Sanchita Borah

ABSTRACT

The race to become a great power in Asia is not only confined to controlling crucial waterways in the South China Sea but also to control Asia's freshwater. About four billion people depend on Asia's water, on which its control lies in China's hands. However, the impediments faced in maintaining the water security of every nation emanate from multiple factors involving population explosion, rapid urbanization, industrialization and environmental degradation. These barriers intensify the rarity of water, which leads to a steady increase in international disputes over it. Such a dispute relates to the Brahmaputra, which has become a point of friction in the Sino-Indian relationship. It is anticipated as a political weapon of China supplementing its water scarcity by controlling the river water. This river originates in the Himalayas and runs through Tibet as the Yarlung Tsangpo, on which China has been constructing hydrological dams causing detrimental effects to the lower riparian countries like India and Bangladesh. The objective of this paper is to comprehend the strategic relations of China and India in the context of the Brahmaputra river dispute through the international theory of constructivism. The theory argues that along with material or economic spheres, notable features of international relations are structured by ideational factors that are historically and socially constructed. The main argument of this research is to envisage how the dispute over the river water has been historically, politically, and economically constructed that redefines the strategies of international security agendas threatening international relations between nations. Attempts will be made to provide transboundary settlement mechanisms to pacify an impending war over water.

Keywords: *water security, strategic relations, constructivism*

Introduction

Water is one of the most vital resources on Earth. It is not only indispensable in sustaining life; it also brings people together as communities, maintains sustainable health, socio-economic well-being, and revitalizes every life on our planet. However, about 97.5 per cent of the total water is either salty or polluted. Seventy per cent of the remaining 2.5 per cent of water remains under glaciers or frozen ice caps. Only 0.01 per cent of water is available for humankind in the form of rivers, lakes, reservoirs, and easily available aquifers (Levy, 2011). The scarcity of water has become one of the greatest challenges in the 21st century. A large population of the world lives in places where the demand for water is significantly more or where its poor quality decreases its use. Insufficiency of water and unequal use, access, and management of available water can endanger human life, harming the quality of life and limiting human development (Gehrig, 2009). With population increasing to almost triple in the last century, all governments are encountering major hindrances in accessing clean water. Environmental degradation, hydrological discrepancy, rapid urbanization, and industrialization have exasperated the challenge. These challenges are distinctively alarming for developing countries because, with the rise in population and growth of urbanization, the per capita availability of water has become limited (Salman, 2006), as a result of which, water scarcity creates an environment of distress and discontent which becomes a precursor of vicious conflicts (Wolf, 2001).

This paper analyzes how the current problem of water shortages has forced the two Asian giants, India and China, to 'securitize' their water, which has ended in a state of contention. The history of Indo-China relations is rather pessimistic, with various territorial tensions emerging, but in recent times, water has become a key security issue that has the potential of becoming a root of a persisting discrepancy between the two. The Brahmaputra is a major concern for India, China, Tibet, and Bangladesh as it flows through them, forming a significant water resource for them. The first section of this article will delineate how water has become the main catalyst of various disputes between countries because of the increasing demand and scarcity of available water through the international relations theory. The second section will try to analyze how the Brahmaputra has become a major source of contention between India and China relations with the potential of becoming a strategic water war in the future. Both India and China's concerns over the Brahmaputra form an important segment to delineate the conflict that forms the third section. The fourth section attempts to exhibit procedures for the resolution that can be replicated for various water disputes of the world. The argument of this article lies in forming water as the main stimulant of various disputes around the world that can reconfigure the security agendas of countries jeopardizing the balance of the international world order.

The Advent of Water Disputes

Disputes over resources arise due to competing demands over their use, and this spreads over local, regional, provincial, national, and international areas. International water disputes have become increasingly perceptible and interwoven with domestic requirements and utilities. In the recent world, the use of shared water by one country might have repercussions on the other sharing the same watercourse, whether it is ground or surface water. More than 300 rivers, 100 lakes, and large numbers of unidentified aquifers are shared by more than one state, which can become a cause of conflict and also a catalyst for cooperation (Salman, 2006). Indeed, this has become the present scenario globally, particularly since the last decade. Historical evidence shows that water was used as a tool by the military to fight wars, whereas the current scenario has transformed into the water itself being the main constituent of a war. The frequency with which water disputes have arisen is listed in Figure 1.

In international relations, water disputes can be examined through the theory of constructivism. The theory accentuates a variety of intangible, ideational values where historical, social, and cultural factors stimulate particular forms of meanings that are to be given to various actors and their intentions (McDonald, 2008). Constructivism has two suppositions: the positions of the agent/structure are analyzed as building blocks in the reality of the international sphere, that is, social, ideational, and material. The formation of these material aspects is formed by 'the social context through which they are interpreted' (Checkel, 1998) and (Jackson, 2003). Second, the interconnection

Figure 1: Water Conflict Events, 1930 to 2018

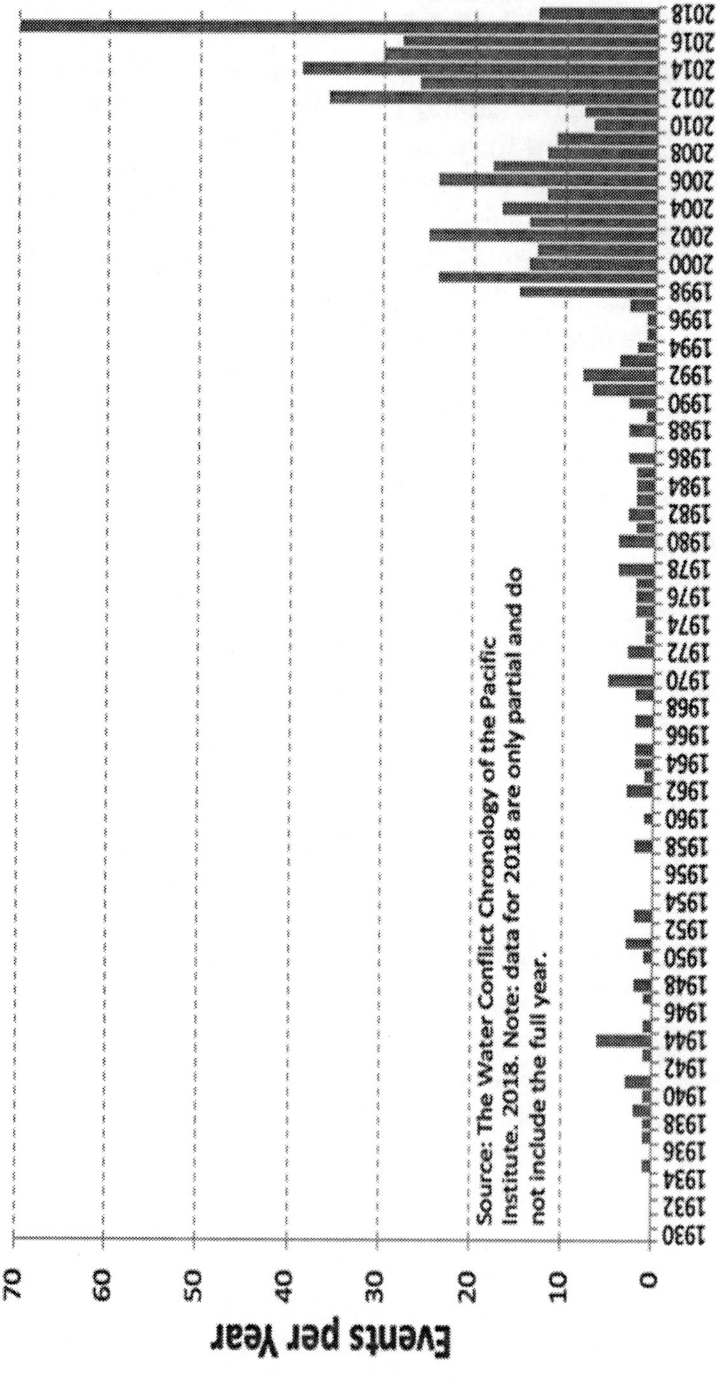

between agent and structure is constructivism. Constructivism examines that social structures and human agents or states are mutually organized in the sense that the existence of human agents depends on the social environment and clustered principles of meaning (structure), social structures that reproduce, create, and alter themselves through the knowledgeable applications of purposeful agents (Shafique, 2011). The Brahmaputra water conflict will be analyzed through this lens of constructivism.

The Mighty Brahmaputra: China-India's Struggle for its Control

The Brahmaputra originates from the Angsi glacier near Mount Kailash, located on the northern side of the Himalayas in Tibet's Burang country, where the river takes the name the Yarlung Tsangpo. For 1,625 km, it flows eastwards through Southern Tibet and, at the easternmost tip, it takes a spectacular U-turn known as the Great Bend or Shuamatan point. After this point, the Yarlung Tsangpo enters the eastern-most state of India, Arunachal Pradesh, where it is known as the Siang. After accumulating water from various rivers, it transforms itself into the Brahmaputra in the state of Assam. After the river snakes leisurely through Assam, it enters Bangladesh, where it is known as the Jamuna. The Jamuna is joined by the Ganga and is known as the Padma and the Meghna. The amalgamation of these three rivers forms the world's largest delta, after which it empties its water into the Bay of Bengal (Ramachandan, 2015). Thus, the Brahmaputra river basin has maintained a balanced ecosystem rich in biodiversity with tremendous potential for irrigation development and infrastructure-related operations like navigation and dams while providing livelihood to China, Tibet, India, and Bangladesh. The dispute over the river is alarming because of the sustained growth in water and demand for energy, with the construction of dams hindering its natural flow, water-diversion, and inter-basin water transfer programs. The river basin has massive fluctuations in water availability due to extremely wet monsoons and dry winter seasons. The incongruous combination of population growth, increasing economic aspects, and escalating demand for energy resources are propelling China and India to lay stress on hydropower projects (Ratha, 2016). Organized hydropower

Figure 2: Map of Brahmaputra Basin

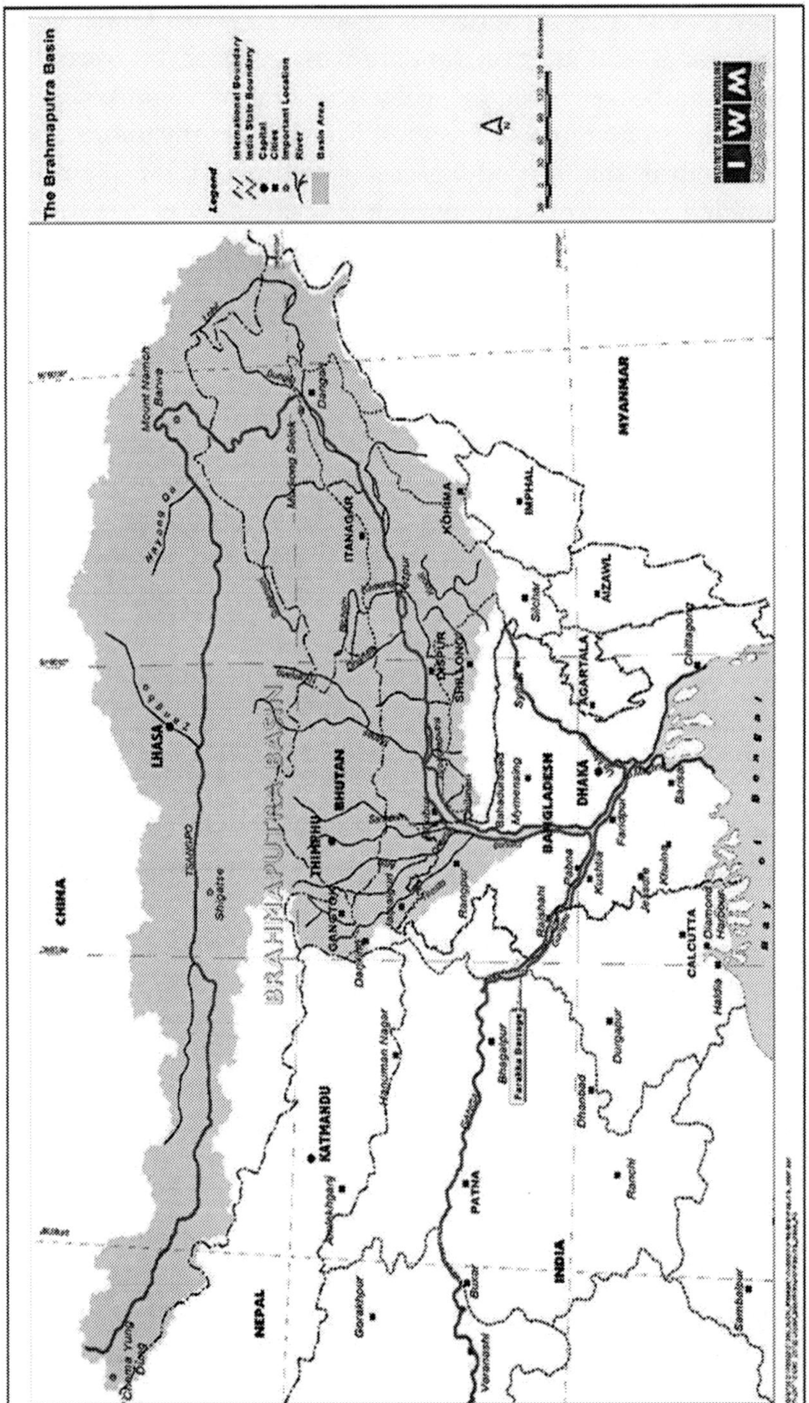

Source: Institute of Water Modelling, Bangladesh

plants and water diversion projects, combined with increasing water security concerns, make a substantial impact on relations between China and India.

Constructivist Understanding of the Brahmaputra Issue

In general, constructivists not only emphasize economic or material aspects but also highlight the importance of historical, social, political, and ideational factors that construct a particular issue. This section will try to describe these factors to understand the nuances of the dispute over the Brahmaputra that stand as a major hindrance in bilateral relations between India and China.

Scrutinization of **historical** factors portrays a sense of pessimism that China and India share in their histories. Both countries are involved in post-independence conflicts: the Sino-Indo war of 1962, the 1967 Chola incident, and the Sino-Indian skirmishes of 1987 that have developed a sense of mistrust (Christopher, 2013). The People's Republic of China's new assertiveness towards the Northeastern state of Arunachal Pradesh, along with the Chinese media's defamatory attacks on India, creates a sense of worry for India. Moreover, China's relations with Pakistan create suspicion for India. Under these circumstances, China's planned construction of hydropower dams and water diversion schemes on the Yarlung Tsangpo, along with increasing water insecurity, has resulted in India's worrisome relations with China (Mahapatra, 2015). These events have neither created a sense of trust nor a transboundary mechanism for mitigating the issue.

From a **political** standpoint, analysts have claimed that China has used the Brahmaputra issue as a political weapon against India. The people of North-East India, mainly the state of Assam, primarily depend on the river for agriculture that sustains the livelihood of many. Structuring huge hydro-electrical dams on the Yarlung Tsangpo would hinder the natural flow of the river leading India to live in perennial distress. China has already built the \$ 1.2 billion Zangmu dam and various other dams on the Yarlung Tsangpo without giving prior notification to India. If China limits the water flow from the river in the upper stream, there will be an adverse effect in the lower riparian states for agriculture and industrial activities. When the key to discharge water remains in the hands of China, it nurtures a political and economic pressure that changes the power dynamics between nations (Mahapatra, 2015). In all probability, China would interfere in the dry season and discharges in the wet season, thus putting pressure on the Indian Government resulting in India remaining at the mercy of China. Since China has been building dams on the river, there is an immense probability that a mammoth-sized reservoir of water would flow, which would devastate the lower riparian states.

On the other hand, **economic** factors always play a significant role in every dispute. In the Brahmaputra river dispute, there is an increasing demand for water resources and energy by both India and China. Until recent times, China's objective towards the Himalayan region was particularly employed in sustaining a power relation with India while maintaining a defensive approach towards Tibet. China's commencement of major plans like the West-East Electricity transfer project (Xi Dian Dong Song) and the Western China Development Strategy (Xibu Da Kaifa) foresees that the People's Republic of China (PRC) posturing Tibet as the major trading hub in the Himalayan region (Svensson, 2012). China's interest in developing the western region is mainly to indulge in natural resource extraction from Tibet that would boost the economic motor of eastern China and also develop 'backward' Tibet. Moreover, the construction of hydropower projects would help China to lower the income gap in the eastern province of China and the region in the west. Tibet's Autonomous Region (TAR) is rich in untapped water resources, which is one of the main objectives of China that would stimulate economic security and consolidation (Svensson, 2012; Mahapatra, 2015). Under these circumstances, China's strategic interest in building hydropower dams will be examined.

China's Strategic Interest in the Brahmaputra

As already discussed, the Himalayan region was earlier designed to maintain a power relation with India and a defensive approach towards Tibet. While recently, its interest shifted towards the Yarlung Tsangpo river to extract the energy and water resources of the region. The People's Republic of China (PRC) campaigned for 'opening up the West' for extraction of Tibet's natural resources and fueling up the economic ladder of Eastern China and moving the otherwise 'backwards' Tibet forward (Svensson, 2012). The Tibet Autonomous

Region's unexplored water resources have become an important objective of the PRC that would promote economic integrity and stability. It is in this context that China's ambition of becoming a 'hydro-hegemon' would be studied.

China has continuously stressed building hydropower plants in the western region of the Tibetan hinterland. The entire river basin of Yarlung Tsangpo has a potential of 114 GW of hydropower potential, of which 79 GW would originate from the main river. China's main hydropower project is the Zangmu hydropower station of 510 MW, while more are being initiated, namely, Lengua, Zhongda, Langzhen, Jiacha Jeix dam and Jiexu hydropower station, Dagu dam and Dagu hydropower station, Bayu hydropower station, Lalho dam, and Lalho hydroelectric project (Svensson 2012). China has claimed that these projects are 'Run-Over–River' projects, and it has fully considered the consequences downstream. However, every construction in a river has an adverse effect on the downstream region when it interferes with the natural flow of the river.

In the Shuamatan or the Great Bend on the Brahmaputra/Yarlung Tsangpo, China has initiated a proposed water diversion plan known as the "Great Western Route". A plan of channelling 200 billion m^3 of water and a proposed link with the eastern and central routes of the south to north water transfer projects has been initiated by damming the river (Svensson, 2012). Moreover, assumptions have been made that building a dam at the Great Bend, which is 30 km from Arunachal Pradesh, would help China to assert its claim over the state. A book, *"Tibet's water will save China"*, has explicitly prescribed rerouting the Brahmaputra northward (Chellaney, 2009). China has openly rejected the possibility of such a rerouting, while experts have been making a blueprint of the proposed project (Holslag, 2011). There has been no declaration officially for the construction of a dam, but it has been a matter of great debate. The initial plans for water diversion projects were started in the late Eighties, assisted by the military establishment. Many researchers and scholars of China have explained the importance of the Great Bend dam. In 1997, a scientist and a member of the Chinese People's Political Consultative Conference, He Zuoxiu, declared that the western route could expand approximately 133 million hectares of arable land of China, resolving agricultural problems and employing

160 million people (Holslag, 2011). In 2005, Li Ling, a second military artillery corps officer, published the extensively-read book *"Saving China Through Water From Tibet"* (Xizang Zhi Shuijiu Zhongguo), which classified various causes and options for tapping the Yarlung River. An article in *People's Daily* stated that the western route might be delayed but not cancelled. Opinion leaders like He Xuoxiu and Li Ling have claimed that constructions like the western route are affairs of subjugating nature to human interest. He Xuoxiu has famously declared that "Man need not revere nature" and "Sometimes it is necessary to destroy the environment and ecology a bit or transform nature in the interests of human beings." (Holslag, 2011). Thus, along with various scientists and opinion leaders, China has been keen on exploiting the rivers for an economic boom of its own.

Figure 3: The Prudent Interest of India over the Brahmaputra

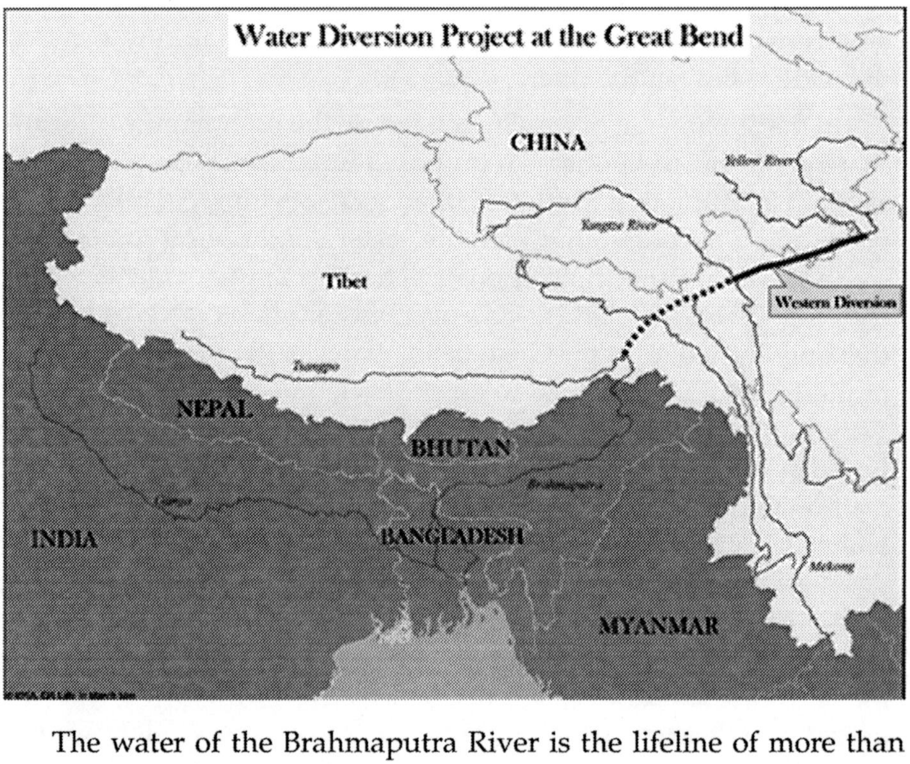

The water of the Brahmaputra River is the lifeline of more than one billion people downstream. If the diversion at the Great Bend is made, the environmental condition of India's north-eastern plains will be devastated. North India would be famished without its lifeline. Also, India is witnessing a massive water crisis issue. According to the Ministry of Water Resources, the per capita water consumption in the country remains at its low level of 1,545 cubic metres as of the 2011 census. This figure is much lower than international standards of 1,700 cubic metres per person per year (Maria, 2017). Under this circumstance, India majorly depends on the Brahmaputra. Thirty per cent of the river accounts for freshwater resources and around 40 per cent for potential hydropower projects of the country (Zhang, 2016). Diverting the water from the river in the Great Bend to the dry north of China would cause serious implications on agriculture and fishing in the middle and lower riparian states. Many environmentalists and analysts have warned that China's diversion project would, in the long run, ruin the livelihoods of millions living downstream. Even the scientific community in China has warned the government about the consequences of the diversion project in the future (Maria, 2017).

Ramaswamy Iyer (2015) has described three reasons how the construction of dams is dangerous for India and Bangladesh. First, the exact position of the river is not clear, and figures vary. In the lean season, the river's flow from Tibet might have a profound significance in the lower riparian countries. Second, 30 per cent change in the flow is not a matter of little concern because even 10 per cent diversion will have a devastating effect. Third, it is not only a concern of diversion of the river, but other serious consequences will follow like hydrological, ecological, climatological, and morphological impacts on biodiversity (Iyer, 2015).

China's assurance that ROR projects would be done with no diversion or storage is quite sceptical because these projects do have some serious consequences. Apart from impacts caused by building dams in ROR projects, there are two special characteristics: a break on the river between the point of diversion to the turbines and the returning point of the water to the river. This break can be substantially longer, in some cases even 10 km or 100 km in some cases, and such breaks would be followed in the cascade of projects ahead. Second, in ROR projects, the turbines function sporadically following the demand of the electricity market, which indicates that the waters are reserved in bondage and released when the turbines are required to function.

As a result, there are huge variations every day from 0 per cent to 400 per cent in a day in the downstream flow. There are cases in which the river is dry for almost 20 hours, and in the remaining four hours, there is an eight-metre wall of water rushing down the river. In these circumstances, no aquatic life or riparian population could survive that artificial rush (Iyer, 2015).

China has tried to use water as a political weapon against India, which has become an imminent threat to India's water security (Mahapatra S.A., 2016). The river projects are built for the management of water, which is not for storage but results in deadly flash floods. The soil of these regions is enriched with nutrient-rich sediment that would be held back in the reservoirs and prevented from reaching the river's delta. China's water delegation approaches and discrete water utilization are equally exasperating. Brahma Chellaney (2009), a strategic expert, has warned that the dams, irrigation systems, barrages, and canals in the upstream could administer water as a political weapon that can turn into a war or indistinctly, in peacetime, signal dissatisfaction among other co-riparian states.

"Even denial of hydrological data (which India and China share in particular seasons) in a critically important season can amount to the use of water as a political tool" (Ramachandran, 2015). Co-riparian states are never consulted by China before starting any geopolitical developments. It lacks in accumulating the nuances of the effects that will be caused by upstream hydro-power projects in the lower regions. China has used water as a political tool to attain unbeaten water hegemony in the entire region. India's distinguished edginess springs from China's non-transparent positions (Mahapatra and Ratha, 2016).

Mitigating Future Hostilities

Both China and India are cursed with water shortages and limited drinkable water. The scarcity of water in both countries poses greater challenges to food security. India's capacity to impede China in dam construction is impracticable because it is on the verge of becoming a hydro-hegemon. The need of the hour is that India should now mainly focus on bringing China to the negotiation table to ink potential binding treatises with the lower riparian regions. Bestowed with high-altitude glaciers, the Tibetan plateau is the fountain of multiple rivers, including the Brahmaputra, the Sutlej, the Mekong, the Indus, and the Salween (Maria, 2017). About 2 billion people are served by these rivers in 11 countries (Christopher, 2013). China is located on the upper reaches of all these rivers forming dominance over the lower riparian states. China's continuous dam construction on the rivers has pressured many downstream countries.

Bangladesh is the most affected country in terms of dam construction by both China and India because India is also building dams over the Brahmaputra for tapping the water resources for its own water security. Bangladesh's High Commissioner to India, Tariq Ahmed Karim, in an interview, suggested establishing a South Asian-level water regulatory and monitoring committee like India's Himalayas River Commission to better supervise water issues in the sub-regions (Maria, 2017).

Be it Vietnam from the Mekong River basin, Thailand and Myanmar from the Salween River Basin, India, and Bangladesh from the Brahmaputra River basin, or other Central Asian countries with whom China shares its rivers, India can become the main catalyst in bringing China to sign legal contracts of cooperation with other co-riparian countries. In the case of transboundary river management, India needs to be very diplomatic in dealing with China. As long as the economic position is a matter of concern, China is more weighted than India. Thus, one alternative to hold back China is by playing the political game of the Tibetan independence caused by India. This is a very sensitive issue, so India's move towards this must be very cautious because a wrong move could lead to a Frankenstein effect. India will create a bond of friendship with the Tibetan people because history recalls the 1959 event when the Dalai Lama quit Tibet and began a permanent exile in India. New Delhi can use this long-standing rapport to influence China. Moreover, India should try to bond with the people of Tibet opposing dam construction in the Yarlung Tsangpo in their autonomous region due to environmental and political concerns (Maria, 2017).

Despite sharing hydrological data for the Brahmaputra by China, a precarious situation arises in cases of dam construction for India because China is much more opaque in its constructions and exploitation of water resources that concern India. Mahapatra and

Ratha (2016) have suggested that China, India, and Bangladesh should plan a comprehensive river basin strategy that can control the geological disasters and impacts of the hydropower projects. Along with the use of resources and technology, an integrated dialogue should be called for managing and reducing disasters. There is an urgent need to undertake coordinated efforts for scientific studies on glacier melting and its ramifications in the flow of its rivers (Gautam, 2012). Bilateral or basin-wide level institutional mechanisms are required as there is no international treaty presently in effect. Based on international norms, inter-country water institutions for fair utilization could help in establishing dialogues and planned cooperation. Although these collaborations are challenging tasks, they can help to sustain water resources, environmental protection, and strategic security (Chellaney, *From Arms Racing to Dam Racing in Asia: How to Contain the Geopolitical Risks of the Dam-Building*, 2012).

The successful joint ventures of Brazil and Paraguay, China and Thailand over the river Salween for peaceful settlement of disputes can become a replica for India-China skirmishes over the Brahmaputra.

Mahapatra and Ratha (2016) have rightly pointed out how water has become the 'Sword of Damocles' for both China and India. There is an urgent need to pacify these precarious circumstances to safeguard the beautiful creation. Efforts should be made to end the antagonism before it takes a violent form. Though India's suspicion is impetuous, given the fact that Beijing is yet to give a green signal to major water diversion projects, the way China and India respond to each other's interests will influence the prospects of stability in Asia. Instead of conflict, water should be the source of cooperation between nations. Moreover, the first right over the Brahmaputra/Yarlung Tsangpo is of Tibet, as it is not just a natural resource or source of electricity, but it is the lifeline of Tibetans who live in permafrost (permanently frozen layer of ice) peacefully safeguarding the region but are now facing the melting of this permafrost. In our greed to exploit natural resources, we must not marginalize the Tibetans. The need of the hour is to have a water treaty that can share information, thoughts, and mutual collaboration between the Asian countries that can tranquillize the discontentment and allow them to prosper with trust, safeguard the river and meet their respective needs.

REFERENCES

Checkel, J. (1998). The Constructivist Turn in International Relations Theory (Review of Essay). *World Politics*, 324-348.

Chellaney, B. (2009). Coming Water Wars. *International Economy*, 38-39.

Chellaney, B. (2012). *From Arms Racing to Dam Racing in Asia: How to Contain the Geopolitical Risks of the Dam-Building*. Washington D.C: Transatlantic Academy Paper Series.

Christopher, M. (2013). *Water Wars: The Brahmaputra River and Sino-Indian Relations.* Newport: U.S. Naval War College Digital.

Gautam, P.K. (2012). Climate changes & conflict in South Asia. *Strategic Analysis*, 32-40.

Gehrig, J.A. (2009). *Water and Conflict: Incorporating Peacebuilding into Water Development.* Baltimore: Catholic Relief Services.

Holslag, J. (2011). Assessing the Sino-Indian Water Dispute. *Journal of International Affairs*, 19-35.

Iyer, R. (2015). India–China–Brahmaputra Suggestions for an Approach. *Economic and Political Weekly*, 13-15.

Jackson, R.A. (2003). *Introduction to International Relations.* New York: Oxford University Press.

Levy, B.S. (2011). Water Rights and Water Flights: Preventing and Resolving Conflicts before they Boil Over. *American Journal of Public Health*, 778-780.

Mahapatra, K.A. (2015). Sovereign States and Surging Water: Brahmaputra River between China and India. *Fondazione Eni Enrivo Mattei* (FEEM), 1-14.

Mahapatra, S.A. (2016). Brahmaputra River: A bone of contention between India and China. *Water Utility Journal*, 91-99.

Map of Brahmaputra River Basin, Source: Institute of Water Modelling, Bangladesh.

Maria, V. (2017). A Check to China's Water Hegemony. *Journal of Political Sciences & Public*, 1-4.

McDonald, M. (2008). Constructivism. In P.D. Williams, *Security Studies: An Introduction* (pp. 63-76). New York: Routledge.

Ramachandan, S. (2015, April 3). Water Wars: China, India and the Great Dam Rush. *The Diplomat*.

Ratha, M.S. (2016). Brahmaputra River: A bone of contention between India and China. *Water Utility Journal*, 91-99.

Salman, M.S. (2006). International Water Disputes: A New Breed of Claims, Claimants, and Settlement Institutions. *Water International*, 2-11.

Shafique, A. (2011). The Case for Constructivism in Analyzing the India-Pakistan Conflict. *e-international relations*.

Source: The Water Conflict Chronology of the Pacific Institute, 2018.

Svensson, J. (2012). Managing the Rise of Hydro-Hegemon in Asia: China's Startegic Interests in the Yarlung-Tsangpo River. *Institute for Defence Studies and Analyses*, 1-50.

Wolf, P.S. (2001). Dehydrating Conflict. *Foreign Policy*, 60-67.

Zhang, H. (2016). Sino-Indian water disputes: the coming water wars? *Wiley Interdisciplinary Reviews: Water*, 155-166.

12

Chinese Aggression on Indo-Pacific Areas post COVID-19

Sandeep Singh

As a geographical concept, the 'Indo-Pacific' has existed for decades. The German geopolitician Karl Haushofer first used it in the 1920s in his academic work *"Indopazifischen Raum"*. Since then, many analysts have intermittently sought to describe the 'geo-economic' connection between the Indian and Pacific oceans. However, in the contemporary context, beginning in the 2000s, analysts began to observe the 'security' linkage between the two oceans. As a political and strategic concept, it has, since 2010, gradually become established in the foreign policy lexicon of some countries, especially Australia, India, Japan, and the USA. However, China seems to be reluctant to identify itself as part of the Indo-Pacific; Chinese leaders believe that the US-led Indo-Pacific strategy aims to contain China. During the Shangri La Dialogue in Singapore in June 2018, our Prime Minister presented India's Indo-Pacific vision. It is rooted in our historical associations with this region and our understanding of its seminal importance in building prosperity in this century. The clarity of our approach was captured thus, "Inclusiveness, openness and ASEAN centrality and unity, therefore, lie at the heart of the new Indo-Pacific. India does not see the Indo-Pacific Region as a strategy or as a club of limited members. Nor as a grouping that seeks to dominate. Moreover, by no means do we consider it as directed against any country".

China is not a littoral state in the Indian Ocean. Nor, historically speaking, did it have a naval presence. Barring a brief three decades between 1405 and 1433, when the Ming Yongle Emperor sent Zheng He expeditions into the Indian Ocean, Chinese naval activity was limited to the East China Sea, the Bohai Sea, the Yellow Sea, and the South China Sea. This by no means suggests that China did not play an important part in Indian Ocean trade; it is to merely posit that such trade, especially beyond the Malacca Straits, was mainly carried on by Arab, Indian and Persian traders. Nonetheless, in today's context, China is the second-largest economy and the world's largest trading nation. The sea-lanes of communication in the Indian and Pacific oceans are vital to its economy and security.

As the COVID-19 pandemic has unleashed a miserable health crisis, social disruption and economic devastation on the world, it has accelerated the combination of forces that were already transforming the international order. One of these trends has been that, contrary to expectations, China's rise and transformation have not been peaceful. As the pandemic spread across the developing nations, the world observed that it had created an opportunity for China to deepen its influence either by the debt trap of the Belt and Road Initiative or by using its political and military power mainly in the Indo-Pacific region. We are witnessing increased aggressive claims of China in the form of military drills, deployed assets and energy exploitation.

However, China claim's it is building a "new model" of relations with neighbouring countries, based on "amity, mutual benefit and inclusiveness".

Media reports indicate that China has been increasing its presence in the US backyard. Earlier this month, it had gone fishing in the Pacific Ocean. Ecuadorian officials have claimed that around 325 vessels have sailed close to their exclusive economic zone on the Galapagos Islands. Made up of 127 different islands, the Galapagos has been declared a UNESCO World Heritage site.

Some of the boats had switched off their satellite tracking systems and were almost nine nautical miles into the waters controlled by the

Ecuadorian government. With so many Chinese trawlers in the waters close to Ecuador, the government of that country suggested that Beijing negotiate an agreement, which would allow inspection of Chinese vessels even outside the EEZ of the Galapagos in international waters. Besides, there are tensions between Vietnam and China over the Paracel Islands, between Indonesia and China over the Natuna Sea and the Spratly Islands have been disputed by China, Vietnam, the Philippines, Malaysia, etc. China's coronavirus mask diplomacy has given way to bare-knuckled geopolitical fistfights with a growing array of its neighbours. In the past few months alone, it clashed with India in one of the worst border flare-ups in decades, escalated standoffs with Vietnam and Malaysia in the South China Sea, pressured Taiwan with night drills in the Taiwan Strait, and threatened Australia with boycotts of wine, beef, barley, and Chinese students.

Strategically, the Indo-Pacific has been seen as a continuum across the two oceans joined by its main trading channel. Like the Straits of Malacca, it contains the world's most crucial sea routes, the world's most populous nations fuelling high-energy demands on its rims.

Beijing's maritime advances have sprawled across the two oceans in a bid to secure its energy requirements and boost its trading ties. China's rise has taken multiple forms. In the South China Sea, its irredentist claims have been showcased through territorial advances. Its growing strides in South Asian waters alongside the string of ports known as 'String of Pearls' facilitate making it a resident power. In terms of connectivity and infrastructure, the Belt and Road Initiative put forward the Chinese-led plan to bind the geopolitical space. China has geographical advantages, which gives control over the water supply of 18 countries. For example, take the Mekong River, which is one of the longest and important waterways. It starts from China and goes on to Myanmar, Laos, Cambodia and Vietnam. On this river, China has 11 dams to gain control over the economic lifeline for around 60 million people of South East Asia. Likewise, on the Brahmaputra River, it has the Sang Mu Dam, and three more are being built. This is a clear indication of hydro dominance or hydro war.

This reflects a pattern of the Chinese government beginning to exercise the same authoritarian mindset externally towards other countries as it does internally towards its people. It shows that, given the opportunity, China's government will treat its neighbours as subjects, not partners. The Chinese government's preference for domineering and unlawful methods and goals is the reason there is tension between China and the rest of the international community.

China's behaviour also reveals a critical pattern. China's government has a history of building power over other states in a given domain while assuring others that it will not use that power against them. Then, when China becomes the dominant player in the domain, China's government abuses that power to coerce or co-opt vulnerable states or multinational corporations.

For example, China built up its economic power over neighbouring states for decades. It framed more profound economic interdependence as win-win solutions and waited until it secured its position as those states' dominant trade partners. Then it used its financial leverage to coerce them. A report by the Centre for New American Security in 2018 detailed some prominent cases: the 2010 rare-earth metals export ban was targeting Japan, the 2010 salmon import restrictions were targeting Norway, the 2012 banana import ban was targeting The Philippines, the 2016 tourism ban targeting Taiwan, the 2016 fees imposed on mining product imports targeting Mongolia, and the 2016 closures of Lotte stores and restrictions on tourism and cultural imports targeting South Korea.

China built up its military power while assuring others that it would not use it to coerce its neighbours. Then, when China's military gained a dominant advantage over its neighbours, it began throwing its military power around.

This pattern is important because, recently, China has been amassing Big Data for information superiority. Further, it is gradually pushing to control other states' digital infrastructure—5G wireless hardware and software, hard-line telecommunication infrastructure, and undersea cables. China assures its neighbours that it will not abuse its power over its infrastructure. We should know how this pattern ends by now. What China cannot hack, it is preparing to be able to sabotage, to obtain what it needs in peacetime or, should it be necessary, prevail in a short, sharp "informationized" skirmish.

The five most important facets of China's total competition

campaign in the South China Sea and Southeast Asia are economic power, information dominance, maritime power, psychological operations, and lawfare.

The information competition is important because it has a domino effect on all the other domains of competition. "Information dominance" is the label we use to discuss China's efforts to harvest data, control digital infrastructure, suppress information and disseminate false narratives, and build up its information-related industries so that it can dominate the information and high technology economy in the future. If China successfully achieves information dominance, it can use that advantage to enhance its psychological operations, its economic leverage, its military and paramilitary activity, and even its efforts to pick apart legal principles and norms. If China is able to dominate this region, then it will exploit not only trade but also geopolitics and natural resources for itself, which will lead it to become a new supreme power in the world.

Countering China

To understand this, one has to know the following aspects of the Quadrilateral Security Dialogue or QUAD; what has been striking about the QUAD thus far, however, is that it has openly resisted identifying China as the primary target it seeks to rein in. Indeed, QUAD press releases from the respective foreign affairs establishments of each country have never once raised the word "China"; neither did the US Indo-Pacific Strategy mention the QUAD directly linking its consultations to addressing China.

What is QUAD?

The grouping of four democracies, India, Australia, the USA and Japan, the Quadrilateral Security Dialogue or QUAD, was first mooted by Japanese Prime Minister Shinzo Abe in 2007. However, the idea could not move ahead with Australia pulling out of it, apparently due to Chinese pressure. The USA has been moving in all directions to make allies to contain China's rise. The attempts to engage more with the East through Obama's 'Pivot to Asia' and now 'Indo-Pacific' partnerships are all strategic actions these countries are taking. All the four nations find common ground of being democratic with common interests of unhindered maritime trade and security.

The first meeting of the group after its 're-organisation' after Australia showed its willingness to join the group was with the aim to counter China's aggressive behaviour in the Indo-Pacific region; this was on November 12, 2017, a day before the ASEAN Summit. Soon after the meeting, India, Australia and Japan issued separate statements listing the Indo-Pacific as the major area of the deliberations and resolved to expand cooperation to uphold a rules-based order and respect for international law in the strategically important region. The dialogue was paralleled by joint military exercises of an unprecedented scale, titled 'Exercise Malabar'. The QUAD met five times in 2017–2019. The organization aims to promote a "free and open Indo-Pacific amid China's aggressive postures in the region". In March 2020, officials from the Quadrilateral met to discuss the COVID-19 pandemic. They were joined by New Zealand, South Korea and Vietnam for the first time.

In July 2020, India, Japan and the USA were in talks to invite Australia for a coordinated navy exercise named 'Malabar 2020', which is scheduled at the end of 2020, owing to the coronavirus pandemic. Australia is most likely to join it.

The QUAD is not a militarized grouping. The areas of cooperation of these countries have ranged from maritime domain awareness, cyber security, counter-terrorism, information sharing, connectivity, and infrastructure.

Australia

Beginning with Australia, perceptions of China have progressively dimmed in recent years. A variety of tensions arising from Beijing's South China Sea and Taiwan policies, promotion of Hawaii in Australia, growing influence in Australian politics and academia, harsh treatment of Hong Kong protests, and threats of economic retaliation amid Australian calls to hold China accountable for coronavirus have all soured the mood among leaders in Canberra. So much so that Australia on July 1 released a defence strategic update and force structure plan that, while reiterating from the 2016 paper the paramount impact of USA-China great power competition on Australian national security, further assessed that "since 2016, major powers have become more assertive in advancing their strategic preferences and seeking to exert influence, including China's active pursuit of greater influence in the Indo-Pacific.

India

India is also a major Asian country with a 3,488-km border with China, which has not been demarcated yet. This places a major constraint on the further development of Sino-Indian relations. The China-Pakistan Economic Corridor (CPEC), which passes through the Indian territory of J&K, has adverse political and security implications for India. The Belt and Road Initiative (BRI) also provides China with an opportunity to expand in India's neighbourhood. China projects the BRI as a "public good", but the reality is very different as more and more countries find themselves in debt distress. The BRI has prompted China to build a new institution like the Silk Road Fund to fund connectivity between China and the neighbouring countries and beyond. India will be affected whether or not the BRI project succeeds. India's neighbouring countries can fall into unhealthy dependency on China.

The security implications of the BRI are considerable as, for instance, in the case of the CPEC, which has brought Chinese presence close to the Indian border, whether in Pakistan-Occupied Kashmir (POK) or in the Sir Creek area. A new security force has been constituted in Pakistan allegedly to protect BRI assets. Border management will become that much more difficult. The implications of a Chinese naval base in Gwadar are self-evident. In the past few years, Chinese submarines have appeared in the Bay of Bengal and Sri Lanka. The Chinese naval base in Djibouti, in the Indian Ocean, is also a matter of security concern for India. The Chinese are also expanding their presence in Duqum in Oman.

India's strategies to counter the second largest economy in the world are currently involved in a standoff along the Line of Actual Control (LAC) in Ladakh. Chinese troops have intruded into the Indian side of the LAC and have set up bases. Galwan Valley and Pangong Lake are the two spots where there is an ongoing tense standoff.

There have been quite a few confrontations between India and China in Ladakh over Sikkim and Arunachal Pradesh. India has been firm on not allowing China to alter Indian territory. At the same time, it has maintained that its priority is peace and tranquillity along the border. While showing military readiness, India has also taken a number of economic and diplomatic steps to confront China. Although the two sides agreed on July 5 to end their military standoff, the damage appears to have already been done following the months-long military standoff in 2017 between them at Doklam, a tri-border junction including Bhutan. Recently, the Chinese spin after the meeting in Moscow between Jaishankar and Chinese Foreign Minister Wang Yi is the latest example of Beijing's relentless pushing of fake news.

In May 2019, India appointed former Foreign Secretary Subrahmanyam Jaishankar to the position of Minister of External Affairs. He was able to persuade Indian Prime Minister Narendra Modi in June 2019 to accede to Japanese Prime Minister Shinzo Abe's request that all the four QUAD country leaders sit together with Chinese President Xi Jinping at the G20—a symbolic, albeit implicit, the show of Indian support for the QUAD that previously would have been unthinkable. India has also responded diplomatically to China's aggression. On May 20, Tsai Ing-wen was sworn in as Taiwan's president for a second term. Two members of India's ruling BJP virtually attended the swearing-in ceremony and sent congratulatory messages. This action was a departure from the past. In 2016, India contemplated sending MPs to Taiwan when Tsai was sworn in for the first time, but, at that time, the trip was put off. India does not have official diplomatic ties with Taiwan. From that angle, India's stand becomes important since it could be perceived as tacit support to Taiwan and its government. India's Act East Policy and focus on its Security and Growth for All in the Region (SAGAR) have resulted in a two-fold approach in its Indo-Pacific initiative. The first part is the creation of Maritime Domain Awareness across the Indian Ocean that aims to provide information on all developments and movements across the Indian Ocean. The second is the expansion of its presence to maximize its outreach and visibility and to increase operational experience across the domain. Its Mission-Based Deployments of ships and aircraft in seven key locations strengthen India's abilities in this region. Recently, India had joint talks with France and Australia to enhance cooperation.

Japan

Japanese support of the QUAD has never been in doubt, namely because it was Abe's idea in 2006 to convene like-minded democratic partners in a quadrilateral format to counter China. Nevertheless, while Australia and India become comfortable with the arrangement, Tokyo is wasting no time to improve its ability to be a better partner within the QUAD framework. For example, late last month, Japan revised its intelligence sharing legislation to allow for sharing with Australia and India (and the UK as well). Japan already regularly shares intelligence with the USA. In addition, last month, Tokyo officially established a new division within its Ministry of Defence to enhance coordination with New Delhi and Canberra on ASEAN and Pacific Island issues. And on July 14, Tokyo released its annual defence White Paper in which it stated, "China has relentlessly continued unilateral attempts to change the status quo by coercion in the sea area around the Senkaku Islands, leading to a grave matter of concern."

USA

The USA, under the Trump Administration, has embraced the QUAD as a mechanism to maintain a "free and open" Indo-Pacific region in the face of rising Chinese assertiveness. Of the four countries, the USA may be the most anti-Chinese as bilateral relations rapidly spiral over a range of challenges, including the coronavirus fallout. Taiwan, the South China Sea, trade, human rights in Xinjiang, Hong Kong, intellectual property theft, press freedom, and others. Indeed, Washington is the only country to directly label China an "adversary" in its National Security Strategy, National Defence Strategy, and Indo-Pacific Strategy Report. However, to date, the USA has resisted the urge to convert the QUAD into an anti-China grouping, probably at the behest of other, more hesitant participants. This looks like it is set to change because the others want to change.

The USA signed a defence framework agreement with the Maldives on September 10 to deepen relations and maintain peace and security in the Indian Ocean.

China's Aggression and COVID-19 Effects on it

On the economic front, China faces several challenges. As a result of COVID-19, supply chains in China have been disrupted. This has led to a number of companies considering shifting their operations out of China. India and ASEAN are among the most favoured destinations for companies moving out of China, and New Delhi is making efforts to lure such companies to set up their operations in India.

Further, in April, India made changes to its Foreign Direct Investment (FDI) policy. As per the new rules, any country that shares a land border with India must get permission from the Central Government before investing in India. These countries cannot invest directly in India. This decision was taken to prevent opportunistic investments from bordering countries, more specifically China, and prevent the hostile takeover of Indian companies by Chinese investors. Over the past few years, China's investments in India have increased. China has invested heavily, for example, in start-ups in India. The new Indian FDI rules and the prospect of businesses moving to India from China will have a long-term adverse impact on China's economy.

The governments of India, Japan, Malaysia, and Australia have taken steps to reduce their economic exposure to Beijing, exploring new efforts to restrict foreign investment rules or shift manufacturing capabilities away from the Chinese mainland. In spite of Beijing's objections, many regional governments have praised Taiwan's highly successful COVID-19 response and offered support for restoring its observer status in the World Health Assembly. The Quadrilateral Security Dialogue between Australia, India, Japan, and the USA is growing stronger and even expanding—with a new "Indo-Pacific Coordination Group" that involves weekly calls between these countries as well as New Zealand, South Korea, and Vietnam.

COVID-19 has increased India's strategic importance in the region. There is little doubt about the emerging role of India, not just as a key player but also as a responsible actor in the Indo-Pacific. Here, India's aid in fighting the pandemic is noteworthy. It lifted its export ban on drugs such as hydroxychloroquine (seen by some as a possible cure for COVID-19) and paracetamol in a bid to supply them to countries such as the USA. It also sent such medicines to the South Asian Association for Regional Cooperation (SAARC) countries, as well as to Mauritius and Seychelles, and provided medical aid to the Caribbean and Latin American countries. India is also levelling its position as a key player in the global supply chain, given the plans of countries to shift production from China.

How do Southeast Asian Countries view Intensifying Geopolitical Competition between the USA and China in Asia?

ASEAN members have discussed other concurrent developments in the region, especially the importance of maintaining peace and stability in the South China Sea amid the contagion. In the context of the Indo-Pacific, it is speculated that the post-crisis world will see an even more hawkish China ready to exploit "free-market vulnerabilities" in order to offset its losses. This may, in turn, lead to further intensification of tensions between China and the USA, with Southeast Asia becoming the theatre of this resurgent competition. Chinese occupation of disputed islands in the South China Sea and the construction of military facilities there, in disregard of the International Court of Justice (ICJ) judgement, is an indication of assertive Chinese behaviour. The ongoing Code of Conduct negotiation between China and the ASEAN is likely to produce a one-sided result because the status in the South China Sea is tilted in favour of China. Indian economic interests and India's relations with ASEAN countries are heavily impacted by the heavy presence of China in the ASEAN. India's decision to keep away from the RCEP, though justified in the context of the lack of competitiveness of the Indian industry, is nevertheless fraught with long-term implications for India's Act East Policy. It opens the field for China to deepen its influence in the ASEAN further. The kind of balance that India could provide in the East Asian region will receive a setback as India has decided to keep away from the RCEP.

Being in the neighbourhood of China, Southeast Asian countries were hit by COVID-19 very early. Having suffered heavily due to the outbreak of the virus, East and Southeast Asian nations like South Korea, Taiwan, Vietnam, and Thailand acted with alacrity, pressing their public health systems into action.

China's efforts to promote its response to contain the virus somehow did not impress the Southeast Asians. Although these nations may not openly criticise China for the coronavirus outbreak, they have shown their loss of confidence in China in a number of ways. The COVID-19 crisis made Southeast Asia look inwards. Cooperation mechanisms such as the ASEAN and the QUAD will no doubt be required to play a vital role in the post-pandemic world while at the same time re-adjusting to probable shifts in economic interdependencies among countries in the region.

The Road Ahead

Despite their differing military capabilities, strategic outlook and risk-taking ability, and the enormous economic linkages with China, cooperation among the QUAD countries are set to deepen as long as it continues to challenge the liberal rules-based order. It can be expected that the QUAD will now work even more closely with countries like Singapore, Vietnam, Indonesia, Malaysia, and the Philippines, so that they are able to assert their legitimate maritime rights consistently in all the zones contested, occupied, and militarized by China on the basis of an illegal "Nine dash line".

The QUAD needs to undertake frequent and regular naval exercises between two or three if not all the partners and clearly and jointly articulate their faith in the freedom of navigation and overflights in the South China Sea. It should pay attention to the redesigning of the China-centred supply chains in the region, thus helping in Indo Pacific economic recovery and creating alternative dependencies. The QUAD needs to take concerted action in dealing with the pandemic, cooperation in health and vaccines, as well as equipment, logistics, movement of their nationals and creating value chains in essentials like pharmaceuticals. Developments in the region have opened up possibilities of enlarging the grouping to involve other like-minded countries in specific cooperation and discussions like the QUAD plus three groupings, which includes the Republic of Korea, New Zealand and Vietnam on dealing with the pandemic. The possibility of a Trade and Investment Agreement between the QUAD countries should be explored. It should cooperate on standard-setting and create a pool of their funds, which they, in any case, have at their disposal for the region. This includes coming together on the 'blue dot' initiative and upholding the voluntary quality Infrastructure Initiative standards advocated by the G20 and offering that as a viable alternative for the ASEAN and other small and vulnerable states in the Indo-Pacific. On the international platform, Germany adopted a new Indo-Pacific strategy against China. The USA is doing large-scale military exercises to provide protection to other small countries. Palau, Taiwan's ally, invited the USA to build a base camp.

To sum up, the challenges before India arising out of China's rise are as follows:

- The rising asymmetry between India and China make it difficult for India to convince China to settle the boundary question.
- China's growing influence in South Asia at India's expense.
- Security implications of the CPEC, Chinese base in Gowanda, Djibouti, etc.
- China's activities to build and take control of ports in different countries in the Indian Ocean.
- China's increasing military presence in the Indian Ocean.
- China's technology edge, particularly in the telecommunications area (5G), which gives its companies like Huawei a hold in the countries of the region in which India also has a strong interest.
- China has used its space capabilities to attract India's neighbours into cooperative folds.
- India's neighbours follow policies of extracting the maximum benefits from the rivalry and competition between India and China.
- China's growing capabilities in education is attracting a large number of Indian and South Asian students to its universities.
- China's dominance in South-East Asia will have an impact on India's Act East Policy.
- India can take several measures. These are as follows:
  - It has adopted a firm position on issues like the BRI and borders (Doklam crisis). This policy should continue, and China should know India's 'red line' clearly.
  - India has promoted the QUAD. This cooperation should continue.

- India should strengthen its Act East Policy. It should keep open its option of joining the RCEP eventually.
- India should strengthen its relations with Russia. It should be a partner with Russia in its Eurasia projects. India's Act, Far East policy, should be implemented expeditiously.
- India has considerable soft power, which can be harnessed to deal with Chinese influence in multiple ways. Civilization, culture and religion bind the people of the region. India has an advantage in these areas.
- In particular, India can be a hub of education, healthcare, and tourism for the people of Asia. These areas should be developed.
- India should pay adequate attention to science and technology, research and development and innovation. Investment in these areas will strengthen India's capability and help development instruments to deal with China.

China is making inroads into Iran, particularly in Chabahar. It has been ahead of India in building railway infrastructure in Iran. India has failed to fully capitalize on the potential of the International North-South Trade Corridor (INSTC). Increase investment and diplomatically overpower China.

It has also been forced to reduce its oil purchases from Iran due to the US sanctions. India will find it increasingly difficult to maintain a balance between Iran on the one hand and Saudi Arabia on the other. So, convince the USA and increase its dependence on India.

Facing the unprecedented health and economic crises spawned by COVID-19, the US and Asian partners will need to coordinate more closely than before. All these incidents after COVID-19 have resulted in a kind of rise of multilateralism. They have a unique chance to build equal and capable regional partnerships and institutions in the long recovery ahead. Hence the politics of the region is open to multiple possibilities.

13

Bilateral Relations between South Asian Nations during COVID-19 Pandemic: A Review

Nancy Puri and Dr. C.R. Akhouri

ABSTRACT

South Asia is one of the most populated regions of the world, marred by political tensions, security issues, and lack of economic development. The region has not been able to establish a strong health infrastructure. With a high incidence of multidimensional poverty throughout the region, it is fighting a major pandemic caused by corona virus disease (COVID-19). The crisis will prove a major economic challenge for every government in the region. The corona virus disease 2019 (COVID-19), which emerged from Wuhan, China, is now a pandemic, affecting the entire globe. Governments of different countries have developed and adopted various policies to contain it, the most common being social distancing and lockdown. Among the South Asian countries, Pakistan and India have the highest number of registered cases of positive COVID-19 patients, followed by Sri Lanka, Afghanistan, Bangladesh, and The Maldives. Nepal and Bhutan have registered a low number of cases of positive COVID-19 patients. In the post COVID-19 world, collective action by the South Asian countries is required to make a more rapid and peaceful exit from the crisis.

This paper will explore the COVID-19 situation and its implications on South Asian nations. The crisis is expected to have a significant economic fallout, and some countries are likely to slide into negative GDP growth that may destabilize the region. This paper will also focus on India's assistance to its neighbouring countries in fighting the pandemic in the post COVID-19 world.

***Keywords**: South Asia, COVID-19, Pandemic, Economy, Health, Cooperation.*

Introduction

In South Asian countries, the rampant corona virus pandemic could affect more than 1.9 billion people—almost a quarter of the world's population. Given the weaknesses of national healthcare systems, the fight against it seems to be lost before it has even begun. The resulting economic damage will increase the levels of poverty and inequality and is likely to exacerbate rather than mitigate a number of existing conflicts. On the domestic front, it is feared that authoritarian tendencies will increase during the management of the crisis. In the regional context, China could expand its influence further at the expense of India. (Wagnar and Scholz, 2020).

There is a need to understand the nature of the pandemic that the world is faced with before we assess its impact on South Asia. As per the World Health Organization (WHO), COVID-19 "is the infectious disease caused by the most recently discovered corona virus. This new virus and disease were unknown before the outbreak began in Wuhan, China, in December 2019." (Bhattacharjee, 2020).

Amongst South Asian countries, Pakistan and India have the highest number of registered cases of positive COVID-19 patients, followed by Sri Lanka, Afghanistan, Bangladesh, and The Maldives. Nepal and Bhutan have registered a low number of cases of positive COVID-19 patients.

The article looks into four main questions:

1. What is the impact of COVID-19 on SAARC countries?
2. How has COVID-19 impacted the economy of South Asian nations?
3. What role has India been playing in SAARC nations during the COVID-19 pandemic era?
4. Will India's initiative be a stepping-tone in the revival of SAARC?

The originality of the study: This paper objectively delves into exploring the impact of the corona virus in the South Asian region and will discuss South Asia in the post-COVID-19 world, thereby providing a real and unique empirical data-based analysis about how the corona virus has altered the economic, political, and social domain of South Asian countries.

Aim and objectives of this paper: This paper will explore the COVID-19 situation and its implications on South Asia. It will also focus on the economic impact of COVID-19 on South Asia and emphasize India's assistance to its neighbouring countries in fighting it.

The discussion of the research paper is as follows: **Section one** reviews the existing literature and methodology used in conducting the study. **Section two** addresses the impact of COVID-19 on South Asia. **Section three** explains the economic impact of the corona virus in South Asia. **Section four** deals with India's assistance to its neighbouring countries during the COVID-19 pandemic era and is followed by **section five,** which describes South Asia in the post-COVID-19 world.

Methods and Approach

A detailed literature review has been done in order to understand the impact of the corona virus on the South Asian region. Most of the information was collected from print, electronic, social media as well as unpublished reports from non-profit organizations. Online databases (PsycInfo, WileyOnline, PubMed, Scopus, Web of Science) were selected to source peer-reviewed texts. Data were collected to examine the impact of COVID-19 on South Asia, comprising more than 1.5 billion population and, further, this paper will explain the impact of the corona virus on the economy of South Asian nations. The current study implies the application of Qualitative Analysis. The high popularity acquired by methods in the social sciences is explained by a number of its features. Qualitative analysis is heavily dependent on the researcher's analytic and integrative skills and personal knowledge of the context. A simple type of qualitative analysis is sentiment analysis—a technique used to capture people's opinions or attitudes towards an object, person, or phenomenon. This paper is conducted in a systematic search across multiple sources of information with reference to political, economic, social and international perspectives among South Asian countries.

Impact of Corona Virus on South East Asia

In South Asia, India is one of the most populated regions as well as the second-largest populated country in the world. To combat COVID-19, India has learnt various preventive measures from China and from other affected parts of the world. In March 2020, it had followed some measures such as checking symptomatic COVID-19 passengers coming from abroad.

India created quarantine centres for those passengers who either showed symptoms or came from COVID-19-affected countries. In March itself, the Government of India closed all public and private schools, colleges, universities, shopping malls, etc. All public and private organization had permitted their employees to work from home. To combat the spread of the virus, nations throughout the world began sealing their borders as well as imposing social distancing norms.

From 25 March 2020, the Government of India suspended all international and domestic flights. On 24 March 2020, Indian Prime Minister Narendra Modi announced a total lockdown all over India. On 30 March 2020, India recorded 1,251 corona positive cases. However, by 6 April 2020, the cases increased to 4,314. (Bhattacharjee, 2020).

In Pakistan, the government imposed travel restrictions for the people. However, for an economically developing country, a total lockdown was not possible. Some doctors refused to be frontline corona warriors to assist patients in getting cured of the corona virus. Clerics refused to close their mosques in the lockdown. (Rehman, 2020).

"We cannot skip Friday prayers because of fears of corona virus", said Shabbir Chand, a trader who attended a packed service in Karachi, the country's biggest city. "Instead, we should gather in even larger numbers in mosques to pray to God to protect us from this fatal disease." (Rehman, 2020).

The Pakistani National Institute of Health (NIH) had followed important protocols to curb and prevent the transmission of COVID-19. (COVID-19, National Institute of Health, 2020). In March 2020, Pakistan lacked testing centres in the region and suspected samples were sent to foreign laboratories. Later, Pakistan received tests kits from China.

Now Pakistan is capable of testing suspected patients at its own NIH Laboratory situated in its own region, though, in Pakistan, there are a few quarantine centres for COVID-19 patients. (Saqlain *et.al*, 2020). After India, Pakistan has the second-highest number of suspected COVID-19 patients. (Paul *et.al*, 2020). "Some quarantine centres were well equipped. At Multan, the quarantine centres were set up in industrial estates for pilgrims returning from Iran." (Nafees and Khan, 2020).

In Afghanistan, the first case of the corona virus was found in a person who came from QOM, the epicentre of the pandemic in Iran. (Mousavi *et.al.*, 2020). "It has been mentioned by the Afghan Public Health Ministry that if serious action is not adopted immediately, an estimate of 25.6 million Afghans will be infected and 110,000 Afghans would die from COVID-19". (Bhattacharjee, 2020).

The Ministry of Health and Education of Afghanistan has shut down all schools and restricted Nowruz (Persian New Year) celebrations in order to prevent the virus from spreading in the country. The population in Afghanistan is 31.6 million, and 71.5 per cent live in rural areas. Currently, the national isolation centre consists of 100 beds. In Afghanistan, there is a lack of laboratories to do diagnostic tests for COVID-19 positive cases. This leads to delay in treating patients in hospitals.

Another issue of concern is the shortage of healthcare workers. There are only 9.4 skilled health professionals with 1.9 physicians per 10,000 individuals in Afghanistan; physicians are disproportionately distributed across the country with 7.2 physicians per 10,000 people in urban areas and as few as 0.6 physicians per 10,000 in rural areas. (Shah *et.al*, 2020). Afghan analyst Ezzatullah Mehrdad stated, "A combination of political rifts, lack of testing, extremely social lifestyles and a war-torn healthcare system led to Afghanistan's failure to contain corona virus".

Bangladesh had confirmed its first COVID-19 case on 7 March 2020. (Anwar *et.al*, 2020). In March 2020, all schools were shut down, and the Government imposed thermal scanner checking at airports. (Hal, 2020). From 16 March 2020, the Bangladesh Government had announced strict quarantine measures for passengers returning from abroad. (Maswood and Chowdhury, 2020).

Bangladesh had postponed all cultural events, including the 100th birth anniversary celebrations of the founding father, Sheikh Mujibur Rahman. (Anwar *et.al*, 2020). It was observed that Bangladesh had not imposed a strict lockdown measure due to which people were not following the norms carefully, and millions of citizens came out on the streets, especially in Dhaka. (Bangladesh Bureau of Statistics, 2020).

There are approx—1.1 million slum dwellers in Dhaka, the capital of Bangladesh. (Bangladesh Bureau of Statistics, 2015). They live in congested areas and are hardly aware of the threat from COVID-19. (Latif, 2020). From the period March to June 2020, there was a rise of positive COVID-19 patients in Bangladesh.

"Along with the slum dwellers, Bangladesh also hosts over a million Rohingya refugees, most of whom are living in close quarters in refugee camps where sanitization facilities are scarce". (Anwar, 2020).

"In South Asia, there are numerous refugee camps holding Afghans, Kashmiri pundits, Rohingyas and the like. It should be noted that the concept of lockdown in these camps or maintaining social distancing is virtually impossible, and they remain susceptible to getting infected in large numbers." (Bhattacharjee, 2020).

In Sri Lanka, the first corona virus case was detected on 10 March 2020. The Sri Lanka Government had already imposed lockdown even before the first case had been detected in the country. To curb the virus from spreading, the Sri Lankan Government followed precautionary measures such as suspending flights from and to China and Saudi Arabia. (*India Today*, 2020).

The Sri Lankan Government announced "work from home" for both the public and private sectors. During curfew hours, traders supplied adequate food and other essential items in door-to-door services. To curb the virus, the Government imposed social distancing measures, self-quarantine, appropriate hygiene activities, etc. It banned all types of mass gatherings such as picnics, pilgrimages, etc. Patients suspected with the symptoms of corona virus were quarantined in regional centres that were under the control of the armed forces. This led to preventing the virus from spreading. (Nanayakkara, 2020).

On 13 January 2020, a 31-year-old Nepali student had returned from Wuhan University, China, with mild symptoms. (Bastole et al, 2020). After that, the Nepal Government decided to shut down all cinema halls, gyms, health clubs, museums and banned mass gatherings of people. The second case of COVID-19 was reported on 23 March 2020. It was a 19-year-old woman who had returned from France on 17 March 2020.

In April 2020, the total positive cases recorded were 57. By the end of May 2020, the number of confirmed cases reached 1,567. The Government had shut down all educational institutions and postponed all national-level examinations. It also imposed restrictions on research in laboratories and ordered them to shut down temporarily. (Pouder et al, 2020).

The pandemic highlighted long-standing problems in government service delivery. Due to a lack of primary health care facilities, many corona positive migrants were put in isolation centres. They were forced to stay in schools that lacked cooking and bathing facilities and were compelled to sleep on floors or on students' benches. (Gill and Sapkota, 2020).

On 6 March 2020, Bhutan detected its first COVID-19 case. On 3 May 2020, had confirmed seven COVID-19 positive cases. The pandemic affected food imports in Bhutan. To make Bhutan self-reliant in food production, the Bhutanese Government wanted to use the crisis as an opportunity to boost the own country production.

On 23 March 2020, it sealed all its international land borders with its neighbouring countries in order to combat the spread of the virus. On 9 March 2020, the Bhutanese Government set up the National COVID-19 Response Fund to control the impact of the corona virus. India had assisted Bhutan, and the country is also supported by other international agencies. (Ranjan, 2020).

"In April 2020, Bhutan and the World Bank signed a fast track US$ 5 million (S$ 7.7 million) COVID-19 Emergency Response and Health System Preparedness Project to help the Himalayan mountain kingdom to prevent, detect and respond to the COVID-19 pandemic as well as strengthen its public health preparedness." (Ranjan, 2020).

The Maldives, the small island state, showed model strengthen in countering the spread of COVID-19. On 7 March 2020, the country confirmed its first corona positive case. Since March 2020, recovery has been reported in 13 out of 17 positive cases. It has been observed that to counter the spread of the virus, the Maldives Government has been taking preventive measures since January 2020.

The Maldives Government imposed a ban on international flights. The Government also set up quarantine centres to treat and check existing tourists on the island. Tourism, which is the major industry for the island country, had declined sharply, and the Maldivian economy was affected by COVID-19. (Bhattacharjee, 2020).

In South Asia, due to the large population, there were more chances of being affected by the corona virus and spreading rapidly except in countries like The Maldives and Bhutan. Currently, each and every country in South Asia is experiencing the community spread of the virus rather than the people who had travelled to infected countries. The countries of South Asia have entered the third phase, where obviously the disease will spread more rapidly.

"South Asia is one of the poorest and most populous regions. Healthcare facilities in this region are also very weak. Each of South Asia's eight countries has one of the lowest numbers of physicians per capita. It ranges from 0.3 physicians per 1,000 people (Afghanistan) to just one physician per 1,000 people (The Maldives, Pakistan and Sri Lanka). At the best of times, there are hardly a few healthcare workers with negligible resources. For such reasons, this region will still be much more vulnerable if severe cases of COVID-19 increase." (Chalise, 2020).

So far, due to this pandemic, no country has gained a winning position; rather, they had faced a loss in the economy, etc. As of now, no government in the world can be said to have come out of the crisis with its reputation or power enhanced. Most of the governments are in basic survival mode. From the future perspective, South Asia will take a long time to come out from the corona virus crisis.

The Economic Impact of COVID-19 on South Asia

International financial institutions such as the World Bank and the International Monetary Fund (IMF) have drastically made downward revisions of their growth forecasts for the countries in the region. The abrupt shutdown of key industries, such as textile production in Bangladesh or the tourism industry in Sri Lanka and The Maldives, will drive up debt and accelerate the threat of recession. The World Bank predicts that 2020 could be the worst business year for South Asia in more than 40 years. (World Bank, 2020).

The pandemic is heavily affecting the poor. In India, the unemployment rate had already gone up to its highest level in decades by 2019. In addition, around 90 per cent of the labour force in the country works in the informal sector. Approximately 450 million people have no social security. On 25 March 2020, when a curfew was imposed in the country, many workers made their way back to their villages. During the lockdown phase, violent clashes broke out between the police and the migrants. Many states closed their borders, due to which many migrant workers were being stranded, and their lack of supplies had become a further problem. (Wagner and Scholz, 2020).

"Migrant workers during the COVID-19 lockdown have suffered many hardships. With economic activities being virtually out of gear due to the lockdown announced by the Prime Minister on 24 March 2020, almost four crore of workers went jobless." (Alok, 2020).

In Pakistan, the government of Prime Minister Imran Khan initially provided $ 8 billion to fight the pandemic. As the country currently has double-digit inflation, Pakistan will have a difficult time obtaining further international aid. The government expects up to 18.5 million people to lose their jobs as a result of the crisis, or more than 30 per cent of the workforce. Another measure has been to expand social programs such as the Benazir Income Support Programme. (Wagner and Scholz, 2020). The pandemic will be a very substantial loss of income for South Asian countries and will lead to severe social consequences for the livelihoods and wellbeing of people." (UNESCAP, 2020).

The situation is further aggravated by the fact that states are losing important external sources of funding. India is the country with the largest volume of remittances from guest workers abroad. In the Gulf region alone, an estimated six to seven million Indian guest workers are employed. For Bangladesh, Nepal, and Sri Lanka, too, remittances by migrant workers to their home countries are important means of economic support.

Since their economic situations vary, individual countries will pursue different strategies to cope with the economic crisis. Countries such as Bangladesh, The Maldives, Nepal, Pakistan, and Sri Lanka are likely to press for rapid integration into the global economy. Not only do they fear for their most important industries, such as textile production and tourism, but they also want to be able to send their workers abroad again as soon as possible. (Wagner and Scholz, 2020).

"Washington has recently announced a welcome relief package for Pakistan. According to US Chargé d' affairs Paul W. Jones, "Since designating Pakistan a priority country for corona virus assistance, the United States has committed nearly $ 15 million in new corona virus response funding to our joint efforts. All of these contributions were identified as top priority needs by Pakistani authorities and are fully paid by the American people." (Chawla, 2020, 5). After four decades, South Asian economies are likely to shrink for the first time.

India's Assistance to Neighbouring Countries in COVID-19 Pandemic Era

India has assured all friendly neighbouring countries of all possible assistance to help them fight the pandemic. New Delhi has also been playing a key role in pushing for a common framework in dealing with the crisis. During a video conference on March 15, Prime Minister Narendra Modi pitched for formulating a joint strategy to fight COVID-19 in the SAARC region and proposed an emergency fund with an initial offer of USD 10 million from India. A 14-member rapid response team was sent to The Maldives last month to help the island nation set up corona virus testing laboratories and train local medical professionals to fight the pandemic. Earlier this month, India sent a 15-member team comprising healthcare personnel from the Army to Kuwait as part of bilateral cooperation between the two countries. India gifted a 10-ton consignment of essential life-saving medicines to Sri Lanka in view of the COVID-19 crisis.

The South Asian Association for Regional Cooperation (SAARC) is a regional grouping comprising Afghanistan, Bangladesh, Bhutan, India, The Maldives, Nepal, Pakistan and Sri Lanka. All the SAARC member-nations are reeling under the adverse social and economic impact of the corona virus pandemic. India had supplied the antimalarial drug hydroxychloroquine to its neighbouring countries, Afghanistan, Bhutan, Bangladesh, Nepal, The Maldives, Mauritius, Sri Lanka and Myanmar.

In South Asia, India is supplying COVID-19 vaccines to its neighbouring countries to maintain bilateral relations among the nations. On January 22, 2021, the Ministry of External Affairs (MEA) said, "Keeping in view the domestic requirements of the phased rollout, India will continue to supply COVID-19 vaccines to partner countries over the coming weeks and months in a phased manner. It will be ensured that domestic manufacturers will have adequate stocks to meet domestic requirements while supplying abroad."

India has rolled out a massive vaccination drive, under which two vaccines—Covishield and Covaxin—have been delivered to neighbouring countries. The Maldives and Bhutan were amongst the first nations to get vaccines from India. On January 22, 2021, India had sent 150,000 doses of the Covishield vaccine to Bhutan and 100,000 doses to The Maldives. The Maldives is the largest COVID-19 assistance recipient in India's neighbourhood, including medicines and food, training and financial assistance of $ 250 million.

Maldivian President Ibrahim Mohamed Solih said, "A short while ago, a flight from India with 100,000 doses of the Covishield vaccine arrived in The Maldives, renewing our hopes for a resolution to the COVID-19 crisis soon. Our heartfelt thanks to PM Narendra Modi, government and people of India for this most generous gift". The Foreign Minister of Bhutan too expressed gratitude. "Our profound gratitude to the Government of India for the generous gift of 150,000 doses of Covishield vaccines that Bhutan received today,"

India officially handed over 2 million doses of domestically produced Covishield vaccines to Bangladesh on January 21, 2021. The vaccines were given at a crucial time for Bangladesh as the nation witnessed a rise in the number of corona virus cases. In an international conference held at the University of Dhaka, Prime Minister Sheikh Hasina said, "I thank Prime Minister Narendra Modi for sending the vaccines (batch) as a gift."

On January 21, 2021, India handed over one million doses of corona virus vaccines to Nepal under grant assistance in sync with its

'Neighbourhood First' policy. During the sixth meeting of the India-Nepal Joint Commission in New Delhi, Nepal congratulated India on its remarkable success in the production of Covishield and Covaxin vaccines and requested for early provision of vaccines to Nepal.

On January 22, 2021, India despatched corona virus vaccines to Myanmar and Seychelles also. While a consignment of 100,000 doses of Covishield vaccines was sent to Mauritius, consignments of 50,000 doses of the Covishield vaccines were despatched to Seychelles. The Minister of External Affairs, S. Jaishankar, said in a tweet, "Indian vaccines reach Seychelles. That's what friends are for."

India will despatch Covishield vaccines in January 2021 to Sri Lanka also. On January 23, 2020, President Gotabaya Rajapaksa said. "We do not have to wait longer than the 27th of this (January) month to receive a number of free vaccines from India." India began its vaccine drive on January 16, and Rajapaksa had tweeted his congratulations to PM Narendra Modi "on the successful roll-out of the COVID-19 vaccine and his generosity towards friendly neighbouring countries" India has always supported its neighbouring countries in each and every hour of crisis. (*The Indian Express*, 2021).

South Asia in post-COVID-19 World

The political, economic, and humanitarian problems in South Asia will continue to occupy the international community even after the corona crisis. In the post-COVID-19 era, trade preferences will become easier for countries from South Asia to return to the world market, though it is believed that governments from the South Asian region face challenges to combat the crisis. However, the nations will emerge stronger than before. In the post COVID era, South Asian nations will exert more pressure on economic development. (Wagner and Scholz, 2020).

COVID-19 is a new phenomenon for the world; both developed and developing countries have been affected equally. For future purposes, developing countries have learnt a lesson that they are more vulnerable as compared to the developed countries, and they lack awareness and education among vulnerable groups, lack good personal hygiene and special transport facility for COVID-19 patients and the dead, etc. (Nafees and Khan, 2020).

Conclusion

South Asia entered the global pandemic with inadequate social protection. Several people have been infected with the corona virus. However, the peak is yet to come in different countries of South Asia. COVID-19 has impacted the socio-economy of South Asian countries. Millions of people have lost their jobs and are being pushed into extreme poverty. South Asian countries need to ensure that the impact of COVID-19 proactively does not target vulnerable and marginalized people. After the COVID-19 era, the problem will not vanish easily. The economies of South Asian countries will become zero or negative this year. Rapid economic growth in the past 25 years has enabled South Asian countries to bring about a significant reduction in absolute poverty, which will now increase once again along with economic inequality. The sharing of accurate information is the best practice in the current situation of COVID-19 and countering the rapid spread of false and sometimes dangerous misinformation. The COVID-19 crisis has given India an opportunity to leverage its image and reputation as a trusted, neutral friend and build on its strong capabilities in key sectors such as pharmaceuticals, medicine, biotechnology, clean energy and humanitarian recovery. Academics and healthcare professionals in South Asia with more than 1.9 billion people must stand together if they have to overcome what is probably the greatest public health challenge of our generation.

Future Scope of the Work

This study opens avenues for researchers, policymakers, scientists, etc., to further investigate the extent and impact of the corona virus on different South Asian countries. More study is needed on the role of various South Asian governments in order to provide measures and procedures to combat the virus and prevent it from spreading around the world.

Limitations of this Study

Time constraint was the main problem in preparing this paper. To better understand the impact of the novel corona virus disease, a detailed research study is needed on a larger scale, including the study of primary sources, as this research paper is entirely based on secondary sources.

REFERENCES

Alok, Anupriya. (2020). Impact of COVID-19 on migrant workers: issues and challenges. *International Journal of Research and Review*. vol. 7, no. 7, pp. 143-152.

Anwar, Saeed; Nasrullah, M and Hosen, Jakir Mohammad. (2020). COVID-19 and Bangladesh: Challenges and how to address them. *Frontiers in Public Health*. vol. 8, no. 5, 1-8. DOI: https://doi.org/10.3389/fpubh.2020.00154

Bangladesh Bureau of Statistics (2015). Slum census and floating population 2014. Dhaka. Available at http://203.112.218.65:8008/webtestapplication/

Bangladesh Bureau of Statistics. Population and Housing Census 2011, National volume 2: Union statistics. Dhaka 2015. Available at http://www.bbs.gov.bd/

Bastola A.; Sah, R.; Morales, A.J.R.; Lal, B.K.; Jha, R.; Ojha, H.C. and Pandey, B.D. (2020). The first 2019 novel corona virus case in Nepal. *The Lancet*, vol. 20, no. 3, 279-280. DOI: https:doi.org/10.1016/S1473-3099(20)30067-0

Bhattacharjee, Dhrubajyoti. (2020). South Asia and Covid-19: The present challenges and upcoming trends.

Chalise, Hom Nath. (2020). South Asia is more vulnerable to COVID-19 pandemic. *Archives of Psychiatry and Mental Health*. vol. 4, 046-047. DOI: https://doi.org/10.29328/journal.apmh.1001018

Chawla, Shalini. (2020). COVID-19 and Pakistan: Dimensions of the surging crisis. Centre for Air Power Studies. (CAPS).

COVID-19 and South Asia, 2020. www.unescap.org (accessed 20 September 2020).

COVID-19, National Institute of Health Islamabad. https://www.nih.org.pk/ (accessed 6 September 2020).

Gill, Peter and Sapkota, Raj Janak. (2020). COVID-19: Nepal in crisis. *The Diplomat*. Thediplomat.com/2020/06/covid-19-nepal-in-crisis/ (accessed 25 August 2020).

H.A.L. Javed. (2020). Passengers from Europe Land in Dhaka despite ban. DOI: https://www.dhakatribune.com (accessed on August 25, 2020).

Latif, Binte Mahmuda; Irin, Anjuman and Ferdaus Jannatul (2016). Socio-economic and health status of slum dwellers of the Kalyanpur slum in Dhaka city. *Bangladesh Journal of Scientific Research*. vol. 29, no 1, pp. 73-83. DOI: https:///doi.org/10.3329/bjsr.v29i1.29760

M.H. Maswood and S.L Chowdhury. (2020). Bangladesh bans travellers' entry from Europe. https://www.newagebd.net/article/102202/bangladesh-bans-travelers-entry-from-europe (accessed 30 August 2020).

Mehrdad Ezzatullah, "How Afghanistan failed to contain COVID-19", *The Diplomat*, March 27, 2020. DOI: https://thediplomat.com/2020/03/how-afghanistan-failed-to-contain-covid-19 (accessed August 28, 2020).

Mousavi, Sayed; Giang, Hoang Ali; Al-Ahdal and M. Tareq. (2020). The first COVID-19 case in Afghanistan acquired from Iran. *The Lancet Infectious Diseases*. vol. 20, no. 6, 1. DOI: https:doi.org/10.1016/S1473-3099(20)30231-0

Nafees, M. and Khan, Farukh. (2020). Pakistan's response to COVID-19 pandemic and efficacy of quarantine and partial lockdown: A review. *Electronic Journal of General*

Medicine 17, no. 6: em 240, pp. 1-4. DOI: https://doi.org/10.29333/ejgm/7951

Nanayakkara Saman, Nakandala Piumi, Nakandala Upuli, and Nanayakkara Indumathie. A Review on COVID-19: A Global and Sri Lanka Perspective. (2020). *American Journal of Multidisciplinary Research and Development* (AJMRD). vol. 2, no. 8, 63-70.

Paul, Abhijit; Chatterjee, Samrat and Bairagi, Nandadulal. (2020). medRxiv. 1-3. DOI: https://doi.org/10.1101/2020.04.08.20055095

Pouder, Kritika and Subedi, Pramod. (2020). Impact of COVID-19 pandemic on socio economic and mental health aspects in Nepal. *International Journal of Social Psychiatry*. vol. 66, no. 8, 748-755. DOI: https://doi.org/10.1177/0020764020942247

Ranjan, Amit. (2020). COVID-19 crisis in Bhutan: An opportunity to boost agriculture. *Institution of South Asian Studies*. www.isas.nus.edu.sg

Rehman ur Zia, Habib; Abi, Maria and Mehsud, Tipu Ihsanullah. (2020). God will protect us: Corona virus spreads through an already struggling Pakistan, *The New York Times*. https://www.nytimes.com/

Saqlain M.; Munir, Muddasir M.; Ahmed Ali; Tahir Hussain Azhar and Kamran Sohail. (2020). Is Pakistan prepared to tackle the corona virus epidemic? *Drugs and Therapy Perspectives*. vol. 36, no. 5, pp. 1-2. DOI: https://doi.org/10.1007/s40267-020-00721-1

Shah Jaffer; Karimzadeh, Sedighe, Ali, Al–Ahdal; M. Tareq; Mousavi, Hamed Sayed; Zahidullah Shafi and Hey Tien Ngeyen. (2020). COVID-19: the current situation in Afghanistan. *The Lancet*. vol. 8. 771-772. DOI: https:doi.org/10.1016/S2214-109x(20)30124-8

Sri Lanka announces first corona virus case, *India Today*, March 11 2020. https://www.indiatoday.in/world/story/sri-lanka-coronavirus-italian-1654323-2020-03-11 (accessed August 23, 2020).

Wagner, Christian and Scholz, Tobias. (2020). South Asia in the Corona Crisis. *Stiftung Wissenschaft und politik*, no 19, pp. 1-4.

14

Multilateralism in Nepal's Foreign Policy: Need of the Hour in Post COVID-19 Asia

Sandhya Rani

ABSTRACT

When the COVID-19 pandemic broke out in China and became a global menace, little did the economies of the world think that it would affect the big and small economies alike. Nepal, one of the Least Developed Countries (LDCs) in South Asia, having an open border with India and China, has been badly affected by the pandemic too.

When the pandemic became severe, the first reaction of the nations was to shut their borders for all activities. The countries adopted a protectionist attitude towards the pandemic, but the question arises: Is it possible to protect oneself unilaterally against this pandemic in this way? This question needs to be answered, especially in the context of Asia, where the two biggest economies, China and India, are facing each other on their borders. Amid this situation, there also exists an uncomfortable situation between India and Nepal when the latter has expressed its territorial claims over Limpiyadhura, Kalapani, and Lipulekh areas.

Few major factors that have helped in accelerating the rate of infection in these SAARC countries can be no proper screening, monitoring or quarantine facilities at airports, and lack of preparedness and prior management even though it appeared first in different regions/parts of the world: hence, giving more time for the virus to spread at enormous speed. Now, when the virus has spread fully, there is a shortage of test kits as these South Asian countries are densely populated, leaving many infected and vulnerable to this dreaded disease.

One thing is evident that in this integrated world, uncoordinated unilateral responses will not help in overcoming the economic depression of this pandemic;

hence, a multilateral approach is the need of the hour. The major actors of international development cooperation need to take action soon to create targeted international support measures involving factors such as food aid, market access of exports, availability of vaccines, concessional financial flow, debt cancellation, etc.

In this context, this paper aims to argue that in the post COVID-19 world, Nepal needs to adopt a multilateral approach in its foreign policy towards the two very close Asian neighbours, i.e., India and China.

Keywords: *Multilateralism, pandemic, foreign policy, Nepal, India, China.*

Introduction

As the virus originated in Wuhan, China, the immediate impact was on travel, tourism and other related industries. Restrictions and bans on visitors from China, flight suspensions, travel advisories, and a more cautious approach to travel owing to a fear of contagion have all led to a sharp drop in the economies of countries through the tourism sector, both foreign and domestic.

Be it a superpower, a rising power, an emerging power or small powers, none were left out by the pandemic. In fact, since globalisation took off, COVID-19 has been the first pandemic that the world has experienced badly without knowing how to cope with it. The USA, India, Italy, Spain, the United Kingdom and France have been the most affected countries so far (Lee, 2020).[1] Even international institutions are not immune to 'virus' geopolitics. Though there had been many heated trade debates among the global powers, fortunately, US and Chinese hospitals and doctors had been in close contact and initiating long-term cooperative projects, which can be taken as mutual benefitting agreements between the two countries. (Yu, 2020).[2]

As of the month of September 2020, in Nepal, the total cases were 69,301, with a recovered population of 50,411 and deaths accounting for 453 (Worldometer, 2020).[3] It should be noted that this number might be even more as Nepal is a developing country with no availability of test kits, and many deaths may go unnoticed among the people who remain unchecked or reside in the interior regions of the country. India, with its huge population, is unable to control the COVID-19 infection too. One aspect that is very striking is that the infected patients comprise young populations in SAARC countries, which show that their ratio is more when compared with the older generation in these countries. There are many workers who do not have written job contracts, and there is a practice of improper hiring and firing of employees in many factories, mills, and companies in this COVID-19 environment. Also, it is the young population that works as daily labourers and hence are more exposed to infections, infecting themselves as well as others. Based on the population scale and the COVID-19 tests are done, it is India, Pakistan and Bangladesh where the infected population is more, and the death toll is high. This also shows that all age groups are susceptible to infection.

The South Asian countries affected by COVID-19 and the status of the major power is shown in Table 1. It shows that the pandemic is a global emergency (Ibid).[4]

Table 1

Sl. No.	*Country*	*No. of Infected Cases*	*No. of Infected Deaths*	*Tests/Million Population*
1	Afghanistan	54,672	2,385	6,057
2	Bangladesh	531,799	8,023	21,469
3	Bhutan	855	1	541,201
4	India	10,668,674	153,508	138,603
5	The Maldives	14,993	51	706,557
6	Nepal	269,450	2,001	69,274
7	Pakistan	534,041	11,318	34,394
8	Sri Lanka	58,430	283	74,248
A	China	89,115	4,635	111,163
B	USA	25,783,220	429,490	900,568
C	World	99,783,220	2,139,229	

The total cases worldwide, as of now, has reached 99,783,220, where the recovered population accounts for 71,776,716 (97 per cent) and the death toll accounts for 2,139,229 (3 per cent) (Ibid).[5] The South Asian Association for Regional Cooperation (SAARC), a COVID-19 Emergency Fund, is to support countries like Bangladesh, Bhutan, and Nepal. Nevertheless, the challenge is to see how effective it can prove in this pandemic, as SAARC has been unsuccessful for so many decades.

Nepal's Foreign Policy for India and China

The term 'foreign policy of a nation', according to the Research Staff of the Brookings Institution, refers to the complex and dynamic political course that a nation follows in relation to other states. It is more than the sum total of foreign policies (throughout courses of action to achieve objectives) and also includes its commitments, the current forms of its national interests and objectives and the principles of right conduct that it professes.

Nepal is not only one of the least developed countries but is also a landlocked country; hence, it is more dependent on its immediate neighbours. Also, India alone provides it with a sea route. Irrespective of their size, population and varying levels of development, India and China are close friends with Nepal. Hence, the geographical topography of a country becomes a major factor for determining its history, culture, economy, demographic composition, eco-system, and the basic parameters of its foreign policy. Nepal is abundant in water resources, and through this enormous availability of water, it can overcome its poverty status by providing electricity to various parts of the country. According to records, lack of electricity is one of the major factors that creates a loss of job opportunities and loss in industrial development; many other sectors lag behind because of electricity scarcity.

Nepal gradually opened up since the 1950s and followed a policy of neutrality and non-alignment (Muni, 1973: 59).[6] In 1973, at the Non-Aligned Movement summit in Algiers, King Birendra proposed the idea of Nepal being considered as a Zone of Peace, and since then, for quite a long time, this has been the main theme of Nepal's foreign policy. With the endorsement of India and the former Soviet Union, many United Nations member countries have accepted Nepal as a Zone of Peace at the global forum. Nepal has been an active member of the United Nations and is also a founding member of the South Asian Association for Regional Cooperation (SAARC). Because of its geographical proximity and historical links with India and China, Nepal's foreign policy has been to focus mainly on maintaining close and friendly relations with both these countries along with safeguarding its national security and independence.

Prime Minister K.P. Sharma Oli, during his visit to Beijing in June 2018, made it very clear that they want Nepal to be a land-linked country between the two neighbours and do not want to hold on to the status of a land-locked country as it has been known for a long time in the past. This policy of Nepal to act as a bridge between India and China can be a welcoming one because no matter what the location of these countries is, it is unchangeable. To overcome these insecurity concerns because of porous border problems or to decrease the influential position of China in Nepal, India now has to look for ways to solve these controversies and seriously take firm steps in terms of supplying trade facilities, connectivity improvement, hydropower projects, and infrastructure development. As Nepal is a sovereign country and also one of the least developed countries, it does look up to someone friendly or whoever can facilitate it with its national needs. It is very well known that China's engagement in Nepal is not new and would increase in the days to come, which makes India insecure and uncomfortable because of its geostrategic location (Bhattarai, 2018).[7] India is aware of China's unmatched economic power that makes it more insecure. However, this insecurity is of no consequence unless India is able to challenge China, which, as of now, seems to be a time-taking race. India also has to manage its own border and political issues with Nepal first. Otherwise, it may very soon lose the privileged position it has in Nepal. On the other hand, Nepal is very clear in its stand as Prime Minister Khadga Prasad Sharma Oli, on his first visit to India and then to China, mentioned that it wants to keep a balanced relationship with both these Asian countries.

The factors responsible for Nepal's shift towards China can be India's reluctance towards hydropower projects, the trade and transit crisis (blockade of 2015) and border area issues. Nepal signed the Belt and Road Initiative (BRI) in 2017. The recent visit of President Xi to Kathmandu clearly manifests China's attempt to secure the space that India occupied in Nepal. Twenty agreements were signed between Nepal and China, including one for Nepal's support to BRI. This will not only prove a great asset to China to make its presence felt in different parts of Nepal but will also help China to have access to the Indo-Nepal border through Nepalese territory (Jha, 2019).[8] China's main objective of trilateral trade to use Nepalese territory as a transit point is to target the vast Indian market, mainly in Bihar and Uttar Pradesh, whose population is over ten times more than Nepal and would come true through the BRI without involving India much. This will not be beneficial for India.

Fig. 1: The Planned Extension of the Qinghai-Tibet Railway to Kerung (Gyirong) and into Nepal

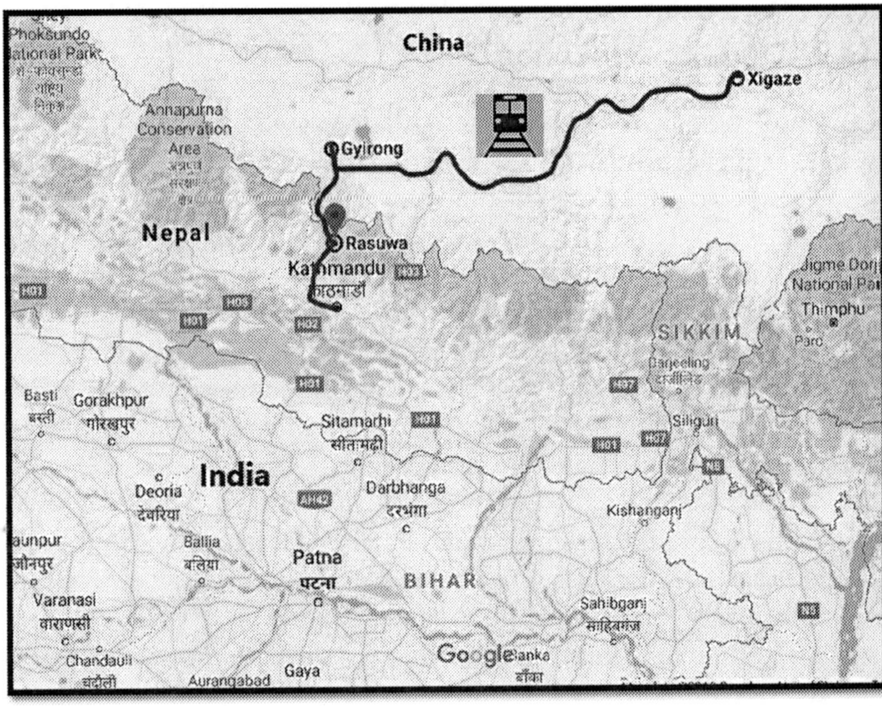

Source: Google maps

The Chinese Qinghai-Tibet railway is operational up to Shigatse and is expected to reach Nepal through the border (Rasuwagadi) in Gyirong. From there onwards, a 100-kilometre-long railway would run up to Kathmandu (Khatri, 2020).[9] China has already started sending cargoes on freight trains from Lanzhou to Kathmandu via Shigatse, where merchandise is loaded on trucks; a combined transportation system comprising rail and truck via that route reduces the journey substantially. It takes only ten days by this route that earlier used to be 35 days through the maritime route via Kolkata. Hence, the Chinese railway in Kerung can thus increase Sino-Nepal trade and commerce, which would be a compulsory and necessary requirement post-COVID-19.

Also, the economic viability of the Gyirong-Raxaul (India) route is a dilemma as India wants its own centrality in the project, whereas China prefers to reach out to the Gangetic Plain via Nepal. Nepal, at the same, is looking at this opportunity to boost its tourism sector post the pandemic. The visits of Chinese pilgrims and tourists to Lumbini, the birthplace of the Buddha, will no doubt enhance the tourism sector, which has been badly affected during this whole year. Nepal cannot afford more of this as it would be one of the best opportunities to boost its economy through the tourism sector.

Fig. 2: Nepal's East-West Railway Network and the Kathmandu-Pokhara-Lumbini Network will be Linked to the China-Nepal railway at the Rasuwagadi-Gyirong Border

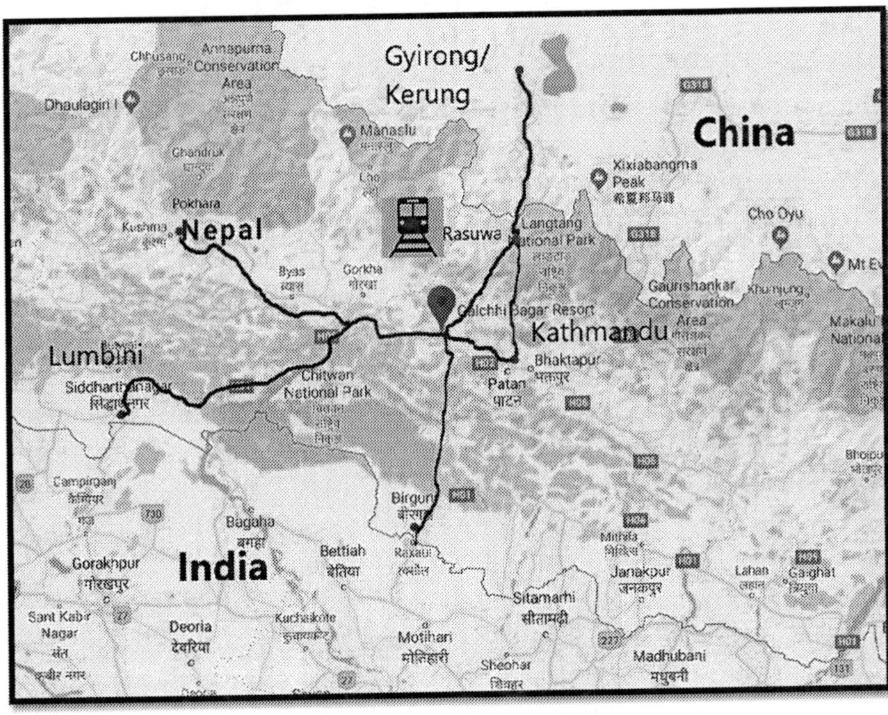

Source: Google maps

The Nepal Prime Minister's comment in May 2020 that the "Indian virus looks more lethal than the Chinese and Italian now" has been a very controversial one which points towards the country's state of mind during the pandemic, i.e., is Nepal behaving like this under the influence of China or is it taking advantage of the pandemic crisis. The two countries should work on these issues as it will be helpful for India to solve its insecurity over China's presence in Nepal. It is well known that trade and commerce are not only made easier for Nepal, but China also takes advantage of this porous border. Thus, the statement by the Prime Minister is a controversial one (as the world knows that the virus originated in the Wuhan province of China), and both these countries are seizing leverage of the porous border and playing the blame game that will not be positive for either country's relationship. Moreover, the countries need to be supportive of each other during these COVID-19 times; it does seem that Nepal is trying to take advantage of this pandemic situation, supposedly in its own way and not knowing how beneficial it would prove for Nepal.

India and China, the Present Status

India's unresolved territorial issues with China have played a major role in creating an unstable relationship between them. China's attempt to prevent United Nations Security Council sanctions against Jaish-e-Mohammed (JeM) founder Masood Azhar, one of the alleged masterminds of the attack on India's Uri military base in 2016, had destabilised their relations in the past. Recently, the construction of a village across the Line of Actual Control (LAC) in Arunachal Pradesh has added to the number of disputed issues between these two Asian giants (Krishnan, 2021).[10] Its heavy infrastructure building exercises in India's neighbourhood, such as ports, bridges, railways and interconnecting roads through the BRI (in which India is not yet a participant), represents its multiplying engagements and influence at India's periphery, creating geostrategic tension for it. In 2017, when Sri Lanka was unable to repay the Belt and Road loan, it handed over the Hambantota deep-sea port to China for 99 years, and if a similar situation through the BRI arises in any other country in the periphery of India, it would certainly create a very disturbing situation for India (Jha, 2019).[11]

In spite of this behaviour of China, the leaders of both these countries met informally in April 2018 at Wuhan, followed by meetings of the Shanghai Cooperation Organization (SCO) summit in June at Qingdao and the BRICS summit in July 2018. This shows that when India has always been ready for communication and development, then why not join hands for post-pandemic development. As China may recover faster than most other pandemic-hit countries because of its economic efficiency, India's image as a reliable partner cannot be ignored by the rest of the world. Hence, India could be a coalition bridge with the rest of the countries through a regime of incentives and sanctions required in this pandemic situation. This approach of cooperation with some like-minded countries and decoupling with other countries (China) may shrink at the personal level, but it would provide more stable ground to the health of citizens health and other security issues. This multilateral approach could be more beneficial for India and Nepal amidst this pandemic crisis.

Role of International Institutions

In 2005, after the SARS outbreak, the World Health Organisation (WHO) revised its International Health Regulations (IHR) to strengthen its independent disease surveillance capacity. Following these guidelines, the WHO was supposed to foster a network of domestic healthcare systems across borders and offer standard guidelines to national health authorities. However, there was much delay in drafting these technical guidelines when COVID-19 hit various regions.

The pandemic, no doubt, has evolved from a global health crisis to a global financial, global economic and geopolitical crisis. Many countries have been claiming to wage war against this COVID-19 virus, but none has shown any positive, united effort to overcome it. Moreover, a course of rising nationalism and hostility can be noticed in the behaviour of countries such as the USA and China. However, at the same time, the pandemic has given the global or big powers the opportunity to find a common cause and purpose to demonstrate global leadership and join together to bridge their significant scientific resources for the benefit of all humankind. China, after controlling the pandemic outbreak first in its own region, stretched out its hand with medical equipment for hard-hit countries like Italy, Iran, Iraq, and South Korea. It should have shown close attention to Nepal too.

In producing the needed test kits, medicines, and vaccines,

governments must be ready to take responsibility to make sure that they are available to all the common people. At the same time, the vaccines should be affordable and accessible on a global scale and on digital platforms to eradicate this virus as quickly as possible.

To address the COVID-19 health crisis and its social and economic implications nationally and internationally, the implications must be guided by the principles of the 2030 Agenda for Sustainable Development and respect the pledge to leave no one out and safeguard human rights (Committee for Development Policy, 2020).[12]

BIMSTEC and ASEAN to Promote Multilateralism

Reimagining multilateralism in South and South-East Asia through BIMSTEC, ASEAN and SAARC can be taken as a positive perspective as well as a reviving technique.

The Bay of Bengal Initiative for Multi-Sectoral Economic and Technical Cooperation (BIMSTEC) was formed in 1997. The member countries at present are Bangladesh, India, Myanmar (1997), Sri Lanka, Thailand, Nepal, and Bhutan (2004). It was founded in June 1997 in Bangkok with the primary goal of technical and economic cooperation. There are 14 priority areas where the member-countries lead, i.e.:

1. **India:** (a) Transport and Communications, (b) Tourism, (c) Environment and Disaster Management, and (d) Counter-Terrorism and Transnational Crime (CTTC).
2. **Sri Lanka:** (a) Technology.
3. **Bangladesh:** (a) Trade and Investment, (b) Climate Change.
4. **Bhutan:** (a) Cultural Cooperation.
5. **Myanmar:** (a) Energy, (b) Agriculture.
6. **Nepal:** (a) Poverty Alleviation.
7. **Thailand:** (a) Fisheries, (b) Public Health, and (c) People-to-People Contact.

The BIMSTEC region accounts for 1.5 billion people and comprises almost 22 per cent population of the globe. This population provides for 2.7 trillion of the Gross Domestic Product (Sharma and Rathore, 2015, pgs. 5-7).[13] The global maritime shipping routes of the Bay of Bengal contribute to one-fourth of global trade, and the energy resources of this Bay are yet to be fully exploited by BIMSTEC member-states (Karan, 2018).[14]

The fourth Summit was held at Kathmandu in August 2018 to promote institutional reforms, and the signing of an MoU among the member-nations to establish the BIMSTEC Grid Interconnection was a necessary step (Palit and Tieri, 2019).[15] The 5th Summit to be held in Sri Lanka in January 2021 (it was supposed to be held in September 2020) to establish the BIMSTEC Development Fund for research and planning and financing projects, and increasing the number of directors from three to seven are very progressive steps (Ibid).[16] BIMSTEC completed 23 years on 1 June 2020. So, it is quite an old organisation now and since its inception has evolved into a mature regional organisation with the expansion of its members. The presence of all seven members in the online conference stresses the importance of strengthening institutional mechanisms and rationalizing BIMSTEC areas of cooperation, keeping in mind the challenges posed by the ongoing COVID-19 pandemic point to the sincerity of the members (Bhuiyan, 2020).[17] The Foreign Secretary of the Government of India, Mr Harsh Vardhan Shringla's visit to Dhaka on 18-19 August 2020 to discuss and take forward cooperation on matters of mutual interest such as India-Bangladesh connectivity and power projects is one of the boosting initiatives for this region. India's assistance for COVID-19 and capacity building training for Bangladeshi medical personnel was another main objective.

ASEAN

The total population of the Association of South-East Asian Nations (ASEAN) accounts for 620 million, and its aggregate economic size stands over US$ 2.5 trillion (i.e., the third-largest economy) and the intra-region trade accounts for 25 per cent (ASSOCHAM, 2016).[18] Brunei Darussalam, Indonesia, Malaysia, The Philippines, Singapore and Thailand have eliminated 99 per cent of their intra-regional tariffs. The Less Advanced members, i.e., Cambodia, Laos, Myanmar and Vietnam, have eliminated this to 90 per cent (Ibid).[19] This fact is mentioned here is to emphasise that the SAARC and BIMSTEC need the same attitude in order to succeed like the ASEAN. In these COVID-19 times when the entire economy is dead, the ASEAN can be one to harness the benefit for all the other regions as it is one of the richest regions in the world in terms of natural and mineral resources. All the areas such as energy, transport, trade, investment and communications are hindered by this pandemic, and this region could play a major role in linking the region as well as opening it up to South-East and East Asia. The announcement of $ 1 million to the ASEAN COVID-19 Response Fund at the 17th ASEAN-India Summit held virtually in November 2020 shows Indian support to the international community (Chaudhury, 2020).[20] Mutual trust, prosperity for all, stability and peace for all is the demand of post-pandemic times, and unity alone can resolve this vast economic and trade gap.

Revival of SAARC for Multilateralism

The video conferencing of SAARC member countries can be seen as a positive engagement towards multilateralism promoting regionalism and coordination. Despatching a 14-member medical team from the defence forces, including doctors and paramedics, to the Maldives to assist in fighting the pandemic is another very important step (Datta, 2020).[21] The meeting of senior health professionals of SAARC countries through the video conferencing to exchange experiences of combating the spread of COVID-19 can be considered as another helpful engagement. One of the reviving steps taken by SAARC during this pandemic is the creation of a COVID-19 Emergency Fund based on voluntary contributions from all the SAARC member countries in the month of April 2020. It can be used by any of these countries to meet the cost of immediate action and medical requirements (Mishra, 2020).[22] It may be mentioned that success lies if only the platforms of these organisations are actively used to overcome this global crisis, which has been prevalent for quite a long time.

Table 2: Contributions by SAARC Member-Countries (Ibid)23

Sl. No.	*Country*	*Contribution (million)*
1	Afghanistan	US$ 1
2	Bangladesh	US$ 1.5
3	Bhutan	US$ 1
4	India	US$ 10
5	The Maldives	US$ 2
6	Nepal	US$ 1
7	Pakistan	US$ 3
8	Sri Lanka	US$ 5

SAARC countries account for about 21 per cent of the world's population and comprise the poorest population. About 33.4 per cent population lives on or less than US$ 1.90/day income. Most of this population is uneducated, underprivileged, ignorant about health issues and careless about the government's directives with regard to their safety. However, they cannot stay in their homes for months, even during lockdown times, as they have to make their living somehow during these COVID-19 times. So, after a few months of strict laws and regulations, this poor population has been unable to survive in various South Asian countries and perforce had to expose themselves for daily wages and to the virus. Now, as the economy has failed badly, the government is slowly opening various public facilities, although the virus spread is still at its peak. Hence, financial aid and support become a must for them.

Nepal hosts the SAARC Tuberculosis and HIV/AIDS Centre (STAC). It was established with the vision of a TB and HIV/AIDS-free generation in the SAARC region. It started functioning as SAARC TB Centre in 1994 and was renamed as SAARC Tuberculosis and HIV/AIDS Centre in November 2007. The laboratories must join hands with global institutions, NGOs and regional institutions to overcome this pandemic. The healthcare in these countries is not developed adequately to tackle such a pandemic, and even hospitals are not well equipped with even minimum requirements like oxygen supplies, ventilators and ICUs for COVID-19 patients. Various sectors and departments formed must now jointly come together and implement the required projects.

Lack of Implementation and Integrated Plans for the Proper Management of COVID-19 in SAARC Countries

The private sector can play a major role here, but none are moving ahead with government plans as of now. The ruling and opposition parties should set aside their personal political games for some time as the pandemic is dangerous for the whole of humankind. Corruption in the administration at various levels is another major factor in the deterioration of the country's economic condition. Different ministries such as Health, Disaster Management and Relief, Home Affairs and Defence must work together in full coordination as any loopholes would only promote the pandemic further. Various local organizations like Epidemiology and Disease Control Division (EDCD) of Nepal, National Centre for Disease Control (NCDC); Institute under the Indian Directorate-General of Health Services, Royal Centre for Disease Control (RCDC) of Bhutan, Institute of Epidemiology, Disease Control and Research (IEDCR) of Bangladesh, Pakistan National Institute of Health (NIH) and the Epidemiology Unit of Sri Lanka are working closely with governments and coordinating and updating awareness action plans in accordance with the World Health Organisation (Sultana & Reza, 2020).[24] However, monitoring and implementation of these various institutes are not up to the measures required to contain the pandemic at the global level. In 1985, for greater economic and cultural cooperation, the South Asian Association of Regional Cooperation was founded in Dhaka, comprising India's immediate neighbours with China still at the Observer status. It may be expected that the time has come to make it successful in this post-COVID-19 situation.

Few Actions to be followed at Unit/Internal Levels

1. Making use of a face mask is a regular basic habit, and remaining indoors must be taken as a 'must-do' action to prevent virus transmission from one human to another human. It is a very effective and cheap method as recommended by the WHO.
2. Radio, television, online newspapers and social media must be used effectively for disseminating various information related to the COVID-19 pandemic as people tend to normalize situations very quickly, which at ground level is not the case with this pandemic. Celebrities must come forward as people listen and are attracted to them.
3. After almost a year of this pandemic eruption, there are areas that are not safe for people; hence, identifying such clusters of COVID-19 hotspots must be strictly monitored.
4. Must be prepared with more quarantine centres such as factories and sports complexes. Managing workplace hygiene and avoiding large gatherings for longer durations is necessary as the temples, malls, churches and marketplaces have started to operate.

Few Multilateral Approaches

1. Government/international institutions must provide food, medicines, disinfectants and essential commodities to labourers and workers. Financial security and optimal health facility must be provided to the general public.
2. Trade multilateralism or open and free trade, i.e., to keep borders devoid of restrictions only for smooth trade flow and also of lifesaving equipment, can be another step to tackle this pandemic quickly.
3. The World Food Programme (WFP) deployment of various aircraft, cargo aircraft and smaller passenger planes for infected patients for transporting aid workers is one major multilateral approach. The UN, a COVID-19 Supply Task Force initiative run by the WHO and the WFP in various countries such as China, Malaysia, Belgium and Ghana, is the other important step to overcome this pandemic. The solution lies in the fact that SAARC, BIMSTEC and ASEAN should also keep on organising similar supply chains for remote places so that the newly-arrived COVID-19 vaccine reaches all regions of the world smoothly.

The Arrival of the COVID-19 Vaccine

The COVID-19 vaccine manufactured by the Serum Institute of India is a huge relief for the people of India as well as for SAARC countries. According to the latest news, over 16 lakh healthcare workers across India have received shots of the COVID-19 vaccine. India shipped vaccine doses to Bhutan, Bangladesh, Nepal and the Maldives. Sri Lanka, too will receive it soon. This move of India has been applauded by the Bureau of South and Central Asian Affairs in the US State Department (Dwivedi, 2021).[25] Globally, around 63.41 million shots have already been given to citizens. South Korea and Taiwan are countries that managed to control the devastation with the help of rapid tests and targeted solutions at the beginning of this pandemic would also be now benefited by the vaccine. China, the most populous country with the help of digital technology, contained the spread of COVID-19 in most of its major cities. The common factor here is the application of digital technology such as Artificial Intelligence and Machine Learning (AI-ML) to contain the transmission of COVID-19 and also share data and information on it quickly (De, 2020).[26] Presently, the supply of medical goods and vaccines are needed to be provided by these various regional institutions with a multilateral approach. A firm commitment for inclusive development of the whole region with a unit multilateral vision can only lead to overcoming this pandemic paralysis, which has to be understood by various global and regional organisations.

NOTES

1. Lee, Jong Sook (2020), "Covid-19 infects international organisations", *East Asia Forum*, 21 April 2020.
2. Yu, Ye, (2020), "Triple headed crisis calls for global cooperation", *East Asia Forum*, 29 April 2020.
3. Worldometer, (2020), https://www.worldometers.info/coronavirus/country/india/, accessed 23 September 2020.
4. Ibid.
5. Ibid.
6. Muni, S.D. (1973), *Foreign Policy of Nepal* (1st edn.), New Delhi: National Publishing House.
7. Bhattarai, Kamal, Dev, (2018), "The China-India-Nepal Triangle: Will India Agree to cooperate with China in Nepal's Development?", *The Diplomat*, 25 April 2018.
8. Jha, Hari, Bansh, (2019), "Xi Jinping's visit to Nepal: A diplomatic victory for China?", *Observer Research Foundation*, New Delhi, 23 October 2019.
9. Khatri, Raunab, Singh, (2020,) "BRI and trans-Himalayan connectivity", *Nepali Times*, Kathmandu, 9 August 2020.
10. Krishnan, Ananth, (2021), "China defends new village in Arunachal Pradesh amid border construction push", *The Hindu*, New Delhi, 21 January 2021.
11. Jha, Hari Bansh, (2019), "Chinese Investment in Nepal in the Context of BRI", *Vivekananda International Foundation*, New Delhi, 11 October 2019.
12. Committee for Development Policy (2020), *Development Policy and Multilateralism after Covid-19*, United Nations, July.
13. Sharma, Aparna & Rathore, Chetna K., (2015), *"BIMSTEC and BCIM Initiatives and their Importance for India"*, Discussion Paper, Jaipur: CUTS International.
14. Karan, Rahul, (2018), "Acting Beyond Borders-An Action Plan for Reorienting BIMSTEC", *Chennai Centre for China Studies*, Chennai.
15. Palit, Amitendu & Tieri, Silvia, (2019), "BIMSTEC: Prospects for reconnecting the Bay of Bengal", National University of Singapore.
16. Ibid.
17. Bhuiyan, Humayun K., (2020), "Bimstec Charter finalized 23 years after inception", *Dhaka Tribune*, 2 September, 2020.
18. The Associated Chambers of Commerce and Industry of India, (2016), *India ASEAN Trade and Investment Relations: Opportunities and Challenges*, ASSOCHAM, New Delhi.

19. Ibid.
20. Chaudhury, Roy D., (2020), "India announces $1 million aid to ASEAN Covid-19 Response Fund", *The Economic Times*, 13 November 2020.
21. Datta, Dr. Sreeradha, (2020), "BIMSTEC Should Address the Common Covid-12 Crisis: Preparatory Mechanisms need to be put in place", *Vivekananda International Foundation*, New Delhi, 17 March 2020.
22. Mishra, Dr. Vivek, (2020), "SAARC's Resurrection: Leadership in the Time of Covid-19", *Indian Council of World Affairs*, New Delhi, 1 April 2020.
23. Ibid.
24. Sultana, Farhana & Reza, Mahmud Hasan, (2020), Are SAARC countries prepared to combat Covid-19 to save young working-age population? *Public Health*, North South University, Bangladesh, 1 July 2020.
25. Dwivedi, Sukriti, (2021), India Vaccinates 10 lakh people in six days, faster than US, UK: Centre, https://www.ndtv.com/india-news/covid-vaccination-drive-india-vaccinates-over-15-lakh-in-a-week-after-slow-start-2357234
26. De, Prabir, (2020), "COVID-19, New Normal", *The Economic Times*, 9 April 2020.

15

New Bipolarity: A Bliss or a Curse for the Future of India

Haridass S.

Welcome to the 21st century, an era of bipolarity. Since the beginning of the 21st century, the Chinese economy has been growing at a rapid speed. The Chinese GDP in 2007 was growing at a speed of 12.7 per cent, which helped the country to face the 2008 economic crisis with a budget surplus at a time when all the other nations of the world, especially the West, was facing a budget deficit thanks to the Chinese export-driven economy. This surplus revenue that was available to the socialist government of China helped the country to come out of the crisis aggressively with a stimulus package of US$ 586 billion. This reprisal of the Chinese economy out of the crisis questioned the century-long Washington Consensus related to market leadership, which failed to give solutions to the East Asian crisis and caused the subprime crisis, whereas the Beijing Consensus based on authoritarian ruling and state intervention in the economy got prominence. This change and the rise of a new consensus laid the foundation for the new bipolar world.

Consequently, in 2008, China became the largest foreign creditor to the USA; the Chinese gave credit to the USA in return for the US market, which led to China becoming the second-largest economy in the world in 2010; this phenomenon was informally called Chimerica.

This Chimerica, in the long run, became a threat to the US economy. In 2016, the US trade shortfall rose to US$ 375.6 billion from US$ 103.1 billion in 2002. All these led to the trade war between the two, and their altercations began to spill over into the global system. The consequent decoupling of the two created a world system with two dominant players competing to enlarge their footprint in the world. In this new great game between the two poles, most of their geo-strategy is directed towards the South Asian region and, most importantly, India. This was majorly due to two reasons. First, the country's geographical positioning at the heart of India's ocean through 70 per cent of world trade and 90 per cent of oil trade passes. Among the other nations in the Indian Ocean rim, India has the potential to control this region, which it is already doing with the IORA and similar other actions. Along with this, India's close geographical proximity with the new rising super power, China, shares a large portion of its borders. Second, India is now among the fastest-growing economies of the world, and it is estimated that by 2030 it will be the third-largest. India is the second-most populous country in the world with rich human capital; the majority of its population in the middle age category serves as a rich resource, and they are the biggest market for the world. Being at the centre of the new great game, India now has an opportunity to utilise this great decoupling between the poles to satisfy its national interests. However, it can also become prey to the great game at the same time.

India's Relations with the USA and China

India is the pivot of the South Asia region. Unfortunately, it never had a cordial relationship with either of the contemporary poles—the USA and China. Two important elements—trust and mutual interest—were always missing between the two and India. With China, since the independence of both the nations, they have been fighting over the borders, beginning from the Sino-Indian war to the present-day standoff in the Ladakh region. The major reason is the conflict of interest, born at almost the same time. Both the nations are vying to be Asia's undisputed superpower, and they are suspicious about each other's intentions. If China is dominating the world with its manufacturing potential, India is overpowering China in services. In technology, India was ahead of China, but in the recent decade, the latter has overtaken India and moved towards attaining global dominance. In the overall sense, in the recent decade, China has overpowered India. However, this does not end here, as both the nations are nuclear powers with large armies. China has always been a strong ally of Pakistan, and with the CPEC, it got intensified. Similarly, the continuous support India has given to the Tibetan refugees and monks vexed China. These actions of both nations create a sense of insecurity and trust deficit between them.

When it comes to the USA, since the time of India's independence, it has been a strong ally of Pakistan during the cold war. Even though India remained non-aligned, it had close bilateral relations with Russia, which supplied India with capital machinery as part of India's First Five Year Plan. This proxy support by both the powers deepened with the first India-Pakistan war of 1965 when the USA indirectly supported Pakistan. This close proximity of the USA with Pakistan was witnessed multiple times thereafter, even during the 1971 war. This USA-Pakistan relation got more intensified with the 1979 Soviet invasion of Afghanistan, where the USA, with the help of Pakistan, instilled instability in the region with the creation of the Taliban, which indirectly impacted the Kashmir region with the inception of the Mujahideen. All these things together instilled in the minds of Indian leaders that America could never be trusted. India's relationship with the USA has always been cautious.

The year 2014 is the year of a paradigm shift as many new changes in the world that we are seeing today began then. When China became the second-largest economy in 2010, the USA became cautious. In 2011, the USA announced its Pivot-to-Asia policy to counter China and, finally, in 2012, it realised the rising trade deficit when it reached an all-time high of 295.5 billion dollars. This ignited the spark between the two, which erupted in 2015 in the South China Sea before the start of a trade war in 2016. In 2014, the Afghan issue dried up. The USA started withdrawing its troops from Afghanistan; this shift in US national interest has limited the need for Pakistan. The new strategy for the USA is to counter China. For that, it needs India rather than Pakistan as a strategic partner. However, the India-USA relationship is not restricted to satisfying each other's strategic interests but to bolster each other's economies, as mentioned earlier. Since the LPG reforms of 1991, the Indian economy has grown today to become the fifth-largest economy and as the second-most populous country of the world, becoming, in the process, the biggest market for US products after China.

In the same year, India's domestic politics shifted from an idealistic to a neo-realist leadership. When Prime Minister Modi came to power in 2014, his first objective was to work hard towards the development of India. For that, India needed to bridge ties with both powers that would help the country to come out of the slowdown that we witnessed, develop the country and finally make India a regional hegemon. For this, the support of both the poles is a necessary element for India. The defence partnership between India and the USA intensified at the same time as the economic partnership with China grew. China in 2015 pledged 20 billion USD investment in the Indian economy.

However, things started changing. In 2016, the rift between the two poles began to have a spillover on the world arena in the form of a trade war between the two large economies—this consequent decoupling between the two divided the world into power blocs. At the same time, the Chinese expansionist policy that India always saw as a threat reached the Indian borders with China's ambitious BRI and String of Pearls initiative. This encircled India from all sides and increased its strategic presence in the region. This, combined with China's close relations with Pakistan, which got upgraded with the CPEC, made the Indian administration more insecure. From the Doklam standoff in 2017 till the recent standoff in the Ladakh region, the Chinese aggression across the Indian border necessitated the need for India to have a close tie-up with the USA. This insecurity has become a common ground for both the USA and India to cooperate.

This great decoupling between the two is a blessing in disguise for India. When the USA decided to move away from China, which used to be the biggest trading partner of the USA, it necessitated the need for the USA to find an alternative power and market in the world that had the potential to equate with China. As mentioned earlier, India is the best alternative for China. India, since 2014, also undertook various measures like Make in India and Made in India that made sure that

India is all set with the necessary infrastructure in place required to attract the world's nations. These measures paid off today as the USA is working towards making India the next generation manufacturing hub starting from the technology sector.

Bliss of Bipolarity

This trade war started in 2016 to overcome the trade deficit of the USA with China and to take care of IPR violations by the Chinese. In early 2020, there was a great decoupling between the two largest economies, which opened up new opportunities for India in terms of Investment and Market. Late in 2020, this trade war moved into the technology sector. As we all know, this is the decade of technology, the fourth industrial revolution, working towards integrating the biological, digital and physical spheres, which, when fully completed, will alter the world at the fundamental level. Among the many technologies of the revolution, 5G is the most important one that will facilitate other technologies like IoT, etc. When China began to lead in that role, it became a big threat to the USA. To stop this rise, the USA undertook various measures to impede the growth of China. It imposed various bans on one of the leading companies of China—Huawei—starting from naming it as a threat to national security to banning the sale of special microprocessor chips needed for 5G networks. However, these measures, in the long run, will hurt the USA and its allies also if they do not find alternatives. Thankfully, the launch of Jio from the Indian side helped India to gain the confidence of the West; many US-based companies like Google, Qualcomm and others have invested in it to boost their own 5G infrastructure development. Qualcomm said it would invest $ 97 million in Reliance Jio platforms to acquire a 0.15 per cent equity stake. Besides, other US and European companies have invested in India; Apple has started manufacturing phones in India. Foreign Direct Investment (FDI) from the USA to India has crossed the $ 40 billion mark so far this year. The outcome of all this is visible already; the Indian forex reserve has reached an all-time high of US$ 523 billion because of huge investments and a drop in imports. High forex reserves help in strengthening the Indian currency, which will increase the confidence of foreign investors and the inflow of investment. Apart from becoming an alternative destination for

Western investments, the USA-China tariff war, which increased the price of Chinese products in the American market, made the American market more competitive for other players like India. An Indian Commerce Ministry report in 2019 stated that India had gained US$ 755 million in additional exports to the USA dominated by three sectors—chemicals, metal ores, and electrical manufactures. Overall, these new opportunities will help India to increase its share of exports from the current 2 per cent to 5 per cent in the next five years.

Political Benefits because of Bipolarity

The economic benefits that India would receive from the Western powers will surely help India to become a strong economy, but these benefits could be obtained from China as well. In fact, in 2016, both the USA and China approached India to establish 5G infrastructure in India. The important aspect of the USA-India relationship is the political relations or benefits that India will receive by allying with the USA, that is, to be the regional hegemon replacing China. This is something China can never give India. Since 2014, the USA has been trying to make India a net security provider in the Asian region, the outcome of which was seen with the visit of Obama to India and the renewal and updating of the India-USA defence agreement. This renewed agreement took the country's defence cooperation to the next level; in the past five years, India has become one of the major importers of American weapons. According to data from the Stockholm International Peace Research Institute, exports of American weapons to India from 2013 to 2017 increased 557 per cent over the previous five-year period. American arms sales to India currently stand around $ 18 billion, with high-level defence cooperation like 2+2 dialogue and increased defence exercises in the Indian Ocean region. The USA and India signed a joint agreement in 2019 called the exercise Tiger Triumph. It is a tri-service exercise between the two. So far, India has conducted such exercises only with the Soviet Union. Today, according to the USA, India's role in the Indian Ocean as the net security provider has moved to the next level. The Americans want India to rise above China and become the regional hegemon. US Secretary of State Mike Pompeo said the two oldest and largest democracies of the world should work together to face the challenges posed by the authoritarian Chinese

Communist Party. His comments came on a day when the USA announced the closure of the Chinese consulate in Houston amid strains in Sino-Indian ties following last month's clashes between their troops over their border dispute in eastern Ladakh that left 20 Indian soldiers dead. These activities across the Indian border also pushed India further away from China. The Indian government is actively participating in Quad 2.0, which India was so hesitant about earlier and planning to invite Australia to the Malabar Exercise, which India did not do in 2018 out of consideration to Beijing; an invitation this year would signal a major shift in position. Such close cooperation between the two democracies is needed to challenge the strong Chinese in the Asian region to satisfy their mutual interest that is to challenge China.

Bipolarity as a Curse

This bipolarity can also be a curse for India, whose greater inclination towards the USA, undermining China, in the long run, might turn India into a pawn in this great game between the USA and China. Washington is trying to get India to capitalise on its decoupling trend, with China and India, utilising the rising tension along the Indo-Chinese borders. The USA, from time to time, portrays China as the enemy here.

As mentioned earlier, the benefits that India will attain from the USA is happening in parallel with the decoupling between China and India. India in early 2020 scrutinized all the Chinese investments and clamped down on them, making prior government clearance mandatory for all forms of investment, even indirect ones, from all countries sharing land borders with India. This multilayered scrutiny of Chinese investment is to protect India's national security and to limit the increasing footprints of Chinese investment in India. However, these restrictions are costly for India as well. Chinese tech investors have put an estimated USD 4 billion of Greenfield investments into Indian start-ups. India followed up its relooking by banning Chinese apps, which coincided with the Clean Network campaign that intensified their decoupling. The restrictions placed by the Indian government on Chinese investment, if not replaced by alternatives, is a big threat to the Indian economy as well. India imports more capital goods than consumer products from China. These are used to make goods that are a substantial part of India's exports. If China decides to impose restrictions on these imports, it will pose a threat to India. Of course, it is true that India can depend on the USA, but such unilateral dependency is a curse for India, as heavy dependency makes the nation indebted to one particular nation. This, in future, can place the country in a vulnerable position, making it a pawn of another specific nation.

Thankfully, India is well aware of the pitfalls of relying too much on the USA for India's security. It is well aware of the history of US external orientation and how it shifts its orientation based on its national interest of the time. It is also conscious of the current turbulence in US domestic politics and the prospect of quick shifts in US external orientation. This is why US-India cooperation, even at such a high level, is based on mutual interest and not trust. This distrust is also an important reason for retaining a steady relationship with our long-term ally, Russia, and carefully managing the difficult and increasingly asymmetric relationship with Beijing. That is, from the beginning, when the USA was trying to meditate on various issues with Pakistan and China, India rejected the American offer outright, stating it could manage its internal business on its own. However, India took the issue to the SCO rather than bring the USA into Indian domestic policy.

Considering all this, it can be said that India can become a pawn but, so far, the way India is playing the game of trying to be an ally, which is sovereign, strong, and independent.

16

SAARC Charter Article 10 Needs Revisiting

Lobzang Dorji, Paljor Galey and Tashi Jamtsho

ABSTRACT

The failure to hold a SAARC summit sometimes offers a new insight to look at the regional organization from a new dimension. Although SAARC has a pivotal role to play in building mutual trust and, bring together political leadership and government machinery among its member states, frequent cancellations of the summit has hindered its progress. Further, bilateral and contentious issues are excluded from deliberations in the summit. Decisions are taken based on unanimity. As a result, the regional body is shifting its choices to a sub-regional grouping from the SAARC regional organization. Using qualitative research, this paper is an attempt to explore the factors limiting the commencement of the SAARC summit and to explain the issues of SAARC Charter Article 10.

Keywords: *SAARC, Article 10, BIN, Unanimity*

Introduction

The regional organization, South Asian Association for Regional Cooperation (SAARC), was established on December 8, 1985, with seven member-states mainly located in South Asia, i.e., Bangladesh, Bhutan, India, the Maldives, Nepal, Pakistan and Sri Lanka. In 2007, Afghanistan joined as a member. Although, the objectives of the SAARC Charter aim to promote and strengthen regional cooperation and economic integration among the member-states. Batra, A. (2012) asserts that South Asia today is among the most unstable regions in the world, riddled with both intra and inter-state conflicts. At present, the frequent cancellation of the SAARC summit prevents leaders of South Asia to meet and interact directly to resolve bilateral issues and issues. As a result, the regional body is shifting its choices from SAARC to a sub-regional grouping like the BBIN.

SAARC, since its inception in 1985, has held only 18 summits in the last 31 years since it was established. Nazzer, M. (2018) states that the prevailing political problems and bilateral disputes of SACs have mainly caused delays. Further, India and Pakistan are the main variables to hold the summit periodically. Burki, S.J. (2011) makes a comprehensive technical analysis of the trade-conflict relationship within the region and explores how South Asia demonstrates underperformance of its potential for economic integration, which is also a problem for the region. However, the lack of written records and documentation hinders it from finding a place in documented history. Therefore, this piece of writing would not only be a source of information but would also be a reminder to the present generation and as well as to future generations about the importance of such summits. Thus, this study will explore the reasons for the cancellation of summits and explain the limitations caused by Article 10 in SAARC's Charter.

Method

Among various research methods, this study employed a qualitative method as the main goal of this research was to explore, describe and interpret the failure of SAARC Summits using secondary to fulfil the aims and objectives of this paper.

Discussion

SAARC, as a regional organization, was set up in 1985. According to Kumar (2009), only 18 summits have been held since then, i.e., 10 in the first 15 years (1986-2000) and eight in the next 15 years (2001-2016). However, the trend of cancelling summits over the last 14-15 years—1989, 1992, 1994, 1996, 1999, 2000, 2001, 2003, 2006, 2009, 2012, 2013, 2015 and 2016—is worrisome. It explains the credibility and complacent nature of a regional organization failing the mandates of its Charter. Significantly, the cause of the failure to host summits was bilateral disputes, contentious issues, and political problems among the member states.

Historically, both India and Sri Lanka have been under the imperialistic rule of the British. Although they share borders in the region, both the countries went through three phases of turmoil between the Sinhalese ethnic majority and the Tamil-speaking minority in 1983 at Jaffna, Sri Lanka. Hagerty, D. (1991) asserts the first phase lasted until July 1987 and New Delhi tried to resolve the growing civil unrest by mediating between the Sri Lankan government of President J.R. Jayewardene and the Tamil separatists who were gaining increasing control over Tamil-dominated areas in the northern part of the island. Secondly, in July 1987, the two countries signed the Indo-Sri Lankan "Peace Accord" that allowed the Indian Peace Keeping Force in Sri Lanka. Hagerty, D. (1991) mentions that under the terms of the agreement, the Indian Army was charged with guaranteeing and enforcing the "cessation of hostilities" in Sri Lanka, while the Indian government pledged to "take all necessary steps to ensure that Indian territory is not used for activities prejudicial to the unity, integrity and security of Sri Lanka". Consequently, in 1989, India agreed to withdraw the Indian Peace Keeping Force from Sri Lanka. In the light of this evidence, the involvement of India in the domestic politics of Sri Lanka failed to build mutual trust bringing together their political leadership and government machinery. This event led to the cancellation of the SAARC summits in 1989 and 1990.

The Maldives is an archipelagic nation situated in the midst of the Indian Ocean. After independence from Britain in 1965, its relationship with India had generally been stable, although Kumar, A. (2016) states that its strategic location straddling important SLOCs and its proximity to Diego Garcia, where the US Central Command base is positioned, has aroused the interest of important world powers including India. In 1988, a coup d'état against President Maumoon Abdul Gayoom saw the involvement of Sri Lankan Tamil militants in the Maldives is trying to secure power for Abdullah Luthufi (*The Economist*, 1988). India, however, saved the Maldives from the coup. However, President Gayoom did not give any special privileges to India. In the later part of his regime, he tried to play China against India, as a democratic movement started to gather momentum. President Gayoom probably feared that democratic India might not support him as strongly in the face of a democratic upsurge in his own country (Hagerty, D., 1991). As a result, insecurity prompted the Maldives to rely increasingly on China to maintain a balance of power against India. These events hindered the hosting of the summits of 1988 and 1990.

The seventh SAARC summit scheduled in Dhaka in 1992 was delayed due to Indo-Bangladesh strained relations and the tense regional environment. Both the countries engaged in domestic politics, weakening the bilateral ties in the region. Pant, A. (2012) states that the summit was postponed when the Indian Prime Minister, P.V. Narasimha Rao, refused to attend following the strong reaction in Bangladesh, including demonstrations and eruption of communal violence, over the demolition of the historic Babri Mosque at Ayodhya, Uttar Pradesh, in India by extremist Hindus in 1992. It was the first occasion that India refused to attend a summit, and this was a severe blow for the SAARC process. The root cause of the problem also existed within Indian domestic politics, which was being increasingly polluted due to growing extremism, communal violence and religious outbursts that threatened the lives, property of minorities and their sacred places, spreading fear and anger throughout the region, more so in Bangladesh (Naazer, M., 2012). The Dhaka Summit was deferred, and after a delay of about five months, it was held on April 10-11, 1993. Moreover, in February 2005, India refused to attend the Thirteenth Summit scheduled in Dhaka to pressurise Bangladesh. Initially, India announced that it could not attend the Summit due to the prevailing security situation and political conditions in its neighbourhood, i.e., Bangladesh and Nepal, respectively.

The eighth SAARC Summit was deferred because of the strained ties between India and Pakistan.

Obino, F. (2009) asserted that the delay in holding the SAARC Summit in 1994 was due to Kashmir-centric issues such as Pakistan's concerns over the grave and massive human rights violations by the occupied forces in India-Held Kashmir (IHK). Both the countries engaged in a blame game accusing each other; Pakistan of sponsoring militancy and the Indian refusal to include the Kashmir contentious issues in bilateral talks. The dialogue was suspended for seven years (1990-1997). Naazer, M. (2012) states that in the second decade (1996-

2005), the SAARC Summit was delayed because of the soured Pakistan-India relations and national issues in the host countries. Pakistan wanted to host the Summit in April 2013. However, when it announced the postponement, India accused Islamabad of sabotaging the event. Finally, after a year's delay, the Islamabad Summit was held on January 4-6, 2004.

The organisation of the Summit suffered due to internal weaknesses and domestic problems of the SACs in the third decade. No summit was scheduled for 2006. Rather, the Association decided to convene the Fourteenth Summit in India in 2007, marking that it was the only one that was held as planned. The Fifteenth Summit was to be held in the Maldives, which later expressed its inability to organise it due to its upcoming General Elections in 2008. Sri Lanka volunteered to host the event that coincided with its sixtieth independence anniversary (*Daily Star*, 2009). Naazer, M. (2012) asserts that the Colombo Summit held in 2008 agreed to convene the next meet in the Maldives in September 2009, which the Maldives again declined due to the ongoing economic recession. On Bhutanese request, the venue of the Summit was shifted to Thimphu, where it was held in 2010 (*Deccan Herald*, 2009). Finally, the Maldives agreed to host the Seventeenth Summit in its country in 2011. Subsequently, the eighteenth SAARC Summit was held in Nepal after being deferred for two years in 2014. The nineteenth summit scheduled in Pakistan was deferred following New Delhi's decision to remain absent after an attack by militants on an Indian Army camp in Uri, India. Bhutan, Bangladesh and Afghanistan also decided not to attend (Panda, A., 2016).

Conclusion

SAARC, since its inception, has held only 18 Summits. Many of them were postponed or cancelled due to bilateral disputes, contentious issues, and political problems. The paradoxical nature of member-states engaged in the creation of a sub-regional grouping in a region has also hindered the summits. India and Pakistan play a key role in a regional organization. However, both countries have undermined the summit process. As a result, the only hope for smaller states in South Asia is to await an improvement in Indo-Pak relations in the region. In future, SAARC will face new challenges with Chinese and US diplomacy traits maintaining their presence in a region. Given those constraints, SAARC will have to revisit the structural problems of its Charter Article 10: "Decisions at all levels shall be taken based on unanimity" and "bilateral and contentious issues shall be excluded from the deliberations". The unanimity section of the Article empowers the freedom of any member-state to franchise any proposal. Consequently, there is no platform among the member-states to resolve their differences. Accordingly, clauses prohibit bilateral and contentious issues to deliberate in a summit which further creates a gap to resolve the issues in a region. Thus, the rectification of SAARC Charter Article 10 provides an opportunity to move SAARC, a regional body, to new heights. However, pragmatism among the leaders in these countries raises a question of doable or not in the region.

REFERENCES

Batra, A. (2012). *Regional economic integration in South Asia: Trapped in conflict?*. ProQuest Ebook Central https://ebookcentral.proquest.com

Burki, S.J. (2011). *South Asia in the new world order: The role of regional cooperation*. ProQuest Ebook Central https://ebookcentral.proquest.com

Hagerty, D. (1991). India's Regional Security Doctrine. ProQuest Ebook Central https://ebookcentral.proquest.com

Naseem, A. (2015). The Honeymoon Is Over: Maldives as a Growing Security Threat in the Indian Ocean. ProQuest Ebook Central https://ebookcentral.proquest.com

Obino, F. (2009). *SAARC*: The Political Challenge for South Asia and Beyond. ProQuest Ebook Central https://ebookcentral.proquest.com

Pant, A. (2012). The Truth of Babri Mosque. ProQuest Ebook Central https://ebookcentral.proquest.com

Reed, A. (1997). Regionalization in South Asia: Theory and praxis. ProQuest Ebook Central https://ebookcentral.proquest.com

Sharma, K. S. (2011). South Asian regionalism: prospect and challenges. ProQuest Ebook Central https://ebookcentral.proquest.com

Index

*

40 YEARS WITH
ABDUL KALAM
Untold Story

40 YEARS WITH ABDUL KALAM

Untold Story

A. SIVATHANU PILLAI

Foreword By

Shri Pranab Mukherjee

Former President of India

PENTAGON PRESS LLP

40 YEARS WITH ABDUL KALAM: ***Untold Story***

By A. SIVATHANU PILLAI

ISBN 978-93-90095-15-5

First Published in 2020

Published by
PENTAGON PRESS LLP
206, Peacock Lane, Shahpur Jat,
New Delhi-110049
Phones: 011-64706243, 26491568
Telefax: 011-26490600
email: rajan@pentagonpress.in
website: www.pentagonpress.in

Printed at Aegean Offset Printers, Greater Noida, U.P.

This book is dedicated to my Father and Mother, my Teachers, and Dr. A.P.J. Abdul Kalam with whom I spent more than 40 years, for making me what I am today.

सत्यमेव जयते

Pranab Mukherjee

8th August, 2020

FOREWORD

My association with Dr. Sivathanu Pillai, whose contribution to India's prominent Defence and Aerospace Missions has been substantive, goes back long. During my tenure as Defence Minister, I personally witnessed the strong resolve and the indomitable spirit with which Dr. Pillai led the prestigious Indo-Russian Joint Venture—BrahMos, as its Founding CEO & MD. His Mission-centric leadership and unique communication capabilities at BrahMos resulted in extraordinary success in the design, development and production of the world's best supersonic cruise missile, and induction by all three wings of Indian Armed Forces. BrahMos is a shining example of how success of Projects in strategic sectors carried out in Mission Mode, can place India into the elite group of technologically developed and advanced nations.

The book ***'40 Years with Abdul Kalam',*** provides truly amazing insights into the life of Dr. APJ Abdul Kalam—India's much loved former President. Dr. Pillai's long association with Dr. Kalam in ISRO and DRDO has helped him bring out the multitude of experiences through which he evolved himself to become one of India's leading Defence and Aerospace technologists. Dr. Kalam's famous words—'Strength respects Strength' provided an invaluable setting to India's journey as a leading nation in Defence technology. The experiences that the book recounts through its firsthand account of various untold incidents are highly inspirational and the values it promotes are more relevant today than ever before. Leadership styles of Nation Builders and India's eminent Visionaries have been vividly documented.

Dr. Pillai strove for the importance of "Make in India" in Defence and the role of Space Industries—present and future. The book sends a powerful message about how collective Leadership can contribute to India's development and to reclaiming our rightful place among the league of developed nations. Dr. Pillai has very well brought out the underlying Vision and the action path towards achieving this Mission. I wish Dr. Pillai all success in his future endeavour. I hope the book will be of great interest to all readers.

Pranab Mukherjee

Contents

Acknowledgements

During my 30 years with the DRDO, I received tremendous support from the heads of the organisation, top leaders of the Governments of India, Russian Federation. President Vladimir Putin and President Dr. A.P.J. Abdul Kalam who gave me outstanding support and constant encouragement, and played a significant part in the success of the joint venture, BrahMos. Visits by Presidents, Prime Ministers and Defence Ministers of both the countries to our missile centres were a great source of motivation for the project. I am indebted to them.

In my 20 years at the ISRO, I got guidance and support from many space leaders at VSSC and HQ, especially from Professor Satish Dhawan and Dr. Kalam, with whom I worked in my prime. I am greatly indebted to them. Chevalier Shri A. S. Kiran Kumar, former chairman, ISRO, gave me an opportunity recently, to contribute as an Honorary Distinguished Professor at ISRO HQ to evolve a management structure for industry consortium for increased production of PSLVs and satellites.

I am greatly indebted to Shri Pranab Mukherjee for going through the draft and giving 'Foreword'.

My mentors and visionaries, Dr. Kalam, and Dr. H.A. Yefremov, Head of DRDO and NPOM, respectively, guided the formation of BrahMos on the fast track through constant interaction and advice. Secretaries to Government, Ambassadors of the Indian and Russian embassies, and officials from Russia's Federal Service for Military-Technical Cooperation have been a constant source of encouragement. The Chiefs of Staff of the three wings of the Indian Armed Forces continuously gave outstanding support to attain higher levels of performance of BRAHMOS. Dr. A.G. Leonov, Dr. A.A. Dergachev, Mr.A.B. Maksichev, the Late Mr. A.N. Semaev, the Late Mr. A.N. Strakhov, Mr. V.M. Kiselev and many scientists from NPOM and partner Russian industries gave their all-out support to the programme. They shared their experiences at every point of the growth trajectory of BrahMos, making the project a shining example of international cooperation. Shri R. Ramanathan made a path-breaking contribution in the formation of BrahMos and Shri. P. Venugopalan, as Project Director, gave leadership to the technical requirements. Dr. Sudir Mishra continued the legacy as the present CEO & MD and progressed the JV. Shri/S Prahlada, S. Som, K. Srinivasa Rao, Atul Rane, Sharad Kumar and Col. J.P. Uniyal made outstanding contributions to the JV at different times. I am thankful to them for all their help. The dedication and hard work of Team BrahMos, scientists, technicians and staff from DRDO and NPOM helped to shape the joint venture. A number of industry meets, partnership programmes and flight tests from ships and shores, as well as interaction with administrators and Service personnel became inputs for this book.

I acknowledge the support given by Dr. S. Christopher, former chairman, DRDO, and Dr. V. Natarajan, Director, RIC, DRDO at IIT (Madras) Research Park, for providing me support in the last two years. I must thank Shri Y. S. Rajan and Shri Vijayanand for reviewing this book and giving guidance at ISRO to shape my thoughts. I gratefully remember my teachers in schools, colleges, universities and at Harvard Business School for imparting knowledge and morality.

While writing this book, many of my friends from industry, Dr. A. Kalanidhi, former Vice-Chancellor, Shri V. Ponraj, Shri H. Sheridon and R.K. Prasad, shared their experiences. Shri Hariharan, Shri Vishal Narain Dar, Col. Anil Mishra, Shri Kamalanath, Shri Surender Kumar and Shri Rajan Arya gave extraordinary support to me for improvising this book.

My special gratitude to Shri G. Sundaravadivelu, Shri G. Ratnavelu, Shri S. Mothakalathran and Shri Parimanam Thangappan, Secretary General, Indo-Russian Chamber of Commerce and Industries, for giving me valuable suggestions and help to complete this book.

My wife, Seethalakshmi, has given me constant support throughout my long years of work at different places. She has been my strength in the long journey.

Finally, I thank all my colleagues and friends from RIC, DRDO, ISRO, PMA, industry and academic institutions for their valuable support to me during the last 50 years.

Dr. A. Sivathanu Pillai

Preface

I was contemplating to pen down some of the interesting events, mostly untold ones, related to Dr. A.P.J. Abdul Kalam, who shared them with me over the course of our four-decade-long association. Over these years, I had the opportunity to work with him closely in the development of the SLV-3 at VSSC in Thiruvananthapuram, PSLV mission and configuration at ISRO HQ Bengaluru, missile programme and combating control regime at DRDL, Hyderabad and Defence R&D missions at DRDO HQ New Delhi. I had several opportunities to interact with him when he was the President of India, almost daily. I had assisted him in all his efforts to make a technologically strong India. He was always my mentor and he shaped me as a worthy son of Bharat.

Many books are available on Dr. Kalam, some of them authored by him and many by others who have been witness to his achievements. I also wrote two books jointly with him—*Envisioning an Empowered Nation* and *Thoughts for Change-We can do it*. But this book is quite different, as it highlights some close interactions with senior leaders in the corridors of power. The COVID-19 lockdown gave me time to recollect the past and write this book.

Kalam often used to say,

> *"History has proven that those who dare to imagine the impossible are the ones who break all human limitations. In every field of human endeavour, whether science, engineering, architecture, technology, medicine, sports, arts, politics, or societal service, the names of the people who imagined the impossible and achieved are engraved in our history"*.

In this beautiful life, which is a one-time opportunity, one must be remembered for one's achievements. Kalam emphasized that every child must think to be 'UNIQUE' to create a page in the history book.

Immediately after the sudden demise of Kalam, I reached out to many children and youth at schools, colleges and public meetings to share the agony with them. In one such gathering of 8,000 rural students of different age groups, organised by Mother Teresa Foundation at Thanjavur, the agitated and troubled children asked me many questions. One little girl from a nearby village asked me in Tamil "Uncle, Dr. Kalam advised people, when he was President, to donate eyes and other useful organs after death. I was wondering why Kalam Sir did not write a will to donate his organs after death". I was puzzled to hear the little girl's question. The whole crowd was thrilled with the question and looked at me with curiosity. Without losing a minute, I spontaneously answered in Tamil:

"All of you would like to ask this question. Dr. Kalam had a brilliant mind and he was affectionate to children. His brain all the time worked for you. He wanted to share with you his dreams and thoughts. His brain had 86 billion neurons. He distributed the billions of neurons to all Indians, particularly to children. Normally one organ can be given to one person. He wanted to give to all of you in one stroke. He kept his brain alive at the time of his instantaneous death, while teaching. You asked that question, because you are one of his ignited minds and he has already entered in your brain". What an ovation this answer drew from the young ignited minds. They all felt happy because Abdul Kalam has entered in their brains. The agitated minds became calm.

Virtues of Kalam

Kalam was one a rishi scientist, with many admirable virtues. He was also the best human resource manager of the modern world and he could read the minds of others. Without any ego, he could adapt himself to the situation to win over the person in front of him or would instantly become a captivating communicator to the audience. Every one, irrespective of age, position or religion, who met him on different occasions, celebrates him as a friend. Another interesting feature about him was that he never treated anybody with contempt. He could develop the little goodness within the person and make him feel wanted. By doing so, he could transform an ordinary person into an extraordinary one. This required patience, tact, adaptation and an analytical mind. Kalam was an expert in this, as I witnessed in many instances. Many of his associates, friends, peers and even superiors could express good ideas, but Kalam had the unique gift of spreading those ideas and convincing other people. He had the perseverance to follow up. Examples are Developed India Vision, PURA (Providing Urban Amenities in Rural Areas) and River Networking, to name a few.

I worked with Kalam directly in ISRO and DRDO, and **we shared difficulties**, failures and successes. I was always in frontline projects of national importance, because of him and was attuned to work for 14-16 hours a day, all seven days, without taking leave or a holiday. Kalam wrote in his book *"Ignited Minds"* in 2002, **"Dr. A. Sivathanu Pillai has worked with me for a long time and his contribution has been both timely and invaluable in giving shape to ideas and thoughts. I am fortunate to have his friendship"**.

Sarabhai envisioned a wide spectrum of development in the country through space research for the benefits to reach the common people. Dhawan focused on accomplishing definite missions and services. Sarabhai used Kalam for the RATO (Rocket Assisted Take-Off) project and put him in the missile panel, kindling Kalam's mind towards Defence, while the mission-driven Dhawan did not want any diversion from Kalam's goal of the SLV-3 and ISRO's missions. Both of them protected Kalam, when the tests failed. They saw his genuine hard work to achieve results. Kalam gave extraordinary leadership to bring out the innate talent in Indian youth when the country was challenged due to control regimes and technology denials by the industrially developed countries during the development of missile technologies. During those difficult times, youth achieved great things through their enthusiasm and vibrancy.

This book brings out some of my unique experiences with Kalam, highlighting some untold crucial events and incidents. I had the opportunity to participate in many official meetings and visits when he was President of India. **It was a long and unique journey for me with the most appreciated true Indian, KALAM—the Brahmarishi.**

A. Sivathanu Pillai

ONE

Introduction

Kalam as *'Brahmarishi'*

Brahmarishi refers to the highest class of human rishis in Hinduism. It is a title given to a rishi who is said to have realised Brahma, the Creator.

A rishi (seer) sees the fine fabric of consciousness. Just as a physicist explores particles and frequencies in Nature, a rishi explores the frequencies and fluctuations of consciousness. So a rishi hears and sees the sounds/impulses of the Vedas. Anyone who sees from that level has achieved "Patanjali Rishi consciousness". The rishi's name is expressed in the form of his cognition.

One thing is to know, see and hear the Veda, but most essential is to put that knowledge to use. A Maharishi is one who takes that vision and knowledge of Natural Law and can create transformation in the world. Maharishis are teachers and Vedic engineers who use techniques to transform their students (and the world) by putting the principles of consciousness into practice. Even their Consciousness is catalytic in this transformation. Rajarishi is a maharishi as adviser to the king, like Chanakya.

Sage Vishwamitra was a Kshatriya king. As he had lost to sage Vashishta in battle, he wanted to attain the stage of Brahmarishi like Vashishta. Later, he did intense penance and acquired the titles of Rajarishi, Maharishi and Brahmarishi. Lord Brahma appeared before Vishwamitra and said, "I am pleased with your austerity, and you are a

Brahmarishi". Vashishta, who neglected him earlier, appeared before Vishwamitra and said, "Indeed you are a Brahmarishi."

A Brahmarishi is one operating from the level of Brahmand, who is transforming and administrating the universe. This is the reason Brahmarishis are considered administrators of the universe. Their Consciousness is operating from that level of intelligence, which manages the universe.

A rocket man (not a Brahmin), known in his earlier days at Thumba as KALAM IYER, was given a sounding rocket project, called MENAKA. This project was discontinued and gave birth to the multi-stage rocket project. Got a boon SLV3. (Padma Bhushan-Maharishi). Went into tapas after SLV3 for 2 years (1981-82, left ISRO). Got a boon–AGNI. (Padma Vibhushan). Went into tapas again in 1990-92, decided to leave DRDO. Got a boon- Chief of DRDO and Scientific Adviser to the Defence Minister (Rajarishi). He persisted with nuclear tests—I.K. Gujral, like Brahma, silenced Kalam by giving him the Bharat Ratna (Brahmarishi). Conducted thermo-nuclear tests—Went into tapas during 2000 to 2002. Vajpayee (Vashishta) called Kalam to make him President of India and just as Vishwamitra, a Kshatriya king became a Brahmarishi, Kalam, the missile man, too became one.

"I have no house, only open space,
Filled with truth, kindness, desire and dreams;
Desire to see my country developed and great,
Dreams to see happiness and peace abound"

—A.P.J. Abdul Kalam

Religion Graduating to Spirituality

A Brahmarishi is the ultimate expert of religion and spiritual knowledge known as 'Brahmagnana'. Kalam was instrumental, with the help of Y.S. Rajan, for the Surat Declaration on Spirituality by all religious heads. Kalam said that religions are like beautiful ISLANDS, giving a good message; but they need to be graduated to become SPIRITUALITY.

This Book

"Spring arrived in February giving its usual magical touch to the Delhi weather, with beautiful flowers in full bloom, like a heavenly yard. Children began going

back to school dressed in colourful uniforms, birds chirped merrily, and then suddenly the clouds from the north rumbled and thundered, with fierce lightning and fire as coronavirus came from the dragon's mouth; not sparing young or old, death took its toll."

The lockdown following the spread of Coronavirus provided an opportunity to write this book on Kalam and myself. My life has been intertwined with Kalam's, like a river and the sea. This book brings out some aspects of my professional life that I shared with Kalam, and our adventures. The chapters include 'Fire in the Belly', Kalam's scientific 'Ups and Downs' in ISRO and DRDO, his life as President of India, especially his difficult times in Rashtrapati Bhavan, Unleashing the power of Brahmastra, and Strategic Industries. Readers will enjoy some untold events on Kalam.

TWO

Fire in the Belly

Shaping Mission of Life (1947-1972)

> *"I was always looking outside myself for strength and confidence, but it comes from within. It is there all the time."*
>
> —**Anna Freud**

KANYAKUMARI

The President of India, Dr. A.P.J. Abdul Kalam landed at Thiruvananthapuram airport in his special IAF Boeing flight on 21 September 2006. He had a series of programmes in Kerala. On the next morning, there was a programme for him at Kanyakumari. His helicopter was to take off at 0835 a.m. I was to join him since he was visiting my native place. The previous day I was at Cape Town in South Africa on BrahMos work, and to join him, I took a flight to Bahrain at night and a connecting Gulf Air flight to Thiruvananthapuram, and landed there at 0750 in the morning. The airport manager arranged for my quick immigration and took me to the guest room. I got ready, dressed up, skipped breakfast and reached the helicopter spot at 0840. His Excellency had come at 0830 and waited for me to board the helicopter. None, including the Governor, Shri R.L. Bhatia and others, knew why the President was waiting. On seeing me rushing to the spot, the President told them, "Pillai was coming from his official tour to South Africa to join me for the visit to his native place, Kanyakumari. Therefore, I had to wait for him".

From the helicopter, we looked at the beauty of Kanyakumari district, full of coconut trees, plantain trees, lakes with lotus flowers, waterfalls, hillocks, temples, narrow roads, beaches and small ports. I showed him the scenic destinations—Thirparappu waterfalls, Marthanda Varma's palace, our family temple Kumarakoil Murugan, Thirunainarkurichi, the birthplace of Saint Thiruvalluvar, Nagercoil town and the tower of Suchindrum Thanumalayan temple. I also showed him a medicinal hillock called Marunthu vazh malai, supposed to be a small portion of Dronagiri hill brought by Hanuman, when he was taking the medicinal hill with the Sanjeevni plant to Lanka to save Lakshmana, and a large lush green patch of paddy fields, as we reached Kanyakumari. This district is a unique place having an amalgamation of Kurinchi (mountainous region), Mullai (forests), Marudam (cropland), Naithal (seashore)—the type of landscapes described in Tamil Sangam literature. While landing we saw the three different colours of water in the Arabian Sea, Bay of Bengal and the Indian Ocean merge at this point.

President Kalam, Rajan and I, then went by boat from the jetty to the Vivekananda Rock Memorial, accompanied by the District Collector. On this rock, Swami Vivekananda had meditated for two days in December 1892 and attained enlightenment prior to his famous Chicago trip to take part in the 1893 'World Religious Conference'. A blend of the Tamil Nadu and West Bengal style of architecture is palpable from the design of the Memorial. While its mandapam resembles that of the Sri Ramakrishna Temple at Belur, West Bengal, the design of its entrance features the architectural styles of Ajanta and Ellora. It houses a life-size bronze statue of Swami Vivekananda standing in his famous 'Parivarjak' posture that was made by the famous sculptor, Sitaram S. Arte.

We spent some time in meditation at the Memorial. The adjacent rock is called *'Sripada Parai'* as it is believed that Goddess Devi Kumari blessed the place with the touch of her holy feet and performed tapas in devotion of Lord Shiva. In reality, the rock has a projection that is brownish in colour and resembles a human footprint. This projection is considered and referred to as *Sri Padam* (foot) and the shrine is called 'Sri Padaparai Mandapam'. The rock memorial attracts thousands of visitors round the year.

From this fascinating rock memorial, we moved to another nearby rock by boat to pay our respects to Saint Thiruvalluvar represented by a 133-foot (40.6 m) tall stone sculpture, representing 133 athikarams—the chapters of the *Thirukkural*.

Dr Kalam felt positive vibes at this spot, as Thirukkural guided him all times. In fact, he established a one-metre tall bronze statue of Thiruvalluvar in Rashtrapati Bhavan and wrote his version for 20 selected kurals, describing how to live as a good human being. He then suggested to the district collector, "I will write and send 10 of the best verses of Thiruvalluvar. They can be written here on the rock and everyone visiting the memorial read them and pledge to follow one of the 10 verses in their day to day life". The President wrote in Tamil in the visitor's book at the memorial. While coming back to the shore in our boat, we saw the beautiful panoramic view of the mainland, from the sangam of three oceans. We saw the Goddess Kumari temple, protecting the whole of India, Gandhi Mandapam, a gigantic Church, Koodankulam atomic power stations at a distance and the Vivekananda Kendra. Dr Kalam whispered to me that, just as he hailed from the holy Rameswaram, I too was a blessed person to be born in this holy place of Kanyakumari. My name Siva thanu came from Thanumalayan, the main deity Shiva at Suchindram, close to Kanyakumari.

MY FATHER—A SAINT

I was born on 15 July 1947 in Nagercoil town of Kanyakumari district, a month before India got freedom. My father, Aapathu Kaathan Pillai (meaning one who protects others from difficulties), was a saint and specialised in Siddha, Ayurveda and Raja yoga. After a very late marriage to my mother, Ponnammal, they had a daughter and son (me). My father was 54 years old, when I was born. He became a family man leaving all his mystic powers. He continued Yoga, Siddha and Ayurveda. Our house had a large number of trees of different varieties of bananas. Nowhere on earth can one find nearly 200 varieties of plantains as one can see in Kanyakumari district. My father never sold plantains to any one, so we had many of them ready-to-eat at any time. My food was 100 tastiest *matti palam* (a very small deliciously sweet fruit having medicinal value) a day and one litre of fresh cow milk. My mother took care of four cows and our earning was through selling milk. I started going to a government primary school at the age of five (1952), in the first standard. There was no concept of nursery in those days and children were free to play until they were five years old. My mother was very keen that I go to school so that one day I could become a Government officer. That was her dream. My father had a different plan for me.

My father wanted to make me a saint. He taught me mantras and ways to achieve higher powers. He never went to any temple in his life to worship God. He said God is within every human being. We should pray to Him internally

Rajayoga

I used to sleep with my father in a double cot. When I was asleep, he used to sit in Raja Yoga and soon, there was no normal breathing. He used to breathe inside himself and stay in that posture for long hours. He told me once, that this was the ultimate state of consciousness—to go for jiva samadhi, like Siddhas. He had one disciple, who was also practicing Raja Yoga. He used to make sculptures for temples. Once he was working at Kuttalam (about 100 km from Nagercoil) in a Shiva temple and used to stay there due to the long gestation period required in making sculptures. There he practiced yoga. One day while practicing Raja Yoga, he could not bring back his normal external breath. Unaware of his practice, the workers thought he was dead. The message reached my father late at night through another person, who came to inform him. In those days, the means of communication were poor. My father rushed and reached the place early morning the next day, but unfortunately, the person's son had already completed the formalities there itself and had consigned the body to the flames, the night before. My father was very upset, as he could have brought his friend back to normal consciousness. He knew the process of bringing back the breathing, in the Raja yoga practice.

When I was 6 years old, people started coming to me to locate ornaments stolen from their house or lost. After 10 minutes of mantra with closed eyes, I used to see a monkey coming and writing on a black board. I used to utter what was written on the black board and that would give the necessary hint to the distressed persons.

Siddha to Cure Cancer

One day, around seven in the night, a car drove up to our house. A person neatly dressed in a white suit got down from the car and enquired from the shop next to our house, whether he could meet Shri Aapathu Kaathan Pillai. The shopkeeper took him inside our house and introduced my father. My father was sitting on a bench and I was standing next to him. The well-built man, after removing his shoes, came inside and touched my father's feet. He introduced himself as a leading auditor based in Madras. With tears pouring from his eyes, he pleaded for help to save his wife who was suffering from blood cancer. He said that she had undergone all possible treatments including blood transfusion. The doctors had given up all hope and had told the auditor that she would die in the next 15 days.

Agonized by this situation, the auditor had gone to his native place, Tirunelveli, to meet his sisters and close relatives to inform them about the expected sad end. On hearing this news, the mood was full of sorrow. There he met his uncle, a highly respected Brahmin, who was a close friend of my father and used to have many common spiritual discussions with my father. His uncle advised him to immediately rush to Nagercoil and meet my father, to save his wife. He told my father about the various efforts he had made to get her treated and how he had lost all hope, as none of them had been successful. My father told him that he needed to see his wife immediately. He put on his white half sleeve shirt and a towel; did not tell anything to us and left with the auditor. Both travelled in the car and after an overnight journey reached Madras the next day.

My father talked to the woman with compassion and knowing her condition, decided on the type of siddha medicine, diet and pooja. The auditor helped him to get all the items needed. He administered medicines in the correct dose, prepared and gave food to her with utmost care, did evening pooja, and gave her mental strength and positive attitude. After 7 days of treatment, he could see a definite improvement in her. He told the auditor that his wife would be normal in a week's time with the medicines and food prescribed by him and instructed that nobody should disturb her. The auditor tried to persuade him to stay on, but my father told him that his task was over and that he would like to go to Tirunelveli to meet his Brahmin friend. He boarded the evening train and reached Tirunelveli the next morning. After staying there for two days, he reached home. In the meantime, we were worried as there had been no communication from my father. On seeing him back, my mother and I asked him what had happened. He told us about the events that had taken place during his stay in Madras.

Ten days later, I was playing kuchi pillai game in the compound with my friends with a half pant and no shirt when I saw the same car. The auditor had come to see my father with a briefcase in his hand. I took him to my father. After removing his shoes outside, he went near my father, and lying prostrate, touched his feet. With tears in his eyes, he said that his wife had been cured and the doctors had informed him that her cancer had subsided. He had rushed to meet my father to pay his respects and express gratitude. He requested my father to accept the brief case. When asked what the case contained, he opened it, which was full of currency notes. **My father said *"All my life I have only given to others and not received anything in return from anybody. Moreover, this was a godly service to cure a person from a dreadful disease. If I expected anything in return for my service, I would lose all my powers to cure others. Therefore, spend the money to support orphanages or for providing food to needy poor people"*. I was witnessing the morality of my father and his strong mind to reject wealth. It left a deep impression on my mind and inspired me to live a simple and transparent life, even during difficult times.**

Saint vs. Government Officer

While there were many good things happening, my mother did not like my being drawn towards a saintly life and following my father's example. Often she used to get very angry and had big fights with my father. She used to say that like other boys I should study and become an officer. She advised me not to follow my father's path and save my life. She said that she would sell milk to earn money for my studies. Her dreams for me were big. There used to be frequent arguments between my parents almost daily. She used to send me to collect money for the milk supplied in the morning to divert my attention and start saving.

School

At school, I was a brilliant boy in studies, getting 100 per cent all the time in all subjects, during my primary school days (1952-1957). I never studied at home, as there was no need. Moreover, there was no electricity at home. I used to finish the homework in the evening itself. I was a good boy to all my teachers. I was taught Mathematics by Shri Shanmugam Pillai and Science by Smt. Alagammal. There was no fees, no expenditure on studies except for books and a slate, both costing less than five rupees a year, and a pair of shirts and shorts. In 1957, at the age of ten, I joined DVD Higher Secondary & Training School for my middle and high school education. It was 2 kilometres from my home, a half hour walk. I used to take a small tiffin for lunch. I used to like idly and rasavada from a woman vendor named Chellamma, who served food to me like her son. She was a widow and her earning was through selling idly in the morning time. There was a lot of rush for her food because of its good quality and low cost. I never had to wait in the queue, as she used to say that I had to reach school on time. I liked her idly very much, as it had the love of a mother.

Desika Vinayaga Devasthanam High & Training School in Kottar was one of the top schools in Kanyakumari district, well known for its highly qualified teachers, in Science, Mathematics and Tamil Literature, in addition to its good laboratories. It was a great time for me to interact with my teachers, who were very fond of me. Shri Thankaraj used to wear full suit on all days and taught Composite Mathematics superbly. He was a strict disciplinarian and carried a stick in his hand. Great teachers—Thiruchitambalam, Vallinayagam, Madevan Pillai,

Chudalaimuthu Pillai, Sivaramakrishna Iyer, Santhanraj, and Chidambarathanu Chettiar—taught me and shaped my life. After seventh standard, it became necessary for me to study until late in the evening. I used to study sitting close to the Thiruvilakku, the big oil lamp to light the house. My maternal uncle, Subbaiya Pillai, was an electrical contractor. One day, my mother went to his house and requested him to get us an electric connection and provide one bulb to enable me to study at home. He did that and later provided one more bulb at the first floor for my studies. This act of my mother and my uncle gave a big boost to my efforts to study more hours at home. I concentrated on my class work. My father realised that I had drifted away from his way of life. He did not force me thereafter. I stood first in school in all standards, year after year and passed SSLC/XI with top scores in the school to earn a National Merit Scholarship. I was the only one in my school to receive the scholarship, in 1963. I was fortunate to study in DVD school, which fostered in me a love for Mathematics. I remember enjoying my school days very much. It was a great time, 1957-1963 at this school.

Later, on my request, President Kalam visited DVD school and gave a motivating speech to the students. He recognised the efforts of my teachers, named all of them and acknowledged their valuable contribution to shape leaders like me. He paid glorious tributes to my school. It was a great day in the history of my school.

S.T. Hindu College

After 11th standard, I moved on to Pre-University (1963-1964) at the South Travancore Hindu College, Nagercoil. There I took up Mathematics, Physics and Chemistry, with the focus on getting a seat in an engineering college in the next year. For the first time in my life, I started wearing rubber chappals and a dhoti, as I was a grown-up boy and going to college. I had to walk 3 kilometres to reach the college and used to buy for lunch, a curd-rice packet for 20 paisa. It was tough competition and I was the only one to get 100% in Mathematics and above 95% in Physics and Chemistry and was the first in my district for the engineering college seat. In addition, I was overall first in the college and district.

Importance of Education

Former President, Dr. S. Radhakrishnan defined education as the instrument of social, economic and cultural change for the balanced growth of an individual. It is the process of facilitating learning, acquisition of knowledge, skill, values, beliefs and habits. By imparting value based education, which is a fine art of moulding the consciousness of students towards noble and fine living with righteousness in the heart, institutions must emerge unique and excel in academics and co-curricular activities in India.

Kalam strongly advocated that students acquire knowledge. He said,

Learning gives Creativity,
Creativity leads to thinking,
Thinking provides Knowledge,
Knowledge makes you great

Thirukkural couplet 421 highlights the importance of knowledge, as below:

அறிவற்றங் காக்குங் கருவி செறுவார்க்கும்

உள்ளழிக்க லாகா அரண்

Knowledge is the weapon for the welfare of one's entire life; even enemies cannot destroy this fort.

THIAGARAJAR COLLEGE OF ENGINEERING (TCE), MADURAI

I applied for an engineering college seat with preference to join TCE Madurai, which was the nearest engineering college from my place at that time. However, there was resistance from both my parents about my going that far to study. Instead, they wanted me to study Science in Nagercoil itself. However, my heart lay in engineering. This was because of two reasons. One, I was fascinated by the vibrant and highly intelligent S. Nambinarayanan, who stayed in the house opposite ours and guided me later while I was studying engineering at TCE, and the other reason was that I wanted to become an electrical engineer and give light to the homes of all those school children who were deprived of electricity. I was left with Rs. 200 from the National Merit Scholarship and I had to spend that for two sets of cotton pants, shirts and shoes (it was the first time that I wore a pant and shoes), required for the workshop. Left with no money to pay my fees of Rs. 346, I was looking towards my father for help.

He asked me to come with him to Tirunelveli to meet his Brahmin friend. We went there and spent a night at his house.

The next day, I bathed in the holy Thamarabharani River. Its cold medicinal water flowed right down from the Pothigai hills where Saint Agastya had lived for thousands of years and enunciated the Siddha formula on palm leaves. It was so refreshing that I forgot all about my fees. When I reached the Brahmin's house, I had a surprise in store. I got money for my fees from Sahitya Akademy winner Shri Srinivasa Raghavan, the Principal of VOC College, Tuticorin, a highly reputed personality and a friend of my father. We took the night train to Thirupparamkuntram, one of the renowned six temples of Lord Muruga, where the deity had married Theyvanai, the daughter of Devendra, after killing demon Soorapadman at Thiruchendur. We reached there at 4 a.m.; it was dark and I could bath under the open tap, which was anyway leaking. I went to the college, finished all the formalities and joined the class on the opening day. In the evening, I went straight to the hostel at Thirunagar and settled down.

I had both National merit and Merit-cum-means scholarships, but I had to choose one. Despite the amount being lower, I chose the Merit-cum-means, because it was paid on a monthly basis. Of the Rs. 100 scholarship amount, the college took Rs. 75 for boarding (vegetarian food), lodging, and Rs. 25 was given to me for my expenditure. All books were free given to me by my seniors, and my classmates were very friendly and supportive. I got my favourite Electrical Engineering branch and studied hard to excel. Fortunately, Prof. Maria Louis, an outstanding teacher, took the main subject. I was a good student and did well.

Turning Point

We were in the fourth year BE, when a science exhibition was held at the newly formed Madurai Kamaraj University in 1968. Students were to make projects to display to visiting scientists. My friend Manisankar and I made **an innovative gadget** getting some input from *Popular Electronics*. At that time, there was no knowledge about processors. We worked day and night for a month, and made a circuit board that operated chosen multiple devices at different times. To us, it looked like an electronic toy. It was fascinating. We demonstrated the gadget at the exhibition.

We had distinguished visitors. **Nobel laureate Sir C.V. Raman** came to see the exhibits of the students. He listened carefully to my explanation and appreciated our effort with a powerful voice and a pat on my back. Both Manisankar and I were thrilled to be appreciated by a Nobel Prize winner.

Meeting Dr. Sarabhai

After a few minutes, **Dr. Vikram Sarabhai** came to us, with a mesmerizing look. He was in the limelight at that time, as the Father of Indian space research. We saw him with reverence. I explained to him about the device. Showing curiosity, he started asking questions on the design and functions. He was satisfied with our explanation, put his right hand around my shoulders, and said, ***"You have a great future"*** and moved to see the next exhibit. A current passed through my body. For some moments, I was not in my senses. My friend kicked me to bring me back to reality. We thanked God for giving us such a wonderful opportunity in life to meet great men of Indian science. That day I made a commitment to myself that I would work for ISRO. After passing out in 1969 with high grades, I applied, attended an interview and was able to get a placement at ISRO.

Bringing R&D Culture at TCE

I did not forget my Alma Mater, TCE. After many years, when I was in a good position in DRDO, I went to my college. I met Professor T. Mohanram and requested him for arranging my talk to the faculty and students, which he did. I saw my teachers, new faculty and students. I spoke about the current technologies at ISRO and DRDO, and opportunities available for academic institutions and students. I emphasised the need for R&D culture in college and participation in national projects. They all liked my talk.

I made my four professors visit missile laboratories at Hyderabad to expose them to advanced research. They were impressed and made some proposals. As these did not meet our requirement for funding, I, along with Dr. S. Sundararajan and some alumni went to the college and prepared project proposals. We encouraged many young faculty to come forward to work for the projects. Many scientists from DRDO labs started interacting and arranged funding for projects. When Prithvi missile flies, TCE has a contribution in it, because of the outstanding work of Prof. Anbarasu. This is only one of the examples. There are many more.

At one time, there were seven projects and Smt Radha Thiagarajan, Chairperson at that time, arranged a review meeting at Kodaikanal, not only to give incentive to both teams, but also to highlight the importance of research projects to the faculty. Professors V Ramamurthi, Abhai Kumar, Valliappan, Manjunatha Rao, Raju, Kannan, Krishnan, Thiruvengadam, Anbarasu, Salini, and many others participated in projects. We also made some incentive packages and availability of latest software for them to use in the projects. By the grace of God, my initiative worked out well. Karumuthu Kannan, Chairman took keen interest and gave full support to research activities. Prof V. Abhai Kumar, the current Director is an outstanding researcher himself. He led the research teams. Many research projects came from different departments, other than DRDO. A new culture emerged in the college. **Today, I am proud that my college is well known as one of the top institutions in the country. Dr. Kalam, fascinated with what I told him about college, visited it twice and talked to students, once, as President of India. He even stayed in the guest house attached to the hostel, where I had lived during my B.E.**

Golden Meet

The 1969 batch students of TCE from all three branches have completed 50 years of passing out from the college. Many classmates with their families, including grandchildren, celebrated the golden jubilee in a big way at Madurai in July 2019. We could see the warmth of friendship among us, in what was the best event in my life. Thanks to

R. Venkatasamy, Ravindran, V. Thalai and other core team members who put in mammoth effort to find and reach out to the alumni and bring them together with their families. I had lost touch with almost all of them, except N. Sivasubramaian, as we worked together at ISRO. We had many things in common and used to meet at functions in school, college and industry.

In the golden jubilee function, I met many friends, after 50 years. I was thrilled to meet my classmates T.D. Srinivasan, P.S. Sundaram, Rajaram, Visvabharathi (a big shot in the USA, came all the way to meet us). Another good friend of mine, and classmate from Pre-University, Dr. T. Karunakaran, took keen interest in the TCE golden meet, but it was sad, that such a strong nationalist died suddenly of cardiac arrest, just a few days before the get-together. A Gandhian by nature, he propagated PURA—(Providing Urban Amenities in Rural Areas) scheme, when he was Vice Chancellor at Gandhigram Rural University at Dindigul near Madurai. President Kalam was very impressed with his dedicated efforts for rural upliftment, when he went to the University to deliver the convocation address. It was a great loss to me, personally. The golden meet went off well, except that we were sad to lose some of our friends. Our families really enjoyed the various events and overall it was a pleasant function to cherish for a lifetime.

In December 2019, Ravindran and family arranged a function at their new Ashvattha School near Madurai. I went with my wife to meet some of my golden friends. It was a happy moment to see the next generation—Ravindran's son and daughter-in-law—managing the school very efficiently with a determination to make it the top school in Madurai.

Space Science & Technology Centre (SSTC)

I joined SSTC on 29 December 1969 in the Systems Engineering Division. The same day, Dr. Sarabhai addressed the Indian Rocket Society Symposium on his vision for future space missions. In the teatime, I met Sarabhai, introduced myself in a humble voice and informed him that I had joined SSTC. He wished me success. I started my work on Systems Engineering for Launch Vehicles, initially on a technology project—Thrust Vector Control of rocket motors. 1970 and 1971 were the golden years, full of activities, as narrated in the next chapter.

THREE

Abdul Kalam, The Rocket Scientist

> *Before I formed you in the womb, I knew you,*
> *Before you were born, I set you apart,*
> *I appointed you as a prophet to the Nations*
>
> **—Jeremiah 1:3**

TURNING POINT

Many of us would have read 'WINGS OF FIRE'—an autobiography of Abdul Kalam. We are aware of his early life at Rameswaram, studies in school, in St. Joseph College, at MIT (Diploma in Aeronautics), his interview while joining DTD&P (Air), and his unsuccessful attempt to join the Indian Air Force. Not getting through the IAF Selection Board at Dehradun, he was depressed to the core, as that was the end of his long-cherished desire to fly. The turning point was his meeting with Swami Sivananda at his ashram in Rishikesh. Swami Sivananda made him cool and said,

> *"Accept your destiny and go ahead with your life. You are not destined to become an Air Force pilot. What you are destined to become is not revealed now; but it is predetermined. Forget this failure, as it was essential to lead you to your destined path. Search, instead, for the true purpose of your existence. Become one with yourself, my son! Surrender yourself to the wish of God"*

This spiritual advice had a deep impact throughout his life. Kalam often used to tell me **"God conspires for one's success".**

At DTD&P (Air), Kalam was assigned the task to make grounded aeroplanes airworthy. Later, he worked at the Aeronautical Development Establishment (ADE), at Bengaluru in the Hovercraft project. He put in hard work to realise the prototype. However, the project was mired in controversies and was finally shelved. This was Kalam's second disappointment in life. **I have assessed his life; there were a number of upsets in his life. However, every failure in his life had a turning point. I will bring out the details later.**

At ADE, Kalam did not know what he should do further on the Hovercraft project. To his surprise, the Director ADE Dr. Mediratta brought Prof. M.G.K. Menon and showed him the Hovercraft. Kalam gave a short ride to Prof. Menon in it, moving at a few centimetres above the ground. Menon was visibly happy. After a week, Kalam got a letter for a rocket engineer's post at INCOSPAR (Indian Committee for Space Research). He was interviewed by Dr. Vikram Sarabhai and Prof. M.G.K. Menon and selected as a rocket engineer.

KALAM AS ROCKET ENGINEER

Kalam moved to Thumba Equatorial Rocket Launching Centre, which was established in the later part of 1962 at Thumba near Thiruvananthapuram. It may be noted that Thumba is the only place in India where the Earth's magnetic equator passes through and is the ideal place for upper atmosphere studies. Kalam started working on the design of rocket payloads and nose-cone jettisoning systems at the office established at St. Mary Magdalene church.

Soon, Dr. Sarabhai decided to send a team to NASA. Kalam got an opportunity for a six-month training course in the USA at NASA's aerospace centres, Langley Research Centre in Virginia, Goddard Space Flight Centre in Maryland and Wallops Flight Test Facility in the East Coast. This provided a great exposure to Kalam in understanding design, development, assembly and flight-testing of sounding rockets. This also gave a very important exposure into the **Scout** Satellite Launch Vehicle—a four-stage rocket to put a satellite into orbit.

On his return, Kalam worked on the American rocket Nike-Apache integration and together with Eswaradas and Aravamudan launched the rocket successfully on 21 November 1963. This was the first rocket launch in India. The next day, Sarabhai outlined his vision to build our nation's own Satellite Launch Vehicle (SLV).

Sweat Creates Fire

Kalam started working on preparing payloads for various scientific experiments. He and his colleagues, V. Sudhakar and R.N. Bhattacharya were preparing a sodium and thermite mix in the remote payload preparation facility. It was hot and humid, and they were sweating. A drop of sweat fell on the mix and suddenly fire engulfed the room and blocked the door. They rushed to the other side to escape. There was no safety escape in the room. There was a fixed glass window, without iron bars. With presence of mind, Sudhakar broke open the window with his elbow and pushed Kalam through the opening, before getting out, himself. For Kalam, it was almost like getting a second life. Sudhakar fractured his hand, while Bhattacharya got severe burns. They were hospitalised for several weeks.

Nose Cone Experiments

At TERLS, Kalam used to prepare the payloads and assemblies inside the nose cone. This payload assembly is part of the rocket, fitted with the propulsion. The nose cone has two halves, assembled with a timer and a pyro device for longitudinal separation at the desired altitude to make a sodium vapour cloud, required for upper atmosphere study. This particular experiment was an international collaborative programme. Kalam and his colleagues gave importance to this experiment. During one of Sarabhai's visits to Thumba, Kalam wanted to show the jettisoning of the nosecone operation, without the payload part. Every aspect of the test was verified and fully ready. Sarabhai came at 9 in the night. The countdown started. 10, 9, ...2, 1, 0; however nothing happened. Sarabhai smiled and said he would come again at 11 p.m. Kalam was confident he would rectify and demonstrate a good test. Sarabhai came again later that night. The countdown started once again 10,....2,1,0. This time too nothing happened. (Later the device worked). Kalam and his team were upset at the failure. They worked the whole night and analysed the circuit to locate the defect. The next morning, Sarabhai asked Kalam to see him at 9.30 a.m. at his office.

Kalam with the analysis and drawing went to meet Sarabhai. He was nervous, expecting harsh words from Sarabhai. He opened the drawing to explain. Sarabhai looked into Kalam's eyes and gave him a paper. Kalam was hesitant to read it. Sarabhai smiled and asked him to read it. Kalam glanced through it to see his promotion to the next grade with an increment. He thanked Sarabhai and promised to work hard. **Sarabhai realised the extraordinary power that resided in Kalam.** Sarabhai gave him a new task of developing a defence system, RATO (Rocket Assisted Take Off) for military aircraft to give an additional thrust required for a short runway take-off. In a meeting at Delhi, he introduced Group Captain V.S. Narayanan of Air HQ, who would coordinate with Kalam on this project. Narayanan later became Director of DRDL. This action of Sarabhai connected Kalam with the Air Force, in a different role and eventually, the DRDL.

This interesting project, RATO, had many new technologies, indigenously developed high-energy propellant, composite casing, canted nozzle, pyro-based separation system and event-based ignition. The team worked hard with special powers and realised the first RATO firing in the twelfth month. Then followed 64 static firings to establish high reliability, as this was to be used in man-rated defence missions. Kalam proved his worth to Sarabhai. However, the indigenously developed RATO was not accepted by the IAF.

Sarabhai created Rocket Propellant Plant with M.R. Kurup as the manager and Rocket Fabrication Facility with D. Eswaradas, to support the Sounding Rocket Programme. H.G.S. Murthy was the Director of TERLS. Kalam was made Head of the Rocket Engineering Division and Aravamudan was the Head of Instrumentation. All of them were very capable in their tasks, even though they did not have doctorates or PhDs.

Sarabhai brought Indian-born highly-rated technology experts working in NASA, universities in the USA and UK, and highly qualified professionals from India, and created the Space Science & Technology Centre (SSTC) at Veli hill, adjacent to TERLS, for R&D. All of them were PhDs from reputed universities. Dr. Sarabhai himself was the Director of SSTC. Politics started between SSTC on one side and TERLS, RPP and RFF on the other. Sarabhai encouraged competition for technology development. Sarabhai's strategy started yielding results. Dr. Vasant Gowarikar and his team developed an indigenous propellant for the

Rohini-75 rocket, which flew in 1967. This was a remarkable achievement. Many technology-proving flights followed.

Dr. A.E. Muthunayagam was the Head, Propulsion and Mechanical Engineering. All designs of rockets came from his team. He led the Multistage Rocket project. At this point of time, Sarabhai added a large number of engineers and scientists, 1,000 per year for three years, and formed many technology development projects, which would lead to a launch vehicle.

Kalam established laboratories for composite FRP rocket cases and Pyro-Mechanisms. Later, they grew into big centres. REPLACE (Reinforced Plastics Centre), which produces all composite hardware like rocket motor cases, was his brainchild. He was made Project Leader for the Menaka multi stage rocket (RH-125+ RH-125 S). However, after three flights, this project was closed.

Space Profile

Around this time, in 1969, I joined as a young trainee-engineer to start with after completing my electrical engineering degree in the Systems Engineering Division. Initially, I worked in the Thrust Vector control technology project. Soon an opportunity came. I was fortunate to become a member of a small team to assist Sarabhai to prepare a **"ten-year space profile for India".** The visionary leader unfurled his ideas and asked us to give them proper shape and draw up a plan. Without any experience, we debated amongst ourselves and made a draft plan. Sarabhai's faith in youth was very visible. He appreciated the work and asked his secretary to integrate the plan with the Atomic Energy Profile. The document, Atomic Energy and Space Research: A Profile for the Decade 1970-1980, was released at the AEC office in the last week of May 1970.

Sarabhai's vision was to launch an SLV in 1974 and place in a near circular orbit an about 400-km satellite of about 30 kg. This was to be followed by a powerful launch vehicle capable of putting a 1,200-kg satellite into synchronous orbit by 1980. He was a truly a time machine. He could think far ahead of anybody else. No one could match the way he thought of doing things. His aim was to catch up with the developed world in providing satellite services to the Indian population in communication, meteorology and remote sensing. His real concern was the upliftment of common people and establishment of sustained development for the nation, using space technology. He established multiple institutions for design, advanced technology development and testing and new centres for management and human resource development. In ISRO, he introduced Systems Engineering for the first time in India to network all stakeholders and analyse projects in an integrated way. He integrated all the centres into one organisation, ISRO.

Various configurations for an SLV for a 30-40 kg satellite to be placed in a near Earth orbit of 400 km circular orbit were presented to Sarabhai. In consultation with senior engineers and Heads of Divisions, he decided on the SLV-3 configuration with four stages and open loop guidance system. He selected Sriharikota Island having an area of 44,000 acres for establishing a launch station on the east coast for SLVs. There was all-round progress in all the areas of space research, technology development, sounding rocket production, flight testing in Thumba, building a big launch station on the east coast, new centres for large size propellant production, rocket motor static test facility, tracking and telemetry stations, and a Space Applications Centre. He initiated many international co-operations with NASA, ESA, ISAS, the USSR and others. They included Satellite Instructional Television Experiment (SITE), using the US ATF-6 satellite connecting 2,400 remote villages and Satellite Telecommunication Experimental Project (STEP) using the Franco-German satellite, Symphony, connecting with a national network.

DESIGN PROJECTS FOR SLV-3

Sarabhai appointed 11 design project teams for SLV-3, after approving the SLV-3 study report submitted by Dr. Y.J. Rao. The design projects were for an overall LV, four-stage guidance system, heat shield and rocket systems, launcher, telemetry, telecommand and the Rohini satellite. Gowarikar was for DPS-1 (First Stage), M.R. Kurup for DPS-2, A.E. Muthunayagam for DPS-3 and Kalam for DPS-4.

I worked on DPS-1 with Gowarikar, who was an excellent team leader. The first stage was designed with a sophisticated three-segmented rocket motor, with nearly three tons of solid propellant in each segment and two types of controls, composite nozzle and igniter. Making it in three segments was necessitated due to limitation in the propellant casting facility at RPP. Dr. S. Srinivasan, a specialist structural engineer, who joined SSTC after his PhD from the USA, designed the 15CDV6 high strength casing with a novel tongue-and-groove joint, for the three-segmented rocket motor. I am mentioning this point specifically because the Space Shuttle, in its 25th mission, had blown up after take-off, because of a faulty segment joint design of the strap-on boosters killing seven astronauts. Srinivasan's design was classic and there was no failure, as the rocket motor is being used in the PSLV as strap-ons and in the AGNI missile.

Kalam and his team worked very hard and brought out the documents of DPS-4 faster than expected. In the status review, Sarabhai appreciated the progress made by Kalam. Soon, Sarabhai brought Prof. Curien, the President of the French Space Agency, CNES. The focus of discussion was to see the feasibility of using the SLV-3 fourth stage as an upper stage of the just-started DIAMANT BP4 launch vehicle. This was a great visionary thinking of Sarabhai. Kalam with his hard-working innovative team brought in compatibility by suitable modifications to the fourth stage design. The upgraded stage resulted in 600 kg and 650 mm diameter, from 250 kg and 400 mm. The advantage was that the SLV 3 could carry a heavier payload and the stage was compatible for the Diamant BP4 Launch Vehicle. Based on initial agreement in 1971, Kalam put in huge effort to realise the design document within a year and started the initial development activities. But the French Government dropped the Diamant BP4 project and therefore the Indian fourth stage was not needed for them.

The Diamant BP4 (4th stage) was yet another, in the series of disappointments faced by Kalam. The others were nose-cone separation, RATO, Menaka, Hovercraft and his rejection by the IAF. Nevertheless, looking back, each disappointment gave him a positive mindset. Not being selected in the IAF brought him closer to spirituality and allowed things to happen in a way ordained by God. The Hovercraft project took him closer to M.G.K. Menon and led to his selection in ISRO. Failure in nose-cone jettisoning made Sarabhai realise his talent to get him an out-of-turn promotion and new assignments. RATO brought him closer to defence and made him a member of the Missile Panel at DRDL. The DiamantBP4 requirement later helped ISRO to configure the Apogee Boost Motor for the APPLE satellite and successfully integrate with the ARIANE rocket. Most importantly, all of them shaped him into a tall leader. He proved his calibre through hard work and building an excellent team.

The Gowarikar team prepared the DPS-1 design report in October 1971. I am happy to have worked for the SLV-3 SI rocket motor design and development, as this is the only system of the SLV-3 being mass produced for PSLV and AGNI in the last 40 years and will be there for many more years. Design projects were completed by December 1971 for review and approval by Chairman ISRO.

Tragedy Struck

On 28 December 1971, Dr. Sarabhai was with us in SSTC to review the design documents. He approved the SLV-3 design, attended other reviews until late night, and went to Kovalam guest house to rest. He had some more meetings the next day at Kovalam over lunch and dinner. It was a great shock for the nation on the 30th morning to hear that he was no more. There was a sense of gloom everywhere. All of us were at Thiruvananthapuram airport to pay our last respects to the departed leader. I had also gone. I did not know what would happen to ISRO without the tall visionary leader, the Father of the Indian Space Programme.

1972

Prof. M.G.K. Menon was interim Chairman, ISRO, for a few months in 1972. Prof. Satish Dhawan became Chairman, ISRO, on 1 June 1972, in addition to his directorship of the Indian Institute of Science. ISRO HQ was established at Bengaluru. ISRO came under the Department of Space (DOS). Prof Dhawan himself was the Secretary of the Department and Chairman of the Space Commission. A highly qualified aeronautical engineer, Prof. Dhawan gave due respect to the position, after Sarabhai. Dr. Brahm Prakash, an outstanding metallurgist from BARC, was appointed as the Director of the newly-formed Vikram Sarabhai Space Centre (VSSC), integrating SSTC, TERLS, RPP and RFF at Thiruvananthapuram. Both Dhawan and Brahm Prakash decided on the appointment of Kalam as the Project Manager of SLV-3, integrating all design projects. Their choice of project manager for the integrated SLV 3 raised many eyebrows among the elite group of PhDs. Dhawan and Brahm Prakash selected Kalam because he could get along well with all and could put in hard work. Kalam organised the SLV-3 team of his choice. **He chose me to work with him as a core team member, along with others.** My **association with Kalam started then, in 1972.**

SLV-3 PROJECT

The first task of Kalam was to evolve a Management Plan, translating the project objectives into a work breakdown structure and tasks of realising 44 major sub-systems, programme management and integration and checkout. These tasks of the project were then linked to technology groups in a matrix form. Decision-making process, advisory committees, infrastructure build-up and development plan became part of the report.

Many innovative solutions came up during propellant development and processing by Dr. V.R. Gowarikar and M.R. Kurup, composite nozzles and propulsion systems by A.E. Muthunayagam, composite motor casing by C.R. Sathya, guidance scheme by Dr. S.C. Gupta and launch complex by Dr. Y.J. Rao. Prof. Dhawan and Dr. Brahm Prakash empowered the project by integrating the efforts with focus and dropping all other non-SLV-3 technology projects. Prof. Dhawan told Kalam that *once the Project Manager was appointed, even the Chairman of ISRO would work for him.* His words were a great source of inspiration for Kalam and our team members.

Dr. S. Srinivasan, Deputy Project Manager, core team members, the entire SLV-3 team, technology groups and technicians had put in their best efforts for the success of the project. It was quite an accomplishment for me to be part of 54 static firings of four rocket motors, qualification testing of 10 sets of rocket systems and establishment of heat shield reliability. The other achievements were dynamic firing of the control packages and in-flight evaluation including RH560 launches, the realisation of guidance system, and establishment of huge integration and the SLV-3 launch complex at SHAR. All these tasks proceeded with the dedicated efforts of the teams from the project and technology centres.

In order to ensure a collaborative climate within the core team, Kalam constituted a PRM team. Project Review Meetings (PRM) were held every Tuesday and gave enormous dynamism to the thinking and decision-making process. Kalam tactfully created constructive differences among the core team members, 14 of us, that led to vigorous arguments. Mostly, these issues ended in a serious exchange of words. This is "Management by Conflicts" and it is a clever tactic to get the best out of differences. After listening to various viewpoints, Kalam used to give his final decision. As convenor of PRM, R.A.D. Pillai issued the decisions taken and the action plan. His meticulous work enabled to put things in order. Everyone followed the decisions strictly to progress the project in the leader's way. All personal comments were forgotten. Each one in the SLV-3 team gave their best contribution.

An important quality of Kalam was that he never said, "You don't know" and treated everyone as an equal. He had no 'likes and dislikes'. He could develop the little goodness within a person and make him feel wanted. By doing so, he could transform the team to contribute. All his decisions were by consensus.

A Bolt from the Blue

In consultation with Prof. Dhawan, Rajan and other staff officers of the Chairman ISRO, Dr. Brahm Prakash, introduced an innovative re-organisation of the Vikram Sarabhai Space Centre in 1976 to focus all the efforts of the centre on the SLV-3. This was a masterstroke, which made a great impact with all the great minds working together to review each of the system performances and achieve results. He formed technology groups, designating the heads as group directors and promoted Kalam to Project Director, from Project Manager. He revamped the Space Centre Council (SCC) and included Kalam as a member, giving him equal status with veterans and the elite. Kalam used the SCC to his fullest advantage due to the presence of Brahm Prakash. The Director's review once a month on a Saturday was another mechanism to control the events and put the project on course.

Kalam was tactful to bring in all the seniors as chairmen of system reviews, making them participate in the midterm review of the SLV 3 in 1976. This turning point united all forces towards achieving one goal. The working environment became conducive to the SLV-3. Activities started moving fast towards an SLV experimental flight.

Thinking of Missiles

In the meantime, Kalam asked me and Raju, an aerodynamic engineer in the project, to configure ballistic missiles using SLV-3 stages. We looked at various combinations S1+S2, S1+S3, S1+S2+S3, S1 alone, S1+1/3S1, S2+S3 and S2 alone and did a performance analysis and made a report. Kalam prepared a letter addressed to Dhawan, which contained a brief on the possible IRBM to be realised. He asked me to take the classified report to Bengaluru and meet the Chairman. I went by flight so that I could reach faster and hand over the document safely to Dhawan.

In the mornings, Dhawan used to be at the IISc and in the afternoons at ISRO HQ at Cauvery Bhavan. I went to the office of Director IISc, and handed over the sealed envelope to Dhawan. He looked at me with a strange look and opened the cover. On glancing through the report, he became furious. He said, "Go and tell Kalam, not to prepare such documents; not even in his dreams. ISRO stands for the peaceful application of space". So saying, he put the report aside.

With disappointment, I started my return journey to Thiruvananthapuram by bus. When I told Kalam about Dhawan's reaction, he gave a sarcastic smile. I realised that he was expecting this. He had sent me because he did not like to face Dhawan directly.

I thought Sarabhai envisioned a wide spectrum of development through space and Dhawan focused at accomplishing definite missions. So Sarabhai used Kalam for the RATO project and put him in the missile panel, kindling Kalam's mind towards defence, whereas Dhawan did not want any diversion from Kalam's task of the SLV-3 and ISRO's missions. Considering the multiple activities in the early stage and the focused SLV3 project in the Seventies, both leaders were right in their own way.

During the period 1974-78, E.V.S. Namboodiri and myself, became very close to each other, worked together with technology groups and completed all ground tests for the four types of rocket motors (S1, S2, S3, S4) and high-altitude test firing of the fourth stage motor. It was not a smooth journey, though there were failures in the initial tests.

Life during the SLV Days

During the SLV-3 days, Kalam and some of us used to go home very late in a jeep. Kalam used to drop me first, being a family man. My son, about two years old, not seeing me for many days, used to ask my wife, "What happened to father? Where is he"? They had to adjust themselves to the routine. My parents and wife knew that I was working on a very important project. They did not trouble me at any time. This continued throughout my life. Unless the family is co-operative, one cannot have peace of mind to put the best effort into difficult projects.

Rocket Motor Testing at SHAR

We had a failure of S1 (one-metre diameter, 10 metre long S1 with 8.66 t of propellant) static test due to a higher rate of ablation of the nozzle, before burning was completed at 49 sec. It needed a change in the design of composite ablative layers with suitable metal back up. Rajaram Nagappa and his team carried out the design modification and analysis, after elaborate thermal analysis.

The S2 motor had to be shortened to 3/4ths in length due to the constraint of the propellant casting facility, called S2 (3/4) at RPP. This motor was prepared for static test. The hardware had a defect. After an excellent analysis by Dr. Srinivasan and structural experts, the project was required to go for the static test. But the Test Article Review Board did not clear it, due to possible failure at 80 per cent of burning time of the test. Srinivasan wanted to go for the test based on his analysis. We suggested to Kalam to get clearance from the Director. Kalam raised the matter at the Space Centre Council, being chaired by Dr. Brahm Prakash, to clear the test supporting Dr. Srinivasan's arguments. The SCC members did not agree for the test. Dr. Brahm Prakash, one of the outstanding metallurgists of our country, knew the defect patterns in the steel type 15CDV6 structure and crack propagation under stress. He told the meeting that he needed some more time to take a decision. He worked hard the whole night, all by himself, went through all the documents and analysed the risk involved in carrying out the test. The next morning, Kalam got a phone call from him to go ahead. Kalam used to say that Dr. Brahm Prakash was a man of a few words but a great decision maker. Everyone held him in high esteem when he gave his decision. All the SCC members, although expressing differing views, accepted his decision. We went ahead with the test and it was successful.

The S3 problems were due to the slotted propellant grain design, and needed a collapsible mandrel. After cast-cure, the six segments of the collapsible mandrel were to be removed one by one through the opening at the head end of the motor case, carefully. There was a theft of two segments of the mandrel from RPP and progress was stalled.

Fabricating a new mandrel and Teflon coating would take months. The S3 rocket motor was in trouble. We changed over to machining of the propellant grain with specially designed non-sparking tools with necessary safety precautions and established a separate facility for the machining.

The S4 problem was associated with the composite casing, which expanded during static testing. This led to debonding between the propellant grain and insulation. The introduction of a Loose Flap between the casing and propellant solved the problem. These were some of the issues during development. After review of the test results by a committee chaired by Dr. Muthunayagam, we prepared the flight motors with stand-by systems for the E-01 launch. The Flight Readiness Review (FRR) team for rocket motors approved all the four rocket motors for flight integration, meeting the quality standards.

Kalam asked me to work with M.K. Abdul Majeed, on rocket systems such as Separation between stages, Destruct system to be used if the SLV deviates from its path and FRP heat shield to protect S4 and the satellite and separate in two halves once they had cleared dense atmosphere. This was in addition to rocket motors. The development of rocket systems was the responsibility of the project team. Majeed, who had worked with Kalam for many years at TERLS, along with six engineers, took up the development of the systems and mechanisms. A great out-of-box thinker himself, Majeed was a great contributor to SLV-3. We had RH-560 flights for proving some control, guidance and rocket systems. His systems were proved in all the tests.

S2+S4 Flight

In the SLV3 programme, we envisaged intermediate flights. Two flights of S2+S4 sub-orbital flights were planned to prove S4 high altitude ignition, heat shield, separation system and avionics. The S2 was converted for ground level performance by suitable modifications. Still the control stability was a question mark. In one of the PRMs in a Tuesday meeting, Majeed put forth a proposal to cancel the S2+S4 flights, the reason being (a) there could be many technical problems in such a flight like controllability and it would not be possible to ignore failures and proceed further with the SLV-3, leading to considerable delay and (b) cancellation at this stage will help to divert all resources to accelerate our main mission of SLV-3. This brilliant idea was further debated in many fora. D. Narayanamurthi prepared a detailed analysis of the pros and cons. The SLV Board discussed and decided to drop the S2+S4 flights. Our focus was now on SLV3-E-01. Majeed saved the SLV3 schedule by at least one year.

Schedule more Important than Pain

During the development of the control system, an accident happened in 1979. An eighteen-member team of engineers and technicians was preparing the complex second stage control system for static test and evaluation. One of the twelve valves did not respond during checkout. Driven by anxiety, the members of the team went to the test site to look into the problem. Suddenly, the oxidizer tank filled with Red Fuming Nitric Acid (RFNA) burst, causing severe acid burns to the team members. It was a very traumatic experience to see them suffering, some of them serious. All the injured were rushed to the Thiruvananthapuram Medical College Hospital. Kurup and Kalam came and talked to the doctors, and met the injured. Hearing about the accident, a large number of employees reached the hospital and stayed there the whole night attending to the injured. Seeing a large number of people in the ward, the hospital authorities got annoyed and discharged all the injured the next day itself, though injuries to some of them were serious and they were in acute pain. Our attempt to keep them in the hospital did not succeed. P.S. Nair, our Sr. Administrative Officer, quickly made necessary arrangements in a private hospital and took care of them.

Sivaramakrishnan Nair, leader of the team in charge of the control system was among those who had received severe injuries. The acid had burnt his body at a number of places. By the time we got a bed in the hospital, he was in severe pain. Kalam kept a round-the-clock vigil. Around 3o-clock in the morning, Sivaramakrishnan regained consciousness. His first words expressed regret over the mishap and assured Kalam that he would make up for the slippage in schedule caused by the accident. His sincerity and optimism, even in the midst of such severe pain, touched everyone. He was also shifted to a private hospital the next day and taken care of.

Flight Transponder Dearer than Life

Another event we recall was the action by Shri Sivakaminathan while bringing the C-band transponder from Thiruvananthapuram to SHAR (Sriharikota Rocket Launch Complex) for integration with the SLV-3. The SLV-3 launch schedule was dependent on the arrival and integration of this equipment. On landing at Madras airport, the aircraft in which Sivakaminathan was travelling, skidded and overshot the runway. Dense smoke engulfed the aircraft. Everyone jumped out of the aircraft through the emergency exit and desperately rushed out to save themselves—all except Sivakaminathan who stayed in the aircraft until he removed the transponder from his baggage. He was among the last few persons to emerge from the smoke and he was holding the transponder close to his chest. This was the level of dedication and attachment to the project. This incident was testament to his outstanding level of accountability with regard to his project. He rushed to SHAR and the package was integrated for flight.

SLV3-E-01 FLIGHT ON 10 AUGUST 1979

We shifted our work to SHAR for flight preparations for the launch campaign. The 44 subsystems were under preparation and testing. QA teams were closely monitoring, recording and giving clearance. A last-minute study showed that aerodynamic heating necessitated thermal protection on the outer structure between stages. Cork with a resin-based thermal cover needed to be put on inter-stages. Kalam asked me to get the materials and execute the work fast, as this had become critical suddenly. All panels were removed one by one and two of us did the work round the clock at SHAR. This was not a big technology, but was crucial for launch preparation.

Dhawan issued orders on mission management, appointment of key executives for launch and formation of a Launch Authorisation Board (LAB). Kalam was the Mission Director and Srinivasan was the Vehicle Director. Dr. Brahm Prakash was the Chairman LAB. The countdown started. More than 400 engineers, technicians and journalists were waiting to hear the satellite injection into an Earth orbit. I was at the Blockhouse, without sleep for several nights during the campaign. One by one, the events were happening, as per the countdown manual.

It was 10 August 1979. The countdown for India's first experimental launch of the SLV-3 (SLV-E01) had been progressing at the SHAR Centre of ISRO for the last 36 hours and we were at T-1 hour for the launch. Every subsystem was given the green signal in the checkout consoles, indicating its perfect health. Everyone present was thrilled to see the display as the countdown progressed, and with great anticipation awaited the result of the seven-year effort of putting together technologies, skills and products to inject the Rohini satellite into a near Earth orbit.

Kalam was sitting in front of Mission Director's Console at the Control Centre, 8 km away from the launch pad. Srinivasan was at the Block House, 500 metres from the launch pad. I was sitting in the Block House, looking at the Vehicle Director's console. Tension started to build up as the countdown progressed to the important phase of final checks at T-8 minutes. At that time, the reaction control thrusters that were housed between the first and second stages were given the warm-up pulse, by mixing the Hydrazine propellant and the Red Fumic Nitric Acid (RFNA). The warm-up was necessary for the thrusters to be ready for the final operation of the control system. However, the solenoid valve in the oxidiser loop, which was supposed to close after the pulse, did not. The RFNA started leaking as red fumes at T-8 minutes, depleting the tank before T-0. Unfortunately, there was no colour monitor at that time to give the necessary indication of the red fumes to the Mission Director's console. The main camera was focussed to the bottom of the launch vehicle at the S1 nozzle to see the ignition. But the inside pressure of the oxidizer tank was dropping. During automatic checkout at T-6 minutes, the checkout computer put a "hold" on to the mission. Madhavan Nair, Dr. Ananthram, and other experts met at the Block house and opined that the pressure of the tank, although low, was sufficient for the control system performance and advised the Vehicle Director to progress the launch faster. Accordingly, Dr. Srinivasan informed Mission Director to lift the hold. The Mission Director gave an overriding command to go ahead for the launch.

Lost the Mission

At 0758 a.m., the SLV-E01 took off perfectly and the first stage performance was as predicted, and SLV-3 was on course. After separation of the first stage, it was a smooth transition to the second stage motor ignition. We were spellbound to see our hopes flying in the form of the SLV-3. However, suddenly we saw the vehicle did not go as per the trajectory and went out of control. The whole system tumbled and fell into the Bay of Bengal, 560 km off Sriharikota at 317 sec. Thus, in one stroke, the seven years of hard work of many scientists, engineers and technicians came to naught. The incident caused profound disappointment. I was upset and frustrated. I was trying to go near Kalam, but many people had surrounded him to know what had happened. Kalam took the responsibility on his shoulders, as he was the Mission Director. However, the magnanimous Dhawan shielded him. Showing remarkable composure, Dhawan stated to the press, ***"most of the systems have worked, and the mission is partially successful. But we have not fallen flat"***. As Head of the organisation, he took the responsibility, without pointing to the Mission Director, Kalam. It was a mood of mourning in our hostel. In the evening, Kalam went for a walk near the guest house. Suddenly, he felt someone touching his shoulder. He looked back. It was Brahm Prakash, who gave him comfort and told Kalam, **"Don't give up"**.

Detailed Post Flight Analysis by a committee chaired by M.R. Kurup brought out clearly that a 40-micron particle had prevented the solenoid valve from closing. Careful assembly in a clean room with appropriate filters would be introduced for the future.

Lost my Father

After the failed launch of the SLV3-E-01 on 10 August 1979, I returned to Thiruvananthapuram on 12 August 1979. Shocking news awaited me. My father, 86, was unwell and had been admitted for prostate surgery. I rushed to the hospital at Nagercoil. I met the doctor who told me that they were waiting for me to come to proceed with the surgery. On 15 August, he was operated on. He became normal, as recovery was fast. On 3 September 1979, he participated in the Onam feast and then, all of a sudden, he left us in sleep that night. I was in terrific shock. We did the formalities. What a great soul he was! He lived for others giving all his time and wealth, helping in difficulties and utilising his knowledge to cure dreadful diseases. He is still living with me and blessing my family and me.

In the *Bhagavad Gita*, Krishna tells Arjun, **"See the flower. How generously it distributes perfume and honey. It gives to all, gives freely of its love. When its work is done, it falls away quietly".**

SLV-3 E02 FLIGHT

The VSSC and SLV-3 teams worked hard for the SLV E-02 launch. Constant reviews by the Space Centre Council, chaired by the new Director, Dr. V.R. Gowarikar helped to progress the tasks faster. All the sub-systems went through reviews by FRR teams. Dr. S.C. Gupta chaired the overall flight readiness and cleared the launch. We moved all the systems to SHAR, before the monsoon started in Kerala.

The launch campaign is an interesting period for people involved in space projects. They forget everything. It is a charged situation. For every mission, we pray to God for success. Many new technical problems cropped up during launch preparation and they were solved completely.

A Moving Experience

During the early stages of the launch preparation, powerful bolt of lightning during a thunderstorm struck the Block House, which housed all the electronic systems that gave connectivity to the launch vehicle on the launch pad. This led to the failure of all the electronic connectivity and crashing of computers and corrupting of the connected software. More than 45 young scientists/engineers (hardware/software) worked continuously for 36 hours and restored all the instruments and computers to their original configuration leading to the early resumption of the launch operation. The ever problem-solver and action-man in the front, Madhavan Nair, took the lead for this task. This shows how youth can rise to the occasion and overcome a challenge.

Umbilical Connectivity

Another incident happened during the launch of SLV-3 D1. The countdown sequence was proceeding smoothly. There were two operations to be carried out on the launcher —one for release of the spacecraft umbilical and the other to release the arms holding the vehicle. Both these systems were pneumatically operated remotely controlled from the Block House. The arms were released as expected. However, the spacecraft's umbilical release system failed to respond to the command. This held up the countdown automatically. There was suspense on how to go about it and the launch managers huddled together to find a solution. Shri M.R. Kurup and Kalam were on the spot to solve it. Seeing the situation, a young tradesman of SHAR, Shri Pappaiah, volunteered to climb on to the launcher and release the mechanism manually. After clearance by the Range Director, he accomplished this marvellous feat and the vehicle was launched that day. No one would forget such committed individuals who have been the backbone of ISRO.

Determined Strivers

"Men like Sivakaminathan, Sivaramakrishnan Nair, Pappaiah and the band of young engineers who restored the power supply in record time are a breed apart. They are the strivers, always reaching higher than the previous time. And with their social and family life welded to their dream, they find the rewards of their drive overwhelming—the inherent joy of being in the flow. These events greatly prove that the committed ISRO teams would stand like a rock in success and in failure".

The Launch

It was a smooth countdown and there was no hold by the checkout computer. SLV3-E-02 launched on 18 July 1980 and was a total success, injecting the Rohini satellite of 40 kg in a 308 km × 915 km orbit around the Earth.

I witnessed jubilation all around at VSSC, SHAR, ISAC and other ISRO centres at the successful SLV3-E-02 mission. **India became a member of Space Club**. All senior Technology Directors, who were the chairs of FRR, made excellent contributions. In fact, every one among the VSSC, SHAR and ISAC scientists, technicians, and support staff and ISRO HQ were worthy of recognition. Dr. Brahm Prakash provided extraordinary guidance for SLV-3 management, Dr. V.R. Gowarikar, who became Director after

Brahm Prakash in 1979, gave full support in progressing the tasks at VSSC for the E-02. He really chased everyone to perform. SCC members and Group Directors contributed significantly to review and certify the flawless performance of individual systems. **Dr. S.C. Gupta chaired overall FRR for the total mission, went meticulously through all the details, and gave clearance to the flight**. It was without doubt a great contribution to the success. Everyone who chaired and prepared the system put their heart and soul into the success and deserved to get recognition. Kalam got a Padma Bhushan in the 1981 Republic Day announcement. He, being the Project Director, who led the project from the front, was no doubt, fully deserving of this national recognition. However, this created heartburn in VSSC, particularly among the seniors, without whom the SLV-3 systems could not have been realised.

Difficulties at VSSC

In the meantime, Kalam submitted the Project Closure Report, heralding that the original objectives had been achieved. Kalam and I prepared a confidential report on the lessons learnt from SLV-3 and proposed a new management structure for future launch vehicles, especially for PSLV, in a multiple project environment. The report was submitted to Dhawan. Our suggestion to create system-level projects was later implemented by ISRO HQ. The SLV3 team was dismantled into SLV-C, ASLV, PSLV study team and into technology groups. V.P. Sandlas became PD SLV-C, M.S.R. Dev became PD ASLV, S. Srinivasan was made Study Director, PSLV, Madhavan Nair was moved to the Avionics Group and so on. Kalam was sidelined. He was made Group Director Aeronautics. Gowarikar offered me the position of DPD ASLV. But I preferred to be with Kalam. From among the entire SLV-3 team, I was the only one to move with Kalam to the Aeronautics Group, in his difficult time.

I recall the conversation between Kalam and me when the two of us were travelling in a jeep, sitting face to face in the back seats. He advised me not to join him in the Aero Group and instead accept what Gowarikar had asked me to do. He said he would somehow manage things by himself, and find his way out. "You have many years ahead and you cannot go against the Director". I told him that over the last eight years that I had worked with him, I was able to bring out my hidden talents and had adapted myself to suit his frequency of thinking and doing. It was like a RAM-and-LAKSHMANA relationship. *Lakshmana followed Rama to the forest.* I recited one Thirukkural. *Gold will shine and shine only when it is subjected to repeated heating. In life, difficulties will become opportunities.* He did not agree, as he thought there would be a revenge action on me. I could notice that he was sad. However, I remained adamant.

Finally, I joined the Aeronautics Group as a senior engineer, reporting to Kalam, with the approval of Gowarikar, and got a separate room in the main building, next to Kalam's room. We proposed a new division for Launch Vehicle Design, along with Aerodynamics, Aerospace Structures, Applied Mathematics divisions and Aerospace Mechanisms. Dhawan was closely following the dynamics at VSSC and thinking of some corrective measures. The Aero Group was renamed Aerospace Design and Dynamics Group (ADDG) with a charter of Integrated Design of Launch Vehicles. Kalam became the Director, ADDG.

Kalam Wrote in 'Wings of Fire'

"Meanwhile, I carried out an analysis of application of SLV-3 and its variants with Sivathanu Pillai, and compared the existing launch vehicles of the world for missile applications. We established that SLV-3 solid rocket systems would meet the national requirements of payload delivery vehicles for short and intermediate ranges (4,000 km). We contended that the development of one additional solid booster of 1.8-metre diameter with 36 tonnes of propellant along with SLV-3 subsystems would meet the ICBM requirement (above 5,000 km for a 1,000 kg payload). However, the proposal was never considered by Dhawan. It nevertheless paved the way for the formulation of the Re-entry Experiment (REX), which much later on became Agni".

Kalam's mind was engrossed with missiles and he started establishing contacts. In January 1981, Kalam went to the Defence Institute of Work Study (DIWS), a DRDO lab at Mussoorie and gave a talk on SLV-3. He attended a conference at the High Altitude Laboratory (now called DEAL (Defence Electronics Application Laboratory) at Dehradun. Dr. Raja Ramanna, the then Scientific Adviser to the Defence Minister & Chief of DRDO was at both places and inaugurated the conference at DEAL. They had private meetings at both places, over tea. These were planned meetings and Air Commodore Gopalaswamy, who was earlier in DRDL and later in IAT Pune, was instrumental. Dr. Raja

Ramanna explained the problems at DRDL in missile development that was reeling under persistent apathy. He wanted Kalam to take over the reins of developing advanced missile systems for the Armed Forces, as Director DRDL. He advised Kalam to talk to Dhawan and inform him for further action.

Kalam witnessed SLV3-D1 flight on 31 May 1981 from the visitors' gallery—for the first time he was outside the control room. He was feeling horrible, as he was not in the theatre of action. But the media locked on to him. This added fuel to the fire in some quarters. Noticing the difficulties Kalam was going through, Dhawan gave him an additional role at ISRO HQ, as Director Launch Vehicles/Systems Programme Office, reporting to Chairman ISRO, while he continued at VSSC as Director ADDG. I was also working at both places. We arranged a major review of ADDG, chaired by Dhawan, with a profile of future tasks. This review brought in a holistic approach to the integrated design of launch vehicles, consolidating the tasks carried out by different groups. It also proved that it was very difficult to contain a hard working person like Kalam. Every time he brought a new dimension to his work.

PSLV Propellant Choice

In the meantime, I supported Srinivasan in PSLV configuration studies. He made me convener of the Steering Committee, with senior scientists from VSSC and SHAR to evaluate different propellants in 1/3S1 (one segment of SLV-3 first stage rocket motor), to decide the choice of propellant for the PSLV booster, by conducting static tests. We conducted several static tests, made detailed analyses comparing Polyol, PBAN and HTPB-based propellants and decided on an indigenously developed propellant with HTPB (Hydroxyl Terminated Polybutadiene) binder, with a high percentage of aluminium powder.

Integration Complex at Valiamala

Abdul Majeed wanted a separate Aerospace Mechanisms complex for zero G test of explosive-filled separation systems, requiring an isolated hillock. We went on a search, visiting several places in Thiruvananthapuram district. Majeed, Natarajan, Gopalakrishna Pillai and I located Valiamala, saw the beautiful forestland covered with young anjeli trees (*Artocarpus hirsutus*) and liked the area at first sight. All of us, including Srinivasan, worked with the administration on the formalities to acquire the land. We made a project report for the Aerospace Mechanisms Centre and later included the Integration Complex and Test Centre. In the meantime, Muthunayagam wanted to establish a separate Liquid Propulsion Centre. His wanted Valiamala, as he desired to be away from VSSC. Kalam also wanted to set up the Launch Vehicle Integration Centre, amalgamating all LV Projects. Eventually, Muthunayagam succeeded. The LPSC was set up in Valiamala.

New Launch Station for PSLV

Another important task I undertook on the directions of Srinivasan was to locate a site for the Polar Launch Station. The PSLV polar launch from SHAR, due to range safety considerations, had to go around Sri Lanka in a dog-leg manoeuvre, losing nearly 30 per cent of its payload capacity. Sriharikota was a better launch site for geo-synchronous missions, needing an eastern launch. For a direct southern launch, we required a safe location. The European Space Agency used to go all the way to Kourou in French Guiana, South America, for a due south launch for polar missions and due east launch for geo-synchronous missions. **Therefore, the launch site is an important consideration for cost effective missions.**

In 1981, I visited several areas in the southern part of Tamilnadu, with some of my colleagues and we identified Perumanal (close to Kudankulam), as a possible location, for a due south launch of the PSLV, to get additional satellite weight.

Being from Kanyakumari, I knew the place well. We worked with the State administration, carried out a survey and prepared a preliminary feasibility report for Srinivasan. An ISRO committee was set up to study further on possible locations—Near Cape, Balasore, Odisha and Kutch, Gujarat. The committee submitted its report in the above order. So a visit was arranged, and Chairman Dhawan, Seshan, Kalam, Gowarikar, Muthunayagam, Y.S. Rajan and others including myself visited Mahendragiri for a liquid engine test facility and to Perumanal, in the hot sun, for a PSLV station. It was a large piece of barren land. A few fishermen's hutments were on the shore. It was an ideal place for a launch station.

I explained the site details to Dhawan and possible locations of the launch pad with assembly tower, control centre and tracking & telemetry locations. Everyone liked the place. The local Bishop garlanded Dhawan and took him to the Church. In front of everyone assembled inside, he said that the local people were not willing to set up the launch station, there. Dhawan felt humiliated by the words of the Rev. Father and left the church along with us. **I felt that we had lost a golden chance.** Dhawan, in anger, informed us that the Polar Launch Station would be located in the National Test Range with Defence at Odisha. It was the Chairman's decision and we followed his direction. We even stopped persuading the Bishop. **I was upset at this decision. If Sarabhai could persuade Rev. Fr. Peter Pereira to get the fishermen's village of Thumba, including the church, that too in Kerala, for space activities, this could have been a much easier task.** Many of ISRO colleagues felt that this decision would result in 30 per cent of payload capacity loss for every PSLV for polar launches.

In the same place, near Perumanal, Kudankulam nuclear power station has now been established. So we lost the place. The National Test Range at Baliapal, Odisha never came due to people agitation. Instead, Kalam obtained Wheeler Islands for the DRDO and built the Agni Launch Pad. Biju Patnaik, while sanctioning the islands, got an assurance from Kalam that **ICBMs** would be launched from these islands. They are now called Dr Abdul Kalam Islands. All PSLV launches continue to take place at Satish Dhawan Space Centre, SHAR for polar missions, going around Sri Lanka and losing payload capacity.

PSLV CONFIGURATION

The VSSC finalised the configuration of the PSLV after presenting it to the Space Centre Council. It comprised two large solid strap-on boosters and a core rocket motor, each carrying 100 tons of solid propellant, liquid propellant of 33 tons with a Vikas engine as the second stage and two upper stages—solid+liquid, weighing 400 tonnes. Gowarikar, as Director VSSC, submitted the PSLV project proposal to Dhawan, Chairman ISRO.

As Director, Launch Vehicle Programme Office (LVPO), Kalam was asked by Dhawan to work out any other more reliable configuration for the PSLV and to study the performance and cost effectiveness of future launch vehicles. I worked on Mondays and Tuesdays at the VSSC, travelled on Wednesdays by train to Bengaluru, worked on Thursdays and Fridays at ISRO HQ, and would return to Thiruvananthapuram on Saturdays. This was my routine during 1981-82.

Dhawan, a highly reputed aerodynamic engineer, with a sound background of mathematics and systems engineering, studied the VSSC proposed configuration carefully and suggested Kalam to look at a reduced number of stages, core vehicle without big strap-ons, increased reliability, growth potential and so on. He illustrated his ideas on the blackboard in Kalam's room adjacent to the Chairman's office. K.A.P. Menon, Dr. N. Sundararajan and me followed his directions and generated A3-size charts to show the results and presented them to Kalam and later to Dhawan, on various options and technologies. I also prepared the trends in the space-faring nations on future launch vehicles.

There was a lull in the VSSC, as the proposal sent from there had not yet been approved. Gowarikar came a few times to HQ and enquired and was told that the report was under study.

To make a high-performance booster, with increased propellant loading and operating at high pressure, we needed very high strength steel, instead of the 15CDV6 steel used in the SLV-3. We looked at Maraging steel knowing well about the import difficulties and its high fracture toughness. MAR+AGING implies martensitic transformation in Fe-Ni matrix and its subsequent ageing in the presence of other alloying elements, in different grades 200, 250, 300 depending on yield strength. The Chairman set up a high-level committee with Brahm Prakash as chairman, and members including Dr. V.S. Arunachalam, a top metallurgist of the country and Director of Defence Metallurgical Research Laboratory, to choose the material. The expert committee recommended the choice of M250 Maraging steel for the booster. The DMRL and VSSC undertook the development of M250, to be produced by Midhani Defence Production Unit. The new configuration had S1 with 125 tonne HTPB propellant loading, second stage with 37.5 t UDMH+N2O4 Vikas engine, 6t solid third stage, 2t solid fourth stage (later changed to twin engine liquid fourth stage) and 6 SLV-3 S1 stage as strap-ons could meet the objective of PSLV mission. Total weight of the PSLV was 275 tonnes (against earlier configuration of 400 tonnes). Technology requirements, cost estimates, development plan were prepared. Dhawan approved the revised configuration and asked VSSC to submit a comprehensive report for the PSLV. Over the years, optimisation has been done with increased propellant loading (S1 with 139 t propellant, S3 with 7t loading and S4 twin engine with 2t propellant). Further changes have been made depending on the missions. Maraging steel became the mainstay for boosters of PSLV, GSLV and variants.

We started giving shape to the REX Project (IRBM) at ISRO HQ. G. Madhavan Nair worked out the details of guidance and control scheme for REX. Sundararajan prepared an integrated design document. I prepared technology requirements, development strategy and cost for the project. Kalam prepared a hand-written letter to Dhawan, making it clear that his heart was in missiles and requested approval to undertake the project in ISRO. I read the letter and told him that it would annoy Dhawan and the project would be turned down. He said, "Yes, Let me see his reaction". After meeting Dhawan, Kalam was happy to tell me that for the first time Dhawan had listened and said that he would talk to the DRDO, so that Kalam could do the project there, and not in ISRO.

DRDO

Dr. D.S. Kothari was the architect of DRDO. He was a student of eminent physicists, M.N. Saha and Ernest Rutherford at Cambridge University. His theory of pressure ionisation brought him laurels from the international scientific community. He was an outstanding physicist, an educationist with a vision, an inspiring teacher, **the father of Defence Science in our country** and, above all, a great human being who symbolised the noblest traditions of Indian culture. He combined in himself profound scholarship, simplicity to the point of asceticism, humility, warmth, enlightenment, tolerance, as well as a passionate and abiding concern for the welfare of humanity. On 12 July 1948, he took charge as the first Scientific Adviser to the Minister of Defence. The Defence Science Centre later became the DRDO on 1 January 1958. Dr DS Kothari continued up to 1961.

Prof. S. Bhagavantam, Director IISc, followed him (1 July 1961-13 October 1969). Dr. Nag Chaudhuri, credited with building India's first cyclotron, from Calcutta University was the DRDO Chief from 1 July 1970 to 1 July 1974. He was a firebrand and wanted to make the ICBM, as demanded by Indira Gandhi. He told the DRDL scientists in a meeting that if the DRDL could not build an ICBM in four years, the lab would be closed down. Of course, he was not realistic. Hectic activity started at the DRDL to build a large engine called Valiant. Excellent infrastructure for fabrication and testing was established in liquid propulsion. Prof. M.G.K. Menon followed Nag Chaudhuri (17 August 1974-1 July 1978). After these stalwarts, Dr. Raja Ramanna, a nuclear physicist who played a key role in the development of the country's nuclear-weapons programme and 1974 nuclear test, and an inspiring leader, became Chief of the DRDO. He wanted Kalam to take up the development of missiles and started the process. After him, Dr. V.S. Arunachalam became the new Scientific Adviser to Defence Minister (SA to RM) in February 1982.

Arunachalam spoke to Dhawan about the formalities for Kalam's taking over the DRDL. But things were not moving with Dhawan. Shri R. Venkataraman, the Defence Minister, after the visit, requested Dhawan to give Kalam to the DRDO for taking over as Director DRDL. Dhawan yielded to the Minister. Dhawan told Kalam that for a month Kalam could be at ISRO Hq, and in turn, ISRO would process the deputation papers to DRDO. Kalam was transferred to ISRO Hq from VSSC in May 82 and during this one month, he stayed at IISc guesthouse. Kalam and I made an updated report on 'Performance and Cost Analysis of ISRO Launch vehicles'. In the evening of May 30, 1982, Kalam presented this report to the ISRO Council. Dhawan announced Kalam's leaving ISRO and joining DRDL as its Director. I was also present. This was followed by a farewell dinner hosted by the ISRO Council.

In the evening of May 31, I went with Kalam to Bengaluru airport. For the first time he allowed me to carry his lone suitcase. He hoped that very soon I would join him at the DRDL. He said he would come to see me, and persuade Dhawan to release me to the DRDL. Kalam joined the DRDL, the missile laboratory of the DRDO, as Director on 1 June 1982.

AT ISRO HQ (1982-86)

At ISRO, Dhawan decided that I must be at HQ dedicatedly, and support him in launch vehicles. I joined ISRO HQ on 1 July 1982, after spending 13 years at VSSC, Thiruvananthapuram. To rent a house Bengaluru, one had to pay ten months' rent as advance. This was a handicap for me. I had to pay Rs. 6,000 as advance. I could mobilise about Rs. 3,000. Kalam came to know about this and gave me a loan of Rs.3,000. I started living in Rajaji Nagar, Bengaluru. Later I returned the loan. My only son, Bhagavath Kumar, got admission in the sixth standard at National Public School. Life took a different turn. Suddenly, it was less stressful, but I was not comfortable.

At ISRO Hq, Y.S. Rajan, Scientific Secretary to Chairman, was the Administrative Head of all personnel working in the HQ. T.N. Seshan was the Additional Secretary, taking care of the Department of Space. Dhawan gave importance to me. He asked me to meet him every Tuesday at 3 p.m. to discuss launch vehicle-related issues. My work began at HQ on ASLV/PSLV technology upgradation, studies on new technologies, cryogenics, world LV performance analysis, replies to letters/ proposals from VSSC and SHAR and attending review/Hqr meetings. This generated a number of documents and system analysis reports.

Government approvals came for ASLV and PSLV. I attended Board meetings and the actions required were followed up. In one of the meetings in the ASLV Board, the Project Director reported a delay in clearance of files by the Financial Adviser (FA), despite Board having approved them earlier. The FA did not attend the meetings. Every file had to go to him, but he would not clear it. I met Gowarikar, Director VSSC, and requested him to review the position with the FA. He said he would not intervene. When I told this to the PD, he felt unhappy and said that he would not like to continue, as the people responsible to support the project were themselves refusing to help. It was a difficult situation, as the FA was not yielding. It looked to me that he enjoyed controlling everyone.

I rushed back to Bengaluru and went straight to Dhawan. On seeing me in a rush, Dhawan realised that something was wrong. I said, "Projects are terribly delayed at VSSC, due to indecision, as the FA holds up all the files without any reason. It looks to me that he enjoys delaying projects". On hearing my views, he pressed the intercom and said "Seshan, come". As I was sitting in the chair opposite Dhawan, Seshan with his heavy weight came running inside and said, "Yes sir". He was standing. Dhawan said, "Remove the FA in the VSSC". Seshan defended the FA saying that he was the best FA and that he had brought him from the Railways with great persuasion, and he would ensure correcting the situation. Dhawan said he was not prepared to listen to any reasoning and instructed "FA must leave ISRO tomorrow. You can go now".

The FA's deputation was cancelled the next day by an express order from Seshan. This sent a shockwave across the VSSC. It was a terrific action by Dhawan. Seshan was a firebrand and I thought he would smash me. Instead, he became soft and friendly. I realised that he accorded huge respect to Dhawan. The Project Directors were relieved. After this episode, Gowarikar came to my room in Bengaluru and said some good words. He also became friendly. I could give good support to VSSC and SHAR. After many years, in 2007, when I received the LOKMANYA TILAK award at Pune in a public meeting, Gowarikar recalled many such incidents. He also recalled my PhD from Pune University in 1996, when he was Vice Chancellor.

Kalam used to come to Bengaluru on most Sundays and discuss the issues at the DRDL. His new problems were the regimental attitude in the system, engineers afraid to talk and put forth their views in meetings, PAC review on DRDL, and that many scientists were aged. There was a need to bring in a new culture in the DRDL. He wanted me to come and spend some time during finalisation of missile projects. Dhawan did not agree to my getting involved in the work of the DRDL. He said he went to the DRDL on Kalam's invitation recently and reviewed the work that was going on. He concluded that it would take considerable time for Kalam to bring in a new culture. However, I knew 'the never give up' attitude of Kalam and was confident that once he decided something, he would achieve it by persistent follow up.

Kalam's request for supply of SLV-3 first stage, to be the booster for the Agni missile was not favourably considered by Dhawan. Kalam asked me to approach Dhawan. I put a note to Dhawan on our surplus capacity at RPP to make segments and recommended four S1 in the 12 segments to be given to the DRDL, at cost. Dhawan sent the file back and asked me to speak. I explained him our capacity and supply of segments schedule and criticality of the issue. I made him recall the REX project and that Dhawan had stated that Kalam could do at the DRDO and not at the ISRO. Since the DRDO did not have one-metre diameter facility, the S1 system supply was justified. That did not mean ISRO was making missiles. He looked at me for some time. Both of us did not talk. Finally, he signed the file agreeing for four SLV-3 S1 to be provided to the DRDL for development tests, with a proper MOU and payment as per ISRO formula. An MOU was to be agreed by VSSC and HQ. It was a breakthrough for Agni development flights. Kalam was happy, as it was the mission of his life to realise the IRBM. My continuing in ISRO HQ helped the cause. Now he would concentrate on the design of the AGNI missile with re-entry control and guidance, and most importantly re-entry structure.

Kalam and I discussed the progress of the evolution of missiles at the DRDL and the need for mobilising many institutions to overcome technology denial. He talked of selection of project directors. He made Col. R. Swaminathan (later he became Major General) who was Director Planning, to explain to me Dr. Ranga Rao's management structure. I said that the three-tier management structure was well conceived and that it would work.

Back at VSSC, Srinivasan consolidated the design documents, integrating system level projects, and preliminary design review took place. PSLV development started. I participated in the project meetings in deciding on industry mapping, contracts, MOUs with system projects, documentation and so on. When Srinivasan had a health problem, Madhavan Nair stepped in as Associate PD, and later became PD PSLV. Srinivasan became the Chief of the LV Projects and Integration Complex at Valiamala. His significant contribution was in establishing the reasons for failures in ASLV flights and corrective measures. Srinivasan became Director VSSC and died while in service. I have great regard for Srinivasan for his knowledge, progressive thoughts, commitment and contributions. Madhavan Nair became Director LPSC and VSSC, and later became Chairman ISRO. **The mission to the Moon was his initiative.**

In the meantime, there was intense discussion at HQ on the PSLV launch pad at SHAR. I presented my views to Dhawan on launch facilities, as I had worked earlier on the Polar Launch Station near Cape. I insisted that since SHAR would be the station for polar and geo missions, we needed to consider that (A) Modular mobile launch tower with 5 metre extra length to accommodate GSLV with cryogenic stage, replacing the present third and fourth stages; (B) Possibility of due east GSLV launch overflying a small part of the land of Malaysia and taking into account trajectory design for range safety. Y.S. Rajan asked me to send these documents to Col. Pant, Director SHAR Centre. My suggestions were accepted.

Visit to Launch Facilities

Dhawan decided to send a team to study all the launch stations and test facilities of all countries for getting inputs for our PSLV launch complex. R.D. John, Chief Engineer, led the team, which included Chandran and me. Construction engineers Ramalingam, Rangarao. Y.S. Rajan and Chandran worked out a detailed plan and got the necessary approvals. It was my first visit abroad, that too for 41 days covering the entire globe during March-April 1984.

To start with, we visited Viking liquid engine and cryogenic engine test facilities at SEP Vernon, near Paris, Ariane integration complex-Aerospatiale, environmental test facilities at Toulouse in France and high-altitude test set up at Stuttgart, Germany. We also visited the MBB satellite complex at Munich. My interest there was to meet the famous D.E. Koelle, who was an authority on designs of futuristic launch vehicles and performance-cost analysis. We recognised each other and discussed global trends on cost effective launchers. He gave me a good lunch and agreed to send me all his publications. From Munich, we went to ESTEC facilities in the Netherlands, particularly those required for satellites, such as thermo-vacuum chamber and vibration, acoustic test set-up.

R.D. John, Ramalingam and I returned to Paris, via London. We proceeded to the ESA launch station at Kourou in French Guiana, South America. It was a long flight over the Antarctica. We studied the first launch pad used for Ariane flights, some for ISRO's communication satellites such as APPLE, INSAT series and the new launch pad being built for Ariane 5 (for heavy satellites like INSAT4, GSAT). We also looked at the total infrastructure required for vehicle preparation, propellant storage, satellite checkout and launch, in this remote facility. It again confirmed my view that Polar Launch Station at Perumanal, near Kanyakumari, must be followed up for direct south launch, like the ESA station at Kourou. I believed we must have an arrangement with MALDIVES to use GAN Island near the Equator, for getting maximum advantage for polar and geo missions. I believed that it was still not late to progress this idea to hire one of the islands near the Equator.

My visit to Kourou was a memorable one. We saw Devil's Islands in the Atlantic Ocean not very far from the shore. The significance was the remote prison- French penal colony. I remembered reading the book *Papillon* by Henri Charrière, an autobiographical novel, first published in France on 30 April 1969. The novel details Papillon's heroic deeds during his incarceration between 1931 and 1945 and his subsequent escape from French Guiana, through the Atlantic Ocean. A film was also made on this hero's story, which I had seen earlier. I remembered many heroic deeds on seeing Devil's Island.

During President Kalam's visit to South Africa in September 2004, I went with him. We had gone to Robben Island prison, where Nelson Mandela served 26 years in prison. We sat in the cell for some time. It was a great visit to meet him later at his residence in Johannesburg.

John, Ramalingam and I proceeded from Kourou to Miami, USA, overflying the West Indies and Cuba. Then we left for Orlando. D. Narayanamurthy joined us during our tour of the USA. Our next visit was to the John F. Kennedy Space Centre. Mr. Philip, Director Engineering, took us to the space shuttle launch pad 39A and 39B and explained every aspect of its design. We went through the Vehicle Assembly Stack, Mobile Service Structure, Flame Deflector, Launch Control & Fuelling, Sound Suppression Water System and Transporter. The same pad was used for the Saturn V launch for Apollo mission to send a human to the Moon.

The next day we spent our time in studying the DELTA pad, especially to understand the jet deflector to avoid any backlash during the PSLV launch. Philip gave me a NASA document on "design criteria of jet defector" (which I shared with Srinivasan and the SHAR team, and the inputs were used in the PSLV Launch Complex). We went through all the other pads, infrastructure, instrumentation, exhibition centre and so on. NASA took good care of us.

We went to the Shuttle Main Engine Test Centre at New Orleans, then proceeded to Washington to visit the Goddard Space Flight Centre, where Kalam had had received his initial training. My desire was to see the painting in the reception lobby of the space centre that Kalam had described to me. It was a battle scene of Tipu's men firing rockets against the British during the

Srirangapatna war. What a glory for India to convey to the world that it was the first country to make proper rockets and use them in war to

defeat the British. After a few years, I went to the Woolwich Artillery Museum in London on a Sunday, made them open it and saw Tipu's rocket, beautifully decorated with golden letters stating that Tipu had used it in large numbers during the Srirangapatna war in 1792 that ended in the surrender of the British. There was a British video giving the same message. **We see other countries celebrate India's achievement in building the first war rocket.** In Washington, we went to the Air & Space Museum and saw the abundant cherry blossoms along the banks of the Potomac River. The statue of Abraham Lincoln was majestic and inspiring.

We went to New York and to Niagara Falls, proceeded to Los Angeles and went to the Western Test Range, the long runway for shuttle landing and other military launch facilities. We went to McDonnell Douglas Delta manufacturing centre and studied the processing of large-sized honeycomb structures. The production line of Delta was very impressive. **On seeing the Delta roll out, I desired that one day, a large number of PSLVs would roll out from our Space Industry Complex. My dream would come true soon. (Recently, I got an opportunity at ISRO to evolve the management structure for production of PSLV in large numbers with industry consortium.)**

Coming back to the narrative on visits, we then proceeded to San Francisco and stayed at Palo Alto. Our work was at Ford Aerospace. INSAT-1A, 1B were already integrated and launched in Delta and Space

Shuttle, respectively. We saw INSAT-1C, which was getting integrated for flight in Ariane, at Kourou. We consolidated the requirements for satellite assembly and testing in a clean environment. I went around Stanford University campus to get a feel of the great institution. We saw the engineering marvel—Golden Gate Bridge. We then flew to Tokyo via Honolulu, over the Pacific Ocean. Due to time difference, we lost one day. Four Seasons Hotel near the Indian Embassy was our place of stay. We went to Kagoshima Space Centre of Japan. Studied the launch facility and rocket systems with regard to the Kappa, Lambda and Lambda-4 rockets that set the stage for small satellite missions. From Tokyo we returned to Bengaluru.

Our team's report contained valuable suggestions for ISRO facilities and plans. Reports on design information, future of cost effective launchers, design of a launch pad for the PSLV and for future tasks were shared with the teams at VSSC and SHAR.

Life at Bengaluru was quite different from Thiruvanthapuram. Instead of running around and pushing activities, it was more about learning, acquisition of knowledge and analysis. I could give more time to thinking and exploring the future of the space programme. I assisted Prof. Dhawan by providing analysis reports on the proposals coming from the centres and on policy matters. We had a good team at the HQ, that would come up with out-of-box ideas all the time. From a hard life at Thiruvanthapuram, I came to a softer life at Bengaluru. My Tuesday meetings continued with Dhawan, including the alternate Sunday meetings with Kalam at Woodlands hotel over lunch.

ISRO HQ had excellent thinkers like Rajan, Siddhartha, Sudharsan, Shetty, Chandran, Prabhu, J.P. Singh and me as technical advisors to Dhawan. This team was the think tank, with outstanding capability in several fields. The HQ was vibrant and abuzz with new ideas, in order to establish a strong foundation for ISRO. T.N. Seshan, as Additional Secretary, provided administrative leadership. The HQ was active in giving policy directions and in helping the centres to progress technology development and trojects. The organisation got streamlined in procedures, decision-making process and mission management. Sarabhai's great vision of building 'Technology and Teams' on a fast track with targets ahead in a healthy competitive mode made ISRO get a kick-start. Dhawan's outstanding organisational leadership and focused mission management led ISRO to become a top class institution in the country. The legacy continued and ISRO maintained its lead among R&D establishments.

Prof. Satish Dhawan retired on 30 September 1984 and Prof. U.R. Rao became Chairman from 1 October 1984. Dhawan continued as Senior Adviser for one year and later as Adviser. I used to meet him quite often and he advised me to prepare a report on Future ISRO Launchers, comparing all the launch vehicles of space-faring countries, launch stations, missions and critical technologies. I did so, matching with the 15-year profile prepared by Dhawan. He corrected the report. My report (ISRO/ILV/S:TN:32:85/S), submitted in 1985, stressed ISRO to embark on Cryogenics immediately as a project, to develop as an upper stage, to get ready for due east geo missions, to acquire land for a Polar Launch Station, to make a common launch pad for PSLV and GSLV, and to bring in a space industry complex. I presented this report to U.R. Rao. He appreciated it and took the report to Delhi, met Prime Minister Rajiv Gandhi, and got his approval for the Cryogenic Programme. Dhawan's fatherly affection continued. He wanted to see the progress of work at SHAR and VSSC. He told U.R. Rao to send me with him. I took care of him while travelling together to Madras, Thiruvanthapuram and Valiamala. He recollected many of the events that happened at ISRO. He narrated his life story. I told him to write an autobiography. He said his people like Roddam Narasimha, Rajan, Kalam and others should write. Those four days with Dhawan were the most memorable days in my life. He continued to come to HQ and we used to share the latest technology information. Listening to him was a boon for me.

Let us go back to ISRO HQ with the new Chairman, Prof. U.R. Rao.

Kalam made a demand for an additional six S1 for the Agni missile. U.R. Rao passed on the letter to me. I made an analysis of the request with respect to internal demands. The S1 was a hard commodity for ISRO, as it was required for the ASLV, each needing core plus two strap-ons, and for the PSLV, six PS0 strap-ons. For two sets annually, 54 S1 segments would be required. With augmented facilities at RPP and SPROB, additional segments could be prepared; but it would be better to provide Technology Transfer Documents on the S1, along with six S1 stages, to the DRDL. I requested the Chairman's approval which was approved. The VSSC team was involved with HQ DRDO scientists to carry out the task.

This action led to the establishment of a big propellant production facility at the DRDL at Jagadalpur later on based on ISRO expertise.

Kalam tried with U.R. Rao to send me on deputation to the DRDO. As it was not coming through, an advertisement was issued by the DRDO to all departments. My application was forwarded by ISRO, with the approval of Y.S. Rajan. Based on this, Dr. Arunachalam sent a request letter to U.R. Rao. After a lot of persuasion by Kalam and with the support of Rajan, an annoyed U.R. Rao relented. I left ISRO after 17 years of service at VSSC and HQ, and joined the DRDO on 1 July 1986. I returned to ISRO on 1 July 2015 as Hon' Distinguished Professor for 3 years with a very important assignment given by Shri Kiran Kumar, the then Chairman ISRO. In all, I served this great organisation for 20 years.

My Family

I got married in Aug 1971. My wife Seethalakshmi is a homemaker and cooks delicious food. She belongs to a very famous family in Travancore and her father VS Arumugam Pillai was a close associate of Diwan Sir CP Ramasamy Iyer, in Travancore State. He worked in different positions as Inspector General of Registration, Textile Commissioner and so on. We were in Thiruvananthapuram in a rented house, while working at VSSC. I got Government loan for constructing a house at Thiruvananthapuram. Before the house could be completed, we shifted to Bengaluru, as I was posted at ISRO HQ.

In 1982, I joined ISRO HQ. My son Bhagavath Kumar joined National Public School in sixth standard. He adapted himself to the new school and curriculum that included Sanskrit as a subject. When I joined DRDL in 1986, the family had to move to Hyderabad. We got a one-room accommodation in the Scientists Hostel and after a year shifted to a good accommodation in the Quarters. Getting admission in tenth standard was a problem in CBSE at that time. After persuasion and written test, Kumar got admission in DRDO Lab School. He came out with top score in the school and was the only one from the school to get NTSE scholarship. He completed his higher secondary at KV and got medical college admission at Madurai. He continued with MS in Coimbatore Medical College and MCh at Stanley Medical College, Chennai in microsurgery. He studied all through with merit scholarship. We shifted to Delhi in March 1996 in Government accommodation at Chanakyapuri, when I moved to DRDO HQ.

FOUR

Strength Respects Strength

Integrated Guided Missile Development Programme

Dr. Kalam, as Director chaired the Missile Study Team (MST) at DRDL Hyderabad, in 1982, the team was to develop the missiles required for the Army, the Navy and the Air Force. The team, which included members from R&D, production and the Services, zeroed in on five projects—SS-150, SAM-X, tactical core vehicle, third-generation anti-tank missile and re-entry technology demonstrator—to be undertaken as part of the Guided Missile Development Programme (GMDP). Kalam prepared a feasibility study report and presented it to Dr. V.S. Arunachalam, the Chiefs of the Armed Forces and Defence Minister Shri R. Venkataraman. The

The Five Projects of the IGMDP

SS-150: A tactical surface-to-surface missile (150-km range) for the Army; later named **Prithvi.**

Multirole tactical core: A multirole missile system for the Army, the Navy and the Air Force; later named **Trishul.**

SAM-X: A surface-to-air missile (25 km) with multi-target handling capability for the Army and the Air Force; later named **Akash.**

ATM-3: An advanced third-generation anti-tank missile for the Army; later named **Nag.**

RTV: A re-entry test vehicle to develop re-entry technology; later named **Agni** (the technology demonstrator was later developed into a full-fledged weapon system).

Defence Minister instructed that the missiles be developed concurrently instead of sequentially. Hence, the project name was modified to Integrated Guided Missile Development Programme (IGMDP).

The Government formally sanctioned the programme in July 1983 for a period of 12 years, with Rs.388 crore.

THE OBJECTIVES OF THE IGMDP

As delineated by Kalam, once the missile was developed, it should demonstrate contemporary performance at the time of deployment and should have the following features: a) futuristic in terms of concept and technology; b) possess different capabilities (multirole); and c) be of practical value to the Army, the Navy and the Air Force (multi-user).

Futuristic Concept

The sad history of the Devil and ATM projects at DRDL was not to be repeated. In their case, the technology was already obsolescent when the development started. When the development ended and a weapon system matured, they had ultimately become obsolete. By working on a futuristic system, the Indian Armed Forces would get a superior and contemporary system at the time of deployment of that weapon system. It meant that there was a need to leapfrog technologies, deviating from the beaten path, for which new concepts, design methodologies and management approaches had to come together.

Multirole and Multi-user

A single system can be used for various missions. This benefits both the producer and the users. The user can maintain a large force level and need not use different systems for different missions. The training and maintenance aspects become simpler. Instead of maintaining different types of systems in the inventory, a single type can be maintained.

Kalam decided that all the five missiles must have multirole capability. For example, the Trishul missile had three roles: of being an anti-aircraft missile (ground-to-air), an anti-sea skimmer (missile fired from a ship against anti-ship missiles), and an anti-radar missile (air-to-ground). In fact, this is how it got its name, meaning the three-bladed 'trident'.

Similarly, Prithvi—so named because it is a surface-to-surface missile—has field-interchangeable warheads, where the users can choose the type and fix them in the field according to the type of targets to be neutralised. Prithvi can be used from a mobile launch system on ground by the Army and Air Force and from a ship by the Navy against land targets. It has a manoeuvrable trajectory to deceive the enemy about its target. This was the first time this concept of a trajectory design was used in a ballistic missile.

The medium-range surface-to-air missile Akash is on tracked and wheeled vehicles and suitable for use by the Army and the Air Force, respectively. Advanced software and capability to intercept multiple aircraft, using the command guidance by a phased array radar, made Akash a unique air defence system. It was so named as the theatre of war is in the sky (*akash*).

Nag is an advanced technology anti-tank missile that can be launched from a tank or from a helicopter. This is a fire-and-forget class third-generation missile, using Imaging Infrared Guidance. It takes a cobra trajectory to make a top attack on the turret of an enemy tank.

The long-range Agni has to go into space and re-enter the atmosphere in order to cover the distance to the target. At the re-entry point, the missile payload module carrying the special warhead experiences a very high temperature of more than 2,500°C—which is equivalent to *Agni Pravesh* and hence the name Agni.

Programme Management: The Key to Success

Kalam brought with him rich experience of managing technology projects from his 20 years of working in the ISRO. Sarabhai, Dhawan and Brahm Prakash had moulded him with leadership qualities. The SLV3-E-01 failure taught him courage to convert failure into success. Jealousy of his peers at VSSC, after getting the Padma Bhushan, removed his ego completely. His ambition to make a Long Range Missile to show the strength of India was his prime objective to come to the DRDL. In the first year, he went through many challenges, including a liquid engine for Prithvi and second stage of Agni. I reminded him of the REX report of SLV S1+S1(1/3) as a better configuration. He talked about the overwhelming confidence on liquid engines and the large resources available at DRDL. Moreover, he did not want to make Agni with all

ISRO stages. ISRO would not support giving both stages. He talked to me about the five projects under IGMDP. Being from the launch vehicle field, I did not understand then anything about Trishul, Akash and Nag. He shared his feelings in our Sunday meetings at Bengaluru, about whether these projects would come through. He was determined to see the success of Prithvi and Agni. He asked me to prepare Dhawan for giving four S1 boosters for Agni.

I suggested that he go in for an organisational renewal with large-scale induction of fresh engineers and fusion with selected experienced technology leaders from outside DRDL, in order to bring in a new culture. We discussed the three-tier structure proposed for IGMDP and I acknowledged that the proposal was excellent. The ISRO experience was to have two level boards—Programme and Projects. Having an Apex Board, GMB, was a brilliant idea, to bring all stake-holders together, particularly top-level Armed Forces officers, as users and secretaries and finance as members, to take on-the-spot decisions. The details are as follows:

At the DRDL, Ranga Rao, Swaminathan and a few others evolved the management plan, capturing Kalam's experience. The IGMDP was a classic multi-project missile development programme, undertaken for the first time in the DRDO, with a three-tier management structure.

1. **Guided Missile Board (GMB)** with SA to RM as Chairman, members at the level of Secretaries to Government, Vice-Chiefs of the three Services and a Programme Chief. This was the highest decision-making authority with delegated financial powers. In the prime period of the IGMDP (1983-92), Dr. Arunachalam was the Chairman. I had witnessed the charged and powerful GMB meetings, conducted by him with dynamism and a command over language and an uncanny presence of mind. He mesmerised everyone, like a music director, to take all critical decisions to progress IGMDP at greater speed, as a collective body, discontinuing red-taped files. Project Directors, sitting at the back, and I had to be on our toes to give flash answers to rapid-fire points, most of the time forgetting our breathing. Kalam tasked me to prepare the agenda and give the key points to him during the meeting, which he would pass on to Arunachalam, so that the course of the meeting led to the required decisions. Every GMB meeting was a programme

milestone. Although it was a strain on me, I enjoyed the GMB meetings. I used my learning from his style of conducting GMB meetings, and adopted a similar style in BrahMos. Salute to Dr. Arunachalam.

A PMB meeting in Progress

2. **A Programme Management Board (PMB**) was formed with Director DRDL as the Chairman and directors of system laboratories, Armed Force representatives, Financial Advisor, chairman of production Management committee as members. Kalam was Chairman and I was the Member-Secretary. We focused on project priority in each of the laboratories, resolving critical decisions, setting up achievable milestones, etc. Directors had their own projects in their lab, which were a priority for them. The conflict was resolved making the lab representatives as system managers, with a separate group under them. Kalam gave importance to the Directors, glorified them and visited their labs periodically. Moreover, PMB meetings were conducted in critical labs to get a commitment from that lab. The PMB could also witness the physical progress that lab had made.
3. **Project Management Boards (PJB**) for each of the five projects and for RCI. Respective Project Directors chaired the Board meetings. System managers from concerned labs called work centres were members, along with the Dy. Financial Advisor. Project milestones, progress, problem areas, schedule, budget and requirements were discussed in the meetings. Kalam used to come for a short time and participate in the discussions. This motivated the system managers who came from the labs. They used to tell him the big picture of what they did in the lab to impress him. This is normal everywhere. After he left the meeting, Project Directors discussed the actual status.

Organisation Renewal

When I joined the DRDL on 1 July 1986, I brought with me the ISRO experiences of Mission Planning, Task orientation, Review Process, Criticality Management in progressing projects, and Energising actions for achieving milestones, and also knowledge of launch vehicles. With new technologies envisaged in projects to make them contemporary to the systems of the developed world and the task of developing five missiles simultaneously and within a short span of time was not easy. Until 1986, it was mostly design work that progressed, whereas Trishul had reached the initial flight trial stage. It required a great deal of reorganisation within the DRDL to change the culture. During this critical period, I became the Director of Planning and Programme Analysis, DRDL. The purpose was to give a new accelerated thrust to technology development, networking among groups as well as programme management for the five projects. I was required to help Kalam to restructure DRDL into a unique matrix set-up. This reorganisation was very close to what Brahm Prakash did in VSSC in 1976. In this new structure, project directors were empowered with more administrative and financial powers, as prevailed in ISRO. Deputy Project Directors were made full time, taking them out from Technology Directorates. New Directorates for Advanced Composites and Quality Assurance were also formed.

Programme Control

My ISRO experience and working closely with Kalam and a short period with Dhawan came in handy to evolve an effective programme management system that could help to streamline the critical technology development process. In a multi-project environment with limited resources and conflicting interests, programme management was very much essential to achieve the objectives of the IGMDP.

I will highlight some of the techniques used to progress IGMDP. We introduced different strategies for critical technology development, monitoring of large activities through a home-grown Computer-Aided Schedule Monitoring System and critical activity monitoring scheme with clear-cut milestones. Another important technique that was evolved was PACE (Programme, Analysis, Control and Evaluation) for critical activity control and conflict resolution in a multi-project environment. Issues were addressed every day in the PACE chamber, where all inputs from work centres at multiple locations were available for analysis and decision. Programme control included a structured review system, flight trial mission management, infusing technology skill, capability

build-up, large-scale induction of scientists reducing the average age of the organisation, continuous renewal by re-organisations in 1986, 1989 and 1992, creating task teams for problem solving, networking with industries, special procurement and stockpiling of critical components and so on. The above activities introduced a new culture and a faster movement to achieve results in the missile programme. The seeds laid 25 years earlier in DRDL, have resulted in many young scientists managing huge missile projects and they have grown as Directors of laboratories today.

We introduced the IGMDP fellowship scheme through which we could get 30 engineers every year, fresh from top institutions. Fellowships were given to selected M. Tech. students, and they were made scientists after project orientation in critical technologies. We also inducted young scientists through electronics fellowships for one year at IAT, Pune. Thus, nearly 200 scientists were added to reduce the average age of DRDL staff. Work output increased through a task plan, detailed schedule, review and control. Kalam brought in a culture of, opening out, participation and discussion. I promoted orientation, solving problems, time management and resource allocation. Things started taking shape, but there was still a long way to go.

Constraints to Progress: Technology Uncertainty

The Devil and ATM did not go through user acceptance, as they were not state-of-the-art systems, by the time they were ready. Understanding the Armed Forces dynamics, Kalam and the team selected appropriate futuristic technologies and concepts beyond the thinking of developed countries. It became a vast technology realisation programme intertwined with missile development. This intertwining brought in uncertainties in development milestones. The technologies were new and futuristic. However, the technology base at DRDL itself was very limited. So the need was to build a partnership, to make IGMDP a national programme. We started identifying partners. While today we have the Internet that brings all the information to the table, back then computers were primitive with monochromatic monitors displaying green fonts in a black background and these could be operated only in air-conditioned rooms. We had to find various industries, research laboratories and academic institutions manually, through reports, conference proceedings or personal contacts.

MISSILE TECHNOLOGY CONTROL REGIME (MTCR)

It is the 'technology denial regime' enforced by First World nations. MTCR is an informal and voluntary association of various countries to prevent the proliferation of unmanned delivery systems capable of carrying a 500-kg payload (read nuclear warheads) up to 300 km. MTCR seeks to coordinate restrictions in exports of complete rocket systems, unmanned air vehicles and related technology.

Unfortunately, some of the systems and technologies having greater civilian applications are also denied or come with a strong end-user agreement that it would not be used for any military purpose. The MTCR was originally established on 16 April 1987 by Canada, France, Germany, Italy, Japan, the UK and the USA.

The MTCR has a long list of technologies and systems that are banned for export. Some common systems like the computerised tomographic scanning systems (commonly known as CT scans) come with user certificate. If the system is found to be used for military purpose, that organisation will be blacklisted and denied further imports. Many of the military-grade computing processors are also restricted by this regime. However, all such transfers are considered on a case-by-case basis (read: nations that are supported by the big powers can import these technologies and proliferate their missiles).

India was not a signatory to the MTCR and many other controversial treaties like the Non-Proliferation Treaty (NPT) and the Comprehensive Test Ban Treaty (CTBT). Hence, many technologies/systems that could have been easily procured from abroad were denied to us. When some technology or equipment is available, it makes sense to use it straightaway. On the other hand, developing the same is time-consuming and uncertain. (India has recently become a signatory to the MTCR).

In hindsight, what must have seemed to be a curse at one point turned out to be the proverbial 'blessing in disguise'? India developed the required technologies, fully understanding and turning the situation into a classic case of **'technology denied is technology gained'**.

Combating MTCR: Critical Technology Development

To begin with, nearly 200 technology packages were identified to be developed for the success of the IGMDP. All these packages were to be developed for the first time in India. Failure to develop them would directly result in the failure of the project of IGMDP itself. Building critical technologies was full of challenges, because they were new and the base knowledge was insufficient. Knowledge, manpower, infrastructure and industrial support had to be made available in the required manner, according to the technology being developed and its relevance in the IGMDP. The progress of the development had to be constantly reviewed and problems had to be solved in real time.

DRDO Scientist of the Year (1988) award given in the 1992 Directors' Conference by the Prime Minister

Technology empowerment became possible through a consortium approach and through collaborative partnerships among the identified partners from R&D labs, academic institutions and industries. These activities had to be planned and strategically managed in order to realise the critical technologies. Above all, these measures had to be innovative. When we went off the beaten track, success came to us like a fruit falling into our laps.

Industry Participation

Colonial rule had kept India away from the Industrial Revolution. This had serious implications in terms of non-availability of suitable industries in India for taking up major missile development programmes. The post-1962 Indo–China War era was the licensed production era. Only knowledge necessary for manufacturing would be passed on by the producer-nation to defence public sector units. This meant that the industry would have only 'know-how' capability, not the 'know-why' capability. The only encouraging factor for India was the thrust given by Dhawan for industries to participate in the space programme. ISRO's contribution to create a minimal base for aerospace technology products would prove valuable for the IGMDP. At one point of time, as the launch vehicle projects took shape, with a large-scale participation by industry, Dhawan said **India could now walk on two feet.**

Kalam invited Dhawan to Missile complex to review the status of missile projects. I received Dhawan at the airport and took him to Taj Krishna. He was very relaxed. We went for dinner. I asked him why he put dye on his hair. It spoiled the beauty of a royal shining and majestic appearance. He touched my hand and said, "Pillai, I would like to be younger". He ordered for a glass of beer for himself and said that at this stage of his life he wanted to be different. I said, "Sir, Your high moral standards all through your life and leadership style had been an education for generations. People like me want to follow in your footsteps". He laughed and thumped on the table. He said he had achieved everything in life and was satisfied. He talked about his son and daughters, and how they shaped themselves in acquiring special capabilities in life. He further said that he had looked inwards and asserted he had been true to himself. He never wanted to project himself for any achievement of ISRO. He talked in many forums like a Professor. He said he was happy with his life's journey. I was quiet. We had dinner. I went to him the next day morning to pick him up for the meeting. He said that after many days he had slept well because of the beer. I did not know whether he was pulling my legs or whether the beer really helped. Anyway, I kept quiet. In the evening, we went together to the airport and I saw him off. He was satisfied with the visit and enjoyed my company.

Leap-Frogging through Innovations

Let me take the reader through two important technology developments in India—combating the MTCR, namely, re-entry heat shield for Agni and a guidance system for Prithvi. These developments ultimately raised our technological capabilities to international standards, paving the way for respect to our scientific community.

Re-entry Heat Shield for Agni

When a ballistic missile payload re-entry vehicle comes from a higher altitude towards its target and reaches the edge of the atmosphere (an altitude of 85 km), at a speed greater than 10 Mach (1 Mach = 330 m/s), it experiences stiff air resistance and due to the resulting friction it gets heated up to a mammoth 2,500°C.

The warhead contains explosives that may be conventional or nuclear material. So, thermal insulators are required to protect the warhead from heating. I hope one will never forget what happened to Kalpana Chawla. She and her crew were returning to the Earth in the space shuttle *Columbia*. At the time of re-entry, a small crack in one of the ceramic tiles of the thermal insulator resulted in blasting of the shuttle and the tragic loss of all the crew members. The camera at the base of the Shuttle had captured the crack, while the Space shuttle was taking off. When the astronauts were in space, NASA formed an expert committee to analyse the effect of the crack. The committee concluded there was no criticality. In the next Shuttle mission, the camera located the same crack at take-off. NASA told the astronaut to come out and replace the tile, in space. It was done and the astronauts returned. Due to the design fault, the Space Shuttle missions were closed.

Now, how to develop such thermal insulators? Since metals generally melt and evaporate at these high temperatures, such insulation is possible through carbon-based composite materials for the structure and carbon-

carbon composite material for the tip. This material has the ability to ablate at high temperatures and high velocity in a uniform manner. Due to this, the flight trajectory is maintained, protecting the warhead by maintaining the temperature at less than 50°C. This technology is essential for long-range missions like intercontinental ballistic missiles (ICBMs) or manned space missions. Re-entry technology is therefore a highly guarded secret for the few nations that possess it. In India, a team of scientists headed by Mrs. Rohini Devi with guidance from Project Director R.N. Agarwal, took it up as a challenge and successfully developed the carbon-carbon technology.

While developing any flying machine, how can we know about its aerodynamic behaviour? One option is to test the scaled-down model in wind tunnels. In the tunnel, the model is kept stationary and air is blown on it at the speed with which that vehicle is expected to fly. The flying conditions are simulated at various speeds at which the vehicle is expected to fly. Various aerodynamic performance parameters like the drag at particular spots on the body are studied to validate the design.

Now recall the trajectory of a ballistic missile; the vehicle re-enters Earth's atmosphere at hypersonic speed. To validate the aerodynamics of the nose tip, we needed a hypersonic wind tunnel–one that would blow air at hypersonic speed. We did not have such a facility.

When Agni re-enters the atmosphere after a long travel in space, it experiences a high enthalpy with almost burning temperature of 3,000 degrees C around the heat shield. The DRDL then designed a structure using Carbon-Carbon, which can withstand this high temperature and protect the vital nuclear warhead, which can withstand only 50 degrees C. The problem we encountered was to simulate the external aerodynamic flow in the subsonic, supersonic and hypersonic speed regimes and optimise the shape of the heat shield to guide it to the target accurately. Aero thermal analysis for the flight regime was carried out at IIT, Madras. Prof. Pandalai, mentor of Kalam, led the team at IIT (M). In the 1980s, we did not have a hypersonic wind tunnel facility and for the AGNI class of missiles, none of the developed nations would allow their hypersonic tunnel to be used. The other option was to arrive at the optimum shape through Computational Fluid Dynamics (CFD), which would help to validate the aerodynamic design of the heat shield. The aerodynamic design comprises hundreds of thousands of grid points for each configuration. Assume these grid points to be nodes in the skeletal structure. There were many shapes. Therefore, a large number of iterations were required.

CFD was then a new field. In India, CFD groups were in the formation stage at various institutions. Prof. S.R. Deshpande of the IISc (Indian Institute of Science) and 10 members of the DRDL (Defence Research Development Laboratory) formed the CFD team. When it was formulated initially, the computational time in an IBM computer was nine days for each iteration of the grid point. At that time, we neither had super computers in India nor adequate time. We approached the problem in two ways. One was to make available a super computer and the second was to improve the software.

Dr. Arunachalam and Kalam went to Washington and made a request to William Perry, US Dept. of Defence to permit the use of the existing CRAY X-MP supercomputer at IMD, Delhi for weather predictions under a separate agreement or agree to sell a new one for R&D purposes. Mr. Perry praised the two great scientists from India and gave them a good lunch. He said he could give a good dinner also, but not the supercomputer. Returning with empty hands, Dr. Arunachalam established the Advanced Numerical Research and Analysis Group (ANURAG) with Prof. G. Venkataraman deputed from the Indira Gandhi Centre for Atomic Research (IGCAR), Kalpakkam, as the leader to design and develop a supercomputer for undertaking the Agni re-entry module design. The time given was 24 months.

Imagine the scenario some 30 years ago. That was a time when the Indian public treated ordinary calculators like computers. When there was no indigenous capability to develop even an ordinary computer, could we hope to develop a supercomputer?

Well, Dr. Venkataraman, Dr. Neelakantan and 14 youngsters developed a hypercube-based parallel processing supercomputer for CFD analysis. Finally, in the assigned 24 months, a 32-node parallel computer called PACE+ was developed with a capacity of 1.7 gigaflops. Roughly, one flop can be compared to one calculation. PACE+ was capable of executing 1,700,000,000 floating-point operations per second. It was 20 times faster than the Cray X-MP that was refused to us. In the meantime, the CFD software team evolved what is called 'kinetic energy split methodology'. The problem arising from very high computer time was solved with the time being reduced to 1/10th of the initial time, using elegant methods by suitably segmenting the algorithm.

With the combination of PACE+ and the new software codes for CFD, each iteration was reduced to just five minutes from the earlier period of nine days.

The irony was that after the development of our supercomputer, the USA offered us their Cray X-MP. The offer was promptly declined. Today, we have mastered the re-entry technology and Agni has various versions with ranges from 700 to 5,000 km. Thus, innovatively developing the supercomputer and the use of home-grown software paved the way for combating the control regime.

CFD ADVANCEMENTS

ANURAG developed PACE 128, with one Terra Flop capacity for advanced CFD solutions. The CFD team, under Prof. Deshpande's guidance, progressed international partnership for the evolution of grid computing, which has a tremendous potential in connecting multiple locations and utilising the computing power from different institutions. Data-intensive computing is a class of parallel computing applications, which use a data parallel approach to processing large volumes of data, terabytes (TB) or petabytes (PB) in size and typically referred to as Big Data. Data-intensive computing describes applications that are I/O bound. Data-intensive science relies on the collection, analysis and management of massive volumes of data. Such applications devote the largest fraction of execution time to movement of data. They can be identified by evaluating "computational bandwidth"—the number of bytes of data processed synonymous to the "number of oating-point operations carried out". Collection of inter-connected stand-alone computers working together as a single integrated computing resource known as "shared nothing" approach is considered suitable for data-intensive computing. The problems are separated into a number of parallel tasks and there is no dependency or communication required between the tasks other than their overall management. These types of data processing problems are inherently adaptable to various forms of distributed computing including clusters, data grids, and cloud computing.

Over the past decade, a new paradigm for scientific discovery is emerging due to the availability of exponentially increasing volumes of data from large instruments such as large space telescopes, colliders and light sources, as well as the proliferation of sensors and high-throughput analysis devices. This is the **Key to Knowledge discovery—the fourth paradigm in computer science.**

Inertial Guidance System for Prithvi

Prithvi is a uniquely designed short-range ballistic missile. It is not that we were the first to develop a short-range ballistic missile. Many countries had achieved that much ahead of us. So then, what makes Prithvi unique?

- Manoeuvrable Trajectory in ballistic missiles for the first time in the world. Guidance algorithm developed by Jadavpur University, with lead from Prof. T.K. Ghoshal. (As the course of the missile will be continuously changing in horizontal and vertical directions, the enemy will not know where the missile is heading. No interception is possible by the enemy, as he will not have any reaction time.)
- High accuracy to reach the target, with a guidance system using advanced software using available low-grade sensors by RCI.

Such guidance systems are entirely dependent on high-precision navigational sensors. Again, this was not available to India. Without the super sensors, there was no possibility for developing a high-accuracy guidance system. Kalam had an idea. He chose four young scientists and gave them the task to come up with a solution that would help attain better accuracy using the rudimentary gyroscopes that were being produced at Hindustan Aeronautics Limited (HAL) Korwa Division.

The group of young scientists had brainstorming sessions and studied the sensor details and the mission. They did several mission runs in computers and 5-axis motion simulators to characterise the sensors, and calculated the errors at various stages of flight. The simulation of the trajectories including many perturbations and failure modes was carried out to estimate the error bands. The idea was to compensate the error in real time by making the guidance computer compensate for the error and update the trajectory. Injecting software in hardware was the innovation of the young minds. The system was validated in hardware-in-loop simulation and later in the flight trials. The innovation of compensating the hardware-induced error through software played a key role in realising an excellent inertial guidance system, using low-grade sensors. I recall our daily evening meetings to review the progress of hardware-in-loop simulations, with J.C. Bhattacharya chairing. The Prithvi was accepted, meeting the quality requirements of all the three Services and inducted. Later, this highly accurate inertial guidance system became the DRDO's process stock, when we formed BrahMos. Accuracy was further improved by incorporating data from multiple GPS, including GLONASS, IRNSS (NAVIC). This was a great contribution by the RCI team led by Dr. G. Satheesh Reddy.

Indian youth demonstrated enormous talent when they were challenged by the control regimes and technology denials during the development of critical missile technologies. During difficult times, the enthusiasm and vibrancy of the youth helped to achieve greater things. We effectively combated MTCR, taught a lesson to the developed world and proved that Indian minds are very powerful.

Agni Flight Trial

The Agni launch campaign was a special one, full of challenges of a technical, managerial, social, and administrative nature. Agni was all set to make its first test flight in April 1989 after six years of laborious effort in the development of various subsystems and a large number of ground tests. The launch campaign commenced on March 31, 1989. A special launch complex was made operational at the Missile Test Range at Chandipur with many instruments for tracking and telemetry. The mission control links range safety, Block House, SHAR Range, down range stations and naval ships. Dr. Kalam led a team of nearly 450 scientists and technicians for the major launch campaign with multiple organisations participating. A mission management structure was evolved and a Launch Authorisation Board was constituted with Dr. Kalam as Chairman. The launch countdown started on April 20, 1989. At T–7 minutes, the missile was put on its internal power through the actuation of batteries, pyros fired and the umbilical connector was pulled out. At T–1 second the launch was aborted due to hold management procedure. It required a detailed review of all the power packages before the go-ahead command could be given. There were many important visitors—the Defence Minister, Cabinet Secretary, Defence Secretary, three

Chiefs of Staff, and many others. Everyone was disappointed not to seeing the missile take off. Dr. Arunachalam was upset and there was a heated exchange of words. I was with Shri T.N. Seshan. Before chaos could take over, Dr. Kalam took control of the situation. A detailed analysis of the failure was carried out on the same day and rectification started. The system was ready once again within 10 days and another launch was attempted on May 1, 1989. Again, during the countdown at T–3 seconds, there was a failure in the first stage control system as one of the SITVC injection servo valves gave way, leading to pouring out of the secondary injectant, strontium perchlorate, and the missile did not take off. There was a crisis. The Government was very unhappy because of the failure of the missile to take off in two attempts. In spite of all the problems, Dr. Kalam was not deterred. He showed calmness and extraordinary determination. He had seen earlier the SLV-3 failure on August 10, 1979, and had all the experience needed to face a major failure and convert it into a success.

After a detailed failure analysis of the control system, I was given the task of taking the base-shroud assembly to LPSC, ISRO, at Valiamala near Thiruvananthapuram, rectify it and bring the accepted assembly for flight at the earliest. I led the team and rushed immediately to the work centre, 2,000 km away from the launch pad carrying the vital control system package of Agni in a special aircraft. Due to my ISRO connections and my close association with Shri N. Sridharan Dhas, Group Director, LPSC, the team could work round-the-clock for 12 days. A detailed analysis of the component failure of the proportional injection valve by the Sudhakar committee, new design, fabrication and, qualification by the Sridharan Dhas team of nearly 40 engineers and technicians of LPSC, QA review and acceptance of the valves for flight, were carried out systematically. In the meantime, VSSC and LPSC teams refurbished the Base-shroud jointly. New fin tip control was assembled in a clean room, and functionally tested. The Secondary Thrust Vector Control (My first project in 1970 at SSTC) assembly was tested for system performance and QA acceptance. The Base-shroud with both control systems as an integrated assembly went through system level vibration test in flight conditions. A Flight Readiness Review was conducted by Madhavan Nair at Valiamala and the system cleared for transport to ITR for assembly with the first stage of AGNI.

The highly motivated teams could do all these in 12 days, which normally would have taken 60–70 days. This was because of the tremendous support of technologists of ISRO, NAL, and the urge of the scientists to ensure success. It was amazing to observe that many scientists and staff members could work continuously and ensure system readiness with all acceptance tests in 12 days' time.

All 12 days, an aircraft was waiting at Thiruvananthapuram airport. The system was loaded in it; we flew to Hyderabad first for me to get off, and the aircraft then went on to Kalaikunda for subsequent action.

I rushed to Kalam at the DRDL Director's office and showed the report of system acceptance. He laughed for a while. I did not understand him. Then he said, "You guys did a good job; but there is no Agni flight. Rajiv Gandhi put it on hold, because of two failed attempts and all-round criticism. Dr. Arunachalam is threatening to resign if the flight is not cleared. I don't know what to do." I said, "There cannot be any problem, this time. The S1 never failed. The Base-shroud is fine. Please meet the Cabinet Secretary (Shri Seshan) with details." He said, "The problem is between Seshan and Arunachalam. Let us do so. Prepare some presentation material." I went to my table and prepared charts that would explain the reliability of the system and the success of the flight.

Kalam went through the charts and was satisfied with the system reliability. He spoke to Seshan and assured him of success of the flight.

The launch campaign started once again in the midst of continuous criticism from the Press and other external pressures. The newspapers of those days were full of cartoons depicting Agni sarcastically as IDBM (Interminably Delayed Ballistic Missile). The final launch date was dictated by the hostile weather conditions including a threatening cyclone. The Meteorological Department and all partner institutions worked together as ambient conditions created great anxiety. All work centres were connected through Satcom and HF links. For the 50-day campaign, Indian Airlines and Indian Railways with just one request had arranged movement of hundreds of members for the launch campaign without any advance reservations. The Air Force came to the rescue with its continuous support by providing aircraft and helicopters. The Navy through ship-borne stations and the Army through its medical facilities also helped.

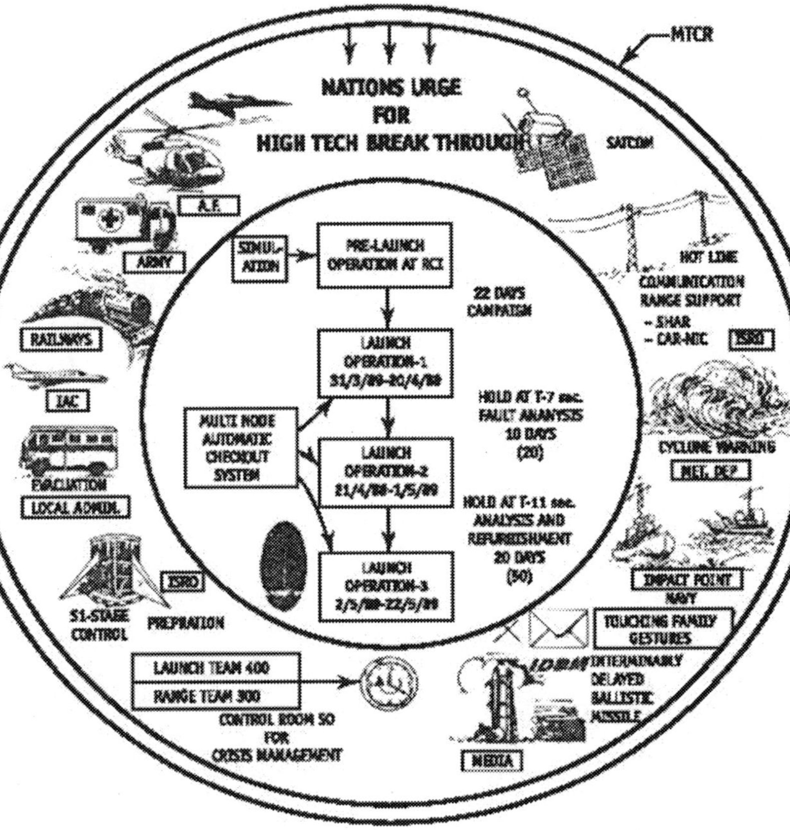

Nation's Urge for Agni Flight

At the ITR range, about 12,000 people had to be evacuated for safety reasons from an area of about 3.5 km radius from the launch pad. A combined effort was made with the local administration to move people, give them proper shelter and food, and make necessary arrangements for their safety.

The launch campaign was in full swing. The team was in high spirits. Clearance for the launch was given. Countdown progressed. All dignitaries were present. On May 22, 1989, Agni took off at 07.10 a.m. and completed its mission successfully. The criticism, abuse, and de-motivating actions for the delay in the launching now turned into praise and the whole country rejoiced in success.

The message from the above examples is that **when there are problems and failures, the leadership must take control of the situation**

and transform the failures to success. The leader must have the courage to face criticism and to have the indomitable willpower to succeed.

Kalam's Retention in DRDO

When we were at the ITR for another mission, a call came to Kalam from Cho Ramasamy, editor of a Tamil magazine *Thugluk*. He wanted Kalam's concurrence to be nominated for the vice-chancellorship of Madras University. Kalam, nearing his 60th birthday, thought it would be better to go in for a change, as he was not comfortable after the Agni launch. He told Cho Ramasamy to give him some time to think it over. Some friends and I objected to the very idea of his going out of the DRDO. But he had a reason, which he shared with me. Kalam wanted to open a school for under-privileged children. The news must have reached Dr. Arunachalam. K.N. Singh called and asked me. I said that Kalam should not leave DRDL. He then suggested that I make a proposal for three years extension of service to Kalam. I knew Kalam would not agree, as he was already organising himself to move. So I did not ask him. I sent the extension proposal for Kalam on my DRDL letterhead and faxed it. The file was then processed based on my request and Dr. Arunachalam got it approved by Shri Chandrasekar, the caretaker Prime Minister at that time. Arunachalam wrote a beautiful letter in golden ink conveying Kalam's extension in the DRDO for three years. Kalam called me, put the letter on the table and asked me to read it. He did not like the way HQ decided without taking his concurrence. He said he had made up his mind to leave. I informed him that it was I who had sent the proposal for his extension; otherwise, it would had been big loss for DRDO. While his face changed from hatred to anger, I said, *"GOD CONSPIRED FOR YOU"*. He then laughed and kept quiet.

Spin off—Light-Weight Callipers

This was a pet project of Kalam, funded by the DST, DRDO, and the Ministry of Social Justice and Empowerment. Big support came from Prof. P. Rama Rao, Secretary DST, for this project.

At DRDL, we were busy realising a lightweight calliper of 300 grams against a conventional calliper of 3 kg and at a reduced cost. The idea was mooted by Dr. B.N. Prasad and later followed up by Dr. L. Narendranath of the Nizam Institute of Medical Sciences, Hyderabad.

They approached Kalam for reduction of the weight to help polio patients using the composite material used for the Agni heat shield. G.V. Rao, B. Shankar Rao and Mayank Dviwedi started working on this at the Composite Centre. I was Chairman of the PRC (Progress Review Committee). Mayank, a brilliant scientist of the DRDO, had worked earlier with Dr. P.C. Sethi of Jaipur Foot fame, and had a fair idea of the FRO (Floor Reaction Orthosis) process evolved by Prof. Lakkad of IIT, Bombay and Dr. Sethi. Our aim was to standardise the FRO, so that availability and fitment time could be reduced to one day instead of the regular process of Sethi taking one month. Based on measurements taken on 1,000 children from different regions using an Anthropometric Device, we classified them into seven sizes and the DMRL evolved the computerised design of moulds for manufacturing the knee, upright, foot in separate parts, using missile materials. Pilot-scale production started at DRDL Composite Centre and later the process was transferred to ALIMCO for production. More than 50,000 children were fitted with these callipers through camps organised at different parts of India.

A girl student, Meha, studying in the eighth standard wrote to me, "Uncle, I got the highest marks in the class. You know why. Earlier when I was coming to school, I dragged my polio-affected left leg because of the heavy shoe I was wearing. Every one stared at me. I was disturbed and not attentive in class. Now I have a lightweight calliper fitted in my leg at the camp at Hyderabad. I am walking freely with the same size shoes on both my legs. No one looks at me. I got confidence. I concentrated on my studies. Thank you, Mayank Uncle and Dr. Narendranath".

When a child asked Kalam, what gave him the most happiness, he replied, "*When SLV3 placed a Rohini satellite in an Earth orbit, India became a member of the Space Club. That gave me happiness. When we launched Agni IRBM and conducted five nuclear tests, India became a strong nation. That also gave me happiness. But when I saw a crawling child begin to walk after fitment of a calliper made of Agni missile material, and happy tears rolling out from the child's parents, I got BLISS.*"

KALAM AS DRDO CHIEF

Kalam became the Scientific Adviser to the Defence Minister in 1992 at the age of 61. He continued in this post until November 1999.

Followed by extraordinary leadership given by Arunachalam to build the DRDO as a front-line organisation, Kalam started consolidating with the background of IGMDP and commanding respect from all quarters. In every DRDO council meeting on Mondays, he focused on results. Labs got a chance to be reviewed by the council regularly. Directors participated with senior engineers in these meetings. He got good support from Sharad Pawar (RM until March 1993), who came with his wife to Chandipur-at-Sea and witnessed the Prithvi launch. Narasimha Rao, who was RM and PM (until May 1996) came to RCI Hyderabad and reviewed the missiles readiness. Mulayam Singh Yadav and George Fernandes also gave excellent support. Many new programmes started coming in during his tenure. To name a few—Longer-range Agni, Dhanush (Naval Prithvi), Electronic Warfare Systems, Naval sensors, Naval Weapons, Laser as a weapon, Military satellites, Cyber Security and BrahMos. Most importantly the visibility of the DRDO and respect for the organisation improved. He brought the DRDO on par with Space and Atomic Energy Departments, and the three heads managed to provide maximum benefits to scientists and technicians. I moved to DRDO HQ as Chief Controller (R&D) Missiles and concurrently CEO&MD, BrahMos.

Nuclear Test Preparation

Kalam was regularly meeting Prime Minister Narasimha Rao about the work being carried out in weaponisation. The IAF conducted dummy drop tests at Chandipur Range, evaluating the triggering system of the DRDO. Flight tests of Prithvi and Agni incorporated the payload functional tests at the terminal stage. The results were evaluated based on data recorded by telemetry. These were necessary to establish completeness of weapon delivery to the right place in the right manner. TBRL, Chandigarh did excellent work on assembly of triggering mechanism which was tested in these flights. In 1994-95, hectic work went on for conducting tests at Pokhran, as directed by Narasimha Rao, even though he was facing continuous pressure from the USA. The book, *Engaging India* by Strobe Talbott is testimony of the Big-Brother attitude of USA towards India. Satellite photographs by the CIA were shown to the PM about the progress of activities in the desert. He was cautious. He did not want to upset the apple cart, at a time when economic revival was in progress.

At the same time, China came out with new solid propellant long-range missiles and transfer of technology to Pakistan for nuclear payload preparation and integration with its missiles, Ghauri (Nodang missiles from North Korea were renamed Ghauri) with 1,300 km range and Chinese M 11 missiles with a range of 600 km (Shaheen 1). China also transferred know-how for M 9—a two-stage missile with a range of 2,000 km (Shaheen 2) and helped to establish solid propellant manufacturing facilities. A. Q. Khan sold nuclear technology to North Korea for the 10 Nodangs he received. The triangular nexus posed a considerable problem for India. The 'string of pearls' strategy by China and pumping support to India's neighbouring countries was definitely a pressure tactic.

With hostile nuke neighbours, the PM had many meetings with Kalam and Chidambaram, weighing the pros and cons. One of the considerations was the Parliament election in a few months. If the tests were conducted before the election, Narasimha Rao thought he would be accused of trying to gain political mileage. Secondly, if he lost the election, it would be unfair to place all the repercussions on the new Government. It seems he told the team, **"You can't gamble on the nation for the sake of political gain."**

Kalam and Chidambaram wanted the tests to be done. Now they had to wait. They kept everything ready, under the care of the Army's 58th Regiment of Corps of Engineers so that the tests could be done in a short time. In Kalam's words," I still remember a scene during May 1996. It was 9-o'clock at night. I got a call from the Prime Minister's House that I should meet the Prime Minister Shri P.V. Narasimha Rao immediately. I met him; it was just two days before the announcement of the General Election results. He told me, 'Kalam, be ready with your team for the N-Test and I am going to Tirupati. You wait for my authorisation to go ahead. DRDO-DAE teams must be ready for action".

In Kalam's words, "Of course, the election result was quite different from what Shri Narasimha Rao anticipated. I was busy at the Chandipur missile range. I got a call saying that I must immediately meet the Prime

Minister-designate Shri Atal Bihari Vajpayee with Shri Narasimha Rao. I witnessed a unique situation. Shri Narasimha Rao, the outgoing Prime Minister, asked me to relate the details of the N-programme to Shri Vajpayee, so that a smooth takeover of such a very important programme could take place. This incident reveals the maturity of leadership and professional excellence of a patriotic statesman who believed that the nation is bigger than the political system".

Both these leaders had the courage to take difficult decisions, even though the consequences of such a decision had great national and international significance.

Real leaders think of the nation first, not political considerations. Both Narasimha Rao and Vajpayee, talked less, listened more and made great decisions. *I am saying this as I had the opportunity to interact with both of them, with Kalam, when they were PMs.*

Kalam and Chidambaram organised the teams and the work progressed. But the Vajpayee Government survived for only for 13 days. Vajpayee told Kalam to wait for the decision of next government.

Shri H.D. Deva Gowda, the new PM, was fully briefed. He appreciated Kalam and Chidambaram for their outstanding work but did not agree for the test. He came to our lab at Hyderabad and familiarised himself with the missile projects. He consulted his ministers, I.K. Gujral and P. Chidambaram, about conducting the test. They advised him that the priority for the nation was economic progress, not the test, which would lead to sanctions. Persuasion on Kalam's part was of no avail.

Kalam achieved one thing during Gowda's prime ministership. Technology Vision 2020 documents were submitted in 1996 by Kalam, the Chairman, TIFAC committee, in a gathering of 500 scientists, who worked for two years to generate 17 documents giving a road map for Developed India. The PM praised Kalam and the team for generating the vision for the nation. Presentations by experts continued for nearly an hour, covering all the areas in the road map. During the entire meeting, Shri Deva Gowda was like Maha Vishnu. At the end he said, "I approve". The PM approved Developed India Vision 2020.

Shri I.K. Gujral became PM in April 1997

Gujral, a polished diplomat, was not in favour of a nuclear test. However, he asked the team to dig one more shaft so that low-yield thermonuclear tests could be done, if it was not possible to carry out a big test.

He came to the RCI and we showed him the readiness of the Prithvi missile system and the status of induction. He saw the Agni missile. He was impressed with the progress and praised the team.

Ballistic Missile Defence

The nuclear neighbours became stronger with the development of new missiles capable of targeting the major cities of India. The DRDL evolved a credible two-layered missile defence system against possible threats—M-11, M-9 and Nodang, acquired by Pakistan and a modernised CSS-5 of China. The idea was to intercept at high altitude about 100 km (exo-atmospheric) using hypersonic missiles and intercept an escaped missile at a lower altitude of about 25 km (endo-atmospheric) using improved Akash missiles. Kalam submitted the proposal to Defence Minister Mulayam Singh, who made a special recommendation note to PM I.K. Gujral.

Gujral Government approved the ballistic missile defence proposal. This is a two-layered system, realised after many experimental interceptions and is superior to any system available in the world, compared to THAAD, Patriot, SM-3 of the USA, S-400 of Russia and Arrow-2 of Israel. The long-range radars, missiles, control systems, software—all requirements had been established.

Gujral's far-reaching decision enabled is to have a credible defence against incoming nuclear missiles. Because of this capability, ASAT mission Shakti was successfully carried out to intercept a satellite.

ASAT-Shakti

Another breakthrough India made was the complex Shakti-Anti-Satellite experiment—ASAT, carried out on 27 March 2019. The Interceptor developed for Ballistic Missile Defence with augmented boost capability successfully destroyed a live satellite at 278 km. The mission involved tracking the satellite trajectory and its speed, real time computation of the interceptor missile trajectory along with command, control, communication, computer and intelligent system and perfect destruction of the satellite in a low Earth orbit to reduce the damage expected to be caused by the debris. This proved the capability of the Indian scientists at the DRDO for complex missions, executed precisely.

Chemical Weapon

Gujral not only refused permission for the nuclear test but also asked Kalam to remove all chemical weapons based on the UN Chemical Weapons Convention, of which India was a signatory.

The Convention aims to eliminate an entire category of weapons of mass destruction by prohibiting the development, production, acquisition, stockpiling, retention, transfer or use of chemical weapons by states Parties. States Parties, in turn, must take the steps necessary to enforce that prohibition in respect of persons (natural or legal) within their jurisdiction. The Convention was drafted on 3 September 1992 and opened for signature on 13 January 1993. It became effective from 29 April 1997.

The Organisation for the Prohibition of Chemical Weapons (OPCW) implements this Convention. It has its headquarters at The Hague, Netherlands. The CWC has 192 state-parties and 165 signatories.

India signed the treaty in January 1993. Thereafter, the Chemical Weapons Convention Act, 2000 was passed in Parliament to implement the CWC.

This herculean task of destroying chemical weapons was performed with great care. All reactors were also destroyed to the satisfaction of International OPCW Inspectors.

Reward

Mulayam Singh, the Defence Minister, had a soft corner for Kalam. Both he and Gujral, the Prime Minister, admired Kalam for his contribution to SLV3, Agni and Prithvi, for his persistent stand on nuclear tests and for his prompt direction on destruction of chemical weapons. Kalam's reputation in the scientific community, industry, and academic institutions was high. In addition, the international community was highly appreciative of the DRDO's transparency on chemical weapons. RM and PM wanted to honour Kalam without allowing him to conduct the nuclear test. Gujral made his recommendation to President K. R. Narayanan, who approved it. The Government announced a Bharat Ratna for Kalam on 3 November 1997.

Raj Chengappa in his book *Weapons of Peace* says, "Gujral believed that if he honoured Kalam, who was a prominent symbol of India's effort to produce weapons of mass destruction, he would be sending out a powerful message. A message not just to his countrymen but to the entire world, on the importance India placed on its security. And yet India would not have to face the damaging consequences of an actual test". Gujral proved his diplomatic skill.

On 28 February 1998, in the rehearsal for the award, I substituted for Kalam. In the Durbar Hall, I was sitting next to M.S. Subbulakshmi on the seat meant for Kalam. I had a good time with the famous Carnatic singer, talking to her in Tamil. She sang one line for me *'Kaatrinile varum geetham.'*

Kalam awarded Bharat Ratna in 1997

The next day, on 1 March 1998 at the investiture ceremony, we had special guests—Prof. Satish Dhawan and Kalam's elder brother. My task was to take care of Dhawan. My wife, Seethalakshmi, being a great admirer of M.S. Subbulakshmi wanted to be with her for some time.

I received Prof. Dhawan on 1 March 1998 at Rashtrapati Bhavan, when Kalam got the Bharat Ratna. He was very pleased to see his disciple getting the highest civilian award. Prof. Dhawan was exceptional in not having a trace of jealousy of his junior receiving an

award greater than what he had received. He never tried for anything for himself. Such was the greatness of the person. I feel excited and proud to work with such a tall leader.

We witnessed Kalam being decorated with the Bharat Ratna by President Narayanan. It was the happiest moment for me, for those who worked with him, for his friends and many from the younger generation. Of course, there were a few exceptions in the scientific community.

Cabinet Minister Offer

In the 1998 election, the BJP, with other parties, formed the Government. On 18 March 1998, Kalam got a phone call from Vajpayee, the PM-designate. Vajpayee told Kalam that he would like to make him a cabinet minister with a ministry of his choice. Kalam wanted some time to think over it. Vajpayee asked him to see him in the morning at his residence, as the ministry was being formed at 11 a.m. on 19 March 1998. Kalam summoned some of his close friends to assemble at the DRDO guesthouse at Asiad Village. We analysed the pros and cons of the proposal. All of us objected to his becoming a minister. He talked to his brother at night, who also expressed the same view. It was a unanimous view. The problem was how to tell Vajpayee. We thought of an idea.

The next morning, Kalam went to Vajpayee's residence. After pleasantries, Kalam told him, "Sir, you know about the nuclear test we were preparing for, when you were the PM earlier. Now we can proceed to assemble and carry out the tests. I have to mobilise the teams and work there with secrecy. I will be able to do this only if I continue as head of the operation, from the DRDO. As a minister, I will not be able to do the test. Sir, you want the test or my becoming minister." Vajpayee laughed, understood and said, "The test is more important than your becoming a minister. How many days do you need?"

Kalam said he needed one month. He wanted a meeting immediately to decide the date. Vajpayee met Kalam, Chidambaram and his Principal Secretary Brajesh Mishra and discussed the details of five tests and the weaponisation with missiles. Vajpayee asked them to get ready. They met again on 9 April, after Ghauri was tested by Pakistan on 6 April. This time they fixed the date as 11 May 1998, taking into account the activities and President's availability in India, after a foreign tour. Raj

Chengappa covered the whole episode in great detail in his book '*Weapons of Peace*'.

Preparations for the Test

Continuous surveillance by US satellites of the test site was a concern. The CIA had been keeping an eye on Indian test preparations since 1995 and the satellite photographs were sent to PM Shri Rao. Therefore, this time, preparation required complete secrecy. The 58th Regiment of Corps of Engineers was responsible to prepare the test sites. Fortunately, six shafts had already been prepared.

The Defence Lab, Jodhpur, did an excellent work in providing a camouflage net to avoid any detection by spy satellites. Moreover not anticipating any quick action by the new Government, the CIA used only one satellite hovering over India between 8 a.m. and 11 a.m. So our teams carefully avoided this slot and all movement was mostly done during the night, and equipment was returned to their original place to give the impression that it had never been moved. Kalam, Chidambaram and others were in Army uniforms, not to give any clue.

The DRDO was responsible for designing, testing and producing components for the bombs, including the advanced detonators; the implosion and high-voltage trigger systems and the camouflage net. The nuclear devices from BARC were flown in an Indian Air Force AN-32 to Jaisalmer on 1 May. They were transported to Pokhran in an army convoy. They were delivered to the device preparation building. On the night of 10 May, the devices were lowered to the designated depth, as under:

The first group consisted of the thermonuclear device, with fusion-boosted primary with design yield of 45 kt (Shakti I) to 200 m depth, the fission device 12 kt yield (Shakti II) to 150 m, and a 0.3 kt non-weapon grade device (Shakti III). The second group consisted of the remaining two sub-kiloton devices 0.5 kt (Shakti IV) and 0.2 kt (Shakti V) Thorium/U-233.

Tests

The first group of three devices was tested simultaneously on 11 May at 3.45 p.m. and the second group on 13 May at 12.21 p.m.

Announcement

Following the Pokhran-II tests, India became the sixth country to join the nuclear club. Shortly after the tests, Prime Minister Atal Bihari Vajpayee made the following short statement:

> *"Today, at 15:45 hours, India conducted three underground nuclear tests in the Pokhran range. The tests conducted today were with a fission device, a low yield device and a thermonuclear device. The measured yields are in line with expected values. Measurements have also confirmed that there was no release of radioactivity into the atmosphere. These were contained explosions like the experiment conducted in May 1974. I warmly congratulate the scientists and engineers who have carried out these successful tests".*

Pakistan followed with five fission tests on May 28, 1998, with yield of 30-36 kt and one more test on May 30. Pakistan did not have a hydrogen bomb. India is way ahead in nuclear technology, having mastered thermonuclear devices, with high yield.

Nuclear Doctrine of India

India had demonstrated to the world community that it is a responsible country and its nuclear warheads are just to ensure the sovereignty and boundaries of the country and not to invade any country.

The basic principle of India's nuclear doctrine is **"No First Use".** According to this policy, nuclear weapons will only be used in retaliation against a nuclear attack on Indian territory or on Indian forces anywhere.

India needs to build and maintain a Credible Minimum Deterrent. This includes; Sufficient and survivable nuclear forces to inflict unacceptable damage to the enemy; Nuclear forces must be operationally prepared at all times; Effective Intelligence and Early Warning Capabilities and Communication of Deterrence Capability to the enemy.

The right to take nuclear action against an enemy will only be taken by the elected representatives of the people, i.e., the political leadership of the country, although the cooperation of the Nuclear Command Authority will be necessary. In other words, the bureaucracy of India is not authorised to take a decision of a nuclear attack on the enemy. If there is any chemical or biological attack against India or Indian security forces, then India will keep the option of nuclear attack open in its response.

India will continue to support the global initiative to create a nuclear-free world and will push forward the idea of discrimination-free nuclear disarmament.

The Nuclear Command Authority (NCA) comprises of an Executive Council and a Political Council. The Chairman of the Political Council is the Prime Minister. It is the sole body that can authorise the use of nuclear weapons.

The Executive Council is headed by the National Security Advisor (NSA). It provides inputs for the decision by the Nuclear Command Authority (NCA) and executes the instructions given to it by the Political Council.

AWACS Accident

The DRDO was proceeding with an Airborne Surveillance Platform at CABS, Bengaluru. The surveillance platform was a rotodome mounted on an Avro aircraft. It was a good project. A number of trials had been carried out by flying and recording data. During the manoeuvrable trials on 12 January 1999 at naval air base Arakkonam, a mishap happened. The radar mounting broke. The aircraft tumbled. All eight members, (2 from LRDE, 2 from CABS and 4 officers from IAF) sacrificed their lives. This incident shattered Kalam and he dashed to Bengaluru. Air Chief Marshal A.Y. Tipnis also reached there. They met the grieving family members in the community hall, in the Township. It was a painful scene; the young wives and their parents were crying. The young scientists and officers sacrificed their lives for a national mission. It was a black day for the DRDO. Kalam often told me that this was the most tragic event to happen to him in his life.

Kargil Conflict (May-July 1999)

When spring ended in April 1999, Indian soldiers, patrolling inside the Line of Control (LOC) in Kargil District of Kashmir were ambushed by intruders firing from high atop the snow-laden peaks of the mountain range. They entered Indian territory and occupied many military posts in the Dras, Mushkoh, Kaksar, Batalik and Chorbat La sectors. After several weeks, Indian Intelligence discovered that the intruders were the trained Pakistan's Northern Light Infantry (NLI) and it was a well-organised surprise attack. It was a failure of Intelligence on the part of

India. Intense fighting started at high altitude and both sides lost hundreds of soldiers.

The Indian Army was later supported by the Indian Air Force and recaptured a majority of positions on the Indian side of the LOC infiltrated by the Pakistani troops. Facing international diplomatic opposition, the Pakistani forces withdrew from the remaining Indian positions along the LOC in July. This particular operation was given the code name 'Operation Safed Sagar.' (Operation White Sea). The conflict is referred to as 'Operation Vijay'.

The conflict was the most recent example of high-altitude warfare in mountainous terrain and, as such, posed significant logistical problems for the combating sides. It is also the sole instance of direct, conventional warfare between two nuclear countries.

Soon after the conflict, the Indian Government set up a high-powered committee chaired by eminent strategic affairs analyst K. Subrahmanyam to analyse the causes of failure of Indian Intelligence and to recommend suitable remedial measures. The committee's final report led to a large-scale restructuring of Indian Intelligence. It, however, came in for heavy criticism in the Indian media for its perceived avoidance of assigning specific responsibility for failures over detecting the Kargil intrusions. Gen. V.P. Malik, in his book, specifically asserted that the conflict was due to 'Strategic and tactical intelligence failure'.

Kargil Fallout

The Chiefs of the three wings of the Armed Forces met Vajpayee and briefed him about the inadequacy of modern weapons, cumbersome procedures and terrific delay in development of systems by the DRDO. At this rate, they feared there would be more losses of men, if Kargil type of conflicts were repeated. After a series of discussions, they requested for a more proactive DRDO. Vajpayee and Mishra decided to request Kalam to step down, as he was already 68. Vajpayee wanted an honourable exit for Kalam, with a respectful position of an advisory role to the Prime Minister. Kalam discussed with Rajan and me, and we suggested requesting the PM for the post of Principal Scientific Adviser to the Government, with cabinet minister rank with a suitable office and funds to enable independent functioning. The PM agreed to the request.

PRINCIPAL SCIENTIFIC ADVISOR TO GOI (PSA)

Kalam quietly left the DRDO and became the PSA. He was also Chairman of the Science Advisory Committee of the Cabinet. Y.S. Rajan joined him as his Scientific Secretary. Dr. M.S. Vijayaragavan came on deputation from DRDO. Sheridon joined him to manage the office and Kalam's programme. The office of PSA was established at Vigyan Bhavan. K.N. Rai, the then Chief Executive of Civil Works DRDO made the office in proper shape.

Promoting Developed India Vision

As PSA, Kalam got an excellent opportunity to promote the Developed India Vision. As mentioned earlier, the Vision had been evolved by TIFAC (Technology Information, Forecasting and Assessment Centre) of the Department of Science & Technology. With Kalam as Chairman and Y.S. Rajan as the Executive Director, TIFAC came out with an action plan for Developed India Vision based on reports by 11 specialist committees. Five hundred top specialists from all over India participated in the committees, suggesting phased actions for achieving developed status by 2020. Prof. U.R. Rao and I prepared the report on Strategic Industry and Critical Technologies.

In transforming the nation into a developed country, five areas in combination have been identified based on India's core competence, natural resources and talented manpower for integrated action to double the growth rate of GDP and realise the "Vision of Developed India".

- **Agriculture and Food Processing**: Aimed at doubling the present production of agricultural and food processing.
- **Education and Healthcare**: Directed towards literacy, social security, and overall health of the population.
- **Information and Communication Technology**: For increased e-governance to promote education in telecommunication, and telemedicine.
- **Infrastructure with reliable electric power:** Providing urban amenities to rural areas **(PURA),** and increasing solar power, hi-tech science and technology areas and **River networking**.
- **Critical technologies and strategic industries:** The growth of nuclear, space and defence technologies. Development of industries for boosting economy.

The drivers for Developed India will be a) reduced poverty level of less than 10 per cent; b) high literacy rate of more than 95 per cent;, and c) GDP growth rate of 10 per cent constantly.

Helicopter Accident: A Turning Point

Kalam focused on visits to schools, research labs and industries. His visits to schools, with the background of a Bharat Ratna, Agni and nuclear tests, made him popular with students. On 30 September 2001, he went to Bokaro by helicopter from Ranchi in Jharkhand. While landing, the helicopter crashed and fell with a thunderous noise. All on board had a miraculous escape. Grateful to God but unfazed by the incident, he went ahead with the school programme. At night, a panel of doctors persuaded him to take a tranquillizer to alleviate the shock and pain. He was all right the next day and returned to Delhi. I met him.

He said that he was 70 and an early warning signal had come. I said his health was fine and he would have many years, like his father and family members. He had to work for Developed India. He said the time had come to meet saints and seers. He discussed with Y.S. Rajan and wanted to meet great men.

He recalled his meeting with Pramukh Swami Maharaj of Swaminarayan Sanstha at Ahmedabad on 13 June when the Swamiji had called him a rishi, like the sages of the past who gave us science.

He went to Ajmer Dargah Sharif of Khwaja Chishti. There the teachings and message of Khwaja Garib Nawaz on universal love and peace inspired him. He believed that one who possesses the magnanimity of the river, the kindness of the Sun and the humility of the Earth, is close to God. Chishti sufis who succeeded him continued the tradition set by him. They were truly the pioneers of national integration.

In October 2001, Kalam visited Mata Amritanandamayee's ashram at Kollam, in Kerala. It was a remarkable experience. The message was how one can take him or her close to God. Her audiences, from many countries, crowded around her to hear her message. She had set up higher learning institutions, hospitals and housing schemes for the economically weaker sections. She appreciated PURA as it connects the capabilities of the services initiated by her. Meeting her gave Kalam inner strength and an urge to serve society through PURA.

After attending a function at Christ College at Rajkot, Kalam went to the Ramakrishna Mission and met Swami Nikhileswarananda. When he reached there in the evening, it was time for bhajans, so he sat with them and meditated for some time.

Next, on 6 October, the Shankaracharya of Kanchi organised a gathering of farmers from hundreds of villages to launch integrated knowledge empowered rural development. Political leaders were also there. Kalam later told us that everyone listened to the spiritual leaders, who could focus on national development programmes. He said he had sold the concept of PURA to the acharyas and farmers. He also visited a nearby mosque, which had been saved once by a Paramacharya. In the mosque, he saw 50 students learning the Holy Quran. They recited *Alhamdu*, the *surah* that embodies the Quran, like the 18th chapter of the Bhagavath Gita—the Path to Liberation through Renunciation.

Kalam went with Prof. Rama Rao next to the Sri Sathya Sai Institute of Higher Learning at Whitefield. When they reached there, a prayer session was going on. The theme was how to remove hatred from our hearts by removing the ego. Sai Baba came during the prayer and blessed Kalam and Rama Rao.

These meetings with seers brought Kalam closer to spirituality, as he was not averse to any religion. From his childhood, his parents and teachers in the holy town of Rameswaram had brought him up. He studied in a Christian College. He met all religious leaders and said that all religions teach good things; but they are islands, as Swami Vivekananda had said in his address at Chicago—'religion is a frog in the well'. Kalam quoted the *Quran*,

> *'O Prophet, you proclaim to the people,*
> *Who do not accept your preaching;*
> *What you worship, I do not worship,*
> *And, What I worship, you do not worship,*
> *The result of your actions belongs to you,*
> *The result of my actions belongs to me'.*

Every religion gives a clear message of high value. We need to respect each one of them and upgrade them to spirituality. I remembered my saint father, who taught me, "*There is a higher self within you that*

***transcends the limitations of the physical world*". I saw my father practicing this.**

Yellow Heaven Group of Kalam

When Kalam was staying in Asiad Village, he had three friends who walked with him in the mornings for 75 minutes. They christened them as Yellow Heaven Group. H.L. Bajaj (power sector), Sudesh Prabhakar (architect) and Pawar (advocate) were from diverse fields and were Kalam's walking friends.

They always had something to share to unwind themselves. There was enough time for each of one to relate different episodes to Kalam, whom they fondly addressed as Guruji. Their popular spot in the Asiad Village Sports Complex was a yellow flowery plant. Kalam would stand near it and say, "When I see this beautiful flower, beauty enters into me and travels through my body". And saying so his face would glow and spread happiness all around him. That was his charm. The Yellow Heaven Group members resolved that Kalam would address 100,000 school students to instil patriotism and righteousness in them; the architect would design low-cost housing for the poor; the power-man would enable additional 150,000 MW generation capacity in the country and the advocate would provide free counselling for the poor.

Whereas walkers would enjoy blossoming flowers, Kalam would look for the gardener Babu Lal to thank, encourage and bless him for maintaining a beautiful complex. Almost every walker would greet Kalam and he would acknowledge greetings with a smile and reciprocate by enquiring about their health. Never was he seen in a hurry and ignore the affection and respect that people reposed in him. The group established great friendship. Kalam once introduced me to his three friends. They became my family friends and we used to get together several times at Asiad and at Rashtrapati Bhavan. Bajaj taught me golf and he, his wife and I used to play together at RB golf course.

Kalam Resigns from PSA Post

The position of PSA was a decorated one created for Kalam without power. Vajpayee used him for a nuclear test. The purpose was over as for as he was concerned. The elite scientists in their heart of hearts did not like Kalam, as he was the only one to get a Bharat Ratna and was the

Chairman of SAC-C. But Kalam thought he must continue to contribute to the nation. He formed a group to work out a comprehensive security plan. He and the team gave a presentation of the Document on Comprehensive Regional Security Plan to PM Vajpayee. I was also present along with the team that prepared the document. Air Commodore Gopalaswami presented it. With respect for Kalam, the PM listened; but there was no action. 'It is like our saying, hear through one ear and let it pass through the other'. But Kalam was active. Unfortunately, as PSA, Kalam did not get much attention of the PM to various proposals from his office.

Feeling that he could not make any breakthrough in that position, Kalam sent a letter on 4 July 2001, expressing his intention to resign. He started discussions with ISRO and IISc to get a suitable position, so that he could be at Bengaluru. ISRO gave him the position of Brahm Prakash Distinguished Professor. Balakrishnan tried to progress the case to find an accommodation on IISc campus. As there was no response from the PMO to his resignation letter of July and to the remainders, Kalam gave a formal resignation letter from his PSA position in November 2001 and went to Bengaluru to stay in the IISc with an ISRO Professorship.

On reaching Bengaluru, he received the shocking news that the doors were shut for him and that the IISc elites did not want him on the campus. Stranded, Kalam did not know what to do. He made calls to many of his friends. Dr. Kalanithi, Vice Chancellor of Anna University, who had earlier offered a Chair Professorship to Kalam at the University, came to his rescue.

Professor in Anna University

Kalam took up academic pursuits as Professor, Technology & Societal Transformation at Anna University, Chennai, from November 2001 and was involved in teaching and research tasks. Above all, he took up a mission to ignite young minds for national development by meeting school students across the country. Over the next decade, despite being in his seventies, he addressed more than five million youth below the age of 17 and inspired them to become active participants in India Vision 2020. Kalam was passionate about bringing rural prosperity through PURA (Providing Urban Amenities to Rural Areas), in which science and technology had a key role to play. Based on his diverse experience he had been propagating the concept of a World Knowledge Platform through which the core competencies of organisations and nations could be synergised to innovate and create solutions and products for the challenges of the 21^{st}century.

He took 12 classes on Developed India and Technologies for an Empowered Nation. Every weekend, I used to go to Chennai to help him. Sivakumar and I prepared the material for the lectures. We consolidated all of them into a book. Kalam and I jointly wrote the book 'Envisioning an Empowered Nation'—Technology for Societal Transformation, based on his lectures.

We also started writing the book "Ignited Minds" sitting in the Anna University guest house. Krishan Chopra of Penguin/HarperCollins helped us.

On 3 February 2002, Kalam had an extraordinary spiritual experience when we went to the headquarters of the Brahma Kumaris at Mount Abu. Kalam came from Chennai to Ahmedabad and I went from Delhi to Ahmedabad on the evening of 2 February. Dr. W. Selvamurthi also reached there. We went to the Brahma Kumari ashram at Ahmedabad, had food and rested for some time. The three of us went in a car to the base camp of the spiritual academy at Mount Abu. Early morning on the next day, there were spiritual lectures from elder Brahma Kumaris. Kalam then gave a talk in the school and interacted with the children. We visited the Global Hospital where they carried out a DRDO project to demonstrate Raja yoga to cure heart disease. In six months' time, the patients were free from heart diseases, by practising yoga, life style modification and controlled diet.

In the evening, 16,000 Brahma Kumaris from many countries assembled to feel Shiva Baba descending on a senior Dadi, Gulzar. The three of us were sitting in the front row seats to witness the godly event. Dadi's face became radiant; her voice became deep like the voice of Baba, as she talked about the **four treasures—Knowledge, Yoga, Virtue and Service.** Dadi explained each one of them in detail. She blessed all the 16,000 Brahma Kumaris with eye contact with everyone.

Dadi called Kalam, Selvamurthy and me to the dais. We went and sat near her. She asked Kalam what was his wish. Kalam said that 500 scientists made a vision for India to become a developed nation; we see poverty and suffering of people. Will things change? Will prosperity come? Dadi said in a godly voice, "*Bharat will become the most beautiful land on Earth. Your wish will be fulfilled. You will soon be placed in a position from where you will progress the vision.*" Dadi blessed Selvamurthy and me and said, "You would assist Kalam in the Vision". It gave us a great feeling that something would happen. But what happened later in May, was something we had never anticipated.

Kalam became very popular with youth, leaders of technology, industry and academic institutions. He emerged as a well-known youth icon.

GOD CONSPIRED FOR KALAM

Kalam's name started floating in public as a possible candidate for the post of President of India. Many proposed his name. News media gave coverage. He started receiving feelers. Chandrababu Naidu and Mulayam Singh Yadav were prominent among them to promote Kalam's name and they discussed with Vajpayee. NDA leaders met. Vajpayee consulted some of his colleagues and finally made up his mind. On 10 June, Naidu told Kalam that he would get a message from the PM and he should reply in the affirmative. Vajpayee telephoned Kalam, who consented.

Suddenly Anna University had many visitors including Chief Minister Jayalalithaa, Dr. M. Karunanidhi and others. To reporters, Kalam recited a verse from the *Bhagavad Gita*.

> *"Whatever happened, happened for the good.*
> *Whatever is happening, is happening for the good.*
> *Whatever will happen, will also happen for the good."*

In the meantime, the Congress Party also endorsed his candidature, as Mrs. Sonia Gandhi had known Kalam as a member of the Rajiv Gandhi Foundation. Kalam's active participation in the technical proposals of the Foundation had impressed her. Shri A.K. Antony, Chief Minister of Kerala, supported Kalam's name. Being an apolitical candidate, there was support from Congress Party, though nominated by BJP. On 10 June 2002, Pramod Mahajan came to Chennai to escort Kalam to Delhi. I also went with them. The Indian Airlines pilot announced "Good morning. This is the captain from cockpit. Today we are honoured. A.P.J. Abdul

Kalam, who is the candidate for President of India, is travelling with us. Please welcome and cheer him." All the passengers clapped and waved their hands. On arrival at Delhi airport, George Fernandes, the Defence Minister, received him.

All the leaders were together to submit the nomination papers. Kalam stayed in the DRDO Guest House at Asiad village. Sheridon managed the office. Kalam wrote to all Members of Parliament, Assemblies and political leaders requesting support. Many political leaders came to see him. Prominent among them was Shri Mulayam Singh Yadav. The Communist parties fielded their candidate, the well renowned Smt. Lakshmi Sehgal, a member of the INA and close associate of Subhash Chandra Bose and a freedom fighter. The election took place on 15 July 2002. The result was announced on 18 July. Kalam got about 90 per cent of the votes and was elected.

On 25 July 2002 Dr. Avul Pakir Jainulabdeen Abdul Kalam assumed office as the eleventh President of India. Many dignitaries and 100 school children attended the function in the Central Hall of Parliament. President Kalam hosted a lunch for the students and teachers.

After Kalam became President, my routine also changed. Every day, Monday to Friday from 0930 to 1700, I spent at DRDO HQ; from 1730 to 2200, I was at the BrahMos office and at 2230, I attended meetings in Rashtrapati Bhavan. Major Gen. Swaminathan (Retired) and Ponraj were Kalam's sources of strength. Our meetings went on up to 02 a.m.. Then the four of us would have dinner. I would reach home at 3 a.m. I spent Saturdays full-time in the BrahMos office. On Sundays, I was at Rashtrapati Bhavan for a morning walk with Kalam in the Mughal Garden and had breakfast with him. Then to the BrahMos office. On most of his tours in India and abroad, Rajan, Swaminathan and I accompanied him as officials. **Our Ram-Lakshman relationship continued till the end.**

FIVE

Eleventh President of India

Swami Vivekananda in his speech on 11 September 1893 at the Parliament of Religions, Chicago, said, *"I will quote to you, brethren, a few lines from a hymn which I remember to have repeated from my earliest boyhood, which is every day repeated by millions of human beings:*

> *"As different streams having their sources in different places all mingle their waters in the sea, so, Oh Lord, the different paths which men take through different tendencies various though they appear, crooked or straight, all lead to Thee."*

I have assessed Kalam's life. There were a number of upsets in it. However, every failure in his life had a positive turning point for him. Obviously, an extra force was acting on him. To start with, his ambition to become an IAF pilot landed him in Swami Sivananda's Ashram in Rishikesh. Swami eased his disappointment and said,

"Accept your destiny and go ahead with your life. You are not destined to become an Air Force pilot. What you are destined to become is not revealed now; but it is predetermined. Forget this failure, as it was essential to lead you to your destined path. Search, instead, for the true purpose of your existence. Become one with yourself, my son! Surrender yourself to the wish of God".

Finally, Kalam landed as the Supreme Commander of the Armed Forces.

PRESIDENT OF INDIA

Bharat Ratna recipient Dr. Abdul Kalam served as the President of India from 25 July 2002 to 24 July 2007. He was the first scientist and the first bachelor to occupy Rashtrapati Bhavan.

The then Hon'ble Prime Minister, Shri A.B. Vajpayee described Kalam, during the release of Ramanathan's book '*Who is Kalam*' on 12 June 2003, thus:

"After his election to the august office, Dr. Kalam has brought immense grace to it, and also a new sense of purpose that is all his own. Place and position do not make a man. A man is made of samskaras.

Besides discharging his constitutional responsibilities with dignified quietude, Dr. Kalam has made Rashtrapati Bhavan the karmabhoomi *for his pet concerns, which are also the nation's major concerns—issues such as education, development of Science and Technology, rural development, and all-round development of our children, who are our most precious asset. From there he has been transmitting the dream of how to make India a Developed Nation.*

Dr. Kalam has been emphasising a spiritual approach to solving the nation's problems. This does not mean adopting the path of any particular religion. Rather as Gandhiji used to remind us, it means learning the human core of every faith. He considers the spiritual traditions of all religions as his own. This is serva panthsamabhava. *This is genuine secularism. In the Indian context, this is also genuine patriotism."*

Spreading India's Glory Abroad

As President, Dr. Kalam personified dignity and optimism throughout India and abroad. His stirring speeches at the European Parliament and the Pan-African Parliament were among the best ever delivered. His simplicity in oration and action were applauded and made him dear to all. The foreign dignitaries who came on official visits returned with a great feeling of India's glory. During Dr. Kalam's visits to many countries, he spoke on the warm relationship and suggested several joint missions. He was regarded in every country as a strong promoter of friendship and knowledge. I had the opportunity to go with him on his official visits, abroad and in India. I witnessed the respect for India through him.

Vibrant Rashtrapati Bhavan

Dr. Kalam had an extremely good relationship with the two prime ministers, Shri Vajpayee and Dr. Manmohan Singh, which was based on mutual respect. They discussed issues with an open mind. Dr. Kalam shared with me some of the discussions. I have given some of the issues here, but not all.

Our old colleague in ISRO at Thiruvananthapuram, Shri P.M. Nair was a great administrator. As Secretary to President, he brought discipline in the President's office and made it efficient. He gave impartial and timely advice to the President on all critical issues. Established cordial relations with his peers in the ministry and the cabinet secretariat. He made the estate tidy and established new facilities. Dr. Kalam made me visit the golf course and initiated me into playing golf. He said that as CEO, I must play golf. The golf course got a facelift and I became a player.

DAY one (Photo)

Dr. Kalam brought in many innovations and changed the style of functioning of the presidential palace. He encouraged biodiversity in the garden, nurtured medicinal plants and created a herbal and "spiritual" garden in the sprawling Mughal Gardens, which attracts thousands of visitors every year. He had a soft corner for handicapped animals and went out of his way to help them. Kalam was concerned not only for human beings but also for the fauna. I recollect an incident that had happened in the garden of Rashtrapati Bhavan. A two-year-old fawn from the deer enclosure in the presidential estate had been rejected by its mother. Kalam asked his staff to adopt it and told the veterinary doctors at Rashtrapati Bhavan to treat and correct a defect in its foot. No doubt, that he was a noble soul.

We generated Vision for each state, in the form of display charts. Dr. Kalam invited MPs to the Mughal Gardens and explained to them the value, core competence, development schemes, etc., of their states. The idea was to mobilise the parliamentarians to participate in the development of their respective states. Dr. Kalam went to State assemblies and presented the Vision for the respective state. He went to schools, colleges and universities to tell them their tasks for creating a new India.

Dr. Kalam opened up Rashtrapati Bhavan to children and the public. Earlier, Rashtrapati Bhavan was used to host only official delegation meetings. Many new things such as establishment of new galleries, which displayed important happenings in history, scientific discoveries, etc,. attracted children. School children used to visit and take away memories by way of sketches made on the computer with Rashtrapati Bhavan in the background and they standing in front of the computer system. Requests poured in from schools for the visit of their students visit Rashtrapati Bhavan. Dr. Kalam used to meet students of every group and interacted with them. The affection showed by such students can be seen in the form of cartoons made by them. Some of them are displayed at the Mission of Life Exhibition Centre at BrahMos Hqrs Complex.

Exhibition for Kalam at BrahMos Hqrs.

Dr. Kalam never kept his medals, certificates, mementos and other decorations. Some were with me, but many were not traceable. I decided to trace them and get them to display his life as an exhibition so that the children could emulate him. I got four acres of army land from the

Ministry of Defence and constructed the BrahMos HQ in the Cantonment area at Delhi. I made a display hall for exhibiting BRAHMOS and a separate 'Mission of Life' hall for Kalam. I kept all his original medals, including the Bharat Ratna, certificates of doctorates from universities from all over the world and mementos in the special hall at BrahMos HQ, in Delhi.

President Putin inaugurated this HQ on 4 December 2004. Shri Pranab Mukherjee, Defence Minister and Shri Natwar Singh, Minister of External Affairs, were present. I showed them Dr. Kalam's chamber. Putin was amazed to see the laurels of Dr. Kalam. His respect for Kalam went up and he said "Genius". I briefed Kalam that evening. He wanted to see the exhibits himself.

Kalam as President of India visited BrahMos HQ on the very next day, the 5 December 2004. He thanked me profusely for creating this 'collage' dedicated to his life. He immediately took me in his President's car and said, 'You deserve a cup of tea'. He did not allow the staff to pour the tea. He did so himself. I told him, that this was just a small gesture. He recited one Thirukural, meaning **'If you give a little help in the right time, it is as big as the globe'**. He was my mentor for 40 years and I was in a position to do this only with the help of my teammates. Many students have come from all over India and the Gulf to see their Kalam Sir in the BrahMos office. I also made a centre of Kalam's achievements in the first floor of the renovated solar powered 'Kalam House' in Rameswaram, called 'MISSION OF LIFE'. For me, this is small, the real thing was my support to him at ISRO and DRDO in difficult times.

Students visit the Mission of Life Gallery at BrahMos Hqrs

Dr. Kalam during the inauguration of Mission of Life at Rameswaram

Lifetime Ambition Achieved

As Supreme Commander of the Armed Forces, he used to be with all the three arms of the Armed Forces. He travelled to the North, Siachen Glacier and Western borders to be with our men in uniform. I travelled with him to some places including Uri in the west and Tawang in the east.

The Navy conducts the Presidential Fleet Review once in the five years of a President's term. During the ninth Presidential Fleet Review at Vizag, he created history by becoming the country's first President to undertake an undersea journey in INS Sindhurakshak, a Russian-origin kilo class submarine. He released my book on *'Ocean Warfare'* in the submarine and the first copy was given to the Chief of Naval Staff and the second to the Deputy Chief.

Release of **Ocean Warfare** *by Dr. Kalam in INS Sindhurakshak*

Kalam flew in a Sukhoi 30 aircraft in supersonic speed. Wing Commander Rathore took the flight to about 7.5 km above ground level and flew at 1.25 Mach (one-and-a-quarter times the speed of sound). "The President took control of the flight for roughly five to ten minutes. He had absolute control over the flight in mid-air," Wing Commander Rathore said. His lifetime mission to be a pilot was finally achieved at the age of 74!

Dr. Kalam addressing the Press immediately after the SU-30MKI Flight

Release of book 'Envisioning an Empowered Nation'

RELATIONSHIP WITH PRIME MINISTERS

Vajpayee conducted a cabinet meeting in Rashtrapati Bhavan to discuss the Developed India vision and action. On several occasions, Shri Vajpayee had lunch with Dr. Kalam. His special dish was curry with king prawns. Being a vegetarian Dr. Kalam used to share with him only poems and not the prawns.

Dr. Kalam told me that in one of his conversations with Shri Vajpayee, the PM had told him, "Normally the Prime Minister, as Chief Executive of the country is more popular with the people. But what my party people tell me is that you are travelling extensively to all places and people like you more. So I want to request you to reduce your travelling, not all of a sudden, but slowly. That will make things better." Dr. Kalam said that he would reduce his travelling.

After the PM left, I told Dr. Kalam, "The PM is right. I also felt that way. His party has to face the people for winning elections. After all, he brought you. He was so kind to you all the time, maintaining a very cordial relationship". Dr. Kalam started reducing his movement for the next few months. However, as more requests started pouring in, he could not follow the guideline strictly. The visits started increasing.

The relationship with Dr. Manmohan Singh was built on mutual respect for each other from earlier days when Dr. Singh was Finance Minister and Dr. Kalam was Chief of the DRDO. They were very transparent with each other, and maintained an excellent relationship. There were many delicate conversations that Dr. Kalam had with both the prime ministers during their respective terms. Both the PMs were under severe stress, due to internal and coalition politics, to the extent of even wanting to resign. Dr. Kalam consoled them with frank discussions. He narrated some of such instances to me.

These three reputed leaders, Shri Vajpayee, Dr. Manmohan Singh and Dr. Kalam were great assets of the nation and raised the glory of India in the international arena, without yielding to any country's pressure.

When we think of Shri Vajpayee as PM, we remember the Pokhran nuclear tests conducted in May 1998, changing the trajectory of the country's relationship with the world; the Delhi-Lahore bus to show

the initiative to make peace with Pakistan; winning the Kargil conflict; the Golden Quadrilateral and National Highways Development Project to change the economic face of the nation; Telecom Policy—hyper growth of communication; 8 per cent GDP growth rate making India shine.

When we think of Dr. Manmohan Singh as PM, we remember the Indo-US Nuclear Deal, GDP growth rate of 10.08 per cent, NREGA (National Rural Employment Guarantee Scheme), Special Economic Zone Act 2005 (SEZ), RTI 2005 and Right to Education.

Right to Education

The Constitutional Amendment of 2002 included Article 21A in the Indian Constitution making education the fundamental right of every child between the ages of 6 and 14. This amendment, however, specified the need for a legislation to describe the mode of implementation of the same, which necessitated the drafting of a separate Education Bill. A draft of the bill was composed in 2005, which was referred for legislation by the President. This was the happiest moment for Dr. Kalam. The Bill was set in motion during his tenure.

The Bill was approved by the Cabinet on 2 July 2009. The Rajya Sabha passed it on 20 July 2009 and the Lok Sabha on 4 August 2009. It received the Presidential Assent and was notified as law on 26 August 2009 as 'The Children's Right to Free and Compulsory Education Act'. It came into effect from 1 April 2010. A law was brought into force for the first time with a speech by the Prime Minister. In his speech, Dr. Manmohan Singh, Prime Minister of India, stated: "*We are committed to ensuring that all children, irrespective of gender and social category, have access to education. An education that enables them to acquire the skills, knowledge, values and attitudes necessary to become responsible and active citizens of India.*"

Two constitutional points often discussed in Dr Kalam's presidentship were the most difficult issues for him. 1. President's Rule in Bihar; 2. Office of Profit Bill. Though I am not a legal expert, I knew what was happening. I got the impression that the position of the President of India was fragile. In a democracy, we need honest politics and respect for constitutional provisions and positions. I was with Dr Kalam as a subordinate, friend, adviser, speechwriter, action man, promoter, fellow traveller, forecaster and Lakshman. So I thought of writing my impressions as a citizen of India on two issues, on which Dr. Kalam was hurt. These views are purely personal.

Dr. Kalam described these two issues in his book—*Turning Points*.

1. Decision to Impose President's Rule in Bihar on 23 March 2005

Within hours of the curtains coming down on the UPA government's celebrations of completing one year in office, the Cabinet at an emergency meeting reviewed the evolving situation in Patna in the wake of Bihar Governor Buta Singh's report and recommended dissolution of the State Assembly. Close to midnight on 22 March 2005, Prime Minister Manmohan Singh spoke to President Kalam, who was in Moscow on an official visit.

At midnight, the Secretary to the President brought the paper containing the decision of the Cabinet to dissolve the Bihar Assembly that had been received by him, and he requested President to sign it. We were having our South Indian dinner. Y.S. Rajan, myself and others were with Dr. Kalam, for the dinner. As the Bihar problem came to the table, food lost its priority. We were not legal experts, so we advised Dr. Kalam to get a legal opinion in the morning or after going to Delhi. All of us told him not to sign the paper that night in a hurry.

The PM called again, saying that he was waiting in the office and requested him to sign the paper. Dr. Kalam said he wanted to consult legal experts and that it would take some more time. The PM pleaded that many were waiting and asking for his assent to proclaim President's Rule before dawn. All of us there in Moscow, that midnight, advised him not to sign blindly. Rajan and I made it clear to him that his clean record as President would be shattered if he signed, because we did not have full details of the political gamble and did not know the consequences. Dr. Kalam was in two minds. The PM was still waiting in his office. P. M. Nair, who was receiving calls from Delhi, advised him to sign, as this was a Cabinet decision. Dr. Kalam told us that he must give weightage to Dr. Singh. He took the pen. Our team was watching with sad faces. I went to the extent of holding his hand and not allowing him to sign, and telling him it would be a black mark on his presidentship. He said that there was no other way. He waited for me to let go his hand and he signed reluctantly, giving his assent to the Union Cabinet's recommendation to impose President's Rule in Bihar under Article 356 of the Constitution.

It was later challenged in the Supreme Court whose five-judge Constitution

Bench, headed by Chief Justice Y.K. Sabharwal, gave an interim order on October 7, 2005 stating that "the proclamation of May 23 dissolving the Bihar Assembly is unconstitutional."

On January 24, 2006, the Supreme Court gave its full judgement that the dissolution of the Bihar Assembly was illegal and unconstitutional. It did not direct status quo ante and the revival of the assembly. *"The drastic and extreme action under Article 356 cannot be justified on...whims and fancies of the governor...The Council of Ministers should have verified the facts stated in the report of the Governor before hurriedly accepting it as gospel truth. Clearly the Governor has misled the Council of Ministers."*

Since the Home Ministry is the nodal body that recommended the Governor's note for approval by the Cabinet, it was clearly its job to verify the contents of Buta Singh's note before passing it on to his Cabinet colleagues.

The Supreme Court verdict was a black mark in the tenure of Dr. Kalam, as he was caught unawares in the political game. If he had signed a second time, after declining the first time, his reputation would have gone up further. He repented having given his assent. He wanted to resign. He made out a letter of resignation, addressed it to the Vice- President. He had a meeting with Dr. Singh and showed the letter. Dr. Kalam says in his book that the scene was touching and a startled Dr. Singh pleaded with him not do it at this critical time. Dr. Singh convinced Dr. Kalam that as President he had given his assent only to the cabinet decision. If it was a wrong decision, the cabinet was responsible and not the President. Emotional, Dr. Singh said, "I am responsible for requesting you to give approval to the cabinet decision. Let us not have any constitutional break down by resigning. As a result of the furore that would be created, even the Government may fall." Next day Dr. Kalam decided not to resign. Even after many years, Dr. Kalam felt sad for the Bihar issue.

2. Office of Profit Bill: Provision in the Constitution

An office of profit means a position that brings to the person holding it some financial gain, or advantage, or benefit. It may be an office or place of profit if it carries some remuneration, financial advantage, benefits, etc. The term is used in Article 102 (1)(a) of the Indian Constitution which bars a member of the Indian Parliament from holding an office that would give its occupant the opportunity to gain financial advantage or benefit. India had the Parliament (Prevention of Disqualification) Act, 1950, 1951, and 1953 exempting certain posts from being recorded as offices of profit. All these Acts were replaced by the Parliament (Prevention of Disqualification) Act, 1959. By virtue of section 3 of the said Act, certain offices did not disqualify their holders from being Members of Parliament.

The representatives cannot hold an office of profit under section 9 of the Representation of People Act and Article 191 (1) (a) of the Constitution.

Few Instances

In 2006, Indian National Congress President and Member of Parliament Smt. Sonia Gandhi resigned from several posts under pressure from the political opposition that asserted that the posts were 'offices of profit' and thus unlawful. The Bill was triggered by a court petition relating to Jaya Bachchan's election to the Rajya Sabha while being Chairman of the UP Films Development Federation. The complaints received by the President from MPs were referred to the Election Commission that ruled that she was in fact holding an office of profit. Jaya Bachchan was disqualified from the Rajya Sabha. Two Uttar Pradesh Legislative Assembly members, Bajrang Bahadur Singh and Uma Shankar Singh, were also disqualified in January 2015 because they were holding government contracts.

It is a term used in a number of national constitutions to refer to executive appointments. A number of countries forbid members of the legislature from accepting an office of profit under the executive as a means to secure the independence of the legislature and preserve the separation of powers.

The New Bill Passed by Parliament

The Bill is known as the Parliament (Prevention of Disqualification) Amendment Bill 2006. The Bill provides in essence that members who are currently holding offices of profit under the Central Government or any state government (individuals holding known and listed "offices") shall not be disqualified from being members of Parliament since Parliament has retrospectively declared by law that the office of profit they so hold would not disqualify the holder.

Parliament rushed through the Office of Profit Bill, for very specific cases involving prominent persons. It was not at all comprehensive, and was hurriedly passed without much consideration. The BJP had strongly criticised the Bill and had walked out of the Lok Sabha during its passage.

All UPA allies including the Left and the Samajwadi Party had supported it. The Bill was sent to the President by Parliament for assent.

President Dr. Kalam held detailed discussions with many legal experts and former CJIs. It was a continuous process for him. None of the experts agreed with the form in which the Bill was put up.

An Expert View

In a newspaper article, former MP and eminent jurist Fali Nariman had sharply criticised the provisions of the legislation that aims to prevent the disqualification of parliamentarians holding offices of profit. Specifically, Nariman said, it violated Article 102(1) of the Constitution. Nariman said that the first part of the Article was founded on the need for establishing and maintaining neutrality and impartiality in public service while the latter part required Parliament to make an "objective assessment" of what construed an office of profit.

Nariman suggested that the Bill would enable members who already hold such offices of profit to continue to do so with impunity as it is to be implemented retrospectively. Nariman called it a "legislative sleight of hand" to justify, rather than correct, a Constitutional transgression. Nariman had urged President Kalam not to sign the Bill and the court to "strike it down as wholly arbitrary and impermissible".

It was known that if the President returned the Bill, it would cause embarrassment to the ruling coalition. The PM met the President. Dr. Kalam indicated that the Bill had many anomalies and needed redrafting in a comprehensive manner, instead of finding ad hoc solutions for some individual cases. However, Dr. Singh insisted that the President give his assent to the Bill in its existing form.

Kalam considered all the relevant issues including the circumstances of its passage and the widespread criticism of the elements of the Bill that constitutional experts had opined. After deep thought, he returned the Bill to the Secretary General of the Lok Sabha and Rajya Sabha, with a letter requesting redrafting in a comprehensive manner, mentioning the criteria for exempting a particular office from the provisions of the Bill, which should be fair and reasonable in consultation with constitutional experts, debated and passed by Parliament.

The Congress Party would not have liked this action of the President. The PM informed that a Joint Parliamentary Committee (JPC) had been formed by Parliament to go into details. As action was initiated and the pressure mounting, President approved the Bill. After a few months, the JPC submitted the Bill in the same way without giving any weightage to the views of the President following which Parliament approved the Bill. We knew on that day that the chances of his second term as President were now over.

Dr. Kalam wrote in his book *'The Turning Points'*

"The return of the Office of Profit Bill clearly establishes how at the Parliament level, practices that cannot meet the standards of public probity are not debated and reviewed with the seriousness they deserve. That can be considered as a starting point for accepting wrong practices that will lead to compromises in formulating and practising a national standard".

SURAT DECLARATION

Towards Enlightened Citizenship

God has created human beings with brains and the ability to think. He has commanded His creation to use this ability with reasoning to reach His image. This is the Mission of Human Life.

Spirituality is a special quality God has bestowed upon human beings, whose duty is to discover and use it for the benefit of all. In whatever field we work, be it science, technology, medicine, politics, policing, theology, religion or judiciary, we have to remain in the service of the common man, whose well-being is central to all human knowledge and endeavour.

On 15 October 2003, spiritual leaders from all religions met in at Surat and signed the 'Surat Spiritual Declaration' on 'Unity of Minds' and for creating 'Enlightened Citizens; in the presence of H.H. Acharya Mahaprajna and presented it to Dr. Kalam, Hon' President of India.

India is a unique nation, constantly communicating the highest value of unity among diversity to the world. There may have been ripples here and there, now and again, but in an overall analysis, "India is India". When we talk about a nation and its greatness, everyone in it has to be a responsible citizen. Every individual needs to create a value system and contribute individually and collectively to its growth.

Next President

On 20 June 2007, Kalam expressed his willingness to consider a second term in office provided there was certainty about his victory in the 2007 presidential election. He told this to Dr. Manmohan Singh, who in turn politely told him that his party was not in his favour. Probably, the office of profit issue had damaged Dr. Kalam's chances, though the popular sentiment of the people of India was for him to continue. Two days later, he decided not to contest the Presidential election again stating that he wanted to avoid involving Rashtrapati Bhavan in any political processes.

TECHNOLOGY INITIATIVES AND INTERACTIONS BY THE PRESIDENT

Nano Technology

The President being an eminent scientist, a full-day conference was organised by us at Rashtrapati Bhavan on the status of nanotechnology in India. Science departments of the government, academic institutions, industry and experts participated and reviewed 22 research projects. Prof. C.N.R. Rao gave an overview of the development and futuristic needs, including the focus areas of research and funding. We divided the participants into four groups based on the applications and gave a growth profile. A senior director from the Planning Commission participated and agreed to provide funding for the finalised developments, through a review process by Prof. Rao. Research outputs from Delhi University on drug delivery system and from Banaras Hindu University on carbon nanotube filters were some projects that benefited through this funding.

Pan-African Satellite

Dr. Kalam addressed the Pan-African Parliament in South Africa attended by presidents of 53 countries of Africa. There he offered the setting up of a Pan-African e-Network at an initial cost of $ 50 million. The satellite and receiving ground network were to be provided by India, for tele-education and tele-medicine, connecting Indian hospitals. Many of the African countries are benefited. V. Ponraj played a key role in implementing this project.

CERN: Finding the God Particle

CERN, the European Organisation for Nuclear Research, is one of the world's largest and most respected centres for scientific research. Its business is fundamental physics, finding out what the universe is made up of and how it works. Dr. Kalam visited CERN. I accompanied him. Anil Kakodkar was there to receive the President along with top scientists. When we entered, we saw a big statue of the dancing Nataraja, representing the cosmology.

Scientists are carrying out experiments on the Large Hadron Collider at CERN, to understand the formation of the universe and the particles, which move faster than light. I recalled the work of Dr. E.C.G. Sudhersan who proved TACHYON particles are faster than light. These experiments are vital for the scientific community to get a clear idea about the universe, which was formed 13.7 billion years ago. CERN's main function is to provide particle accelerators and other infrastructure needed for high-energy physics research. As a result, numerous experiments have been conducted at CERN through international collaborations.

The main site at Meyrin, near Geneva, hosts a large computing facility, which is primarily used to store and analyse data from experiments, as well as simulate events. Researchers need remote access to these facilities, so the lab has historically been a major wide area network hub. CERN is also the birthplace of the World Wide Web. Artificial Intelligence will have a greater role in the future in data analysis of several experiments to understand the God particle.

Technology Vision 2020

Developed India

In India and abroad, Dr. Kalam had met about 17 million students and interacted with them on the Developed India vision. He travelled the length and breadth of India and promoted the salient aspects of the Vision and action plan. Prime Minister Vajpayee, while addressing the nation on Independence Day, had announced that the Government would implement the Developed India Vision 2020. Dr. Kalam hard-sold the PURA scheme to the Government and many projects were implemented. Still a lot more PURA projects have yet to come up. Dr. Manmohan Singh, while addressing Governors, promoted Vision 2020.

The freedom movement was the first vision of India. The need of the hour is to make India a developed nation and regain its past glory. This becomes our second vision for the nation. The objectives of the second vision were to be self-sufficient in food production, achieve a sustained GDP growth rate above 10 per cent, reduce poverty below 10 per cent and achieve 100 per cent literacy. In order to achieve the above vision of a developed nation, TIFAC (Technology Information, Forecasting and Assessment Centre) of the Department of Science and Technology undertook a study of Technology Vision 2020 to identify the specific areas for development and produce a road map to achieve the desired results. Detailed action plans were outlined in 17 volumes and five key result areas were identified based on the core competence of a developed nation.

The five areas identified in Technology Vision 2020 are: (i) Agriculture and food processing; (ii) Education and Healthcare; (iii) Information and Communication Technology; (iv) Infrastructure: Reliable and Quality Electric power, Surface transport and Infrastructure for all parts of the country, PURA; and (v) Self- reliance in critical technologies correlated and progressed in an integrated way that will lead to overall national progress and development.

These sectors are closely interlinked and can together strengthen the economy and national security. Integrated action in the above areas, if implemented, will result in a GDP growth rate of more than 10 per cent from the present level and sustainable in the same range for at least 10 years, bring down the number of people below the poverty line to less than 10 per cent and increased literacy and employment.

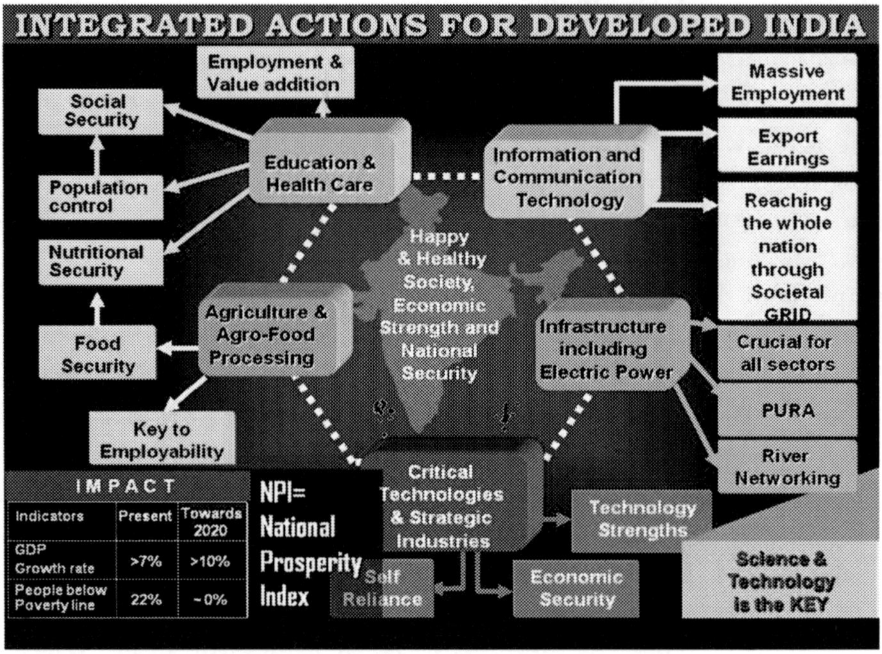

Integrated Action for Developed India

India began its journey of economic progress by concentrating on non-strategic sectors like agriculture, dairy, pharmaceuticals, telecommunications, power generation and cars because these were the dire needs at that point of time. With continuous efforts, India became self-reliant in these non-strategic sectors. The development of these sectors paved the way for the ultimate growth of connected sectors comprising infrastructure development, strategic sectors and other high technology areas. Government of India approved the road map outlined in Technology Vision 2020 in 1996. A vigorous action plan will have a great impact on sustained growth of the economy. Instead, Government funds are being used in popular schemes, which will have only a temporary effect.

Developed India action

India must focus on bringing sustainable development through rural and urban infrastructure, quality education, healthcare, environmental up-gradation, bringing vibrancy in public institutions for better and enhanced delivery of essential public services on time, reforming the financial system for better global integration and a proactive regulatory system. It is critical to the success of India becoming a Global player.

PURA: Providing Urban Amenities in Rural Areas

Dr. Kalam spearheaded a socio-economic movement named PURA, which is vital for realising Developed India. The components of PURA are: Physical connectivity of 20-30 villages in a cluster; IT-enabled Electronic connectivity; education-driven Knowledge connectivity and industry-linked Economic connectivity. This will enhance rural prosperity of the clusters. PURA is a good model for public-private partnerships to use technology innovation for sustainable development of six hundred thousand villages.

1. Villages must be connected within themselves and with main towns and metros by good roads and wherever needed by railway lines. They must have other infrastructure like schools, colleges, hospitals and amenities for the local population and for visitors. Let us call this physical connectivity.

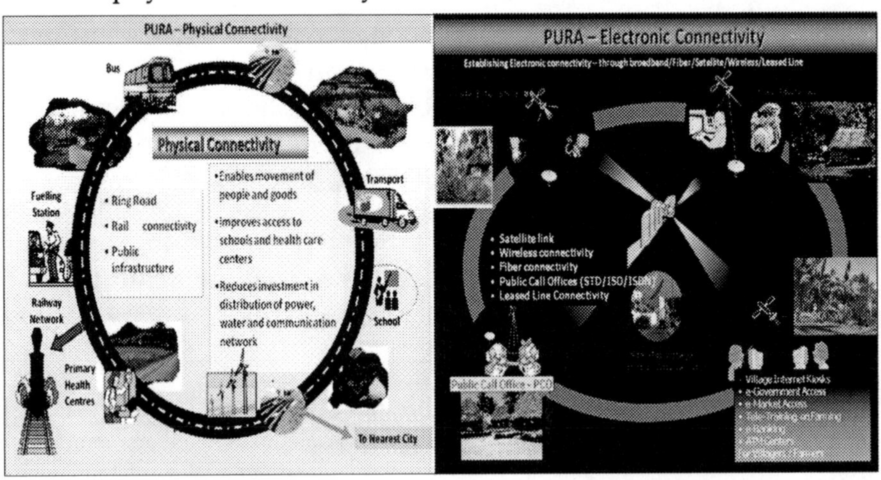

2. In the emerging knowledge era, native knowledge has to be preserved and enhanced with the latest tools of technology, training and research. Villages have to have access to good education from the best teachers wherever they may be, must have the benefit of good medical treatment, and must have the latest information on their pursuits like agriculture, fishery, horticulture and food processing. That means they have to have electronic connectivity.

3. Once physical and electronic connectivity is enabled, knowledge connectivity is enabled. This can facilitate the ability to increase productivity, utilise spare time, be aware of health welfare, ensure a market for products, increase quality conscience, interact with partners, get the best equipment, increase transparency and so on.

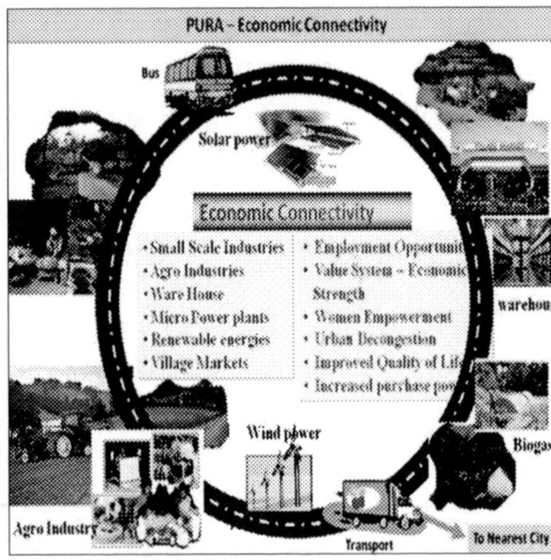

4. Once physical, electronic and knowledge connectivity is ensured, it facilitates economic connectivity. In short, when we Provide Urban Amenities to Rural Areas (PURA), it can lead to the upliftment of rural areas, can attract investors, and effectively introduce useful systems like rural BPOs, Micro Finance, etc.

Thus, if we take up PURA as a mission, we can make villages prosperous knowledge accumulation centres and villagers entrepreneurs. Is this possible? Can we make PURA as an enterprise? This is what management experts must work out.

Missions for prosperity can be achieved only through their spreading based on core competence to village clusters.

The number of PURA projects for the whole of India is estimated to be 7,000 covering 600,000 villages where 750 million people live. Similarly, about 30,000 PURA complexes would be required to convert the 3 billion rural population of the world into a vibrant economic zone and bringing sustainable development to rural areas. *There are operational PURAs in India initiated by many educational, healthcare institutions, industry and other institutions such as Periyar PURA in Tamil Nadu, Loni Warana Valley PURA in Maharashtra, and Chitrakoot PURA in Madhya Pradesh.*

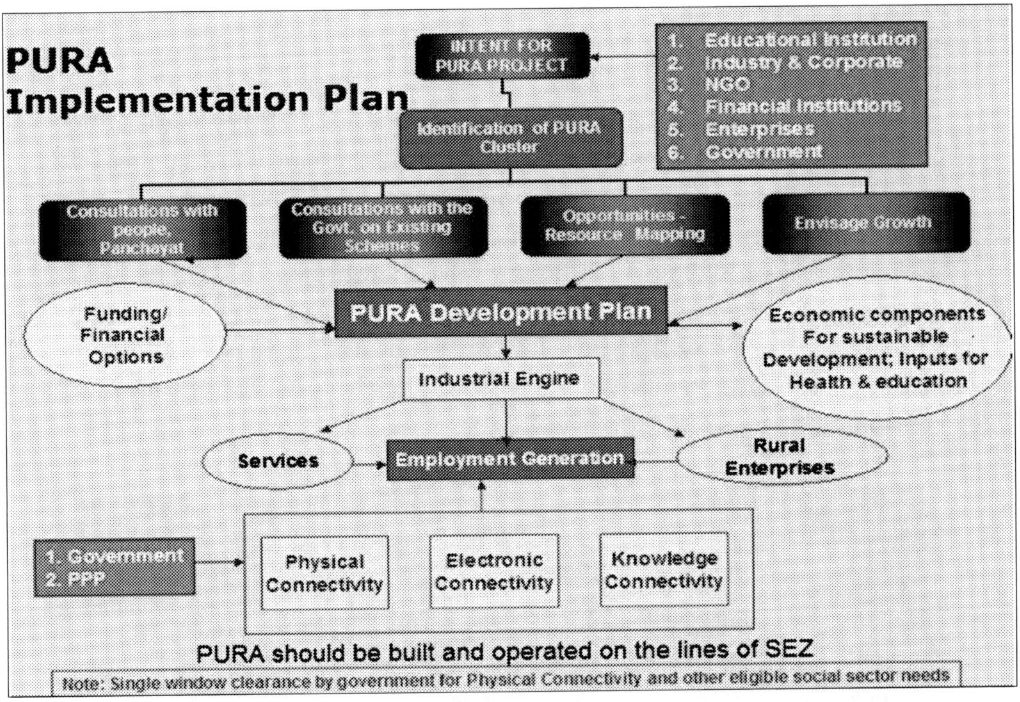

The Government of India already went ahead with the implementation of PURA on a national scale across several districts of India with an outlay of Rs.1,500 crore in a public-private partnership model. Kalam discusses all these examples of rural development through PURA along with international experience in the book, *Target 3 Billion*. Simultaneously, we have to enhance the rural and urban infrastructure through the establishment of PURA complexes and Smart cities spread in different parts of the country. The mission of PURA is employment generation with value-added skills through connectivity. The investment in these areas will not only provide value-added employment to our citizens but will generate higher growth in economic activity. Innovation has to come into action to strengthen the economy and progress the development of the nation.

World Knowledge Platform

The concept of a "World Knowledge Platform" can be utilized by organizations for integrating their capabilities spread in different work centres, synergising the unique competence available in other likeminded companies, both within the country and abroad for vertical domains for collaborative research, development, production and marketing of products and systems using the Global Sourcing approach.

Initially, the mission of the World Knowledge Platform is to connect and network the R&D institutions, universities and industries using fibre broadband from the partner nations for selected R&D missions. The underground fibre cable infrastructure already exists between many partners. It is only waiting to be put into operation with state-of-the-art optical networks and ignite the minds of knowledge workers. This knowledge GRID will support a multitude of seamless connections supporting both synchronous and asynchronous communication, carrying either text, audio or video.

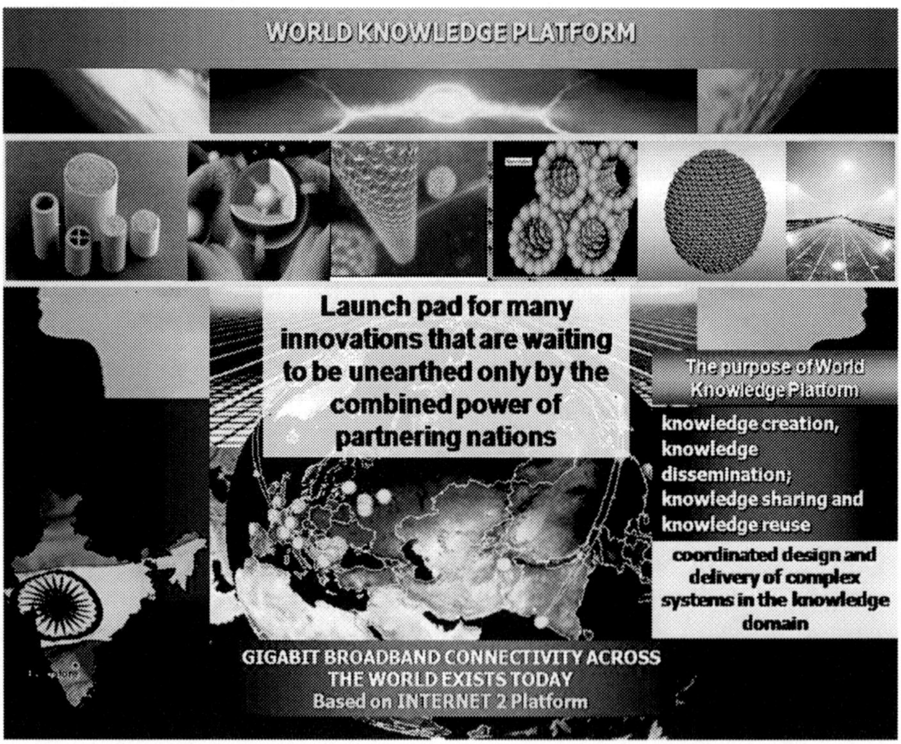

We can then use this network in academic environments to teach courses online and share expensive equipment remotely. In an industrial environment, it can be used to design complex systems—even ones that are as complex as an aircraft in a collaborative way using virtual prototyping concepts in cyber space.

Missions of World Knowledge Platform: The convergence of Bio, Nano and IT is expected to touch every area of concern to humanity. The "World Knowledge Platform" will take up missions in some of the areas (discussed further) which are of utmost urgency to all of us in order to make our world a safe, sustainable, peaceful and prosperous place:

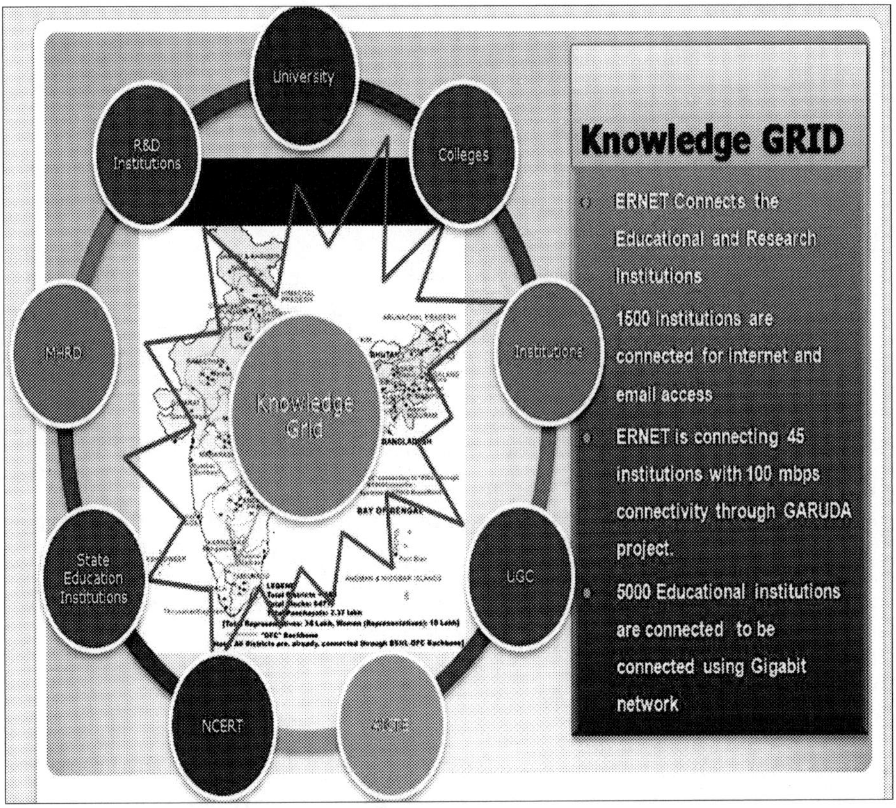

Knowledge Grid

1. **Energy:** Exploration, Storage, Production and Conversion
2. **Water:** Desalination of sea water using solar energy, channelisation, networking of rivers, cost effective safe drinking water
3. **Healthcare:** Diagnosis, drug delivery system, development and production of vaccines for HIV/TB, corona virus, malaria and cardiac diseases, detection and cure of diabetics
4. **Agriculture and Food Processing:** Increased production of foodgrains in an environment of reduced land, reduced water and reduced man-power; preservation of food; food processing; cost-effective storage and distribution

5. **Knowledge products:** Hardware, Software and Networking and storage products including handheld micro and nano electronic devices
6. **Transportation systems:** Fossil fuel-free transportation systems using renewable energy safety systems, hardware and embedded software integration
7. **Habitat:** Energy efficient, water efficient, pollution free habitat
8. **Diamonds:** Exploration, conflict-free sourcing, mining, processing, polishing, production and state-of-the-art jewellery designs
9. **Disaster Prediction and Management:** Earthquake forecasting, assessing in advance the quantum of rain for a particular cloud condition
10. **Capacity Building:** Quality human resource development for all the above areas including the development of personnel with world-class skills.

In this situation, the World Knowledge Platform is a suitable mission. The number of academic, research and production institutions within India and abroad can form a consortium for the vertical missions of the World Knowledge Platform in the above-mentioned areas with public-private partnerships. In short, the Knowledge Platform would be a launch pad for many innovations that are waiting to be unearthed only by the combined power of multiple institutions.

KALAM'S 80TH BIRTHDAY

Dr. A.P.J. Abdul Kalam attended Dr. Kumar's marriage at Thiruvananthapuram on 28 May 2000 and blessed the young couple, Kumar and Gomathi. My daughter-in-law is a computer engineer. They were based in Delhi and Kumar worked at Apollo Hospital for one year. Later they moved to Chennai, as Kumar was doing MCh in Hand Surgery at Stanley Medical College. My grandson Sivathanu Kumar is a smart boy and used to talk to Kalam on phone. When Kalam was President, they used to meet him at Raj Bhavan, Chennai and at Rashtrapati Bhavan, Delhi.

Kumar and his family moved to Hersey, Penn. State and then to Little Rock, Arkansas USA for his Fellowship in Micro Vascular Surgery. He had the opportunity to get guidance from Dr. Gazi Yasargil, Microsurgeon

of the Century. I met this great surgeon during my visits to Little Rock and as advised by him, I gave a talk on Nano technology for neurosurgery to all doctors of the University Hospital. I visited the nanotechnology laboratory established by Prof. Vijay Varadan and his pioneering research work on devices. Dr. Varadan was my senior in TCE and from my native place. We jointly wrote a book on Nanotechnology for Engineering. Kumar's family was in the USA for 4 years. Our daughter-in-law completed her MS in Computer Science at Arkansas University. Our granddaughter Meenakshi was born at Fayetteville, when Kumar was in the University of Arkansas for a few months, before moving to India. They came back in 2008 and settled at Coimbatore. Dr. Kumar joined Ramakrishna Hospital as Consultant in **Micro and Hand Surgery**.

On 15 October 2011, Dr Kalam visited our house at Coimbatore on his **80th birthday**, and had dinner with us. People in the surrounding neighbourhood assembled in large crowds to have a glimpse of Kalam. It went on until midnight. It was a great honour for us to host Kalam on his 80th birthday.

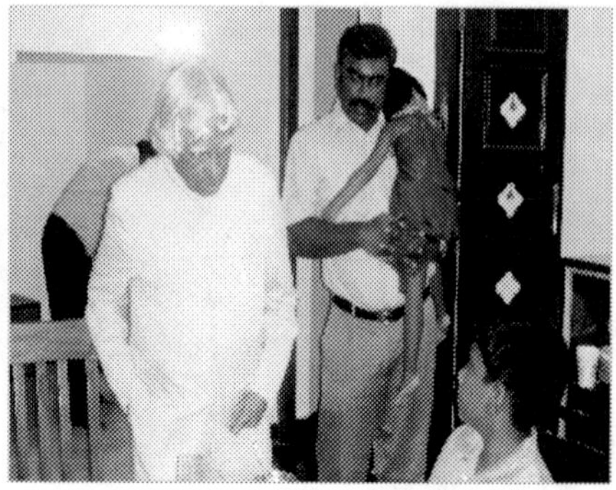

Now, Siva is doing his Electronics & Communication Engineering at Amrita Vishwa Vidyapeetham, Coimbatore and Meenakshi is in the seventh standard.

SIX

The Brahmastra

The Mind without Fear

CAN INDIA BE NUMBER ONE IN THE WORLD

> *Everyone holds his fortune in his own hands,*
> *like a sculpture fashioned into a figure from raw stone.*
> *The skill to mould the material into what we want*
> *must be learnt and attentively cultivated.*
>
> **—Von Goethe**

Many times Kalam and I discussed about when Independent India would become Number One in the world. Two thousand years ago, India dominated the world in every aspect—Knowledge, Culture, Noble thoughts, Trade, Civilisation, Science, Medicine, and Arts. Spiritual wisdom and culture have been our strength. We have survived as a nation, in spite of foreign rule, but lowered our aims and expectations and settled down to a lower mind-set.

Many eminent leaders emerged during the freedom movement, who tried to boost the spirits and minds of the people in their attempts to recapture the greatness of Indians. It is time now that we regain our heritage and wisdom, to enrich our lives in the coming years. Therefore, we need to evolve our own model of development, based on our inherent strengths, to reiterate to the world that Indians are remarkable.

George W. Bush

When President George W. Bush came to India in March 2006, President Kalam introduced me to him. Bush said, "Dr. Pillai, I have heard about your successful cooperation with Russia called the BrahMos missile. Why not the USA?" I replied, **"Excellency, any deep technology joint effort to make a product for the first time in the world on an equal partnership only will make India and America long-standing friendly countries".**

He said, "You made a good point. We will work on it". He then introduced me to his wife, Laura, with some good words. Ambassador D.C. Mulford sent a letter to me enclosing a photo of me with President Bush, signed by the President himself.

Pentagon Reception

In 2008, I led a delegation for visiting US Defence labs to work out cooperation in naval materials. Vice Admiral B.S. Randhawa Chief of Material (COM), Indian Navy and DRDO Directors were members of my team. During our visit to the USA, the Naval HQ at Pentagon received us. The Fleet Commander of all naval ships of the US Navy, in the rank of Vice Admiral, welcomed us with nearly 30 officers inside. Behind me, our Vice Admiral was standing. I thought the commander would be more interested in our COM. The Admiral welcomed me by name with pleasant words and held my hand. He kept on pressing and did not want to leave the hand. I told him to meet COM. Surprisingly, he opened my palm and showed it to his officers. "Officers, this hand is powerful and can destroy all our 220 warships." It was a shock to me. I promptly said that we had come for a cooperation programme. He said, "I know you are a friend of the USA. What I meant was you have a powerful weapon

BRAHMOS. We know its capability and we do not have any missile to match it. We respect you." Afterwards, he met our delegation and our cordial discussions started. He gave clearance for our team to visit some of the very critical technical centres. I remembered Kalam saying often that **strength respects strength**.

P5 must become P6 with India

When we go to temples to worship gods and goddesses, we surrender to them. Such a god who is all powerful, why show weapons of different kinds in multiple hands. This is to demonstrate that god is powerful. All our stories are about gods killing demons. That means we respect valour and weapons. That is why if we have to live in a country of value, we need military strength coupled with prosperity. Shri Vajpayee demonstrated the strength through nuclear test and proved to the world that India is a responsible nation by declaring **'no first use'**. Sanctions were imposed; yet nothing happened to us. The USA cancelled the LCA contract on control algorithm development. But we realised it by forming a National team. The Indian mind is reactive in nature. If someone says we cannot do it, we will prove him wrong. So, we must keep the pressure on, to get the best out of our youth. This was the mantra Kalam used to develop critical missile technologies, which were denied to us. **Technology denied is Technology gained**.

USSR (now Russia), the USA, France, the UK and China are the five Permanent Member countries in the UN Security Council, because they have Inter-Continental Ballistic Missiles (ICBM) and a large number of nuclear weapons. We have demonstrated our nuclear capability. We must have an ICBM with 14000 km range to reach any point on Earth. We are capable of doing it. Bharat Karnad in his book *'Nuclear Weapons and India Security'* strongly advocates ICBM and clout (megaton thermonuclear weapons). The big Powers will then come and offer the sixth seat in the UN Security Council, with veto power (permanent membership), as we have demonstrated that we are a responsible nation. P5 will become P6.

President Putin, during the inauguration of BrahMos Hqrs on 04 December 2004 declared that Russia would strongly put forward and support India's permanent membership with veto power.

God Conspires

When Kalam was Director DRDL at Hyderabad, after the Agni launch in 1989, we were preparing his lecture. He asked a question, "India was the leader in knowledge, science, medicine, mathematics, cosmology, trade, civilisation, and many others, 2000 years back. Can we tell the world now that we are the first in at least one system?"

While we debated this issue for many days at DRDL, Hyderabad, an opportunity came to me in 1990. Dr. Arunachalam and K.N. Singh proposed to send me to Harvard Business School for a twelve-week advanced management course, starting in February 1991. HQ obtained necessary approval. **Kalam told me that I must use this break to come up with new thoughts on how India could become the Number One country.** It was a good task given to me. He advised me to take care of myself, as February would be cold in Boston, and gave me some dollars that were left with him for my immediate use as I would be getting my allowance only at the Indian Embassy in Washington.

I joined Harvard Business School in February 1991. It was a great time for me to understand the business world and successful entrepreneurs. I was fully immersed in a transformational live-learning experience, networking with executives from around the world, and engaging in programmes led by experienced HBS faculty. Some of the faculty like Michael Beer, Michael E. Porter and Nitin Nohria were truly outstanding. Many stalwarts, like Steve Jobs, Sam Walton, and others shared their experiences in the evening lectures. I enjoyed talking to them. Competitiveness, Organisational Effectiveness and Leadership were the focus areas for me. From case study discussions and small group projects to simulations and dynamic lectures, all these provided many opportunities to deepen knowledge, broaden skill set, and collaborate with peers. It was a "life-changing experience." I went to the nearby MIT a few times and gave a lecture to Indian students, many whom were doing their doctorate. The MIT's environment for research-oriented learning was truly impressive. I visited the labs to acquaint myself with new developments. I enjoyed walking on the sides of the beautiful Charles River in the evenings. It was most refreshing.

During my stay in the USA, the Gulf War was in full flow. I closely followed the war updates on CNN daily, analyzed the Iraq war and the

dominance of the Tomahawk cruise missile. More than 500 cruise missiles were launched from the Persian Gulf. They flew at very low altitude and destroyed the anti-aircraft radars in Iraq. It was a deliberate attack to destabilise the enemy by removing the air defence sensors. Cruise missiles were very effective as a front line weapon. Particularly when India has 'no first use' in place, we need cruise missiles.

THOUGHT ON INDIAN CRUISE MISSILE

It was during the Gulf War that I thought that the time had come for the development of an Indian Cruise missile. Unlike the Tomahawk, I realised that it had to be a supersonic missile capable of travelling at high Mach (speed two to three times faster than sound), suitable for future wars. Similarly, we needed Ballistic Missile Defence using Akash, like the Patriot engaging Scud-D. I spoke to Kalam on these two points. He wanted to progress these two areas after my coming back from Harvard. I knew 1990 and 1991 (after the Agni launch) were not good years for Kalam. He wanted to leave the DRDO. So he asked me to come fast.

After my successful completion of the executive programme at Harvard, I came back in May 1991. I met Dr. Arunachalam at Delhi, briefed him on what I had learnt at HBS, and thanked him for sending me there. At DRDL, I made two notes on Cruise missile development and BMD for India. My idea was to use Akash variants, ramjet technology for the Cruise missile and a suitable seeker for BMD. Kalam asked me to discuss it with Vice-Admiral Bharat Bhushan, Director General ATVP. Bhushan told me of possible procurement of 3M-54 Klub Cruise missiles from Novator Design Bureau, Russia, for equipping submarines. It was not interesting to me. That proposal was later dropped. I participated in the discussions at ATVP office on design consultancy with NPOM Russia. That was on underwater launched missile for ATVP. Bhushan told me to lock on with NPOM, as they were pioneers in Cruise missiles.

At DRDL, Kalam started discussing the BMD programme with a larger team based on Akash and Prithvi in extended versions. Saraswat, Prahlad and the Prithvi team carried out preliminary studies on BMD; they called it Air Defence (AD). Kalam took interest in BMD, because there was a need for protection against incoming nuclear missiles. The AD programme needed long-range radars, and command and control stations. But work went on a low key as we got involved in getting orders for Prithvi, documentation, training the users and technology transfer to BDL for production. We had got over a major hurdle for Prithvi earlier in 1989. Let me go back to 1988-89.

Tochka vs Prithvi

The Army made a proposal to buy Tochka surface-to-surface missiles from Russia. Arunachalam put up a strong case for Prithvi and did not support buying Tochka. Kalam formed a committee with Prof. I.G. Sharma, Air Cmde. Gopalaswami and others to make a statistical analysis of the performance of both the systems. The committee brought out an excellent report with a clear analysis of the Prithvi's superiority. Arunachalam asked Kalam to come to Delhi to give a presentation on the report. Kalam took me with him. In the Army Ops room, Prime Minister Rajiv Gandhi was taking a review on operational readiness. Arunachalam introduced the Prithvi discussion in the meeting. Kalam and I participated. Knowing Rajiv would be interested in computer presentation, I prepared the material for Kalam and also took the Sharma committee report. T.N. Seshan was present as the Defence Secretary. I briefed Seshan just before the meeting in order to get his support. Rajiv went into greater details on war strategy with Tochka and Prithvi. Arunachalam was giving spontaneous answers on many issues in a convincing manner. Fortunately, I had the report. Kalam showed the performance graph. Rajiv locked on to the report. He took a pencil, started writing on it, and clarified the points. The Army pointed out that Prithvi had one test only and had not been proven. Arunachalam's presence of mind was so powerful, he talked about nuclear warheads. He made Rajiv say that Prithvi was the choice and promised that the system would be proved in a year. The Chief of Army conceded. Rajiv said to the Army to forget about Tochka and buy Prithvi. I witnessed Arunachalam clinching the deal for Prithvi. Kalam showed to our team at Hyderabad, Rajiv's handwritten portion in the report deciding on Prithvi. We started planning for special procurement and stock piling of critical components.

Army HQ said they did not have funds to advance Prithvi production. They demanded additional allocation. DG Artillery Gen. Khosla, a strong supporter of Prithvi, was fighting for funds. Kalam wanted the Army to give a Letter of Intent with an advance so that everything would be in stream. It was not coming through due to heavy shortage of funds.

T.N. Seshan as Defence Secretary (1988-89)

Seshan and Prithvi

Having worked together in the Department of Space, Seshan was very friendly with Kalam and me. But Arunachalam and Seshan did not see eye to eye. They had problems with each other all the time, even in the Guided Missile Board and the Directors' Conferences. For Prithvi, I went to Seshan directly, explained the issue and requested his help for funds. In my presence, he called up the Additional Secretary, made out a letter for reallocation, and provided Rs.69 crore additional funds to the Army as a special provision only for Prithvi, non-transferable to any other head. Allocation was made on the spot. That was Seshan. One should surrender to him. He would go to any extent to do what we think is impossible. The Army transferred the funds to the BDL in March 1989 as an advance, with a letter of intent. The BDL nicely put it fixed deposit in the bank. Thus, the Prithvi order was sealed. But a lot of work remained for more flight tests, user trials and production.

Seshan and Akash

Seshan came to RCI and was acquainted with the missile projects. I told him about the problem we faced in getting clearance for the Akash and Trishul propellant plant at the Ordnance Factory, Itarsi. He asked me to see him at his office in Delhi. Kalam told me that the issue was complex, as DRDO HQ was putting heavy pressure on this issue to get environmental clearance. Seshan, when he was Secretary, Environment & Forests, before becoming Defence Secretary, did not help. The issue was to cut 11,000 Angely trees, to establish the propellant complex for missile projects at OF, Itarsi. The MP Government did not issue permission for construction, due to non-clearance by DG, Forests, under the ME&F. I was the Co-Chairman with DG, Ordnance Factory Board to progress all installations and technology transfer from DRDO labs for all explosives in 13 factories for missiles and we were given funds from IGMDP for civil works and equipment. It was my task to progress facility readiness.

Bandarkar, Chairman OFB, and me went to Seshan and explained the situation, as everything was held up. Seshan talked to the Secretary E&F, Geetha Krishnan and both decided to find a solution. DG Forests was called. The map was spread on the table, and the area calculated. Seshan made out a letter to Secretary E&F, expressing the urgency of the issue to help missile projects, committing double the area of defence land from MP state and expenditure for planting double the number of plants. He wanted an express order permitting OF Itarsi to cut trees and commence construction within a week. He told me to meet him after a week to review the situation. Bandarkar was astonished to see what was happening. Seshan solved the problem that had been pending for years in one stroke. I had to go over my leaders, as I did not want Akash and Trishul production to suffer. All the required permissions came and the plant was established at OF, Itarsi. Akash went through all the flight trials and was successfully inducted in service.

T.N. Seshan as Cabinet Secretary (1989)

Seshan and Agni Missile

Seshan came for the Agni launch on 20 April 89. I escorted him. He sat in the control centre along with Defence Minister Shri K.C. Pant. The countdown continued. When Agni did not take off, the Minister, Arunachalam and Kalam went to the Block House and the Launch Pad, and then drove to the guest house, where the Minister was staying. In the meantime, an annoyed Seshan asked me to take him to the Minister. We reached the guest house and I took him to the room. There were heavy verbal exchanges in front the Minister. Arunachalam was furious with Kalam, for the mishap. The Minister was trying to pacify them.

When we entered, the arguments stopped. Seshan told the Minister that the Americans had sent a high-power microwave from the air to jam the communication link and therefore the missile could not take off. (His reason was that a reconnaissance aircraft was flying in that region monitoring the range). Everyone laughed and the situation eased. The Minister asked Seshan how he had arrived at the conclusion. Seshan quipped that his expert, Pillai, had told him. I got a shock. I had never told him anything like the microwave. Fortunately, Arunachalam (Arunachala is Shiva at Thiruvannamalai, TN) did not have a third eye. In his anger, he would have burnt me up. I went out of the room thinking that more damage would happen. Kalam kept quiet, as he felt very bad that day, not because Agni did not take off, that could be solved, but because of Arunachalam's reaction. Seshan came out with the Minister and both left by helicopter.

On 1 May 1989, Agni again did not take off. Seshan put up a note to Rajiv Gandhi and stopped further attempts to launch it. Details of further developments are given in the previous chapter. My information was that Seshan put up a note again, after making sure, everything was in order, to clear the flight on 22 May 1989 and Rajiv signed it. After the launch, Arunachalam communicated the success. Later, the PM made an announcement about the launch. Though both Arunachalam and Kalam got Padma Vibhushans, Kalam was not happy to continue in the DRDO. Added to this, the second launch of Agni, AE-02, was a failure. Yet, Arunachalam looked at the organisation, gave an extension to Kalam in October 1991 and later, recommended him to be the next chief of the DRDO in early 1992.

Cruise Missile

Let us come back to the Gulf War in 1991. It gave a clear message that the first-level attack on the enemy had to be by low altitude flying cruise missiles with high-precision engagement to remove his assets. Our intention was to possess an advanced cruise missile system in the least possible time. What would help us to leapfrog and lessen the time from drawing board to front-line deployment, while ensuring operational effectiveness of the product and customer satisfaction? That was the question before us.

Through IGMDP, we had established higher levels of capability in manufacturing of airframe, solid, liquid and ramjet rocket motors, inertial navigation system (INS), on-board computer (OBC), avionics and software, and mission management. We had expertise in system integration and programme management. Now we required a new engine capable of providing supersonic speed. We had expertise in solid propellant ramjet engine technology, as demonstrated in the Akash project. For the long-range cruise missile and for its growth potential, the optimum choice was the liquid-fuelled ramjet engine, which was two times more energy-efficient compared to a solid-fuelled ramjet. Therefore, we needed a liquid ramjet engine.

At DRDL, the design of the Sagarika submarine-launched missile was taking shape through the design consultancy with NPOM, initiated by Bhushan under ATVP. Kalam appointed S.P. Kukillaya, an aerodynamic engineer, who joined from ISRO, as the project director of Sagarika. Kalam asked me to participate in the design discussions for Sagarika in Russia. Kukillaya and team had gone before me. I left for my first visit to Russia two days later.

At Moscow, I was received by a Russian lady from NPOM and Cdr Jungare, a retired naval officer who could speak Russian fluently. They brought a luxury car called GAZ **Chaika**, which means 'gull', a luxury automobile from the Soviet Union made by GAZ, used for VVIPs. From the airport, we went to Moscow University and Red Square. Jungare and I took the night train to St. Petersburg and reached the next morning. I spent two days with the team in the reviews on the critical control system for launching from submarine and homing seekers for missile guidance at factories in this beautiful city. Then I came back to Moscow to participate in the design review at NPOM. It was a great experience with Russian designers. What we discussed was regarding underwater launch technology for missiles. I met Dr. Yefremov, Director General of NPOM, a top missile scientist of Russia and Lenin Medal awardee. He gave me a long lecture about Chelomey the originator of NPOM and the capabilities in remote sensing and possible collaborative work with ISRO, missiles in general and cruise missiles in particular. I told him our interest was in supersonic cruise missiles. He listened and did not react then.

In February 1992, Kalam became Scientific Adviser to the Defence

Minister, Secretary, Department of Defence R&D and Director General DRDO. Lt. Gen. V.J. Sundaram became the Director of DRDL & RCI. I continued my work with missile teams at Hyderabad. Kalam made me Programme Director, IGMDP. I was also Associate Director, DRDL. Kalam had a settled mind and wanted to make sure more indigenous systems were inducted into service.

The frequency of my visits to NPOM, Russia increased on account of Sagarika. During one of my visits, we lost Kukillaya, who died at Moscow. With the help of the Indian Embassy, I brought his body back via Frankfurt, as there was very poor connection to Moscow from India. Vice Admiral Bhushan joined me at Bombay to transfer the body to a local flight to Hyderabad. Life was very difficult during the early 1990s in Russia after the collapse of the Soviet Union. We were not able to move outdoors. The police grabbed dollars at gunpoint. Doors were broken in the hotel and thieves took away our belongings. So we shifted to the NPOM guest house near the plant, with a security guard in place. It was a difficult time until 1998. We were not used to the very low temperatures. Once I went with Chakraborty, the next Project Director of Sagarika after Kukillaya, to a test site to witness missile ejection from a canister. It was bitterly cold at minus 35 degrees C. We had special protective suits given to us by the Russians. Still it was uncomfortable to bear the cold for more than 15 minutes. Every 15 minutes we would go to a hot chamber and then come back after sometime to the test site.

During this visit, I discussed with Dr. Yefremov the possibility of helping in cruise missile development. He said it would be possible. He whispered in my ear that he would make the Indian cruise missile supersonic, with an engine available at NPOM. Later, NPOM showed Venugopalan and me the supersonic ramjet engine developed just before the breakup of the Soviet Union. I was amazed to see the engine. After learning the specifications, we realised that there was no equivalent available in the world. Upon realising that this engine could do miracles, we were filled with a feeling of great satisfaction. Dr. Yefremov agreed that there was a strong possibility of collaboration in supersonic missile capability.

I went straight to Kalam after returning to Delhi and reported the availability of the engine. I told him that a supersonic cruise missile was now within sight. He called Bhushan and Ramanathan to work on engine technology transfer. As I was part of DRDL, it was decided that the file noting would be from Ramanathan, Additional FA & Joint Secretary and DG ATVP. Ramanathan requested Kalam to form a team to discuss further with NPOM. Kalam asked Ramanathan, Venugopalan and me to go as a three-member team to discuss the modalities with NPOM. We had several meetings at NPOM to arrive at a possible cooperation model. By end December 1994, the team concluded that the best way to work together was by a joint venture. On return, Ramanathan prepared a detailed note on the advantages of engine technology transfer, the need for forming a JV and the funding methodology. I led a team with more specialists, including an engine expert from GTRE to NPOM and the Strella plant at Orenburg where the engine was manufactured. The purpose was to understand the fabrication at the parts level and to assess our capability to reproduce.

After assessing the overall characteristics of the engine, our team started looking at the shape of the missile. We realised that the combustion chamber of the engine could accommodate the booster. Thus, it would become a booster-sustainer combo, enabling reduction of the length of the missile. Further discussions revealed that Russian experts had worked out a prototype configuration of the missile and conducted wind-tunnel tests on the model. NPOM had already carried out initial flight tests of the prototype to establish the propulsion system. The project could not progress further due to shortage of funds in the 1990s. It so happened, that in Russia most of the design bureaus and R&D Centres started losing their best brains as those people migrated to other countries, especially to China. Having worked with Russian specialists, I felt that it was a great loss if specialists leave at that critical juncture. A collaborative arrangement with NPOM for the cruise missile would help to retain the best work force with them. Yefremov was convinced with this fact. Kalam strongly supported this viewpoint of working with NPOM. A preliminary note was put up to Shri Narasimha Rao, PM/RM. He approved further action to form a joint venture.

In the meantime, the Russian Government sent a team with Mr. Sepenov, Chief of Russian Defence Industries, to assess the capabilities of DRDO labs, technology status and industry support for JV formation. We took them to DRDO labs at Dehradun, Bengaluru and Hyderabad, apart from Delhi. We showed them Akash booster-sustainer test on ramjet propulsion, Nag imaging infrared guidance, Prithvi inertial guidance, Hardware-in-simulation and radars, in order to convey the impression that that the DRDO had mastered missile technologies and could be an equal partner in the JV. The team reported to the Russian Government on its positive recommendation on formation of the JV. The joint team and DRDO and NPOM, signed the feasibility report, after hectic negotiation from $ 1,400 million to $ 250 million, hard cash contribution of 49 per cent instead of only technology from the Russian side and the headquarters of the JV in New Delhi. When we reported this progress, Kalam was happy with the task performed by Ramanathan, Venugopalan and me. He visited NPOM in February 1995. Yefremov and he became thick friends and signed an agreement to form the JV, endorsing the feasibility report. Based on this agreement, a note was sent to the PM (as RM) for approval of the JV with $ 250 million as equity 51 per cent of India (49 per cent for the DRDO and 2 per cent for financial institutions) and 49 per cent for Russia. The PM (as RM) approved it. Somehow, I did not prefer a third party like ICICI getting in with 2 per cent to keep 49 per cent for the DRDO. They would come to know about the project. Keeping 51 per cent and making it a government company was also not a good idea. Ramanathan and I debated this issue. We finally hit upon the idea of 50.5 per cent for India.

FORMATION OF BrahMos JV

Triggering point for joint Venture
(September 1993)

Signing of Agreement for JV
(February 1995)

FORMATION OF JV

Ramanathan and I worked out the details of the JV and financing in discussion with the Secretaries of Finance and Company Affairs. When both of us met Finance Secretary Montek Singh Ahluwalia, he appreciated the progressive nature of the JV with equity share of 50.5 per cent for India and 49.5 per cent for Russia. We reported to Kalam, who agreed to the proposal for the JV to be a private company. We went through the approvals of the Defence and Finance Secretaries. Maximum support came from Ahluwalia in support of 50.5 per cent, as a non-government company.

Kalam wanted to meet Finance Minister Dr. Manmohan Singh to get the file signed. Dr. Singh asked Kalam to come to his house the next morning. Kalam took the file and went to his house. He saw a bald-headed person in a dhoti watering the plants. Kalam told him he had come to meet the Finance Minister and requested the gardener to inform him. The man doing the gardening gave a big laugh and said he was Manmohan himself. Kalam felt ashamed that he did not recognise the FM without his usual turban. Both of them went inside, had breakfast and the file was signed, after the FM went through the comments of the Finance Ministry.

Kalam and I met Shri Narasimha Rao, the Prime Minister holding the Defence Ministry, at 7, Race Course. We presented the details of the project, formation of the JV, financial outlay and execution methodology. When I said that we would become the first in the world through this JV, we saw an unconvincing smile spread across his face. Kalam quipped that we would be trying to become the first, adding that others also would come in by the time we achieved readiness. I told the PM that the JV would be a private company, based on a shareholding of 50.5 per cent of India, for operational efficiency and flexibility in the decision-making process (referring to his earlier approval of 51 per cent). The Russian contribution (49.5 per cent) would come to the JV by diverting a part of the loan India was paying back to Russia every year for the credit purchase of weapons. He listened very carefully and said, "It is a new model, must be tried out." and approved the proposal. I saw a modern-day Chanakya, with a high level of concentrated listening, internal analysis and decision-making process in the interest of the country. I told Kalam that he had made a big task look so simple.

Shri Narasimha Rao was an exceptional Prime Minister who could take such a courageous decision to form a JV despite the risk of the Soviet Union collapsing, uncertainty of equity fund from debt-prone Russia, forming a private company with government funding and approving a futuristic unknown cruise missile. In an half-hour meeting and seeing Kalam and me, he could foresee what BRAHMOS would be. What a great leadership. **He believed in Kalam and Kalam believed in me.** That was the equation.

On the recommendation of Kalam, Narasimha Rao appointed me as the Founder CEO & MD, on a salary of one rupee. The JV company was incorporated as a closed private entity in December 1995. From Hyderabad, I shifted to Delhi as Chief Controller (R&D) and CEO&MD of BrahMos. The company started functioning from a rented building in Vasant Vihar, New Delhi with a small team. We had a wonderful Company Secretary, Shri Krishnamurthy, who took care of the formation of the JV along with the legal framework and registration. Venugopalan, Som, Atul Rane and Srinivasa Rao took care of the technical documentation and task planning between partners. I got tremendous support from Srinivasa Rao and Hariharan in preparing government papers and analysis reports, and from C.K.N. Rajashree for providing secretarial assistance for all the preliminary tasks. The major challenge was to get the approval of the Russian Government, signing of an Inter-Governmental Agreement (IGA) and equity share of $ 125 million from them. The responsibility was largely with Yefremov.

Ronen Sen, an outstanding diplomat, was the Indian Ambassador in Moscow. He put his officers, Sunil Mitra and Sandip Nayyar, in the embassy to help the process. The proposal had to go through nearly 200

desks before it could reach the Prime Minister and then the President. It was the most difficult time in Russia. So Yefremov had a tough time convincing the Russian government about the JV. Boris Yeltsin, the then President, got a heart attack twice and changed five prime ministers. The proposal had to go through the process repeatedly. Yefremov, with his team of Kromoshkin, Strakov and Leonov had the worst time. Whenever I met Yefremov, I could see his brave face and determination. It was a life and death situation for him to get funds through for this JV to retain his best experts. The scientists were getting very small salaries, not even sufficient for meeting their food requirements. They cut down on their noon meal. It was difficult to get bread. We gave them additional work for the Akash missile, which was witnessing repeated failures. They solved the propulsion problem in the solid fuelled ramjet engine. We kept the pressure on for getting the JV through with the Russian government. In India, we got a small fund to start our design activities and worked out DRDO tasks. As I was simultaneously holding the post of Chief Controller of Missiles, I could get the support of DRDL, RCI and R&DEE to formulate the design details from the DRDO.

Finally, President Yeltsin signed and issued a decree forming the JV in February 1997. We started working on a draft Inter-Governmental Agreement (IGA), taking support from Ronan Sen and the embassy. Yefremov and I met Mr. Pakhomov, the Deputy Minister of Defence. We knew each other. We finalised the draft IGA. Clearance from the MEA was taken. Shri I.K. Gujral was the PM and Shri Mulayam Singh Yadav was the Defence Minister (RM) at that time. A detailed file was prepared for the RM and PM about the JV, seeking approval for the IGA and authority for the Secretary, Department of Defence R&D to sign on behalf of the Government. Both of them approved it.

The Secretary, Department Defence R&D, Dr. A.P.J. Abdul Kalam and the Deputy Minister of Defence of the Russian Federation, Dr. Mikhailov signed the IGA on 12 February 1998 at the Indian Embassy in Moscow forming the JV for design, development, production and marketing of anti-ship supersonic cruise missiles. The cost of $ 250 million capital would be contributed as equity, at 49.5 per cent by the Russian Federation and 50.5 per cent by India. The DRDO, on behalf of the Government of India and NPOM on behalf of the Russian Federation would be the shareholders and partners of the JV. A supervisory council with members from both the governments would oversee the performance of the JV.

The major activity we undertook was to finalise the responsibilities of the DRDO, NPOM and BRAHMOS. $ 250 million was demarcated for tasks to be performed. This Tripartite Agreement was signed by Abdul Kalam for the DRDO, Yefremov for the NPOM and me for BrahMos. This document was vital for streamlining responsibility, tasks, contracts and fund flow, without any dispute.

The essence of the tri-partite agreement was not to have any ambiguity during execution of tasks between partners. The hidden point was that the NPOM had to work and deliver design documents and subsystems, including engines, to the JV to get their portion of 49.5 per cent. In other words, we got systems for flight trials at their cost.

Financing JV

The next step was to get the contributions from the DRDO and Russia. We divided $ 250 million into year-wise four tranches based on task distribution and contractual obligations for each shareholder. Maj. Gen. Swaminathan made the DRDO allocation of the requirement in the annual budget and year-wise transferred it to the BrahMos account.

The problem was to get the Russian part of the contribution. The situation was precarious in debt–ridden Russia. There was no way to give even salaries for the armed forces and ministry personnel. The NPOM could not penetrate the Finance Ministry. Ramanathan and I went to meet the Finance Minister. At the reception, a stout woman talked to us in Russian and asked us to get out, even though the visit had been arranged by the Embassy. The reason was the agony and desperate situation in Russia. I sought the help of Ambassador Mr S.K. Lambah, who had joined after Ronen Sen. He fixed a meeting with Deputy Minister Finance, Kudrin. Both of us met Kudrin. It was a cordial meeting. He knew every detail of the JV. We proposed that the Indian side had no objection to divert a portion of the loan repayment in kind against the weapons purchased on credit. He asked us to come after two weeks. Ambassador Lamba and I met Kudrin, who had now become the Finance Minister. This time the heavyweight woman was soft and talked sweetly. She took us to Kudrin and served tea to us. We communicated the progress from the Indian side. Kudrin was happy to inform us that he had got the proposal cleared by the government. Very soon, the other formalities would be completed. Lambah hosted a dinner at the embassy for Russian government officials, Yefremov and NPOM senior scientists to mark the occasion.

Mr. Semaev, in charge of Finance in the NPOM, showed us a flow chart indicating many activities that still needed to be gone through. This included an agreement between the two government on the financial arrangement and an agreement to be signed between the NPOM and the Russian Government to ensure repayment by the NPOM with interest to the Russian Government. We went through a hectic and painstaking process.

Lambah told me to get all the necessary approvals from the Indian Finance Ministry. Ramanathan and I met Vijay Kelkar and he issued a letter to Kasyanov, First Deputy Minister of Finance, on diversion of the loan repayment and confirmation of the draft agreement on 19 March 1999, based on the detailed guidelines worked out by both sides.

Sri George Fernandes became the Defence Minister. It was a good time for us. He liked the BrahMos Project. Kalam and I met him a number of times. He approved progressing the design and deputing of scientists to Russia for it. We generated a note for the RM, FM, and PM, and got the necessary approval for diversion of the loan repayment in four tranches as the Russian contribution, waiving off any reference to the Joint Commission.

The whole process took many months with vigorous following up, visiting Moscow numerous times. It was achieved through sheer willpower and determination. While Ramanathan and I concentrated on formation of the JV, Venugopalan led the teams on design. Finally, the Indian Ambassador to Russia and the Deputy Minister of Finance from Russia signed the IGA for financing.

I got a letter issued by Special Secretary Mr. B.K. Chaturvedi to the RBI about the approvals for provision of funds for the JV, for the Russian contribution. I spoke to Mr. Gandhi, Dy. Governor, who appreciated the project and assured us of all help. I sent Srinivasa Rao to RBI, Bombay with all relevant approvals to meet the deputy Governor of RBI, Mr. Gandhi. In the meantime, the Russian Finance Ministry directed the Russian Vnesheconom Bank to sign an agreement with the RBI for the final arrangement to fund the JV in rupees, equivalent to each tranche in dollars and adjust against loan repayments. The two banks signed the documents. The RBI issued the first tranche to BrahMos in July 1999. Now we started the Board meetings and officially, the Design and Development began. In the meantime, Ramanathan got a tax holiday approved from the Chairman, Central Board of Customs and Excise. We got a R&D cess waiver from the Secretary DST, Prof. Ramamurthy, for technology/design documentation.

Design & Development

I started interactions with the Indian Navy for necessary documentation and participation. The initial data on the design of the missile was discussed with the teams. Further optimisation studies were carried out after a preliminary design review (PDR). Slowly, the supersonic BRAHMOS took shape. The universal characteristics of the missile for sea, sub-sea and land launch capabilities encouraged us to freeze the design for anti-ship application for the Navy.

After a detailed analysis, Venugopalan and I decided not to reinvent the wheel but to exploit and augment the missile's capability in a systematic process. Since the Russian missile was at a prototype stage, we were sure that its potential could be augmented with our contribution, especially for land-target engagement and for multiple platforms. The next step was to design the guidance system. We took the state-of-the-art guidance system developed for Prithvi and improvised it. We augmented the accuracy of the guidance system and reduced the reaction time considerably for a quick take-off.

As for the launcher systems, fire control systems, etc., we decided to develop state-of-the-art versions. Today, our land-based launcher systems are fully network-centric in operation and totally developed in India. There is no cruise missile system operating in the world along the lines of the land-attack version of the BRAHMOS, in the form of a universal missile.

Multiple DRDO labs participated in the effort to realise the best design for India. A separate design team was formed to look at a suitable platform system for ships, submarines, road mobile complexes and aircraft. The same missile could also be used against different types of targets so development of systems like fire control and launcher for ship and land were started. Industry partners were identified through a systematic process, involving experts from India and Russia. The Government approved the selection of industries.

In hindsight, the Indo–Russian partnership worked well. Each side decided to respect the strength of its counterpart. The propulsion modules became the process stock of Russia and the guidance and on-board electronic modules became the process stock of India. Over time, our decisions were proved to be correct—a missile that was designed to be an anti-ship missile system evolved into many fascinating versions capable of attacking targets that were earlier thought impossible. Thanks to the high-accuracy guidance system and high-power propulsion system, today we can hit targets anywhere with precision.

Over the years, BRAHMOS took many avatars—mobile land platforms, aircraft and submarines against sea and land targets in a salvo mode for fast and lethal deployment.

I am proud to say that the Indo-Russian joint venture 'BrahMos' was a major break-through in missile technology. The successful development of the missile in multiple formations and induction in our Armed Forces made India the only country to have an operational multi-platform—road mobile launcher, ship and aircraft—supersonic cruise missile for all the three Services. With its supersonic speed, precision and power, BRAHMOS stands first in the world (Russia has only an anti-ship version). This most advanced missile gave India the cutting-edge technology and the spirit to come out of the fifth country syndrome. The emerging battle scenario would largely depend on the effective utilisation of this winner—BRAHMOS. It is really a ***Brahmastra*** for the Indian Armed Forces. **Two things came to my mind: 1) I was instrumental to find the way for India to become Number One in the world; and 2) the courageous Chanakya-like decision of Shri Narasimha Rao yielded results for the formation of the JV.**

In Kalam's words

"A Unique Joint Technological Venture"

The joint venture BrahMos signifies great friendship and trust between India and Russia in high-technology cooperation. The best talents from both nations have been pooled together to turn the dream of the supersonic cruise missile into reality.

It was my lifelong longing to see India become the first nation to possess the most advanced weapon system in the world. As it turned out, with BrahMos, India became the first nation to have a universal operational supersonic cruise missile, thereby also demolishing the 'sixth nation syndrome'. There is no equivalent operational system elsewhere in the world in terms of the speed, precision and power demonstrated by BrahMos. We started BrahMos with a mere $ 300 million investment by both countries. Today the business of the company has crossed $ 6 billion. My desire is now to see the BrahMos business going beyond $ 10 billion and achieving a unique status in the world, connecting the oceans and making new strategic partners beyond the borders.

It is a long story—about how we could make the BrahMos a reality. The path-breaking joint venture was not easy to arrive at. My friend, Dr Yefremov, the then director-general of NPO Mashinostroyenia, became convinced of the feasibility of a joint venture after visiting the DRDO laboratories. The result was a unique joint venture in a ratio of 50.5:49.5, giving full empowerment to the JV company. This enabled the underlying concept to negotiate its course from mind to market. BrahMos is a fine example of courage and leadership and, of course, system design, system engineering, system integration and system management. Different versions, continuous product improvement and integration of the user at every stage make the weapon system user-friendly. All the three wings of the Indian armed forces cherish the BrahMos as a prime weapon. And yet, it is not all about BrahMos. The results show that this successful model can be—and must be—replicated in many other areas, both military and civil.

Dr. A. Sivathanu Pillai, distinguished scientist and chief controller research & development, DRDO, and also the founder CEO–MD of BrahMos Aerospace, was my colleague for more than three decades—from the SLV-3 days to the IGMDP days and beyond. He made significant contributions in the launch vehicle programme of ISRO and in realising critical missile technologies for DRDO's guided missile programme through a network of academic institutions and industries, thus effectively combating the technology control regime. Dr. Pillai's great leadership in fulfilling the BrahMos dream, integrating the best brains in the respective fields in India and Russia, and bringing together multiple institutions and industries to build up a world-class product is commendable. BRAHMOS missiles have been inducted in the Indian Armed Forces to their complete satisfaction. ***BrahMos has earned its page in the history of the world and Dr. Pillai is synonymous with BrahMos.***

s/d A.P.J. Abdul Kalam,
28 February 2014

MANY CONTRIBUTED TO THE SUCCESS OF BRAHMOS

I was CEO& MD of BrahMos from December 1995 to July 2014, brought it from concept stage to a great institution, with an outstanding of product. Kalam, Yefremov and Ramanathan were my main sources of inspiration and their positions as Chief of DRDO, NPOM and Financial Adviser, respectively, helped the process of JV formation with their deep involvement. Venugopalan, Adm. Mohapatra and Srinivasa Rao were always with me. No one expected this level of growth for BrahMos. Many great persons were part of this long journey.

I came across Indian and Russian Presidents, Prime Ministers, Defence Ministers and Chiefs of Staff of the three Services during the BrahMos Programme in building the institution. Also interacted closely with Indian and Russian Ambassadors, Secretaries to Government and policy makers and officers. Each one of them made significant and some path-breaking contributions to the success of BrahMos. On every possible occasion, President Putin and President Kalam talked about BrahMos.

Many of the very senior officials had said 'this project will not come through, you do not take it, and it will be an utter failure, do not believe the Russians and so on'. Some were envious of me because of the way the project was taking shape. Sheer determination to go from MIND TO MARKET—zero stage to build large infrastructure, making 205 Indian industries to work on high-tech products with their investment to build infrastructure and with 20,000 engineers and technicians working full time and building a team of young engineers and work force with BrahMos integration complex in multiple locations yielded results. The best part was constant interaction with the three Services and meeting their difficult user specifications. I received outstanding support from the Government, all ranks of the three wings of the Armed Forces, industries and media throughout the project.

Support from Defence Secretary & Secretary Defence Finance

Shri Shekhar Dutt, Defence Secretary, gave me constant guidance and support at the right time to progress the project. Even after becoming Governor of Chhattisgarh, he continued to guide us. Shri Yogendra Narain participated many times in the reviews in Russia and also gave land for the BrahMos HQ in Delhi Cantonment. As Secretary General, Rajya Sabha, he arranged a review by the Standing Committee on Defence that gave an excellent report on BrahMos. Shri Sivasubramanian, Secretary Defence Finance, was the force behind BrahMos getting special powers from the Finance Ministry. Shri Sunil Verma, Additional Financial Adviser after Ramanathan, gave continued support as a board Member. Shri Vinod Misra, former Secretary Finance took a full review of the financial management of BrahMos and streamlined the system. As requested by Shri A.K. Antony, Defence Minister, Shri Vinod Rai C&AG reviewed the BrahMos Programme Management, Accounting & Audit System, Administrative & Procurement Procedures, Financial arrangement between DRDO and NPOM, Contracts with the Armed Forces, Deliveries, Cost structure, Board proceedings, and Overall performance. It was a full-day review and at the end, he expressed his full satisfaction about the system. He gave a report to RM that the system followed was highly adequate and satisfactory.

The Rajasthan Government gave 210 acres of land at Pilani for Re. 1 to set up a BrahMos facility with full infrastructure to cater to the need for a deployed missile system in readiness for war fighting. The Kerala Government gave a precision fabrication facility KELTEC with a trained work force and 16 acres of land in a prime location from for Re. 1 to make missile assemblies. Lt Governor, Andaman and Nicobar, allotted two islands for BrahMos testing. The Defence Ministry provided four acres of Army land in Delhi for the BrahMos HQ.

The Armed Forces supported with the deployment of more than 5,000 Army, Navy and Air Force personnel at different launch sites and at sea, along with decommissioned ships, a number of which were used as targets. Just by word, industries came forward to commit their funding, to create needed machinery, even before getting any production order. The DRDO civil works team constructed large infrastructure/technical positions at many locations for the three Services, to make the BRAHMOS weapon system fully ready for deployment.

George Fernandes—Defence Minister (March 1998-March 2001 & October 2001-May 2004)

George Fernandes, the Defence Minister, periodically reviewed the project. In 1998, even before funds came, he approved bulk sanction of deputation of DRDO engineers and naval officers for carrying out the design work at Moscow. Both he and Kalam gave me a free hand and separate funds for the design of the missile and a shore-based mobile launch complex. Because of this action of the RM, we saved nearly one year in the schedule. Later, he visited NPOM Russia with me to review BrahMos work, mainly to motivate the Russian team. Goan fish curry and rice was arranged for his lunch at NPOM. In any meeting of officers, he locked on to me. One day we were together at the missile range, waiting for the helicopter. He was in a good mood after a successful launch of Agni. He told me one big news, as informed to him by Shri Vajpayee, the PM.

The President of Russia, in a meeting with Shri Vajpayee at the Kremlin told him *that the President of China requested Putin for supersonic cruise missile technology, like an arrangement with India. President Putin refused.*

RM said that from a strategic point of view, such an important missile must be given to Vietnam, for which he would arrange a credit line of $ 250 million. (George Fernandes had a soft corner for Vietnam). I told him that I would do so.

India was fortunate to have the most dynamic defence minister, fast decision maker and firebrand who gave outright support to projects, lived simply with two pairs of dress washed daily by him and lived as an example for others. His concern for jawans at high altitudes was well known. He posted the Finance Director in Siachen for two weeks to understand the problems our Army men face at high altitude war theatres. He despatched cakes to our men at Siachen every Christmas from Bengaluru.

He approved placement of a production order for the Navy after a successful flight trial from the flagship of the Indian Navy, INS Rajput, in 2003.

Jaswant Singh—Minister, External Affairs & Defence (March 2001-October 2001)

We were preparing for the first launch of BRAHMOS at ITR, Chandipur, in June 2001. So far, BrahMos had been a secret programme. I requested RM and PM to give permission for the launch and make an announcement of the JV to the outside world. Permission was granted. Shri Jaswant Singh was Defence Minister at that time. He witnessed the first flight of BRAHMOS on 12 June 2001 at ITR. Dr. Yefremov came from Russia. It was a perfect launch.

Chief of Air Staff Anil Tipnis piloted an IL-76 from Kalaikunda for RM to reach Delhi. I came with him on the flight. I requested a joint announcement by RM and Russian Ambassador Mr. Kadakin. Both of them wanted me to announce it. I thought a government announcement would be better. I followed him to his Foreign Ministry office and again requested him to do so. He said, "Believe me, we want you to make the announcement". I called a press conference and announced the flight test and importance of BRAHMOS. The news was flashed across the whole world. *"India launched Supersonic Cruise Missile"*.

Dr. Singh came to Moscow for the meeting of the Indo-Russia Joint Commission for Military Technical Cooperation and both the defence ministers highlighted BRAHMOS. In a short period, he became part of BrahMos.

He approved construction of the head office for BrahMos, allotment of land and fund.

Pranab Mukherjee—Defence Minister (May 2004-October 2006)

The RM showed keen interest in the project. He joined President Putin in the inauguration of the BrahMos head office at Delhi Cantonment. He visited our partner, NPOM, with me.

BRAHMOS to Chile

Chile made a request for the BRAHMOS for their naval ships. The RM wrote to his Russian counterpart and got clearance from Russia to sell to Chile. Our team had completed the technical and financial details. Chilean Navy Chief Admiral Rodolfo Codina visited India in October 2005, spent time at the DRDO and BrahMos HQ and saw the system fitted on INS Rajput at Vizag. He held discussions with the Indian Navy. The RM delegation and I travelled together to Chile for the final meeting with the President of Chile.

The meeting with the Defence Minister of Chile and their Chief of Navy went on well. But when we met the President, she said that due to political reasons, she was told not to buy BRAHMOS. We were upset to hear this, especially when the Defence Minister had come all the way to India to discuss the sale. I understood from Navy Chief Adm. Codina that there was an offer of $ 50 million worth of the latest block of Harpoons on deferred payment. He told me that this was a political decision. He had seen the system fitted on the Indian naval ship and BRAHMOS was an ideal system for the Chilean Navy. Now we would have to wait for a good time. Similarly, HAL's attempt to sell ALH also did not go through.

Antarctica

The RM delegation, Indian Ambassador Sushmita Thomas and Chilean Air Force officers went to Antarctica on a CAF flight and landed on ice at the Base Camp of Chile. It was a fantastic journey. We went out in the cold, very well dressed. Suddenly the RM felt thirsty. He asked for water. I gave him a glass of fresh coconut water. Like a child, he was looking around. Everywhere he could see only ice. He asked me, "Pillai how did you get fresh coconut water, when there is no tree here." "Sir, this is DRDO technology. I am going to give you fresh hot chapattis with your favourite chicken curry for lunch." The Ambassador told him that I had brought a good load of ready-to-eat food from DRDO's Mysore lab and we got special Customs clearance due to the strict rules in Chile. Shri Pranab Mukherjee was very happy and called up the Congress President saying "Soniaji, I am now in Antarctica, drinking fresh coconut water. Very refreshing. Thanks to DRDO and Pillai. We came here by a Chilean Air Force flight. Wonderful". Everyone including officers of the Chilean Air force enjoyed Indian chicken curry at lunch.

We went round in a snow scooter and met scientists and their families from different countries staying for a long time and doing research. I went inside the house of a Russian scientist. He, his scientist wife and a boy were staying there. He explained how difficult life was in the weather. Still, they were happy because of the exotic research work and warm friendship with Chilean scientists.

We saw penguins, seals, and albatrosses, roamed around in snow scooters, in tractors and enjoyed being there until evening. We flew back to Punta Arenas, a beautiful sprawling metropolis on the edge of the Strait of Magellan, at the bottom of the Americas. It was good weather—the sun shone through the rain. Christopher Columbus had landed here and declared that he had discovered India. At that place, there is a huge statue of Columbus. We stayed in the port city near the Air Force station.

BRAHMOS for the ARMY

Gen. J.J. Singh, Chief of Army Staff witnessed BRAHMOS flights at Pokhran piercing targets. The second test was conducted on 31 May 2006 and the temperature was 52 degrees C. Very hot; all our systems exposed to summer desert war condition. Every system worked well and it was a perfect launch. We rushed in a helicopter to the target site. It was a bull's eye hit on target. On seeing two successive successful flights, the excited General told the gathering, "I will send BRAHMOS to Gen. Musharraf's bedroom, through the window". He asked me to come and give a presentation to all the corps commanders of the Army.

The next week, as promised, Gen. J.J. Singh arranged a meeting with all Lt. Generals—Corps Commanders/Vice Chief/Dy Chiefs. I entered the hall and all of them clapped. I gave a PowerPoint presentation on the Army version of BRAHMOS with war simulations. After I had answered their questions, the Chief said, 'We will now discuss and inform you'. I said, 'Sir, I need a decision now'. "Ok. You can wait in the opposite room for five minutes". I went out.

Exactly after five minutes, I was called inside amidst more clapping. The General said, "The Army has decided to have BRAHMOS; but you must process the file and get the approval from the Government. If we process the file, it will take a minimum of a year. We know you will get it done fast. Will you please do it?" I said, "the Government approval would come in a week". The next day, I prepared a file based on the Babur (DH-10 Chinese cruise missile) just launched by Pakistan and the urgent need for a land mobile supersonic cruise missile for land targets. I went to the Chief of Army Staff and requested his signature to confirm the need. He said he would sign only the backup internal file. Government files would go from the Vice-Chief. I insisted on his signature. In a beautiful handwriting in red ink, Gen. J.J. Singh emphatically wrote the need for BRAHMOS to be with the Army on an urgent basis.

I straight went to Shri Pranab Mukherjee, RM. I explained the situation as it was. He was only staring at my eyes. He saw the force in me to get BRAHMOS inducted into the Army. I asked for a sanction of Rs.5,000 crore for some BRAHMOS regiments. He signed. He called up FM Shri P. Chidambaram on the intercom and told him that Pillai would come now with a very important file.

I went to Chidambaram who smiled at me and asked what the important file was. I showed it to him. He read it for about 10 minutes and then said that it had not been seen by any finance officer. I explained that the file was not for spending the money from the very next day itself. It will accelerate the process of acquisition by the Army. He said, "You answer my question. We all know the USA is a powerful nation; technologically advanced. You are claiming only India has a supersonic cruise missile. No developed country has. How can I believe this?"

I said, "Sir, the USA has the Tomahawk subsonic cruise missile. Very successfully deployed in the Gulf war. The guidance is from American GPS, with military codes enabling high precision. It is terrain guided by GPS matching stored data in the on- board computer of the missile. The flight is initially guided by the Inertial Navigation System and near the target guided by satellites to very great accuracy. Subsonic speed is ideal giving time for data processing for scene matching. The Tomahawk system with its fire control and launcher have been placed on 145 warships and more than 24,000 have been produced and elaborate storage and maintenance facilities have been in operation since 1983. The USA made a study on the FASTHAWK missile and dropped it in view of the new technology and cost involved.

> *"In our case, we have no GPS with accuracy codes. Therefore, we went for RF seeker. This radar-guided seeker can work at supersonic speed. Our inertial guidance with advanced software developed in the DRDO gives a 2-metre accuracy and with homing by the RF seeker, we ensure hits on targets. Supersonic speed to the missile is given by a Russian engine, the equivalent of which is not available in the USA. Supersonic speed gives nine times more energy to destroy targets."*

After this explanation, he signed the file as approved. He placed a condition that the Finance Ministry must vet the contract document when ready.

Then I rushed to the PMO and met the Principal Secretary. The PM was in Goa meeting British PM Tony Blair. The next afternoon I got the PM's approval. I met RM and showed him the file. **It is because of Shri Pranab Mukherjee that the Indian Army is today the only land force in the world to have a supersonic land attack cruise missile for multiple missions, as demanded by them. The Indian Army has its BRAHMASTRA.**

After Shri Pranab Mukherjee became President of India, I went to see him. He remembered the coconut water. On another occasion, he gave me the Lal Bahadur Shastri National award and spoke for 10 minutes about my association with him in the Defence Ministry. It was my good fortune to work with such a great leader.

When I narrated the above details of the BRAHMOS induction into the Army to Kalam, he said with pride,", You have beaten me". I said "It is all your training".

Shri A.K. Antony—Defence Minister (October 2006-May 2014)

IGA Extension: JV was formed in February 1998 through IGA signed between the two goverments. It would be in operation for fifteen years. Therefore, the IGA needed to be extended from February 2013. After detailed discussions, both sides suggested a suitable formula to retain the JV, with an automatic extension every year without going to the Governments again. The IGA would get extended automatically every year, if there is no denial from either side. There was a requirement to get the approval of both the governments before signing the amendment to IGA.

Shri A.K. Antony took special interest to sustain the JV; otherwise, it would have affected the production of BRAHMOS in India and its induction in the Armed Forces. He talked to his counterpart during the Inter-Government Commission meetings so that approval activities could be speeded up. He visited NPOM and reviewed the BrahMos work in Russia. He got the proposal cleared from the Indian Cabinet Committee on Security on a fast track. All preparations were made for signing of Amendment of IGA. But the Russian team came with a last-minute correction from the office of the Russian President. The variation needed to go through another cycle in India. This put the JV in difficulty and legally it would not exist if the amendment to IGA was not signed on that day itself. I rushed to RM for his help. It was late in the evening. The Defence Secretary and other team members analysed the issue and found a way out. The RM waited in his office till late night and approved signing the modified IGA. What amazed me was the high level of commitment of the Defence Minister to support our Armed Forces to have an advanced technology weapon system.

Land for BrahMos Product Support

We created several technical positions in the western regions for deployment of missiles. Any requirement of maintenance must be attended to quickly. So there was a need to build a large set-up at a vantage location. We decided on Pilani for upkeep of the system, ever ready for war. Our team—Col. J.P. Uniyal and Col. Anil Misra surveyed the site and told me to see it. I saw the place but did not like it. I wanted another location. The Rajasthan Government officers showed me another area of 210 acres. I told them that it was ideal. They said the court had put a hold on its use. I told them we would sort it out.

I briefed the RM and requested a letter addressed to the Chief Minister of Rajasthan for the land. We sent it by hand to deliver to the CM. Col. Anil Misra fixed a meeting for me with CM Ashok Gehlot. We went by the morning flight to Jaipur. Anil got a message that the CM had cancelled all appointments, as he was unwell and running 104-degree temperature. Doctors had advised him rest. I said nothing doing. I wanted to see him for the project work to help Rajasthan. The message was passed on to him. He agreed to meet me at his house.

We went to the CM's residence. To our surprise, the Chief Secretary and Principal Secretaries of Finance, Revenue, Legal & Company Affairs and Industries were also present. Quickly a Powerpoint presentation was kept ready for me. The CM came with a shawl around his shoulders and a cap. He looked very tired.

I thanked him for giving appointment despite his being unwell. I conveyed the greetings of the RM and the letter he had written. I made a presentation on the project and the need for land, investment and employment potential, tax revenue to State, etc., and presented a model of the Army version of BrahMos to him. He said he was very happy to know the progress of the prestigious BrahMos and it was a good thought to set up a plant in Rajasthan. He saw the revenue map and the location of the requested land.

Regarding the court order, he said that as this was a defence requirement, a cabinet decision on it could be sent to the High Court. He said there could not be any objection. Everyone agreed. Any unauthorised houses constructed on the site could be removed by giving notice. He asked me whether I was happy with the discussion. "Not yet", I said. I told him that BrahMos being a JV with the Russians, any land given to the company would have a share for them too. So, the land will not be owned by BrahMos JV. "This is an exclusive facility built for the Army and managed by BrahMos. The ownership would be with the DRDO, Ministry of Defence", I added. But DRDO will not give fund for the joint venture. I requested the CM's approval for a notional payment of Re. 1 for the land, and conveyed my gratefulness. He asked the views of the secretaries. They were impressed by the project and wanted to support the activities in that area by creating an industrial hub. CM agreed to the proposal. I said," Now, I am happy". Though he was not well, he came up to the car, opened the door and said good-bye. I was deeply impressed by such a wonderful CM. Anil Misra stayed back and got the letter issued for the allotment of 210 acres of land to the DRDO for Re. 1. I showed the letter to the RM. He could not believe that a State government could give 210 acres for Re.1 and issue an allotment order within two days. I told him that his letter had helped and that the CM was a simple man.

Air Chief Marshal Fali Homi Major, after taking over as Chief of Air Staff in 2009, visited the BrahMos office. On seeing the land attack capability of BRAHMOS launched from a mobile launcher, he thought there was a necessity to deliberate this capability at Air HQ. I went with my team and gave a detailed presentation to the senior officers. The IAF decided to induct a land mobile version, in addition to Air Version specifically for IAF targets. It decided to have a land version of BRAHMOS also. Now a clash started between the Army and the IAF, because BRAHMOS had been in service with the Army. I knew I was responsible for this clash. I briefed the RM to resolve it. In the Defence Acquisition Council, the two chiefs were arguing; the Army Chief said 'the land launched BRAHMOS weapon belongs to the Army. The IAF cannot have it.' The IAF said, 'We have specific AF targets to destabilise the enemy quickly. It is an independent operation and we would need minimum squadrons'. RM decided that both would have BRAHMOS land versions and in addition, the IAF would have an air-launched version also. He amicably resolved the flash point.

BRAHMOS AIR VERSION

Shri Antony, RM, took a decision in support of the IAF to integrate the BRAHMOS missile with SU30MKI and got it approved in CCS. Details are discussed under a separate section in the next few pages. Even before development, the Government approved funding from the IAF to BrahMos for integration of the missile including modification of two aircraft and a production order for missiles. Such was the level of confidence! All the three Services now have the BRAHMOS.

GREAT CONTRIBUTIONS OF INDIAN DEFENCE MINISTERS FOR BRAHMOS

Shri Mulayam Singh Yadav approved Draft IGA on formation of JV.

Shri George Fernandes approved BRAHMOS induction in NAVY.

Shri Jaswant Singh approved First flight test of BRAHMOS and Announcement, Land for HQ.

Shri Pranab Mukherjee approved BRAHMOS induction in ARMY.

Shri A.K. Antony approved induction of BRAHMOS Land Version and Air Version in Indian AIR FORCE and IGA for Indefinite Extension of JV. He also got CCS approval for establishing large infrastructure for Armed Forces and DRDO to store, maintain and deploy the BRAHMOS missile system at different locations.

PRESIDENT PUTIN AND BRAHMOS

Now, I must talk about the contribution of President Putin for BrahMos. I met President Putin with President Kalam in Rashtrapati Bhavan when he visited Delhi in October 2002.A one-to-one rapport was established. In December 2004, he inaugurated the BrahMos HQ at Delhi Cantonment, and saw the exhibits and special gallery set up to honour Kalam. He was extremely delighted, and said that BrahMos would be the right model for Indian and Russian projects. He spent 40 minutes in our complex. Defence Minister Shri Pranab Mukherjee and Foreign Minister Shri Natwar Singh were also present during the visit. That visit made a deep impression on President Putin. He declared to the Press that India must become a Permanent Member of the UN Security Council, with veto power.

President Putin Inaugurates BrahMos Complex

President Putin always wanted to help NPOM, our BrahMos partner. He waived NPOM's loan arrangement for the Russian Government's contribution to the JV.

In the BrahMos joint venture, we had eliminated all the bottlenecks to progress the project faster. We could eliminate Rosoboronexport in our project. Our partner NPOM informed us that President Putin had issued a new decree stating that all contracts related to defence would go through Rosoboronexport, withdrawing special powers given to some big industries. NPOM felt that the new procedure would delay the project and lead to cost increase. I went that time to Moscow along with President Kalam. I was at Kremlin and got a chance to talk to President Putin. I told him about the recent decree issued by him and how his favourite BrahMos would be affected. I requested him to issue an exemption for BrahMos. He assured me he would take action. President Kalam told me it would be difficult for Mr. Putin to do it in a short time, due to the Russian bureaucracy. Much to our surprise, a decree was issued within a week, exempting BrahMos from Rosoboronexport.

President Putin was the guest for the 2007 Republic Day. He was sitting with President Kalam and witnessing the parade. Both were happy on seeing theBrahMos moving along as part of the parade. In the evening 'At Home' at Mughal Gardens, I went with my wife to meet Mr. Putin. Due to security reasons, no one was allowed to meet Putin, who was surrounded by three-ring security. We just went in; no one stopped us. Both Presidents stood up to greet us. Putin, Kalam and I had some interesting discussions for more than ten minutes. I could sense the power of his friendship with India.

Later, when Putin was Prime Minister (for a short period), in a Rostec Technology Exhibition at Moscow, he came to see hypersonic engine development—a joint effort of by 5 Russian institutes. He located me standing at a distance in the BrahMos pavilion. He changed his direction, rushed to me and hugged me, while everyone looked on in amazement. He was with me for 15 minutes and asked about BrahMos progress. This entire interaction got flashed across all TV channels. (Rostec is the State Corporation for Assistance to Development, Production and Export of Advanced Technology Industrial Product). He asked me to discuss the hypersonic development with the institutes and work out a joint proposal.

Dr. Pillai with President Kalam and President Putin at Rashtrapati Bhavan

Aircraft Su-30 MKI based Weapon Complex

In the original feasibility study for supersonic cruise missiles, in 1995, NPOM and our team envisaged an air platform with design optimisation

with reduced weight missile. We were considering different aircraft operated by the Navy IL-38, Tu-142 and by IAF SU-30MKI. After many deliberations, the IAF showed interest to fit the BRAHMOS-A in the SU30MKI for both ship and land targets. Our intention was to fit three missiles, but it could not be done due to the weight of the missile, each weighing 2.5 t. Even fitting one missile in the central fuselage needed structural modification of the airframe. I discussed with HAL, Nashik division, where the SU30MKI were produced, regarding technology transfer from the Sukhoi Design Bureau (SDB). Mr. P.V. Deshmukh, Managing Director of HAL, was very dynamic and progressive in his thinking and strongly supported the idea of indigenous effort. He agreed to take up the task. But HAL did not have the design details of the airframe and load bearing structures.

Dr. K. Tamilmani, Chief Executive, CEMILAC, DRDO advised me to create the design from the product. From the available drawings, dimensions were taken. We got one Su30 aircraft from the IAF, instrumented it extensively, flew for different manoeuvres and measured all load information. A very accurate model was prepared, put through wind tunnel tests at different speeds, and the data was corroborated through CFD analysis. The design document was ready and given to HAL to undertake modification of the structure for taking the missile load. HAL came out with a good design documentation. Opportunities and drive make people perform better. We got full support of Dr. RK Tyagi, Chairman HAL to progress the task at HAL, Nashik division. I put that documentation through a review committee of aircraft designers. Modifications were carried out by HAL. Another expert committee reviewed the modified report and the design was cleared for prototype manufacturing.

In the meantime, the IAF finalised the PSQR and we jointly took the decision to realise the project with indigenous effort. The IAF agreed to give two aircraft from the production line at HAL, Nashik.

Push from Russia for Air Version

Our partner NPOM made necessary modifications in the missile with a shorter booster, new structure, nose cap, tail fins, etc. A prototype of the air version and technology missiles were realised.

Rosoboronexport—Russia's export arm, proposed to carry out missile integration with two HAL-made SU30 and flight-testing at Russia. The Russian authorities would give certification. The proposal was for $ 250 million. Two HAL-made aircraft were to be certified for flight, disassembled, packed, insured and sent to Russia. Then, at Russia, India was to custom clear the packages, aircraft to be assembled, flight certified to Russian requirements and handed over to them. The SDB was to make the modifications with no design details given to us. Missiles on order from us would be delivered to SDB by NPOM. SDB would conduct flight trials with Russian pilots. On proving the success with a number of missiles, the modification would be certified and drawings issued to HAL. The two modified aircraft would be received from SDB and all processes like packing, customs, etc., would be repeated, as when sent to Russia.

The Russian team of SDB designers, retired Generals and officers of Rosoboronexport, 20 of them in all, came to meet my team. DRDO, HAL, IAF, BrahMos, CEMILAC and me participated. SDB gave important lectures for more than two hours, saying that India had no design documents, and that HAL would fail in making design changes, it was not possible to make software changes in the sealed mission computer, we had no experience of new missile integration, and aircraft safety during firing the missile, etc. I made it clear that our mission was to carry out the complete task in India only. I told them that Indians would rise to the occasion and overcome all deficiencies, and thanked them for coming all the way. The disappointed Russians then went to the Chief of Air Staff who directed them back to meet me. He asserted that we would do the task ourselves. They tried all channels, but did not succeed. They went to the Defence Secretary. He too did not say anything.

In the meantime, we geared up our responsibility in a systematic manner with necessary approvals from the Defence Minister and progressed all the tasks for total indigenous effort. Gp Captain Srivastava, deputed by the IAF, was helping me. We had total support of DRDO, IAF, HAL, CEMILAC—the certifying agency, SDI—unit of IAF and NPOM. BrahMos Board approved all our actions and gave us a free hand.

Rosoboronexport did not want to yield. It was not only about $ 250 million. They wanted to take control of BrahMos, which they had lost out in the land version and also in the lost opportunity of sale of Klub missiles to the Indian Navy. They sold SU30MK versions to Malaysia, Vietnam, Indonesia, Venezuela, Algeria, Uganda, Russian AF and a version of SU30 to China. Countries like Malaysia, Vietnam and Indonesia already approached us for the air version BrahMos. Rosoboronexport saw big business for SU30 fitted with BrahMos. It was a game plan to use Indian money, develop the system, sell to India, and export to other countries.

After all their efforts were unsuccessful, SDB and Rosoboronexport approached Mr. Dmitry Medvedev, President of Russia. for discussion with Dr. Manmohan Singh, Prime Minister of India. in the annual summit at Moscow. Mr Shivshankar Menon, NSA was also present during the meeting. The soft-spoken Mr. Medvedev in a firm voice told Dr. Manmohan Singh that Russia only would undertake the installation of BrahMos in SU30 due to technical issues, which could be solved only by

Russian experts. It would be a failure if this was attempted by the Indian side. If this was not resolved, Russia would reconsider the supply of spares for SU30 production in India.

Mind Without Fear

On his return, an annoyed PM asked NSA to discuss this issue. NSA Shri Menon called for a meeting with Defence Secretary Shri Shashi Kant Sharma, Chief of Air Staff Air Chief Marshal Browne and myself. NSA briefed the above about the directive of PM, saying that the issue was so serious that it was better to go with the Russians, because BrahMos should not control other strategic issues. I took half an hour to explain the whole game plan of Rosoboronexport. I explained how we were confident that we could do without Russian help. I wanted Indian pilots to launch BrahMos in India to show the world our might. The Russian proposal was to launch BrahMos by Russian pilots, in Russia, with no details available to us. I explained in detail the progress made and assured success. It was a great opportunity to prove our worth. The Air Chief said, "As per the contract signed with Russia, we could carry out weapon integration; even there is a need to modify structure. Therefore, our executing this work in India is within the framework of obligations. Seeing the dynamism in carrying out the task already, Air Force is confident of BrahMos team. I go by what Pillai said". The Defence Secretary added, "I am convinced that we must take it up, as outlined by Mr. Pillai. We will induct air version BrahMos in Su30MKI, ourselves." The NSA summed up, accepting that India would be responsible for BrahMos integration with SU30MKI. "I will generate a note to PM and take his approval. Pillai must work with Russians to see there is no repercussion". I said that I would do it.

Just when I was working out how to handle SDB and Rosoboronexport, it was my good fortune that Mr. Vladimir Putin became President again, after Mr. Medvedev in 2012.

The top officers of Russia were well aware of my relationship with President Putin. The Rosoboronexport and SDB did not want to approach their President. Instead, the team came back to BrahMos office and said they would like to participate in the missile integration in any form. I suggested to them to verify the design of structural modification made by HAL. They agreed and requested for $ 2.6 million for support to HAL, for the design verification and follow up for six months. I agreed and signed the contract. ($ 250 million saved along with pride for the nation!)

Simulation, Software Validation

The IAF has a special unit called Software Development Institute (SDI) at Bengaluru. The commandant is of the rank of Air Vice Marshal. We posted a team at SDI. On request, the IAF assigned an officer of the rank of Group Captain on deputation. I identified four fresh engineering graduates and posted them to work with Gp Captain Rath to carry out simulations in the SU30 rig at SDI. They designed launch operations, sequencing events such as target identification, missile readiness, positioning aircraft in the slot and launch; cockpit display; and simulated all the operations in the SU30 simulation rig, using modified software. One more aspect was alignment of aircraft Inertial Measurement Unit with missile guidance at RCI. I was pleased to see the performance of the team, working round the clock. Initially the team was inside SDI and later, Dr. Christopher gave office space at CABS, in the building next to SDI. Once in two weeks, I was in Bengaluru to progress this work jointly with the Commandant AVM Sood. I got full support from Air HQ.

Wind Tunnel Tests

During this time, NAL was carrying out wind tunnel tests for the aircraft with missile, release at different flight regimes, angle of attack, and manoeuvres with a large number of blowdowns in the Trisonic tunnel. In one of the discussions, the Russian side asked for collecting data for dynamic release of the missile from aircraft. NAL had never carried out this activity. NPOM specialists helped NAL to identify one of the low speed wind tunnels already available in NAL. With minor modifications, this tunnel was used to simulate dynamic separation of the missile from the aircraft.

Launcher

The launcher for the missile is held at the fuselage in the modified locations or hold points. This launcher is unique to hold a heavy missile. I gave this task of fabricating the launcher to BrahMos Aerospace Thiruvananthapuram Limited (BATL). They made this 5-metre long Al alloy launcher and the test set up for release of a dummy missile, till reliability was established for simultaneous release at both points. (BATL was earlier the Kerala Government-owned sick KELTEC, with excellent skills. It was taken over by BrahMos.)

Flight Sequence

The aircraft has its own computer—the flight computer—as the centrepiece of its avionics. The flight computer gets inputs from all sensors and communicates with the pilot through displays. From the movement of various pilot controls (throttle stick, etc.), it understands the intentions of the pilot regarding the flight path. Accordingly, it actuates various aerodynamic features. Actually, it is only the flight computer that flies the aircraft, but it flies according to the pilot's instructions, which he gives through his flight controls. The missile has its own on-board computer (OBC) that directs the missile to the target. This computer needs the location of the target, which is supplied by a peripheral control device (PCD). The PCD communicates with the missile's OBC and the aircraft's avionics. The pilot in a typical anti-shipping mission will get the target coordinates from the naval sensors that are then fed in by the pilot in the cockpit. The target coordinates are then passed to PCD. The PCD feeds the target coordinates into the missile's OBC. When the pilot squeezes the launch trigger, the missile is released from the launcher. After release, the missile stabilises itself to fire the booster. Then the routine programmes in the missile's OBC are executed. The IAF has the land version of the missile also.

Audacity of Vision

Today, air-launched missiles for ship and land targets are operational. In all three missions, the missiles hit the targets with precision. IAF pilots launched the missiles, hitting the targets accurately. Bold decisions taken that India take up full responsibility without yielding to pressures, helped India master the BrahMos with SU30MKI—a *Brahmastra* in the air! and resulted in saving of more than $ 250 million, our own design capability and launch operation by IAF pilots. India became the only country to have a powerful supersonic missile from a refuel-capable deep strike aircraft.

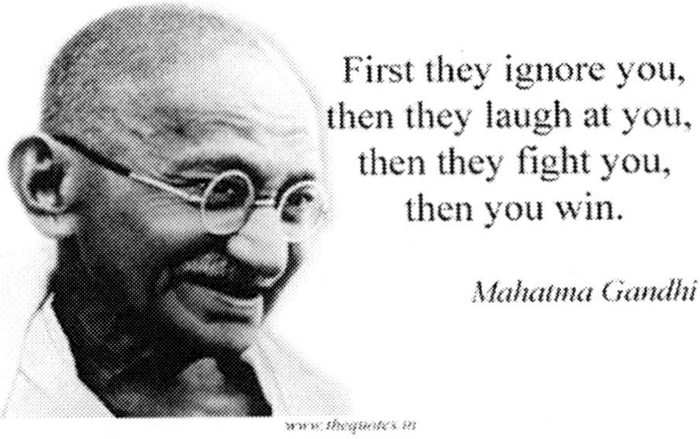

EXPORT OF BRAHMOS

BrahMos Aerospace participates in international expos. In an exhibition at Abu Dhabi, a delegation headed by a **Major General from Pakistan**, visited our stall. The leader of the delegation politely asked whether we could explain about the BRAHMOS system. As it was an exhibition, we were obliged to display the normal presentation material to highlight the importance of BRAHMOS and its capabilities. He expressed his happiness at the openness and wished good relations between the two countries. He however whispered to me whether India is prepared to sell BRAHMOS to his country. I could not resist my temptation to respond to his question. I told him **"BRAHMOS is a free delivery item to your country"**. The General felt bad having asked that question. He left immediately.

BRAHMOS FORMULA

- Robust design with unique excellent capabilities of the missile (best in the world).
- Systematic validation of systems, simulation, checkout procedures and reviews, quality standards establishing reliability at every stage of development.
- Consolidating gains from IGMDP with dynamic management and incorporating the lessons learnt through earlier experiences of Prithvi and Agni, and thinking a step better in the product performance.
- Continuous performance improvements, upgradations and new versions for customer delight, utilising experts from India and Russia.

- Strong customer loyalty to the brand.
- Consortium of industry partners keeping design, integration and management with JV. All stakeholders networked with integrated management system and transparency in operation.
- Establishing a sense of urgency and faster execution of the tasks due to autonomous operation of JV and empowerment in the decision-making process.
- Utilisation of young energetic talent force with pride in working for excellent missiles for the nation.
- Anchoring new approaches in the culture.

A Fusion of great minds—President Kalam's visit to NPOM

When President Kalam visited Russia in 2005, he made a point to go to NPOM and met his friend Dr. Yefremov. They discussed BRAHMOS-2, a hypersonic cruise missile. Dr. Yefremov and I signed a MOU on possible collaboration in Kalam's presence. Based on this, the BrahMos Board decided to fund from the profits, the establishment of the Hypersonic Centre at IISc.

The First Flight Trial

The design of the missile was decided by the time the company became operational. Initially we did not have the facilities to integrate the missile in India. So all the necessary components from the DRDO were sent to Russia and they were integrated with the remaining Russian components. A special transport aircraft secretly brought the final missile. Even the crew was clueless about the contents of the container. At that time, only the top brass of the three Services, top bureaucrats in the Defence Ministry and the DRDO knew about the project. A date was fixed for the trial; it was 12 June 2001. In Russia, the date is celebrated as Russia Day!

We were both confident and nervous. Mr. Jaswant Singh (the then Minister of Defence as well as External Affairs), the three Service chiefs and top brass from the DRDO and NPOM had assembled at the Integrated Test Range (ITR), Odisha. The countdown began and everyone's attention was on the monitor in the blockhouse. At T0, the missile came out of the launcher. A new era in missile warfare had begun.

The JV so far was a secret project, but any flight trial conducted at ITR would come into the limelight. Hence, it was necessary to get the permission of the Government for the flight trial and release the news on the results. **The then Prime Minister, Atal Bihari Vajpayee, a man of wisdom, who was in complete knowledge of the BrahMos project (I had briefed him earlier) approved the announcement of the joint venture** programme and release of the news about the flight test. **The whole world was stunned by the successful launch of a supersonic cruise missile by India.**

From that day onwards, the company grew exponentially and every month there has been steady progress.

Courage in rough seas ***"There are no secrets to success. It is the result of hard work, perfection, learning from failure, loyalty and persistence."***— Colin Powell

There were difficulties for us and we had to put in all our efforts to overcome them. For the uninitiated, the nerve-racking moments we faced during the flight trials would be beyond the realms of imagination. So, let me take you back in time.

Flight Trial Locations

Generally, missile flight trials are conducted at the Integrated Test Range (ITR) at Chandipur-on-Sea near Balasore, Odisha. It is a beautiful place for tourists. The Bay of Bengal recedes four kilometres during low tide and the waves are in full blast during high tide. This happens twice a day and is an interesting sight. During low tide, one can walk on the sea with bare feet and collect shells. The British had located this site to try

out the firing of shells (ammunition) from artillery guns. This establishment is today called Proof and Experimental Establishment (PXE) and has completed more than one hundred years.

At the Integrated Test Range, whenever we launched Agni, we needed to evacuate nearly 3,500 residents from the nearby villages in order to have the required safety clearance. While the villagers obliged without any problem, there were considerable difficulties. We needed a safe range. That was the time we were also looking for a land target for the Prithvi flights, as we had to prove the accuracy of impact to the Army. The Wheeler Islands, off Damra (in Odisha) could give a 70-km range from ITR. The Prithvi launch took place successfully, impacting close to the target on the Island, as part of the user acceptance trial.

Today, Agni-V is launched from the Wheeler Islands, now called **Dr. Abdul Kalam Islands.**

1. Though the Missile Fell

As we prepared for the first launch at the ITR, we started loading the missile in the static vertical launcher exclusively erected for the BRAHMOS system. For the loading, it was necessary to lift the missile to double its length and slide it inside. The missile was being lifted by a crane with a special lifting device holding the nose cap. When the missile reached 15 metres above the ground level, the holding device inadvertently yielded and broke. The live missile fell down, back on the corsette—the transport trolley, making a loud noise. It was a pathetic scene and the operating personnel ran for safety. A live missile is terribly dangerous even if it is without any warhead. Everybody held their breath. Slowly some of them gathered courage to approach the missile for observing any abnormality. We got the information and swiftly acted to isolate the live missile for a detailed examination by experts. Our Russian friends suggested that we destroy the missile by following a procedure. That was what they did in their country.

For the flight test, we had prepared two missiles: the main and the standby. With the main missile in an accident, we did not have time to lose and loaded the standby missile after taking corrective measures for the loading fixture. The launch was successful as explained earlier.

Next, we studied the fallen missile and made an elaborate plan to check each subsystem carefully and analyse the results. We were satisfied with the health of the missile and decided to go ahead with a flight trial instead of destroying it. Conventional wisdom said a dropped missile could not be flight-tested as there was the possibility of an internal failure. But the Indian team took this up as a challenge and after careful review of risks decided to carry out the launch. After detailed review, system wise, we decided to test in the inclined mode, as per the requirement for the Navy. Russian specialists had reservations about the launch. When I said I take the responsibility, they agreed to the launch. The launch (FT 02) was hundred per cent successful and our scientists were even more jubilant than they were after the first successful flight. Such was the robustness of the BRAHMOS. What was equally important was the decision making process and not afraid of failures. It paid off immensely.

2. Launch from MAL

No machine is complete unless the man using it is competent. As a military machine is used in adverse and frequently changing dynamic situations, the man operating it should be highly competent. He plays a significant role in exploiting its full capabilities. Yet, human interface with the war machine is the last in the chain of proving a system. This is because the safety of the system has to be proved by successive trials.

So, the missile was to be test-fired from the ITR to validate its operation from a mobile launch complex with an advanced guidance system and manoeuvring trajectory meant for the Indian Army. Several activities were going on at full throttle in preparation for the launch from a mobile autonomous launcher (MAL). The launch team had to be in the MAL driver console. The Army had posted a specialist team to take over the missile group and it was headed by Col. Bishnu Ram.

I still remember the indomitable spirit of the Colonel as he volunteered to launch the missile from the MAL itself. Normally, till the time the system design is frozen and development is complete, such an adventure is not advisable. In this case, the safety concerns were huge as the missile was to fly over his head. It was loaded with hundreds of kilograms of propellant. A mishap would result in a catastrophe and failures were a part and parcel of flight trials. Even developed nations like the USA and the USSR had faced failures in flight trials and had lost their astronauts and cosmonauts. You may be aware that Yuri Gagarin was the first man to reach space. He was a test pilot and he died when he was test-flying an aircraft. So accidents can happen at any time.

The Colonel here said, "Sir, my organisation has placed me here with some purpose. This system belongs to us and I have grown with the system. I must launch the missile from the MAL as per the ultimate configuration." I was overwhelmed by the courage and faith of the officer in the system. He showed the finest traditions of the Army, 'displaying selfless devotion and leading from the front.'

Eventually, his confidence convinced us to go ahead with his plan. I knew the worth of the system, but the thought of the one-in-a-million possibility of failure was at the back of my mind.

Meanwhile, the head of the FCS division, Mr, V.S.N. Moorthy, volunteered to join the Colonel in firing the missile. Here, I have to laud his guts and grit. Normally, a scientist thinks twice before taking a risk. Although our Russian friends advised us to opt for a remote launch, by then I had decided to go ahead with the launch with our men inside the MAL. I spent sleepless nights pondering over the issue of the MAL launch with our men. I was worried because it was the first such experience for our missile team. If any mishap were to occur, it would be a disaster and the end of the induction of BRAHMOS into the Army. But the sheer grit and courage shown by our men was negating the risk and helped us to overcome the worries. I mounted a big contingency plan at the launch pad to face the worst. I remembered the famous statement of Astronaut John Young, "*Anyone who sits at the top of the largest hydrogen-oxygen fueld system in the world, knowing they are going to light the bottom, and does notget a little worried, does not fully understand the situation.*"

The designated time had arrived. After praying, I broke a coconut in front of the missile and wished both men good luck. They stepped into the MAL at the scheduled time. I remembered the Apollo 11 mission in July 1969, when Neil Armstrong, Michael Collins and Edwin Aldrin walked into the Lunar Module LM 5. In the same style, our friends walked into the MAL. Both officers were calm and showed no sign of hesitation. The launch pad was evacuated and we settled in the Block House in front of the consoles. The CCTV cameras were inside the FCS cabin of the MAL to monitor the crew conditions. The crew with their smiling faces comforted us and the countdown was initiated. The atmosphere inside the Block House was tense. Our lips went dry as the final few seconds came. Till that time there was no glitch and everybody sat with their fingers clenched and crossed. An emergency vehicle was waiting outside the blockhouse for me to rush to the launch pad, in case of an emergency. The teams were alert to face any eventuality. The countdown reached the final ten counts. My heart started beating fast.

10... 9... 8... 7... 6... 5... 4... 3... 2... 1... Zero!

The command was given. There was an ear-shattering thunder. If any of you live near an airport, you must have complained about the noise of the flying aircraft. The level of noise that a missile launch creates is exponentially higher and is hard to endure. Amidst that thunder, the missile came out of the canister like a shining sword coming out of its scabbard. It rose high, rolled, pitched and started its supersonic journey right above the firing team. The Block House broke into applause and tears of joy. Yes, the launch was a success! The capability of the MAL was proved beyond doubt. I rushed to the launch pad to look at the courageous firing team, which emerged victorious without a single scratch. Their victory smile still shines in my eyes and will remain forever. I recalled to them the words of Neil Armstrong, "That's one small step for man, one giant leap for mankind. **The Indian Army would be the first land force in the world to have a land-attack supersonic cruise missile".** The fire team was thrilled to be the first-ever crew to fire a supersonic cruise missile for the land force.

Col. Bishnu Ram commanded the first ever BRAHMOS regiment for the Army and Mr. V.S.N. Moorthy, a DRDO scientist, became Project Director of BrahMos. These men have certainly made their proud place in the history of BrahMos for firing a supersonic missile over their own heads. Now, it is routine practice since all our Army-version missiles are launched from the MAL. The same MAL is being used by the Indian Air Force as well.

3. A Cyclonic Trial

One of the flight trials was conducted at the ITR in June, the south-west monsoon period. We intended to launch the missile to test some of the crucial parameters including advanced software and guidance. Unknown to us, Mother Nature wanted more from the missile. She wanted the missile to prove its all-weather capability.

All the requirements were met and launch procedures were carried out systematically. Then, almost out of nowhere, a severe tropical cyclone had formed in quick succession in the Bay of Bengal and was supposed to cross somewhere around the eastern coast. When we reached the ITR, the sea was rough and roaring to its full might—a scary sight for us. It is known that wind and sea conditions during a cyclone are not at all favourable for launch of missile. In our case the wind was roaring with a speed of around 150 km per hour, as reported by the ITR's meteorological set-up.

During any flight trial, we follow a set of procedures to clear the flight tests based on what is called flight readiness review (FRR). We were in the middle of the FRR meeting on the cyclone day and debated whether to conduct or postpone the mission due to the Met warning. Some were in favour of the launch and many others were against it. There were strong winds and chances of heavy rain in the next morning when the launch was scheduled. We decided to wait for a minimum level of favourable weather on the next day; if there was no improvement, we were to pack our bags and go to Hyderabad because the meteorologists had reported a storm approaching.

That night, I could barely sleep due to the apprehensions about the next day's flight trial. It could prove to be an ultimate test for men and machine. So many thoughts were battling in the mind. The missile had to prove itself with tall mission objectives and which would be a proof for us. The rain started to pour as if in chorus to the whistle of the gusting winds. I was not able to sleep due to the anxiety and opened the windows of my room from where I was able to see the sea. Indeed, it was a fearsome sight to see the roaring sea. Like the waves of the sea, my thoughts were also oscillating and I discovered that my colleagues were also spending sleepless nights.

Why I am stressing over this is due to the fact that war is not a cricket match that can be called off due to rain or whose result can be decided with the Duckworth–Lewis method. War may erupt at any time and weather is an important feature that militaries take advantage of. Think of a similar situation at sea when ships are subjected to heavy roll and pitch in different conditions. Still the men in uniform on the ship have to fight the war. They have to launch the missiles to attack the enemy ships. All the resources, men or machine, must be in fighting fitness even in adverse conditions. So, while one cannot escape proving the efficacy of the system in adverse conditions, it may not be advisable to take risks during development tests to prove new objectives.

Next day, early morning, I went out to have a look at the sea waves and the fury of the wind. I met many of my team members at the seashore. I went to the new guesthouse where the Russian specialists were staying. The door could not be opened as the wind from the opposite side was blowing in full throttle through the door that was kept open by them. All our Russian colleagues were on the balcony looking at the sea. When I went inside, one of them exclaimed, "Nature treats everybody equally!" Ripples of laughter started shaking the room due to this timely comment.

It was raining like anything; imagine how the cyclonic rain together with gale winds would feel in a coastal area. Amid this, there was a sudden clearance in the weather though it was far from favourable. Yet, it was the only concession that nature seemed to offer for our launch. We did all the preparations in quick succession. Vice Adm. Arun Prakash, the then Vice Chief of Indian Navy, joined us to witness the launch. As the user arrived, we saw a sudden patch of light as the clouds gave way. The sun appeared. We acted fast and took the decision of going ahead with the launch.

The countdown reached its most crucial last phase. In that short period of time, we felt as if we are going to receive the question paper of some practical examination—students of science and engineering disciplines can understand the problem very well! Even for experienced professionals, the last phase of countdown is a test for patience and endurance. Then, as the wind started increasing its speed, a warning came that a cyclone might be crossing through that area very soon. The mission was held back from launch as the range director did not consider the situation conducive for the launch.

A decision had to be taken—whether to conduct the trial in high wind speed or to call off the mission. I asked the Russian team, but they were not sure to launch. I checked the wind parameters. I told the Admiral that we were going ahead. Gave clearance to my team to go ahead with the launch and not to worry about the wind speed, which had just reached its extreme limit of 10m/s. The then project director Mr Venugopalan and the MAL team signalled their readiness. The hold was lifted. The countdown started.

At the count of zero, the missile took off. It rose up into the sky and then carried out its journey in what was a textbook performance. The take-off picture clearly showed how severe the wind was. Even to move the exhaust of the booster to one direction was a herculean task. We realised that the missile was so robust in its control system design and structure that it could withstand such severe weather conditions. In particular, the inertial navigation system of DRDO technology performed beautifully. It was a great experience of decision making with risk. I had the feeling that God was a partner to the BrahMos project!

The astonishing performance of BRAHMOS was understood by Adm. Arun Prakash and other user friends who witnessed the launch. This boosted the user confidence tremendously which resulted in a quick letter of intent for BRAHMOS in multiple ships for the Navy, signed by Vice Adm. Arun Prakash, the then Vice Chief of Naval Staff. The Admiral was totally supportive of BRAHMOS.

4. The Andaman Launch

An Island, Please!

We had to prove the land-attack capabilities of our missile when launched from a ship to a land mass having a target. This would enable the Navy to use the missile for coastal targets. Therefore, we decided to conduct a flight trial in the Andaman Islands, as it was not possible for us to locate land target in the mainland of India. Lt Col. Anil Misra, another hero, and I, planned to carry out an aerial reconnaissance of the 572 islands of

Andaman and Nicobar to locate our island for positioning a target. We had the help of the Navy and the Combined Command of Andaman & Nicobar (A&N). Many believed it would not be possible to get environmental clearance from the Prime Minister's Committee to carry out a missile launch on a land target at Andaman and Nicobar Islands. The reason was the presence of rare species of flora and fauna in most of the uninhabited islands as well as islands occupied by the tribal natives. Still, we decided to first conduct the survey and choose the appropriate island to position the target for the BRAHMOS missile to be launched from a ship sailing in the Andaman Sea. After the survey we chose Meroe, Trak and Treis islands for BrahMos missions. The administration gave necessary approvals after going through all procedures to clear the proposal.

A five-member team consisting of Col. Misra (BrahMos), Rane (DRDL), Dhir (TBRL), NS Srinivas (RCI) and Satyanarayana (RCI) had to construct a target on the island, make necessary alignments of the target taking into account the trajectory of the incoming missile, and place high-speed cameras at suitable locations to capture the target destruction. It was a wonderful launch hitting the target precisely with a 290 km range. When I met the members of the target-erection team at Port Blair after the successful mission, my eyesight got blurred with tears. Those men had blisters all over the body, sunken eyes, and unshaven faces stuck with sand, but their eyes glittered. I have seen this light in the young scientists hardened by determination, working tirelessly in the labs and missile integration buildings, unmindful of time–space boundaries. I have seen this light in the eyes of people who burst into tears after seeing through the missile meeting its mission objectives. Once I had visited the frontiers, I saw the same light in the eyes of our soldiers who fought with the enemy disregarding the bad terrain, weather conditions, and other personal emotions. This light of determination, courage and dedication keeps the nation on the track of development. What a great Nation we belong to and the men of action when there is need! Hats off to my friends! They are the heroes of BrahMos.

5. Launch from INS Rajput: Clenched Fists

It was Navy's foresight to possess such a powerful weapon onboard their warships. Upon seeing the first flight trial, Vice Adm. John DeSilva, the then FOC-in-C of Eastern Naval Command, thought of finding an opportunity to get a ship for fitment of BRAHMOS. Fortunately, INS *Rajput* was on re-fitment. He advised Adm. Sushil Kumar, the then Chief of Naval Staff, to give this opportunity to BrahMos. When the Admiral asked me over telephone, I immediately accepted and gave an accelerated schedule to match the refit time and install BRAHMOS. It was a great boon for us.

It was the first time that a missile of this size was being launched by the Navy and the concerns were well understood. Risk is involved everywhere, but we were not afraid of them. A careful intelligent analysis is necessary to overcome any risk. With this determination, we cleared the launch. The launch was a great success. Now, the Navy got a big boon that a long range supersonic anti-ship cruise missile was installed on-board the flag ship of INS *Rajput*—a historical moment for India.

6. Combat Launch: One Shot, One Kill

Having seen the successful flight trials with full user participation, a request came from Admiral Arun Prakash, who had then taken over as the Chief of Naval Staff, to conduct a combat flight trial during their annual naval exercise. Normally, trials do not include testing with warheads. Assuring us of giving production orders and that no more trials would be conducted, Admiral Prakash demanded successful destruction of the target ship by BRAHMOS, like in a war. I accepted the demand though it was a deviation from our plan. Our Russian friends said that this test must be conducted by the Navy on a missile to be declared as delivered. The Navy accepted the condition.

We quickly mobilised ourselves to conduct a test with a live warhead in combat mode, off the Goa coast. INS *Rajput* was loaded with a combat missile and ex-INS *Sindhudurg* was chosen as the target ship. On 15 April 2005, I was onboard INS *Virat* along with Admiral Arun Prakash, Vice Admiral Sureesh Mehta, the then DCNS and other officers from the Navy. Our team with Venugopalan was onboard INS *Rajput*. The Navy carried out the launch with a precise hit on the target, which split into two parts and sunk. All happened in no time. After the launch, the Admiral and I boarded a helicopter and went to see the condition of the target. When we reached there, the vessel had sunk completely. Only traces of the

vessel's debris were found. We saw a boat nearby from which naval divers were waving their hands.

The naval divers had recorded the video of the missile hitting the target with a big bang; the target ship was split into two and had sunk. Later, they said the event happened so fast that the missile came and hit the vessel and it sank within minutes. The disturbance caused by the sinking of the vessel made it difficult for the divers to maintain the stability of their boat. Nevertheless, the videos displayed the enormous kinetic energy and the power of the missile. There was no match for the BRAHMOS. Admiral Arun Prakash kept his word and placed production orders to fit the BRAHMOS on multiple ships. He also authorised funds to design and develop the universal vertical launcher module for fitment in future ships. Indeed, it was a great partnership with the Indian Navy.

Induction of BRAHMOS in Indian Navy

7. Desert Launch—Converting Anti-Ship into Land-Attack Missile

The BRAHMOS was originally designed to perform as an anti-ship missile with a radar seeker. In order to make a new version for the Army, it had to be used as a land-to-land missile. In other words, the missile had to be launched from a mobile launcher equipped with a command-and-control system. The typical targets are ammunition dumps, missile bases, missile or ammunition factories, railway yards, airports, communication centres, critical bridges, and so on. A suitable seeker is required for homing in on these types of land targets. Generally, the option is to go for terrain mapping and a GPS-guided system. We improved the present RF seeker.

Flight Trial in the Desert

We conducted two consecutive successful trials for proving the land-attack version of the BRAHMOS. These trials are carried out at the Pokhran Field Firing Range (PFFR). Both the flights were witnessed by General J.J. Singh, the then Chief of Army Staff. Incidentally, the second trial conducted on 31 May 2006 became a summer trial. The Rajasthan desertis known for its heat, and in summers the temperature easily exceeds 52°C. The conditions were such that work had to be started very early in the morning and stopped by 10 AM. Only after 5 PM could work resume. Here I must mention the willpower of our Russian partners. When we declared the launch, they wanted to participate even though the temperature did not suit them at all. In their country, –20°C is a normal ambient temperature. They withstood the harsh weather.

Target Hit

General J.J. Singh reviewed the preparedness for the launch. He went through the mobile command post, the mobile autonomous launcher loaded with the missile, its standby, and the command centre. The countdown began and, as usual, at T0 the missile took off beautifully, vertically, turned towards the direction of the target, and quickly disappeared from our sight. The General and I quickly rushed to a helicopter to see the effect on the target. We found that the missile had finished its job much earlier. We built a helipad near the target for the General. From the helipad, we went in a four-wheel drive vehicle on the desert and looked at the target. With a glowing smile, the General congratulated me and the team. He asked me to meet him in Delhi to present the details to all his Generals.

8. Taste of Failure and Regrouping

We had successfully inducted the first regiment in 2007. The Army now wanted a next version of the BRAHMOS, which would discriminate a particular target from among a group of targets. This needed surgical precision to locate and hit the target. More intelligence needed to be incorporated in the missile on-board computer and guidance system. We required a GPS receiver that would be compatible with multiple global navigation satellite systems as also a seeker tuned to home in on non-radio-contrast targets. This requirement was quite challenging and we started developing the system as BRAHMOS Block II. The first launch of Block II was scheduled for 20 January 2009. General Deepak Kapoor, the then Chief of Army Staff, came to witness the launch.

In the Pokhran range, a group of five targets was constructed. They were not reflecting radar energy (low signature) constructed with a thin sheet.

After short count down, the missile took off and headed towards the actual target. To our disappointment, the missile did not hit the target; it just passed above it. General Kapoor was dissatisfied with the performance and the Army informed the media that the flight trial was a failure. The media took it very seriously. In the history of BrahMos, this was the first incident of a missile not hitting the target. Moreover, it was a crucial time for our country since it was immediately after the 26/11 Mumbai attack. There was a huge outcry. On their part, the Army maintained an indifferent posture by saying that further induction would be carried out only after successful flight trials of Block II. I assured the Government, Army and the media that we would find a solution to the problem and that within a month the next launch will take place.

COURAGE TO SUCCEED

When I returned to New Delhi, I saw pale faces in the office. For the first time my team had tasted failure. The critical comments had left them extremely hurt. I called for a meeting in the evening and declared, "We will conduct a successful flight trial in a month after re-tuning the software."

I had already seen a major setback when I was at ISRO, during our first attempt to launch the SLV-3 on 10 August 1979. The same thing happened in the fourth launch of Prithvi in 1989 and the second launch of Agni in 1991. Dr Kalam used to say 'Failures are grounds for a lot of learning if we carry out the analysis carefully and draw the conclusions correctly'. The second launch of SLV-3 on 18 July 1980 was a great success and further flights of Prithvi and Agni were consecutive successes. Having narrated my Agni experience, I told my dejected team members, **"The factor between us and success is just a matter of time; the challenge is to compress the time."** The entire team geared up and everybody regardless of his or her work profile was ready to contribute.

We carried out a detailed analysis with all the concerned engineers and chalked out a programme along with the Russian specialists to validate the new software and to carry out necessary simulations. The corrective measures included more sensitivity to the seeker to track low-radar energy from the target with dynamic computations to give error details to the on-board computer and logic for correction with the INS. All these problems do not occur with a long-range mission, which is the real application. Here, in the desert, the range is very limited and the time of flight is short and the speed is supersonic. The software corrections were incorporated taking into account these factors and the whole mission was simulated for a number of times. This time we were quite sure that the target would be hit. Hence, we informed the Army that we were ready.

Sujan Dutta and GS Mudur wrote about the success of the BrahMos in *The Telegraph* on 3 April, 2009.

Missile Man Pierces Army Apathy

How a tenacious technocrat put the supersonic BrahMos back on track

New Delhi, April 3: India can stake claim to be among the first in the world to be ready with a supersonic land-attack cruise missile because of the tenacity of an unheralded Missile Man whose pet project was almost written off for aiming too high.

Sivathanu Pillai, a technocrat whose bald pate is not covered by berets, whose chest is bereft of medals and shoulders of epaulettes, dared the Indian Army by claiming he would arm its artillery divisions with a missile the world had not seen.

The Army was hesitant. There was new pressure to look at alternative imported systems. Disregarding all apprehensions, we proceeded with the desert launch with great confidence. The launch took place on 4 March 2009 and the missile hit the target. This time, the Deputy Chief of Army Staff had come to witness the trial.

Sivathanu Pillai, a technocrat whose baldpate is not covered by berets, whose chest is bereft of medals and shoulders of epaulettes, dared the Indian Army by claiming he would arm its artillery divisions with a missile the world had not seen.—***The Telegraph***

The Army said they wanted one more launch to establish the reliability of the missile. I smiled and immediately agreed. Multiple targets were created in the desert. The target chosen was the least signal-emitting thin sheet. This was a real challenge. On 29 March 2009, the flight trial was conducted in the presence of the Director General of Military Operations. The missile discriminated the specific target among the group of targets, flew straight towards it, and hit it precisely. We declared the Block II readiness to all. **Soon thereafter, we got a production order for two more regiments of the Army.**

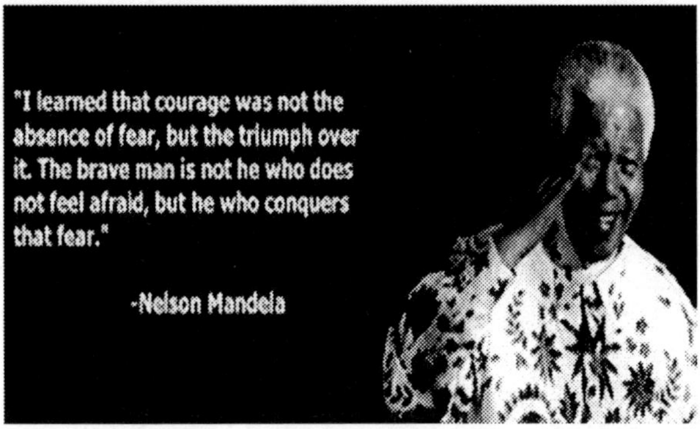

Failure is an inherent part of any high-technology development, particularly when trying to achieve new missions and stretching the potential of the weapon. Failures give better understanding of the system and contain lessons for the future.

There were many, many special experiences that the BrahMos team has gone through and shared. On all occasions during the last 15 years, the members displayed a high degree of integrity, commitment, courage and value. I was fortunate to have such a wonderful team with me. This was acknowledged by the great men who participated in the celebration that marked the completion of 15 years of BrahMos—as Aardhik Diwas (Partnership Day)—on 19 February 2013. All the three Services highlighted the importance of BrahMos for the Armed Forces.

First Delivery of the Land-based System

Dr. Kalam, after becoming the President of India, earned great fame as "The People's President." By 2007, our land attack version for the Army was ready and the production process was in progress. We organised a ceremonial function on 21 June 2007 to mark the beginning of delivery of systems. It turned out to be a huge function attended by the Defence Minister Mr. A.K. Antony who declared that the day marked a historic one for the Indian Army. Gen. J.J. Singh who received the missile from the Supreme Commander of the Armed Forces expressed his happiness to possess the most potent missile for the Army. **President Kalam declared that BrahMos has made India the first and has broken the Fifth Nation Syndrome.**

Army Chief Receiving BrahMos from the Supreme Commander

PUBLIC–PRIVATE INDUSTRIAL CONSORTIUM

The BrahMos team evolved a policy to retain system design, system engineering, system integration and system management with the company and go for partnership MOUs with leading industries for production of subsystems, components and materials. The contractual obligations are fulfilled and industries produce and deliver the products well in time, which ensures smooth functioning of the missile integration and its timely delivery to the user.

The integration of public–private industry partnership in the production of the BRAHMOS missile was a unique concept. The criteria for the identification of industry partners had been laid out and was carefully reviewed and verified. The criteria for selection of partners was based on (a) their willingness to invest own funds to support or sustain the capacity and also to increase quantity on requirement basis, necessitating a modular approach; (b) their experience in aerospace technology products; (c) their ability to absorb state-of-the-art technology with a high level of knowledge competence; and (d) high governance indicators. The joint specialist team from both countries assessed the manufacturing and production capabilities of various industries and shortlisted the ones that could be partners to BrahMos. This report was presented to the board of directors. The board appointed a specialist committee with board members to scan through these industries.

Based on the final list, Government approval was obtained for the consortium of public and private industry partnership. The best part was the industries came forward, enhanced their infrastructure by funding from their own source, and manufactured subsystems for an advanced supersonic cruise missile. They made exclusive production set-ups for the missile subsystems.

Many other small private industries either provided support to BrahMos directly or became subcontractors to major industries. In all, 20 major industries and more than 200 small- and medium-scale industries became partners to BrahMos. All these tasks were carried out in record time in a concurrent manner, without knowing the number of units to be produced as there was no production order with us at that point of time. It was amazing to see the overwhelming response of the industries expressing full confidence in the leadership. They were confident that the missile would be produced in large numbers. In many other cases where the industries participated in development, product acceptance by the user took many years; by that time the technology would become obsolete. Finally, only PSUs were given the production orders. In course of time, industries lost interest in participating in the development of defence equipment. BrahMos reversed this trend. Human resources comprising more than 20,000 specialists, technicians and engineers have been engaged in the manufacture of BRAHMOS subsystems at different industries.

The most important points to be noted are: (a) visible focus on results; (b) work plans and responsibilities to achieve; (c) constant review and problem solving; (d) tuning the organisation structure to meet the defined tasks; (e) networking with partners to outsource more; (f) total control on system design, system engineering, system integration and system management; (g) encouraging employee-development activities with good HR management; (h) instituting appropriate performance-measurement systems; and, above all (i) expression of courage in decision making.

Partnership Forums

Be it individuals or industries, recognition is vital for growth and motivation. Forums are platforms for partners to express and share their views and allow them to take ownership in the project.

On 19 February 2013, BrahMos organised *Ardhik Diwas* (Partnership Day) celebrating 15 glorious years of friendship, trust and achievements since the signing of the Inter-Governmental Agreement for the joint venture. On this occasion, all who had contributed to the formation and growth of the joint venture were felicitated. Shri Ronen Sen, former ambassador to Russia said BrahMos had truly become a pioneering joint venture built on trust. Air Chief Marshal N.A.K. Browne, Chairman COSC & Chief of Air Staff and Admiral Arun Prakash appreciated the tremendous dynamism, innovation and imagination shown by the leadership to establish a model that works for weapon projects.

Dr. Kalam escorted to the stage by Dr. Pillai and Shri Shekhar Dutt

Dr. Kalam and Shri Shekhar Dutt, Hon Governor of Chhattisgarh, participated in the special award function to celebrate the partnership day.

On 30 July 2013, an industry meet was organised at Hyderabad to highlight the vital contributions made by public and private industries in making the BRAHMOS missile an excellent and formidable weapon system. It was an occasion to recognise the contributions of 205 Indian industries and seven Russian industries that are associated with the project. The dedication showed by the industries towards delivering high-quality systems/subsystems is commendable.

The former president of India, Dr. A.P.J. Abdul Kalam graced the grand event and described the BrahMos JV as a fine example of courage and excellent leadership.

HYPERSONIC CENTRE AT IISc

While work was continuing to progress technologies for BRAHMOS-II, We initiated collaborative effort with the Indian Institute of Science to set a hypersonic centre funded from the profits of the BrahMos JV. Dr. A.P.J. Abdul Kalam inaugurated this Centre of Excellence on Hypersonic Technology on 8 November 2011 at the IISc. Brilliant scientists were selected to work in research areas.

Signing of the Memorandum of Understanding and Inauguration of the Centre of Excellence

This Centre has undertaken focused collaborative research in high-speed aerodynamics and associated interdisciplinary areas, under the guidance of Prof. G. Jagadeesh. They include hypersonic flow control, new concepts in aerodynamic configuration, design of typical Scramjet engine and numerical simulation. Special materials/coating for hypersonic flight, next generation control and guidance strategies for hypersonic speed regimes and chemical kinetics associated with fuels in scramjet engines are the other areas of research. Excellent output has come from the centre. Likewise, the BrahMos JV signed a MOU with Moscow Aviation Institute (MAI) for development of high temperature materials, which have been developed and given to NPOM.

Post BrahMos Assignment (2014-20)

I was Distinguished Scientist & Chief Controller (R&D) DRDO and Founder CEO&MD of BrahMos Aerospace till 31 July 2014.

I joined Indian Institute of Science (IISc) in the Aerospace Engineering Department on 1 August 2014 as Hon' Visiting Professor for Hypersonic Research. About the same time, I was Hon' Professor at IIT, Delhi, from 1 January 2015. I was also Chairman of the Governing Board of National Institute of Technology (NIT) Kurukshetra (2012-15).

Dr. Kalam, the Chief Guest for 12th Convocation of NIT Kurukshetra being received

ISRO (2015-2018)

On request from Shri Kiran Kumar, the then Chaiman ISRO, I joined ISRO as Hon' Distinguished Professor, at HQ on 1 July 2015 for a 3-year assignment to evolve Management Structure for large scale industry partnership for production of PSLV and satellites. Details are in the chapter on Strategic Industry.

DRDO (2018-20)

On completion of my task at ISRO, I joined Research & Innovation Centre, IIT (Madras) Research Park, Chennai as DRDO Dr. D.S. Kothari Chair. I supported DRDO in Research Tasks for Naval Systems, Electronics and Combat Ground Vehicles, being undertaken by RIC at IITM, Anna University and other nearby institutions. My main interest is still in Hypersonics. I was the Chairman of a sub-committee to evolve a new management structure for fast realisation of Advanced Medium Combat Aircraft. I am chairing the Flight Readiness Review of Rustom II, a medium-altitude long-endurance unmanned aerial vehicle (UAV), being developed by ADE.

PMA (2015—)

Currently I am the President of Project Management Associates, India, which is a Member Association of IPMA (International Project Management Association), a network of 72 countries. I am also member of the Board of Governors of Thapar University, Patiala and MS Ramaiah University, Bengaluru.

Receiving Padma Bhushan from Shri Pranab Mukherjee, Hon'ble President of India

Receiving Padma Shri from Shri KR Narayanan, Hon'ble President of India

Receiving Lal Bahadur Shastri Award from Shri Pranab Mukherjee, Hon'ble President of India

With Dr. Manmohan Singh, Hon'ble Prime Minister at BATL, Thiruvananthapuram

Receiving Technology Leadership Award from Dr. Manmohan Singh, Hon'ble Prime Minister of India

Order of Friendship Award Government of Russian Federation

SEVEN

Strategic Industries

The Way Ahead

"In modern warfare, a large army is not sufficient; it needs industrial potential behind it.

If the army is the first line of defence, the industry is the second."

—Field Marshal K.M. Cariappa

DEFENCE INDUSTRY

In geopolitics, only a strong nation can advocate peace in the world. The strength of a nation comes from economic prosperity and military power, which in turn comes from technology, knowledge and innovation to make competitive products and systems. The nations that enslaved us used our raw materials and built a strong industrial base in their country, to become economic powerhouses. In economic terms, manufacturing is a very important component for prosperity. Therefore, realising the development of infrastructure and industrial base is vital, India took the initiative to establish a **'Defence Industrial Corridor'**. We must progress further, add value to our own raw materials using innovative processes and make the products competitive in the globalised world.

Military Industry in the West

When the Industrial Revolution started in Europe, many new industries were commissioned. Individuals were encouraged to develop new machines to augment production of trade commodities. This paved the way for research and development efforts to be carried out and feats once considered impossible became possible. In time, machines started replacing human beings in every sphere of production. Not only commodities, even military weapon systems were produced with the help of machines. When arms and ammunitions began to be manufactured through machines, people found that they were able to produce at an unimaginable rate. In a war, the rate at which the fighting forces are supplied with ammunition is a crucial factor. The European nations, Russia and America established dedicated military industries just to produce arms and ammunition. Suddenly, even the small countries realised that they were capable of supporting the war fighters and started exporting. Thus, the race to establish, run and maintain military industries began.

During WWII, approximately 280,000 armoured vehicles (tanks, armoured personnel carriers and other armoured vehicles), 105,000 artillery systems (howitzers, field guns, rocket launchers), 730,000 military aircraft (all sorts of fighter, bomber and transport aircraft), 700 warships (frigates, cruisers, battleships), and 1,500 submarines were collectively produced by the USA, the USSR, the UK and Germany.

Just imagine how much steel, coal, diesel, gasoline and manpower would have been used to produce so many weapon systems. All these steel, petroleum and coal industries needed support systems like mining industries and processing and refining industries. Also, imagine the machineries required for these industries, logistics, etc. I have not included the trucks, jeeps and other vehicles that also played a huge role in combat effectiveness.

During WWII, Wernher von Braun demonstrated the V2 missile flight test to Hitler. Realising its potential in the war, Hitler ordered its deployment. He asked von Braun how many he could produce. The scientist politely told him that he would produce 250 missiles in a year's time. Hitler roared, "You will produce 250 missiles per month from next month onwards. You are empowered to use any industry for that purpose." From then on, Germany produced 250 V-2 missiles per month and deployed 5,000 in war. This revolutionised the war theatre with the entry of guided missiles and a military industry complex to produce them. When von Braun came to ISRO in 1972, we asked him about the V2 and he told us, 'The industrial production capacity for missiles was a challenge. In defence, the requirement is large and sudden. So, industry should be fully equipped with capacity and technology'.

I visited a missile industry in a place called Orenburg, Russia. This Strella plant, a partner to BrahMos for manufacturing supersonic engines, was once producing 3,000 ICBMs a year. This is only one type of ICBMs. Many such similar production plants were in Russia. I visited a number of similar manufacturing plants in France, Korea, Israel and Sweden. It was amazing to see the scale of production. Industrial capacity is vital for defence and aerospace products, in view of the demand.

Indian Scenario

At the time when the Industrial Revolution started, India was under the tight grip of slavery. India was kept away from the developments elsewhere, as the British needed raw materials from India for their industries to run. This denial resulted in the limited growth of Indian industrial infrastructure. Pre-Independence saw two great stalwarts, as visionary leaders of industry in India. Jamsetji Nusserwanji Tata had a vision for value addition industry—iron ore to steel, water resources to hydro- electric power, research—Indian Institute of Science, Taj Hotels and cotton yarn. Walchand Hirachand for Hindustan Aircraft Factory, Hindustan Shipyard, Walchand Industries, Premier Automobiles, Cooper Engineering and many more. It is worth recalling a statement made by Walchand in August 1943.

> *"I long for the day when we shall have India made motor cars, locomotives, railway coaches, tramways, buses, aeroplanes, ships, electrical goods, machinery, and thousand and one things for which we have to depend on imports. When that consummation is reached, I assure you, there will not be anyone in our country who will go to bed hungry, poverty would have been outdated and standard of living will be that of prosperous countries."*

After Independence, public sector units were formed for military equipment production. After the 1962 war, India resorted to Technology Transfer and Production in the PSUs. The incompetence on the part of the PSUs, to fully absorb technology, made our nation lock to this route and we became ever dependent on those countries for spares, materials and support.

Large industrial infrastructure is available with Indian defence PSUs for specific product lines to support Armed Forces (Su-30MKI, T-90s, radars, missiles and ships). At the time of establishment, the main motive was to produce defence systems to cater to the immediate requirement, looking for technology inflow from outside. This has resulted in production expertise and not the technology know-why due to low absorption of technologies. Low R&D effort in the industries has further worsened the situation. Technological obsolescence and the non-upgradation of machineries to suit modern manufacturing techniques led to low productivity and quantity of production, which has in turn resulted in the high cost for products. Moreover, dire requirement of equipment and systems by the Armed Forces forced them to go for **imports** due to the exorbitant delay in delivering the products by the industries.

PROBLEMS IN IMPORTING WEAPON SYSTEMS

Presently, India is one of the leading countries for import of defence equipment. The following are the difficult conditions caused by importing a weapon system.

Inferior Systems

First, a foreign nation will never sell a weapon that is in service in its own armed force. There will always be an export quality weapon. In non-military business, an export quality material is a superior one, whereas in military businesses it is just the opposite. An export quality weapon will always be inferior to the ones used by the parent country. If we are buying a military aircraft, critical sensors like radars or associated weapons will be downgraded.

Sky-high Cost

Any weapon system purchased from a foreign nation comes with a sky-high price tag. They follow Machiavelli's ideas. They would have spent considerable money in developing a system. They intend to retrieve that money by selling inferior systems to the importer and that too in the first lot of order. In other words, a sky-high price tag for an inferior system and an advanced system for their military at our expense!

Unreliable Support during Crisis

In spite of paying huge amounts, during crisis time embargoes may be enforced thus blocking the arterial supply of necessary spares that are required to continue the war effort. India is not new to such embargoes!

Subversive Tracking

There exists a contemporary technology called Radio Frequency Identification (RFID) tags. This tag will emit a radio frequency signal, when it receives a particular signal from a checking system. Each RFID tag can be given a unique code to reply. In such a way, these tags are used to track the movement of goods and serve as an important tool in the logistics industry. But those same RFID tags can be installed in the weapon systems by the seller. Then through some clandestine means, those RFIDs can be queried and the RFIDs will reply. By identifying the geographical location of the reply, the location of the weapon system could be easily found out.

Unacceptable Terms and Conditions

Sometimes, the seller nation may impose a condition called end-user agreement. That agreement may even demand that those weapon systems should not to be used for offensive purposes. The seller country may even send some of its experts to verify whether we had used the system for any offensive operations!

Sabotage

Assuming that we purchase a weapon system under the 'end user' condition, a natural question would arise about how the other nation will react if that that condition is violated. As mentioned in the previous point, they can track the location of that system. If the seller senses a violation, then there is a possibility that a small part of the weapon system could be turned off by the seller nation through satellites at times of war.

However, such instances have not occurred but there is no way to deny the existence of such a possibility also!

Ever Dependent on the Seller

If the purchased weapon system requires a solution for some teething problem that involves a design level modification, then we have to depend on the seller. The seller may even put some conditions that if with our ingenuity we introduce the required modification we cannot claim Intellectual Property Rights (IPR) for our knowledge.

Delay and Poor after-sales Support

If, for some reason, the seller delays the deliveries it is we who will have to pay the price by way of a reduction in fighting capability! There is every possibility that the seller nation may make up many stories for the delay. Every after-sale support comes with a heavy price and delay.

Indigenous Customisation Impossible

The seller never gives the source code of a critical system's software so that the buyer may not be able to modify the system according to his own requirement. Even for this, we have to depend on the seller to make the modification, thereby revealing our intentions.

Bending with the Seller Country

Above all, the seller nation's foreign policies will affect us. We may be required to support the countries that are against Indian policies or oppose countries that are friendly to us because of persuasion from the seller nation.

Job Creation/Loss

Recently a new concept called 'job creation' has emerged. If a selling nation clinches a bulk purchase order, then that nation will generate an enormous number of jobs. For example, if we are buying 10 transport aircraft from a country, then some 30,000 jobs will be generated in that country. One can imagine the number of jobs that would result from Rs. 4,50,00,000 crores worth of weapons purchased in the near future. If those purchases are made from India itself, then those jobs will be carried out by Indians for Indian companies. Ultimately, the money spent would circulate within India thereby improving our economy, apart from job creation.

Corruption, Aggressive Marketing and External Pressure

Corruption is inherent in an arms deal. This exists not only in India, but it is a trend the world over. But in the Indian perspective, it has more weightage. When a weapon system is sourced from abroad, it usually evokes reactions from various quarters stating that corruption was involved. In addition, aggressive marketing by the seller nations can become irksome and too much to bear, resulting in delays in decision making. The seller nations create an extraordinary politico-diplomatic pressure on us and higher level visits to buy their systems.

Myth of Import

Dr. V. Siddhartha an Emeritus Scientist who has served in DRDO, ISRO, DST, MEA, is an authority on export control and security matters. Now he is Adjunct Faculty in the International Strategic and Security Studies Programme. With all his credentials he once said,

> *"(a) No country parts with the best product. So what is sold to us is only with second grade technology. (b) Design knowledge is not shared and the product is sold under licence, recovering the cost spent on development. (c) The seller country controls through spares and critical inputs and makes us ever depending on them".*

Do we need to continue import of weapons and equipment for ever? How do we improve our self-reliance ratio? How do we mobilise indigenous talents to produce the best of the products?

Even when a system could be developed to our specifications, production posed a challenge. This led to misunderstanding and mistrust. Product competence comes from performance excellence, cost effectiveness and large production on demand. Unfortunately, this was not forthcoming. Due to the high risks in getting orders for defence equipment, private industry never came forward for investment. Over time, thePSUs have become white elephants. They need to be cut to size, as they block progress.

GRADUATION OF INDIAN INDUSTRY

Dr. Arunachalam, the then Chief of DRDO initiated large programmes, like IGMDP—Missiles, ATV, LCA, Radars, Sonars, and follow-on Projects Electronic Warfare systems, Aerial Early Warning systems, Software Radios, Rockets and Engineering systems like bridges, launchers, different electronic hardware, UAVs and life science systems during the 1980s and 90s with larger participation of the industries. This initiative propelled many industries to participate with full involvement to compete to get the status of a Strategic Partner to DRDO. Some industries attained the stage of Build-to-Specification and System Integrators. Thus, a mature defence industry base has been realised in the country through DRDO effort.

Many private industries have now come to support indigenous production, with their capex plan, only looking for commitment and production orders. R&D departments think small about capabilities of industries and give development orders based on their design. I broke this mind-set in BrahMos. I fully believed the specific industries on proper evaluation based on their core competence. This belief led to industries putting in their funds even without any production order. There were many such instancesof a private industry asked to develop a prototype in the development of subsystems and on successful realisation, the production orders were given to PSUs. In recent times, there are a few cases where the developer got the production order. In BrahMos, the production orders were given only to those those industries that had developed the prototype. When BrahMos got large orders, they were all benefitted.

SELF-RELIANCE

Dr. Siddhartha once said:

> *"The nation's ability to provide its own security and to conduct an independent foreign policy is dependent on the degree to which the nation is able to underpin self-reliance in defence and defence systems".*

While we have excellent government-funded infrastructure in public sector units, they alone will not be able to form the military industry complex. Even now, the import content for defence systems is more than 60 per cent. If we have to increase the self-reliance index, we have to produce weapons and equipment in large quantities in Indian industries. Realising the need for larger participation from industries, Defence Ministry is also in the process of naming strategic industries. This could be the first step towards an MIC in its real form, helping the nation to be self-reliant. MIC for India should be a consortium of both public and private industries.

Shaping the Procurement Policy towards Self-Reliance

Government has, as part of its 'Make in India' programme, given a new impetus to the development of defence production in the country—both for its own need and for exporting to friendly countries. Several initiatives have been taken in the last three years to promote greater participation of industry. These include revision in Defence Procurement Procedures to introduce 'Make-I' and 'Make-II' processes, introduction of a Strategic Partnership Model, increase in FDI through the automatic route to even 100 per cent restricting licensing requirements for critical items and identifying several items previously produced only by OFBs for production by the industry. The Government of India has shaped up the procurement policy in its draft Defence Procurement Policy (DPP) 2020. The main objective of DPP is to increase the indigenous content by giving a boost to Indian defence industries, both public and private. Capital acquisitions are of three types: a) buy; b) buy and make (India), and c) make. Buy means outright purchase of an equipment. It emphasises a minimum of 30 per cent indigenous content on cost basis.

The offset helps the participation of a large number of medium-scale industries. Acquisitions covered under buy-and-make (India) cover systems are developed by a foreign industry and technology provided for production by Indian industry. This must have a minimum 50 per cent indigenous content on cost basis. Acquisitions covered under make (India) will include production of strategic, complex and security-sensitive systems (no possibility of imports); systems designed, developed and produced indigenously (DRDO + industry or consortium of industries or one industry); and systems jointly designed, developed and produced under JV (for example, BrahMos). There is a minimum of 30 per cent indigenous content on cost basis. The thrust given on the offset policy with increased indigenous content for production of systems will increase the participation of more Indian industries in national development.

THE BRAHMOS WAY

IGMDP started building up core competencies in production of ferrous and non-ferrous alloys and composite materials, precision fabrication of components and large sized structures, electronic systems, avionics, sensors, radars, chemicals, cables, connectors, etc., from the raw materials stage to systems like launchers, checkout equipment and many more. The industrial base therefore was strong enough for better utilisation in the realisation of BRAHMOS missile and ground systems. We needed to build around the capability and suggest augmentation of capacities of these industries and make such partnerships, which infuse such a confidence in them that they would be partners during large-scale production.

Through our experiences at that time, in 1999, we were aware that it would be extremely difficult to give the total production responsibility to one industry, which can coordinate with all other agencies, integrate the system and deliver it to the user. Hence, it was decided to set up an integration complex by DRDO and operated by the JV to produce all the components and subsystems through industrial network. Moreover, being a joint effort between the two countries, a considerable amount of coordination was required to put things together to ensure timely delivery of quality systems to the users. Hence, the JV did the system integration and delivery.

BrahMos JV kept system design, system engineering, system integration and system management with itself. All stakeholders networked with integrated management system and transparency in operation. JV carried out continuous performance improvements, upgradations and new versions for customer loyalty to the brand, utilising experts from India and Russia. BrahMos works with 205 partner industries from India with 20,000 engineers and technicians working full time and 7 industries from Russia, thereby creating the 'industry consortium' capable of producing weapons and weapon systems at the required level. BrahMos has set up a model of industry consortium that can be replicated to bring together both public and private industries to form a military industry complex.

Present Ambience and Requirements

An important factor prevailing in the present context is the absence of coherence and discrete relationship between the stakeholders, viz., Government; Armed Forces; R&D organisations and industries. This has resulted in the large import of weapons and equipment due to which there has been continuous dependence on other countries for spares/ equipment. There is no effective coordination between the R&D organisation and industry resulting in a lack of unison and an absence of "Mind to Market" thinking. There are both advantages and disadvantages associated with each of these four categories of stakeholders. Identifying the bottleneck areas and resolving them and by unifying the strengths of the stakeholders will bring synergy in developing products in the niche areas of technology.

The Government has progressively improved the Defence Procurement Policy to boost the indigenous production of systems and equipment. Moreover, the offset policy guidelines outlined will induce active participation of industries in the development of systems.

What the Government can do further is to give a Long-term Defence Strategy and Vision for self-reliance and defence industry growth, involving large number of private industries as production partners and trimming PSUs to size. Government should insist that renowned global companies collaborate with Indian industries for the flow of new manufacturing techniques and state-of-the-art technologies to be shared with our industries. This will in turn result in the realisation of high quality technology products. Allocation of more funding by Government for R&D and infrastructure for establishment and nurturing advanced research labs and foundries. This will strengthen our indigenous R&D capability to help the industries. As in many countries, legal provision for "Use only Indigenous Weapons" will definitely necessitate the growth of indigenous industries and their investment in R&D and going for JVs in high technology products. Defence PSUs, OFs and major identified private industries should become a single entity.

Our highly committed Armed Forces need contemporary, state-of-the-art weapon systems to fight the enemy in the process of protecting the nation. No country gives the best of its weapons and equipment to other countries. When it comes to the development of systems indigenously using home-grown technologies, there must be better acceptance procedures for these systems. At the time of formulation of Qualitative Requirements (QR), the user must consult the developer to formulate specifications. The QR once formulated should be final and there should not be any change midway. This will definitely affect the schedule since change in QR affects the entire chain right from design to process to production to validation. United effort is essential like in the case of BRAHMOS to realise Indian systems to the requirement.

MILITARY INDUSTRY COMPLEX

> *"It was surprising that whereas every country wanted to produce her own war material, in India, even very senior officials and ministers wanted to remain dependent on foreign countries and governments for military hardware and would not take any initiative for local production. These people did not understand that a country must not remain for ever dependent on another country for her military requirements as, in the event of a war breaking out, that country could stop supplies, putting the receiving country in dire difficulties when her need would be the most acute."**
>
> **—Pandit Jawaharlal Nehru, *B.N. Mullick, "My Years with Nehru 1948-1964"** (Allied Publishers, 1972, p. 130)

This utterance shows that even the Prime Minister was helpless; the system controlled him. Shri Narasimha Rao told DRDO directors in the meeting in 1992 that Prime Ministers of some countries had told him that India was blessed with a strong R&D team. This knowledge team could make India produce its own weapon. He was happy to hear these comments. As of now, DRDO could translate developed products to large-scale production to the order of Rs. 2.5 lakh crore. But the problem lies in the delay in executing projects leading to cost over-runs and technology obsolescence.

Even today, we depend on imports for most of our requirements. Self-reliance to the level of 70-80 per cent and export of defence equipment would be achieved only if we decide on a Military Industry Complex and R&D integrated with industry, like in other countries. MIND TO MARKET SHOULD BE ONE ENTITY. It means from concept level, to design, to production, to marketing of defence system which must be the responsibility of one agency. The need is bold decision by Government—'No import of defence equipment'and all defence requirements will be met by a strategic industry complex. The result will be astonishing. We will see a new India emerge. This is my firm view based on my experience with many vital projects of DRDO, including BRAHMOS. We need Indian leadership at different levels with responsibility and accountability. My strong belief is that if we depend on major industries to form clusters, better results will come with MIC in place.

Need of the Hour: Strategic Industries form Military Industry Complex with MSMEs Partnership

The need of the hour is to establish a Military Industry Complex (MIC) at the national level enlisting large and medium industries to be the partners along with Defence PSUs as members of MIC. Procedures are to be formulated which will enable participation of clusters of industries to respond to RFP to design, develop and produce the systems (irrespective of private or public). More thrust has to be given for Government funding of R&D even to private companies to strengthen the indigenous R&D capability. Regulations and control procedures like in USA need to be implemented in managing the private industries for manufacturing of defence systems. **Creation of an MIC Authority** helps to oversee building up production capability and capacity within India. Encouraging high technology tie-ups/JVs between Indian and other global defence industries will not only achieve competitiveness, but will also envisage the product for export. India cannot afford to lose any more time in pondering over the issue. Indian Military Industry Complex with MIC Authority as regulatory body is an absolute necessity.

This will change the world's perception on India from an importer country to an exporter one.

SPACE INDUSTRY

Indian Government recently announced a policy framework for the Indian private sector to come in as co-traveller to ISRO, in the space programme. Finance Minister said,

> *"India already has the benefit of an extraordinary institution like ISRO, but now lots of private players are also coming in with innovative space*

technology. We will allow private players to benefit from ISRO's assets and give them a level-playing field to boost India's space sector further.

Many geospatial data is available in India. Currently start-ups and private companies have to go abroad, but that will now change. This is a sensitive area and will follow strict guidelines, but will make information available to start-ups and private firms."

The announcement is in the line of future course. Commenting on this, Narayan Prasad, an innovative start-up promoter said, "I hope they consider creating an independent regulator who can conduct systematic reviews and reforms on a continuous basis rather than the Ministry of Finance or the Prime Minister's Office getting involved in every single decision."

Opportunity

Space represents an asymmetrical advantage to the nation in terms of technological capability in fulfilling the needs of the people, security of the nation and ultimately financial advantage. We have seen how in World War II, there was a surge in space capabilities in the developed nations in civil and strategic levels, developing the requisite industrial and technological base through national policies with competitive spirit. This in turn generated huge manufacturing capabilities and higher level of technological skills for undertaking advanced space missions. The growth of large industries contributed to the economy and to the capability to build large space systems. As space has become essential for every country's development, economy and security needs, those space-faring countries now attempt to capture their own economic development, while at the same time making other countries to depend on them.

In this context, the world has seen India emerging as a new player in the space market, but due to limited industrial capability and capacity it is not able to compete with other nations in getting a sizable share. Therefore, the need is to build an industry complex for space sector, under Make-in-India programme for sustained industrial production. The vital resources and expertise of ISRO can work on futuristic missions and technologies, so that India can be one of the lead nations in space ventures.

Emergence of ISRO

ISRO has taken major strides in indigenously creating threshold technologies and associated indigenous supply chain to build space assets for the sovereign right of the nation over space. These assets have been invaluable for our nation in meeting its scientific, communication, weather and other economic/strategic requirements. What is even more creditable is that this progress was attained against the backdrop of repeated long-term technology sanctions and denial regimes. Currently, the task of positioning space assets into their orbits is achieved with the help of two classes of launch vehicles, viz., Polar satellite Launch Vehicle (PSLV) and Geo Synchronous Launch Vehicle (GSLV). The Indian Space Programme has reached a significant status with accomplishment of 78 launches and orbiting 119 Indian, 319 foreign and 10 university satellites. Today, India has matured as a self-reliant space-faring nation with operational launchers, satellites and scientific missions, and with infrastructure and experienced human resources.

We have reliable launchers (PSLV with more than 50 successive successful missions), more than 60 national satellites (with a total mass of 50 tonnes), 10 university and 319 foreign satellites (with a total mass of 7 tonnes)/Services/Ground Segments, attracting the other nations and thereby opening up market opportunities. The mission to the Moon and Mars proved to be a demonstration of the robustness and cost effectiveness of PSLV and GSLV for undertaking scientific missions. It has been an outstanding performance. It is heartening to note that in such a short time, space technology applications are contributing to nationwide development in terms of Earth resources, communication, navigation, weather forecasting and disaster warning. ISRO has also drafted a 15 years' vision document outlining programmes in Space Transportation Systems, Space Infrastructure, Space Science and Capacity Building.

The major thrust of space research is to merge with the development schemes for the society and nation building. It is also essential for ISRO to make India stand equally with the developed world in technology and space exploration, by networking with academic institutions and industries for capacity enhancement.

The global space market is entering an exciting phase with revenues of about 360 billion dollars in 2018 and a constant growth of 8-9 per cent.

ISRO Strategy

Realising the necessity for larger capacity to produce launch vehicles and satellites to meet the increased requirements, Shri Kiran Kumar, the then Chairman ISRO/Secretary DOS constituted two steering committees for launch vehicles and satellites, respectively. Based on the deliberations in the steering committees and the presentations, ISRO decided to go in for PSLV as the first product for serial production by an industry consortium. An industry meet was organised to express ISRO's intent and to solicit industry cooperation to form a consortium to undertake end-to-end production of PSLV. Subsequently, as decided in the industry meet, the then Chairman ISRO/Secretary DOS constituted a Composite Implementation Team (CIT), with industry participation, to evolve a management structure for the industry consortium, identifying the partnership pattern, financial plans, legal issues, schedule and cost aspects, in order to increase PSLV production capacity to 12 per year, to meet the overwhelming requirement of launching multiple satellites in polar orbits. The CIT arrived at a possible management structure for the joint venture between ISRO and the industries along with a business plan, bringing out the partnership pattern, financial plans, infrastructure requirement, and quality management.

In line with the experiences of BrahMos, PSLV can be produced end-to-end by an Industry Consortium formed with DOS/ISRO as a joint venture, registered as a private limited company with the Government of India holding a share of 50.5 per cent and a group of industries holding 49.5 per cent. Gestation period for industry to absorb technical details from ISRO for independent operation is five years. Production target per annum will be a minimum of 12 for Government of India and could go up to 24, depending on the production orders for satellites received from other countries. The first launch of PSLV (to be produced by industry consortium) is to take place in five years, after the formation of JV.

Segments of Market

- Launch Services
- Satellite Manufacturing
- Downstream Application
  - SATCOM market
  - EO market
  - Satellite navigation market
- Ground Stations and Satellite Networks
- Small satellite ground stations

Small Satellites

In the area of Earth observation satellites, the market has been very sensitive. Presently, low cost small satellites are widely used internationally for defence and strategic applications. These small satellites with a weight of around 100 to 150 kg, use commercial-off-the shelf (COTS) components, allowing them to be manufactured at 1/3rd to 1/5th the cost of a large satellite of the same functionality. These small satellites usually have a mission life of two to five years. They also have the additional advantage of minimal logistics support and provide augmentation and reconstitution of resources at an extremely rapid pace. They can be designed for theatre-specific ops and are agile fall-back options in tactical warfare.

In addition to the above, the survivability of satellites during ASAT attack can be easily managed. Loss of any one of the satellites due to age, malfunction or accident will not affect the overall performance of the constellation.

It is expected that 2,000-2,500 small satellites are to be launched in the next five years, more than four times the number launched in the last decade. Asia will witness strong growth as more and more countries are coming forward to launch small satellites for two main reasons: National sovereignty and security, and technology acquisition.

Satellite constellations are also on the anvil. One Web planned to launch 648 communication satellites in non-GSO, Ku band; each weighing ~175 kg to be deployed in 1,200 km non-stationary orbit with small, low-cost user terminals to talk to satellites in the sky, emit LTE, 3G and Wi-Fi to surrounding areas.

India has emerged as a potential player in the space market with growing opportunity for PSLV. Space market presents a challenge for competition, coupled with government tax and duty subsidies, national ownership and pride, and the huge opportunity to prove India's emergence as a global player. We need to be responsive to the economic forces that drive the commercial market, barriers to market entry, economic payoffs, financial incentives to industry for capacity building, and must stand up to the competition, while also estimating the risk associated with the venture.

PSLV's Edge

The above scenario provides a strong commercial footprint, especially for the PSLV, in acquiring a sizeable global market of launch vehicles. PSLV is in a unique position in the competitive world because of its highest reliability index and cost advantage. It has demonstrated launch capability and re-ignition of fourth stage for different orbital injection of multiple satellites in a single mission. The global scenario dictates that future satellites will be smaller in size and form constellations, which will bring an ideal situation for PSLV to capture a good market for many satellites in every launch. The maturity level of the industries participating in PSLV systems/hardware gives an opportunity to step up production level. The increased market potential for commercial satellites, civil and military requirements make it necessary to look at increased production. The competitors of PSLV from the USA, Russia, Europe, and China do not have the same standing in terms of reliability, cost, insurance premium, comfort level, etc. Many satellite industries prefer Indian PSLVs due to their outstanding capability and reliability, proved in successive missions.

The present mode of realisation of PSLV by ISRO involving support from industries for fabrication of structures, components and electronic packages limit the availability of PSLVs to 5-6 per year, which is grossly inadequate to meet the demand even for national missions. Hence, there is a pressing need for enhancing the production capacity of PSLVs through a conducive industrial set up, with required flexibility in management. If the PSLV load is off the main stream of ISRO's programme, future missions of ISRO such as operationalisation of GSLV MK III, Heavy Lift and Reusable Launch Vehicles, Human Space missions, Advanced Research in Planetary expeditions can progress adequately with necessary priorities.

Strength of Indian Industry in Space Sector

ISRO, over four decades, has been pursuing a conscious policy of building up and nurturing the industrial capabilities in the country to maximally support launch vehicles and satellite programmes. The industries produced motor cases and structures with special materials and processes, precision manufacturing of engines and control components and different types of electronic packages. Investments have been made from ISRO to create special infrastructure and capability enhancement to enable them to produce nearly 80 per cent of hardware as contracted items from industries. Indian industries have proven themselves. Enhancement in rate of production of PSLV can be achieved by leveraging the development partner industries by forming a Space Consortium of Indian Industries to scale up the production of PSLVs. Therefore, a strategy is needed to evolve an exclusive structure as a consortium for ensuring seamless and speedy production of PSLVs. This will enable ISRO to utilise the specialist manpower and core competencies for future missions to obtain space leadership at par with the developed countries, through innovative culture and environment.

Some of the critical subsystems are being produced only at ISRO. These include composite motor cases, nozzles, control components, inertial systems, sensor packages and to test them using in-house testing facilities. In addition, stage level integration is being carried out at specially created ISRO facilities. There is an absolute need to transfer technology to identified industries and equip them to produce the required quantity to overcome the limited production capacity of 4-5 PSLVs per year, and schedule clashes with GSLV and future launch vehicle programmes. Hence, production of PSLVs must be addressed separately and off-loaded fully from ISRO, with only Quality, Configuration Control and Mission planning being retained with ISRO. The lead role of integration and checkout of PSLV and launch operations can also be given to the consortium of ISRO + industry. Similar arrangement will be needed for Small Satellite Launch Vehicle (SSLV).

Even though ISRO has been talking about allowing the private sector in its various missions and projects, it has so far seen limited success.

Industrial production needs volume to make it attractive. With missions such as Chandrayaan 3 and Gaganyaan in talks, it will not give business potential for the private sector, except pride to be manufacturers of space systems.

Suggested Business Model

A study of existing global models, viz., Arianespace, United Launch Alliance and Space X reveals that Government plays a very critical role to make these entities financially, strategically and operationally viable. Government, besides providing tax breaks, can provide all infrastructure facilities for conduct of launches. In case of Arianespace, the Government body also supports performance of range operation and mission control. NASA provides all their facilities to SPACE-X. These organisations essentially exploited their existing facilities.

This lightens the operations by saving capital servicing costs (depreciation and interest costs) to make the operations competitive.

In view of the complexities in PSLV technologies, technology transfer from ISRO to selected industries must be through a non-disclosure agreement. The envisaged bottlenecks between ISRO and the industries need to be overcome by specialist inputs and continuous handholding by ISRO to ensure smooth production at the industries. This can be a systematic process during the gestation period of first five years.

Industry for Satellites

There are three types of satellites needing large-scale production. (1) Communication satellites of large size and weighing more than 4 tonnes, require an annual production of about five. (2) Medium size of less than 2 tonnes for remote sensing, navigation and for scientific satellites, require more than 20 per year for civil and military needs. (3) Small satellites of 100-500 kg class needed as constellation or scientific experiments require 2,000-2,500 numbers per year.

ISRO has built a large Satellite Production Centre with all types of test facilities. Electronic industries have been shortlisted for limited partnership for the medium class. There are many industries that can build and test small satellites for meeting large requirements. ISRO can integrate and test large-size satellites for communication and planetary missions, as the numbers are limited.

Satellite Imaging

As per the market survey by Allied Market Research, the commercial satellite imaging market is valued at $ 5,256 million by 2026 with a growth rate of 11.2 per cent. Imaging is required for different applications such as disaster management, town planning, agriculture crop management, farmer crop insurance, energy resource planning, rural development, surveillance and security, defence and Intelligence, and so on. New emerging technologies include remote sensing with high-resolution cameras, Light Detection & Ranging (LiDAR), etc.

Communication

Satellite communications play a vital role in the global telecommunications system. Approximately 2,000 artificial satellites are orbiting in GEO. Russian satellites are placed in inclined orbits due to a larger spread in the northern sphere. Ground stations on Earth relay analog and digital signals carrying voice, video, and data to and from one or many locations worldwide through satellites orbiting at a speed synchronised to a particular region. Satellite communication has two main components: the ground segment, which consists of fixed or mobile transmission, reception, and ancillary equipment, and the space segment, which primarily is the satellite itself.

Satellite communication is going through new trends, due to technology fusion. The increase in small satellites, their constellations and their communication networked in space in different orbits, cost reduction in launches by reusability and use of 5G, the Internet of Things (IoT) and Artificial Intelligence are some of the most important developments to come.

Overall

The Space Industry is emerging as one of the most lucrative industries globally. The space industry, is valued at US$ 360 billion in 2018 and is projected to grow at a CAGR of 5.6 per cent, to reach US$ 558 billion by 2026. Larger investments are also expected in space-faring countries. Demand for nano, micro and small satellites, small SSLVs and re-usable launch vehicle systems will be the need of tomorrow.

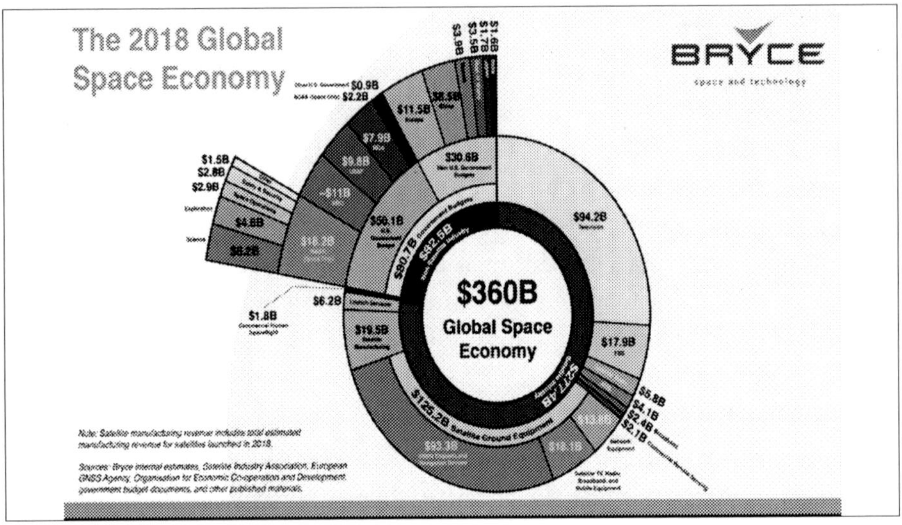

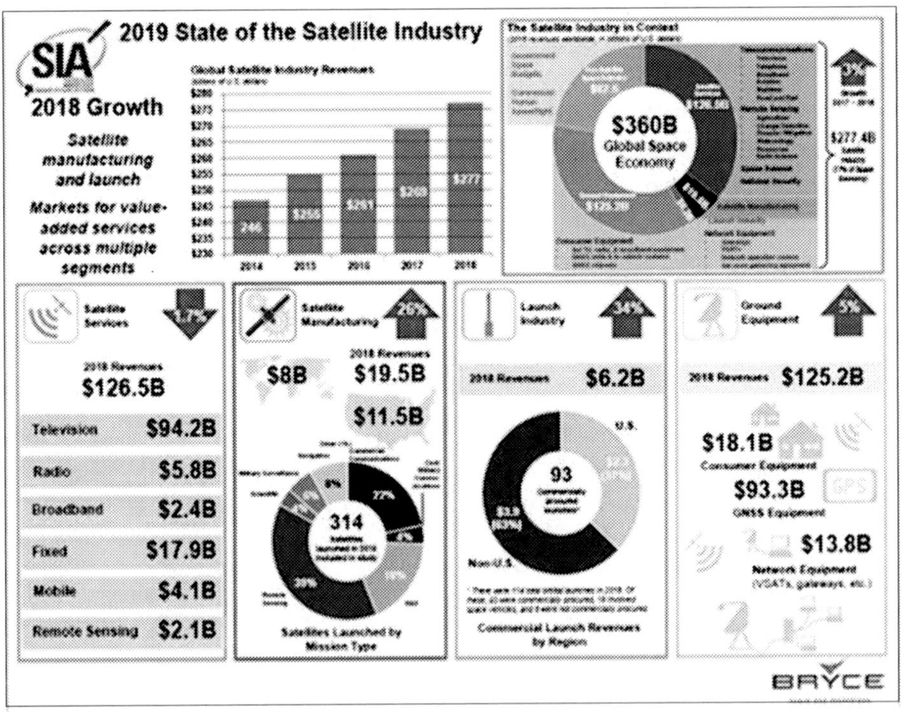

SPACE INDUSTRY ON MOON

Insights about lunar resources gained from orbit and sample-return missions have greatly enhanced the understanding of the potential for *in situ* resource utilisation of the Moon. The natural resources could be exploited in the future. Potential lunar resources may encompass processable materials such as volatiles and minerals, along with geologic structures such as lava tubes that together, might enable lunar habitation. The use of resources on the Moon may provide a means of reducing the cost and risk of lunar exploration and beyond.

Lunar materials could facilitate continued exploration of the Moon itself; facilitate scientific and economic activity near both the Earth and the Moon. Million tonnes of Regolith is the most important material for many products like Helium-3. Also, it can provide radiation and micrometeoroid protection as well as construction material by melting. Oxygen from lunar regolith oxides can be a source for metabolic oxygen and rocket propellant oxidizer. Water ice can provide water for radiation shielding and life-support.

Solar power, oxygen, and metals are abundant resources on the Moon. Elements known to be present on the lunar surface include, among others, hydrogen (H),oxygen (O), silicon (Si), iron (Fe), magnesium (Mg), calcium (Ca), aluminum (Al), manganese (Mn) and titanium (Ti). Among the more abundant are oxygen, iron and silicon. Daylight on the Moon lasts approximately two weeks, followed by approximately two weeks of night, while both lunar poles are illuminated almost constantly. The lunar South Pole features a region with crater rims exposed to near constant solar illumination, yet the interior of the craters are permanently shaded from sunlight, and retain significant amounts of water ice in their interior. By locating a lunar resource processing facility near the lunar South Pole, solar-generated electrical power would allow for nearly constant operation close to water ice sources.

Solar cells could be fabricated directly on the lunar soil by a medium-size rover with the capabilities for heating the regolith, evaporation of the appropriate semiconductor materials for the solar cell structure directly on the regolith substrate, and deposition of metallic contacts and interconnects to finish off a complete solar cell array directly on the ground.

The atomic oxygen content in the regolith is estimated at 45 per cent by weight. At least, twenty different possible processes for extracting oxygen from lunar regolith have been described, and all require high energy input: between 2-4 megawatt-years of energy to produce 1,000 tons of oxygen.

Water

NASA's Moon Mineralogy Mapper (M3) spectrometer onboard India's Chandrayaan-1 orbiter has taken images showing the distribution of surface ice at the Moon's South Pole and North Pole. Cumulative evidence from several orbiters strongly indicate that water ice is present on the surface at the Moon poles, but mostly in the South Pole region. It has been determined that the cumulative area of permanently shadowed lunar surface is 13,361 km^2 in the northern hemisphere and 17,698 km^2 in the southern hemisphere, giving a total area of 31,059 km^2. The extent to which any or all of these permanently shadowed areas contain water ice and other volatiles is not currently known, so more data is needed about lunar ice deposits, its distribution, concentration, quantity, disposition, depth, geotechnical properties and any other characteristics necessary to design and develop extraction and processing systems.

The water ice must be in the form of small ($< \sim 10$ cm), discrete pieces of ice distributed throughout the regolith, or as thin coating on ice grains. Water may have been delivered to the Moon over geological timescales by the regular bombardment of water-bearing comets, asteroids and meteoroids or continuously produced *in situ* by the hydrogen ions (protons) of the solar wind impacting oxygen-bearing minerals.

The lunar South Pole features a region with crater rims exposed to near constant solar illumination, where the craters' interiors are permanently shaded from sunlight, allowing for natural trapping and collection of water ice that could be mined in the future.

Hydrogen

Water molecules (H_2O) can be broken down into its elements, namely hydrogen and oxygen, and form molecular hydrogen (H_2) and molecular oxygen (O_2) to be used as rocket bi-propellant or produce compounds for metallurgic and chemical production processes. Just the production of propellant alone was estimated by a joint US panel of industry, government and academic experts, to have a near-term annual demand of 450 metric tons of lunar-derived propellant equating to 2,450 metric tons of processed lunar water, generating US$ 2.4 billion of revenue annually.

The solar wind implants protons on the regolith, form a protonated atom, which is a chemical compound of hydrogen (H). Although bound hydrogen is plentiful, questions remain about how much of it diffuses into the subsurface, escapes into space or diffuses into cold traps. Hydrogen would be needed for propellant production, and it has a multitude of industrial uses. For example, hydrogen can be used for the production of oxygen by hydrogen reduction of ilmenite.

Travel to Moon

The ESA plan describes an interest in regolith, which is lunar soil rich in specific elements. However, the U.S.'s interest seems more closely linked with building sustainable settlements on the moon, which NASA's Artemis Programme plans to do beginning as early as 2024. Scientists and researchers are busy working out the possibility of getting building materials for life-sustaining shelter, water and even renewable fuel for people staying on these celestial bodies.

A launch pad on the Moon will be ideal for travel to Mars and deep space, due to lesser gravity compared to Earth (1/6). Use of high-speed nuclear rockets is possible. Russia and China will follow soon. The European Space Agency (ESA) also plans to mine the moon, but when, it is not clear. India will plan its way. In 2030, there will be a MOON INDUSTRY.

The 1967 (deep breath) Treaty on Principles Governing the Activities of States in the Exploration and Use of Outer Space, including the Moon and Other Celestial Bodies, outlines the way the world agrees to behave in space. The world's spacefaring nations have so far stayed out of a 1979 treaty that says nations will refrain from mining on the Moon. Now, there is a new wave.

Once the idea of moon traffic becomes more commonplace and less abstract, world powers will have to grapple with space policy again, because any group will eventually need to make rules together and decide what to do with people who violate the rules. Indeed, when it comes to the law of space, this is just the beginning. The political reality of space could end up being more like Antarctica.

Helium-3: The Future

Man's quest for perennial sources of clean energy such as solar and other renewable energies and thermonuclear fusion would be filled through mining/exploration on the Moon. Large deposits of Helium-3 in the

Moon provide a solution for future energy demand. A 100 kg of Helium-3 would have a coal equivalent value of $ 140 million. Access to lunar helium-3 at competitive cost potentially offers an environmentally benign means of helping meet an anticipated nine-fold or higher increase in energy demand by 2050. Samples collected in 1969 by Neil Armstrong during the first lunar landing showed that helium-3 concentrations in lunar soil are at least 13 parts per billion (ppb) by weight. Levels may range from 20 to 30 ppb in undisturbed soils. But at a projected value of $ 1,410 per gm, 100 kg of helium-3 would be worth about $ 141 million. The highest concentrations are in the lunar Maria; about half the He-3 is deposited in 20 per cent of the lunar surface covered by the Maria. It is believed that there are large deposits of He-3 that have been deposited by solar winds in the lunar soil. Since the lunar soil has been stirred by collisions with meteorites, the possible availability of He-3 in the Moon would be down to depths of several metres. Nearly 1 million metric tonnes of He-3, reacted with deuterium, would generate about 20,000 terawatt-years.

The use of He-3 for electric power needs Fusion Technology. He-3 being non-radioactive, safety requirements are minimum.

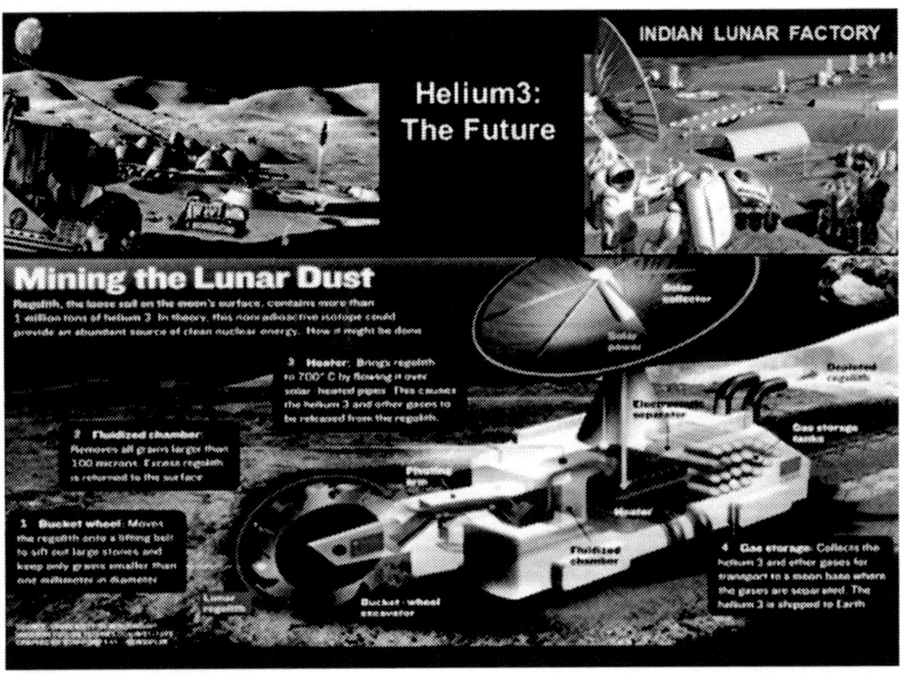

Space Consortium for the Future

ITER PROJECT: THE ROAD TO FUSION POWER

ITER (An acronym of International Thermonuclear Experimental Reactor) is an international nuclear fusion research and engineering project, which is currently building the world's largest and most advanced experimental nuclear fusion reactor. The ITER project aims to make the long-awaited transition from experimental studies of plasma physics to full-scale electricity-producing fusion power plants. The project is funded and run by seven member-entities—the European Union (EU), India, Japan, China, Russia, South Korea and the USA. ITER will produce about 500 MW output power in nominal operation with an input heating power of 50 MW and hence the power amplification is 10. ITER is based on the doughnut-shaped "Tokamak" concept surrounded by coils that produce an intense magnetic field. The first plasma is expected to be produced in 2025. According to the ITER Project, after the successful construction of the first electricity generating plant, the reliable commercially available electrical power from fusion would be available in partner countries around 2045. The long-term aim of fusion is to create power station prototypes taking into account operational safety, environmental compatibility and economic viability.

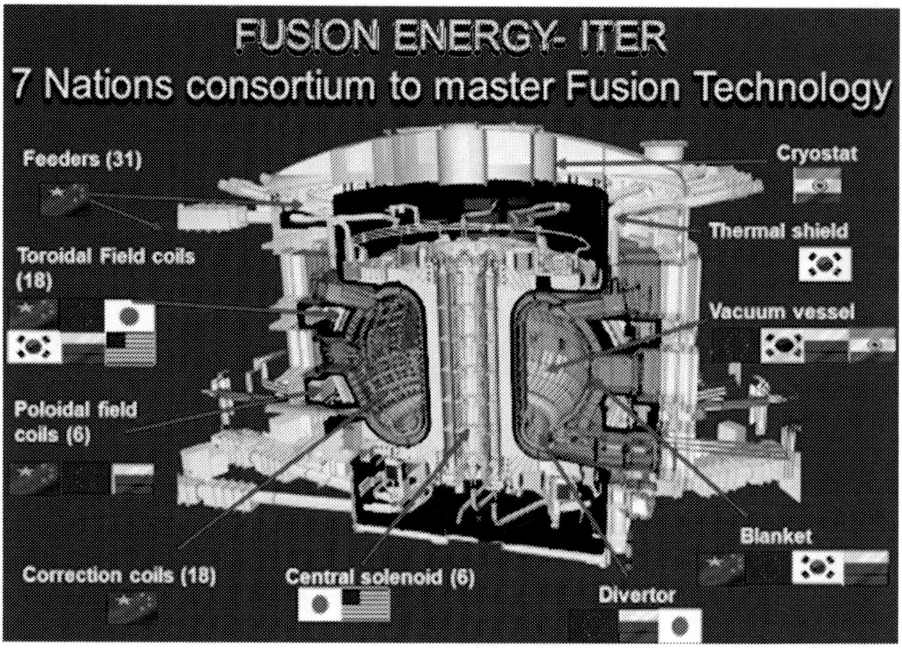

It is required to concentrate on technology developments and concept improvement for realisation of a commercial electricity-producing reactor. The Institute of Plasma Research is responsible for ITER-India to absorb the technology and build our own plant to produce safe energy. I was in the ITER-India Empowered Board to progress the contribution from the Indian side for the Fusion Reactor-Cryostat, Vacuum vessel, Cryolines, RF heating and Neutral beam heating, all manufactured through industries. Our scientists are working on site in the integration of the reactor.

The power of the nucleus is mighty and the future of humanity lies in harnessing it in a safe and efficient manner. In the years to come, it will fuel not only our Earth-based needs but also our space missions and perhaps even our civilisation's reach to other planets for habitation. Our current nuclear projects will expand into better and safer materials, like Thorium, and later on, into better reactions like fusion, which once completely developed, will be able to generate hundreds of times more power than current fission methods. Affordable, clean and abundant energy provided by He-3 is our gateway to a future, that will span deep into space and cross the boundaries of current human imagination.

Strategic Industry in TIFAC Report

Prof. U.R. Rao and I worked out the vision for the strategic industry portion of the Technology Vision 2020 document, which elaborated the requirement of System-level Strategic Industries to be identified for the defence sector. Large portion of space segment needs to go to industry, especially production, application and marketing. Government is in the process to give a boost to strategic industries.

As a follow-up, industry partnership was evolved by a committee appointed by then Chairman ISRO, with the guidance of Shri Y.S. Rajan and Shri Vijayanand, former Additional Secretary of Department of Space. I chaired the committee with directors of ISRO centres as members, as detailed earlier.

EIGHT

Immortality

POST-PRESIDENCY OF DR. KALAM

I climbed and climbed
Where is the peak, my Lord?
I ploughed and ploughed
Where is the knowledge treasure, my Lord?
I sailed and sailed
Where is the island of peace, my Lord?
Almighty, bless my nation
With vision and sweat resulting in happiness.

This poem by Dr. Abdul Kalam focuses on the vision and hard work to bring peace and prosperity to the people through knowledge

After leaving office of President of India, Kalam continued to spread his ideas and vision to create a peaceful and prosperous India. His efforts were targeted at motivating India's youth, as he ceaselessly engaged with the student community to inculcate in them the beliefs and values that would make them worthy contributors to India's great future.

Kalam was Visiting Professor at

- Indian Institute of Management, Shillong
- Indian Institute of Management, Ahmedabad
- Indian Institute of Management, Indore
- Honorary Fellow of Indian Institute of Science, Bengaluru

- Chancellor of the Indian Institute of Space Science and Technology, Thiruvananthapuram
- Professor of Aerospace Engineering at Anna University
- Adjunct at many other academic and research institutions across India.

He visited many leading universities and research labs all over the world.

Dr. Kalam was the recipient of honorary doctorates from 48 universities.

A.P.J. Abdul Kalam: THE LAST DAY

On 27 July 2015, Dr. Abdul Kalam was delivering a lecture at IIM, Shillong. He collapsed due to heart attack and his condition became critical. He was shifted to Bethany Hospital, where he was declared dead. Brahmarishi Kalam reached the abode of God.

Memorial

The DRDO, under the then Chairman Dr. S. Christopher, has built a memorial to Dr. Kalam at Rameswaram, at the place where his last rites were done. Various models of rockets and missiles are displayed, representing the work of Dr. Kalam. Acrylic paintings about his life are also displayed along with hundreds of portraits that depict his life.

At the entrance of the memorial, a statue of Dr. A.P.J. Abdul Kalam is placed showing him playing the veena, a musical instrument.

The DRDO civil works group with Ajay Singh and Col. Choubey made a remarkable contribution to build this wonderful memorial.

Presidents may come and go, every five years. But Kalam established a unique place in the hearts of Indians as the 'People's President'.

Even today, if you ask a villager who is the President of India, he/she will answer 'Abdul Kalam'

A new bacterium, discovered by researchers at the NASA Jet Propulsion Laboratory to be used as filters of the International Space Station (ISS) was named *Solibacilus kalami* to honour the late President. Dr. Abdul Kalam.

Kalam was uniquely combined a simple lifestyle with a strong will and a bold vision for a developed India. He lived an illustrious and successful life, and his legacy will continue to inspire people around the world for years to come.

Kalam is living in the hearts and minds of all Indians. He *will remain one of the finest human beings to have ever lived. As a Brahmarishi, he is immortal.*

"Life Tree". In this poem, God's message proclaims His race.

You, the human race is the best of my creation,
You will live and live.
You give and give till you are united,
In human happiness and pain;
My bliss will be born in you.
Love is continuum.

—A.P.J. Abdul Kalam

Epilogue

யாதும் ஊரே யாவரும் கேளிர்
I belong to the world; Every place is mine,
Everyone is my kith and kin.
—Kaniyan Poongunranar

The Pride of the Nation

India achieved great strides through self-reliance in strategic areas, nuclear, space and missiles. The significant turning point was the audacity of vision of political and scientific leaders in the free nation, steering for a strong and respectful India. Scientists Homi Bhabha, Vikram Sarabhai, Satish Dhawan, D.S. Kothari, Arunachalam, Kalam, and others contributed in the strategic areas to make the nation strong to face threats. Agriculture, milk, industry, pharma, IT & ITES, auto, defence equipment, infrastructure, metro rail, etc., have also seen excellent leaders who have made a difference on the economy map of India. Some political leaders have made far-reaching contributions to the growth of the nation.

India carried out many technologically complex missions. The most recent one was Shakti—an Anti-Satellite ASAT, destroying a live satellite at 278 km using an interceptor developed for Ballistic Missile Defence. In the Space Programme, there were two long-duration missions. Five orbit-raising manoeuvres and trans-Mars injection in the Mars Orbiter at 380 million km spread over 300 days and Chandrayan Mission2 orbit raising, separation of the Lander from the orbiter and landing Manoeuvres, supersonic cruise missile-BRAHMOS, the fastest, precise, powerful and non-interceptable unique system in the three Services of the Armed Force, made India the first in the world to possess the war winner. The project used advanced algorithms for precise command, control, communication and computing large data in real time for operations in achieving the desired missions. In Kalam's words, 'the success of BrahMos was the courage to travel in unexplored paths, determination to achieve the mission and creative leadership, to make India Number One'.

India is a great nation, a powerhouse of knowledge. We all belong to a great gene of civilisational heritage. India's requirements are large. To meet them and for India to become a global leader among the top three countries, we need organisations and industries that are world class. We must take on and grow further from the strong foundation that our great leaders have so assiduously created.

In the 20th century, the great themes were the atom, the computer, the rocket and the gene. The 21st century will witness an understanding of the mind, DNA code for every one, artificial intelligence, quantum dot computers, autonomous vehicles, fusion energy, space tourism and factories on the Moon and Mars, and eventually a new Earth for humanity. We must energize our youth with a high level of skill to achieve big missions. In addition, collaborations among nations will give extra-ordinary results in achieving the above missions.

Concern of the World

Today, humanity is devoting more attention to COVID-19, economic turbulence, climate change, energy, water and international terrorism, which are concerns for the entire world, solutions of which are beyond any individual nation or a group of nations. Thus, the need has arisen for the whole world to work for a common mission for the welfare of all.

When we recover from COVID-19 and peace prevails, people can concentrate on national development with united and focused efforts to solve poverty, illiteracy, unemployment and undertake development projects.

Youth Power

My experience in working with space and missiles shows that the Indian youth has enormous potential talent, which springs up when the nation is challenged. Wherever I go and interact with students, I see them highly enthusiastic and vibrant to achieve greater things in life. I see a different India, one that is poised to become a global leader, if we can transform the youth into creative leaders. Our institutions can play a great role to build a cadre of creative leaders. Young scientists and the technological community must take it upon themselves to make India move forward from strength to strength, with the firm belief that nothing is impossible.

So every youth of India must keep this in mind,

> *"If we are expected to Achieve Results never before Accomplished,*
> *We must employ Methods never before Attempted,*
> *But with utmost honesty".*

India today is in a unique position in the world attracting all developed countries to look at it because it is the best resource hub of young, talented, intelligent minds. The history of India dominating the world during its past civilisation is set to repeat itself as society has moved from being agriculture and manufacturing dependent to become knowledge-based. This is a time of great advantage for all of us, as it provides an opportunity for India to become an economic power with military might equal to the developed world. We must leapfrog for faster growth, employing disruptive and innovative methods. The key is in the value-based education system promoting skill and creativity.

The future of India is in the hands of its 700 million youth. In this context, it is worthwhile to recall the words of **Sir C.V. Raman** during his address to students.

> *"I would like to tell the young men and women not to lose hope and courage. Success can only come to you by courageous devotion to the task lying in front of you. I can assert without fear of contradiction that the quality of the Indian mind is equal to the quality of any Teutonic, Nordic, or Anglo-*

Saxon mind. What we lack is perhaps courage, what we lack is perhaps driving force, which takes one anywhere. We have developed an inferiority complex. I think what is needed in India today is the destruction of the defeatist spirit. We need a spirit of victory, a spirit that will carry us to our rightful place under the sun, a spirit that can recognize that we, as inheritors of a proud civilization, are entitled to a right place on this planet. If that indomitable spirit were to arise, nothing could hold us from achieving our rightful destiny."

—Sir C.V. Raman

References

1. Kalam, A.P.J. Abdul, and Y.S. Rajan, *India 2020: A Vision for the New Millennium*, Viking Penguin India.1998.
2. Kalam, A.P.J. Abdul and A. Sivathanu Pillai, *Envisioning an Empowered Nation*, Tata McGraw Hill Publishing Co. Ltd.
3. P.V. Manoranjan Rao, P. Radhakrishnan,"*A Brief History of Rocketry in ISRO.*
4. Pillai, A. Sivathanu, '*Future ISRO Launchers –A Study*' (Report No. ILV/S: TN: 32: 85/S).Kalam, A.P.J. Abdul and A.S. Pillai, '*Performance of Cost Effectiveness of ISRO Launchers*' (Report No. ILV/S:RN:03:83).
5. Pillai, A. Sivathanu, *102 Launch Azimuth for Geosynchronous Mission from SHAR* (Report No. ILV/S:TN:83).
6. Pillai, A. Sivathanu, *PSLV—A Launch for Indian Meteorological Satellite.*
7. Pillai, A. Sivathanu, '*HQ Analysis of PSLV Configuration Options*' (Report No. PSLV: MRLCHR: 06: 91).
8. Kamath, M.V., *Milkman from Anand – The Story of Varghese Kurien*, Konark Publishers Pvt. Ltd.
9. Kalam, A.P.J. Abdul, and Arun Tewari, *Wings of Fire*, Universities Press.
10. FICCI. "Footprints of Enterprise", *Indian Business through the Ages.*
11. "The Uncommon Vision of J.N. Tata", *Financial Express*, May 19, 2004.
12. Swaminathan, M.S., *Time Magazine*, Vol. 154, No 7/8, August 23-30, 1999.
13. Gopal Raj, *Reach for the stars—The Evolution of India's Rocket Programme*", Viking, 2000.
14. Mahanti, Subhodh, "H.J. Bhabha—The Architect of India's Nuclear Programme", *Vigyan Prasar*, January 2000.
15. Lala, R.M., *For the Love of India– The Life and Times of Jamsetji*, Tata Viking Penguin India.
16. Swaminathan, M.S., *New India Digest*, Vol. VI/3, No.8, May-June 2001.
17. Roddam, Narasimha, *Rockets in Mysore and Britain*, 1750-1850 A.D., Project Document DU 8503, National Aeronautical Laboratory, Indian Institute of Science, Bangalore.

18. Kalam, A.P.J. Abdul, 'The History of Indian Rocketry, Hazrat Tipu Sultan' Shaheed Memorial Lecture, November 30, 1991.
19. www.meddev.nic.in/science/policy.htm
20. Huber, George P., *The Necessary Nature of Future Firms*, Response Books, 2004.
21. Hesselbein, Francis, Marshall Goldsmith, and Richard Beckhard, *The Leader of the Future*, Josey Bass Publishers, 1996.
22. A.P.J. Abdul Kalam – *Forge your Future.*
23. R.P. Shenoy, *DRDO 1958-82.*
24. Mark Lipton, *Guiding Growth* HBS Press, 2003.
25. History of Leadership Research, SEDL – *Leadership Characteristics that Facilitate School Change, Internet Source.*
26. Tedlew, Richard S., 'Giants of Enterprise', *Harper Business*, 2003.
27. Kouzes, James M., and Barry Z. Posner, *The Leadership Challenge.*
27. Mistry. Dinshaw, "Containing Missile Proliferation", *Strategic Technology, Security, Regimes, and International Cooperation in Arms Control*, University of Washington Press.
28. Mallik Amitav, "*Technology and Security in the 21st Century*, SIPRI Research Report No. 20.
29. www.reachingcriticalwill.org
30. McGraw-Hill, *Encyclopaedia of Science and Technology*, Seventh Edition, Vol. 18, p. 151, 1992.
31. Mar, B.W., Newell, W.T. and Saxberg, B.O., *Managing High Technology. An Interdisciplinary Perspective*, 1985.
32. Ford and Ryan, *Journal of Projects Management*, 1981.
33. Subba Rao, A., *Management of Technology Change*, Global Business Press, 1994.
34. Barth, R. and Steak, R., (eds), *Interdisciplinary Research Group: Their Management and Organisation*, Seattle, University of Washington, 1980.
35. Abernathy, W.J., *Industrial Renaissance, Producing a Competitive Future for America*, Basic Book Inc., New York, 1983.
36. Larson, E.W. and Gobeli, D.H., 'Matrix Management: Contradictions and Insights', *California Management Review*, 29(4), 1987.
37. John A. Kuprenas, 'Implementation and Performance of a Matrix Organisation Structure', *International Journal of Project Management*, 21, 2003.
38. Scott McCutcheon & Bobbi—*Space and Astronomy—The People behind Science*, 2007.
39. John Adair—*Inspiring Leadership*, 2003.
40. Nuclear Weapons & Indian Security.

41. Strube Talbott, *Engaging India.*
42. Vikram Sarabhai Science Policy of National Development.
43. DRDL—*Dare Devil Days.*
44. Memories; Incredible Kalam DESIDOC.
45. A.P.J. Abdul Kalam & A. SivathanuPillai – *Some Project Management Experiences from SLV-3 Development.*
46. A.P.J. Abdul Kalam – *SLV 3 Applications – A study report.*
47. The Nuclear War file.
48. The Shots Heard Round the World.
49. Ashok Kapoor—*Pokhran and Beyond.*
50. G. Venkatraman—*Bhabha and his Magnificent O0bsessions.*
51. Kanti P. Bajpai and Harsh V. Pant,*India's National Security – A Reader.*
52. A.P.J. Abdul Kalam—*Ignited Minds-– Unleashing the Power.*
53. A.P.J. Abdul Kalam—*Turning Points.*
54. A.P.J. Abdul Kalam & A. Sivathanu Pillai – *Thoughts for Change – We can do it.*
55. A.P.J. Abdul Kalam & Y.S.Rajan – *India Beyond 2020.*
56. A.P.J. Abdul Kalam—*My Journey.*
57. Jain Vishva Bharati Institute—*Towards Enlightened Citizenship* – Surat Spiritual Declaration.
58. V.S. Arunachalam—*From Temples to Turbines – An adventure in two worlds.*
59. Peter R. Lavoy—*Asymmetric Warfare in South Asia – Kargil Conflict.*
60. Pillai, A. Sivathanu—*The Path Unexplored.*
61. Pillai, A. Sivathanu—*Success Mantra of BrahMos.*
62. Nuclear India in the 21st Century.
63. Robert Hutchinson—*Weapons of Mass Destination.*
64. 'The Bomb', *National Geography.*
65. S.C. Gupta, *Growing rocket system and the team.*
66. Lynn Eden, *Whole world on fire – Nuclear weapon devastation.*
67. Amrita Shah, *Vikram Sarabhai – A Life.*
68. Rajiv Narang & Devika Devaiah, *"Orbit Shifting—Innovation".*
69. Rajaram Nagappa. DESIDOC—*Evolution of Solid Propellant Rockets in India.*
70. Arun Maira, *Remaking India.*
71. Carmine Cerallo, *Secrets of Steve Jobs.*
72. C.K. Prahalad, and N.S. Krishna, *The New Range of Innovation.*
73. Pillai, A. Sivathanu, *Revolution in Leadership – Building Technologies.*
74. DESIDOC, *IGMDP.*
75. Pillai, A. Sivathanu, *Technology Leadership.*

76. Raj Chengappa, *Weapons of Peace.*
77. Chandra Shehani, *Vision to Mission.*
78. A.P.J. Abdul Kalam and S.P. Singh, *Target 3 billion.*
79. A.P.J. Abdul Kalam and Y.S.Rajan, *The Scientific Indian.*
80. P. Jagadish Gandhi, *Dr. Kalam's PURA Model and Societal Transformation.*
81. Prof S. Dhawan, *'Star Wars' 5 July 1986 - Arms race in space.*
82. AEC Atomic Energy and Space 1970 Research – *A Profile for the Decade 1970-80.*
83. *Thirumandhiram* Vol. I.
84. Michael Dowd, *Thank God for Evolution.*
85. William E. Rothschild, *The Secret to GE's Success.*
86. Michael J. Neufled, *von Braun-Dreamer of Space, Engineer of War,* Tata Mc Graw Hill.
87. Jeffrey A. Krames,*The Welch Way.*
88. Dr. Haridwai Singh, *Science OS Technology of Solid Propellants.*
89. John P. Kotter—*The Heart of Change.*
90. James W. Robinson, *Jack Welch and Leadership.*
91. Michio Kaku, *The Future of Humanity.*
92. E.D. Regis, *The Biology of DOOM.*
93. Michio Kaku, *Vision.*
94. Ivan Bakey, *Advanced Space system concepts as Technology.*
95. ISRO/SC/CIT/8/16 Report of PSLV Production.
96. Indira Chowdhary & Ananya Das Gupta, *"A Masterful Spirit – Homi Bhabha".*
97. Chalah et al. *The Brain.*
98. Eve Glaxta, *The Book of Life.*
99. Clayton K,. S. Chun, *Thunder vs Horizon - from V2 rockets of Batholic Missile.*
100. Amit Goswarai, *God is not dead.*
101. Brian Cox, *Human Universe.*
102. AeSI, *Development of SLV 3.*
103. Lewis Dartwell, *Origins.*
104. Rhonda Byrne, *The Secret,*
105. Arun Maira, *Remaking India.*
106. Number of inputs from internet, Wikipedia, Dr Kalam's lectures, website through Mr. Ponraj.
107. Dave & others, 'Results-based Leadership', HBS Press, 1999.

Abbreviations

ADDG	Aerospace Design and Dynamics Group
ADE	Aeronautical Development Agency
ADOC	Air Defence Operations Centre
ADS	Air Defence Systems
AEC	Atomic Energy Commission
ANURAG	Advanced Numerical Research and Analysis Group
ASLV	Advanced Satellite Launch Vehicle
ATM	Anti Tank Missile
ATV	Advanced Technology Vessel
AWACS	Airborne Warning And Control System
BARC	Bhabha Atomic Research Centre
BATL	BrahMos Aerospace Thiruvananthapuram Ltd
BMD	Ballistic Missile Defence
CABS	Centre for Air Borne System
CEMILAC	Centre for Military Airworthiness and Certification
CFD	computational fluid dynamics
CJI	Chief Justice of India
CNES	Centre national d'études spatiales
COM	Chief of Material
CTBT	Comprehensive Test Ban Treaty
CWC	Chemical Weapons Convention
DEAL	Defence Electronics Application Laboratory
DIWS	Defence Institute of Work Study
DMRL	Defence Materials Research Laboratory
DOS	Department of Space
DRDL	Defence Research & Development Laboratory

DRDO	Defence Research and Development Organisation
ERP	Enterprise Resource Planning
FA	Financial Advisor
FCS	Fire Control System
FRO	Floor Reaction Orthosis
FRR	Flight Readiness Review
GDP	Gross Domestic Product
GMB	Guided Missile Board
GSLV	Geostationary Satellite Launch Vehicle
GTRE	Gas Turbine Research Establishment
HAL	Hindustan Aeronautics Limited
HILS	Hardware-in-loop Simulation
HSTDV	Hypersonic Technology Demonstrator Vehicle
HTPB	Hydroxyl Terminated Polybutadiene
IADS	Integrated Air Defence Systems
IAF	Indian Air Force
IAT	Institute of Advanced Technology
ICBM	Inter Continent Ballistic Missile
IDBM	Interminably Delayed Ballistic Missile
IGCAR	Indira Gandhi Centre for Atomic Research
IGMDP	Integrated Guided Missile Development Programme
IMD	India Meteorological Department
INCOSPAR	Indian National Committee for Space Research
IOC	Intercept Operations Centre
IPMA	International Project Management Associates
IPR	Intellectual Property Rights
IRBM	Intermediate Range Ballistic Missile
ISAC	ISRO Satellite Centre
ISRO	Indian Space Research Organisation
ITER	International Thermonuclear Experimental Reactor
ITR	Integrated Test Range
KV	Kendriya Vidyalaya
LAB	Launch Authorisation Board
LCRT	Lunar Crater Radio Telescope
LCSV	Light Combat Support Vehicle

LOC	Line of Control
LPSC	Liquid Propulsion Systems Centre
LRDE	Electronics and Radar Development Establishment
LVPO	Launch Vehicle Programme Office
MAL	Mobile Autonomous Launcher
MCP	Mobile Command Post
ME&F	Ministry of Environment & Forests
MIT	Madras Institute of Technology
MMI	Man–Machine Interface
MOU	Memorandum of Understanding
MRV	Mobile Replenishment Vehicle
MST	Missile Study Team
MTCR	Missile Technology Control Regime
NCA	Nuclear Command Authority
NDA	National Democratic Alliance
NLI	Northern Light Infantry
NPT	Non-Proliferation Treaty
NREGA	National Rural Employment Guarantee Act
NSA	National Security Advisor
NTSE	National Talent Search Examination
OBC	On Board Computer
OFB	Ordinance Factories Board
OPCW	Organisation for the Prohibition of Chemical Weapons
PAC	Public Accounts Committee
PBAN	Polybutadiene acrylonitrile
PCD	Peripheral Control Device
PD	Project Director
PFFR	Pokhran Field Firing Ranges
PJB	Project Management Board
PMA	Project Management Associates
PMB	Programme Management Board
PMO	Prime Minister's Office
PSA	Principle Scientific Advisor
PSLV	Polar Satellite Launch Vehicle
PURA	Providing Urban amenities to Rural Areas

QA	Qualitative Assurance
RATO	Rocket Assisted Take Off
RCI	Research Centre Imarat
REX	Re-entry Experiment
RFF	Rocket Fabrication Facility
RFID	Radio Frequency Identification
RFNA	Red Fuming Nitric Acid
RIC	Research & Innovation Centre
RPP	Rocket Propellant Plant
RTI	Right to Information
SA to RM	Scientific Advisor to Raksha Mantri
SAM	Surface to Air Missiles
SCC	Space Centre Council
SDB	Sukhoi Design Bureau
SHAR	Sriharikota Ranges
SITE	Satellite Instructional Television Experiment
SITVC	Secondary Injection Thrust Vector Control
SLV-3	Satellite Launch Vehicle 3
SOC	Sector Operations Centre
SPROB	Solid Propellant Space Booster Plant
SSLV	Small Satellite Launch Vehicle
SSTC	Space Science Technology Centre
SSTO	Single Stage To Orbit
STEP	Systematic Training and Education Programme
TBRL	Terminal Ballistic Research Laboratory
TCE	Thiagarajar College of Engineering
TERLS	Thumba Equatorial Rocket Launch Station
TIFAC	Technology Information, Forecasting and Assessment Centre
UPA	United Progressive Alliance
UVLM	Universal Vertical Launcher Module
VSSC	Vikram Sarabhai Space Centre
WHO	World Health Organisation

INDEX

About Author

Born on 15 July 1947, Dr. Pillai graduated in Electrical Engineering from Madras University in 1969, underwent Management Programme at Harvard Business School, 1991 and obtained PhD from Pune University (1996) and D.Sc. from Tumkur University (2012). Dr. Pillai's **fifty** years of experience in ISRO and DRDO under the great visionary leaders Dr. Vikram Sarabhai, Prof. Satish Dhawan and long association with Dr. APJ Abdul Kalam made him a Technology Leader in the field of Satellite Launch Vehicles, Guided Missiles and Aerospace Systems.

Dr. Pillai's contributions to the successful development of SLV-3 as a core team member and evolution of PSLV configuration for ISRO have been remarkable. His skills in networking multiple institutions for the development of critical missile technologies overcoming technology denial regimes imposed by developed nations, and innovative Programme Management techniques enabled realisation of Agni, Prithvi, Nag and Akash missiles under the IGMDP, as its Programme Director and Chief Controller R&D of DRDO.

BrahMos Aerospace is a unique Joint Venture, first of its kind between India and Russia to design, develop, produce and market the most advanced supersonic cruise missile. His outstanding leadership qualities, as CEO & MD of Brahmos Aerospace, made India proud to possess the fastest, highly precise and the most potent missile BRAHMOS which is now inducted in multiple platforms, in all the three services of Indian Armed Forces. BRAHMOS is a world leader in the family of Cruise Missile surpassing those in the development countries.

As the Architect and Founder CEO&MD of the Joint Venture, Dr. Pillai established a role model for future joint ventures between India and other countries.

Well known as aerospace and defence technologist in the world, Dr. Pillai has been recognised by many prestigious engineering and management institutions with fellowships. He has received Honorary Doctorates from **fifteen** reputed Universities of India and Russia. The Moscow University of Security, Defence and law Enforcement honoured Dr. Pillai with the **"Order of Peter the Great"** and the Academician of the University. Dr. Pillai has published more than one hundred papers in the international and national journals and Conference Proceedings, Keynote addresses and chaired many technical and strategic management sessions.

Dr. Pillai has written eight books including **The Path Unexplored-Success Mantra of BrahMos, Revolution in Leadership, Co-authored Nano Science and Nano Technology for Engineering and Ocean Warfare. He co-authored with Dr. Kalam, the books (a) Envisioning an Empowered Nation and (b) 'Thoughts for Change – we can do it'.**

Dr. Pillai is a recipient of various prestigious awards including Technology Leadership Award, Dr. Vikram Sarabhai Research Award, OISCA – Organisation for Industrial, spiritual & Cultural Advancement, International Award from Japan, Raja Rammohan Puraskar, Lokamanya Tilak Award, Performance Excellence Award from Institution of Industrial Engineering, Lal Bahadur Shastri National Award by the President of India and most importantly **Padma Shri (2002) & Padma Bhushan (2013) by the Govt. of India** for his contribution to Aerospace, Missile and Defence Technologies and **"ORDER OF FRIENDSHIP"** by the Govt. of Russian Federation, the highest Russian Award for foreign citizens.